Sociology

Sociology
The Study of Man in Adaptation

JOHN T. DOBY
ALVIN BOSKOFF
WILLIAM W. PENDLETON

Emory University

D. C. HEATH AND COMPANY
Lexington, Massachusetts   Toronto   London

Preface

There can be a great deal of disagreement over what the emphasis of a single course (semester or quarter) in introductory sociology should be. Certainly, the stock of theoretical and empirical materials available is much too large and fragmented to be encompassed in one volume. Therefore, organization and selection are necessary. The guiding ideas underlying the organization and selection of materials for this text are set forth below.

To try to introduce the student to the entire waterfront of sociology in one course is foolhardy. Instead, we have chosen to concentrate on major intellectual issues and problems in the field. The problem areas selected for analysis are organization, socialization, stratification, population, power and authority, technology, innovation, and social change. While an adequately integrated theoretical scheme for unifying the data on these does not exist, a workable degree of conceptual unity can be found in the evolutionary framework for the analysis of social systems. This framework is the perspective provided in this book.

The social system *is* man's system of adaptation to both the social world and the physical and natural environments. The evolutionary processes of continuity and change in the social world are controlled by four interrelated cultural systems. These four are systems of knowledge, systems of technology, systems of social organization, and systems of ideology. The concepts of knowledge, technology, organization, and ideology in conjunction with the concept of adaptation constitute the conceptual focus of the book.

As a discipline matures, its connections with adjacent fields become more apparent. The study of human social behavior involves several levels of determinants, ranging from biology, anthropology, economics, political science, physiology, and history, as well as sociology. From our perspective, human evolution and individual development are mutual and interdependent systems. The fact that man is unique in the animal kingdom as a culture-bearing and culture-creating animal is of considerable interest from the point of view of biology, as well as anthropology and sociology.

Through cultural and social inventions, man adapts to and develops control over his environments, including the cultural and social ones. In other words, man invents or develops the systems to control his environment, and through man's adaptation and socialization, these systems in turn regulate man's behavior. Some of man's inventions may be false or mythical, but they are just as binding, and sometimes more so, on his behavior than if they were true. In other words, as W. I. Thomas so clearly stated, "if men define things as real, they are real in their consequences." [1] The power of ideas to control human behavior is astonishing. Moreover, if men believe certain things will or can happen, their subse-

---

[1] W. I. Thomas and Dorothy S. Thomas, *The Child in America* (New York: Alfred Knopf, 1928), p. 572.

quent actions tend to insure that they do happen. Therefore, there is a "self-fulfillment" element in human behavior that is, of course, not present in any other aspect of reality (for example, the physical sciences). The social system is dynamic in the sense that man can, as needs arise, intervene and modify his own system through creativity and the diffusion of its applications. Thus the study of continuity and change in the social world is one of the principal areas of intellectual concern in sociology. Systems are by definition made up of interdependent parts, and, in regard to human systems, the actors or individuals are also interdependent on each other as role members. Accordingly, another consideration in the choice of topics for this book is that individuals are highly dependent on others for rewards and punishments, and they are highly dependent upon others for information about themselves and their environments. The processes set into motion by consideration of the two basic social conditions of continuity and change lead to consideration of the broad areas of human socialization, social control, and social organization.

In a very substantial sense, the book, as a whole, is the collective effort of three authors. Each participated in the conceptualization and each has made significant suggestions to the others' chapters. The chapter division of labor is as follows: Chapters 1, 2, 3, 6, 12, and 16 were written by John T. Doby; Chapters 4, 5, 8, 13, 15, and 18 by Alvin Boskoff; and Chapters 7, 9, 10, 11, 14, and 17 by William W. Pendleton.

Finally, we appreciate the helpful criticism and advice from Dr. W. Clark Roof, Department of Sociology, University of Massachusetts, who read and criticized the entire manuscript. Dr. Roof's comments were particularly helpful in enabling us to clarify portions of the manuscript and to correct various shortcomings in our own arguments. Any remaining errors are, of course, the responsibility of the authors alone. In addition, we wish to express our appreciation to Mr. Michael Zamczyk, Editor for D. C. Heath and Company, who has facilitated our efforts at every phase of the work.

John T. Doby
Alvin Boskoff
William W. Pendleton
Emory University

Contents

viii Contents

PART V
Continuity and Change:
An Overview of Broad Patterns
in Social Adaptation

16 Cultural and Social Change in Modern Societies 479
17 Creativity and Innovation:
Potentials for Human Adaptation 521
18 From Innovation to Social Change: Problems of Integrating
Adaptive Solutions with Existing Structures 541

Introduction and Overview

Currently, people throughout the world are disturbed by numerous and profound difficulties (poverty, war, racial conflicts, abuse of the environment, social inequities, family disruption, political corruption, inadequacy of public services, the dissatisfaction of youth, and so on). Perhaps the most gnawing aspect of this deep-seated concern is the enormous gap between man's capacity to deal with these problems (based on accumulated knowledge, technology, and wealth) and his pitiful record of actual "solutions." But this dilemma is not as unique as some would believe. In fact, virtually every generation in history—from the ancient Hebrews to our own perceptive and dedicated social critics—has viewed its era as one of crisis and perilous social inadequacies. A crucial difference, however, distinguishes our own age of rapid communication; that is, today critical and conflicting evaluations of our problems are spread rapidly to vast portions of the population. This development tends to intensify dissatisfaction, stimulate mass reactions, and create a heightened sense of disaster.

It would be inaccurate to conclude that humans are simply bumbling animals with delusions of grandeur, or that humans dissipate all their energies and talents in waves of ineffectual criticism and in emotional orgies of substitute satisfactions. Though many persons have always lived "the unexamined life" (which, to Socrates, is not worth living), one of the distinctively human achievements of the last 3000 years or so is expressed through an irregular line of specially motivated individuals who have sought to understand man as a phenomenon (rather than as a catastrophe) and to use that understanding in constructive attempts at improvements and progress. In retrospect, these tasks were perhaps the crucial aims of early theologians, historians, and philosophers—whatever we might think of the validity of their individual conclusions.

Without underestimating the significance of these pioneers in human understanding, we can identify the decided shift toward the various social sciences as a vital step in the development of an architecture of social interpretation and responsible analysis. This shift may be dated from the latter decades of the 18th century in the western world, when the foundations of modern science and mathematics were likewise readied. In fact, from approximately 1820 to the present, the following specialized social fields emerged: political economy, which split into economics and political science (and seems to be developing as a composite once more); anthropology; psychology; and sociology.

The diversity of the "sciences of man" may be viewed in several ways: as a reflection of confusion, as a result of competition between stubborn thinkers, or as a series of tentative concentrated studies of selected aspects of human experience. One might well consider, however, that these diverse approaches—which are more complementary than competitive—are necessary to encompass the complexity of man as a creator and creature of varied and changing societies.

"Where did we come from . . . who are we . . . where are we going?" by Paul Gauguin.
(Courtesy Museum of Fine Arts, Boston.)

All social sciences are important, in their own ways, because of their focus on the development and (in varying degrees) the use of their respective categories of knowledge about humans. Several social sciences have studied man from intentionally narrowed vantage points, with rather striking results. For example, economics has dealt with the more rational processes of organizing production and distribution of goods and services in fairly complex societies. Political science has largely concentrated on the varied structures and operations of public authority in community or national decision making. Physical anthropology has pursued a very different approach to man—by tracing long-term changes in man's physical structure and by comparing variations in the physical structure of human populations to find their relevance to the operation of human communities.

But human society cannot be adequately described—or understood—by these otherwise valuable disciplines. Man is not simply a biological entity, nor a producer of goods, nor a manipulator of public rules. He is creator, participant, beneficiary, and sometimes a challenge to distinctively human collectivities in which numerous activities, needs, desires, and possibilities interact with amazing (but not mysterious) complexity. To encompass that complexity is no easy task. Yet this has been the underlying purpose of two related social sciences—sociology and cultural anthropology. The latter has generally devoted its attention to simpler or preliterate communities and societies. Sociology, on the other hand, studies primarily the operation of human societies with well-developed technologies and rather complex patterns of social interaction.

Since the archeological and historical records indicate that humans have survived more than 2 million years, and prospered for perhaps 7000 years, the study of man's achievements in nature is far from simple. But a major consideration for sociology is the pervasive fact of *differences*, both in human products (material and valuational) and in difficulties or frustrations. Throughout history, and in various environments, humans in their societies have created—and changed—solutions to collective problems of survival and meaning, and then in varying degrees, to problems of environmental control and change. Furthermore, since biological changes seem quite limited during most of this long period, these achievements could only be explained in terms of cumulative efforts and creative experience—in short, by culture and social organization.

Biological explanations of human behavior, as is the case for explanations from any other single discipline, are inadequate. While man must adjust to his environment—as must other animals—it is much too simple to try to link his behavioral systems to either environmental and/or genetic factors alone. Man's behavior is largely based on customs that develop in the context of specific social and environmental conditions. In other words, his major behavioral adaptation is culture; and variations, either cultural or biological, are all subject to selection through the action of the environment.

Man's capacity for culture is rooted in biology; yet culture frees man to an unprecedented degree from strictly biological controls over the development and maintenance of his behavioral systems. Consequently, this book opens with the evolutionary and biological bases of culture and proceeds to analyze man's adaptation through his systems of behavior that are guided and conditioned by culture.

The fundamental concern of sociology is to understand the operation of human society as an indispensable link between man as animal and man as exploiter–creator. More specifically, sociology begins with the undeniable fact that man is an effective adaptor first to physical environments and then to various social environments. Logically, the first sociological question becomes: how does human adaptation (in varying degrees) result from the operation of and change in social mechanisms, given the underlying functioning of biological systems? Such a question, of course, cannot be answered without a set of more specific and more manageable inquiries. Sociology has, perhaps, advanced to the point where we can delineate recurring and basic problems or questions in the following way:

1. How do human groups develop efficient means of acquiring and allocating skills and responsibilities for adaptation of humans to a given setting? *(The problem of social specialization.)*

2. How do human groups produce and sustain proper practice of such skills in their members (both old and new)? *(The problem of socialization.)*

3. How do human groups deal with the personal and social inequalities that accompany the use of specialized skills and resources in social adaptation? *(The problem of stratification.)*

4. In what ways are different social skills and responsibilities (and their practitioners) connected with one another to ensure effective adaptation? *(The problem of social regulation and order.)*

5. How do difficulties in collective and personal adaptation generate attempts to create new or different adaptive solutions? *(The problem of innovation and variation,* both in accepted and unaccepted forms.)

6. Finally, in what manner are innovations integrated with ongoing forms of adaptation to produce new levels of collective adaptation? *(The problem of social change.)*

This set of practical problems of human societies has come to be the central concern of sociologists during the last 50 years or so. However, in order to study and understand the operation of human societies as complex adaptive systems, it is necessary to take into account a considerable variety of societal experiences throughout man's recorded history. This requires sociologists to adopt an intelligible framework for ordering this variety in human achievement—one that is faithful to human social experience and also to our knowledge of subhuman animals. We believe this concern for orderly comparison over extended time periods is well served by the evolutionary approach, which in its essentials deals with the mechanisms and consequences of adaptation by particular species in time and space.

Evolution, it must be emphasized, does not necessarily mean "progress" or a single direction of development. An evolutionary approach instead searches for *changes* in the capacity to adapt or survive—whether this capacity derives primarily from natural selection (as in plants and animals) or from social selection (as in human societies). For the sociologist, an evolutionary approach focuses on the ways in which human effort and ingenuity are employed in solving the five practical problems we have outlined at the beginning of Chapter 4. Significantly, the sociologist studies social adaptation (and its changes over time) by careful analysis of the major components of human effort (and thus of social selection). As we shall see later (in Chapters 1 and 2), these components are knowledge, technology, social organization, and ideology.

In this book, we try to provide a basic outline and survey of the functioning of human societies (mainly "modern" societies), as viewed from the perspective of general sociology. However, the key problems of society (and of sociology) present a fundamental and characteristic difficulty: they occur simultaneously (or almost so) and they are intimately interrelated with one another—yet we can only discuss them in some detail as separable matters. In addition, the four components of human adaptation (knowledge, technology, social organization, and ideology) are in practice combined in somewhat different ways in different societies and in the five problem areas. This calls for more complex discussions and interpretations than are feasible in this work. Therefore, we have organized our discussions into five parts that focus on social adaptation and related sociological problems in the following basic scheme:

Part I analyzes the major features of the evolutionary approach and establishes the essential continuity between biological and social evolution. The key adaptive problems of human societies and the components of human adaptation are presented as a backdrop to more detailed discussions in remaining parts.

Part II focuses on problems of specialization and socialization, with considerable emphasis on the contributions of all four components to the operation of these two processes.

Part III gives special prominence to technology and its impact on specialization, socialization, and stratification in modern society. While the other three components of adaptation are historically extremely important, the recent role of technology in human affairs suggests a fundamental alteration in human capacities and in the practical problems of social adaptation.

Part IV deals with the perennially difficult problem of social regulation, particularly as a consequence of achievements in specialization and stratification.

Part V completes the spectrum of sociological concerns with analyses of innovation and social change, and with the implications of the shift from gradual, unforeseen processes of change to the more conscious, controlled, or planned processes of social change and adaptation.

For convenience, the accompanying figure summarizes the major objectives of this work by indicating the interconnections of (a) fundamental human problems, (b) major tools of human adaptation, and (c) the set of key intellectual problems with which sociology seeks to understand the functioning and evolution of human societies.

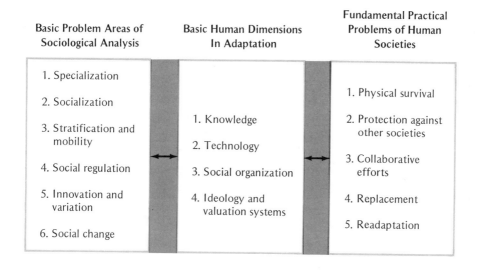

Basic Problem Areas of Sociological Analysis	Basic Human Dimensions In Adaptation	Fundamental Practical Problems of Human Societies
1. Specialization		1. Physical survival
2. Socialization		
3. Stratification and mobility	1. Knowledge	2. Protection against other societies
	2. Technology	
4. Social regulation	3. Social organization	3. Collaborative efforts
5. Innovation and variation	4. Ideology and valuation systems	4. Replacement
6. Social change		5. Readaptation

Part I

Human Adaptation: Biological and Ecological Bases of Social Organization

1

A Biosocial Evolutionary Perspective

INTRODUCTION TO SOCIOLOGY

Like other forms of life, the human species has undergone a long course of evolutionary change. Improved adaptability, broadly speaking, has been brought about through processes of natural selection. But in order to study the sociology of man and of human adaptation, it is necessary at the outset that we understand the nature of the human species both biologically and socially.

A basic level of adaptation in humans, as well as in other animal forms, is (1) **biochemical,** or the process through which life is maintained and perpetuated. (2) A second level of adaptation is **behavioral** and consists of the *individual* responses of an organism to its environment. Individual acts of food gathering, fear, or hostile responses to members of its own kind or other species are examples. (3) A third level of adaptation is the *coordinated responses of two or more* members of the same species, that is, **social** behavior. The coordinated acts of nest building of birds and the division of labor between the sexes in human beings, or the play interaction of children are a few of the many examples of this third level. (4) A fourth level of adaptation consists of the *coordinated responses of several groups, whole communities, or even societies* through culturally regulated forms of social organization. **Cultural adaptation** (level four) is apparently peculiar to man and is well illustrated by systems of technological, economic, and political organization.

Sociology is primarily concerned with the third and fourth levels of adaptation. We begin the discussion of these levels from the perspective of biological evolution. Since level four is unique in man, there must be biological bases for his potential for cultural adaptation. This chapter considers the biological evolution of man's capacity for culture and the applicability of the evolutionary perspective in discussions of the development of human social adaptation.

One of the profound results of organic evolution is increased genetic diversity and improved adaptability through natural selection. If this were not so, species could not long survive since environments vary greatly in time and space. Man is no exception to this; in fact, he is a part of the great unfolding drama of life. However, in the process of man's evolution he has achieved a state of evolutionary uniqueness. It is this singularity in adaptation that makes the sociology of man different in a fundamental way from the sociology of other animal societies. In this regard, this chapter has two main purposes. First, to describe the adaptational framework and second, to examine how it applies in general to human evolution.

AN INTRODUCTION TO THE EVOLUTIONARY FRAMEWORK AND ORIENTATION

Though humans are members of the primate order, they differ enough to be placed in a separate family, the *Hominidae*. Some of the characteristics that distinguish man from the other primates are (1) man's brain is larger, being two and one half to three times as large as the gorilla's; (2) man's nose has a prominent bridge; (3) man has a jutting chin and apes have none; (4) man's great toe is not opposable, but is in line with the others; (5) the human foot is adapted for carrying weight by the construction of its arch; (6) man has a true erect posture; (7) man is capable of true speech; and (8) man is a language-using primate. Seven of these differences are biological, while the last is cultural and the prime basis for human adaptation.

As George G. Simpson has noted,[1] culture is man's major adaptive characteristic—a species-specific adaptation. Culture is the evolved system of rules, guidelines, knowledge, and beliefs that

---

[1] George G. Simpson, "The Biological Nature of Man," in S. L. Washburn and Phyllis C. Jay (eds.), *Perspectives on Human Evolution* (New York: Holt, Rinehart & Winston, 1968), pp. 9–13.

define and guide human interaction. It is learned and symbolically transmitted among generations. This is a unique and important distinction that clearly separates the adaptive *capacity* of man from other species. However, this does not mean that the general evolutionary model is less applicable in describing human adaptation than it is for any other species-specific adaptation. What is suggested instead is that man's culture-creating capacity is a fundamental breakthrough in the long course of evolution.

Systems of behavior that employ culture differ significantly from systems of behavior that do not, and therefore, some new terms are necessary to describe the cultural aspects. What follows is a brief presentation and discussion of the general theory of evolution as a framework that includes human behavior and culture. Implicit in the above list of eight characteristics that distinguish man from other primates is the fact that the biological theory of evolution includes the development of human behavior and culture. The evolution of man's *capacity* for speech and language is what made culture possible.

Evolution is an adaptive process by which species respond and adjust to continuous environmental pressures. The key elements in the process are **genetic variation, organic continuity, organic extinction,** and **natural selection.** Variation provides the new genetic raw materials and new responses for natural selection; continuity provides stability of the organism and the external adaptive system; extinction eliminates responses and characteristics that are dysfunctional and maladaptive; and natural selection provides a better environmental fit and establishes new adaptive trends. Rough logical cultural parallels exist for three of the above four organic processes. These are (1) cultural innovation; (2) institutional and organizational continuity; and (3) cultural and social change. The fourth, natural selection, has no logical parallel unless it is unconscious or unwitting social selection. Innovations and social change are analyzed in Part V and institutional continuity is discussed in Part II.

New types of adaptive responses in a society may develop from four sources, two of these are cultural and two are biological: (1) from modifications of the existing response repertory by innovation or invention; (2) by cultural diffusion or borrowing from another society; (3) by mutation from the genetic pool; and (4) from differential survival of alternative alleles in the population.[2]

---

[2] The terms *gene* and *allele* are sometimes used interchangeably. More specifically, the allele is a contrasting inherited condition. For example, the gene B for brown eyes is said to be an allele of b for blue eyes. This implies that there are two or more alternative kinds of genes located at a specific point or locus in the chromosome. *Natural selection* thus is defined as the differential survival of alternative alleles.

The Concept of Adaptation

How does one recognize an adaptation? This is a difficult question to answer because neither biologists nor sociologists have developed the principles or operations that permit a precise evaluation of a behavior pattern and its functional consequences. The answer to the question—"What is a function?"—is equally obscure. It has generally been assumed that function or functional design can be comprehended intuitively by an investigator and communicated to others for judgment and test.

In practice the answer to the related question of whether something is functionally adaptive is often provided by analogies between biological structures and human artifacts. For example, we can understand a structure such as the human eye as a mechanism for transmitting light and suitable for vision, if we speak of the lens of the eye as analogous to the lens of a camera. An examination of the structure of the eye provides a plausible demonstration of a design in relation to a goal (seeing). But the presence of a structure, or even its observable effect, should not necessarily be interpreted as an adaptation. It must be demonstrated that the effect is a *function* of the design of the structure and not a chance effect or a mere statistical summation. In other words, one should never imply that an effect is a function unless it can be shown that it is produced by a design and not by coincidence. "The mere fact of the effects being beneficial from one or another point of view should not be taken as evidence of adaptation. Under these rules it is entirely acceptable to conclude that a turtle leaves the sea to lay eggs, but not that a lemming enters it to commit suicide." [3]

In biological evolution there are two forms or modes of adaptation—internal and external. The internal adaptation depends upon the existing capacity of the organism to tolerate variation and adjust to it. Human beings, for example, are capable through physiological ventilation of adjusting to considerable temperature variation. The same is true of tolerance of variations in oxygen supply in higher altitudes and in many other conditions. These inherent flexibilities are as much the product of evolution as are the transformations that occur over long time periods and affect the evolving of the species. External adaptation refers to the organism's responses to the environment in which he lives—for example, temperature control through air conditioning technology. In other words, an organism is made up of a number of subsystems—*internal* adaptation is the coordination of changes in these subsystems and *external* adaptation is the correlation of the organism's responses to its external environment.

---

[3] George C. Williams, *Adaptation and Natural Selection: A Critique of Some Current Evolutionary Thought* (Princeton, N.J.: Princeton University Press, 1966), p. 261.

In the case of human beings, as opposed to any other form of animal life, there is an added external system to which the individual must adapt. This is the man-made environment or *culture*. Thus there are two types of external adaptation in man. One is biological external adaptation, which is transgenerational in origin (for example, communication by speech). The other is cultural external adaptation and is intragenerational in origin (for example, the invention of a new system of transportation such as the airplane). Not only must the newborn individual or the immigrant adapt to the behavioral environment of others, but his responses to the physical world are mediated by culture.

Obviously internal and external adaptation are complementary and are two different aspects of the general process of adaptation. In other words, internal adaptation is that response adjustment within individuals that occurs during their own lifetimes. And external adaptation refers to individual responses and cultural system changes that occur through environmental selection. Thus it is possible for a species or a population within a species to be well adapted to its environment, but for certain individuals in the population to be poorly adapted. Similarly, a cultural system may be stable, well adapted, and functional, but many individuals within that system may have serious adaptive personal problems. For example, an industrial plant that is automated may be a very efficient system of production, but many individuals working in the plant may have serious psychological problems of boredom in trying to adapt to the working conditions. More will be made of this distinction in Chapter 14 (Social Conflict). The distinction between individual and system adaptation is particularly important with respect to human behavior because of the varying effects a system may have on different individuals who occupy different positions in the organizational or societal systems.

These two forms of adaptation (internal and external) can be more fully appreciated if a distinction is made between the **origin** and **function** of traits in an adaptive system. For example, the origin of the capacity for speech in man is genetic and this capacity is transmitted through the reproductive process. The origin of mathematics is language and is culturally transmitted.

However, independent of the questions of origin or cause of the species' traits is the related question of function in a system. For example, how does speech, once it has developed in a person, function to affect perception, cognition, and social behavior? Human beings are born with a generally undifferentiated and uncoded behavioral potential, which becomes patterned through acquiring speech, language, and culture. Of all the animals, man is behaviorally the most flexible—a point that is underscored by the human capacity to adapt in a great variety of environments.

Once it is recognized that the concept of evolution refers to *process* rather than to some end, object, or organism, then it is as easy to conceptualize processes of cultural adaptation in man as it is to recognize processes of instinctual adaptation in the insects. This implies that although the capacity for culture in man resulted from biological evolution, the specific forms which culture takes reflect the pressures of environment and the mental makeup of a particular population or society. In other words, the development of culture is the result of the *functioning* of human capacities and systems with respect to problems of social interaction and social adaptation. Therefore, the development and *operation* of a system can be analyzed quite apart from the origin of or the evolutionary capacity for the system. The organic capacity of man made possible the development of his cultural system of adaptation; the distinction between capacity and development has enabled us to view human behavior and culture as being included within the general framework of biological evolution. To be more specific, we have asserted that man's biological capacity for language made culture possible; therefore, the interaction of man through language and in relation to common problems of adaptation results in culture. *Culture can then be analyzed as a static system peculiar to a particular population in time and space or it can be analyzed as a dynamic system of adaptation that evolves.* In any event, the mechanisms of the system exhibit properties that are characteristic of any system that is produced, operated, and maintained by living animal organisms.

Properties of Evolutionary Systems

Analogies can be useful logical devices if properly applied. However, they are more often misapplied, particularly in the realm of biological and cultural evolution. Obviously, analogies are not explanations. In this text when analogies are used they will be used not as explanatory devices, but as aids to exposition.

Using the approach of Alland,[4] we have discarded analogue models of evolution in favor of the biological model and an analysis of the problems of adaptation in terms of this model. Viewing evolution as a process, Alland breaks the theory of evolution down for purposes of analysis into what he calls **process statements, process mechanisms,** and **process-outcome statements.** He defines *process statements* as statements about the interaction of organisms and environmental conditions. *Process mechanisms* are defined as acting to maintain the stability of the system or to bring about innovation in it, which in turn can lead to system transformation. Process mechanisms include, of course, mutations and other genetic

---

[4] Alexander Alland, Jr., *Evolution and Human Behavior* (Garden City, N.Y.: The Natural History Press, 1967), pp. 195–199.

factors, as well as nongenetic phenomena such as culture, innovation, and social organization. Finally, *process-outcome statements* refer to changes that occur across generations as a result of the interactions between systems and environmental conditions; for example, social and cultural changes are process outcomes. These outcomes may have neutral adaptive results, adaptive value, or non-adaptive or even maladaptive effects.

Alland correctly notes that empirical testing of generalizations derived from the foregoing three types of statements assumes that they refer to specific environmental contexts. Furthermore, the investigator must specify (1) the state of the system under investigation; (2) the parameters affecting the system; (3) the process mechanisms that are operating; (4) the new variables, if any, that occur; and (5) the potential outcomes as measured in terms of selective factors.[5]

While the evolutionary process may be the same for all species, the rules and conditions of process operation are not. Obviously the evolving of culture traits occurs under different operating rules and conditions than the evolving of biological traits.[6] As Alland notes, this is precisely why analogies between biological and cultural mechanisms fail, if pushed too far. All that the theory of evolution requires is that the system contain mechanisms of variation and mechanisms of continuity to maintain the system, and that the system be subject to environmental selection. Thus, there is no requirement that these mechanisms be specifically biological in nature, and accordingly, except for semantic reasons, the distinction between biological and cultural evolutions disappears.

The viewpoint presented up to now has been that there is only one evolutionary process—adaptation, viewed both as a biological and a cultural process. A corollary to the biological and cultural modes of adaptation is the important distinction to be made between individual and group adaptation.[7] These two are differentiated in terms of the origin of the mechanism of adaptation. A change in the fish fauna of a lake, for example, illustrates potential would-be group evolution. Group selection would yield a biased representation of those produced by genetic selection or organic adaptation. That is, adaptation produced by group selection would systematically alter random genetic selection and favor the direction of the characters expressed in the group adaptation. The conceptual

[5] Alland, *ibid.,* p. 196.

[6] John T. Doby, "Man the Species and the Individual," *Social Forces, 49* No. 1 (1970).

[7] There are several proponents of this two-way view, but three of the best known ones are W. C. Allee, V. C. Wynne-Edwards, and Sewall Wright. See for example, W. C. Allee *et al., Principles of Animal Ecology* (Philadelphia: W. B. Saunders Co., 1949); V. C. Wynne-Edwards, *Animal Dispersion in Relation to Social Behavior* (Edinburgh: Oliver & Boyd, 1962), and Sewall Wright, "Tempo and Mode in Evolution: A Critical Review," *Ecology, 26* (1945), pp. 415–419.

distinction, as Williams indicates, is that of the difference between a population of adapted individuals and an adapted population.[8] In a sense the definition of group adaptation is a residual one as indicated by Williams' statement that "any feature of the system that promotes group survival and cannot be explained as an organic adaptation can be called a biotic adaptation." [9]

Another way of describing these differences is to note the summated or cumulative effect of individual fitness that accrues to a population and the fitness that accrues from some adaptive organization of the group itself. Williams provides in the following an excellent hypothetical illustration of the above distinction.[10]

Benefits to groups can arise as statistical summations of the effects of individual adaptations. When a deer successfully escapes from a bear by running away, we can attribute its success to a long ancestral period of selection for fleetness. Its fleetness is responsible for its having a *low probability* of death from bear attack. The same factor repeated again and again in the herd means not only that it is a herd of fleet deer, but also that it is a fleet herd. The group therefore has a *low rate* of mortality from bear attack. When every individual in the herd flees from a bear, the result is effective protection of the herd.

As a very general rule, with some important exceptions, the fitness of a group will be high as a result of this sort of summation of the adaptations of its members. On the other hand, such simple summations obviously cannot produce collective fitness as high as could be achieved by an adaptive organization of the group itself. We might imagine that the mortality rates from predation by bears on a herd of deer would be still lower if each individual, instead of merely running for its life when it saw a bear, would play a special role in an organized program of bear avoidance. There might be individuals with especially well developed senses that could serve as sentinels. Especially fleet individuals could lure bears away from the rest, and so on. Such individual specialization in a collective function would justify recognizing the herd as an adaptively organized entity. Unlike individual fleetness, such group-related adaptation would require something more than the natural selection of alternative alleles as an explanation.

The characterization of the herd as an adaptively organized entity with a specialized division of labor illustrates a prime characteristic of human society. But is this social characteristic of *Homo sapiens* always a form of group adaptation? This question is difficult to answer. It appears that some types of human groupings are instances of organic evolution and some are forms of group adaptation and selection. For example, friendship groups could very well be the result of an extension of man's capacity for love, sympathy, and affection. It takes little imagination to recognize that altruism among primitive people would have produced mutual aid efforts that would have greatly facilitated survival. But such efforts

[8] George C. Williams, *Adaptation and National Selection: A Critique of Some Current Evolutionary Thought* (Princeton, N.J.: Princeton University Press, 1966), p. 108.
[9] George C. Williams, *ibid.*, p. 108.
[10] George C. Williams, *ibid.*, pp. 16–17.

would be the result of the extension of the trait for friendship, thus a gene-related trait, and as such would be an example of organic adaptation.

On the other hand, the development of specialized roles for research in bacteriology and immunology led to organized health facilities for the purpose of controlling communicable diseases through artificial immunization. Certainly a group or human population that is so adaptively organized would increase its population survival relative to one that did not. This fact is well illustrated in Chapter 12, "Technological Developments and Problems of Social Adaptation," where it is shown that in 1650 people of European ancestry made up about one sixth of the population of the world. By 1959, they constituted about one third of the world's population. It is true that this result could be interpreted as a consequence of genic selection, that is, the summated results of individual contributions. But such an interpretation could not account for the additional population gained by the creation of specialized social agencies which, for example, assure that the entire population of newborns is inoculated. Nor would it take into account instances such as the following preventive measures taken by the 1972 Georgia Legislature, which passed a bill requiring a premarital examination to determine if the marriage applicants are carriers or victims of sickle cell anemia. Early detection of this sort allows genetic counseling and the prevention of offspring who would be additional victims.

Williams is skeptical about the existence of group or biotic adaptations. The reasons for this skepticism derive from the many claims of group adaptation that upon closer examination have turned out to be more easily explained as instances of organic adaptation. As a consequence, he warns that "in groups of organisms an effect should be ascribed completely, if possible, as the fortuitous summation of individual activities, unless there is evidence of coordinated teamwork for producing the effect, or mechanisms for producing group benefit by individual self-sacrifice. One should postulate adaptation at no higher a level than is necessitated by the facts." [11] This is a sound principle and the likelihood of coordinated teamwork occurring in nonhuman populations other than among the social insects seems rare. Nevertheless, culture, the fundamental basis of human adaptation, is a *group* property.

In spite of all the difficulties inherent in demonstrating a functional relation as the result of a group form of adaptation and the shifting meanings of the term "organization," it is the point of view of this text that this mode of adaptation is a major force in *human* evolution and survival. Each group must be examined separately to determine whether its characteristics make functional sense

[11] George C. Williams, *ibid.,* p. 262.

at the group level in addition to being characterized by some statistical summation of individual characteristics. In other words, it is our contention that *human adaptation* is a function of both organic adaptation and group adaptation and that the latter is organized by culture and changes *within* a generation, as well as *between* generations, whereas changes in organic adaptation can occur only between generations.

In the human social system, there are several sources of behavior-variation-producing mechanisms that can potentially affect social adaptation. Some of these mechanisms derive from creativity and innovation, which are manifested in the development of new knowledge and technology. Some derive from diffusion of innovations from other societies through intersocietal contact. Continuity and system maintenance are produced through processes of social organization and processes of value orientation. And, at least one measure of the quality of adaptation in the human system is the quality of human reproduction and the system's capacity to maintain or increase the population size. Accordingly, the sources of the process variables for analyzing human social adaptations as conceptualized in this book are **knowledge, technology, organization,** and **ideology,** and three of the processes of social selection are education, competition, and conflict. The processes of knowledge, technology, and ideology are unique to man.

EVOLUTIONARY UNIQUENESS OF MAN

One of the results of the process of evolutionary diversification of forms of animal life is the increased complexity of the nervous systems associated with the higher animal forms. An important corollary of this process is that some forms of animal life have evolved a capacity to modify and control aspects of their environment rather than to be wholly controlled by it. Because of the potentialities of culture, it is this characteristic that, of course, most distinguishes man.

Man is so different with respect to his impact on the natural environment from even his closest primate forms that natural selection operates in an entirely different way on man than on nonhuman forms of life.[12] Nonhumans adapt *only* through natural selection, but man, as a species, adapts through both organic and *cultural* evolution. Cultural evolution is an extension of the forms of organic

---

[12] See, for example, George G. Simpson, *The Meaning of Evolution* (New Haven: Yale University Press, 1949); Theodosius Dobzhansky, *Mankind Evolving* (New Haven: Yale University Press, 1962); Bernard Campbell, *Human Evolution: An Introduction to Man's Adaptations* (Chicago: Aldine Publishing Co., 1966); and Anne Roe and G. Simpson (eds.), *Behavior and Evolution* (New Haven: Yale University Press, 1965).

evolution in the sense that man had to evolve an organic capacity for cultural adaptation before it could arise.[13]

Spuhler suggests seven interrelated biological prerequisites to the development of man's capacity for culture. These are (1) finely coordinated binocular vision giving supervision to manual manipulation; (2) upright bipedal locomotion; (3) prehensile and coordinated hand manipulation; (4) omnivorous diet; (5) cortical control of sexual behavior; (6) speech; and (7) expansion of the cerebral cortex.

It should be clear that man is the product of two kinds of *interdependent* evolution—the biological and the cultural. As the student will learn later in the course, this has profound implications for the growing concern about the quality of man's sociocultural–ecological environments. But let us focus for the moment on the concepts of biological and cultural evolution. The latter will be our principal concern in this book because it is the basic difference that separates man from the rest of the animal kingdom. Nevertheless, cultural evolution as an adaptive system for *Homo sapiens* will be viewed in the perspective of adaptive capacity.

In biological inheritance and evolution, man is not basically different from other species, whether these be submicroscopic viruses or complex animals.[14] In all living beings, inheritance depends upon the generation to generation transmission of genetic information that is necessary to the continuity of the species and life. The material necessary for this replication is deoxyribonucleic acid, DNA. These nucleic acid molecules, in order to multiply, must have specific cytoplasms. Nevertheless, DNA is the material of which genes are made, and this material, though differing in arrangement, complexity, and cytoplasmic environment of the gene nuclei, is the same for all life. The role of ribonucleic acid (RNA) in gene functioning is not clear. It has been shown to affect the synthesis of protein and in some cases of DNA itself, so its "messenger" or so-called subordinate role to DNA, in the opinion of geneticists, may not be entirely correct. Genes do not act independently of each other; instead the genes of an individual or a population form an interdependent system.

Random genetic drift together with natural selection among isolated subpopulations can lead to evolutionary formation of new gene constellations. Presumably this is the way evolution occurs. The biologists define **species** as genetically closed systems,

[13] J. N. Spuhler (ed.), *The Evolution of Man's Capacity for Culture* (Detroit: Wayne State University Press, 1959), pp. 4–10; also Konred Lorenz, *Evolution and Modification of Behavior* (Chicago: University of Chicago Press, 1965).
[14] See Adrian M. Srb, R. D. Owen, and Robert S. Edgar, *General Genetics*, 2nd ed. (San Francisco: W. H. Freeman & Co., 1965); Isaac Asimov's *The Genetic Code* (New York: Orion Press, 1963); and Ernest Borek, *The Code of Life* (New York: Columbia University Press, 1965).

that is, interbreeding, at least genetically effective interbreeding, is absent between species. In other words, a species is a population that shares a genetically closed pool of genetic information.

It follows by process of logical extension that a *society is a complex mode of adaptation peculiar to species whose members are biologically interdependent.* The formation of societies within a given species depends for development upon geographic isolation, sufficient contact among the members of the subpopulation for sexual reproduction, and a division of labor. Since members of different societies are members of the same species, it is assumed that genetic reproduction can occur between the societies, and likewise communication. However, it is further assumed that such intercourse, whether sexual or social, will be largely confined to members within the society for adaptive reasons or purposes.

Human society is a particular case of animal societies and may be defined as a human population that shares a common culture and social organization. In the simplest form of animal societies, for example, the arthropods (insects, spiders), behavior is guided to a remarkable degree by inherited patterns of response that follow automatically when certain stimuli are present. For example, the digger wasp female, after being fertilized, digs a tunnel in loose soil and makes a chamber at the end. When she completes the tunnel she closes the entrance and flies in circles overhead, apparently to fix its location. She then searches for the caterpillar of a sphinx moth, stings it to paralyze it, and carries it to the hut she has

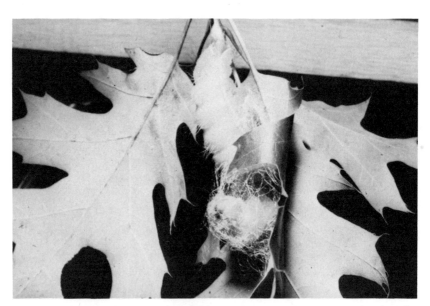

The behavior patterns of some organisms are genetically transmitted as in the case of the Chinese Oak silkworm.
(Courtesy Phil Lounibos, Harvard University.)

The behavior patterns of man, unlike those of the silkworm, are symbolically transmitted by language and by example.
(Courtesy Elsa Dorfman.)

prepared. She opens up the entrance and takes the caterpillar to the chamber at the end. She then lays a single egg and attaches it to the caterpillar, closes the entrance to the burrow, and leaves. When she has another egg ready, she repeats the whole performance. The female dies and the offspring have no contact with the parents, but each egg that hatches a female will upon maturity repeat the same process. Since there is no possibility for learning, we say that their behavior is governed by unlearned patterns of behavior or instincts that are genetically transmitted.[15]

The farther up the scale of complexity of phylogenetic development one goes, the less one finds genetically transmitted response patterns of the type described above. At the farthest end of the scale from the insects is the human species, whose social behavior is learned. This does not imply that man is like putty and can be molded into any conceivable form of behavior. It assumes that his behavior *potential* is genetically determined, and that his actual behavior is determined by the interaction of the environment with this potential.[16] The potential includes the potential for creativity. What the limits are to potential cultural shaping of personality is unknown. Perhaps particular experience and self-interest

[15] For an intensive study of this kind of behavior among honey bees, see Karl von Frisch, *Bees, their Vision, Chemical Senses, and Language* (Ithaca, N.Y.: Cornell University Press, 1950).
[16] Konrad Lorenz, *Evolution and Modification of Behavior* (Chicago: University of Chicago Press, 1965).

channel potential cultural influences and therefore limit them. The poor performance of otherwise able lower-class students suggests this. Moreover, the type and quality of one's behavior is significantly affected by the difficulties he encounters in his environment. The very poor cannot give consideration to their long range self-interest because their physical problems of survival cause them to concentrate on short range self-interests. Man's behavior potential is very complex and varied. It contains some of Rousseau's man as well as some of Hobbes'. He is capable of great goodness, compassion, and altruism, as well as great cruelty, hostility, and selfishness. The capacity of his culture and social organization to meet his basic needs, including the need for affection, are fundamental in determining which aspects of his potential nature are in fact expressed.

CULTURAL ADAPTATION

What kinds of capacities and traits would an animal need in order to be able to reflect on its own behavior as subject matter for analysis? Lawrence K. Frank, on reflecting upon the lateness of man's discovery of culture as a natural process, compared this to a fish endowed with the capacity to self-reflect. He asked what such a hypothetical fish would likely think of last in its efforts to understand its own behavior. The answer was "the water about it," and so it has been with man in his search to understand and explain himself and society. The reasons for this are complex, but one is that cultural accumulation and change were extremely slow during the first 2 million years or so of man's existence; therefore, it would have been extremely difficult to perceive and conceive of cultural transmission.

We have been talking about culture for some time without defining it. It has not been defined precisely and may never be. It is like the term species in that the elements to which it refers are constantly evolving, and therefore, cannot be defined precisely. However, by a process of analogy it can be given a fairly specific meaning. The concept of culture in human behavior serves the same general empirical and theoretical purpose that the concept of *inherited behavior patterns* serves in describing insect behavior. That is, culture refers to those patterns of behavior that are *learned* and are transmitted by communication from one generation to the next, usually by means of language.[17]

---

[17] The authors are well aware of the distinction between *behavior* and *culture*, that is, the conception of culture as the symbolic prescriptions and proscriptions for behavior, including technological prescriptions, and behavior on the other hand as the enacting or acting out of culture with varying degrees of conformity. We will make use of this distinction later, but in terms of a *general* definition of culture at this place in the text, we thought it best not to make the definition any more abstract than necessary.

The fundamental distinction that must be made between instincts and culture is that instincts are genetically formed, regulated, and transmitted, whereas culture is symbolically formed and symbolically transmitted. In other words, biological evolution occurs through population changes in the germ plasm, and cultural change occurs through modifications in the knowledge and beliefs of the population and is symbolically transmitted through learning.

This distinction can be clarified and its significance amplified by applying White's distinction of levels of behavior. He formulated four levels of response complexity and illustrated them as follows. Following White, one of the simplest forms of response is the physiological response in animals that is called the **simple reflex** and in plants is called a tropism. This level of behavior is mechanically determined by the interaction of the intrinsic properties of both the organism and the stimulus. For example, the structure of the human eye is very sensitive to light, and the retina will contract when a beam of light is focused on it. Obviously this type of involuntary behavior does not give the organism power to control its environment—instead, it is controlled by the environmental stimulus.

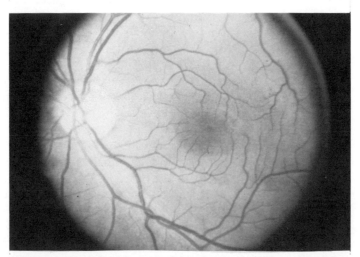

Man is equipped with several levels of adaptation that range from the genetic or mechanical, as in the retina's response to light, to the cultural, as in the utilization of optic lenses to improve and extend vision.
(Courtesy Ed Gadowsky, Massachusetts General Hospital, Boston.)

A second level on the evolutionary scale of response levels is the **conditioned response** or reflex. This type is well illustrated by Pavlov's dog experiments. A hungry dog salivated when it smelled food (the unconditioned stimulus) and was indifferent to a sound from an electric bell. However, when the dog was stimulated by the sight or odor of the food and the sound of the bell simultaneously for a number of times, the sound of the bell alone became sufficient to evoke the salivation response.

The conditioned response is similar to, but not the same as, the simple reflex. Let us label the sound of the bell in Pavlov's study as the secondary or conditioned stimulus, S_2, and the food as the primary or unconditioned stimulus, S_1. The relationship between the organism and the S_2 stimulus, the sound of the bell, is not dependent upon any intrinsic properties. S_2 could just as well have been any other stimulus. In other words, it was not S_2 itself that was important, but the relationship in time and space between S_1 and S_2. As White stated the idea: ". . . the salivary gland-meaning of the electric bell is in no sense intrinsic in the sound waves that it emits." [18] The organism still has not gained any control over its environment; instead, the conditioned response is determined by the paired arrangement of the stimuli in the organism's environment.

The third level of response is very difficult to label accurately with a single term. It is best labeled as **adaptive coping by use of tools.** To find an example, it is necessary to move up the phylogenetic scale of animal development. Level three is best illustrated by Kohler's studies of problem-solving behavior of the chimpanzee. This is the well-known study of the chimpanzee using a stick to knock down a banana suspended from the roof of his cage beyond reach of his hands.

It is important to compare and contrast response levels two and three. First, the organism in both levels is relating simultaneously to two things or events in the external world. Secondly, in the level-three response, the two things that are related or associated are significant to the organism from the start to the finish of the level-three action, for the chimpanzee has already learned beforehand the general idea of the use of things as tools. This is not true for the level-two response, where the association of the bell sound develops only through conditioning. Third, the relationship between the banana and the stick in level three is determined from experience and learning and is directly established, whereas in the level-two response (conditioned reflex) the sound of the bell and the odor of the food were indirectly related within the biochemical and neurological system of the dog. Finally, the relationship in the level-three response resulted from determinant actions taken by the organism, whereas the relationships established at level two were the result of conditions arranged by the experimenter or similar chance arrangements within the organism's environment. These

[18] Leslie A. White, "Four Stages in the Evolution of Minding," in Sol Tax (ed.), *Evolution After Darwin* (Chicago: The University of Chicago Press, 1960), Vol. 11, p. 241.

four points led Professor White to make an important behavioral distinction. Either the organism initiates and revises its responses to a stimulus on the basis of results, or it mechanically responds like a plant that turns toward the sunlight. In the latter, the organism has no alternative; in the former, it learns alternatives. Obviously, to revise one's responses in the light of experience requires an organism with a more complex central nervous system. The dog unwittingly responds to the bell sound as formerly he responded to the food. The chimpanzee *decides* what to do and how to do it. In other words, an organism capable of a level-three response is executing some *control over its environment.* That is, the chimpanzee forced its environment to yield the banana. This is a far cry from creating an environment, but then it is a great leap beyond the blind environmental subjugation resulting from the conditioned reflex level alone.

The chimpanzee's experience with using tools would accumulate to a certain extent within his own lifetime, but no cumulative experience is passed from one generation of chimpanzees to the next. In other words, chimpanzees do not produce a culture of tool using. This level of behavior depends upon a higher behavioral capacity and is found only among *Homo sapiens.* The characteristic that makes culture possible is what White called the level-four response and designated it with the label **symbolizing behavior.**

In level three, the relationship between the stick and the knocking down of the banana was a perceptual one. That is, the organism took elements that already existed in the immediate environment and used them to help achieve an end. Thus there existed a situation with elements in it that enabled the chimpanzee to perceive a functional connection between the stick and reaching the banana. In level four, a symbol for *banana* is the English word "banana." This word sound is completely arbitrary, and the meaning assigned to symbols is arbitrary, and the *symbol* stands for or represents an object, such as a banana, an idea such as freedom, or a relationship such as velocity. In other words, an organism with the capacity for forming words or symbols can *conceive* meaning, maintain and convey meaning by encoding it into a structure of symbols, and implement the meaning through a process of translation of symbolic structure into action, whether that action be mental or physical. This permits the organism to conserve experience in symbols as well as in the neural structure, thus facilitating and freeing memory. It enables the organism to accumulate experience between and among generations, and this is of profound significance in enhancing the adaptive capacity of a species. The storing of experience in symbols and transmitting it from one generation to the next by means of language is a form of adaptation peculiar to man. It is this

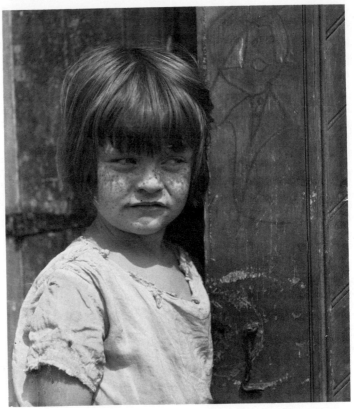

$E = mc^2$ is an example of pure symbolizing. A child's drawing, though less sophisticated and refined, is also a form of symbolizing.
(Courtesy Walker Evans.)

form (symbolic or cultural) that has permitted the steady march of man's increasing adaptive capacity from the beginnings of Lower Paleolithic man's use of fire, to the invention of the plow, metallurgy, and agriculture in the ancient Mideast, to water power, steam power, fossil-fuel power, and to electric power, to the atomic power of the present.

Archaeologists estimate that mankind in earliest forms began at least 2 million years ago. During this long span of time, his culture accumulated very, very slowly until approximately 10,000 years ago. It was not until about 3000 B.C. that agricultural or agrarian societies began.[19] The increase in man's adaptive capacity has been accompanied by physical changes in body form and cranial capacity as Figures 1–1 and 1–2 clearly show.

[19] The student who is interested in the archaeological history of mankind should read V. Gordon Childe, *Man Makes Himself* (New York: Mentor Books, 1951) and Grahame Clark and Stuart Piggott, *Prehistoric Societies* (New York: Alfred A. Knopf, 1965).

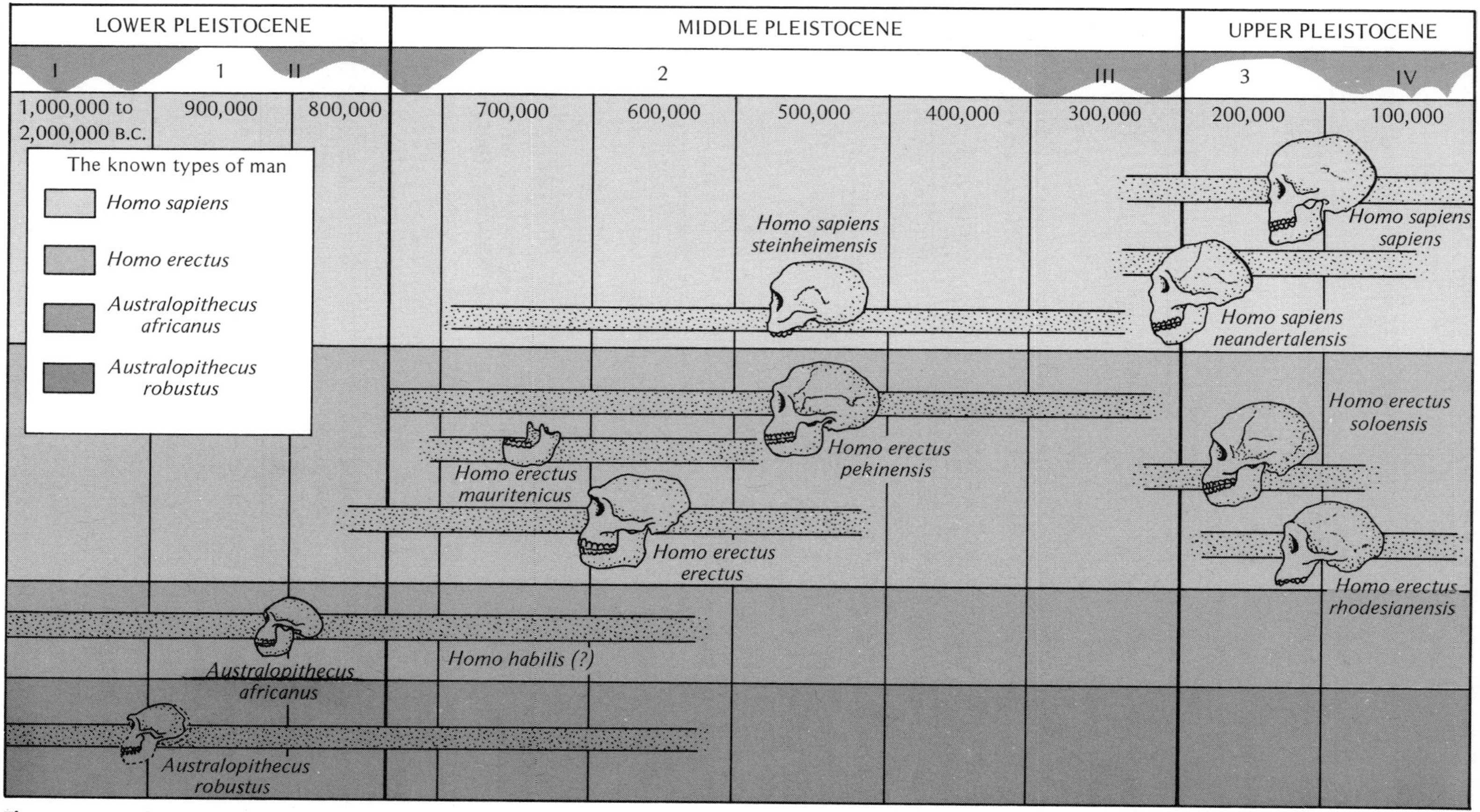

Figure 1–1   The known types of man.
(Skull drawings adapted from S. L. Washburn, "Tools and Human Evolution," *Scientific American,* with permission of the publisher.)

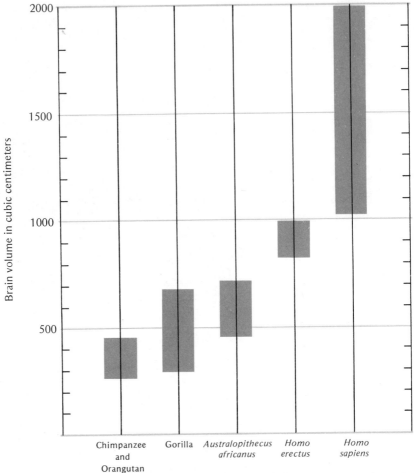

Figure 1–2   The ranges of cranial capacities of the great apes, *Australopithecus africanus, Homo erectus, and Homo sapiens.* **The progressive increase in minima and maxima is evident.**
(From E. Adamson Hoebel, *The Study of Man,* 4th ed. *(New York: McGraw-Hill Book Company,* 1972), p. 128.)

Man's capacity for the invention and use of symbols made it possible for him, through observation, conceptualization, and the pragmatic testing of the conceptualizations, to develop knowledge. The knowledge then could be converted into technology—for example, how to make fire, build a wheel, domesticate plants and animals, produce iron, build ships and airplanes. Equally important, his knowledge could be used to build a social organization and ideology to regulate and control his own behavior more efficiently in keeping with the environmental changes produced by technology.

In other words, through knowledge man changes what he "knows" about the world, and through technology he changes the world he knows and in which he lives. By changing his knowledge

Through observation and analysis man develops information, but it is through his ability to use symbols that he transmits this and expands it into knowledge.
(Courtesy Robert Rapelye, Photography International.)

of the world and through changing the world in which he lives, he changes himself. Man's views of nature, including human nature, have changed as culture and civilization have advanced. Bruno's, Kepler's, and Newton's formulations on the Universe expanded man's image of the Universe, his image of God, and of himself.

It is clear that when man evolved the biological capacity for true speech and language, he had also in the process evolved the capacity to affect his own biological evolution. The uniqueness of man, as was indicated above, lies in this fact. Adaptation by culture is more rapid than adaptation by genes, and in addition, it offers the possibility for planned genetic alteration. The flexibility of man's cultural capacity for adaptation is amply attested to by the expansion of mankind from his origin somewhere in the tropics or subtropics of the old world to his present habitation of the entire globe.

Biological adaptation alone is very efficient, but random genetic changes as Dobzhansky points out "are likely to produce deterioration rather than improvement."[20] It should be remembered that most of the species that ever existed have become extinct, despite the changes brought about by their evolution through natural selection. Presumably, systematic changes brought about

[20] Theodosius Dobzhansky, "Man and Natural Selection," *Amer. Sci., 49* (1961), p. 285.

by knowledge can be directed by knowledge. The danger is that the knowledge in some instances may be incomplete and thus have unanticipated consequences or side effects that could produce new and difficult problems of adaptation. The environmental pollution problem today is such a problem.

An interesting aspect of cultural evolution and cultural adaptation is that it existed for tens of thousands of years without man's explicit awareness of it as such (as illustrated in the beginning of this section by L. K. Frank's comparison of man to a self-reflecting fish whose last consideration in its attempt to understand its own behavior is "the water about it"). Man's beginning awareness of cultural evolution began not more than about four centuries ago.[21] Thus man's knowledge has been affecting his evolution, but it has done so without man's cognizance of the process for the far greater portion of his existence. As Redfield notes "man makes himself . . . in two senses, and the two senses imply a contrast between folk society and, at least, modern civilization. Man is self-made through the slow and unpremeditated growth of culture and civilization. Man later attempts to take control of this process and to direct it where he wills." [22]

The outline and dynamics of biological evolution are becoming reasonably clear. A similarly comprehensive theory of cultural and social evolution awaits another Darwin. In spite of the inadequacies of the views on cultural evolution, it is desirable to fit together as well as possible the current thinking on the problem. We shall attempt to do this using the concept of adaptation as the central focus.

HUMAN ADAPTATION: SOCIOCULTURAL EVOLUTION

Biological Backgrounds

It will help to introduce the problem of this section if we first ask the following question: How does life solve the problem of biological adaptation under the condition of environmental change in time and space? The answer is a twofold one. The first is what Lorenz and others have called **adaptive modification** or plasticity, that is, the elaboration and development of *existing* organic and

[21] The Moslem writer Ibn Khaldun, writing in the 14th century, is a classic exception. His writings had the force of a modern historian. The first Westerner to formulate a systematic theory of social change was Jean Jacques Turgot in his *Discourse on Universal History*. See Howard Becker and H. E. Barnes, *Social Thought from Lore to Science* (Boston: D. C. Heath and Company, 1938), pp. 266–279, 411–415.
[22] Robert Redfield, *The Primitive World and its Transformations* (Ithaca, N.Y.: Cornell University Press, 1953), p. 113.

behavioral potentialities. An example of adaptive modification in man is the development of his physiological ability to maintain a constant internal body temperature despite great external changes in temperature. The brain is the most generalized and plastic organ of the human organism, indeed the most plastic of all organs in any organism, and education is the means for *developing* human plasticity. Hence adaptive modification through learning in man is a result of biological evolution and is elaborated by cultural evolution through education. In other words, the human organism has the capacity for both constancy and change in responding to environmental change.

The second biological means for dealing with environmental diversity is **genetic diversity** within a population. The greater the genetic diversity within a population, the greater potentiality the population has for dealing with a complex environment. In other words, a genetically heterogeneous population has a greater evolutionary potential than a genetically homogeneous population. Accordingly, the trend in biological evolution is improved adaptive modification through evolutionary diversification.

The physical changes that make possible evolutionary diversification are gene mutations and alteration in the **genome** structure. A genome is the characteristic haploid set of chromosomes and genes for a species. In man, each person has two genomes, one from each parent. The zygote (fertilized egg) contains twice as many chromosomes as either gamete (the germ or sex cells). The number of chromosomes per zygote varies in different species. Sex cells or gametes, whose nuclei contain one set of chromosomes, are called the **haploid** set; those such as zygotes, whose nuclei contain two sets of chromosomes, are the **diploid** set. Obviously, if a zygote has twice as many chromosomes as a gamete, there must be some mechanism for halving the chromosome number, or else the chromosome number would double each generation. A special form of division known as **meiosis** results in daughter cells with the haploid number of chromosomes. The meiosis assures the process of organic continuity.

Mutations are sudden, potentially heritable changes in the structure of genetic material. In addition to mutant genes, another source of genetic variability occurs when chromosomes independently segregate from each other. In this process of reshuffling, different kinds of gametes are produced. This segregation and recombination is a process by which original genetic variations such as mutants are developed, incorporated, or discarded, thus producing maximum variability from the gene mutations.[23]

[23] The reader who is interested in the details of this process should consult any current textbook in introductory genetics; for example, see C. Stern, *Principles of Human Genetics*, 2nd ed. (San Francisco: W. H. Freeman & Co., 1960).

Sources of Sociocultural Change: An Illustration

It will help in our efforts to understand sociocultural change if we keep in mind the biological analogues of change just described. Though the forms of organic and sociocultural evolution are different, there are parallel processes that characterize the two.

Let us begin by sketching some instances of sociocultural change across large spans of time. We shall do this by examining the evolution of predominant forms of subsistence and economic goods in human society in different archaeological and historical time periods. Table 1–1 lists some types of societies by characteristic population size and by approximate time periods. These dates and sizes, it must be emphasized, are very crude, but the relative differences are very probably close to correct.

TABLE 1–1
Approximate time and size of societies by predominant source of economic goods.

Source of goods	Characteristic population size	Approximate time period
Hunting and gathering[a]	40– 100	50,000 B.C.–10,000 B.C.
Horticultural	200– 10,000	10,000 B.C.– 4000 B.C.
Simple agrarian	10,000–100,000	4000 B.C.– 2000 B.C.
Advanced agrarian	100,000 and up	2000 B.C.– 1800 A.D.

[a] No effort is made here to develop a refined set of categories in terms of degrees of each as some authors have. The interest is in respect to the overall evolutionary trend and not in precisely describing specific points or segments of time.

The sources of goods described in Table 1–1 [24] depended upon the type of technology in use in the society. The advance of technology, particularly the development and harnessing of new sources of energy, made possible the creation of new products, new patterns of living, and new societal structures.[25] To illustrate, the criteria for differentiating the four types in Table 1–1 are stone chopping, cutting and scraping tools, spears and bow and arrow as constituting the tools for a hunting and gathering technology; following this, a simple technology of metallurgy was de-

[24] Table 1–1 is compiled from several sources, some of which include V. Gordon Childe, *Man Makes Himself* (New York: Mentor Books, 1951); Gerhard Lenski, *Human Societies* (New York: McGraw-Hill Book Co., 1970); and John Buettner-Janusch, *Origins of Man* (New York: John Wiley & Sons, Inc., 1966). An important source for comparative societal data is the "Ethnographic Atlas" published in each issue of the *Journal of Ethnology*.
[25] See "Energy and the Evolution of Culture" in Leslie White's, *The Science of Culture* (New York: Grove Press, 1949).

veloped, particularly bronze and small copper hand tools related to plant cultivation and processing; following this, iron smelting was discovered, and iron tools such as the plow were developed, leading to mature agriculture and the agrarian type society.

The evolution of technology from stone and bone tools to more advanced forms of energy and tools used to harness and exploit the energy is interesting and important in and of itself. The sociologist, on the other hand, is concerned with explaining and understanding social behavior and social adaptation under particular or specified conditions of adaptation. We are now at a point where we can give the reader the overall perspective of the book by analyzing in detail the implications of Table 1–1 for social adaptation.

Universal Problems of Human Social Adaptation

In the broadest sense, every society, if it is to continue, must replace its members and *meet the needs of its population.* Membership *replacement* and *support of the population* are the two areas of adaptation that must necessarily be solved if a human population is to survive or grow.

The *social systems* that constitute the structure of a human society are the organizational means for implementing the above two adaptive functions. The general and special adaptive problems solved by various social systems that constitute society will be discussed throughout the remainder of the book. In other words, human *society* is a system of adaptation, and the study of how it evolves and how it functions is perhaps the most consistently given definition of *sociology* from its beginnings to the present. In the most general sense, the evolution and functioning of human society are regulated by four interrelated societal subsystems. These are systems of **knowledge,** systems of **technology,** systems of **organization,** and systems of **ideology or values.**

A general illustration of the use of these concepts in sociology will now be given, utilizing the two variables of population size and form-of-subsistence organization shown in Table 1–1 and relating changes in these to changes in the four analytical concepts of knowledge, technology, organization, and ideology.

Given the fact that man in hunting and gathering societies did not have an alphabet and a system of writing, then his technology would necessarily be very primitive. This, of course, is still the case in the few hunting and gathering societies that remain and their subsistence knowledge centers around edible fruits, plants, and roots, and strategies for hunting wild game. The division of labor is very simple and based primarily on sex and age differences. There is no class system (though a very rudimentary stratification system is present), and social organization tends to be based on kinship, revolving around the nuclear and extended families. Since there was a minimal division of labor and no formal status system, power was determined by personal characteristics; that is, it was based on superior performance of activities centering around hunting and knowledge of hunting. Moreover, there was always a shortage of food, and when available, it spoiled quickly; anyone who had been extremely fortunate and secured a good catch always shared it with others in the clan. This sharing was an important source of social insurance.

Internal strife such as murder, theft, and other forms of crime against persons and property were probably very rare. If we understand the environment of Paleolithic or Stone-Age hunting and gathering man, the reasons for the lack of such crimes are not difficult to find—they are found in the constraints of the environment of hunting and gathering man and in his social system.

First, he lived in a hostile and niggardly environment, and cooperation was literally necessary for survival. Secondly, everyone knew everyone else, and crimes or deviation were easy to observe and detect. Thirdly, a violator could not leave the clan because to do so meant death by a hostile tribe or by starvation. And fourthly, punishment for a crime was left up to the one who had been mistreated and/or his close relatives, and these were swift, certain, and severe. However, beginning with early horticultural societies and moving to the present, tribal warring and warfare have been rampant.

As food became too scarce in a given area, the clan or tribe moved as a whole to a more bountiful source of supply. As technology advanced, however, his social organization and ideology changed. For example, following the discovery and development of techniques for metallurgy, it became possible to cultivate plants more effectively and to domesticate plants and animals. This in time increased the supply of food and eliminated the necessity for a nomadic form of life.

Later, with the discovery of iron smelting and the development of iron tools and weapons, horticulture, and then agriculture were developed. This generated an enormous amount of sociocultural change. Archaeologists chart the beginnings of civilization with the development of agriculture. The reasons are that agriculture enabled ancient man to produce not just enough food, but a surplus as well. This meant that for the first time a new division of labor or increased social differentiation beyond sex and age could take place. For example, with a surplus, consumer goods could be exchanged for producer goods, that is, for tools or services. Once this exchange process developed, it was easy for it to multiply to the vast system of production and distribution associated with a modern industrial society, assuming the continued parallel expansion of the necessary energy supply.

   With the increase in the division of labor and the increase in the population, new problems of control of the population arose. The division of labor was accompanied by differentiation of skills and changing attitudes toward social roles among the members of the population. For example, a merchant and artisan class arose, a religious priesthood developed, as did a governing class with a central ruler, or king. Accompanying the increased division of labor, social classes arose and social stratification became more marked.

As the urban populations grew, specialization or division of labor resulted in a division of classes. The split between the classes gradually widened and differences in their life styles, values, and morals became apparent— often expressed by disdain.
("Morning" by William Hogarth. Courtesy Museum of Fine Arts, Boston.)

The economy of production and marketing dictated a concentration of populations, where those persons engaged in the reciprocating processes of producing and exchanging goods could function more efficiently. Herein were the beginnings of urban society. Accordingly, agricultural production with its surpluses stimulated the rise of the cities and the subsequent emerging of greater sophistication of ideas, manners, and skills of the urban people, and a resulting condescension and disdain by the urban population (small as it was) of the rural population. As the development of the cities has proceeded from antiquity to the present, the proportion of the total population that is rural has decreased, while the urban proportion has increased through migration.

Problems of tax collection and protection of the cities against external aggressors prompted the ruler to create a specialized military force. The availability of an economic surplus made this possible. In time, this enabled the Chinese, Egyptian, and Mesopotamian rulers to unite their peoples under one ruler and form an empire. Not only were these armies useful for internal defense and control, but they came to be useful forces for increasing the wealth and goods of a society by conquest. In other words, economic expansion by foreign conquest originated with the ancient mideast and eastern civilizations that arose through the evolution of agrarian societies.

With the emergence of cities in agrarian societies, new social classes formed out of the earlier social differentiation resulting from the increased division of labor. These systems created sharp cleavages between the ruling class and the merchant and artisan class, with the peasants separated from both of the former; in other words, *systems* of social stratification were formed. These systems increased competition and conflict within society and therefore increased the pressure for altering and recombining elements of the social structure. Hence, such systems were prime factors in sociocultural evolution. This point will be discussed further in the section "Processes of Human Adaptation: A Conceptualization."

As would be expected with population growth, class differentiation, and expansion by conquest, the dependence of the old ruling organization upon relatives, as in the hunting and gathering societies and horticultural societies, would become inadequate. Consequently, formal systems of state organization were developed and the government became populated by "trained" bureaucrats. In respect to conquered territories, local rulers were co-opted and placed in charge of the conquered group as a state subdivision. This was a typical form of government employed by Rome with respect to conquered territories.

It is not our purpose in this chapter to develop and apply formal theories to explain social behavior. Rather, we are concerned with illuminating some of the central problems of sociology and describing some social changes that have occurred in human history. Towards these ends, we have employed certain concepts that will be used in a more elaborate way in subsequent chapters to describe and explain sociocultural developments, when explanation is possible.

Motivating Courses of Action

One final point should be noted relative to the illustration involving the application of the concepts of knowledge, technology, organization, and ideology to help explain sociocultural change and adaptation. We have contended that new knowledge leads to new technology, which in turn affects the social organization of the society, but we have not connected this with ideology. Clarification of this is now necessary. We are defining *knowledge* as composed of information, ideas, concepts, and theories, and distinguishing this from the *implementation* of these, which we have called *technology*. New knowledge may or may not be implemented or transformed into technology. This is itself an interesting sociological problem. What determines whether given types of knowledge are implemented? Irrespective of the answer to this question, it is true that before certain types of technology are possible, the basic knowledge underlying it must first exist. This is especially true of modern technology, though early man's technology was more related to his everyday practical problems. Once a given type of technology and social organization are chosen, how are these justified in the face of opposition and criticism? One means of justification is to appeal through ideology or belief systems.

Until quite recently, man's technology has been designed to control the physical world and bend it to his needs for production. In other words, technology has been geared to production, and organization has centered around the factory system and related problems of administration and political control in the larger society. Ideology or the belief systems have served to motivate man and to obtain the support of the consumer, production, and governmental systems. For example, the ideology of sharing in the hunting and gathering society had to give way to a money economy in the agrarian systems; that is, the ideology justifies and musters support for chosen courses of action.

The technology of modern advanced industrial societies has become so complex, and the human and industrial waste resulting from the system has become so immense and in some cases so toxic, that technology itself has become a problem of adaptation. Accordingly, the populations in such societies have become concerned with the problem of environmental pollution resulting from modern technology. This implies that the older attitudes and values toward technology are giving way to new ones concerned with regulating technology itself as a means for controlling new adaptive problems. In other words, we have come full circle in our description of sociocultural evolution. That is to say, a multiple feedback or interaction type of relationship between knowledge, technology, organization, and ideology, with technology playing the most determinant role, appears to be the central process involved in shaping sociocultural evolution from Paleolithic man to industrial man. However, post-industrial man is faced with adaptive problems generated by his own adaptive technology and is forced to consider developing a rational system of feedback controls on aspects of his technology.[26]

PROCESSES OF HUMAN ADAPTATION: A CONCEPTUALIZATION

Many animals are marvelously adapted to their environment by having physical characteristics that enable them to meet their needs effectively. Darwin asked in 1859, "Can a more striking instance of adaptation be given than that of a woodpecker for climbing trees and for seizing insects in the chinks of the bark?"[27]

Man's body is not characterized by its specialized forms for adapting. Rather, man is noted for his possession of a highly generalized brain by means of which he depends upon learning as his principal method for adaptation. If the results of the learning were not organized and stored in *symbolic* form as *culture*, then man's *cumulative* growth in adaptive capacity would be no greater than that of an intelligent great ape.

The storing of the results of experience in symbolic form enables each generation of mankind to begin with the heritage of the preceding generations. This not only prevents the repetition of some errors of the past, but it permits experimentation, change, and future cumulative growth.

Man would never have evolved in his adaptive capacity beyond that of an agrarian society without the development of new sources of energy beyond manpower and animal power. These

[26] We realize, of course, that systems of belief or ideology have to some extent always affected man's search for knowledge—even his emphasis on given kinds of technology, though this has not been the predominant *direction* of the influence. The point is that the degree of *interaction or joint effects* of technology and ideology have tended to increase in postindustrial society. The *problems of adaptation* have always determined a society's perspective toward knowledge and technology; therefore, it would follow that when technology itself generates problems of adaptation that new technology would be produced to regulate the undesired side effects of the old technology.

[27] Charles Darwin, *On the Origin of the Species by Means of Natural Selection* (1859), Chap. 6, cited from Verne Grant, *The Origins of Adaptations* (New York: Columbia University Press, 1963), pp. 93–95.

sources of energy were steam power and fossil-fuel power. This points to the enormous importance of increased knowledge, both theoretical and technological or practical, as a process in man's adaptation. It is true, as Leslie White indicates, that energy without tools to consume and direct it is useless to man, but a strong case can and has been made for viewing the new sources of energy over which man has gained control as stages of real evolutionary progress in man's sociocultural world. Mutation as a source of biological evolutionary variability is analogous to the combined role of *discovery and invention* in sociocultural evolution. We shall therefore speak of discovery and invention as the source of new systems of technology that increase the adaptive capacity of a *society*. This, of course, includes new educational and health technology, which improves the adaptive capacity of *individuals* to use the systems of technology.

Just as genetic recombination in biology ensures the extracting of maximum variability from gene mutation, a functionally similar social process is performed by *social movements*, which achieve reallocation of power and resources and by *advertising and diffusion* of new practices to the entire population through communication and influence processes.

It must be remembered that for change to take place, either biologically or sociologically, *continuity* of structure must also be achieved for change to have a stable environment and structure in which to take root. In life, this continuity is controlled by meiosis and "genetic copying," and in the human social world it is approximately achieved by stability of *institutional structures* and through *educational* and *socialization* "copying."

In biological evolution or variability, there is continuity, mutation, and extinction, and in sociocultural evolution, there is continuity, discovery and invention, and extinction. The functioning of the social system maximizes the evolutionary advantage afforded by discovery and invention by transforming knowledge into technology and by rearranging the vested interests inherent in existing forms of social organization and ideology by the pressures and conflicts generated by social movements and social revolutions.

As in the case of biological mutations, not every social or cultural change that occurs is adaptive. Most are maladaptive, or of no positive adaptive value. Natural selection eventually arbitrates the value of a biological mutation and, in the long run, a similar process occurs in social innovation. In regard to social inventions, movements, and revolutions—how is their adaptive value determined? Many, of course, have no significant impact, and some, such as ideologies that foster hate and prejudice, are maladaptive and lethal, and the question remains. The student is invited to develop an answer.

Jeremy Bentham (1748–1832) formed an answer based on the idea of a calculus of felicity of "the greatest happiness of the greatest number." This intellectual or rational formulation does not suggest or imply a mechanism or process for determining such a state. The trouble is that there is no way of determining such a state *before* the fact. The reasons for this are quite clear and simple. To achieve such a state would be to imply that change and evolution had stopped. This is not so either by definition or by fact. There is no such phenomenon as continuous 100 per cent accurate production and transmission of any system, biological or social. It is for this reason that Darwin's notion of natural selection has served biology so well. In other words, evolution is an on-going system, and new conditions determine the natural selection in the future. So it is with the social system. In other words, the anvil of pragmatic test and guidance by prior experimentation is often the best arbitrator of change available.

SOME IMPLICATIONS OF THE FOREGOING SOCIOCULTURAL PERSPECTIVE FOR IMPROVED BIOLOGICAL ADAPTATION

If we look again at Table 1–1 and note the simple technology and division of labor and the very small population associated with a hunting and gathering society, certain implications for biological evolution become apparent in light of the discussion in the previous section.

First, it is clear that the potential range of genotypes in a human population of 40 or 50 is much, much less than in a population of 40 or 50 million or greater. Secondly, the more complex the division of labor and the overall societal system, the greater the probable variation in the phenotypic expression of the genotypic range. In other words, a very heterogeneous environment increases phenotypic variability and a homogeneous environment decreases it. We know, therefore, that one way to increase adaptive capacity of a population is to increase the range of genotypic and phenotypic variability. These yield a greater potential for improvement of adaptive selection through social organization and social competition. Individual creativity and innovation are sources for increased social variability and potentially increased social adaptive capacity. Presumably, increased genetic variability, if properly cultivated, leads to increased social variability and potentially increased adaptive capacity. The problem of innovation will be considered in detail in Chapter 17.

It seems to follow, then, that at least historically technological advance results in increased population growth and increased sociocultural complexity to support the population, which in turn, through adaptive selectivity, increases the range of phenotypic variation and hence increases the adaptive potential of the population. All of this, of course, presupposes educational and economic opportunity systems, which enable all members of the population to develop their biological potential. This points to the basic importance of the cultural systems as means for adaptation—a problem to be discussed in Chapter 2.

Summary

The behavior of each species of animal life is determined, to a significant extent, by its particular species characteristics. This chapter has emphasized the evolutionary uniqueness of man as necessary to understanding man's social behavior and social adaptation. For example, the evolution and modification of behavior of all other species of social animals is explicable by the laws of genetics or biological evolution. In man, the same evolutionary laws are a part of the explanation of man's behavior evolution, but not all. For example, man's biological evolution has produced an organism with a neurological and anatomical structure capable of true speech, and therefore the development of language. This in turn permitted the development of culture, that is, the relative standardizing of learned behavior patterns across a span of generations, and hence the accumulation and improvement of these through experience.

Changes in these culture patterns result from the social interaction of individuals. These changes in turn affect man's natural selection, and in time his genetic drift and biological evolution.

It follows, then, that as man learns to direct and influence cultural and social change, he has to that extent learned to control his evolution. The principal means by which this second source of evolution is determined are *knowledge, technology, organization,* and *ideology or values.* Consequently, the psychological and social similarities of contemporary man can be analyzed by a comparative analysis of his systems of social organization, and finally, his systems of values. To the extent that accurate information on these systems is available from man's past, a reasonably accurate picture of his past behavior can be retrospectively inferred.

Exercises

1. Discuss the evidence for the proposition that the biological theory of evolution, when properly modified, includes human behavior and culture.
2. Compare and contrast instinctually and culturally controlled social behavior.

3. Distinguish and illustrate organic adaptation and group adaptation. Is it difficult to demonstrate genuine cases of group adaptation? Why?

4. Distinguish biological evolution from cultural evolution.

5. What is the relationship of biological adaptation to genetic variability?

6. Distinguish a population of adapted individuals from an adapted population.

7. Define the term human society and distinguish it from other animal societies.

8. Compare and contrast biological and cultural adaptation.

9. Discuss the role of technology in cultural evolution.

10. Under what conditions can social conflict and social movements affect cultural evolution? Illustrate.

11. Compare the social organization of different societies with (a) very similar technologies and then (b) societies with different technologies.

12. Discuss the role of ideology in social and cultural change.

Selected Bibliography

Alland, Alexander, Jr. *The Human Imperative*. New York: Columbia University Press, 1972.

Alland, Alexander, Jr. *Human Diversity*. New York: Columbia University Press, 1971.

Buettner-Janusch, John. *Origins of Man*. New York: John Wiley & Sons, Inc., 1966.

Clark, Grahame, and Stuart Piggott. *Prehistoric Societies*. New York: Knopf, 1965.

Dobzhansky, Theodosius. *Mankind Evolving*. New Haven: Yale University Press, 1962.

Harrison, G. A., et al. *Human Biology*. New York: Oxford University Press, 1964.

Howells, William. *Mankind in the Making*. New York: Doubleday & Co., 1959.

McGill, Thomas E. *Readings in Animal Behavior*. New York: Holt, Rinehart & Winston, 1965.

Morris, Desmond. *The Human Zoo*. New York: McGraw-Hill, 1969.

Roe, Anne, and George G. Simpson (eds.). *Behavior and Evolution*. New Haven: Yale University Press, 1958.

Washburn, S. L. *Classification and Human Evolution*. Chicago: Aldine Publishing Co., 1963.

Washburn, S. L., and Phyllis C. Jay (eds.). *Perspectives on Human Evolution*. New York: Holt, Rinehart & Winston, 1968.

2

Biological and Cultural Contexts of Human Adaptation

It should be clear from the preceding chapter that the unit of biological *evolutionary* change is not the individual but the population gene pool, and the mechanisms of continuity and change are genetic processes. It is similarly true that an innovation or change in the behavior of an individual does not have any significant effect on the human social system unless it diffuses and becomes an integrated part of the behavior of the population of the society.

In this chapter, we deal with the interdependence of man's development as a species and the development of his systems of adaptation, both behavioral and cultural. The late Clyde Kluckhohn[1] wrote that man is in some respects like *all* other men, and in some respects like *some* other men, and in some respects like *no* other man. The first part of the characterization refers, of course, to the species or biological likenesses that all human beings share. The second part refers to man's social and cultural similarities, and the third to each person's unique personality differences.

---

[1] Clyde Kluckhohn and Henry A. Murray, "Personality Formation: The Determinants," in Clyde Kluckhohn and Henry A. Murray (eds.), *Personality in Nature Society, and Culture* (New York: Alfred A. Knopf, 1949), p. 35.

All three of these statements are true, and a similar characterization can be made about man and other members of the animal kingdom. For example, the genetic material DNA, which primarily determines human heredity, is chemically the same in *all* organisms. Biological classification of animal and plant form is not as precise as desirable, but it will suffice to illustrate the structural and functional similarities implied in the statement, "Man is like some other animals." The biological unit of classification for both plants and animals is the **species.** This is an imprecise concept, but it roughly means a population of individuals, alike in structural and functional characteristics, which breed only with each other and have a common ancestry. Closely related species are grouped together in the next higher unit of classification, the **genus** (plural, *genera*).

Just as several species may be classified together to form a genus, a number of related genera make up a **family,** and families are grouped into **orders,** orders into **classes,** and classes into **phyla.** Man is a member of the phylum *Chordata,* subphylum *Vertebrata,* class *Mammalia,* subclass *Eutheria* (mammals that have a placenta for nourishment of the developing embryo as contrasted with a marsupial mammal, for example), order *Primates,* family *Hominidae,* genus *Homo,* and species *sapiens.* We may now illustrate our second point, namely, that man is like some other animals in respect to some characteristics. For example, the primate order is composed of lemurs, monkeys, apes, and man. These mammals have highly developed brains and eyes, nails instead of claws, opposable great toes or thumbs, and binocular vision. Finally, in a biological sense, man is like *no* other animal; that is, he represents the species *sapiens,* and his most distinguishing characteristic is true speech, which provided him with the means for producing his most unique adaptive characteristic, namely, language and culture.

A fuller appreciation of the significance of the above evolutionary similarities and differences of man and the other members of the primate order from the point of view of adaptation requires, at least, a brief survey of what we know about the evolutionary development of man. There is obviously a relationship between a species' evolved systems of adaptation and its biological capacity for these systems. From the point of view of adaptation, man is pliable, but he is not infinitely malleable. The interconnections between man's biology, his culture, and his behavior are so important that if he is to survive for long in the future, this survival will depend upon the degree and quality of his knowledge in these *interrelated* areas. Many efforts today toward understanding man are too fragmented and torn by disciplinary chauvinism, which interferes with the development of knowledge in these interrelated areas.

MAJOR EVOLUTIONARY CHANGES IN MAN

Anatomical and Genetic Changes Related to Man's Adaptation

Not all change is adaptive, nor is all adaptation evolutionary. Behavioral changes can occur, and many do, that have no adaptive results or, at least, trivial adaptive consequences. It is doubtful if the changes in the sizes of men's neckties have any adaptive significance. Likewise, *all* instances of adaptation do not mean evolution. "If a clam is perfectly suited to its mud, its food, and the temperature of the water, then it is the perfect clam (for its clamship, food, and water). Natural selection will operate purely to keep it that way. If, however, there is an avenue leading to a better state, natural selection will begin to push and pull in that direction." [2]

Because there is always genetic variation within a species, a species may respond to change through the shuffling and sorting of genes it already has. Occasionally someone points to the success that cattle breeders and dog breeders have had in planned or artificial selection and suggest the same for man. It should be pointed out that if we attempt to direct evolution and make an error in judgment, then the resulting reduced genetic diversity leaves us with reduced adaptive defense. [3] Evolutionary change is slow, but cultural change that exploits existing genetic diversity could accomplish, in a few years, an increased adaptive capacity that would take thousands of years to accomplish by evolution. This statement should not be interpreted as in any way depreciating genetic engineering, if the capacity for culturally controlled genetic change should become available. Rather it implies that we need to protect adaptive capacity by maintaining its diversity instead of decreasing it through the application of dimly outlined genetic goals. The relationship of systematic genetic variation as opposed to random variation as means for organic evolution is presently not clear. Until these alternatives are clear, it seems best not to tamper with the evolutionary process of man.

Because of the gradual and integrated nature of the evolution of human traits, it is somewhat inappropriate to speak of critical or milestone changes in the evolution of man. The fossil data on man's past are incomplete and the many gaps are filled in by inferences and extrapolations from comparative studies among living species and archaelogical interpretations of human remains. Man's place in geological time is also unclear and incomplete and few will venture to develop such a chart on man. The same is true of man's

[2] William Howells, *Mankind in the Making* (Garden City, N.Y.: Doubleday & Company, Inc., 1959), pp. 23–24.
[3] More will be said about this in Chapter 6, "Socialization and Social Competence."

TABLE 2–1
The Pleistocene period and man's place in it. Durations of each period not drawn to scale.

Geochronology	Stratigraphy — Glacial (Europe)	Stratigraphy — Pluvial (Africa)	Estimated age (years B.C.)	Culture	Tool types	Hominid forms
	Postglacial	Postpluvial		Urban Neolithic Mesolithic		
			10,000	Magdalenian Solutrean Aurignacian	Blade tools	Homo sapiens
Upper Pleistocene	Last (Würm) glacial	Last pluvial	70,000			
				Mousterian	Flake tools	
	Last interglacial	Interpluvial	100,000			
	Penultimate (Riss) glacial	Pluvial (?)	200,000			
	Great interglacial	Interpluvial (?)		Acheulean	Biface and flake tools	Pithecanthropines
Middle Pleistocene			400,000			
	Antepenultimate (Mindel) glacial	Pluvial (?)		Chellean		
			500,000			
	Interglacial	Interpluvial				
	Early (Günz) glacial	Pluvial (?)				
Lower Pleistocene			1,000,000			Australopithecines
	Preglacial (Villafranchian)	Prepluvial		Oldowan	Pebble tools	
			2,000,000			

Source: John Buettner-Ianusch, *Origins of Man* (New York: John Wiley & Sons, Inc., 1965), p. 26.

TABLE 2–2
Time scale for the evolution of primates.

Epoch	Approximate years B.P. (before the present)	Types of primates
Pleistocene	10,000– 2,500,000	*Homo sapiens* *Homo erectus* *Australopithecus*
Pliocene	2,500,000–13,000,000	*Australopithecus* *Ramapithecus* *Oreopithecus*
Miocene	13,000,000–25,000,000	*Kenyapithecus* *Proconsul* *Pliopithecus* *Dryopithecus*
Oligocene	25,000,000–36,000,000	*Propliopithecus* *Parapithecus* *Oligopithecus*
Eocene	26,000,000–58,000,000	Tarsiers Lemurs
Paleocene	58,000,000–68,000,000	Prosimians like tree shrews or lemurs

Source: Victor Barnouw, *An Introduction to Anthropology. Volume 1. Physical Anthropology and Archaeology* (Homewood, Ill.: The Dorsey Press, 1971), p. 96.

cultural past, which is further complicated by the fact that different societies enter different cultural periods at different times, and some phases may be skipped altogether by the processes of contact and diffusion of traits from a more developed society to a less developed one. For example, the Lower Paleolithic period ended in Europe about 150,000 years ago; it ended in eastern and central Africa about 50,000 years ago.[4] Given the fact that we will be referring to various time periods later in the chapter it would be helpful to have a rough summary chart of man's cultural evolution in geological time. This is presented below with, of course, the limitations indicated above. One of the best such charts for the Pleistocene period is provided by Buettner-Janusch and is reproduced in Table 2–1.[5] A more extended set of estimates is given by Barnouw in Table 2–2[6] for the entire primate order.

　　　As man's cultural progress has accumulated through geological and historical time, his neurological, physiological, and

[4] See Sonia Cole, *Prehistory of East Africa* (New York: Mentor Books, 1965).
[5] Table 2–1 is taken from John Buettner-Janusch, *Origins of Man* (New York: John Wiley & Sons, Inc., 1965), p. 26.
[6] Table 2–2 is taken from Victor Barnouw, *An Introduction to Anthropology. Volume 1. Physical Anthropology and Archaeology* (Homewood, Ill.: The Dorsey Press, 1971), p. 96.

behavioral characteristics have concomitantly changed. For example, it is estimated that the average cranial capacity of *Australopithecus* (earliest culture-bearing hominids) man was 625 cc and
that of *Homo sapiens* or modern man is about 1500 cc. This evolution of cranial capacity has occurred over a period of about 1–2
million years, and it has major implications for the evolution of
man's adaptive systems. Man's present average cranial size was
achieved about 100,000 years ago, and there has not been any
discernible change since.

    Australopithecus' ability to speak, given his average cra-
nial capacity, has been a subject of debate, but assuming (and evidence indicates such) that he was a culture-bearing animal, then
speech is a prerequisite.[7] Not enough studies have been made on
human infants, but those that have been made indicate an average
cranial capacity around 600 cc in the first 12 months and a jump to
about 950 cc in two years.[8] By four years, cranial development is
about 80 per cent complete. And, of course, infant speech begins in
the second year of development, but it should not be surmised that
the brain size of the average one and one-half to two year child is
the critical threshold of brain size with respect to the origin of
speech. This threshold is not answerable at the present. In other
words, we must be careful to avoid the error of implying that
"ontogeny recapitulates phylogeny."

    As indicated in Chapter 1, Spuhler listed certain biological
capacities that he considered as prerequisites to the emergence of
culture as a mode of adaptation in man. Thiessen has developed a
more refined progression of the evolution of the adaptive capacity
of man, and because of its usefulness it is reproduced below with
slight modification:

1. Bipedal locomotion.
2. Manipulative abilities.
3. Binocular vision.
4. Carnivorous diet.
5. Tool use.
6. Hunting.
7. Communication.
8. Toolmaking.
9. Increased brain size.

All the above advances are evident characteristics of the earliest
Hominidae form, *Australopithecus.* Later developments include:

[7] C. Loring Brace, *The Stages of Human Evolution* (Englewood Cliffs, N.J.: Prentice–Hall, Inc.,
1967), pp. 60–70.
[8] Mischa Titiev, *The Science of Man,* Rev. ed. (New York: Holt, Rinehart & Winston, 1963),
p. 191.

   10. Refined toolmaking.
   11. Language use.
   12. Increased brain size.

   Thiessen notes that these are simply refinements of functions and structures possessed by earlier forms. Though it is significant that as "brain size increased, the brain also became more specialized; there was a disproportionate increase of the frontal lobes and an asymmetrical development of the temporal areas associated with handedness and speech." Finally, in the most recent characteristics, we find:

   13. Advanced toolmaking.
   14. Elaborate cultural organization.
   15. Further increases in brain size.
   16. Extended periods of childhood and adolescence.[9]

   It can be seen from Table 2–1 above that the period of estimated time involved from the beginning of *Australopithecines* to the beginning of *Homo sapiens* is almost 1½ million years, but the period estimated from the beginning of *Homo sapiens* to the present is approximately 100,000 years. There seems to have been an acceleration of evolutionary change as we move from the beginnings of the *hominid* form to the present. Buettner-Janusch recognizes three different, but related criteria for evolutionary change. "First, evolution may be viewed as the change in genetic composition of a population. Second, evolution is the morphological differentiation exhibited by a set of animals. Third, evolution is the progressive diversification of taxa in a larger taxonomic set. Each of these views implies a different criterion or method for determining the rate at which evolution takes place." [10]
   The criteria used in developing the set of 16 characteristics discussed above were morphological and behavioral. Among the set of 16, there are three characteristics that are uniquely human and fundamental to the understanding of the evolution of man.
   Physical anthropologists are in accord that the single most important anatomical change in man is his *acquisition of upright posture and true bipedal locomotion*. *Australopithecus* is the earliest fossil found with upright posture and true bipedal locomotion. The other anatomical changes of importance are coadapted or integrated with this one. These are the prehensile hand and its freedom to function as a tool to explore in conjunction with finely

---

[9] Delbert D. Thiessen, *Gene Organization and Behavior* (New York: Random House, 1972), pp. 119–120.
[10] John Buettner-Janusch, *Origins of Man* (New York: John Wiley & Sons, Inc., 1966), p. 28.

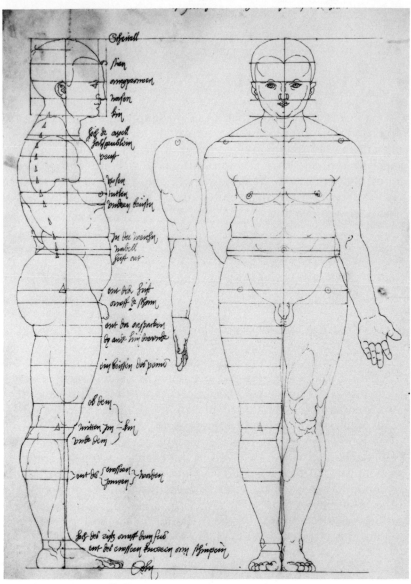

Upright posture and bipedal locomotion separate man as a species from other species.
("Anatomical Studies" by Albrecht Dürer. Courtesy Museum of Fine Arts, Boston.)

coordinated binocular vision and the concomitant expansion of the cerebral cortex. The other two changes are cultural, but could not have developed without the first, namely, the upright posture, bipedal locomotion, and neurological capacity. The two cultural means of adaptation represent an increased attainment of evolutionary capacity within the human species. These two means are *toolmaking and language.* However, the upright posture, prehensile hands, brain/body ratio, and capacity for speech are the anatomical changes that made culture possible.

The making of tools and the use of tools to make tools are essential to the development of material culture.[11] A stone may be used to knock flakes from another stone to make an ax, or a stone may be sharpened into a knife to skin animals and shape the skin into clothing. Very crude but unmistakable stone tools have been found in rock strata containing human fossil remains that were approximately 2 million years old. It is quite likely that man, the toolmaker, is older than this, but it is extremely difficult to authenticate older materials because it is difficult to distinguish rocks that were deliberately manufactured or reshaped by man from those picked up and used in their natural form. Many lower animal forms use natural objects as tools. Chimpanzees and birds may rearrange twigs or straws for use as tools, but this simple behavior is too primitive to be classified as toolmaking.

Man's prehensile hand enabled him to become man the fabricator of tools and implements.
(Courtesy Robert Rapelye, Photography International.)

[11] We are aware of the objections to conceptualizing culture as material and nonmaterial, but some distinction between ideas, behavior, and the tangible products of behavior is necessary to our discussion at this point.

The cumulative growth of tool production by man shows a generally continuous, though slow, progress through prehistory,[12] and a fantastically accelerated growth in historic times. The accelerated rate of growth in man's technology has achieved its presently highest rates of change during the 20th century, although there has been no noticeable or observable change in man's biological capacity. It seems clear, then, that the sweep of technological growth from the Neolithic, or horticultural, revolution (roughly 7000 years ago) to the present era of electronic computers and automation has been an unfolding and extension of the biological capacities of man rather than a development of new biological traits. In other words, this unfolding of increased adaptive capacity was sociocultural in nature rather than genetic.

The march of man's technological progress was slow until the 19th and 20th centuries.
(Photo above, courtesy Robert Rapelye, Photography International; photo below, courtesy Wide World Photos.)

[12] See V. Gordon Childe, *Man Makes Himself* (New York: Mentor Books, 1951).

The increased use of cultural and social modes of adaptation has involved a progressive expansion in the use of natural resources and a concomitant increase in the harnessing of sources of energy, as illustrated in the figure below.[13]

Paleolithic	Mesolithic	Neolithic	Metal Ages
Wild plants	Domesticated dog	Agriculture	Molten metals
Wild animals		Stock raising	Writing
Cold materials		Pottery	Astronomy
		Weaving	Mathematics
			Coinage

While it is true that energy is controlled by technology, improved technology depends upon new or improved basic knowledge. However, basic knowledge is affected by the state of the technology used for obtaining it and by the new problems the new technology raises. Accordingly, knowledge and technology *interact* as do social organization and ideology. Though the relationship between knowledge and technology is more direct, knowledge is also affected by ideology to the extent that beliefs, myths, and values affect what is studied and researched upon in a society. The genetic changes that provided the physical or neurological capacity for the sociocultural adaptation indicated in Figure 2–1 had already occurred hundreds of thousands of years before. In other words, this improved adaptive capacity through cultural evolution utilized *existing* genetic diversity. This is not meant to imply an answer to the controversial issue of whether man's biological evolution has been arrested or is continuing. This question is better left to the biologists. The factual materials presented in this chapter and the implied logic of these data are that biological evolution and cultural evolution in man are both continuing and interrelated. If this is not true, then eventual extinction of the species would be implied. In this respect, it is not heartening to note that most of the species that ever existed are now extinct, although since man adapts primarily by *sociocultural* means, such an observation is perhaps not so devastating in its implications. In any case, it is a basic assumption of sociology, as well as biology, that man's biological limitations impose limitations to the suitability of certain types of environments for survival, and that

[13] Figure is taken from Mischa Titiev, *The Science of Man*, Rev. ed. (New York: Holt, Rinehart & Winston, 1963), p. 374.

natural selection, operating through genetic variability and environmental variability over long periods of time, shapes species evolution. In this respect, the evolution of human technology equips man with a capacity to transcend many of the difficulties and limitations of the natural environment, thus extending his adaptive capacity in a unique way unavailable to any other species.

The underlying biological quality that has made possible this unique process of sociocultural adaptation is the capacity for **true speech** and **language.** Language is unquestionably the single most distinctive and explanatory trait of man. There are two basic factors that underlie the general importance of language to human adaptation and to *knowledge* in particular. The first is the transmission both within and between generations of important information for adaptation. This allows for the accumulation of knowledge across time and for the subsequent evaluation and improvement of the state of the knowledge. In other words, knowledge is symbolically represented by language. This last quality makes language extremely important in the socialization process for the young. The second basic factor is that language is also a means for *constructing* pictures of reality, which in turn become guides for human action, and therefore for all practical purposes represent reality. This includes the representation of scientific constructions of reality, as well as socially constructed systems of meaning in the social world in general. Human institutions are examples of the social construction of systems of meaning, and these are fundamentally possible only through language.

In this ancient Chinese drawing, a solar eclipse is interpreted as a dragon devouring the sun. With the development of language, and particularly the alphabet and the number system, the dependence on knowledge increased, and the improvement of technology progressed.
(Yerkes Observatory Photograph, University of Chicago, Williams Bay, Wisconsin.)

Many laymen and some scientists have confused and obscured the meaning of the word "language" by speaking of the "language of bees and birds," as well as other forms of animal life. In all forms of animal societies, there is some form of communication in the sense that specific signals convey specific information. These signals may be in the form of odors, colors, or sounds. Human language is also a system of communication, but it is much more than this. It has an inherent logical structure and system of *symbols* essential for human socialization. In the words of George Gaylord Simpson, "The difference between animal interjection and human language is the difference between saying 'ouch' and saying 'fire is hot.' "

The origin of language is obscure, controversial, and unknown. Even the most simple cultures existing today have highly complex languages with complicated grammar and large vocabularies. They are, therefore, too remote from earlier language-using human forms to permit significant inferences as to the origin of language. Likewise, the idea of the ontogeny of language, that is, the notion that the acquisition of language by the individual recapitulates the origin of language, is, in the light of modern knowledge, absurd. The child is not uttering primordial language; he is simply learning what is around him. Moreover, the modern child's brain is genetically (through natural selection) quite different from early man's brain, and is hence structured differently for language use. The evidence for this is complex and derives from two archaeological sources. First, the cranial capacity of modern man as we indicated above averages about 1500 cc; by contrast, the cranial capacity of the hominids that lived during the Lower Paleolithic (that is, prior to 500,000 years ago) averaged just over 500 cc. Second, man made rapid cultural progress during the Middle and Upper Paleolithic periods and such extremely slow progress during the Lower Paleolithic period that some experts have hypothesized that Lower Paleolithic man had only a rudimentary speech and language capacity. This appears reasonable since speech and language are controlled by the left frontal cortex, and expansion of this part of the brain corresponded to the later Paleolithic periods. In other words, the production of speech does not depend on the sound apparatus, but on the central nervous system. The parrot and the Mynah bird can be trained to utter simple words clearly, but they do not understand the meaning of any of them.

Noam Chomsky argues that the structure of the human brain contributes significantly to the structure of and the learning of language. He offers as evidence two arguments: (1) the universality of language forms from Australian Bush to modern languages and (2) the fact that children easily learn the structure of language without being taught.

It is quite reasonable on phylogenetic evidence to assume that the human brain determines man's capacity and ability for language, but Chomsky's arguments are hardly sufficient to explain man's language behavior. The fact that children learn the structure of language without being taught is to be expected. They could hardly do otherwise, given their dependence on it and its presence in adult expression. Regarding the first point on universality of language forms, this is true only in a very loose sense. Some languages make great use of all three tenses, and a few use only two tenses.[14] English language and Indo-European language, in general, place great emphasis on time. Much of the mathematics in physics is based on time as an element in its equations. The Hopi have more concern for validity and the Navaho emphasize types of activity, and both have minimal development of the tenses.[15] Therefore, the structure of language varies, but there are still many universals. For example, time only has a small place among the Hopi—not a nonexistent place.

Chomsky contends that linguistic universals are probably the results of innate mental endowment rather than the result of learning.[16] B. F. Skinner, on the other hand, contends that the brain is blank in this regard, and that while man and man alone has the capacity for language, its origin is through learning.[17, 18] At this time, it is sufficient to refer to these divergent views on speech and language. We will compare them in some detail in Chapter 3.

Earlier, Benjamin Whorf[19] formulated a relativistic view of first language acquisition, that is to say, that one's view of the world is relative to the structure and content of his language descriptions of that world. Whorf's hypothesis has been succinctly stated as follows[20]:

The commonly held belief that the cognitive processes of all human beings possess a common logical structure which operates prior to and independently of communication through language is erroneous. It is Whorf's view that the linguistic

[14] Clyde Kluckhohn and D. Leighton, "The Navaho," *The Tongue of the People* (Cambridge, Mass.: Harvard University Press, 1951).

[15] Clyde Kluckhohn and D. Leighton, *ibid.*

[16] N. Chomsky, "Language and the Mind," *Psychol. Today*, (1968), p. 68.

[17] B. F. Skinner, *Verbal Behavior—Language* (New York: Appleton–Century–Crofts, 1957).

[18] A review of the issues separating the innate versus experimental views on language learning is given in a review by Roger Brown, "In the Beginning Was the Grammar" [Review of F. Smith and G. A. Miller, eds., *The Genesis of Language: A Psycholinguistic Approach* (Cambridge, Mass.: MIT Press, 1966)], *Contemporary Psychol.* 13, No. 2 (1968), pp. 49–51.

[19] B. L. Whorf, *Language, Thought and Reality, Selected Writings of B. L. Whorf*, John Carroll (ed.) (New York: John Wiley and Sons, Inc., 1956).

[20] F. Fearing, "An Examination of the Conceptions of Benjamin Whorf in the Light of Theories of Perception and Cognition," *American Anthropologist Memoir No. 79*, 56, 6, part 2 (Dec. 1954), p. 47 (Menasha, Wisc.: American Anthropological Association). Also, published in H. Hoijer, *Language in Culture* (Chicago: University of Chicago Press, 1954).

patterns themselves determine what the individual perceives in this world and how he thinks about it. Since these patterns vary widely, the modes of thinking and perceiving in groups utilizing different linguistic systems will result in basically different world views.

Thus we are introduced to the idea that all qualified observers are not led by the same physical evidence to the same conclusions about reality. In fact, the picture of reality formulated is itself somewhat determined by the linguistic background of the conceptualizer, as illustrated below[21]:

The Indo-European languages have a structure based on substantives and actions (nouns and verbs). They draw an unreal distinction between what a thing is and what it does, and compound this confusion by separating its qualities from the thing itself—as if heaviness had some separate existence apart from the class of heavy objects.

Anderson goes on to point out that Western physicists were led to postulate ether as the substance of space, and that there was no logical reason for this. Since there was no logical reason, there must have been a psychological one, and Anderson suggests that since nouns in the Indo-European languages refer to substantives, then the concept of space must refer to a substance. The idea of relativity of space and the self-contradictory character of "absolute space" did not fully develop until Poincaré, and more precisely, until Einstein. Anderson postulates that the slowness in the grasping of the modern concept of space was probably because the structure of Western language made it difficult to understand.

In the late 1920's and early 1930's, George Herbert Mead, a philosopher and social psychologist at the University of Chicago, formulated a new principle of the development of language and mind.[22] Mead conceived language as the product of brains in *interaction* rather than simply the product of brain action, and argued that the structure of language was conditioned by the larger context of the culture and the structure of experience of the members of society encountering reality. In other words, language is formalized speech. Mead's conception is well illustrated by one of Professor Einstein's famous analogies illustrating the connection between general relativity and geometry.[23]

[21] Poul Anderson, "How Social is Science?" *The Saturday Review* (27 April 1957), pp. 10–11. See also, N. Hanson, *Patterns of Discovery* (Cambridge, Mass.: The Harvard University Press, 1958).
[22] George H. Mead, *Mind, Self and Society* (Chicago: The University of Chicago Press, 1934); and *The Philosophy of the Act* (Chicago: The University of Chicago Press, 1938).
[23] Albert Einstein and L. Infeld, *The Evolution of Physics* (New York: Simon and Schuster, 1938), pp. 236–238.

Let us begin with the description of a world in which only two-dimensional and not, as in ours, three-dimensional creatures live. The movies have accustomed us to two-dimensional creatures acting on a two-dimensional screen. Now let us imagine that these shadow figures, that is, the actors on the screen, really do exist, that they have the power of thought, that they can create their own science, that for them a two-dimensional screen stands for geometrical space. These creatures are unable to imagine, in a concrete way, a three-dimensional space just as we are unable to imagine a world of four dimensions. They can deflect a straight line; they know what a circle is, but they are unable to construct a sphere, because this would mean forsaking their two-dimensional screen. We are in a similar position. We are able to deflect our curve lines and surfaces, but we can scarcely picture a deflected and curved four-dimensional space.

By living, thinking, and experimenting, our shadow figures could eventually master the knowledge of the two-dimensional Euclidean geometry. Thus, they could prove, for example, that the sum of the angles in a triangle is 180 degrees. They could construct two circles with a common center, one very small, the other large. They could find that the ratio of the circumference of two such circles is equal to the ratio of their radii, a result again characteristic of Euclidean geometry. If the screen were infinitely great, these shadow beings would find that once having started a journey straight ahead, they would never return to their point of departure.

Let us now imagine these two-dimensional creatures living in changed conditions. Let us imagine that someone from the outside, the "third dimension," transfers them from the screen to the surface of a sphere with a very great radius. If the shadows are very small in relation to the whole surface, if they have no means of distant communication and cannot move very far, then they will not be aware of any change. The sum of angles in small triangles still amounts 180 degrees. Two small circles with a common center still show that the ratio of their radii and circumferences are equal. A journey along a straight line never leads them back to the starting point. But let these shadow beings, in the course of time, develop their theoretical and technical knowledge. Let them find means of communications which will enable them to cover large distances swiftly. They will then find that starting on a journey straight ahead, they ultimately return to their point of departure. "Straight ahead" means along the great circle of the sphere. They will also find that the ratio of two circles with a common center is not equal to the ratio of the radii, if one of the radii is small and the other is great.

If our two-dimensional creatures are conservative, if they have learned the Euclidean geometry for generations past when they could not travel far and when this geometry fitted the facts observed, they will certainly make every possible effort to hold onto it, despite the evidence of their measurements. They could try to make physics bear the burden of these discrepancies. They could seek some physical reasons, say temperature differences, deforming the lines and causing deviations from Euclidean geometry. But sooner or later, they must find out that there is a much more logical and convincing way of describing these occurrences. They will eventually understand that their world is a finite one, with different geometrical principles from those they learned. They will understand that in spite of their inability to imagine it, their world is the three-dimensional surface of a sphere. They will soon learn new principles of geometry, which, though differing from the Euclidean, can nevertheless be formulated in an equally consistent and logical way for their two-dimensional world. For the new generation brought up with a knowledge of the geometry of the sphere, the old Euclidean geometry will seem more complicated and artificial since it does not fit the facts observed.

The foregoing illustrates beautifully the relationship of language to human interaction and to experience and the evolution of language, concepts, and thinking as experience changes. As the new language evolves, it becomes an important means for linguistically structuring thought for the generations to come, and thus to an extent enabling them to avoid the misconceptions of the past. Thus language structures thought and experience, and new thought and experience modify language.

Indo-European languages have parts of speech, and a sentence is essentially a combination of these parts according to the rules of grammar. Thus, in Western thought, the attribution of properties or characteristics to entities or classes of events and, in turn, the separation of these qualities from the "thing" or entity itself is common, though often confusing. Thus, while language liberates and extends human perception and conception, it also binds each through strong beliefs and habituation. Cognition and sensation are also structured and limited to an extent for all organisms by virtue of the biological organization of the organism as well as the psychological limitations of strong habits. Man is also subject to his biological limitations. For example, he has very crude thermal senses as compared to a snake or tick.[24]

Just as there is a biological relativity of behavior among different animals on the phylogenetic scale, there is a cultural relativity of categories of stimuli and experiences among populations of humans of different cultures. We have already emphasized the dependence of our perceptual world on language; it is also dependent upon cultural themes, values, and ideologies. Hunting societies have a rich vocabulary regarding animals and many cultural themes concerning the place of animals in their life. Industrial societies do not place a similar cultural emphasis on animals, but rather on the products of their industrial society. The experiencing of time varies with the cultural values placed on time in a society. Imagine the necessity for a time punch clock in a hunting or horticultural type of society; yet, in an industrial society, such is essential. In Newtonian physics time flows uniformly; however, in man it is not uniformly experienced, either physiologically or culturally.

Environmental Variation and Evolution

The genotypes of an animal population determine the physiological states and structure of the organisms that make up the species, and the phenotypes are the characteristics of the organisms resulting from the effects of environmental natural selection. Adaptation to an environment is achieved by correlating the behavior or functions of the organism with the conditions, demands, or changes in the environment; therefore, adaptation must occur through phenotypic

[24] For a detailed discussion, see L. von Bertalanffy, *General System Theory* (New York: George Braziller, 1968), pp. 227–232, for his discussion of Yexkiill's concepts of psychophysical organization.

units within the organism. From this it would follow, as Harrison and Weiner have pointed out in respect to a given species, that "since the environment of organisms operating through natural selection determines the phenotype, one would expect forms with the same ecology to become convergent or evolve in parallel without respect to their ancestry." [25]

It would seem that when an evolutionary adaptation that is a general improvement emerges, that is, when a character develops that facilitates survival in many different environments rather than a particular environment, a rapid expansion of the population of the species would result. Such seems to be the case with man in the development of speech and language traits. Through these traits, cultural adaptation became possible, which gave men an unparal-

Language is far more than a means of communication among men. It is a means for thought, memory, self-reflection, and problem-solving.
(Courtesy Robert Rapelye, Photography International.)

[25] G. A. Harrison and J. S. Weiner, "Some Considerations in the Formulation of Theories of Human Phylogeny," in *Classification and Human Evolution,* Sherwood L. Washburn (ed.) (Chicago: Aldine Publishing Co., 1963).

leled source of control over his environment. Language is far more than a means of communication in man. It is a means for thought, memory, self-reflection, and problem-solving activities.

"The common factors that dominated human evolution and produced *Homo sapiens* were preagricultural," [26] says Washburn. The genus *Homo* has existed at least for 600,000 years, and agriculture has been important only during the last few thousand years. Washburn estimates that less than 1 per cent of human existence has been dominated by agriculture. Given the rapidity of man's social development following the development of agriculture as contrasted with the extreme slowness of his development over the preagricultural period, it is important to contrast what little is known about early man biologically with that known about his present-day counterpart. It is assumed that biological progress as well as technological progress was made during this period.

The archaeological evidence of the existence of large numbers of large animals in sites with man-made tools indicates that man as a hunter had a very considerable skill. This skill did not derive from physical strength, but from the use of hand tools and social cooperation. The estimated statures of fossil men fall between 5 ft 2 in. and 5 ft. 10 in.

Recent evidence from primatologists indicates considerable hunting behavior on the part of the great apes. They are handicapped in comparison to early man, whose true upright posture, efficient opposable thumb, and handedness gave him considerable skill in the use of weapons. For example, the bow and arrow permitted the hunter an accuracy by eye sighting and an increased missile range that were formidable. These anatomical skills, in conjunction with tools and weapons technology and the patterns of male cooperation in hunting, made all other animals, irrespective of size, subject to capture by man. This cooperation of man in hunting and food gathering was undoubtedly extended through experience and necessity to other areas of social life, such as caring for the sick and injured, protection, and toolmaking. Such patterns would be expected to build further and more elaborate social bonds through increased human groupings, and thus permit the species to occupy almost every environment in the world, and even to explore environments in outer space as in the present.

The earliest major expansion and proliferation of human social organization and population growth occurred in what is roughly called the Upper Paleolithic and the Mesolithic, or approximately 10,000–15,000 years before agriculture. Progress during this period included, as archaeological records show, the bow and

[26] S. L. Washburn and C. S. Lancaster, "The Evolution of Hunting," in *Perspectives on Human Evolution,* S. L. Washburn and Phyllis C. Jay (eds.) (New York: Holt, Rinehart & Winston, 1968, p. 214.

arrow, grinding stones, domesticated animals (particularly the dog), and boats.

Fossil remains of man found in sites with manmade tools reveal a strong natural selection for greater skill in tool manufacture. The more efficient and symmetrical tools are associated with fossil remains of the larger-brained men. For example, the bones of small-brained men (*Australopithecus*) are never found with finely developed, balanced, and symmetrical tools.[27] Symmetry of tools or weapons is important in enabling accuracy and speed. Irregularities on a tool produce problems of balance and lead to deviations in the path or flight of the tool or weapon.

The natural selection and rapid growth of the larger-brained Paleolithic man's powers for making and using symbols led to the expansion of technology, an increased survival rate of man, and the eventual development of urban societies with their sharply contrasted differences between preagricultural and agrarian societies. Where there is little division of labor, all men learn the same roles and activities. When the population is large, the variations in abilities, skills, and motivation are greater than in small populations; there is a greater chance of innovation and a greater division of labor, and hence greater social differentiation and organization.

CULTURE AS ADAPTATION

At least from the Upper Paleolithic Era to the present, improvements in human adaptation have been clearly more dependent upon cultural and social rather than biological change. Moreover, the rate of change in patterns of adaptation has increased at an exponential rate, and so has the population growth of man. Man formerly lived in small groups and bands of primitive hunters estimated in size from 20 to 60, with a density of 5–10 square miles per person. As a result of the growth of technology and social organization, he now lives in urban populations with a density, in some cases, of a quarter of a million per square mile. This has profound implications, both for human adaptation and maladaptation.

We have argued earlier that the very long period of time involved in the evolution of man in the Pleistocene period (roughly 2 million to 10,000 years ago) resulted in the development of a hominid whose biological traits, drives, emotions, and social organization correlated well with the environmental and ecological demands of that era. Geologists have little doubt that the environment of early man was unstable on a worldwide basis during the Pleistocene period. There were numerous alternating glacial and warmer periods, resulting in significant rising and lowering of the ocean levels. In addition, the evolutionary changes that trans-

[27] S. L. Washburn and C. S. Lancaster, *ibid.*, p. 221.

formed the early hominids into modern man occurred within a relatively brief period—relatively brief in the sense of geological time. If the environmental conditions were quite unstable and the evolutionary selection in the hominids occurred rapidly, then only those forms able to adapt to rapidly changing conditions would be likely to survive. Other things being equal, those hominids with the greater capacity for symbol using would have a superior technology and hence a greater capacity for survival. It was indicated above in the section "Environmental Variation and Evolution" that no symmetrical tools have been found among the fossil remains of Australopithecines (small-brained apelike man).

Modern man's climatic environment has been more stable (last 30,000 years), but during the last 5000 years his social and cultural environments have been rapidly changing and at an increasing rate of change. Concomitant with this has been an accumulation of human waste products, both organic and inorganic, that has reached a dangerous volume for our large population. The average amount of waste per person per day in an industrial society today is estimated at 11 pounds. Some of these products, particularly certain types of chemical pesticides, detergents, and exhaust emissions, are pollutants to the soil, water, and air, respectively. These create problems of physiological adaptation. There are also heavy concentrations of behavioral, emotional, and mental contaminants in modern societies. Some of these are the homicides, robberies, burglaries, rapes, economic exploitation, deliberate deceit, constant exposures to noise, garbage, and litter that occur each day and form part of our total environment. Such constant and widespread exposure is likely to dull the public's sensitivities to a state of acceptance of these conditions as normal.

Is it too much to hypothesize a correlation between the high rates of mental disorder, crimes against persons, and the callous indifference to humanity so often observed in the large urban areas today with the high density of population per square mile, and the highly impersonal and inadequately integrated or regulated urban social structures? This is a thesis of Desmond Morris in his book *The Human Zoo*. It is also a logical implication of the discussion in this section.

Let us further extend this argument by noting some connections between behavior, social structure, and culture with respect to adaptation in man. We can approach this problem by identifying some of the factors that, if they vary, will produce different effects on, or consequences for, human adaptation. One such factor or source of variant consequences is the climate. Another is the abundance or scarcity of natural resources, including soil fertility, in man's geographic environment. These combine with climate to facilitate or hinder adaptation. Another set of consequences derives

A society's level of technological development determines its capacity for supporting a dense or a sparse population.
(Courtesy Wide World Photos.)

from the level of development of the society's culture, particularly of its technology. If the culture, for example, does not contain adequate theories of health and disease control, then the population must rely entirely upon natural immunity to cope with disease. Finally, human behavior itself constitutes the most direct source of consequences for each of us. Many of the things people do (many of their actions) have direct and indirect consequences, not only for those who act, but for many others as well. Because social behavior has potentially harmful effects as well as positive effects, it has to be controlled or regulated for the common good of the members of a society. In other words, attitudes and values are products of social interaction that emerge out of the perceived consequences or potential consequences of certain forms of social behavior. From the point of view of behavioral development, attitudes and values are by-products of behavior in a social system. Once given attitudes and values become a patterned way of feeling among adults, then the expression of these in adult behavior influences the development of similar attitudes and values in the children.

One of the profound differences between animal and human behavior is made clear, by implication at least, in Descartes' famous statement, "I think, therefore I am." This implies a self-fulfillment prophecy, and if true, requires us to think a lot about social evolution. For example, what is the selection principle involved in the evolution of social ideas? Ultimately or in the long run, pragmatic and objective factors are probably paramount, but in the short run (and this sometimes means a century or more), much behavior is guided by myth and misinformation, as well as beliefs and ideology. Statements that are incorrect can induce the behavior that the incorrect statement describes, thus implying the truth of the incorrect statement. Incorrect laws or statements about the physical world would not necessarily produce anything. However, statements of principle about the social world, whether they are true or false, may have a profound impact on people's behavior. John Locke (1632–1704) and J. J. Rousseau (1712–1778) argued (though it had been argued earlier) that the basis of political sovereignty ultimately resides in the people. This was a very revolutionary doctrine at that time, and it did not come to have a successful basis for political action until the 18th century, that is, until it became accepted by a sufficiently large number of the population.

Decision making and judgment among human beings are constantly revised and upgraded as the individual gets new information about the effectiveness of his responses. This new information may produce new problems and responsibilities. For example, prior to modern surgery and immunization techniques, many people died prematurely. These deaths were believed to be natural and inevitable, and hence, no one was charged with a responsiblity for them. Today, however, with modern drugs and medical practice, parents and physicians under certain circumstances can be held responsible for the death of children through illness or certain birth defects. The reason for this is that once it is known that certain things are possible, such as saving a life by surgery, then the use of such skills is demanded by the public. Hence human behavior is constantly evolving and changing to meet the demands of new conditions, and one of the new conditions is new knowledge and new technology.

We may again ask the question—What guides the evolution of behavior systems? The development of planned systems of behavior is very recent in human history, and these have been greatly conditioned by the power structure of the society. Trial and error and natural selection, so to speak, may enable man to adapt reasonably well in a simple type of social system, such as a hunting-type society, but this is hardly sufficient in an industrial society. It seems clear that new knowledge and technology are the prime movers of new modern behavior systems and that the attitudes and

The development of surplus foods in human society was an event that stimulated growth in the division of labor and the emergence of towns and cities.
(Courtesy Russell Lee.)

values toward the new or potential new behaviors are by-products of the behavior rather than causes themselves. These in turn help make behavior predictable, tolerable, and acceptable once the values and attitudes form.

Power to make decisions is assigned to members of a society as a basis for ranking its members on properties believed necessary for the society to best adapt. This does not mean that those who have this power will necessarily use it effectively to ensure the survival of the culture. Obviously, the stability of human behavior assumes an adequate system of behavior control. Stability of the social system is among the conditions necessary for human freedom. The opposite of control is not freedom, but simply a different kind of control. Certain types of control produce an environment where an individual can choose among multiple actions, while others do not. However, an unstable social system, or one without reliable controls, is a system in which an individual will either choose an action, believing it will lead to one end, only to find his expectations frustrated, or he will constantly be forced or coerced to actions by the contingencies of the unstable system. Neither "choice" is a manifestation of freedom. In other words, there is freedom when there are alternatives, but alternatives themselves are binding even though the nature of the bindings differ. There is not freedom of choice, if there are in reality (practical or otherwise) no alternatives.

As indicated earlier, man has only in the last 8000–10,000 years begun the adaptation to agriculture and systems of technology. The larger part of his existence, something near 2 million years, was dominated by man the hunter and gatherer. From the point of view of time, this indicates a rather successful system of adaptation. In reflecting on this, Lee and DeVore recently noted: "It is still open to question whether man will be able to survive the exceedingly complex and unstable ecological conditions he has created for himself. If he fails in this task, interplanetary archaeologists of the future will classify our planet as one in which a very long and stable period of small-scale hunting and gathering was followed by an apparently instantaneous efflorescence of technology and society, leading rapidly to extinction." [28]

The domestication of animals reduced the need for hunting by stabilizing the supply of meat and materials for clothing.
(Courtesy Russell Lee.)

[28] R. B. Lee and I. De Vore, "Problems in the Study of Hunters and Gatherers," in R. B. Lee and I. De Vore (eds.), Man the Hunter (Chicago: Aldine Publishing Co., 1968), p. 3.

In summary, the general conclusion of this chapter is that when man became a biosocial–cultural animal, the latter endowed him with a capacity to affect speedily for better or for worse his adaptive capacity for life chances. The principal sources for this new form of evolution are new *knowledge,* converted into *technology,* applied and put into operation through social *organization,* and guided in its use or misuse by human values and *ideologies.* Ill effects can be modified or eliminated by appropriate changing of the above four interrelated systems. Such possible or probable manipulation presupposes that the leaders of the society and/or societies can muster sufficient consensus of the population as to what the problems are and what needs to be done to solve them. The general problem of behavior control will be dealt with as the principal subject of the next chapter.

Summary

This chapter has shown that the basic nature of man is in broad outline determined by his genetic inheritance and evolution. The specific expression of this nature, his phenotypic traits, are determined by the environment, and particularly by his sociocultural environment. These systems are not only the means by which man increases his adaptive capacity, both within as well as between generations, but also the sources of his new problems of adaptation and the new challenges for future generations.

The development of the foregoing adaptive systems of man was viewed from the perspective of biological evolution across long periods of time. Singled out for special analyses in this respect were anatomical changes unique in man. These were upright posture and true bipedal locomotion, enlarged cerebral cortex, and the capacity for toolmaking and language.

Exercises

1. It is, of course, well-known that there is a strong relationship between the bodily structure of an organism and the organism's principal means of adaptation. Man is no exception to this rule. In the evolutionary history of man, what anatomical changes occurred along the way that contributed to man's development of culture as a mode of adaptation?

2. Discuss the implications of large scale systematic genetic intervention for man's adaptation. Include the social and psychological implications, as well as the biological implications.

3. Discuss the interrelations of knowledge, technology, organization, and energy for human adaptation.

4. In what ways do the making and using of symbols by man enable him to create his own environments?

5. Language liberates but it also binds and blinds cognition. Why is this so?

6. What does Descartes' famous statement "I think, therefore I am," imply for social and cultural evolution?

Selected Bibliography

Aronson, Lester R., et al. (eds.). *Development and Evolution of Behavior.* San Francisco: W. H. Freeman Co., 1970.

Berger, Peter L., and Thomas Luckman. *The Social Construction of Reality; a Treatise in the Sociology of Knowledge.* Garden City, N.Y.: Doubleday & Company, Inc., 1966.

Brace, C. Loring. *The Stages of Human Evolution.* Englewood Cliffs, N.J.: Prentice-Hall, Inc., 1967.

Cohen, Yehudi A. (ed.). *Man in Adaptation: The Biosocial Background.* Chicago: Aldine Publishing Co., 1968.

Cohen, Yehudi A. (ed.). *Man in Adaptation: The Cultural Present.* Chicago: Aldine Publishing Co., 1968.

Hinde, Robert A. *Animal Behavior,* 2nd ed. New York: McGraw–Hill Book Co., 1970.

Hulse, Frederick S. *The Human Species,* 2nd ed. New York: Random House, 1971.

Kluckhohn, Clyde. "The Study of Culture," in Daniel Lerner and Harold L. Lasswell (eds.). *The Policy Sciences.* Stanford, Calif.: Stanford University Press, 1951.

Mazur, Allan, and Leon S. Robertson. *Biology and Social Behavior.* New York: The Free Press, 1972.

Sahlins, Marshall D. "The Origin of Society," *Sci. Amer.,* September 1960.

Ternes, Alan P. (ed.). *The State of the Species.* New York: The American Museum of Natural History, 1970.

Washburn, Sherwood L. "Tools and Human Evolution," *Sci. Amer.,* September 1960.

3

The Development and Patterning of Social Behavior

In Chapter 1, we described the orientation and perspective of *adaptation* and examined its applications to man as a species. In Chapter 2, we continued this perspective by a detailed examination and analysis of the *interdependence* of man's biological, cultural, and behavioral evolution. The primary unit analyzed in these chapters was human population or society. In this chapter, the focus shifts from a consideration of the species and societal characteristics of man to an analysis of both individual and social behavior, although individual behavior *per se* is secondary to our interest in social behavior. Some questions central to the understanding of human behavior are: What are the mechanisms and properties of the human organism that make social behavior of the human variety possible and how is behavior patterned individually and socially? How is human behavior organized and controlled at the individual, group, and community levels?

We begin by defining some terms that are essential to our discussion. We shall regard an **individual response** as one that is *not* directed to another. It may have coincidental, unanticipated, or unplanned effects on another person or persons, but this is unintended. A **social response** is defined as a behavioral response to another. In

A handshake, a gesture while speaking, and a pose of listening are all social responses—behavioral responses to another. An interaction is taking place.
(Courtesy Russell Lee.)

other words, a *social response* is an *interactional* response. Three types of social responses are distinguished: First, there are social responses that are primarily self-facilitating such as the closing of ranks in flight by a flock of starlings upon the appearance on the scene of a falcon. There is a great variety of this sort of individually oriented social behavior among human beings ranging all the way from "confidence games," where individual greed is the motive, to legitimate interpersonal exchange activities such as a sales transaction, where a profit is the motive (although in many cases an automaton may replace equally well the clerk in the sales exchange). In other words, there is much social behavior that is simply personal facilitation as

Floyd Allport conceived it in the early 1920's. This general type of social behavior that is primarily self-serving is given the label **interpersonal relations.** These interactions are characteristically short in duration and personal in motivation. They are further characterized by the absence or near absence of social organization. The key point is that the motivation is personal, and the interaction behavior is determined by trait and/or situation rather than by role or organization. In interpersonal behavior the actors are the central elements, whereas in a social group the roles are the central elements.

A second type of social behavior is called a **social aggregation** or *collectivity,* and the interaction derives either from a common stimulus from the environment or from a common problem of the individuals. The massing of insects around a light at night is an aggregation, since it results from their common attraction to the light. The queuing up of a number of unemployed persons at an employment office as a result of their common interest in employment is another type of aggregation. The crowd at a sports event or the audience at a symphony are other examples.

The third type of social behavior, and the principal concern of this book, is **group behavior.** A group is defined as a set of persons in interaction as a result of occupying *interlocking* social

Individuals seek companionship through interpersonal relations.
(Courtesy Robert Rapelye, Photography International.)

roles. In other words, interaction is brought about by interdependent social responses *to each other* or by a socially defined division of labor, rather than by responses resulting from other factors in the environment or from purely personal motives. We shall not define social role at this point, but it will be defined formally in Chapter 4.

This last type of social behavior, that is, group behavior, is the basic means of adaptation in human society. It is true that self-serving and self-seeking behavior, whether of the aggressive, conniving, exploitative, or altruistic type, has potential survival value. Yet the universal and ubiquitous presence of groups attests to their functional value in adaptation. Etkin points out that despite the difficulty from competition and conflict within a species, that is, among the members of a species, social cooperation and group life among animals is widespread.[1] Perhaps the widespread development of group life results, not in spite of the considerable amount of self-serving behavior, but as a means of minimizing its effects on the survival of the population. Certainly, formal (i.e., socially prescribed) group organization is an important means of controlling conflict within a human society. Interestingly, it can also be used to develop counteraction or power as a means of escaping social control—for example, organized crime. The principal characteristic of a formal social group is the substitutability of persons in given roles, assuming skill competency. In other words, a formal group is a set of social relationships that constitute a behavior system and can be activated by any set of persons with necessary skills and authority. The division of labor in a factory or a baseball team are examples. There is another type of social group that possesses a characteristic of interpersonal social behavior, namely, the *non*substitutability of the actors. Examples of such groups are peer groups, and the family. These have a division of labor and constitute a role system, but the membership is personally determined except in cultures where marriages are prearranged. These types of social groups are sometimes called *primary* groups after the designation given them by an early American sociologist, Charles H. Cooley, in his well-known book on *Social Organization* published in 1909.

Many complex problems of adaptation can be more efficiently solved by social interaction and the proper allocation and combination of a division of labor, and many can be solved *only* by an effective division of labor. For example, social-cooperation systems are used to protect the population against its enemies, to increase the food supply, and in the case of man, to increase his control over aspects of his environment, including his behavioral environment.

[1] William Etkin (ed.), *Social Behavior and Organization Among Vertebrates* (Chicago: University of Chicago Press, 1964), p. 4.

Ironically, mutual aid among human beings, while considerable, nevertheless seems to require a great deal of external motivation or pressure to bring it about. Man in the Paleolithic Age cooperated as a hunter, but cooperation was a clear necessity for survival. He still cooperates today, but he does so with enthusiasm only in times of great threat or crisis. Most other times his cooperation is either from self-interest or from social control. It is probably true that man has not lived long enough under systems of formal government and other elaborate systems of social control for the genetic selection or sociocultural conditioning of a more cooperative type to have yet occurred. This again raises the significant issue discussed in Chapter 1: Does man only adapt individually, while employing social interaction and organization instrumentally as supplemental means for organic evolution, or do some forms of his social organization themselves affect natural selection and survival as forms of group adaptation? It is doubtful if this question can be resolved until we develop criteria for measuring adaptation that are clearer and more precise than those of survival or population growth and stability.

For example, it may be that modern systems of centralized government contribute immensely to human survival and population growth by means hitherto unclear. Government programs for compensatory education, better nutrition for expectant lower-class mothers and their children, and better health distribution programs all improve the quality of life and the net survival of the lower classes. But what if any, are their effects on the gene pool? If the gene pool is not affected, then, accordingly, behavior via genetic transmission would show no effect. But genetic transmission is not the only avenue by which human behavior is selected—another means of selection is cultural transmission. Assuming that the efficient functioning of the central government does enhance the general welfare and that the population comes to perceive this clearly, one could then reasonably assume that such an institution would gain public support, and that its institutional traditions would be strengthened accordingly. But all such strides toward stability can be lost or nullified by failure to socialize the developing new generation adequately, unless strong protective means for internalization of support are built into the socialization process. Lord Keynes' work on *The General Theory of Employment, Interest and Money*, which shows that full employment in a society is not the result of impersonal social mechanisms, but rather the application of deliberate economic and social policy, has only grudgingly been accepted in this country. This does not mean that everyone would want to achieve the goal of full employment. Some may conceive of full employment as socially undesirable for some personal, selfish, or elitist reason, although they would seek to rationalize such a view with loftier motives. Thus the self-interest of some always conflicts with enlightened social interest, and group power struggles are usually the result. The greater the degree of specialization in a society the more self-interests there are to conflict with social interest. Often the adoption of enlightened social policy awaits the pressures of crisis in human social problems.

The need to resocialize each generation brings to mind a newspaper story of a few years ago about a problem experienced by sea gulls at St. Augustine, Florida. A newspaper reported a story about sea gulls starving amid plenty at St. Augustine. There were plenty of fish, but it seems that these gulls did not know how to fish. For generations they had depended on the shrimp fleet to toss them scraps from the nets. The fleet had moved to Key West, and the birds, having learned to feed from the nets, had not taught their off-spring how to fish. As a consequence, these gulls are now having difficulty readapting.

The development of new behavior patterns that meet the demands of environmental change is adaptation. Some organisms already have the genetic potential for the required new behavior, and the new environmental conditions stimulate the development and release of the appropriate responses. Sometimes the needed capacity within the population has to await adaptive mutation, or genetic recombination, and natural selection for development. If the organism is complex, this process takes many generations, and if the environmental changes are critical, extinction may occur in the meantime. Insects, on the other hand, with their large breeding colonies and short life spans, can produce in a brief time a sufficient number of generations for adaptive genetic changes to occur.

Recall that in the case of man we have two mechanisms for adaptive change, genetic and cultural. Assuming that the cultural change can be developed and socially implemented, it is, under certain circumstances, capable of greatly increasing the adaptive capacity of a society in a very short time. Furthermore, for an equally great increase in capacity to occur in man by organic evo-lution would take thousands of years. Cultural change requires the development of the necessary social organization, social control, and cooperation to implement the new cultural products or pro-cedures. It also sometimes takes decades for the necessary con-sensus or control to be achieved. This brings us to the problem of this chapter—*how is human social behavior developed and con-trolled?* We already know from Chapter 2 that individual behavior is neurologically and endocrinologically regulated. However, there is no innate structure to integrate and control human social be-havior automatically. First of all, the appropriate kinds of responses often have to be discovered and developed.

In Chapter 1, four factors were presented as the basic

elements involved in the development and regulation of a social system. These were knowledge, technology, organization, and ideology. However, systems of knowledge, technology, organization, and ideology are inert except when they are activated and carried out by individuals or groups of individuals. The basic problem is what controls the way in which the individual responds to environmental stimuli and internal need. To a very great extent the individual learns responses and solutions that have already been worked out and are a working part of his society's culture. Sometimes he invents *new* responses that are accepted by others but sometimes these responses are rejected. Furthermore, he may by trial and error or by invention produce a new response that is not acceptable to himself. Thus there are at least two rejection screens involved in behavior development: one's personal values and the values of significant or powerful others. The process of behavior development referred to above is the normal behavior of persons and is conceptualized by the following model.

Antecedent conditions stimulate and contribute to the formation of a cognitive awareness in the form of information, beliefs, or opinions. On the basis of these an inference or judgment is formed that produces an *evaluation* or *attitude*. The attitude is a signal for an approach or avoidance response of some sort. The response is given and certain consequences follow that confirm or deny the initial phase meanings. If the response confirms the initial perceptual or cognitive interpretation and related attitude the new response is reinforced. Subsequent experience may contradict the earlier outcomes and the behavior sequence is revised and the person is resocialized in respect to this experience. Figure 3–1 illustrates the behavior development model just described for an individual and for individuals in social interaction.

A_{i-n} represents the antecedent or simultaneous conditions that produce a set of neurological and behavioral phase sequences; S_{i-n} represents the sensory information on the antecedents. C_i is the cognitive interpretation of A_{i-n} and S_{i-n}, which may be in the form of an opinion, belief, cultural definition, or hunch. For the individual this cognitive interpretation leads to an evaluation or attitude toward the significance of A_i; the evaluative attitude implies a response, R_1, consonant to the attitude; the R_1 response generates an outcome or consequence, C_1, which confirms or denies the operations at C_i and E_a. The R_1 response, the cognitive interpretation C_i, and the evaluative attitude E_a are stabilized or revised on the basis of the outcome C_1.

The foregoing model can be modified by introducing the notion of conflict of phase sequences. For example, antecedent conditions may carry information that conflicts with previous antecedent conditions of this type. A girl's date may arrive in a drunken

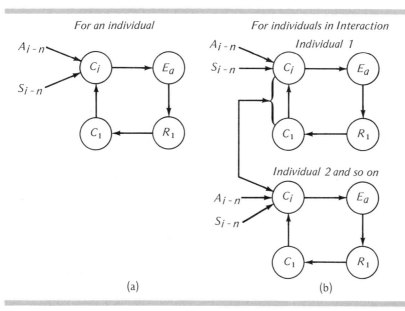

For an individual   For individuals in Interaction

FIGURE 3–1 Conceptualization of behavior development and change as a causal feedback loop.

state to take her out for dinner. She has never before observed him to drink. The present attitude inferred from a particular cognitive interpretation phase may be in conflict with earlier attitudes. Such a conflict in phases would produce an emotional disturbance that in turn could lead to irrational or emotional-type responses. These emotional responses may later be controlled by cognitive redefinition.

There is another type of condition by which the phase sequences may be disrupted; this occurs when one is in social interaction with others regarding the same antecedent conditions as shown in part (b) of Figure 3–1. This is particularly true when the interaction requires coordination and cooperation as in a social system. From this it should be clear that the actions of others in a social situation become significant *antecedents* and *consequences* for defining the actions of each. Even though the individuals as individuals have significantly different phase patterns, these patterns may become very similar and integrated after several rounds of social interaction. Therefore social interaction may be viewed as a process for shaping behavior development and change occurs along the lines suggested in the model in Figure 3–1. Also, when the model is viewed as a function of interacting sets of persons the process of mutual reinforcement of the actors on each others' responses is also the basis for the formation of social norms in a social system as will be shown below.

We shall turn now to a consideration of this question.

BEHAVIOR DEVELOPMENT AND CONTROL

Individual Behavior

Individual behavior was defined as responding *without* regard to others, that is, behavior that is not reinforced by others. A response may have a *positive* reinforcement, a *negative* reinforcement, or no reinforcement at all, that is, a *neutral* outcome or consequence.

Learning is defined as a change in probability of response under certain specified conditions. We shall briefly sketch two kinds of learning that are central to understanding behavior development and change. These are operant learning or conditioning and respondent learning or conditioning.

Operant behavior is behavior that occurs as a consequence of environmental effects and may be modified by environmental change. The key idea is behavior modification as a function of the feedback of the consequences of the immediately previous behavior. If an experimenter wants a pigeon to peck at a certain place, he rewards the pigeon only if it pecks at that place. Operant conditioning, then, is the modification of operant behavior by reinforcement or punishment. This type of conditioning has also been referred to as *instrumental* conditioning.

Respondent behavior is behavior that is elicited by stimuli. For example, salivation may be defined as a respondent in terms of its elicitation either by food or by a conditioned stimulus. Respondent conditioning, then, is the modification of respondent behavior by the *pairing* of stimuli. This type of conditioning has also been referred to as classical conditioning or Pavlovian conditioning.

The reader should not conclude that operant conditioning and respondent conditioning are necessarily exclusive of each other. Many operant responses are made more probable by the presentation of certain stimuli or cues along with the operant. And operant control has been demonstrated over many responses formerly considered exclusively respondent, for example, modification of heart beat rate.[2]

Higher animal forms adapt primarily by means of learning how to cope with environmental conditions and individual needs. The farther down the phylogenetic scale of complexity one goes, the less the organism relies on learning to adapt. The social insects adapt by instincts, which are, of course, genetically regulated. With this mode of adaptation there is no problem or question of "how" the organism should respond to given stimuli or what his behavioral functions are. These are determined for him by his genetic makeup and resulting body structure.

---

[2] Neal E. Miller and L. DiCara, "Instrumental learning of heart rate changes in curarized rats: Shaping and specificity to discriminative stimulus," *J. of Comp. Physiology and Psychology,* 63 (1967), pp. 12–19.

Man, on the other hand, who depends more .on learning to adapt than any other animal, does not have a biologically predetermined behavioral structure, although he does have many social and culturally predetermined behavior patterns that he must learn if he is to adapt. His behavioral structure develops from two interacting sources—namely, contact with the culture of his society, and his unique experience and physiological capacities. Consequently, for man, but not for social insects, a given stimulus may have multiple meanings, which may vary with circumstances. Moreover, a man's place in the division of labor is not determined by his body structure as is the case of the social bees, but it is probabilistically conditioned by competition and his position in the social structure. This will be discussed in detail in the chapter on social stratification, namely Chapter 8. This biological difference is the source of two important problems of adaptation in human populations. These are: (1) how are the positions in the division of labor to be filled, and (2) how is one's responses to these related positions to be controlled and co-ordinated, that is, made socially predictable? Though the answers to the two problems of adaptation listed above will be discussed in several chapters to follow, we will anticipate these discussions by noting that part of the answer lies in the social conditioning that the

The behavior of one individual is a stimulus force on another individual. The responses produced are not biologically predetermined but follow culturally learned patterns.
(Courtesy Robert Rapelye, Photography International.)

individuals receive in their social-opportunity structures, the conditions of social reinforcement in those structures, and the resulting occupational identifications or aspirations.

The variability and flexibility of human behavior is one of the sources of man's adaptive capacity, for if operant behavior is to be differentially reinforced, it must first vary for reinforcement to occur. Although the modification of operant behavior by reinforcement is a solution to the problem of behavioral variability, it is the source of another problem, namely, reinforcement stability of behavior.

For human beings, there are alternative ways of perceiving any given stimulus; thus the possible behaviors that may be exhibited will vary from person to person. This fact is an important basis for selective filling of the positions in the division of labor. Such behavioral variability and plasticity, as well as genetic variability, have implications for the survival of the species. This conception is similar to Lorenz's notion that there is a trend in human evolution toward greater plasticity of adaptive mechanisms. In order to exploit this plasticity and variability effectively, the organism needs to correlate information from several sense sources. In this respect, one of the more important adaptive mechanisms for information processing in man is *cross-modal integration*. This is the capacity to correlate two or more sensory processes. For example, the subsequent selection by sight of a picture previously known only by touch from among several pictures. Correlation of sensory information processing is extremely important to adaptation, and the capacity for doing so varies from species to species. In man, the structure and functioning of the brain and its use of symbols are assumed to be the principal source and means for internal processing and integration of behavior.

Harvey and others postulate two interdependent properties of the structures that process information.[3] He calls the first **dimension** and the second **integrating rules.** For example, an organism can react to a stimulus on the basis of one or more than one dimension. Human beings are capable of perceiving a three-dimensional object. For example, light may be reacted to on the basis of three dimensions: brightness, saturation, and hue. Certain lower forms of animal life are capable of reacting to light on only one dimension. This capacity to respond to a stimulus object in terms of a multidimensional picture of the object is a form of increased adaptive capacity emerging out of man's long evolutionary development and is largely dependent upon the complex development of the human brain. The brain can process many pieces or bits of information at once, and in man it can distinguish between reality,

---

[3] See Harold M. Schroder *et al., Human Information Processing* (New York: Holt, Rinehart & Winston, 1967) and O. J. Harvey (ed.), *Experience, Structure and Adaptability* (New York: Springer, 1966).

imagination, memory, and fantasy. It has developed the capacity to control, at least partially, the very drives and emotions that it activates.

The higher forms of human behavior are controlled by the cerebral cortex. The cortex is extremely rudimentary in lower animals and has evolved rapidly in the mammals. In man, it has become nearly 80 per cent of the volume of the brain. Moreover, in man the brain's capabilities are not determined by biological evolution alone. The development of language has given our species (to be sure the *capacity* for language in man depended upon the evolutionary development of the cortex) the unique capacity to represent and transmit knowledge symbolically from generation to generation, enabling the brain to build, both cumulatively and progressively, upon past learning of previous generations. In fact, man's symbol system is the means for representing, analyzing, storing, and presenting knowledge. This means that as knowledge accumulates, new systems of knowledge and technology become possible, thus changing man's environment and the selective criteria for future evolving and adapting. For example, consider the evolution of energy sources available to man. At first, he had only that energy available from his own physiological capacity or strength, but this was extended through the harnessing of power obtained from domesticated animals, from water, steam, electricity, and atomic energy. These changes resulted in rapid development and differentiation of the human community from small nomadic bands to the large metropolitan areas of today with a million or more people concentrated in a very few square miles.

Such changes were not only biological and cultural, but also ecological in nature and in effect. In other words, the development of so complex a community as a modern urban area becomes interlaced with the whole biosystem of nature as a result of man's dependence upon the biosystem and the feedback of his waste products into it.[4] During such complex development, the community undergoes successive modifications of its *selective* criteria for adapting. In human communities, such criteria are values and goals. Given the fact that these are selective determinants of human evolution (wittingly or unwittingly), then explicit attention should be given to the study of the role of values in the evolution of community systems. This brings us back to the problem of *social* integration and control of social behavior to which we shall turn following a restatement of the integrative controls of individual behavior.

It is the complexity of the human brain that governs the human's ability to piece together and interpret millions of visual

[4] See Howard T. Odum, *Environment, Power, and Society* (New York: Wiley–Interscience, 1971); and Julian Huxley, *Evolution: The Modern Synthesis* (London: G. Allen, 1942).

The seemingly simple act of reading a comic book requires the collection and interpretation of many visual fragments including, hue, brightness, and symbolic expressions.
(Courtesy Robert Rapelye, Photography International.)

fragments and bits of information. It is also the brain that activates, and, in turn, partially controls human drives and basic emotions. The data processing and interpreting functions of the brain are carried out through the structure and organization of the neurons. Almost 90 per cent of all our information comes to us through our eyes, and it is estimated that fully one tenth of the cerebral cortex is required to interpret these visual data. The brain's complexity allows human beings to interpret the data of several senses simultaneously. In addition, the human being carries out multidimensional analyses of these data. That is, he can analyze any property of reality in terms of *n* dimensions of the property. The number of dimensions is determined by the degree of differentiation of conceptual structures. Moreover, the human individual is capable of all the forms of reflex-type responses of any other animal plus one unique type of response, namely, *symbolic* expressions or language. The capacity for language gives rise to systems of knowledge and organization and hence to systems of social regulation and control. The capacity for language expands man's adaptive capacity from one of neurological organization of individual behavior to one linking one man's knowledge and behavior to other men's—hence the cumulative growth and stability in behavior across the generations. This means that the human environment is social and verbal to an extreme degree and, in turn, that the responses of adults in this environment through operant and respondent conditioning have a profound effect on patterning the behavior and the language of children. The first vocalizations of infants are more or less undifferentiated except for cries of pain and discomfort. But these soon become differentiated and patterned because the social environment of the child is patterned through social reinforcement and the child is conditioned by these patterns. Thus the child's language environment is an important source of control over human social behavior.

Development and Control of Human Social Behavior

Just as the human brain has an *internal* electrochemical system of communication and a set of substructures that correlate, interpret, and integrate individual behavior at the neurological level, there must exist, in addition, an *external* system of communication to enable human social behavior to function. This is a system of *symbols*, and the principal means of utilizing these is in speech and language.

Correlating and formulating meaning for one's self is not quite the same as communicating meanings to others, that is, *shared* meanings, and it is shared meanings that constitute the essence of social behavior. How are shared meanings conveyed? No attempt will be made to describe the acquisition of language; instead, language acquisition is assumed.[5] Once a language is learned, it is the principal means for acquiring shared meanings in human society. See Figure 3–1.

Design for Social Communication

All languages have a stock of elementary sounds called **phonemes**. These are the smallest units of speech that characterize a speaker of a language. More specifically, a phoneme is a category of phones, a phone being a particular occurrence of a vowel or a consonant. Phonemes by themselves are meaningless units of sound —that is, they are semantically empty. Phonemes are combined to form larger units, called **morphemes**, which do have meanings.

The number of phonemes in the languages of the world is small, ranging roughly from 15 to 85. The English language uses

[5] For the student who is interested in this problem, the following beginning sources may be consulted: R. Brown, *Words and Things* (Glencoe, Ill.: Free Press, 1958); N. Chomsky, *Language and Mind* (New York: Harcourt, Brace & World, 1968); and B. F. Skinner, *Verbal Behavior* (New York: Appleton–Century–Crofts, 1957). For a detailed statement on language that accords with the view expressed in this book, see Charles F. Hockett, *The State of the Art* (The Hague: Mouton, 1968).

45. The 45 phonemes in the English language can be combined to produce 100,000 or so morphemes, as in the ordinary college dictionary.

As a meaningful linguistic unit, morphemes may be of the *free* form such as "play," "child," or "toy," or the *bound* form, as the "hood" of child*hood* or the "ed" of toy*ed*. No language ever uses all possible combinations of phonemes. In English, there are many thousands of possible combinations of one, two, or three consonants, but fewer than a hundred are actually used. In other words, each language has a characteristic set of linguistic forms.

From morphemes or the smallest units of meaning, words are formed by *morphological* rules, and from words sentences are formed by *syntactical* rules. The morphology and syntax together make up what the linguist calls grammar.

These elements may be illustrated by presenting them in terms of the levels of meaning each represents. The simple diagram below[6] displays a hierarchy of levels from the more complex level of the *sentence* (level 1) down to its ultimate constituents, the morphemes (level 5). The first cut or vertical bar (appearing in level 2) separates subject from predicate. The next bar added (level 3) separates, within the predicate, the verb from its object. The final cuts (those added in levels 4 and 5) break the sentence into the morphemes that are its basic elements (shown by level 5).

1. The dog chased the cats.
2. The dog | chased the cats.
3. The dog | chased | the cats.
4. The | dog | chased | the | cats.
5. The | dog | chase | -d | the | cat | -s.

The invention of the elements of a grammar evolved over very long periods of time and probably in response to problems of accuracy of communication in social behavior. The origin of the grammar of a language or of language itself in the prehistory of the species is unknown. However, the problem of determining or explaining the origin of language should not be confused with the problem of the origin of speech and its expression in language in the preschool years of the child. Learning to speak is essential to the development of competence in social interaction, and particularly the development of the capacity to view oneself from the perspective of others. The capacity for reflexive thought is a distinctively human trait and is therefore species specific. (This capacity and its dependence on language will be discussed in some detail in Chapter 6, "Socialization and Social Competence.")

But how does one learn to speak or talk, to see oneself as a subject of analysis, and thus to view oneself from the perspective of others? Let us first return to the question—how does a child

[6] This diagram is a slightly altered form of a figure taken from R. Brown, *ibid.*, p. 283.

extract from the finite sample of adult speech to which he is exposed the means for generating an infinite set of sentences? Before we discuss attempted answers to this question, it is necessary to make some distinctions regarding theory and data or facts.[7]

Certain statements are called theories because they contain verified ideas that are essential in the scientific activity of a discipline. Certain other statements are sometimes called theories simply because they have not been verified and are not yet facts. No statement of fact is wholly nontheoretical, for evidence is never complete and, therefore, some interpretation or guidance is always necessary. The term theory will be used here to mean an empirically testable statement of explanation that relates one set of data to another. In choosing among competing theories to help formulate an explanation, one should select that theory which, other things being equal, is based on the least number of untested assumptions. This is one aspect of the so-called law of parsimony or Occam's razor.

In broad outline, there are two conflicting theoretical assumptions about how a child acquires a language. One is that the child is genetically equipped with an innate structure that organizes the learning of speech. In other words, the infant is born with a kind of an inherent grammar. The other is that language has evolved from the dim past of early man's interactions and his concomitant efforts to communicate his experiences in the interdependent process of adaptation. This theory assumed that the human brain, particularly the frontal cortex, evolved a sufficient mass to provide the neurological capacity for true speech, but it does not make any further genetic assumptions regarding an innate mechanism for grammatically structuring speech. Thus the former assumption implies a biological evolution of a mechanism that strutures and organizes the learning of speech, while the latter implies a biological evolution of the capacity for speech, but a sociocultural evolution of language, including its structure and its organization.

The work of Noam Chomsky is principally associated with the theory of an innate mechanism or the nativist view.[8] The second point of view, or the environmentalist approach, has many proponents, but the principal one cited here derives from the work of Charles F. Hockett.[9] In his book, *The State of the Art*, Hockett has thoroughly analyzed Chomsky's position. Part of his analysis involved the arrangement of Chomsky's argument into a series of 19 propositions, which he then had Chomsky himself check for accuracy. Certain of these necessary to our discussion are given below.

[7] A detailed discussion of the interrelations of theory, data, and research is found in an article by John T. Doby, in Edgar Borgatta (ed.), *Sociological Methodology 1969* (San Francisco: Jossey–Bass Inc., 1969), Chap. 5.
[8] See Noam Chomsky, *Aspects of the Theory of Syntax* (Cambridge, Mass.: MIT Press, 1965).
[9] See Charles F. Hockett, *Language, Mathematics, and Linguistics* (The Hague: Mouton, 1967) and Charles F. Hockett, *The State of the Art* (The Hague: Mouton, 1968).

Because of the frequent citing of Chomsky's work by social science writers, and since it logically conflicts with the social interaction view presented here, it is given detailed attention. It is especially important for the student to distinguish Chomsky's basic assumptions from those of this book.

Chomsky starts his analysis of the learning of a language with the implicit assumption that the grammar of a language is a well-defined system (i.e., precisely defined), and that only a well-defined system can give rise to a well-defined system—for instance mathematics derived from a language approach. Hockett defines a well-defined system as "one that can be completely and exactly characterized by deterministic functions." [10] However, Hockett also shows, and quite correctly, that no *physical* system is a well-defined system. This statement, of course, would include the brain as a physical system. These ideas should be recalled when evaluating Chomsky's orientation, which is given below in basic outline, except for his propositions concerning the development of a theory of linguistics. (The number preceding each entry is the number assigned by Hockett in his delineation of Chomsky's position into 12 propositions.)

1. The vast majority of the sentences encountered throughout one's life by any user of a language are encountered only once; that is, most sentences are novel.

2. Any user of a language has access, in principle, to an infinite set of sentences. In practice, only a finite subset of these are used.

3. The user knows the grammar of his language, though not in a sense of "know" that would imply that he can explicitly tell others of his knowledge. This body of knowledge constitutes the user's competence. The user's competence *is* the grammar of his language. User's competence means his own personal version, not the language of his speech community in some generalizing or common denominator sense. Also, in Chomsky's sense, the grammar *of* a language is not to be confused with any investigator's explicitly proposed grammar *for* a language.

4. A user's performance—what he actually says and hears—reflects his competence, but is also conditioned by many other factors.

8. The distinction between grammatical and nongrammatical sentences applies to competence not to performance. The degree of acceptability of an actually performed utterance is a different matter.

9. Meaningfulness, like grammaticalness, pertains to competence. But these two are distinct—there are grammatically well-formed sentences that are meaningless, and nongrammatical sentences that are meaningful, at least in the sense that, when performed in an appropriate setting, they convey the information they are intended to convey.

---

[10] Charles F. Hockett, *The State of the Art* (The Hague: Mouton, 1968), p. 45.

10. The grammar of a language is a finite system that characterizes an infinite set of (well-formed) sentences. More specifically, the grammar of a language is a *well-defined system* by definition not more powerful than a universal Turing machine (and, in fact, surely a great deal weaker.

11. At present there is no known algorithm for computing or discovering the grammar of a language.

12. Yet almost every infant performs successfully the task of language acquisition. It must be, therefore, that the infant brings to this task at least the following: an *innate* system for the production of an indefinitely large set of grammars of possible human languages; and the *innate* ability to select, from this set, the correct grammar for the language of his community, on the basis of a small sample of dimly perceived and imperfectly performed actual utterances in their actual settings.[11] Chomsky added this statement to Hockett's formulation of proposition 12: "that the infant's innate system must include much more, for example, an algorithm for determining the structural description of an arbitrary sentence given an arbitrary grammar."

In Chomsky's view this innate grammar-producing system is a well-defined system. The remaining propositions of Chomsky's are concerned with the potential development of a general grammar or general linguistic theory and need not concern us here. Enough has been said to provide an understanding of the basic outline of Chomsky's orientation.

In speculating about how human beings learn a language, certain peculiarities of the process are worth noting from the point of view of possible self-deception. Speech is the first verbal system of communication that we are exposed to and learn. Moreover, we are exposed to it from birth onward. Furthermore, as our language capacity develops, we can examine in a reflective way its sources and development within us, but this introspection is in the same terms and concepts of the language we have learned. Since we are not conscious of the learning process in our acquisition of language as we are in the classroom when learning mathematics, it is reasonable to assume that *we did* the *ordering* of the language we learned rather than having learned it *already ordered*. In other words, as Hockett notes, there are certain fields in which terminology and subject matter, if distinct, are hard to keep apart. This is the case with linguistics.

Let us turn now to Hockett's critique of the innate theory of language as formulated by Chomsky. First, Hockett points out as we did in Chapters 1 and 2 that there are *two* known processes that transmit a child's heritage—its genes and its culture. Chomsky seems to be unaware of the second one. Hockett formulates his criticism of Chomsky's main assumption as follows: "The two main

---

[11] Charles F. Hockett, *ibid.*, pp. 38–43.

known mechanisms responsible for a child's heritage are genes and cultural transmission. These are not determinate, and hence *not* well-defined. Therefore the innate grammar-producing system that the infant brings to the task of language acquisition cannot be either of these, or any part or combination of them; hence there must be some additional mechanism, as yet undiscovered. Furthermore, this additional mechanism cannot be physical, since no physical system is well-defined." [12] Accordingly, if one were to hold on to the concept of a well-defined system, he would be, in effect, excluding linguistics from the empirical sciences.

Hockett proposes a way around the difficulty in Chomsky's formulation by suggesting the abandonment of Chomsky's idea of grammar as a well-defined system. The concept of a well-defined system is the foundation of Chomsky's theory; hence if it collapses, then his whole system collapses—and we believe, along with Hockett, that it does.

Hockett's proposition for circumventing the difficulty is as follows: "We can propose that there are ways in which well-definition can arise from ill-definition and we can look for the step from ill-definition to well-definition at any of three points. (1) Physical genes and nonphysical (but ill-defined) tradition perhaps yield a well-defined grammar-producing system in the child. Or (2) the grammar-producing system of the child is perhaps itself ill-defined, though it characterizes well-defined grammars; or (3) languages may themselves be ill-defined, so that well-definition appears *only* through those special uses of language that give rise to things like mathematics." [13]

In our judgment, Chomsky's principal fallacy is his insistence that the long relative stability of grammar necessarily implies "well-definition" and that this implies innateness. Cultural forces *also* produce stability, especially when they are learned so early in life. As Hockett observed, Chomsky has heard of genes but gives no sign that he knows anything about cultural transmission.

It is our argument that speech is acquired in the same way that any other symbolic content is learned, only it is acquired *first* and as a consequence becomes the vehicle and structure for learning other symbolic systems such as mathematics, moral systems, and legal systems. This means that it is easy to separate language from the other systems since they come later, but it is difficult to detach language from thought and speech because it is harder to keep the terminology separate from the subject matter when the subject matter is language itself.

Hockett notes that "speech is to language as behavior is to habit or skill, as structure is to pattern, as event is to institution, as

---

[12] Charles F. Hockett, *ibid.*, p. 58.
[13] Charles F. Hockett, *ibid.*, p. 59.

history is to sociology, as message is to code." Thus Hockett has reversed Chomsky and concludes: "the linguist seeks theories, which are generalizations from observations, and are about *speech*. They yield predictions, and are corrected by subsequent observations. The linguist is led to posit that the observable regularities of actual speech are a matter of habits, resident in the users of language—rather than, say, a matter of automatic chemical response to impinging sunlight. He (the linguist) calls these habits language. This proposal is part of our theorizing about speech. It makes no sense to pretend that there can be a separate and distinct theory of language." [14]

"Chomsky's views lead him to insist on remarking that there are no algorithms for the discovery of the structure of a language, unless such exists in the innate equipment of the infant. The assertion is true but impertinent; there is no reason for the proviso about infants. Algorithms are to be found only within logic and mathematics. Even there they play a minor role. For example, new mathematics is not invented algorithmically, but presumably by just the same mechanisms responsible for the production of novel utterances in a language. If we turn from logic and mathematics to the world, then there is no reason to separate language from the rest of reality for special treatment. There is no algorithm for the discovery of *any fact about the real world*. There are, at best, discovery procedures: more or less systematized and channeled methods of trial-and-error, not guaranteed to be successful, but the best we have and, by virtue of the fundamental nature of the world, the best we can hope to have." [15]

The perceptual buildup of cognitive structures through learning cumulates rapidly, so rapidly in fact that when the structure is perceived, it appears as if we perceived it as a whole from the beginning. Therefore, it should not, from the perspective of learning theory, appear to be an innate phenomenon when children correctly use the proper progressive inflection for certain verbs. These distinctions are made frequently as general usage in the adult community. The child has to mature to a sufficient age, but this maturity is conditioned with many examples.

Since the infant vocalizes before he learns speech, it is easy to demonstrate the involvement of operant behavior in the learning of speech. For example, the adults are already using the speech they expect the children to speak, and indeed they must speak, if they are to communicate effectively with the adult community. No child talks without being exposed to reasonably fluent speakers, and the language he learns, including the dialect he uses, is precisely the language and the dialect to which he is exposed.

[14] Charles F. Hockett, *ibid.*, pp. 65–66.
[15] Charles F. Hockett, *ibid.*, p. 75.

It is, therefore, more parsimonious to assume that he *learned* the language, *including* its structure, its grammar, and its dialectal form, than to assume the existence of an innate structure that organizes the learning of the languages as the child is exposed. Incidentally, such an assumption does not *explain* language acquisition at all since no one knows what this alleged genetic structure is.

It is not our main purpose here to explain how language is learned. Instead we are primarily concerned with how social behavior is patterned and controlled, and our discussion of this led us to the problem of language, since language is a principal means for social interaction and behavior patterning.

The generalization and discrimination of stimuli are each sharpened and facilitated by language. In addition, language particularly enables one to learn from others, not only from direct observation, but also from talking or reading about others experiences. Thus much social behavior is coordinated by verbal or written communications. If we think of a rule of conduct, a standard of work, etiquette, and so on, as norms for social behavior, we can easily see that these can be verbally stated as well as behaviorly demonstrated. Norms have no force of control in ensuring compliance unless they are reinforced by sanctions.

SOCIAL NORMS AND SOCIAL SANCTIONS

Individuals perform many acts that are rewarded by the nonhuman environment, such as planting a shrub and enjoying its beauty. Moreover, individuals are rewarded by other persons as a result of their responses to each other. Some of these acts are nonrecurring or unique and consequently have no long-range social consequences. Others, however, are forms of action that *recur* and center around important or significant social events, processes, or values, and have socially defined consequences. For example, the exchange of goods or services, care and treatment of the sick, events such as marriage, births and deaths, recreation, selection of political leaders, and an almost endless list of other acts. The fact that some acts or events have *consequences* for others means that if the consequences are to be controlled, then the acts must be defined and regulated. **Social norms** are the rules by which the *interactions* between or among persons are defined and patterned. In other words, a norm is a statement, implicit or explicit of an "ought" or "should" and is socially reinforced by social sanctions.[16] Thus norms are guides to action and are not to be confused with behavior itself. The strength of the sanctions that reinforce a norm is indicated by the rate of compliance or degree of correspondence of behavior to the norm. A norm that is not reinforced is no longer a norm.

[16] George C. Homans, *Social Behavior: Its Elementary Forms* (New York: Harcourt, Brace, and World, 1961).

Some norms are so important to the stability of a society that they are made universally applicable, and some are specific and apply to particular groups doing particular things. Often where norms exist to regulate action among the members of the whole population, some groups will perceive themselves at a disadvantage with respect to other groups and may seek to evade the customary norms and operate by their own norms. This precipitates a normative conflict in interaction; often the conflict is decided by those who have the will and the power to enforce their norms. Organized crime in a community is an example of such a conflict. Of course, the same kind of conflict can occur within a small group or even a family.

The patterning of the actions and interactions is what makes them predictable, and it is the predictability that makes organized social life possible. To ensure the predictability of certain social acts, the norms are reinforced by institutionalized **sanctions;** that is, *sanctions* are socially prescribed rewards or punishments for socially defined behavior. The state or central government is the ultimate source of enforcement in a society.

All behavior that either has or is perceived to have social consequences (that is, consequences for others) is normatively defined. Some behavior that is normatively regulated is more important than other forms for adaptation. Such socially valued behavior is **institutionalized**—that is, it is protected, encouraged, or discouraged through *clusters or configurations of norms* that regulate the socially valued or tabooed activities. Such organizations of norms are called *institutions*. In other words, when specific procedures or organizations are set up to enforce and carry out specific norms a process of institutionalization has occurred. Institutionalization facilitates adaptation by providing ready-made solutions to practical problems for succeeding generations. For example, even though the American constitution has been amended it provides the means for its amendment and, in addition, serves as a source for settling political and legal conflicts among groups in the society.

Many acts or forms of social behavior are short-lived or trivial, but still socially defined or normative, though not institutionalized. Most interpersonal relations are of this variety. Occasionally, an act is normative and not institutionalized, but later its importance is redefined and it becomes institutionalized. This process of social change occurs regularly, as does the similar process by which some norms become obsolete and "fade away," when they no longer have importance in that society.

In institutionalized normative behavior, the behavior is *not directly* rewarded or punished by the immediate actors who are interacting, but by someone whose special function is to do so. This person may be a supervisor, a foreman, or a judge.

In summary, types of significant social behavior that recur will be regulated and the means of regulation and enforcement will be institutionalized.

A poorly coordinated social system that denies a group of individuals the means to achieve success produces negative personal, as well as social, results.
(Courtesy Bruce Davidson, Magnum Photos, Inc.)

One of the problems associated with normative regulation is that the conditions that gave rise to the norms in the first instance change and the norms may then be inappropriate or even in conflict with the needs of the new conditions, but the sanctions may be still in effect. For example, a society with a high infant mortality rate may evolve strong norms against abortion. Suppose that, in time, the society's infant mortality rate is reduced and the society becomes overpopulated. Then agitation may develop for a relaxation of the sanctions against abortion. Thus there may and often does exist a time lag in the replacement of one norm by another when the social circumstances or problems of adaptation change, because others besides the immediate actors are involved. In other words, in institutionalized behavior the system of control has obviously transcended those who are immediately involved. Implicit in the foregoing discussion of normative change is the notion that norms are means for social adaptation and that norms change as the problems of adaptation change.

THE SOCIAL SYSTEM AS A SYSTEM OF SOCIAL CONTROL AND COORDINATION

Social interaction is a very dynamic and delicately balanced process and as shown above its stability does not depend alone upon the *internal* properties of the particular actors themselves. If these were sufficient, there would be no need for *external* forces to be applied by others. The larger the population involved, the more differentiated and complex are the social structures necessary to organize and control the population.

The internal properties of control are the social identification that the participants have with the system and the socialization effects of previous social conditioning, both operant and respondent. The external controls are the sanctions of others, the reinforcements both formal and informal, that is, institutional and noninstitutional. In a sense, social control takes over where impulse control or internalization of norms fails or is insufficient.

How does interaction in groups or social systems affect the behavior of the participants? In the first place, a social system is a system of prescribed action, and the *role occupants* are expected to perform their reciprocal parts. Successful fulfillment and performance of the roles results in the achievement of the group or organizational goals. Social reinforcement is dependent upon the goal achievements of the action systems. For example, the shortstop or the first baseman on a baseball team must field the ball effectively if "outs" are to be obtained when the ball is thrown or hit in his direction. If he fails too often in this role, he will receive not only the scorn of the spectators but of the other team members and management, as well. It is evident that a social system is composed of a set of social relationships, which, when coordinated and skillfully executed, result in achievement of expected outcomes that have positive results for the members, and, when poorly coordinated and poorly executed, produce negative personal as well as social results. In other words, a social system is an adaptive system that simultaneously, and with varying degrees of efficiency, meets the needs of individual members and of the larger society. The reinforcement system is based on the participants successfully contributing to the group goals. This discourages the temptation of individuals to place their own welfare and interests above that of the group or the organization.

From the foregoing discussion of the social system as a mechanism for integrating and coordinating human social behavior, the following two general assumptions are now made explicit. First, sociologists have assumed for almost a century and certainly since the classic work of Charles H. Cooley in his book *Human Nature and Social Organization*, that *man becomes as he behaves and he behaves as his social environment conditions him.* Second, the mechanism of social influence in the organizational and group contexts is the powerful force of the anticipation or expectation of others that we do certain things. These significant *others* (that is, those who control the reinforcements) gear their behavior in ways to ensure that we fulfill their expectations. Failure to perform as expected, if repeated, usually results in some form of social sanction.[17] Actors in the theater may not become as they behave, because human beings can distinguish between real life and fantasy or imagination. But individuals acting in real life do become as they

---

[17] There are, of course, individuals who for various reasons, fail to perform or live up to societal norms. When such individuals are able to come together in groups, they can and do form their own subcultures and adapt within their own subsystems, if they can muster sufficient resources, either legitimately or illegitimately.

The owners of this factory show little regard for the conditions of the people in the village below. Groups as well as individuals take into account the socially negative consequences of their own behavior or policies only when they are effected by the negative results.
(Courtesy Robert Rapelye, Photography International.)

behave. For example, a child's intelligence as expressed in behavior has largely reached stability by age four, and the social interactions with his parents prior to this age are profoundly significant in influencing the development of his intellectual and social skills.[18, 19]

The development of intellectual ability and maternal interaction varies with sex. Kagan has shown in a recent study that the partial correlation between maternal verbal IQ and the four-year old's IQ score, with maternal social class controlled, was 0.39 for daughters, but only 0.15 for sons. The same sex differences emerged even when the analysis was restricted to working-class families. Furthermore, maternal language ability, assessed when the child was preschool age, was a better predictor of reading proficiency two years later in daughters ($r = 0.50$) than in sons ($r = 0.25$).[20]

[18] Benjamin S. Bloom, *Stability and Change in Human Characteristics* (New York: John Wiley & Sons, Inc., 1964).
[19] Jerome Kagan, *Change and Continuity in Infancy* (New York: John Wiley & Sons, Inc., 1971).
[20] Jerome Kagan, *ibid.,* p. 184. Correlation is defined as a measure of the degree of relationship between two or more variables.

Apparently, the cognitive environment in one's social system has a greater impact on girls' readiness for school than on boys' readiness for school. However, this sex difference only held for language and reading skills and not for arithmetic performance. This may be due to the tendency of female children to emulate the mother. Since boys do not generally emulate the mother a cognitive environment created by the mother would be expected to have a greater impact on the female child. Since this environment is predominantly a verbal, language using one, it should not be surprising that the sex difference does not carry over into mathematics, for neither male nor female child would have been exposed to the mother's skills in that area.

It is difficult to tell how much of the sex-related difference in cognitive growth of girls is related to their differing social stimulation and how much, if any, is related to differential rates of physiological maturation. Kagan's research showed that upper-middle-class mothers of daughters were three times more likely than poorly educated ones to chide their daughters for not performing up to a standard held by the mother. There was no comparable class difference for the mothers of sons. Other studies tend to emphasize developmental or maturational factors. For example, Vigotsky, Piaget, and Kohlberg have conducted studies that show that children perform very differently on problems of classification and reasoning from adults and do not operate in a fully mature way on such problems until early adolescence.[21] Children's answers to questions about time are amusing to adults. For example, children two to seven years of age will insist that the time it takes to move one object farther than another object, even though to move each takes the same amount of time, is the longer for the one moved the farther distance. He is focusing on the spatial property and is not able to integrate distance, velocity, and time as an adult can.

Kohlberg and Piaget argue that certain kinds of intellectual processes develop sequentially or in stages. For example, they argue that sensorimotor behavior develops before relational and abstract reasoning, and that the latter depends significantly on the former. The implication of this argument is that cognitive structures (which, in their consideration, except for content and catalytic stimulation, develop independently of social experience) intervene in crucial ways between social reinforcement and behavior development.

Aronfreed criticizes Kohlberg's work for seeming to imply

---

[21] Lawrence Kohlberg, *Stages in the Development of Moral Thought and Action* (New York: Holt, Rinehart and Winston, 1969); L. S. Vigotsky, *Thought and Language* (Cambridge, Mass.: MIT Press, 1962); Therese Gorun Decarie, *Intelligence and Affectivity in Early Childhood: An Experimental Study of Jean Piaget's Object Concept and Object Relations* (New York: International Universities Press, Inc., 1965).

that "patterns of conscience necessarily evolve, through a fixed sequence of qualitative transformations, in the direction of what is considered socially desirable or mature, provided only that certain common forms of social experience are available to the child. Failure of the sequence to reach its terminal point must be regarded as an arrest of the natural order of development . . . . The undertone of these conceptions is unmistakably that of Rousseau's *Emile*." [22]

There is no doubt that there is a maturational basis to behavior development and that certain behaviors develop sequentially, but this does not necessarily imply a built-in innate structure that determines sequence. Rather, a more economical formulation at our present state of knowledge would be that physiological development is a process of increased differentation and that experience interacts to produce different qualitative results at different levels of maturation. From this it would also follow that the outcome of behavioral patterning would vary with variations in both maturation levels and social variations. Thus social class and cross-cultural differences would be expected to produce different behavioral outcomes as would maturational levels.

Scott in commenting on Kohlberg's formulation compares it to two so-called "models of man": the model of Rousseau and the model of Hobbes. "For Rousseau's 'noble savage,' morality is either inherent or at least a strong latent possibility, which society can only frustrate. Evil in this model is a social product, but goodness is presocial (and therefore by implication invariant among societies). The Hobbesian model of man is one of a wholly amoral actor, made moral, if at all, entirely by social processes—usually, in Hobbes' terms through constraints or negative sanctions. Both good and evil are social products in this view and thus vary as societies vary." [23]

We do not know enough yet about how learning and perception occur and cumulatively develop to be able to form crucial hypotheses for testing and resolving the above conflicting formulations. It may be that the results of learning integrate in small bits and rapidly form structures so that the results appear to be the effect of innate structures. On the other hand, very primitive innate organizing mechanisms may play a part in organizing experience—the intellectual chips are obviously not all in. At the present time, however, social reinforcement by means of social institutions and group processes seems the more parsimonious interpretation of how behavior develops and changes.

Despite the limited range of social class differences in

[22] Justin Aronfreed, *Conduct and Conscience: The Socialization of Internalized Control over Behavior* (New York: Academic Press, Inc., 1968).
[23] John F. Scott, *Internalization of Norms: A Sociological Theory of Moral Commitment* (Englewood Cliffs, N.J.: Prentice–Hall, Inc., 1971), p. 162.

Kagan's study, statistically significant differences still emerged during the first year of life and were "unequivocal" by 27 months of age. Kagan observes that "This finding is to be contrasted with the absence of class differences [in behavior] during the first two years on the Piaget Object Scale or the Cattell Infant Intelligence Scale, neither of which focus on distribution of attention to discrepant schemata, but emphasize coordination of sensory–motor systems." [24]

One of the major findings that differentiates lower-class from middle-class parents is the parents' faith that they can influence the child's mental development. The lower-class mothers evidence a greater sense of fatalism and powerlessness in contrast to the middle- and upper-middle-class mother's belief that she can contribute to the shaping of her infant's mind. One of the consequences of this is that middle-class mothers pay more attention to the responses of their children thus reinforcing the child's operant behavior, especially with regard to curiosity and question asking by the child—that is, some children have learned to pay attention because others have given attention to them. Attention span and focus are important conditions for successful learning. This factor would be expected to correlate significantly with school adjustment.

It is clear that the types of behavior of parents, teachers, and peer groups affect the cognitive development of children. To the extent that the functioning of the social system produces better-adapted new members and members who have developed more fully their own potentialities, the system itself will be strengthened by the success these individuals have in improving the adaptive mechanisms in the social system. Hence there is a loop-type relationship between cognitive development, social system organization, and adaptation.

Anthony F. C. Wallace illustrates this mutual dependence in a poignant way. He states that "a group with fire is, in any environment, in a better position to survive various threats from cold, exposure, and predatory animals than is a group without fire and will also be able to live in colder regions than its fireless confreres; second, within the group, any individual who is unable to perform the cognitive tasks necessary to fire control is endangering both himself and his group, and he is apt to be negatively selected by his group if he fails to perform adequately." [25]

This brings us now to a consideration of the organization and functioning of human societies, which is the topic of the next chapter.

---

[24] Jerome Kagan, *Change and Continuity in Infancy* (New York: John Wiley and Sons, Inc., 1971), pp. 187–188.
[25] Anthony F. C. Wallace, *Culture and Personality*, 2nd ed. (New York: Random House, 1970), p. 68.

Summary

This chapter has focused on the development and control of behavior and their relationship to social experience. We considered first the development and control of individual behavior and discussed this in terms of reinforcement theory. A feedback loop model of individual and social behavior was formulated. In this respect, two principal forms of conditioning, namely, operant and respondent were analyzed.

Building on these concepts and relating them to the patterned social nature of the human environment, we analyzed the development and control of social behavior. Speech, language and social sanctions were given a significant place in the development of social behavior in children, and of course, in adults. In this respect, the conflicting arguments of the nativists and the environmentalists were considered with special attention to Chomsky and Hockett, respectively.

Following this, the social system was analyzed as a means for controlling social behavior, and the effects of the system on behavior development were considered. Here the cognitive theorists were contrasted with the learning theorists in assessing these effects. The tentative conclusion drawn is that cognitive development, physiological development, social system experience, and adaptation interact.

Exercises

1. Define and illustrate the three types of social behavior discussed in this chapter, namely (1) interpersonal behavior, (2) collective behavior, and (3) group behavior.

2. Illustrate how social behavior is patterned by operant reinforcement and by classical or respondent reinforcement. How may these processes (operant and respondent condition) affect each other?

3. What is the dependence of operant conditioning upon behavior variability and what is the significance of this for social adaptation?

4. Distinguish social behavior from individual behavior and discuss the problems of learning appropriate responses in social behavior.

5. Compare and contrast Chomsky and Hockett's views on the learning of language.

6. What is the relationship of social norms to the patterning and regulation of social behavior?

7. What kinds of behaviors are likely to be normatively regulated? What are some social conditions that are likely to lead to normative conflict?

Selected Bibliography

Barnett, S. A. *Instinct and Intelligence*. Englewood Cliffs, N.J.: Prentice–Hall, Inc., 1967.

Bernstein, Basil. "Sociolinguistic Approach to Socialization," in Frederick Williams, *Language and Poverty*. Chicago: Markham Press, 1970.

Crothers, J., and Patrick Suppes (eds.). *Experiments in Second Language Learning*. New York: Academic Press, 1967.

Hamblin, Robert L., et al. *The Humanization Process: A Social, Behavioral Analysis of Children's Problems*. New York: Wiley-Interscience, 1971.

Hockett, Charles F. "The Origin of Speech," *Sci. Amer.*, September 1960.

Keller, Fred S. *Reinforcement Theory*, Rev. ed. New York: Random House, 1969.

McHugh, Peter. *Defining the Situation: The Organization of Meaning in Social Interaction*. Indianopolis, Ind.: Bobbs-Merrill Co., 1968.

Phillips, Leslie. *Human Adaptation and its Failures*. New York: Academic Press, 1968.

Sampson, Edward E. *Social Psychology and Contemporary Society*. New York: John Wiley & Sons, Inc. 1971.

4

Basic Organization and Functioning of Human Societies

Human beings—and many animal species—live and survive by means of *societies*. Indeed, human societies are from one standpoint superior adaptive devices, complex mechanisms for assuring life for many human organisms in variably difficult physical environments. But society as a basic form among humans has been developed, refined, modified, and camouflaged in so many ways that the fundamentals of its operation sometimes elude laymen and specialists alike.

Society—that is, *human* society—is a problem-solving (and also a problem-provoking) device that involves fundamentally similar methods for meeting a set of continuing practical problems. Essentially, these problems can be classified in a reasonably orderly way, if we recognize that these problems are (a) roughly simultaneous and (b) interdependent, and that perhaps they reflect an unalterable set of priorities.[1]

[1] Marion J. Levy, Jr., *The Structure of Society* (Princeton, N.J.: Princeton University Press, 1951); Talcott Parsons, *The System of Modern Societies* (Englewood Cliffs, N.J.: Prentice–Hall, Inc., 1971); Kingsley Davis, *Human Society* (New York: The Macmillan Company, 1949), Part I; John W. Bennett and Melvin M. Tumin, *Social Life* (New York; Alfred A. Knopf, 1948), Chaps. 3, 4.

FUNDAMENTAL PROBLEMS OF HUMAN SOCIETIES

1. The first problem is, of course, physical survival of a significant portion of a designated population. From the standpoint of that population, survival is an end in itself and unarguable. But from the standpoint of the social structure devised by that population, survival is a precondition of replacement, since death can be postponed but not evaded. (See Tables 4–1 and 4–2.) While survival depends on coping with the physical environment—through technology—success in this fundamental task is also related to the degree of success with two other problems.

2. A second problem, therefore, is protection against the assaults—actual or threatened—of other accessible human societies or populations. Isolated societies by definition face no such problem. But few societies remain isolated for very long. And it is quite probable that isolation is only a temporary means of pursuing physical survival.

TABLE 4–1

Expectation of life at birth in western countries in the 19th and early 20th centuries.

Year	Males	Females
1840	39.6	42.5
1850	40.3	42.8
1860	41.1	43.4
1870	42.3	44.7
1880	43.9	46.5
1890	45.8	48.5
1900	48.9	56.1
1910	52.7	56.0

SOURCE: *United Nations, Dept. of Economic and Social Affairs; Determinants and Consequences of Population Trends* (New York: United Nations, 1953).

TABLE 4–2

Crude death rates for the United States 1900–1965 (per 1000 population).

Year	Deaths per 1000
1900	17.2
1910	14.7
1920	13.0
1930	11.3
1940	10.8
1950	9.6
1960	9.5
1965	9.4

SOURCE: *Dept. of Health, Education, and Welfare; Vital Statistics of the United States, 1963* (Washington: USGPO, 1965); *Monthly Vital Statistics Reports, 1966* (Washington: USGPO, 1966).

3. A third societal problem is developing and sustaining common efforts among members of a population to assure adequate adaptation to the physical environment. More specifically, this problem takes two forms. First, there is the obvious necessity to manage or reduce aggressive acts between members, not only for moral or ideological reasons (personal dignity, human rights, and so on), but

Human societies require active collaboration. This is particularly true when the technology is underdeveloped or the population is small.
(Courtesy Alfred Eisenstaedt, Life Magazine © 1972, Time Inc.)

because interindividual conflicts greatly interfere with the societal capabilities of survival in hostile or indifferent environments. Second, human societies require active collaboration of efforts— particularly in smaller populations, in difficult environments, and in technologically undeveloped populations. Therefore, an enormously significant problem is the inability and/or unwillingness of significant numbers to cooperate with others in activities designed to produce the means for survival (food, shelter, protection against aggression).

4. A fourth problem was unavoidably mentioned before —and that is replacement. Because of death, disability, or desertion, cooperative efforts for physical survival are periodically threatened by manpower shortages. In short, survival entails consideration of replacements, so that the survivors (or a large proportion) can *continue* to survive. Logically, and to a small extent actually, replacements may come from immigration. Yet this is both inefficient and unpredictable. In more practical terms, replacement is usually better served by human reproduction. Consequently, societies must always establish means for encouraging, controlling, and caring for the fruits of the biological process of reproduction.

5. The final problem for human societies is one that derives from successful solutions to the preceding problems. Indeed, this problem and its attempted resolutions are probably the most distinctive aspects of human society, as compared with the societies of lower animal species. Essentially, societies that survive over some

extended period of time are constantly confronted by the possibility that past adaptations are either partly successful or successful for limited time periods. For example, trial by jury is an old method for insuring adequate defense against arbitrary judgments by powerful leaders. But this technique was based on the existence of relatively small, homogeneous communities. In highly dynamic urban areas— with very complex activities and populations—the jury trial is no longer an effective method of obtaining fair or acceptable judgments in many cases.

Societal adaptation is thus a variable that may be interpreted in terms of two significant and practical challenges:

(a) One adaptive problem results from the fact that experience and knowledge with regard to various facets of the environment tend to be unequally developed. More bluntly, there are areas or situations about which adequate knowledge for direct solutions is not available or is vague and not capable of being put to satisfactory use. These problem situations have included treatment of diseases[2]; understanding of death; understanding deviant behavior of individuals; management of internal conflicts; and control of such natural processes as combustion, atomic energy, and genetic coding. Human societies rarely seem to have ignored their special areas of collective ignorance. Instead, they may adapt by devising compensatory or "symbolic" solutions to such problems. A very old and still current instance is the problem of the socially deviant individual whose behavior is described and explained by the dominant symbolism of specific eras. For example, in the middle ages and in our own colonial period, such persons were symbolized as "possessed" by demons or witches, while in our own time, the appropriate symbolism is often that of "sickness"—though there is considerable uncertainty about causes or conditions. We may conveniently label this general adaptive problem as the "search for social protection against significant unknowns" in the environment. Adaptation, therefore, consists of temporary social camouflage, which serves to protect a population temporarily through symbols (verbal manipulations) rather than by physical techniques.[3]

(b) Societies must also face the recurrent problem of environmental change, whether change derives from physical conditions, from the intervention of other societies, or from the society's manipulation of the environment. It is a truism that most social and

---

[2] See, for example, David Bakan, *Disease, Pain, and Sacrifice* (Chicago: University of Chicago Press, 1948); Leslie Phillips, *Human Adaptation and its Failures* (New York: Academic Press, Inc., 1968); Georg Simmel, *Conflict and the Web of Group-Affiliations* (New York: Free Press, 1955).

[3] Mircea Eliade, *Images and Symbols* (New York: Sheed and Ward, 1961); Mircea Eliade, *Myth and Reality* (New York: Harper & Row Publishers, Inc., 1963); Hugh D. Duncan, *Symbols in Society* (New York: Oxford University Press, 1968), pp. 48–49; V. W. Turner, *The Drums of Affliction* (Oxford: Clarendon Press, 1968).

personal adaptations are oriented to past situations and to the probability that past conditions will recur. But these are questionable—if not dangerous—assumptions for societies that function in complex environments. Therefore, a particularly serious problem is a society's ability and willingness to readapt by devising new or greatly modified solutions to the venerable and enduring problems discussed above.[4] In short, social change is not primarily a political or ideological matter, but, over some time span, a matter of survival or precarious continuity.

FUNCTIONING PARTS OF HUMAN SOCIETIES AS ADAPTIVE MECHANISMS

For the sociologist, human society is not simply an aggregation of persons in a definite geographic area—though society includes both population and geographic location. More appropriately, society refers to the complex, interrelated, and relatively orderly process of interaction among those members that produce collective adaptation to their common environment. These interaction processes and their distinctive products constitute the "working parts" of society—and, most important, they constitute explicit or implicit solutions to the five sets of adaptive problems presented earlier.

As we have already noted in Chapter 1, the basic ingredients of human social experience can be reduced to (1) the amount and quality of *knowledge;* (2) ability to control or manipulate energy, that is, *technology;* (3) control or coordination of human behavior through *social organization;* and (4) interpretations and evaluations of social experience or *ideology.* Societies function and evolve by combining these four ingredients in a limited number of societal subsystems, which are of crucial interest not only to members of society but also to those who are concerned with understanding the complex achievements and difficulties of men and women in their manmade habitats.

Family

Perhaps the first adaptive subsystem we should mention is that ancient and pervasive unit of survival and biological replacement—the family, in its various forms (see Chapter 6). The family system has been an organization of basic technologies (food growing or gathering, environmental protection) and, in varying degrees, a means of transmitting adaptive (and maladaptive) mechanisms, through socialization to a defined circle of participants. In short, the family per-

---

[4] Ralph Linton, *The Study of Man* (New York: Appleton–Century–Crofts, Inc., 1936), pp. 348–355; Oscar Lewis, *The Effects of White Contact upon Blackfoot Culture* (New York: J. J. Augustin, 1942).

Families provide common emotional supports, in addition to the task of meeting physical needs.
(Courtesy Alfred Eisenstaedt, Life Magazine © 1972, Time Inc.)

forms its historic role by providing (1) physical protection; (2) the means for obtaining and distributing or allocating food and shelter; (3) biological replacements; and (4) a focus for the creation and expresson of values, priorities, judgments, and interpretations of individual and collaborative behavior. This multiadaptive potency is truly remarkable. However, much of the social contribution of family systems derives from the absence of other social mechanisms and from the practical monopoly that family systems therefore maintained over the fortunes and allegiances of members in earlier societies.[5]

From the successful operation of family systems came opportunities for additional adaptive devices—not by design or rational plan, but by considerable and unrecorded extensions and trials, which probably stimulated the adaptive solutions now inseparable from society itself. As we shall see, the family has been a seed bed for other, more complex, forms of social organization.

Division of Labor and Its Structural Forms

Though some specialization has always been a feature of family systems, usually in terms of sex and age differences, specialization or division of labor is a widely applicable mechanism in human communities and societies. Essentially, division of labor is a means by

[5] Ralph Linton, *ibid.*, Chaps. 10–12; Paul Bohannan, *Social Anthropology* (New York: Holt, Rinehart and Winston, Inc., 1963), Chaps. 6, 7, 9.

which greater efficiency in adaptation is sought. Because adaptation is both a complex and a continual problem, and because the abilities (physical and acquired) of members are unequal in intensely practical ways, division of labor *permits* (but does not guarantee) an ordering of human abilities that frees most individuals from the intolerable necessity of acquiring and satisfactorily using all adaptive devices.[6] In other words, division of labor makes specialization possible.

There have been varying *degrees* of division of labor in human societies, a phenomenon that has been widely recognized and discussed—from Plato and Aristotle, Aquinas, Saint Simon, A. Comte, H. Spencer, Durkheim, Marx, through such 20th century thinkers as Malinowski, Toynbee, John Dewey, Sorokin, and Parsons.[7] But how does division of labor operate? What are its component parts? First, each segment of a division of labor is characterized by a limited set of knowledge, skills, responsibilities, time and space allocation, and some explicit or implicit immunity from other adaptive responsibilities. Each of these specific items is an *evaluated guide to* social behavior—that is, a *norm*.[8] From an adaptive standpoint, norms must be relatively clear, practical, and within the competence of their enactors. Furthermore, norms not only provide a behavioral solution, but specify (or imply) the way in which the actor interacts with other members (that is, by acting in collaboration, in controlled competition, in antagonism to others, or by ignoring others).

For example, there are in our society specialized norms (in some quarters) for reading newspapers. In some respects, newspapers are adaptive devices; they provide information that is presumably necessary for making choices in the allocation of one's resources (for example, shopping, investing, house hunting, and so on). Thus, we expect businessmen (and dedicated investors) to read the *Wall Street Journal* or financial sections of general newspapers with great regularity, to decipher the otherwise mysterious symbols of stock market reporting and technical financial analysis and to discuss their reading with their peers. Normally, this type of behavior is

[6] V. Gordon Childe, *Man Makes Himself* (New York: Mentor Books, 1951), Chaps. 5–7.

[7] Plato, *The Republic* (New York: Modern Library, 1941); Aristotle, *The Politics* (New York: Modern Library, 1942); Herbert Spencer, *Principles of Sociology* (New York: D. Appleton, 1897), 3 Vols.; Emile Durkheim, *The Division of Labor in Society* (New York: Free Press, 1947); Karl Marx, *A Contribution to the Critique of Political Economy* (Chicago: Charles H. Kerr, 1904), pp. 11–12; Bronislaw Malinowski, *A Scientific Theory of Culture and Other Essays* (Chapel Hill, N.C.: University of North Carolina Press, 1944); Arnold J. Toynbee, *A Study of History,* Abridged ed. (New York: Oxford University Press, 1947), pp. 187–208, 241–246; John Dewey, *Intelligence in the Modern World* (New York: Modern Library, 1939); Pitirim A. Sorokin, *Society, Culture, and Personality* (New York: Harper & Row Publishers, Inc., 1947), Parts III and IV; Talcott Parsons, *Societies* (Englewood Cliffs, N.J.: Prentice–Hall, Inc., 1966), Chap. 2.

[8] John Thibaut and Harold H. Kelley, *The Social Psychology of Groups* (New York: John Wiley & Sons, Inc., 1959), pp. 126–136.

NEW YORK (AP) — New York Stock Exchange final quotations.

	Sales (hds.)	High	Low	Last	Net Chg.
— A—A —					
AbbtLbl.10	98	76⅞	75½	76⅞	+1
ACFInd 2.40	58	43¾	43¼	43¾	— ⅛
AcmeClev.80	20	15½	14¾	15½	+ ⅝
Acme Mkt2b	38	32⅝	32¼	32⅜	— ⅜
AdmsEl.09e	18	13	12¾	12⅞	+ ⅛
Ad Millis 20	27	8⅞	8½	8¾	— ⅛
Addresso.60	138	42⅜	41¼	41¾	— ⅞
Admiral	38	20	19¼	20	+ ⅝
AetnaLfe1.68	235	59¼	58⅞	59	— ¾
AetnaLfpf 2	4	53½	53½	53½	— ⅛
AguirreCo	9	14⅜	14¼	14⅜	— ⅛
AileenInc	38	11¼	11	11⅛	.....
Air Prod.20b	18	70¾	70⅜	70¾	+ ⅜
Airco.80e	119	18⅜	18	18⅜	+ ⅛
AJIndustries	32	4½	4⅜	4½	+ ⅛
Akzonala	10	28⅞	28¾	28⅞	+ ⅛
AlaGas 1.10	15	15⅞	15⅝	15⅝	— ⅛
AlaPpf8.28	z290	105	104	104½	— ½
AlaskaInters	336	45¾	43¾	45⅝	+ ¾
AlbertoC 32	71	26	25½	25⅞	— ⅜
Albertsns.36	25	13	12⅞	12⅞	.....
AlcanAlu.80	26	20½	20¼	20¼	— ⅜
AlcoStand.34	41	11⅞	11½	11½	— ⅜
Alcon Lab.26	37	63¾	61¼	61¼	—2¼
Alexndrs.30e	48	12⅞	12½	12½	— ¼
AllALfe.24e	43	12⅜	11⅛	11⅛	— ¾
Alleg Cp.20e	15	10⅝	10⅛	10⅛	— ¾
AllegLudlm1	52	26⅝	26⅛	26⅜	.....
AllegLudpf 3	12	40½	40½	40½	+ ¼
AllegPw1 40	121	21⅛	21	21	— ⅛
AllenGp1.04t	12	24½	24¼	24½	— ⅛
AlliedCh 1.20	159	29½	28⅝	29¼	— ⅜
AlldMills.75	4	19⅛	19⅛	19⅛	.....
AlliedPd .68	7	19½	19⅜	19⅜	— ⅛
AlliedStr1.40	34	33¼	33¼	33¼	— ⅛
AlliedSuper	36	4⅞	4¾	4⅞	.....
AllisChal.20e	x81	12¼	11⅞	12⅛	+ ⅛
AllrgtAut.48	x7	20⅜	19¾	19¾	— ⅜
Alcoa1 80	87	49½	48⅝	49	— ½
AmalSug1.60	2	26	25¾	25¾	.....
AMBAC.50	79	14⅞	14½	14½	— ⅛
Aer Es1.20	5	25½	25¼	25½	+ ¼
Am Espf2.60	3	44⅞	44⅞	44⅞	+ ¼

Explanation of Symbols

Sales figures are unofficial.

Unless otherwise noted, rates of dividends in the foregoing table are annual disbursements based on the last quarterly or semi-annual declaration. Special or extra dividends or payments not designated as regular are identified in the following footnotes.

a—Also extra or extras. b—Annual rate plus stock dividend. c—Liquidating dividend. d—Declared or paid in 1971 plus stock dividend. e—Declared or paid in preceding 12 months. f—Paid in stock during 1971, estimated cash value on ex-dividend or ex-distribution date. h—Declared or paid after stock dividend or split up. k—Declared or paid this year, an accumulative issue with dividends in arrears. n—New issue. p—Paid this year, dividend omitted, deferred or no action taken at last dividend meeting. r—Declared or paid in 1972 plus stock dividend. t—Paid in stock during 1972 estimated cash value on ex-dividend or exdistribution date.

z—Sales in full.

cld—Called. x—Ex dividend. y—Ex dividend and sales in full. x-dis—Ex distribution. xr—Ex rights. xw—Without warrants. ww—With warrantsm wd—When distributed. wi—When issued. nd—Next day delivery.

vj—In bankruptcy or receivership or being reorganized under the Bankruptcy Act, or securities assumed by such companies. fn—Foreign issue subject to interest equalization tax.

	Sales (hds.)	High	Low	Last	Net Chg.
CentSoya 1	62	26⅜	25⅜	25⅜	—1⅜
CenTelUt.94	59	17⅝	17⅜	17⅜	— ⅜
CerroCp.60e	46	13⅛	12⅞	13	.....
Cert-teed.80	27	54¾	54¼	54¼	—1⅛
CessnaAir.70	26	33¼	32½	33	— ½
ChadbrnInc	58	3	3	3	.....
Chadbrnpf	1	3¼	3¼	3¼	— ⅛
ChampInt.84	111	23¼	22⅝	22¾	— ½
ChmIpf1.20	45	25⅛	24⅝	25	.....
ChampS1.24	34	48⅛	47¾	47¾	— ½
CharterNY 2	68	30	29⅝	29⅝	— ⅝
ChaseManh2	353	56	55	56	+ ⅛
ChaseT3.59e	205	48⅜	46½	48⅜	+ ⅞
CheckerMot	4	21¾	21⅝	21⅝	— ¼
Chelsea.24	46	15½	15⅛	15½	+ ⅞
C emetrn.40	14	25⅜	24⅞	25	— ⅛

	Sales (hds.)	High	Low	Last	Net Chg.
DennyRst.04	75	16	15⅝	16	.....
DentsplyIntl	18	47½	47¼	47¼	— ½
Derecopf A	1	67½	67½	67½	— ¾
Derecopf B	12	68½	68½	68½	.....
DeSotoInc.40	24	17⅜	16¾	17	— ⅝
DetEdis1.40	67	20	19⅝	19⅝	— ¼
Det Edpf9.32	z90	117	116½	116½	—1½
Det Edpf5.50	7	78	77¾	77¾	— ¼
Dexter.24	17	25⅜	25	25⅛	— ½
Dial Finl.52	17	16⅜	16	16⅜	+ ⅜
DiamIntl1.80	93	37½	37	37⅜	.....
Diam Sham1	59	18⅝	18¼	18⅜	— ¼
Dia Sh pfC2	7	30¾	30⅝	30⅝	.....
DiaSpf D1.20	13	17	16⅝	16⅝	— ¼
Dictaphone	94	10½	10	10½	— ⅛

Figure 4–1 A portion of the daily listings on the New York stock exchange. These mysterious symbols and the information they represent are discussed and watched each day by a specialized group of people, and, most probably, at a specific place and time.

principally expected during early morning hours—either at breakfast or on the way to work. In fact, family norms specify whether or not newspaper reading at the breakfast table is appropriate, indicating the *degree of* specialization in time and space that is desirable.

Similarly, we expect an effective search for housing will involve attention to the Sunday papers, in which considerable space is given to available housing in various categories, in clearly identified areas of the community, and in distinctively abbreviated form. For best results, one must read real estate sections early on Sunday in order to reach the owner or agent before other potential buyers (or renters). In some areas, this is made difficult by the church-going inclinations of owners or realtors, which therefore requires information about the time range of Sunday services—normally provided in the Saturday editions of newspapers.

Social Roles as Adaptive Devices

Specialized norms, as has been implicitly suggested, cannot be practiced with efficiency in isolation from complementary or facilitative norms. Specialization, therefore, tends to operate through **sets of**

norms[9] that are focused on different phases of an important and practically separable type of adaptation. These norm sets are called **social roles.** But roles, which are the smallest crucial working parts of societies, are adaptive to the extent that the proper performance of one leads to or facilitates the satisfactory performance of interdependent roles. Role specialization, in short, serves to parcel out or subdivide relevant skills and responsibilities with the presumption that roles (and component norms) are *means* toward some *specific* goal of adaptation—not ends in themselves.

In the roles connected with being a male parent, the relevant norms are so numerous that a full accounting would be long and tedious. But it is clear that the "normal" male parent in contemporary American society must develop certain minimal skills. As husband, he must learn to distinguish and adapt to the legitimate wishes of his mate; as head of household, he must practice the occupational skills required for his job; as father, he must develop skills and norms concerning companionship, training, and discipline of his children. Obviously, these sets of norms deal with the problems of parenthood by separating adaptive issues into neat compartments. However, no parent can adapt successfully by favoring any one portion of these specialized responsibilities.

One of the basic lessons of human experience is that specialization can produce autonomous roles and thus, in time, create serious deficiencies in either physical or social adaptation. Consequently, specialization of roles is expressed in two important patterns. The first is designated the **complementary-role pattern.** Without exception, social roles are found in reciprocal pairs (or trios), since there is normally some *interchange* of service, information, or resources in pursuing a role. The illustrations of this universal regularity are endless: teacher–student, parent–child, husband–wife, producer–consumer, professional–client, entertainer–audience, employer–employee, official–citizen, master–slave, writer–public, criminal–public protector, officer–enlisted man, hero–fan, and so on.[10] The second type is the **sequential-role pattern.** Specialization of

---

[9] Michael Banton, *Roles* (London: Tavistock, 1965); S. F. Nadel, *The Theory of Social Structure* (London: Cohen and West, 1957); S. F. Nadel, *The Foundations of Social Anthropology* (New York: Free Press, 1951); Frederick L. Bates, "Position, Role, and Status: A Reformulation of Concepts," *Social Forces, 34* (May 1956), pp. 313–321.

[10] See, for example, John W. Bennett and Iwao Ishino, *Paternalism in the Japanese Economy* (Minneapolis, Minn.: University of Minnesota Press, 1963); Talcott Parsons, *Essays in Sociological Theory* (New York: Free Press, 1954), Chaps. 2, 18; Gilberto Freyre, *The Masters and the Slaves* (New York: Alfred A. Knopf, 1946); Hugh D. Duncan, *Language and Literature in Society* (Chicago: University of Chicago Press, 1953); Hugh D. Duncan, "Sociology of Art, Literature, and Music," in Howard Becker and Alvin Boskoff (eds.), *Modern Sociological Theory* (New York: Dryden, 1957), pp. 488–494; Eliot Freidson, *Professional Dominance* (New York: Free Press, 1970); Jerold Heiss (ed.), *Family Roles and Interaction* (Chicago: Rand McNally & Co., 1968), Parts 3, 5; Orrin E. Klapp, *Heroes, Villains, and Fools* (Englewood Cliffs, N.J.: Prentice–Hall, Inc., 1962).

roles in time is virtually a human invention. It rests on the implicit notion of degrees of social experience and learning, thereby allowing or encouraging members to succeed to more complex or more valued roles in some predictable time period. An obvious example is the normal movement from children's roles to adult responsibilities—sometimes mediated by the development of adolescent roles.[11] Most organizations (political, economic, educational, religious) have a graded set of official positions—from "member" to secretary, to vice-president, and then to president or chairman—that represents a probable career line of increasing role responsibilities for selected members. Similarly, in an open-class society such as ours, it is widely expected that as resources and experience expand (this simply refers to the popular phenomenon of upward social mobility), individuals will exchange simpler roles (as consumers and active participants) for more difficult and more varied forms of social participation.[12] Sequential-role specialization seems to be a means by which unavoidable (but not necessarily just or rational) social inequalities are made more acceptable and more workable in given societies—in short, it provides social mobility.

Systems of Exchange and Allocation

In addition to the more immediate reciprocities of complementary roles (for example, parent–child, teacher–student), there are extremely important problems in sustaining and coordinating the operation of many simultaneous sets of complementary and sequential roles in human societies. These problems are reflected in many familiar forms: distrust, jealousy, and envy; unbridgeable generational differences; inability to empathize with persons in other roles; the development of "bureaucratic" isolation from unforeseen events; exploitation, or the practice of taking special advantage of the rewards associated with some skill or item of information. Of course, with few exceptions historically, societies have operated with rather limited resources of natural wealth, manpower, and socially defined wealth (approval, esteem, respect, and so on). Under these circumstances, an unrestricted competition between and among various specialized roles can produce considerable imbalance among roles and thus reduce the adaptive efficiency of social specialization itself.

Societies normally develop two related devices that serve in varying degrees as protections against the confusion and conflict

---

[11] Arnold Van Gennep, *The Rites of Passage* (Chicago: University of Chicago Press, 1960); Max Gluckman (ed.), *Essays on the Ritual of Social Relations* (Manchester, England: Manchester University Press, 1962).
[12] Pitirim A. Sorokin, *Social Mobility* (New York: Harper & Row Publishers, Inc., 1927), Chap. 26. See also Barney G. Glaser and Anselm L. Strauss, *Status Passage* (Chicago: Aldine Publishing Co., 1971).

that usually accompany uncontrolled competition for scarce resources. One such mechanism is the invention of one or more flexible "media of exchange." Essentially, the practical problem of
"interchange" rests on two considerations: (a) between which specialized roles is exchange necessary and/or desirable and (b) what
mechanism effectively controls the process of exchange? Generally,
human societies have tended to place greatest emphasis on exchange
between and among "productive" roles, that is, roles whose products are such tangible items as food, weapons, tools, art objects,
and even wives. The earliest attempts at developing workable exchange processes must have been extremely difficult both because
the available supplies of such items were limited and because determining a scale of comparative worth or value was (and is) extremely
tricky and perhaps inherently arbitrary. With a small number of exchanges between and among numbers of a limited population, the
adaptive solution could often be *direct exchange or barter* of needed

**The invention of money as a means of exchange freed every man to par-
ticipate in many phases of society.**
(Courtesy Russell Lee.)

products and even of personal services[13] (such as aid in food raising or house building).

But such complex human societies as the classical civilizations of Egypt, Mesopotamia, Anatolia, Greece, and Rome could not operate with inefficient and idiosyncratic methods of barter. Despite centuries of moral condemnation, *money as a means of exchange* must be objectively viewed as a social invention of the highest importance to human social adaptation.[14] For money—an independent yet commonly valued measure of worth—enables virtually every member to participate in processes of exchange and thereby encourages implicitly the continuation and even the extension of specialization. Thus, at least in part, it brings about greater efficiency in producing items of adaptive value.[15] In recent generations, perhaps, in collaboration with technological developments, money has stimulated production of a great number of nonadaptive and even maladaptive products (such as cigarettes, harmful drugs, and various electrical appliances).

In the last two centuries, but particularly in the past 50 years, money as a medium of exchange has been immensely extended through the invention of *credit*—the relatively dependable promise to transfer money (and therefore some definable amount and range of products) at some *future time* to facilitate exchange of goods or services in the present. Thus, the potentialities of role specialization and exchange can attain a complexity and a liberating effect that our predecessors in the eighth century B.C. could not anticipate in their wildest imaginings. Indeed, as credit was progressively extended to merchants, producers, and then consumers (see Tables 4–3 and 4–4),[16] the ability to choose among a multiplicity of devices and products has paradoxically *increased adaptive capacity* for more people and at the same time fostered a number of critical problems in modern societies that *threaten human adaptation.* (See Chapter 12 for discussions of some of these adaptive problems.)

Social Differentiation of Opportunities

In addition to the mechanism of exchange (which the economists identify as the "market system"), human societies have normally responded to the practical problems of specialization with a system (or systems) of *social allocation of opportunities and rewards.* While specialized roles usually include some clues to the physical and social

---

[13] For example, Bronislaw Malinowski, *Argonauts of the Western Pacific* (London: Routledge and Kegan Paul, 1922); Elizabeth E. Hoyt, *Primitive Trade* (New York: A. M. Kelly, 1926).
[14] Georg Simmel, *On Individuality and Social Forms* (Chicago: University of Chicago Press, 1971), Chap. 5; Max Weber, *General Economic History* (New York: Free Press, 1950), Chap. 19.
[15] Max Weber, *ibid.,* Chaps. 20–21.
[16] A general survey of value is W. F. Oakeshott, *Commerce and Society* (Oxford: Clarendon Press, 1936).

TABLE 4–3

Consumer credit (in billions of dollars) in the United States 1958–1968.

Type of credit	1958	1963	1966	1967	June 1968
Mortgage debt	105.1	167.3	210.1	221.6	228.5
Short and inter-mediate term consumer credit	45.0	70.5	94.8	99.2	101.5
Installment	33.6	55.5	77.5	80.9	89.9
Non-instalment	11.5	16.3	20.0	21.2	23.3
Single payment loans	3.6	6.1	8.0	8.4	9.1
Charge accounts	5.1	5.9	6.7	7.0	7.8
Service credit	2.8	4.2	5.3	5.8	6.4

SOURCE: *Finance Facts Yearbook, 1969* (Washington: National Consumer Finance Association, 1969), p. 42.

TABLE 4–4

Installment credit in 1968 by income level and amount of credit.

Family income	No credit	Install-ment credit	Under $200	$200–500	$500–1000	$1000 and over
All families	52%	48%	8%	7%	10%	23%
Under $3000	83	17	9	4	3	1
$3000–4999	60	40	12	10	8	10
$5000–7499	44	56	10	10	13	24
$7500–9999	38	62	7	8	14	33
$10,000–14,999	40	60	6	7	11	36
$15,000 and over	52	48	3	3	9	34

SOURCE: *Survey of Consumer Finances* (Ann Arbor, Mich.: Survey Research Center, University of Michigan, 1968), p. 50.

satisfactions one can expect, the practitioners of each role tend to view their skills and responsibilities as especially important. Indeed, normal processes of role learning *encourage* a certain degree of chauvinism or magnification of role. But the competition of varied roles (and their practitioners) for limited resources inevitably pro-duces dangerous social conflicts. The practical problem thus be-comes one of controlling competition by developing a system of *socially defined priorities.*[17]

[17] See Chapter 8.

This system of allocation by priorities is generally known as **social stratification,** with emphasis on the part of many analysts and social philosophers on the *inequities* or *inequalities* that characterize stratification. While such inequities are obvious, a more careful analysis indicates that several other considerations or aspects are also important in understanding the operation of human societies. Perhaps the most basic aspect of stratification is regularization through grading of roles and persons—in other words, a **social hierarchy.**[18] Clearly, grading or differential evaluation of roles can be either predominantly arbitrary or somewhat rational, depending on the standards used and the position of the evaluator. The broader consequence, however, is the creation of a diminished competition for relatively scarce resources and a clarification for each level or social category of the resources it can confidently expect. In addition, one or more *social mechanisms* for unequal (graded) allocation can be found in stratified societies. For example, in typically capitalistic societies, the market and its manipulation serve to distribute wealth and goods in classically unequal manner to financiers, entrepreneurs, artisans, and craftsmen, apprentices, and the unemployed.[19] Similarly, the institution of the state as a specialized agency of control explicitly or implicitly channels varying funds and valued services to such different categories as large farm holders, workmen (through unemployment insurance), businessmen (through tax policies), urban middle classes (through federal deposit insurance, guarantee of home loans, and so on). During the late medieval period, the Catholic Church was a major mechanism of European stratification, not only in its system of ecclesiastical hierarchy, but in distributing money, power, and military force to aid or oppose nobles, merchants, workers, and peasants.[20] Finally, in the modern era, formal educational systems indirectly and perhaps unwittingly aid existing inequalities by providing further opportunities for those already best suited to obtain greater amounts of valued resources and experiences.[21]

It is now evident from this range of *stratificational mechanisms* and systems that the practical necessity of social stratification outweighs the often justified criticisms of its particular forms—at least under the technological conditions that exist thus far in human

[18] See, for example, Marc Bloch, *Feudal Society* (Chicago: University of Chicago Press, 1959); Albert J. Reiss, *Occupations and Social Status* (New York: Free Press, 1961); Melvin M. Tumin, *Social Stratification* (Englewood Cliffs, N.J.: Prentice–Hall, Inc., 1967), Chaps. 1–3.
[19] Max Weber, *General Economic History* (New York: Free Press, 1950), Part 4.
[20] Henri Pirenne, *Economic and Social History of Medieval Europe* (New York: Harcourt, Brace and World, 1937).
[21] Patricia C. Sexton, *Education and Income* (New York: Viking Press, 1961); Aaron V. Cicourel and John I. Kitsuse, *Educational Decision-Makers* (Indianapolis, Ind.: Bobbs–Merrill, 1963); James S. Coleman et al., *Equality of Educational Opportunity* (Washington, D.C.: Department of Health, Education and Welfare, 1966). See also the sociological fantasy, Michael Young, *The Rise of the Meritocracy* (Baltimore, Md.: Penguin Books, Inc., 1961).

societal development. On the other hand, it is also clear that systems of unequal allocation have been perceived as difficult but necessary *compromises*. This perhaps accounts for the fact that every stratification system operates with a reinforcing or "rationalizing" ideology—for example, "divine right," the "will of Allah," the compelling needs of the nation, the sanctity of free enterprise, the dictatorship of the proletariat, Aquinas' concept of a "natural necessary world order," "what's good for General Motors is good for the U.S."[22] In some systems—such as our own—there is a special *ideology of potential mobility,* which confirms the existing hierarchy by encouraging aspirations for individual "movement" to levels of greater opportunity.[23]

As we shall see in Chapter 8, the consequences of stratified allocation systems tend to be a mixture of adaptive and maladaptive aspects. However, wherever specialization is a dominant feature, some form of stratification normally develops, perhaps because no alternative solution to the problems of specialization is workable. Consequently, it seems fruitless to debate the merits of stratification as a mechanism.[24] Instead, social scientists and citizens would be more justified in carefully examining the variety of stratification systems in their respective societal settings for clues about (1) the contributions of those systems to adaptation and (2) their costs in human and physical terms for obtaining certain levels of adaptation.

Systems of Symbolic Participation—Ritual and Related Organizations

Thoughtful observers of contemporary societies—and of specific periods in earlier societies—continually point to the phenomena of individualism, of numerous personal and intergroup conflicts, of unsuccessful communication and inadequate understanding. In short, they point out that societies are seriously deficient in sustaining common efforts and active cooperation for adaptation to physical and social environments. But all societies, in varying degrees, have devised social mechanisms that normally produce minimal (or greater) degrees of common purpose, trust, and cooperative attitudes in a substantial portion of their members. The basic form of such mechanisms is found in groups or organizations that directly or

---

[22] Gerhard Lenski, *Power and Privilege* (New York: McGraw–Hill Book Co., 1966); Vilfredo Pareto, *Mind and Society* (New York: Harcourt, Brace and World, 1935), Vol. 3.

[23] John W. Tebbel, *From Rags to Riches: Horatio Alger, Jr. and the American Dream* (New York: The Macmillan Company, 1963); Donald B. Meyer, *The Positive Thinkers* (Garden City, N.Y.: Doubleday & Company, Inc., 1965); Richard Weiss, *The American Myth of Success* (New York: Basic Books, 1969); Irvin G. Wyllie, *The Self-Made Man in America* (New Brunswick, N.J.: Rutgers University Press, 1954).

[24] See Melvin M. Tumin (ed.), *Readings on Social Stratification* (Englewood Cliffs, N.J.: Prentice–Hall, Inc., 1970), Chap. 9; Tumin, *Social Stratification* (Englewood Cliffs, N.J.: Prentice–Hall, Inc., 1967), Chap. 12.

There is a meaningful bond, an emotional kinship, among these Harvard alumni. They share a common feeling of identification.
(Courtesy Jim Harrison.)

indirectly provide repeated experiences of "emotional kinship" and relatively complete immersion in common or collective activities.[25] In short, the essential effect of these social forms is the production of a meaningful and voluntary feeling of fundamental similarity among members of society, despite their obvious differences, rather than a concern for direct problem-solving efficiency or individual striving.

Thus, to take the more obvious instances first, religious denominations provide regular opportunities for "retreats" in isolated areas and "potluck suppers" for sociability and fellowship. Large firms try to create and sustain common feelings of identification through office parties, company outings, honorific social occasions for faithful employees, and "in-house" newspapers. Similar attempts at emotional kinship may also be seen in sports "pep rallies" in high school and college, in enthusiastic spectatorship of professional games (basketball, baseball, soccer, and so on), and in various informal student–faculty conferences in which the usual differences are consciously ignored.

[25] A good general discussion is in David Bakan, The Duality of Human Existence (Chicago: Rand, McNally & Co., 1966). Specific examples can be found in Richard Neville, Play Power (New York: Random House, 1970); William Hedgepeth, The Alternative: Communal Life in America (New York: The Macmillan Company, 1970); Lewis Yablonsky, The Hippie Trip (New York: Pegasus, 1968); Jane Howard, Please Touch (New York: McGraw–Hill Book Co., 1970).

Symbolic Participation

A highly important functional component of human societies is a set of sociocultural inventions that provide some measure of cohesion or integration among their members through **symbolic participation** in a limited variety of social organizations. Symbolic participation, however, is a crucial but subtle aspect of human experience and deserves some emphasis at this point. Essentially, this kind of social interaction is based on the discovery that human satisfactions and needs can be fruitfully pursued not only directly and practically (by immediate application of definite skills), but also by converting concrete problems into more general and nonthreatening forms (that is, situations not requiring immediate, evaluated solutions). In other words, "normal" problems (such as growing adequate food, properly handling strangers, adjustment to some loss, anxiety over personal worth) are depersonalized and are instead represented by "substitute" activities and conceptions (values, ideas). Let us call these "substitute activities" *ritual practices,* and such substitute conceptions *symbols.*[26]

Ritual practices include prevailing patterns of superstition (for example, avoiding black cats or walking around, not under, ladders), the attribution of social difficulties to some culturally defined ethnic category (scapegoating), and conspicuous display—or even destruction—of wealth and property (as in the potlatch of the Kwakiutl Indians). Symbols that serve as "answers" to important adaptive problems may be found in culturally designed material items (for example, flags as symbols of national strength, rings as symbols of marriage bonds), or in widely appreciated names that summarize (and perhaps caricature) an enemy or a problem (for example, "City Hall," "the system," "the Establishment," "Wall Street").

Groups that are marked by the phenomena of symbolic participation seem impractical, unnecessary, or "backward" to the unsympathetic observer. But these judgments belie the amazing tenacity of symbolic participation and ignore the immensely practical (adaptive) role of apparently "impractical" social arrangements. Perhaps the most significant feature of such mechanisms is that they provide for their participants relatively simple, unexamined, and therefore unchallengeable answers to hypothetical (that is, not immediate) problems. By doing so, such experiences promote emotional ease, trust, temporary immunity from the need for actual achievement, and a feeling of community derived from similarly protected experience.

---

[26] Gregory Bateson, *Naven* (Cambridge, England: Clarendon Press, 1936); Suzanne K. Langer, *Philosophy in a New Key* (New York: Mentor Books, 1948), especially Chaps. 6, 7.

Religion and Symbolic Participation. For example, religious organizations typically develop (or confirm) attitudes of belonging or cohesiveness among their believers by creating powerful conceptions of an intangible but meaningful realm of spirits, deities, supernaturals, or some ultimate power. These conceptions are symbolized in religious objects (for example, sacred books, robes, the cross, the star of David) that are believed to represent otherwise unattainable entities.[27] But symbols of this general kind are normally employed in prescribed ways when the members of the group or organization are assembled. Thus, religion, in one important respect, provides symbolic—ritual—bonds that unify those who accept either the *meanings* of the particular symbols or the importance of shared symbols.

The symbolism of religion is captured in the traditional Catholic mass.
(Courtesy Robert Rapelye, Photography International.)

Art and Symbolic Participation. Historically, the arts were primarily concerned with symbolizing religious activities and concepts. But the various arts as independent secular activities likewise serve as forms of symbolic participation for large segments of society. Music, painting, literature (everything from comics to classics to erotica), drama, and aspects of advertising[28] all operate (a)

[27] Emile Durkheim, *The Elementary Forms of the Religious Life* (New York: Free Press, 1947); Anthony F. C. Wallace, *Religion: An Anthropological View* (New York: Random House, 1966); Elizabeth Nottingham, *Religion: A Sociological View* (New York: Random House, 1971), Chaps. 3–5.

[28] Hugh D. Duncan, *Language and Literature in Society* (Chicago: University of Chicago Press, 1953); Frederick Antal, *Florentine Painting and its Background* (London: Kegan Paul, 1947); Vernon L. Parrington, *Main Currents in American Thought* (New York: Harcourt, Brace and World, 1927, 1930), 3 Vols.

Different forms of music attract different audiences but all participants feel the emotional exhilaration and the unifying effect of the occasion.
(Courtesy Robert Rapelye, Photography International.)

with one or more distinct publics and/or assembled audiences; (b) using symbols in the form of current styles or fashions, popular heroes, "sacred" works or memories; and (c) at key production or performance centers (for example, Carnegie Hall, Fleet Street, the "Met"). Ritual occasions of great significance include major exhibitions of art objects, "first night" performances, autograph ceremonies in department store book departments, and personal appearances of prominent artists. The emotional exhilaration of these occasions and the unifying effect of personalized symbols are perhaps best illustrated by the collective screams and moans of teenagers during the performance of rock groups—and in earlier years, the emotional response provoked by an Elvis Presley, a Frank Sinatra, or even a Rudy Vallee or a Rudolph Valentino.

Other Forms of Symbolic Participation.   Religion and the arts, however, do not monopolize phenomena of symbolic participation in modern society.   Many voluntary associations[29]—such as clubs, lodges, brotherhoods, civic groups, and most recently, "sensitivity groups," likewise seem to function without great tangible achievements, despite their formal objectives of service, charity, and social action or influence.   Members enjoy or need the symbolism of the Masons, the Shrine, the PEO (women's educational organization), the Daughters of the American Revolution, the Kiwanis, the Tuesday Afternoon Musical, the "coming out" party.   In addition to their ostensible goals, such organizations enable persons to meet regularly with some range of "strangers" who are often found to be quite similar in basic respects.

Still another form of symbolic participation is the *voluntary primary group,* as distinguished from the inescapable early primary groups (such as one's family of orientation, the circle of close relatives, and the network of intimate neighbors).   Clearly, voluntary primary groups are more likely to occur in larger, more differentiated societies, where contacts with early primary groups are often more difficult and where the major symbolic alternatives are formal voluntary associations and voluntary primary affiliations.   As examples of the latter, we have most obviously newly established families (families of procreation), informal associations of co-workers, adult friendship circles, and the less than fragile patterns of sociability among adult neighbors.   These groups or quasigroups are *predominantly* concerned with interchange of personal subjective values and opinions, with support rather than criticism or evaluation, and with ease rather than specific achievements.   Consequently, ritual occasions (parties, weddings, cookouts) are memorable and necessary links among informally dedicated participants.   And each such group possesses its own focal symbols—the family name and certain valued possessions; "shop talk" and favorite targets for ridicule; special foods and beverages and favorite places for pleasant association; the valued identity of a geographic area and locally significant issues for impassioned discussion.[30]

The diversity and prevalence of symbolic participation forms is not usually apparent to the layman, perhaps because he takes them for granted.   Yet their importance as adaptive devices cannot be overestimated.   Without some satisfactory participation in these universal social settings, individuals fail to acquire indispensable social competence and become social casualties or social burdens to their fellow seekers of physical and social survival.   Indeed,

[29] A good introduction and survey are contained in David L. Sills, "Voluntary Associations: Sociological Aspects," in *International Encyclopedia of the Social Sciences* (New York: Free Press, 1968), Vol. 16, pp. 362–379.
[30] Gerald D. Suttles, *The Social Order of the Slum* (Chicago: University of Chicago Press, 1968); D. C. Dunphy, *Cliques, Crowds, and Gangs: Group Life of Sydney Adolescents* (Sydney: Cheshire, 1969).

lack of contact with such integrative (cohesive) associations often eventuates in the stigmatization of these "deprived" persons as odd, eccentric, or "mental cases." [31]

Systems of Ideational Readjustment

As a final component of human societies, there is the increasingly visible pattern of activities that deal with conscious reappraisal and restructuring of the environment and/or of available social solutions for controlling the environment. Essentially, these activities produce either conceptual or technical innovations that are designed to offer "better" or "more efficient" solutions to crucial problems faced by a group, community, or society. However, innovation is a rather widespread phenomenon among individuals[32]—and much of this innovation is either ignored or rejected. By "systems of ideational readjustment," we mean socially encouraged (or permitted) sources of innovation, which subsequently result in altered kinds of social behavior and achievement.

Warfare and Religion

In retrospect, it is difficult to locate a single, unalterable social or cultural form or source of innovation. Simple societies possess no identifiable social incubator of innovation (though it is clearly inaccurate to conclude that members of such societies are not innovative). But when we turn to "historical" societies of the past 5000 years, the development of alternative structural sources of innovation is unmistakable. In some societies, a primary source of innovation was the *military system* and its related technology, which resulted in more efficient battle formations and the adoption of improved weapons. Classical Persia, Greece in the fourth century B.C., Mesopotamia from 3000 to 1200 B.C., and Rome in the first and second centuries B.C. are some of the relevant illustrations of the dynamism of aggressive warfare.[33] Another innovative source was the *religious sphere,* from which significant moral, ethical, and organizational changes were derived—for example, monotheism, caste systems, notions of human dignity, new role models (such as the selfless intellectual or monk, the prophet, and the crusader–reformer), systems of public charity, and such varied dividends as new architectural forms (the Gothic) and the foundations of classical music.[34]

[31] Georg Simmel, *The Sociology of Georg Simmel* (New York: Free Press, 1951), pp. 43–49; R. D. Laing, *The Politics of Experience* (Baltimore, Md.: Penguin Books, Inc., 1967); Thomas Szasz, *The Myth of Mental Illness* (New York: Harper & Row Publishers, Inc., 1961); Thomas Szasz, *The Manufacture of Madness* (New York: Harper & Row Publishers, Inc., 1970).
[32] H. G. Barnett, *Innovation: The Basis of Cultural Change* (New York: McGraw–Hill Book Co., 1953), Introduction, Chaps. 2, 6.
[33] Max Weber, *General Economic History* (New York: Free Press, 1950), Chap. 28.
[34] Max Weber, *Economy and Society* (New York: Bedminster Press, 1968), Vol. 2, Chap. 6.

Philosophy

A third major matrix of innovation has primarily spawned *intellectual goals* for practical, political change in complex, troubled societies. This is the realm of philosophy, which has traditionally been part of (and sometimes dominant in) the formalized system of higher education. Beginning with the Greeks, philosophy and education have been an enduring seed bed of novel (or attractively refurbished) arguments for cultural or social changes. While philosophers were not regularly successful in promoting new sociopolitical programs during the past 200 years in Western civilization, the realm of philosophy has been responsible for political democracy (Locke, Rousseau, Montesquieu); mercantilist foreign policy (A. Smith); socialism (W. Morris, B. Russell); communism (Marx and Engels, Lenin); experiments in education (Rousseau, Dewey); racist social policy (de Gobineau, Nietzsche); passive resistance movements (Ghandi, Tolstoy); government welfare through deficit spending (Keynes, Galbraith—philosophical economists).[35]

Science

More recently, perhaps from 1920 to the present in the more complex societies, the primary organizational focus of innovation has been *science*—in institutes, universities, private research laboratories, and government-sponsored facilities. The immense flow of new solutions from science—and technology—is too familiar and expansive for any attempt at precise itemization here. Basically, scientific innovations have been technical in character, and have comprised improvements in productivity (food and various luxury products), in ease and extent of communication, in health, and in destructive ability. Certainly, science has also helped in altering man's orientation to the physical world (and to himself as well). He has moved from a relationship characterized by dependence, chaos, and fear, to one of partial and dubious mastery of a complex and still unfathomable order, one in which great potentialities are counterbalanced by the recognition of man's recurrent irrationalities, one in which the practical need for adequate diversity and change is taxing the apparently limited capacity of man to sustain viable societies under rapid and incessant processes of semidigested changes.[36]

[35] See, for example, Bertrand Russell, *A History of Western Philosophy* (New York: Simon and Schuster, 1945). For the relation between philosophy and economic policy, see the following works of J. K. Galbraith: *The Affluent Society* (Boston: Houghton Mifflin Company, 1960); *American Capitalism* (Boston: Houghton Mifflin Company, 1952); *The New Industrial State* (Boston: Houghton Mifflin Company, 1967).
[36] Thomas S. Kuhn, *The Structure of Scientific Revolution* (Chicago: University of Chicago Press, 1970), Rev. ed.

Changes in Innovation

Ideational readjustment has always operated by producing revisions in basic ideals or values, in technical processes, and in forms of social organization. But three tendencies in innovation can be identified in the history of evolving social complexity. First, there is the development of multiple (and partly antagonistic) sources of responsible readjustments—for example, religion, government, the intelligentsia (philosophers, educators), science, technology, and in recent decades, the literary and fine arts. Second, primary responsibility and trust in innovation has clearly shifted toward science, though there is considerable evidence of ambivalence toward science in recent decades and an anxious search either for a widely acceptable substitute (religion, political activism) or an alternative to active readjustment itself (for example, drugs, violence, social withdrawal).[37] Third, until very recently, perhaps greater efforts and more rewards have been connected with technical innovations and their implementation. It is of course erroneous to conclude that innovations in values and ideologies and in social organization have declined to the point of insignificance. Yet there is considerable evidence of old and impractical solutions masquerading as "innovation" in either basic values or forms of organization and social mobilization of effort. Legislation in the areas of farm problems, poverty, housing, taxation, and crime, for example, seems to employ old strategies and mechanisms with new labels—and with continued but more expensive failures.

Part of the pervasive unrest and disquietude of our time —both among the disaffected young and the presumably "established" middle-aged—may be interpreted as a reflection of concern for the feeble attempts at readjustment in values and organization.[38] The crisis of complex society may well be the understandable fear that we have scraped the bottom of the barrel of innovation and that technical proficiency will be *inappropriately* applied to problems of moral and associational alteration. This is not "cultural lag" —the simple retardation of valuational change, as compared with

---

[37] A much cited general discussion is C. P. Snow, *The Two Cultures and the Scientific Revolution* (Cambridge, England: Cambridge University Press, 1959; Rev. ed., 1963). Two critical analyses of science are J. W. Krutch, *The Measure of Man* (Indianapolis, Ind.: Bobbs–Merrill, 1954); Jacques Barzun, *Science: The Glorious Entertainment* (New York: Harper & Row Publishers, Inc., 1964).

[38] Widely read or often quoted works of social criticism in this vein include Lewis Mumford, *The Myth of the Machine* (New York: Harcourt, Brace and World, 1967); Jacques Ellul, *The Technological Society* (New York: Alfred A. Knopf, 1961); Herbert Marcuse, *One-Dimensional Man* (Boston: Beacon Press, 1964); Charles A. Reich, *The Greening of America* (New York: Random House, 1970).

technological advancement—but a reaction to (and fear of) a *perceived technological imperialism* that would enforce a single mode of solutions to a variegated set of societal problems in evolution.[39]

The long quest for human adaptation has resulted in a limited number of recurring social activities or mechanisms, as we have seen in the latter half of this chapter. These adaptive activities depend, not only on biological capacities of human populations, but on the previous experience of similar populations. For convenience, we have discussed such experience as composed of four interlocking aspects—knowledge, technology, ideology, and social organization. While all four are important, the fundamental significance of social organization (the ordering of interactions between and among persons in defined populations) is undeniable. Essentially, social organization provides varied and complementary means of collaboration in applying and changing forms of technology and ideology. In Part II, therefore, we turn to this crucial aspect of human adaptive experience—social organization—with major concern for the operation of organizational components (role and skill types, groups, stratified structures, and communities). The basic theme of Part II—social specialization as a primary source of adaptation—is detailed in Chapter 5.

Summary

In this chapter, human society has been viewed as a series of complex structures that are typically faced with a common set of practical problems. These problems can be conceptualized in various ways, but we have identified them as survival, effective cooperation, replacement, and readaptation. As a consequence of more or less successful attempts at solving these problems, human societies typically develop a limited number of basic human social inventions. Essentially, these "inventions" have become fundamental components of all societies and their study is inseparable from an understanding of how societies operate. Our discussion has focused on universal components: a family system, a structured division of labor, a system of exchange and allocation, systems of symbolic participation and ritual, and systems of ideational readjustment. The nature of interactions of these

---

[39] Classic discussions of lag are found in W. F. Ogburn, *Social Change* (New York: B. W. Huebsch, 1922), pp. 200–213; Howard W. Odum, *Understanding Society* (New York: The Macmillan Company, 1947), Chap. 20.

components, and changes in the way they interact, constitute indispensable means by which we try to develop valid and reliable explanations of human phenomena. In fact, sociology as an intellectual enterprise has evolved as a means of determining and specifying significant questions about the functioning of manmade components in different societies and in different time periods. The remainder of this work will try to show how knowledge of these components (and their interrelations) and understanding of the developments in these components contribute to a fuller appreciation of the nature and achievements of social adaptation among humans.

Exercises

1. Assemble a list of the most important obstacles to social or collective human adaptation to a given environment.
2. What are the advantages and disadvantages of symbols for human adaptation?
3. What are the difficulties one must face in trying to follow any one norm?
4. Evaluate these statements: (a) Equality is necessary for social adaptation; (b) equality of ability is necessary for social adaptation; (c) equality of opportunity is necessary for social adaptation.
5. Why is art in various forms of great interest to any serious student of human society?
6. How can you account for the popularity of sensitivity groups? Of various kinds of counseling services?
7. What seem to be the most needed kinds of social (organizational) innovations for the adaptive problems of modern societies?

Selected Bibliography

Alland, Alexander. *Adaptation to Cultural Evolution.* New York: Columbia University Press, 1970, esp. Chap. 2.
Banton, Michael. *Roles.* London: Tavistock, 1965.
Blau, Peter M. *Exchange and Power in Social Life.* New York: John Wiley & Sons, Inc., 1964.
Childe, V. Gordon. *Man Makes Himself.* New York: Mentor Books, 1951.
Durkheim, Emile. *The Division of Labor in Society.* New York: Free Press, 1947.

Durkheim, Emile. *The Elementary Forms of the Religious Life.* New York: Free Press, 1947.

Parsons, Talcott. *The System of Modern Societies.* Englewood Cliffs, N.J.: Prentice–Hall, Inc., 1971.

Service, Elman R. *Primitive Social Organization: An Evolutionary Perspective.* New York: Random House, 1962.

Part II

Social Organization and Human Adaptation

5

Differentiation and
Social Organization

In 1776, the year of the Declaration of Independence and the beginning of an effective revolution, a Scots philosopher–economist, Adam Smith, published a thick book called *The Wealth of Nations*, which was also revolutionary in pointing out the importance of specialization (division of labor) in manufacturing and, by extension, in human enterprises generally. Of course, Smith assumed that division of labor would be worked out efficiently and rationally, and that people would recognize the benefits of such specialization.[1] However, in the intervening 200 years, Western civilization and other parts of the world have recurrently discovered that specialization is both adaptive and problematical. For example, the development of specialized skills and the growth of specialized concentrations of populations in urban communities have created the bases for (1) extended survival of human populations and (2) more efficient means of harnessing and changing the physical environment in pursuit of biological and acquired (cultural) needs and goals. On the other hand, differentiation or specialization in human society is not without intense practical difficulties or defects in application. In the economic sphere of major nations, we can

[1] Adam Smith, *The Wealth of Nations* (New York: Modern Library, 1937), Chaps. 1, 2.

TABLE 5–1

Number of governmental units in selected standard metropolitan statistical areas, 1962.

Area	Total units	School districts	Counties	Municipalities	Townships	Special districts
Atlanta	84	9	5	45	. . .	25
Baltimore	123	2	. . .	17	59	47
Chicago	1060	340	6	246	114	354
Detroit	241	96	3	80	52	10
Los Angeles– Long Beach	348	141	2	95	. . .	110
Minneapolis– St. Paul	261	86	5	105	51	14
Newark	204	72	3	49	33	47
New York City	555	198	5	132	36	185
Philadelphia	963	331	7	140	199	286
Pittsburgh	806	261	4	189	119	233
St. Louis	439	105	5	163	46	120
San Francisco	398	143	5	58	. . .	192

SOURCE: *The Municipal Year Book 1964* (Chicago: International City Managers' Association, 1964), pp. 40–41.

note periods of high unemployment, crushing debt, poverty, and inadequate or even overabundant production of goods. Clearly, economic differentiation has been recurrently inefficient, in many types of economic order.

Likewise, in the political sphere, the number of specialized government units and jurisdictions in metropolitan areas is so large that it is often impossible to arrive at practical solutions to serious problems in, among others, educational services, airport facilities, adequate water supply, racial discrimination, pollution of air and water, adequate local financing, and health services (see Table 5–1).[2] Though there are many more examples of inadequacies of specialization, it is important to recognize that specialization is a widespread and a variably effective social device. We must therefore understand the nature and dynamics of social specialization more fully than has any previous generation in human history.

A DEFINITION AND SOME DISTINCTIONS

Social differentiation is a necessary and continuing process in human communities and societies through which skills, interests, opportunities, or social experiences are distinguished and assigned (or

[2] John C. Bollens and Henry J. Schmandt, *The Metropolis* (New York: Harper & Row Publishers, Inc., 1965); Robert C. Wood, *1400 Governments* (Cambridge, Mass.: Harvard University Press, 1961).

made available) to different persons—or to different facets of the same persons (that is, their roles). In short, differentiation provides some variety of simultaneous (and sequential) forms of participation in and contribution to a specific social system (for example, to a nation, a corporation, a city, a university, a family, a gang, a hospital). However, at least three issues must be clarified before this definition can be applied.

Specialization and Stratification

First, social differentiation involves only specialization or differences in social participation. It does not refer to additional—and very important—social processes that *evaluate* and *rank* a set of differences or to the persons who can be "located" in different types of activities. Social differentiation, therefore, should not be confused with social stratification, though differentiation is a necessary precondition of stratification.

Differences and Distinctions

Second, we must be very careful to separate **differences** from **distinctions** in the phenomenon of social differentiation. Let us define social *differences* as *objective* variations between and among members of a population, regardless of the sources of these variations (for example, sex, age, physical strength, computational skill, speaking ability, skin color). *Distinctions*, on the other hand, can be defined as products of (a) *selection* from available social and personal differences and (b) *decisions* as to how to apply any such difference. For example, we may ignore all but age differences in the members of a group and then assign specialized tasks to young adults that are quite distinctive from those assigned to middle-aged persons (for example, defense of the community versus decision making on community issues or conflicts). In this hypothetical instance, differences are used as *clues* to a particular form of social differentiation. Yet it should be quite evident that social differentiation itself is not necessarily an accurate or predictable *reflection* of differences. In fact, over time, processes of social differentiation tend to *create* additional differences by providing specialization experiences that generate acquired differences in skill, perceptions, values, and aspirations.

The Basic Character of Differentiation

Third, social differentiation has resulted in such a profusion of forms and types that it is difficult to arrive at a simple conclusion about these important social processes. For example, there is, in principle, a certain rationality or sense in the division of labor. But for a given period and a specific social system, social differentiation may seem rather pragmatic and even arbitrary, with considerable trial and error and very dubious efficiency. This suggests that social specialization should be viewed less as a product of design and conscious fabrication than as a long-term process in which earlier nonrational forms have been increasingly (but not always successfully) challenged by more rational and more efficient modes of social specialization.[3]

Thus, we have the instructive case of the displacement of the neighborhood family-operated grocery store by the national chainstore system, especially since 1950 or so. But the chain stores were not open in the early morning or in the late evening, nor was their location convenient for small, last-minute purchases. In recent years, then, new neighborhood food stores have appeared—with various descriptive names (such as "7–11" to indicate their special hours)—primarily for those persons who are not well served by the dominance of the giant chains. And now, the food chains are extending their hours to meet the competition of the new neighborhood stores. It is a moot question whether food shopping is more satisfactory now than a generation ago.

INGREDIENTS OF SOCIAL DIFFERENTIATION

Social differentiation is an ancient social invention designed to furnish a practical solution to an eternal problem—an abundance of human needs and desires and a limitation of resources, time, and skills.[4] This problem recurs in every regularized human association. However, unlike the human organism—with its genetically controlled specialization of organs, nervous system, bone structures, and so on—the social system must create its collective solution to that problem from the human material at hand. The "solution" must take into account the number of persons involved; the number and relative severity of their biological needs; the number and relative difficulty of nonbiological or acquired needs or objectives; the amount and distribution of abilities, skills, and strength among members of a population; the physical resources of the environment; and the level of technology attained by that population.

DIFFERENTIATION IN SIMPLER SOCIETIES

With these ingredients as major clues, it is feasible to search for an understanding of elementary social differentiation among the simpler societies investigated by cultural anthropologists. While each

[3] Emile Durkheim, The Division of Labor in Society (New York: Free Press, 1947), Book II, Chaps. 2, 5, Book III; Hans H. Gerth and C. Wright Mills, From Max Weber: Essays in Sociology (New York: Oxford University Press, 1946), Chap. 8; Chester I. Bernard, The Functions of the Executive (Cambridge, Mass.: Harvard University Press, 1938).
[4] Emile Durkheim, The Division of Labor in Society (New York: Free Press, 1947), Book II, Chap. 2.

such society is unique in some respects, they share certain fundamental aspects in specialization.[5] First and most obvious, the simpler societies tend to be relatively small in population, somewhat
isolated geographically, relatively limited in technological skills (for
example, in food production, weapons technology, and transportation), and normally confronted by uncertain or scarce food supplies.
Second, though there is some specialization of activities and related
groupings—for example, hunting and/or agriculture, family and
child rearing, religion and magic, recreation, and government—the
social context for most of these activities is the kinship system and
rather complex patterns of descent. Almost every available skill or
cultural symbol is the property of a specific clan, or, if skills are
widely shared, they are transmitted and learned through participation in family settings. Third, and as a consequence of the preceding
features, the practical needs for division of labor and responsibility
are moderate, and can be implemented only in a limited fashion.
Generally, the key specialization is between productive (survival)
roles and symbolic or coordinative roles. In the first category,
specialization involves distinctive skills in growing or acquiring
food, in warfare, and in nurturing children. In contrast, the second
category includes ability to devise or manipulate beliefs and values,
material designs (for example, pottery), and formulas for settling
conflicts. Parenthetically, the second set of skills is thought to have
considerable adaptive value for the members of such societies.

Finally, simpler societies recognize few bases for assignment of specialized roles. Indeed, with few exceptions, *individual
abilities and individual achievements* are not linked with the process
of allocating recruits to specific roles.[6] The two clear exceptions
are the leading warrior roles, based on demonstrated prowess and
bravery, and the religious virtuoso role—*shaman* and similar terms
—which is impressed on any indivdual who naturally possesses the
appropriate psychological properties or who demonstrably endures
certain prescribed personal experiences (the "doctor dream" of the
Northern California Indians).[7]

Apart from these exceptions, specialization is typically
based on easily visible and familiar grounds: sex, age, and family
line. From our standpoint, these criteria may seem arbitrary and
irrational, but, *given the context in which they are selected,* these

---

[5] Howard W. Odum, *Understanding Society* (New York: The Macmillan Company, 1947),
Chaps. 9, 14; Robert Redfield, *The Primitive World and its Transformation* (Ithaca, New York:
Cornell University Press, 1953); Elman R. Service, *Primitive Social Organization* (New York:
Random House, 1962).

[6] Ralph Linton, *The Study of Man* (New York: Appleton–Century–Crofts, Inc., 1936), pp. 115–
131; Margaret Mead, *Sex and Temperament in Three Primitive Societies* (New York: William
Morrow, 1935).

[7] Robert Spott and A. L. Kroeber, "Yurok Shamanism," in R. F. Heizer and M. A. Whipple
(eds.), *The California Indians* (Berkeley, Calif.: University of California Press, 1971), pp. 533–
543.

ascribed criteria are meaningful and manageable. The pattern of differentiation by sex, for example, stems from the presumed necessity of employing males for survival activities away from the household (that is, for warfare, extensive hunting). Therefore, females must assume the no less important activities of child care, food preparation, and *localized* food production. Incidentally, this sexual division of labor probably accounts for the accidental discovery of agriculture, probably by women.[8] Similarly, age differentiation in such societies draws on the greater experience of the elders in societies where skill and wisdom are available only through direct personal communication between old and young. Consequently, such important tasks as contact with and interpretation of the supernatural and decisions concerning the welfare of the kinship group or community are reserved for the older males or females, while the younger males receive some graded series of initiation and training in hunting, fighting, diplomacy, display (as in the *potlatching* of the Northwest Canadian Indians),[9] magic, the prevailing arts, and the selection of marriage partners for younger relatives.

The Limits of Specialization

"Simple," when ascribed to specialization, then, involves a limited number of sharply contrasting skills and operates by developing a few groups or associations and by treating people as members of socially defined categories. Under these conditions, the adaptive capacities of simple societies are clear but limited, are based on past rather than current experience, are largely unchallenged by their members, and generally undergo little attention.[10] For individual members, this kind of social differentiation allows considerable direct contact with different roles, as well as opportunities for predictable movement from role to role (for example, with respect to age). Differentiation is linked in this instance to the individual's life cycle. In this type of society, however, there is little structured opportunity for experimenting with new skills or greater technological proficiency. Consequently, the growth and further development of such societies are normally arrested for long periods of time.

Further social differentiation in these societies usually involves very complex distinctions within the two focal areas of

[8] Melville Jacobs, *Pattern in Cultural Anthropology* (Homewood, Ill.: Dorsey Press, 1964), Chap. 6; Otis T. Mason, *Woman's Share in Primitive Culture* (New York: D. Appleton, 1898), Chaps. 1, 2.
[9] Ruth Benedict, *Patterns of Culture* (Boston: Houghton Mifflin Company, 1934), Chap. 6; Helen Codere, *Fighting With Property* (New York: J. J. Augustin, 1950); Philip Drucker, *To Make My Name Good* (Berkeley, Calif.: University of California Press, 1967); Abraham Rosman and Paula G. Rubel, *Feasting With Mine Enemy* (New York: Columbia University Press, 1971).
[10] See Howard Becker, *Man in Reciprocity* (New York: Praeger, 1956), Chaps. 10, 11.

As technological society grew and became more complex, specialization among skills became more distinct.
(Courtesy Robert Rapelye, Photography International.)

kinship and religion, in ways that seem incomprehensible to the biases of modern man. We tend to approach differentiation from the standpoint of practical efficiency (that is, its consequences for greater or lesser adaptation to the physical environment). But among simpler peoples, an emphasis on *social or relational "efficiency"* is expressed, not in specialization of skill, but in specialization of status or of contrived social relations.[11] Within the kinship

---

[11] Claude Lévi-Strauss, *The Elementary Structures of Kinship* (London: Eyre and Spottiswoode, 1969), Chaps. 3, 8, 9; Sir Henry Maine, *Ancient Law* (New York: Everyman Library, 1917), Chaps. 5, 9. (The original edition of *Ancient Law* was published in 1861.)

system, therefore, are numerous specifically named kinds of relatives —some strictly biological (natural parents or siblings), some through marriage (cross cousins), some through ceremonial creation (for example, treating mother's brother as "father" rather than "uncle").[12]

Social Efficiency and Limited Specialization

How can we account for this intricate and apparently impractical kind of differentiation? One reasonable explanation is Herskovits' theory of **cultural focus,**[13] which asserts that societies tend to devote overwhelming attention to the most highly valued activities, normally by devising more and more complex means of pursuing those activities. It follows that the longer the focus remains central, the greater the play of variations and, assuming retention of most variations, the greater the resultant specialization of roles, statuses, and social mechanisms.

Another explanatory approach starts from the premise that technical specialization is not the only means of adapting to the environment. Indeed, the complexity of kinship systems among many simple societies may be interpreted as a unique type of *social efficiency*, especially important when technological forms of adaptation are quite restricted. More explicitly, the intricate network of kinship relations places every member of the community in a complex web of close physical and emotional "services" that are supplied by each category of relatives. Thus, each member has multiple or alternative sources of built-in support. Isolates, forgotten or socially ignored categories, and so on, are unthinkable phenomena in such a system. In addition, complex kinship systems insure a regular, predictable transmission of property, capital goods, and even valued skills among defined members of a clan or sib, thereby controlling the use of technical means for a locally defined optimum range of "consumers." [14] Monopoly, cutthroat competition, manipulation of a market—with their deprivation of many for the benefit of a few—are consequently avoided.

Similarly, though perhaps not so obviously, the amazingly rich and complex religious and magical systems of simpler societies provide additional, if not complementary, means of adaptation to the environment. From this standpoint, for example, each component of religious practice (fertility rites, rainmaking, black or white

---

[12] A. R. Radcliffe-Brown and Daryll Forde (eds.), *African Systems of Kinship and Marriage* (London: Oxford University Press, 1950), Introduction; Paul Bohannon and John Middleton (eds.), *Marriage, Family and Residence* (Garden City, N.Y.: Natural History Press, 1968); Jack Goody, *Comparative Studies in Kinship* (Stanford, Calif.: Stanford University Press, 1969), Chaps. 3, 4, 8, 10; Nelson Graurn (ed.), *Readings in Kinship and Social Structure* (New York: Harper & Row Publishers, Inc., 1971), Chaps. 8, 11.
[13] Melville J. Herskovits, *Man and his Works* (New York: Alfred A. Knopf, 1948), Chap. 32.
[14] Claude Lévi-Strauss, *The Elementary Structures of Kinship* (London: Eyre and Spottiswoode, 1969), Chaps. 16, 17; Jack Goody, *Comparative Studies in Kinship* (Stanford, Calif.: Stanford University Press, 1969), Chap. 5.

magic) may be viewed as a substitute for (perhaps sometimes as supplements to) some limited technical knowledge.[15] Furthermore, the vast range of practical problems to which religious and magical systems are addressed—with a vivid and impressive variety of solutions and with no room for permissible doubt—reflects a collective necessity to maintain a comprehensive and ready blueprint for meeting, explaining, or manipulating every known contingency in social experience. Death, disease, impotence, famine, childbirth, puberty, menstruation, growth of crops, invasion, warfare, weather, seasonal changes are just a few of the typical objects of religious interest. Each has a specific religious "explanation"; each involves specific and appropriate (that is, adaptive) beliefs, rituals, and materials.[16]

Among the Suku of the Congo, certain medicines, witchcraft, or the displeasure of the elders are taken as causes of misfortune, illness, or death. At crucial points, the proper remedy requires use of a diviner, who, it is believed, can determine which of

Specialization yields an abundance of food and trade.
(Courtesy Robert Rapelye, Photography International.)

---

[15] Bronislaw Malinowski, *Magic, Science and Religion and Other Essays* (New York: Free Press, 1948); Elizabeth K. Nottingham, *Religion: A Sociological View* (New York: Random House, 1971), Chaps. 4, 5.

[16] V. W. Turner, *The Drums of Affliction* (Oxford: Clarendon Press, 1968); Mary Douglas (ed.), *Witchcraft Confessions and Accusations* (London: Tavistock, 1970), Parts 3, 4; J. R. Crawford, *Witchcraft and Sorcery in Rhodesia* (London: Oxford University Press, 1967).

the three causes is responsible for a given case of serious difficulty or illness. The diviner then follows the appropriate set of practices: use of new medicines; public warning or threat to the witches to stop their nefarious practices; or sacrificial ceremonies aimed at placating a disaffected ancestor. Should these remedies fail, the Suku may try another diviner or two. If this measure likewise is ineffective, the difficulty is "explained" as emanating from the unattainable and inscrutable Creator God.

The kind of social differentiation we have just analyzed tends to be self-perpetuating and structurally incapable of much additional specialization. This limited or "conservative" differentiation is fundamentally one of symbols and statuses rather than of technical skills. Consequently, the amount of practical alteration of the environment is virtually fixed (for example, greater or more diversified food supply; greater, or less costly, conversion of resources into socially usable goods; more efficient weapons; greater ability to control natural sources of power). In fact, the unchallenged dominance of symbolic differentiation, exemplified in religion and kinship, tends to inhibit differentiation and specialization in other spheres (government, economic, scientific), perhaps because these forms of specialization present unprecedented and unmanageable dangers to the elders and the religious professionals.

EXTENSIVE DIFFERENTIATION AND ITS SOCIAL CONSEQUENCES

In a significant number of historical cases, symbolic differentiation has given way to another order of differentiation—social differentiation of skills, occupations, value systems, and associations. We normally call these societies "civilizations," with the implication that technical specialization and its complex accompaniments constitute their distinctive features and problems.

The historical and archaeological records of developments in particular civilizations are relatively clear. But how can we *account for* their basic forms, especially since the conservative character of differentiation in simpler societies has already been affirmed? Much attention and much controversy have developed around this fascinating problem,[17] but identification of the most important ingredients of a satisfactory explanation is possible. The key notion is, perhaps, that of an unplanned succession of social interactions and pressures, favorable environmental factors, expanded opportunities, and the dynamics of unleashed innovation.

[17] Arnold J. Toynbee, *A Study of History,* abridged by D. C. Somervell (New York: Oxford University Press, 1947); Pitirim A. Sorokin, *Society, Culture and Personality* (New York: Harper & Row Publishers, Inc., 1947), Part 7; Rushton Coulborn, *The Origin of Civilized Societies* (Princeton: Princeton University Press, 1959); Darcy Ribeiro, *The Civilizational Process* (Washington, D.C.: Smithsonian Institution Press, 1968).

Surplus, Differentiation and Change

There is little doubt that the major precondition of complex social differentiation was an assured and expanded food supply. In a number of cases, the development of food surpluses was due to favorable rainfall or to manageable flooding of key rivers (in Mesopotamia, India, Egypt, China). But the prior discovery of agricultural methods—for wheat, millet, corn, and other crops—was an indispensable condition of a generally adequate food supply, given appropriate climatic conditions. Though food surplus was not always predictable—because of drought or catastrophic storms—surpluses permitted two revolutionary processes in developing societies. First, sizable numbers of people could *focus* their efforts on other significant activities, such as religion, metalworking, pottery, military skills and organization, art and decorative work, reflection on human experience (philosophy), study of natural phenomena (the stars), development of writing and the recording of notable events. Second, surpluses of food and fiber became the bases for trade and interchange between societies. The effects of commerce on social differentiation in both "sending" and "receiving" societies are undeniably crucial for social evolution. For both societies, commerce in surplus goods necessarily involved the development of "new" skills for amassing, transporting, selling, bargaining, storing, and recording, all of which created the *merchant role* and subsequently the *investment or credit (lending) role* in virtually every civilization known to historians.[18]

These two forms of specialization effectively (and perhaps inevitably) broke the mold of simpler and conservative systems of social differentiation. It is difficult, of course, to trace the changes in motives, aspirations, and values that probably developed with the maturation of specialization. Several important social patterns emerged, however, and these are best interpreted as *opportunities* for further differentiation. For example, economic specialization and commerce provided new opportunities for technical innovations (for tools and weapons) and for more concentrated populations (in villages, towns, and then cities)—and, in time, for the efficient warfare that produced the noted empires of ancient history. Though kinship and family connections were tenaciously maintained throughout the first major wave of complex specialization (*circa* 1200 B.C.–900 A.D.), the social categories that emerged were products of apparently irrepressible technical and material achievements. To the basic distinction between citizens and slaves were added the

---

[18] Robert J. Braidwood and Gordon R. Willey (eds.), *Courses Toward Urban Life* (Chicago: Aldine Publishing Co., 1962), pp. 342–355; Robert M. Adams, *The Evolution of Urban Society* (Chicago: Aldine Publishing Co., 1966); Alice Beardwood, *Alien Merchants in England, 1350–1377* (Cambridge, Mass.: Mediaeval Academy of America, 1931).

varied occupations of priests, graded sets of civic-officials, specialized warriors (foot soldiers, cavalry, artillerymen), merchants (at first marginal and then legitimate types; at first foreign in ancestry or status and then recruited from indigenous citizens), artisans, entertainers, prostitutes, concubines, literary men, astrologers, teachers, and sages.[19]

Wherever such specialization developed, the net results were normally reflected in enhanced human adaptation to the environment. This was expressed in growth of population and in the extension of resources (natural and human) that could be brought under conscious human control. However, even more important, processes of specialization and differentiation essentially transformed human experience for an increasingly large proportion of the world's population. Essentially, this transformation has entailed the development of social systems whose major characteristics are multifaceted innovation, prodigious and largely unresolved problems of social coordination, and paradoxically, the prospect of dangerously diminished human adaptation.

Before we can examine the varied fruits of social differentiation in contemporary societies, it is particularly necessary to analyze and evaluate the state of social and cultural complexity that has been achieved—largely during the past 200 years of Western civilization. For convenience, we can organize our discussion around three interconnected means of studying specialization and differentiation: (1) varieties of groups, organizations, and associations; (2) basic differentiation of social skills or role types; and (3) spatial differentiation and specialization.

Varieties of Groups, Organizations, and Associations

One of the most frequently recognized forms of differentiation concerns rather sharp differences in the *character of interactions among members of the society*. Key aspects of social interaction certainly include[20] the number of persons involved; the informality or formality of interaction; the relative strength of emotional (affective) and technical (intellectual) emphases or themes in interaction; limited or expansive interests that are pursued through such interaction; the degree to which participants share responsibilities,

---

[19] Margaret O. Wason, *Class Struggles in Ancient Greece* (London: Gollancz, 1947); Michael Seidlmayer, *Currents of Medieval Thought* (London: Blackwell, 1960); Michael Rostovtzeff, *The Social and Economic History of the Roman Empire* (Oxford: Clarendon Press, 1926); Fustel de Coulanges, *The Ancient City* (Garden City, N.Y.: Doubleday & Company, Inc., 1955), Book 3, Chaps. 9–12. (The original edition of *The Ancient City* was published in 1864.)

[20] Kurt H. Wolff (ed.), *The Sociology of Georg Simmel* (New York: Free Press, 1950), Part 2; Georg Simmel, *On Individuality and Social Forms* (Chicago: University of Chicago Press, 1971), Chap. 18; Pitirim A. Sorokin, *Society, Culture and Personality* (New York: Harper & Row Publishers, Inc., 1947), Chaps. 4–7; Robert M. MacIver and Charles H. Page, *Society* (New York: Holt, Rinehart and Winston, Inc., 1949), Chaps. 2, 17.

knowledge, and rights; and the kinds of control—direct or indirect —exerted on the behavior of actors. A major form of interaction is the **primary group,**[21] which generally includes the small, intimate groups in which persons feel relatively comfortable and of roughly equal worth.

The Range of Primary Groups

Primary groups, however, are far from homogeneous. There are, in fact, several subtypes and versions, each of which supplies somewhat different experiences to participants. For simplicity, we can identify three phases of primary groups.

Early or Childhood Types.[22] The predominant form is of course the immediate (or nuclear) family and, in some instances, a supplementary circle of close relatives (the extended family). In addition, primary group settings can be found among youngsters of similar age—either in the form of play groups or as shifting clusters of friends, buddies, or pals. During the early years of socialization, these primary groups tend to monopolize one's social experiences and generally emphasize basic morality (notions of justice, loyalty, honesty) rather than personal achievement. On the other hand, primary groups at this stage also involve frictions, jealousy, petty differences—perhaps because young children are not yet adequately socialized and have few social alternatives.

Adolescent Types.[23] While family connections persist, adolescence provides a wider range of primary group affiliations than the preschool period. School and church participation normally result in exposure to several peer groups within a narrow geographic area—cliques, gangs, clubs, teams, and so on. It is the rare adolescent who does not find it useful or satisfying to take part in some form of these social circles. However, at this stage, primary groups tend to compete for the allegiance of young people (particularly family and peer groups) and also to develop considerable exclusiveness and defensive distinctions in speech, clothing, hobbies, or geographic identity. Peer groups become larger in size, somewhat more formalized, more specialized in activities and skills, and in some ways more demanding of most members.

[21] Charles H. Cooley, *Social Organization* (New York: Charles Scribner's Sons, 1909), Chaps. 3–5.

[22] Bert N. Adams, *Kinship in an Urban Setting* (Chicago: Markham, 1968), Chaps. 3, 4; Leonard I. Pearlin, *Class Context and Family Relations* (Boston: Little, Brown and Company, 1972), Chaps. 1, 6, 7.

[23] A. B. Hollingshead, *Elmtown's Youth* (New York: John Wiley & Sons, Inc., 1949); James S. Coleman, *The Adolescent Society* (New York: Free Press, 1961); David Gottlieb and Charles Ramsey, *The American Adolescent* (Homewood, Ill.: Dorsey Press, 1964); Ernest A. Smith, *American Youth Culture* (New York: Free Press, 1962); Thomas J. Cottle, *Time's Children* (Boston: Little, Brown and Company, 1971).

Adolescent peer groups, more than earlier primary groups, are microcosms of the outside world. Members experience the struggles, opportunities, and pressures of adult life.
(Courtesy Robert Rapelye, Photography International.)

Friendships (sometimes continued from childhood, but often with new additions) supplement the more formalized primary groups, though the more unspecialized friendships may yield to the pressure of time and the subtle requirements of maintaining a position in one or more "crowds" or cliques.[24] Even more complexity develops when sexual attachments began to blossom into definite dating patterns, going steady, and, as is so frequently the case for 16–18 year olds, marriage.

Peter Willmott's study of teen-age boys in London's Bethnal Green area (*Adolescent Boys of East London*) documents the fluidity and complexity of adolescent primary groups. In addition to the limited circles of informal friendships, these boys take part

[24] Peter Willmott, *Adolescent Boys of East London* (London: Routledge and Kegan Paul, 1966); D. C. Dunphy, *Cliques, Crowds and Gangs* (Melbourne, Australia: Cheshire, 1969); Hyman Rodman (ed.), *Marriage, Family, and Society* (New York: Random House, 1965), Parts 4, 5, 7; Gerald D. Suttles, *The Social Order of the Slum* (Chicago: University of Chicago Press, 1968), Chaps. 9–11.

in neighborhood youth clubs, where peer groups of younger boys tend to congregate. But as boys reach the age of 16 or 17, the appeal of these primary groups alters considerably. In the youth clubs, the simplified contacts and activities that attract 13 and 14 year olds become boring. Girls become a distinctly superior attraction at about 17 years of age, when somewhat serious courting begins. However, in the less formal friendship groups, the single sex character of such groups gives way to inclusion of girls—usually when the boys reach the age of 19. At that age, too, many boys begin to withdraw from former peer groups. Apparently, the desire for primary-like relationships is only temporarily satisfied by any one such group, both in Britain and in the United States.

In short, the adolescent primary groups have several interesting features. They have greater scope and more nearly reflect the opportunities and problems of the outside world than do the family and earliest friendships. They represent the first genuine extrafamilial source of social power, as well as social competition and conflict. And these primary groups help to sort out the goals and aspirations that young people ultimately bring to the specialized associations of later years.

Adult Primary Groups. Marriage and employment provide additional opportunities for primary group contacts. Characteristics of newly established families, which tend to be located apart from the families of either mate, are difficult to summarize. However, it is reasonably clear that the practical difficulties of maintaining satisfactory intimacy in modern families are related to the complex nature of this type of primary group and its competition with other social affiliations. Briefly, the family as a primary group is greatly affected by the divergent roles of the mates and the relatively limited opportunities for shared activities during the routine of the normal week.[25] Likewise, modern families operate with an inherent contradiction between the presumed sanctity of the relationship and the stress on individual choice in establishing and evaluating family experiences. Paradoxically, the family and its complex set of primary-like relationships are sources of great satisfaction and social learning, as well as of an enormous amount of unhappiness, irrational behavior, and personal and social maladaptation to the larger environment.[26]

---

[25] Elizabeth Bott, *Family and Social Network* (London: Tavistock, 1957); Lionel Tiger, *Men in Groups* (New York: Random House, 1969); Helen Z. Lopata, *Occupation: Housewife* (New York: Oxford University Press, 1971); Michael Young and Peter Willmott, *Family and Kinship in East London* (London: Routledge and Kegan Paul, 1957); J. Clyde Mitchell (ed.), *Social Networks in Urban Situations* (Manchester, England: Manchester University Press, 1969).

[26] Raymond Firth et al., *Families and Their Relatives* (London: Routledge and Kegan Paul, 1969); Harold T. Christensen (ed.), *Handbook of Marriage and the Family* (Chicago: Rand McNally & Co., 1964), Parts 4, 5.

Adult experience in primary groups also derives from a very widespread intrusion of primary groups in existing complex organizations—principally the firm or corporation and the church or religious organization. Since the late 1920's, studies have identified and analyzed the operation of informal "work groups" in industrial plants, unions, military organizations, hospitals, offices, and government agencies. Normally, these primary groups develop among those with similar skills and face-to-face working conditions. In general, such primary groups are effective multipurpose systems through which members exchange information, advice, and marks of recognition, and also provide tolerated means of voicing gripes and criticisms of the larger organization.[27]

Secondary Associations:
The Intensification of Specialization

Potentially, and actually, members of societies like our own have quite a variety of primary-like affiliations throughout their lifetimes. But this is far exceeded by the number of available specialized or "secondary" groups in most communities. Each secondary or "voluntary" group caters to a small segment of man's interests and acquired needs—from recreational and aesthetic to weighty economic and political types.[28] For example, there are labor unions, professional and business associations (for example, the American Medical Association), private charitable groups, local and national political parties, country clubs, youth service groups (for example, the Scouts), local nationality organizations, national book clubs, dieting and weight-reducing groups, national Greek letter fraternities and sororities, "nature" groups, organized discussion groups (for example, "The Great Books"), local policy-making boards (for example, in the Office of Economic Opportunity and Model Cities programs), ladies' information and action groups (for example, the League of Women Voters), specialized political action groups (for example, women's liberation, "end the war" groups), and so on. For most people, however, the essential secondary groups are business, agency, bureau, corporation, university, school system, and so on, in which most people find a niche for their respective skills and personal aspirations.

For an individual, the range of accessible secondary groups varies according to his education, style of life, general level of responsibility, and personality. One's major opportunities for

---

[27] Seymour M. Lipset et al., *Union Democracy* (New York: Free Press, 1956); Warren O. Hagstrom, *The Scientific Community* (New York: Basic Books, 1965); Fritz J. Roethlisberger and William J. Dickson, *Management and the Worker* (Cambridge, Mass.: Harvard University Press, 1939); Peter M. Blau, *The Dynamics of Bureaucracy* (Chicago: University of Chicago Press, 1955).

[28] J. Roland Pennock and John W. Chapman (eds.), *Voluntary Associations* (New York: Atherton Press, 1969); Murray Hausknecht, *The Joiners* (New York: Bedminster Press, 1962).

self-expression, creativity, and extended personal impact derive from these groups rather than from the environment of most primary groups. But from the perspective of the community or the nation, the complex network of secondary groups and associations—with their varied capabilities and demands—appears to encourage a stimulating, yet problematic, competition for the considerable but finite resources of modern societies. As we shall see in Chapters 13 and 14, modern systems of power and authority represent variably successful attempts to manage (without stifling) this aspect of contemporary specialization and differentiation. At this point, we may simply point out the inherently two-edged character of social organizations and social mechanisms: their achievements ultimately entail further adaptations or adjustments in order to prevent "diminishing returns" or even intensified difficulties.

Basic Differentiation of Social Skills or Role Types

The Range of Social Skills

The awesome variety of specialized groups and associations in complex society would be impossible without a corresponding variety of socially useful skills for members of these groups. Obviously, persons interact and collaborate for common objectives through appropriate skills that are historically invented and shaped through interaction itself. But how can we hope to understand such complexity and to identify the most important trends and consequences of such complexity? For simplicity, it is possible to reduce the apparent chaos of social skills to perhaps four basic types and, following that, to suggest the limited number of ways in which these skill types are combined in a minimum number of core **social roles**.

Technical Skills. Basically, technical skills—derived from a relevant core of knowledge and/or from learning the proper behavior by example—involve abilities to affect or change aspects of the physical or social environment in some socially approved or useful manner. Obviously, the most important technical skills in any population deal directly with specific problems of survival, such as food, clothing, shelter, protection against menacing forms of life (human or subhuman). Each technical skill is marked by a particular *form of energy* and a specific *goal or product*. Thus, we can distinguish a general evolutionary trend from individual and collective manpower (and womanpower), to animal power, to simple mechanical devices and water power, to complex machines (driven by fuel), to the present machines powered by electricity or atomic energy. These forms of energy have been used for agriculture, warfare, textiles, mining, the production of vehicles, printed works, medicines, flood and fire control.

But technical skills have also been applied to an immense range of acquired needs that are only indirectly connected with survival.[29] For example, there are distinct technical skills in preparing and serving food for the connoisseur, in reproducing and distributing units of the mass media (books, magazines, newspapers, radio, TV programs), in performing each of the major sports (baseball, football, hockey, basketball, soccer, tennis), in expediting record keeping and reporting, in business, and in manipulating physical objects (water, incense, wafers, and so on) for appropriate contact with supernatural entities or powers.

Organizational Skills. The essence of such skills is the ability to obtain some form of coordinated behavior from two or more persons in a definite situation or set of situations.[30] In practice, organizational skills create conditions that directly or indirectly promote a regular and approved social product. For example, one such skill can parcel out responsibility for specific tasks in a group so that (a) each member makes his optimum contribution; (b) no member interferes with the participation of others; and (c) the objectives of the group are efficiently pursued. Another organizational skill is applied to problems of developing workable compromises among members with sharply different values or opinions. We can also mention those subtle skills that recruit a set of willing members into a new organization (for example, a cult, a protest group, or a pressure group). It is important to note that human organizations do not persist *primarily* because of the quality of their values and goals, or because of the interest of their members. More likely, the career of groups and organizations depends also on the effectiveness of basic organizational skills of key members.[31]

Evaluational–Ideational Skills. While the preceding skills deal with manipulation of the environment or of persons, this third variety of skills focuses on the realm of ideas, values, ideals, objec-

---

[29] In the area of food: Elizabeth Wason, *Cooks, Gluttons and Gourmets* (Garden City, N.Y.: Doubleday & Company, Inc., 1962); Magnus Pyke, *Food and Society* (London: Murray, 1968). Techniques of business organization and management: Russell L. Ackoff, *A Concept of Corporate Planning* (New York: Wiley–Interscience, 1970); Joan Woodward (ed.), *Industrial Organization: Behavior and Control* (London: Oxford University Press, 1970). Sports techniques are meticulously detailed for various sports; see, for example, Barry C. Pelton, *Badminton* (Englewood Cliffs, N.J.: Prentice–Hall, Inc., 1971); William S. Talbert and Bruce S. Old, *The Game of Singles in Tennis* (Philadelphia: J. B. Lippincott Company, 1962).

[30] James March and Herbert A. Simon, *Organizations* (New York: John Wiley & Sons, Inc., 1958); James D. Thompson, *Organizations in Action* (New York: McGraw–Hill Book Company, 1968).

[31] Robert Eyestone, *The Threads of Public Policy* (Indianapolis, Ind.: Bobbs–Merrill, 1971); Joseph Nyomarkay, *Charisma and Factionalism in the Nazi Party* (Minneapolis, Minn.: University of Minnesota Press, 1967); Ezra Stotland and Arthur L. Kobler, *The Life and Death of a Mental Hospital* (Seattle, Wash.: University of Washington Press, 1965).

tives, and interpretations.[32] In short, these skills facilitate the creation, criticism, and alteration of crucial guides to behavior and social organization forms. One such skill clarifies or articulates past or present ideals by showing their connection to other ideals and values and to some personal or collective experience. Another skill applies rules of logic to a current or proposed value, with some conclusion about the worth or applicability of that value or idea. Still another ideational skill creates relatively new values or ideals in response to the experiences and problems of some group or social category.

Symbolic Skills. Often these are closely related to evaluational–ideational skills, but a notable difference should be recognized. Evaluational–ideational skills are applied to the *content or quality* of ideas and values. Symbolic skills, on the other hand, concern the expression or communication of values in effective ways to some audience or public. Novelists, for example, may take some value theme that is already available and present it meaningfully and persuasively through their characters and setting. Zola, Flaubert, Conrad, Dickens, and other admired writers seem to have developed such a skill. Similarly, some composers had fine musical ideas that seemed to require development or orchestration by others (Ravel for Moussorgsky, Ferde Grofé for George Gershwin). Of course, sometimes a person possesses or develops both skills (Beethoven, Dvorak, Tchaikovsky, Brahms). However, in recent decades, specialization of symbolic skills is particularly clear—witness the enormous proliferation of speech writers, ghost writers, advertising men, public relations specialists, editors and adapters, and, propagandists.[33]

A Repertory of Social Roles

These social skills (or socially relevant skills) can be distinguished in specific instances of social behavior. But humans in societies do not acquire and practice their skills as single, isolated items. Instead, members learn *complementary sets of social skills* that are approved for use in a recurring set of social situations. This set of skills (and related practice with or for designated persons) is usually called a **social role**. But while social skills are ingredients

[32] See the classic discussions in Florian Znaniecki, *The Social Role of the Man of Knowledge* (New York: Harper Torchbook, 1968), pp. 64–90, Chap. 3 (the original edition was published in 1940); Karl Mannheim, *Man and Society in an Age of Reconstruction* (New York: Harcourt, Brace and World, 1940), pp. 98–108, 149–155; Philip Rieff (ed.), *On Intellectuals* (Garden City, N.Y.: Doubleday & Company, Inc., 1969).

[33] William L. Safire, *The Relations Explosion* (New York: The Macmillan Company, 1963); Alan R. Roucher, *Public Relations and Business, 1920–1929* (Baltimore, Md.: Johns Hopkins Press, 1968).

of social roles, it is not clear whether existing roles encourage the development of relevant skills or emerging skills facilitate new roles or a significant alteration of preexisting roles.

In any case, the normal evolution, development, and growth of most social systems produce fundamental (and perhaps indispensable) categories of specialized social roles, all of which are found with different labels and somewhat different content in virtually all human organizations.[34] Varied investigations—of families, hospitals, business firms, experimental groups, military groups —suggest the plausible conclusion that such recurring roles reflect understandable social solutions to routine practical problems of effective social interaction and social productivity.

Instrumental or Task Specialist Role. One or more of these roles in a group or organization furnishes immediate answers to relatively narrow but important "housekeeping" problems for given groups. In the family, cooking and home repair skills are examples of this type, as are machine maintenance responsibilities in industry, programming skills in computer installations, and anesthesia in surgery. Sometimes survival itself depends on task specialists, but, at the very least, reasonable security, minimum comfort, and effective pursuit of group goals depend on prior contributions from such roles.

Coordinative or Policy-Implementing Social Specialist Role. The prime responsibility of this "administrative" role is to regulate and facilitate the contributions of other roles toward workable solutions of group problems and efforts aimed at collective goals or ideals. The crucial skills are, therefore, of the organizational variety, but social specialists also require skills in interpreting values and norms for technical specialists (that is, some skill in evaluative and symbolic forms). Housewives play this role in setting and following family budgets, and in monitoring the time schedules of each member of the family. Other examples are department heads and deans in universities; executive officers in military commands or posts; ministers in large congregations; such elective officials as mayors and governors; and leaders of group discussions.

Expressive Social Specialist Role. It has been widely observed that the practice of instrumental and coordinative roles creates conditions of dependence and even perceived threats to less capable (or less confident) members of a given system. Consequently, often as a supplement to the coordinative role, there is a subtle but important "social solvent" role that serves to reassure vulnerable

---

[34] Talcott Parsons, Robert F. Bales, and Edward A. Shils, *Working Papers in the Theory of Action* (New York: Free Press, 1953), pp. 144–151; Robert T. Golembiewski, *The Small Group* (Chicago: University of Chicago Press, 1962).

members by providing personal understanding, support, and an approved locus for expressing dissatisfaction. Normally, this role is assigned to persons with relatively high prestige (related to age, experience), or who are held in high esteem (the most generally respected or revered persons), who in addition possess evaluative, symbolic, and some organizational skills. In military organizations, either the commanding officer or his second in command may assume this role, while the other informally accepts the coordinative role. Clearly, the chaplain tries—with variable success—to serve as an expressive social specialist. In colleges, some faculty advisers function as expressive intermediaries between students and intellectual pressures. Businesses, offices, laboratories, and so on, usually have an "old hand" or "sage" who "knows the ropes" and acts as a fount of wisdom and sensitive advice for less experienced members. Recently, the development of the *ombudsman* position—in government and certain complex organizations—offers another structured opportunity for such a role, though the ombudsman also has the authority to translate his expressive role into changes in one or more coordinative roles in that system.[35]

Clown and/or Scapegoat Role.[36] More involved social systems sometimes develop another form of expressive social specialist. In its *positive* form (the clown) this kind of role reduces tensions by acceptable ridicule of either organizational goals, high prestige roles (and persons), or some accessible member. The correct tone is very important—good humor rather than harsh criticism —because it offers a means for informal consensus. Unfortunately, the clown role has not been properly studied, though it must surely involve considerable symbolic and evaluative skills.

The scapegoat, by contrast, is a negatively significant role, one that is played with a socially useful ineptness that evokes or (accentuates) skills in other members. In practice, the scapegoat is either one who carries some stigma (size, weight, facial deformity, and so on) or who made a widely noted (but not necessarily crucial) error in performance, or both.[37] He therefore becomes an accessible, irresistible target for collective dissatisfactions. If the scapegoat role is not really one of skill, but rather an object for the baiter role, then baiting or scapegoating must involve rather subtle social skills— probably evaluative and symbolic.

---

[35] Walter Gellhorn, *Ombudsmen and Others* (Cambridge, Mass.: Harvard University Press, 1966); Frank A. Stacey, *The British Ombudsman* (Oxford: Clarendon Press, 1971).
[36] Orrin E. Klapp, *Heroes, Villains, and Fools* (Englewood Cliffs, N.J.: Prentice–Hall Inc., 1962); William Willeford, *The Fool and his Scepter: A Study in Clowns and Jesters and their Audiences* (Evanston, Ill.: Northwestern University Press, 1969); Erving Goffman, *Stigma* (Englewood Cliffs, N.J.: Prentice–Hall, Inc., 1963).
[37] William F. Whyte, *Street Corner Society* (Chicago: University of Chicago Press, 1943), Chap. 1; Erving Goffman, *ibid.*, Chap. 1.

"If it had not been for these thing, I might have live out my life talking at street corners to scorning men. I might have die, unmarked, unknown, a failure. Now we are not a failure. This is our career and our triumph. Never in our full life could we hope to do such work for tolerance, for justice, for man's understanding of man as now we do by accident. Our words — our lives — our pains nothing! The taking of our lives — lives of a good shoemaker and a poor fish peddler — all! That last moment belongs to us — that agony is our triumph." — Bartolomeo Vanzetti

The Roaring Twenties produced two of the most sensational scapegoats in American history. Nicola Sacco, a shoe-factory worker, and Bartolomeo Vanzetti, a fish peddler, were electrocuted during a wave of anti-Redism. ("Sacco and Vanzetti" by Ben Shahn. Courtesy Fogg Art Museum, Harvard University.)

Innovative (Social Anticipation) Role. All the preceding roles are largely geared to rather immediate and recurring situations. They operate with the capital of past skills and solutions. However, one of the dominant features of complex social systems is self-generated and/or externally presented change. Formally or informally, then, the need for a specially protected or insulated role may be recognized. Essentially, this role is based on immunity from routine matters and freedom to speculate about future needs and problems well before they arise. This role does not involve "tinkering" or inventing better solutions to available problems. It deals instead with locating new problems and new interconnections among existing problems; with devising new goals or objectives; with new or revised explanations or justifications for behavior; with creating new criteria of evaluation.

Innovative roles require perhaps the widest range of social skills—obviously, technical and evaluative skills but also symbolic skills (for interpreting their innovations) and organizational skills (to estimate the impact of innovation on existing organizations and groups). Consequently, the innovative role type is extremely difficult to perform adequately: it demands extraordinary knowledge and ability to withstand considerable frustration and misunderstanding, and it requires a certain isolation from the "contaminating" contacts of normal routine roles and persons.[38]

Social Transmission (Training) Role. For continuity in social systems, the indispensable type of role is surely one that transmits successful skills of varying kinds to successive generations of members.[39] The training role is based on several practical considerations: large numbers of members; great complexity and variety of socially approved skills; and inadequate opportunities for self-instruction in many needed skills. Training or social transmission usually requires some technical skills, in conjunction with the complemenatry use of evaluative and symbolic skills.

Passing on craft skills from generation to generation is a dying tradition in modern society.
(Courtesy Robert Rapelye, Photography International.)

---

[38] Myron A. Coler (ed.), *Essays on Creativity in the Sciences* (New York: New York University Press, 1963); Gary A. Steiner (ed.), *The Creative Organization* (Chicago: University of Chicago Press, 1965). See also the poignant account of literary creativity in Thomas Wolfe, "God's Lonely Man," in his *The Hills Beyond* (Garden City, N.Y.: Sun Dial Press, 1943), pp. 186–197.
[39] See Chapter 6 for analyses of socialization processes. The classic discussion of the importance of socialization is Gabriel Tarde, *The Laws of Imitation* (New York: Henry Holt & Co., 1903).

Spatial Differentiation and Specialization: Human Communities

Since human organization necessarily involves the use of (and adaptation to) the environment, social differentiation is understandably accompanied by some specialization of land use. In simpler societies, with low social differentiation, the relevant land area tends to be small; in addition, there is rather limited variation or specialization in the location of activities within that area. By contrast, as societies emphasize and develop social differentiation, spatial specialization becomes marked in two important respects. First, a given population tends to form several distinct *communities*, each of which exchanges goods, mates, knowledge, and skills with others. Second, some strategically located communities within a society operate and thrive by developing highly specialized units of land in which distinctive skills, resources, social categories, and manmade products are concentrated. This second type of community—the town or city—ultimately becomes the focus and generator of several adjacent communities, all of which interact to form a modern metropolitan community or urban region.[40] (This will be analyzed in considerable detail in Chapter 9.)

CONSEQUENCES OF SPECIALIZATION

Social differentiation and its consequences persist as the central concern of sociologists and of social scientists generally. The reasons for such an interest are not difficult to identify: human societies have largely survived and developed through processes of social specialization; the general trend in specialization has been the creation of a limited set of universal roles (with numerous cultural variations on each) and a consequent specialization of groups and focal activities (political, economic, educational, scientific, religious, artistic, recreational, affectional).[41] In previous centuries—from the classical Greeks to the middle of the 19th century—*explanations* of social differentiation were a consuming interest among students of society. Consequently, we have theories on the impact of population increase and density, war and conquest, cultural contacts, racial contacts, and on the role of favorable geographic conditions.[42]

[40] See Chapter 9. Basic works on communities as foci of specialization include Amos H. Hawley, *Human Ecology* (New York: The Ronald Press, 1950); N. S. B. Gras, *An Introduction to Economic History* (New York: Harper & Row Publishers, Inc., 1922), Chaps. 3–5.
[41] Leslie A. White, *The Evolution of Culture* (New York: McGraw–Hill Book Company, 1959), Part II; Talcott Parsons, "Evolutionary Universals in Society," *American Sociological Review*, 29 (June 1964), pp. 339–357; Talcott Parsons, *Societies: Evolutionary and Comparative Perspectives* (Englewood Cliffs, N.J.: Prentice–Hall, Inc., 1966).
[42] See Pitirim A. Sorokin, *Contemporary Sociological Theories* (New York: Harper & Row Publishers, Inc., 1928), Chaps. 6–8; Frederick J. Teggart, *Theory and Processes of History* (Berkeley, Calif.: University of California Press, 1941); Werner J. Cahnman and Alvin Boskoff (eds.), *Sociology and History* (New York: Free Press, 1964), Part I.

For the past 100 years or more, however, our emphasis has shifted toward the adaptive and maladaptive *effects* of rather well-defined processes of social differentiation.[43] With a few "romantic" exceptions, our thinking accepts social specialization as indispensable or nondiscardable, though we acknowledge the indisputable fact that differentiation generates both social achievements and increasingly severe practical difficulties. Thus, almost all of the remaining chapters of this book deal with the specific effects of differentiation in contemporary societies, or with social experiments in managing these effects. For example, Chapters 8 and 9 analyze the organization of specialization through stratification and community systems; Chapters 10 and 11 are concerned with population and economic consequences of specialization processes; and Chapters 13–15 and 18 focus on the typical social mechanisms that operate as structured solutions to the undesirable by-products of social specialization.

The Dilemma of Mixed Effects

As a prelude to those more detailed discussions, however, it may be useful to suggest a most fundamental sociological observation, which is that *continued and increasingly complex processes of social differentiation have multiple and contradictory consequences for the operation of society and for its members as individuals.* One major result is apparently infinite expansion of opportunities for innovation in almost every sphere of human experience.[44] But this encouragement of innovation occurs mainly in secondary or formal groups and in the realm of technical and evaluational–ideational skills. Consequently, many primary-like groups and affiliations, with their significant but limited capabilities, face difficult problems of adaptation, not only to formal associations themselves, but to the challenges provided by numerous and sometimes bewildering innovations. The net result is a tendency toward reorientation or restructuring of primary groups in complex society—either toward greater insulation and increased emotional security, or toward miniature versions of larger associations. The visible symptoms of these social pressures are numerous: mental difficulties; early marriages; a revived emphasis on the home; marital problems; fragility of friendships; the proliferation of adolescent attachments to a series of vivid, emotional entertainers; the recent appeal of communes; the addictive use of drugs.[45] (See Tables 5–2, 5–3, and 5–4.)

[43] Emile Durkheim, *The Division of Labor in Society* (New York: Free Press, 1947), esp. Book II, Chap. 5; George K. Zollschan and Walter Hirsch (eds.), *Explorations in Social Change* (Boston: Houghton Mifflin Company, 1964), Chaps. 8, 10, 17, 21, 26.
[44] Cf. Alvin Toffler, *Future Shock* (New York: Random House, 1970); Bertram M. Gross (ed.), *Social Intelligence for America's Future* (Boston: Allyn and Bacon, Inc., 1969).
[45] Charles Cooley, *Social Organization* (New York: Charles Scribner's Sons, 1909), Chaps. 11, 30–33; Robert W. Winslow, *Society in Transition* (New York: Free Press, 1970).

TABLE 5-2
Mentally ill in public and private hospitals of the United States, 1955-1968.

Year	Total cases (approx.)	Rate per 100,000 population
1955	1,675,000	799
1965	2,637,000	816
1966	2,764,000	815
1967	3,140,000	834
1968	3,381,000	811

SOURCE: *Statistical Abstract of the U. S., 1971* (Washington: U.S. Govt. Printing Office, 1972), p. 73.

TABLE 5-3
Divorce rates in the United States, 1940-1962.

Year	Per 1000 marriages performed	Per 1000 married females
1940	165	8.8
1945	300	14.4
1950	230	10.3
1952	254	10.1
1954	254	9.5
1956	241	9.4
1958	253	8.9
1960	258	9.2
1961	261	9.6
1962	250	9.4

SOURCE: *Statistical Abstract of the U. S., 1965* (Washington: U.S. Govt. Printing Office, 1966), p. 62; and *U.S. Department of Health, Education and Welfare, Trends, 1965* (Washington: U.S. Govt. Printing Office, 1966), Table S4.

TABLE 5-4
Suicide rates in the United States, 1930-1969.

Year	Rate per 100,000 population over 16 years of age
1930	21.6
1935	20.6
1940	19.5
1945	14.3
1950	15.7
1955	14.6
1960	15.8
1965	16.7
1969 (estimate)	15.9

SOURCE: *Statistical Abstract of the U. S., 1971* (Washington: U.S. Govt. Printing Office, 1972), p. 142.

Both increasing specialization and expanded opportunities for innovation create rather new and formidable strains on the coordinative and control mechanisms of modern societies. A crucial fact must be faced: most of our methods of community and societal control were developed for rather small, technologically simple societies—the classical civilizations and the embryonic nations of the 16th and 17th centuries. These methods included legal systems of prohibition and punishment; the election of a small number of public officials (with much turnover); legislative bodies representing geographic areas and empowered to tax without clear relevance to interdependent public programs or services. All of these implicitly assume simple problems, a relatively static society, and common value systems among members and citizens. But specialization and innovation create a variety of values and interests, a perplexing ambiguity about legitimate behavior and legitimate controls over behavior, a diffusion of energies and resources, and over time a disenchantment with the practicality of effective social coordination.

Obstacles to Effective Control of Specialization

Why has specialization (and innovation) not been followed by appropriate modification and innovation in methods of coordination? In other words, how can we account for the lag in social adaptation? Several reasons can be suggested for thought and further investigation. First, we must reckon with a persisting notion of the 19th century that the implicit, indirect interdependencies of increasing specialization would "naturally" limit the possibilities of irresponsible advantage for any social category. This was the key to liberal economic theory and its expression in the "checks and balances" political theory of *laissez-faire* republican government.[46] To this viewpoint must be added the understandable hostility of the 19th and 20th century to highly centralized and disastrous power systems—for example, the two Napoleons, Imperial Germany, Nazi Germany, Fascist Italy, the Stalinist Soviet Union, and Franco's Spain.

In addition, specialization and innovation—once in high gear—tend to encourage emphasis on technical skills and related roles, with greater rewards reserved for these skills and for those organizational skills directed toward highly specialized social enterprises (firms and corporations in industrial production, banking and finance, and commercial and trading ventures).[47] For generations, training and reward for broad organizational skills were specifically downgraded, with the result that organizational responsibilities on the community and national levels were largely relegated to hack

---

[46] The symbolic figure of this orientation has for a long time been Herbert Spencer. See his *Social Statics* (London: John Chapman, 1851).

[47] Cf. the viewpoints of Thorstein Veblen, *The Engineers and the Price System* (New York: Harcourt, Brace and World, 1963) (originally published in 1921); James Burnham, *The Managerial Revolution* (Bloomington, Ind.: Indiana University Press, 1960) (originally published in 1941); J. Kenneth Galbraith, *The New Industrial State* (Boston: Houghton Mifflin Company, 1967).

The mixed fruits of unplanned urban expansion were obvious to Londoners in 1828. ("Monster Soup commonly called Thames Water, Being a Correct Representation of That Precious Stuff Doled Out to Us" by William Heath. Courtesy Philadelphia Museum of Art. Photograph by A. J. Wyatt, staff photographer.)

politicians, political bosses, military leaders, and affluent business-men. Only in the last decade or two has the need for organizational skills been seriously recognized—in schools of urban and regional planning, in several graduate programs in administrative science, in various business-sponsored institutes for community affairs, and in a few recent and highly experimental programs in urban studies centers.[48]

Finally, until very recently, few people were willing to recognize the growing costs, both material and social, of unhindered specialization and innovation. Such critics as Patrick Geddes, Benton Mackaye, Lewis Mumford, Jacques Ellul, Oswald Spengler, and José Ortega y Gasset[49] were predicting the general nature of our current problems as early as the 1920's, but were ignored by

[48] Harvey S. Perloff, *Education for Planning: City, State and Regional* (Baltimore, Md.: Johns Hopkins University Press, 1957); Melvin R. Levin, *Community and Regional Planning* (New York: Praeger, 1969); Urban Institute, *A Directory of University Urban Research Centers* (Washington, D.C.: Urban Institute, 1969).

[49] Patrick Geddes, *Cities in Evolution*, Enlarged ed. (New York: Oxford University Press, 1950); Oswald Spengler, *The Decline of the West* (New York: Alfred A. Knopf, 1927); Oswald Spengler, *Man and Technics* (New York: Alfred A. Knopf, 1940); Lewis Mumford, *The Culture of Cities* (New York: Harcourt, Brace and World, 1938); José Ortega y Gasset, *Man and Crisis* (New York: W. W. Norton and Company, Inc, 1958); Benton Mackaye, *The New Exploration* (Urbana: University of Illinois Press, 1962) (originally published in 1928).

men in power and by the busy creators and consumers of goods and services. Even the Second World War encouraged little change in orientation toward the march of specialization. The first major pause for reflection came with the awsome realization that atomic power could quickly destroy generations of specialized achievement. Then, in varying degrees, the mounting severity of urban problems led to a new concern for appropriate coordination. Most recently, a growing awareness of the effects of technological and political carelessness on our water supply, our air, and even our food has confirmed the need for coordination in pursuit of the oldest objective of humans—that of physical survival.[50]

The kinds of social specialization we have reviewed in this chapter reflect the most frequent ways in which human societies have devised and embellished this indispensable mode of adaptation. But we have not yet considered an immensely important practical problem: the processes by which persons learn to participate in and use specialized units (roles, groups, communities). The "fit" between individual and society is mediated by the character of the prevailing social organization. But the evolving connections between a given social organization and a generation of human individuals are developed through the complex human phenomena of socialization, the focus of our discussion in Chapter 6.

Summary

Differentiation or specialization is an essential aspect of human social organization because needs and desires tend to outrun available resources and skills. In simpler societies, where knowledge and technology are relatively limited, specialization is based on sex, age, and family line. But such specialization tends to be self-limiting and thus quite constricting in its possibilities for greater levels of adaptation. In more complex societies, where knowledge and technology are considerably more developed, opportunities for social specialization are greatly expanded, particularly in those areas of human adaptation not directly related to problems of survival.

Social specialization in complex societies largely comprises four types. First, there is specialization into several forms of primary groups and secondary associations. A second mode is specialization by types of skills appropriate to given human interactions (technical, organizational, eval-

[50] See, for example, Paul R. Ehrlich, *The Population Bomb* (New York: Ballantine Books, Inc., 1970); Paul R. Ehrlich and Anne H. Ehrlich, *Population, Resources, Environment* (San Francisco: W. H. Freeman, 1970); Frank P. Grad *et. al., Environmental Control* (New York: Columbia University Press, 1971); Richard A. Falk, *This Endangered Planet* (New York: Random House, 1971).

uational–ideational, and symbolic). A third category of specialization is the combination of these types of skills in different ways in a widespread set of specialized social roles (task specialist, coordinative, expressive social specialist, clown/scapegoat, innovative, and social transmission types). The fourth type of social specialization involves concentration of groups and roles into separate and specialized communities.

The consequences of specialization for adaptation, however, are mixed. The adaptive capacities and achievements of secondary groups are considerable for large populations, but may interfere with the adaptive possibilities of primary groups. In addition, specialization tends to develop insulation of specialized parts, thereby placing great pressures on coordinative and control structures of given societies. In short, adaptation through social specialization seems to be efficient up to some optimal range of differentiation; beyond that range, "diminishing returns" and even some degree of maladaptation can be identified.

Exercises

1. Speculate on the probable effects of selecting people for public office on the basis of each of the following: age, sex, race, speaking ability, height, amount of earned income, place of residence, native ability, formal education, and health.

2. Analyze any familiar group (a family, a fraternity or sorority, a club, a sports team) and try to locate differences and distinctions—as defined in the section "Differences and Distinctions." Which are more numerous? Which tend to be more important to the operation of that group?

3. How does increased social specialization lead to more innovation?

4. Show how social specialization tends to generate both very close social interaction and highly limited forms of social interaction, as well.

5. In the early development of a new group, which skills tend to be developed first? Is there any order in the development of the other social skills?

6. If you were responsible for the training (formal and informal) of persons in a given community or organization, would you emphasize the learning of skills or roles? Why?

7. What are the major adaptive problems of primary groups in modern society?

8. James Burnham (in *The Managerial Revolution*) and Thorstein Veblen (in *The Engineers and the Price System* and *The Vested Interests and the State of the Industrial Arts*) analyzed the competition of major social roles in modern societies in somewhat different ways. Whose interpretation is more adequate for the United States since 1945?

Selected References

Braidwood, Robert J., and Gordon R. Willey (eds.). *Courses Toward Urban Life.* Chicago: Aldine Publishing Co., 1962.

Coleman, James S. *The Adolescent Society.* New York: Free Press, 1961.

Golembiewski, Robert T. *The Small Group.* Chicago: University of Chicago Press, 1962.

Hawley, Amos H. *Human Ecology.* New York: Ronald Press, 1950.

Mannheim, Karl. *Man and Society in an Age of Reconstruction.* New York: Harcourt, Brace and World, 1940.

McCall, George J., and J. L. Simmons. *Identities and Interactions.* New York: Free Press, 1966.

Mumford, Lewis. *The Culture of Cities.* New York: Harcourt, Brace and World, 1938.

Parsons, Talcott, Robert F. Bales, and Edward A. Shils. *Working Papers in the Theory of Action.* New York: Free Press, 1953.

White, Leslie A. *The Evolution of Culture.* New York: McGraw–Hill Book Co., 1959.

Whyte, William F. *Street Corner Society.* Chicago: University of Chicago Press, 1943.

6

Socialization and Social Competence

In the previous chapter society was viewed as a composite of many types of social organization aimed at coping with recurring practical problems of social adaptation. One of the major categories of social organization is a division of labor, which may be defined as, essentially, a distribution of tasks and functions related to a goal or set of goals. For example, the organization may be a hospital and the division of labor would comprise the maintenance personnel, the sanitary personnel, the food services personnel, room orderlies, nurses' aides, nurses, technicians, doctors, and administrators. Within each of these categories, there is, of course, a further division of labor. Different positions within the division of labor call for different abilities and skills, though many positions vary only slightly in this respect.

Two important problems of adaptation resulting from specialization in systems of organization are (1) the selection of individuals with the requisite skills, abilities, and motivation appropriate to the positions, and (2) the assurance of continuity within the organizational system. The process of socialization contributes to the solution of these two problems in varying degrees depending upon its success (1) in equipping new members (of society) with the

The questions "Who am I?" and "What will I become?" are answered by the type of social world in which one grows up.
(Courtesy Helen Levitt.)

general and special skills necessary to function in society, and (2) in modifying the skills of older members as their positions change. This chapter will analyze the general problem of socialization. Chapter 7 will follow with a discussion of one specialized institution of socialization, the family. (Another such institution is the educational system. Both the family and the educational system function as important adaptive agencies in the society.)

Despite some differences of approach in the study of socialization, there is general agreement with regard to how individuals learn to participate in society. Brim defines socialization as "the process by which individuals acquire the knowledge, skills, and dispositions that enable them to participate as more or less effective members of groups and the society."[1] We consider this definition a useful focus in the study of the socialization processes.

The study of socialization as an area of interest extends into several fields. Among the disciplines significantly concerned with the field are anthropology, biology, particularly ethology, psychology, and sociology. As might be expected the special concerns or problems of each of these fields tend to color the varying perspectives; as a consequence there is difficulty in integrating the various viewpoints. No attempt will be made in this chapter to

[1] Orville G. Brim, Jr., and Stanton Wheeler, *Socialization after Childhood* (New York: John Wiley & Sons, Inc., 1966).

The development of one's potentialities depends upon the opportunities afforded by the social system.
(Courtesy Elsa Dorfman.)

synthesize the varying conceptions, though some convergences will be noted. Anthropologists have tended to emphasize the role of culture in socialization, while ethologists have emphasized species and evolutionary inputs. Psychologists have emphasized the development and conditioning of perception and learning through interaction with the behavior of others, while sociologists have emphasized the study of processes of social influence and institutional effects. That each of these approaches has its place attests to the many facets of the socialization process.

The different biases that these diverse fields bring to the study of socialization give rise to a variety of theoretical issues that are treated with varying degrees of emphasis. Some of these issues are (1) the relative influence of genetics and experience on behavior —for example, in temperament studies and studies of the development of intelligence; (2) the relative influence of very early experience on personality development as compared to effects of later experiences on behavior; and (3) the relative emphasis on the inherent *psychic unity* of man as opposed to unity based on social forces, that is, the emphasis on universal drives and needs as contrasted to the psychological effects of groups, institutions, and culture as sources for behavior patterning; (4) the relative emphasis of psychological conflicts as opposed to conditions of socialization and social control as causes of deviations from social norms. These differences in substantive emphasis reflect more the differing problem and conceptual orientations of the various fields concerned with socialization theory and research than any real theoretical differences.

In this chapter, we will emphasize the social learning approach, particularly the operant conditioning model, in the context of problems of adaptation that derive from group interaction and institutional arrangements. The key adaptation problems in socialization with respect to the individual are (1) access to socially relevant knowledge and skills; (2) access to socially appropriate social values, attitudes, and beliefs; and (3) access to social roles in relation to one's skills and motivation. There are also three key problems of adaptation from the point of view of society. These are (1) the problem of social continuity, that is, the intergenerational transmission of culture so necessary for social adaptation; (2) the problem of behavioral conformity or social control necessary for coordination and integration of group and organizational action; (3) the problem of social selection and placement of new members into appropriate social roles, including the phenomenon of role aspiration or anticipatory socialization.

We do not seek to provide a complete or detailed treatment of the above set of problems, nor is this necessary for our general objectives or aims.[2] We intend to focus, instead, on three interrelated problem areas, which in turn relate in various ways to the six problem areas outlined above. These are (1) social experience and the development of the intellect; (2) internalization or learning of social norms; and (3) the learning of social roles and related attitudes toward authority and one's self. This chapter will employ a developmental and social learning perspective to examine the processes of socialization with respect to these three areas.

THE SOCIAL UTILIZATION AND ORGANIZATION OF INDIVIDUAL VARIATION IN HUMAN POPULATIONS

Human populations as evolutionary systems depend upon mechanisms of *variation* and *continuity* for their development and maintenance. Man survives not as an individual, but through society. Individuals die, but human *life* continues and the external system (that is, external to the individual) of maintenance is the human social

---

[2] For a detailed treatment, see David A. Goslin (ed.), *Handbook of Socialization Theory and Research* (Chicago, Rand McNally & Co., 1969); and John F. Scott, *Internalization of Norms: A Sociological Theory of Moral Commitment* (Englewood Cliffs, N.J.: Prentice Hall Inc., 1971).

system. The individual, through socialization, learns his positions in the great variety of groups to which he comes to belong; he acquires, as well, knowledge of the behavior patterns of the community and the larger society. These patterns include social skills, techniques, codes of conduct, rights, and obligations. In addition, the socialization process enables the individual, through his interaction with other individuals, to form and develop self-attitudes, sex identity, friendship relations, and some degree of general social competence.

The mechanisms for variation and continuity of population characteristics, as well as of social systems, are, as Alland[3] notes, both somatic and extrasomatic. The somatic elements are the genetic capacities for behavior, while the extrasomatic elements are culture-based behavior systems, such as institutions and systems of technology. The former lead to organic adaptations and the latter to social adaptations.

One of the difficult problems in understanding the development of human behavior, particularly human social behavior, is the fact that the human evolutionary system involves system *properties* that transcend the individual members, whereas the actual somatic and behavioral *bases* for the system are held within the individual.[4] This conceptual difficulty can be reduced by keeping in mind that concepts and theories are meant to explain certain things in respect to *specified conditions* and *levels* of reality, but not in respect to just *any* conditions or levels. For example, the law of falling bodies refers to a vacuum and not the open and variable atmosphere. Likewise the explanation of a person's motivation requires a knowledge of the person's personality and his environmental problems, but the explanation of varying rates of economic growth among societies requires data on the population characteristics at the institutional level of social behavior rather than at the level of the individual *per se*.

The human social system is highly differentiated and specialized, especially in its modern form. The filling of its positions calls for a wide range of behavioral capacities and skills; that these positions *can* be filled presupposes that the capacities exist in the population and that the individuals who possess them will be induced to acquire the skills and be motivated to apply them.

Though the human social system changes within as well as between generations, it is perhaps the new generations that are more motivated to seek institutional and organizational change. Yet, in spite of this, great systems continuity exists between generations. In other words, stability requires a certain continuity thus the *system*

[3] Alexander Alland, Jr., *Evolution and Human Behavior* (Garden City, N.Y.: The Natural History Press, 1967), p. 226.
[4] The student may wish to review Chapters 1 and 3 in this regard.

transcends the individuals and is transgenerational. Each new generation will be slightly different genetically from the previous, but the system will require that it supply the capacities and skills developed and institutionalized by the previous generations. Thus the new generation becomes molded to the systems demands. Similarly, as a new generation, it will face different environmental contingencies that will affect its need and desire to learn certain skills and apply them in ways the system demands. Moreover, this takes place in a context of overlapping generations of adults, that is, from young adult grandchildren, parents, and grandparents. This overlapping of generations is another source of pressure for system change and continuity.

Potentialities or capacities are produced by the process of human reproduction, which by its nature generates a rather wide range of variation in human capacities. This variation is a natural resource and it is brought about by the genetic processes of meiosis and recombination, in addition to the new combination of parental genes at conception.[5]

The genotype is the particular combination or composition of genes that characterize an individual. As implied in meiosis, no human individual transmits his or her genotype. Meiosis and recombination destroy genotypes. Only genes are transmitted, and these are shuffled and reshuffled by meiosis and recombination in each generation. As Professor George C. Williams has expressed it, "Socrates' genes may be with us yet, but not his genotype. . . ." [6] Thus the transmission of genes provides the continuity of the human species; genetic segregation and recombination provide the genetic variety within a species that is so necessary to adapt to changing environments.

Given the great variety of tasks to be performed in the human social system and the varying levels of complexity associated with the tasks, the variety in genetic materials is an indispensable natural resource. Genetic diversity does not express itself directly except in the familiar form of such physical traits as hair and eye color. In social behavior, it always expresses itself indirectly and

---

[5] When two gametes, or sex cells, unite and form a zygote, the zygote has twice as many chromosomes as either gamete; obviously there must be some mechanism for halving the chromosome number so that the daughter cells have the original number or one half. This process of reduction is meiosis. This results in two divisions of the nucleus accompanied by a single division of the chromosomes. All the genes on a particular chromosome constitute a linkage group. During the process of meiosis new combinations of linked genes occur. Mutations are any inherited changes not resulting from the *normal* recombination of genetic materials due to meiosis. Thus mutations also contribute to the diversity of genetic material, though these are usually not adaptive. Estimates of mutation rates for man range from about 10^{-4} to 10^{-6} per generation. (See the section "Human Adaption: Sociocultural Evolution—Biological Background" in Chapter 1, for a brief discussion.)

[6] George C. Williams, *Adaptation and Natural Selection: A Critique of Some Current Evolutionary Thought* (Princeton, N.J.: Princeton University Press, 1966), p. 24.

then as a function of development interacting with experience, which includes nutritional background and cultural background. Consequently, it is unlikely that genotype differences associated with behavioral differences would be detected except in cases where wide genetic differences exist or where the environments are more or less equal. In any event, what group and societal leaders look for in selecting individuals to fill positions are behavioral and attitudinal characteristics that will validate the role requirements of the positions. These characteristics not only vary from individual to individual but within the individual as well. For example, a person may have performed a given set of roles for a given period of time. Having seen him in these roles, his acquaintances will have formed judgments about his personality only to discover an almost "new" personality in him after he is promoted to some new position. It is not that he has changed so much. He had these behavioral capabilities all along, but his former social position did not call for them. Inasmuch as different social roles call for differing kinds of behavior and each person has developed a rather large repertoire of behaviors, it is reasonably easy for most people to move from one role to another, although in some cases additional training may be required.

In a very real sense, the human social system is an "organization of diversity."[7] It is not only an organization of diversity derived from genetic variation within the species and from variation in experience, it is itself a source of further diversity through role differentiation and conditioning. For example, sex differences are genetic differences, but social roles based on sex differences produce behavioral differences that are not biological. The differentiation and patterning of behavior differences caused by social role interaction are sufficiently effective and stable across time to cause many people to mistake the source of such differences as biological rather than social. For this reason, blacks have been labeled as biologically "lazy" and women have been labeled as uncreative for the same reason. Minority groups such as blacks and women that are denied the privilege of serving in certain social roles are thereby conditioned not to seek these roles. Hence after a few generations they may come to think of themselves, and to be thought of by the rest of society, as not being suited for these roles. In fact, in some instances women who have been creative in spite of their cultural handicaps have had to adopt male pseudonyms—as exemplified in the literary world by George Sand and George Eliot.[8]

In Chapters 2 and 3 it was shown that the major evolutionary change that has most sharply separated man and his modes

[7] This term is borrowed from Anthony F. C. Wallace in his book *Culture and Personality,* 2nd ed. (New York: Random House, 1970), p. 23.
[8] For a good selection of readings on socialization and sex roles, see Judith M. Bardwick (ed.), *Readings on the Psychology of Women* (New York: Harper & Row Publishers, Inc., 1972), Part II.

of adaptation from the nonhuman primates is the capacity for language. Language, particularly written language as well as the language of mathematics, has made the creation of complex systems of adaptation and adjustment possible. These symbolic forms permitted the creation of systems (systems of justice, social control, production and distribution, technology and education, and so on) that guide human social interaction and provide tentative but changing solutions to problems of human nature and human adaptation. The successful adaptation of each new generation is dependent upon the social transmission of the available knowledge, skills, and information from the previous generations to the new ones. The process of human socialization is largely responsible for this transmission. In advanced societies, the educational institution is conceived as a special system for social transmission and hence a part of the overall socialization process. Since culture is *socially transmitted* largely through symbolic communication, each new generation is dependent upon the parental generation for the acquisition of culture. In other words, each generation of parents has about 20 years to socialize the newborn or as some would say to civilize them. This has been facetiously expressed as "one generation between civilization and barbarism." Konrad Lorenz has speculated on the importance of the transmission of culture in the following[9]:

Were it possible to rear a human being of normal genetic constitution under circumstances depriving it of all cultural tradition—which is impossible not only for ethical but also for biological reasons—the subject of the cruel experiment would be very far from representing a reconstruction of a prehuman ancestor, as yet devoid of culture. It would be a poor cripple, deficient in higher functions in a way comparable to that in which idiots who have suffered encephalitis during infantile or fetal life lack the higher functions of the cerebral cortex. . . . Man's whole system of innate activities and reactions is phylogenetically so constructed and so "calculated" by evolution, as to need to be complemented by cultural tradition. For instance, all the tremendous neuro-sensory apparatus of human speech is phylogenetically evolved, but so constructed that its function presupposes the existence of a culturally developed language which the infant has to learn. No man, not even the greatest genius, could invent, all by himself, a system of social norms and rites forming a substitute for cultural tradition.

Therefore, if the controlling generations of a society fail to give their children what they need to learn, they will have failed to give their society what it needs to survive.

It should be noted that there are those who would argue that more emphasis should be placed on programs of controlled

---

[9] Konrad Lorenz, quoted in Philip K. Bock, *Culture Shock: A Reader in Modern Cultural Anthropology* (New York: Alfred A. Knopf, 1970), p. 1. For a study showing the effects of extreme social isolation on development, see Kingsley Davis, "Extreme Social Isolation of a Child," *Amer. J. of Sociology*, 45 (1939–1940), pp. 554–565; Kingsley Davis, "Final Note on a Case of Extreme Isolation," *Amer. J. of Sociology*, 52 (1946–1947), pp. 432–437.

genetics rather than on environmental improvement and natural selection as a means for improving the adaptive capacity of a human
society. In other words, some argue that a planned program of artificial selection would speed up the evolution of "desirable" characteristics and eliminate the "undesirable" ones. There is no question
that in the long run we must consider the quality of the gene pool.
In spite of the great adaptive advantage supplied by culture, man is
still dependent upon organic evolution, and organic evolution presupposes sufficient genetic variation to produce some genotypes
capable of surviving unforeseen pressures. Artificial selection has
been widely applied in agriculture. Perhaps the results learned
there may have important implications for considering such a program in man. Gottesman and Erlenmeyer-Kimling[10] have recently
examined this very issue and some of their findings are presented
here.

In the first place, should the artificial selection focus on a
single trait or multiple traits? Some traits are polygenetically determined and several such traits would, of course, involve still further
genetic complexity. But with respect to human behavior we know
very little about what responses are correlated with a given genetic
trait. For example, Kohlberg's studies on moral development indicate very little if any correlation between IQ and moral commitment.[11] If one were formulating a program of artificial genetic
selection for human beings, should one emphasize intellectual traits
or moral traits or both, and/or what others? Furthermore, who is to
decide?

As we have already indicated, multiple trait selection is
complicated; furthermore, it is difficult to foresee the kind of traits
that would optimize adaptation in the future. Certainly, intense selection for a single trait would not provide much insurance for
future adaptation, since such selection rapidly reduces genetic variation and leads to the fixing of undesirable genes in a population.
Gottesman summarizes some of the results of intense artificial selection for a single trait in food production. The result has been the
rapid exhaustion of genetic variation. For example, "Selection for
egg size in chickens . . . led to a reduction in egg production. Selection for broadbreasts in turkeys led to such a reduction in fertility
that breeders had to resort to artificial insemination to maintain the
flocks. . . . The potato famine in Ireland resulted from the low resistance to fungus in varieties that had been intensively selected for
high yield with consequent homogeneity. A recent example involves the loss of 10 per cent of the corn crops in the United States

---

[10] Irving I. Gottesman and L. Erlenmeyer-Kimling, "A Foundation for Informed Eugenics,"
Social Biology, 18 (1971), pp. 51–59.
[11] Lawrence Kohlberg, "Stage and Sequence: Cognitive-Developmental Approach to Socialization," in *Handbook of Socialization Research and Theory*, David A. Goslin (ed.) (Chicago:
Rand McNally & Co., 1969), pp. 347–480.

in 1970 to a mutant fungus. Growers had sacrificed genetic diversity for the high yielding, easily processed, but genetically homogeneous hybrid corn. In some southern states 50 per cent of the crop was destroyed. Species survival requires enough variation in the gene pool to produce some phenotypes capable of resisting unforeseen disasters and perpetuating the harshly selected survivors." [12]

It is true that selection may be based on multiple traits, but there is still a conflict between natural selection in the gene pool and artificial selection. The conflict arises from the excessive genetic uniformity and loss in flexibility that arises out of artificial selection as compared to a randomized gene selection process. What can be done immediately to improve the general adaptive capacity of a society is to improve the prenatal and postnatal environment of the newborn to enable them to realize their potential. This would permit an increase in social competence, which is the principal function of the socialization process. One of the primary elements in social competence is cognitive development and particularly the development of intelligence, to which we now turn.

COGNITIVE AND INTELLECTUAL DEVELOPMENT

Early Experience and Cognitive Development

The research literature on child development rather strongly indicates what might be called critical periods for development. These have been interpreted to mean that a child's psychological or physiological reactions to environmental events are different at different ages and levels of maturation; and that with respect to some behaviors a particular experience or process must occur during a limited critical time period if those behaviors are to develop normally. For example, Piaget in his studies on the moral development of children has shown that a three to five year old child's judgment on the seriousness of an act is quite different from that of a child seven years of age. At the earlier age, the child's more limited powers of abstract thought preclude the taking into account of the factor of intentionally harming someone else, as contrasted with accidentally doing so. The older child can make this distinction and his judgment varies accordingly. The second or stronger kind of effect can be illustrated by the fact that speech in the human child will not develop unless the child is exposed to adult speech. This does not mean that the subject will not develop speech if it is properly exposed to speech patterns later in life. It will—but not as well as it would have if the experience had been earlier.[13] A still stronger

[12] Irving I. Gottesman and L. Erlenmeyer-Kimling, "A Foundation for Informed Eugenics," *Social Biology, 18* (1971), p. S6.
[13] See Kingsley Davis, "Final Note on a Case of Extreme Social Isolation," *Amer. J. of Sociology, 52* (1946–1947), pp. 432–437.

The seriousness of an act is much less evident to a three year old than to a seven year old. Meanings change as their context in society is learned.
(Courtesy Helen Levitt.)

effect is illustrated by the dramatic demonstration by Riesen that patterned light during the early postnatal days of development is necessary for the development of visual capacity.[14]

The human brain accomplishes approximately 80 per cent of its growth in the first three years of life. Research reports coming from several laboratories have recently shown quite conclusively that nutritional deficiency, particularly protein deficiency, interferes with brain development. Malnutrition reduces the amount of nucleic acid in the brain and reduces the quality of brain cells as compared to cells in normal children of the same age.

The normal human infant learns much more during the first few months of life than was formerly believed. Moreover, the learning occurs at a period in the child's life before symbolic means of discrimination (language) have developed, or have only begun to develop. Consequently, learning under the condition of the child's

[14] Austin H. Riesen, "Arrested Vision," in David C. Beardslee and Michael Wertheimer (eds.), *Readings in Perception* (Princeton, N.J.: D. Van Nostrand Co., Inc., 1958), pp. 306—311. Also A. H. Riesen, "Stimulation as a Requirement for Growth and Function in Behavioral Development," in D. W. Fiske and S. R. Maddi (eds.), *Functions of Varied Experience* (Homewood, Ill.: Dorsey Press, 1961), pp. 57–80.

minimal powers of discrimination is very difficult to extinguish.[15] This point helps to explain the psychiatric observation that it is much easier to deal with psychological conflicts deriving from conditions experienced later in life than conditions experienced very early in life. It is much easier to reconstruct the conditions of learning during the later period than during very early life because of the advantage afforded by the language factor. Therefore, it is easier to unlearn and extinguish later learning as compared to learning during infancy.

Kagan points out that the *rate* of change in physical and psychological growth in the infant is dramatic, compared to any other period in life. Given the rapid growth of the brain during this period, early learning becomes of prime importance because of the great plasticity of the child and of the effects of learning during this period on subsequent learning. "The newborn is transformed from a crying, squirming, reflexive creature to a coherent, symbolic, coordinated, and planful child in less than 30 months. And a set of convenient milestones mark the journey—the smile of recognition at four months, fear of a stranger at eight months, crying to separation at ten months, two-word sentences at eighteen months, and conceptual conflict at twenty-four months." [16]

To summarize, early experience is very crucial in launching a child's physiological, psychological and social development. It is crucial because to a very significant extent subsequent development depends upon what happens to a child during the first two to three years of life, including prenatal life. These experiences refer to adequate neurosensory stimulation, adequate nutrition, adequate social interaction and affection from *significant* others.

Early Development of Social Behavior

Concerning socialization the sociologist is especially interested in the development of patterns of social behavior. Some of the important questions of concern are: Is the child's behavior socially oriented to begin with, as Vigotsky contends, or is it egocentric at the start and develops toward a socially oriented perspective following experience with others and with language development, as Piaget contends?[17] What is the degree of permanence of early attributes and what are the effects of differential experience on cognitive development? Does cognitive development in the child proceed in

[15] David C. McClelland, *Personality* (New York: Holt, Rinehart and Winston, Inc., 1951), p. 452.
[16] Jerome Kagan et al., *Change and Continuity in Infancy* (New York: John Wiley & Sons, Inc., 1971), p. 3.
[17] L. S. Vigotsky, *Thought and Language* (Cambridge: MIT Press, 1962) (first published in 1934), and Jean Piaget, *The Language and Thought of the Child* (New York: Humanities Press, 1959) (first published in 1924).

One's self-image develops through social interaction and through observation of the responses of others to one's actions and attitudes.
(Courtesy Elsa Dorfman.)

stages, with sensorimotor development preceding the development of meaning? Or, can meanings develop from the child's experience of simply looking and listening? All these questions and many others need answering if we are to develop a thorough understanding of how social behavior develops and changes. The student of human behavior must keep an open mind on these issues until more adequate data and theory are available to help him form a more valid and comprehensive view than is now available.

In order to get to the base of the problem we need to know the principles that describe and explain the relation between an event and a stimulus and the resulting schema and meaning. This is analogous to understanding the relation between a sensory stimulus and its related neural event.

The term **schema** only loosely defined now, refers to the patterned mental results of perception. In this sense, a schema permits the organism to recognize and assimilate information. Schemata form in varying degrees of completeness; in their early or vague stage the assimilated information may or may not result in a meaningful interpretation.

Kagan defines schema as a representation of an event that preserves the temporal and spatial arrangements of its distinctive elements without necessarily being isomorphic with the event.[18] Piaget, on the other hand, contends that "At birth the only 'organizations' available are the congenital sensorimotor schemata. . . . The reflexive sensorimotor schemata are generalized, coordinated with each other, and differentiated to become the elementary operations of intelligence. . . ."[19] Here we have two contrasting usages of the term schema. The *first* describes what emerges immediately following a perceptual experience and the *second* describes the functioning of an inherent process as it is activated by experience. The differences in meaning are not as great as they seem. Rather these usages appear to have somewhat different points of departure. Kagan assumes that the principles underlying the formation of schema are not known while Piaget assumes they are the workings of inherent biochemical processes. This issue need not concern us here. We will start with the fact that schema are formed and then concern ourselves with (a) the patterns in their formation and (b) whether there is a relation between the schemata and subsequent behavior.

The major function of schemata is to allow the child to recognize and assimilate information. Perhaps an example will

Children learn by formulating images and pictures of experiences.
(Courtesy Stephanie Lodish.)

[18] Jerome Kagan et al., *Change and Continuity in Infancy* (New York: John Wiley & Sons, Inc., 1971), p. 6.
[19] J. McV. Hunt, *Intelligence and Experience* (New York: The Ronald Press, 1961), pp. 113–114.

make this process a little clearer to the reader. Kagan reports his recent study that illustrates this concept. He asked a sample of four year olds to look at a set of 50 pictures. The pictures illustrated many things the children had never seen before. They devoted no more than a few seconds to each picture and looked over the set of 50 in three to four minutes. They were then shown 50 pairs of pictures, one of which they had seen earlier and the other was new to them. They were asked to point out the pictures they viewed earlier. On the average they recognized forty-five out of the fifty and some recognized all of them even two days later. Kagan notes that since some of the pictures represented things the children had never seen before, such as an unusual lathe or an engineer's slide rule, that it is unlikely that this high level of recognition was the result of language labels. The amount of time for scanning was probably too short for well-defined images to form. Kagan concludes, and we think correctly, that neither language, overt action, nor image provide a satisfactory explanation for the children's ability to recognize the scenes with over 90 per cent accuracy. Therefore, he uses schema to stand for the cognitive structure that permitted recognition. Kagan extends his reasoning to the verbal level by noting that in the instance where a child learns the meaning of "stop that" *schema* refers to the process that "permits a child to understand the meaning of that phrase." [20] It is easy to assert that schema is the process that permits this, but schema is not sufficiently defined to allow a specification of this process. Consequently, it might as well have been labeled *X*, except that we do know that we are concerned with the process that determines the meaning of an experience. With respect to social behavior, one person's *response* to another *is* the stimulus to the *other person's* schema, and the effects of the response on the other person significantly determine the meaning of the interaction. The relationship of schemata to response in the context of social behavior is an important research problem, but an adequate means of measuring or indexing schemata will have to be achieved first.

It is assumed that the meaning of *A*'s response to *B* is determined by *B*'s perception of the *consequence* or potential consequence of *A*'s response to him. No attempt will be made to derive the principles that determine one's *perception* of the consequences of another's action or chain of actions, though this is important. We simply assume that individuals develop with varying degrees of accuracy the capacity to judge whether another's actions have positive, negative, or neutral consequences for themselves.

In other words, we assume a Skinnerian model of behavior until more is known about the biochemical and physiological

[20] Jerome Kagan, *et al., Change and Continuity in Infancy* (New York: John Wiley & Sons, Inc., 1971), pp. 7 and 8.

processes that go on inside one's head as a function of external or internal stimulation. That is to say, one can study patterns of social behavior by determining the relationships or covariations between environmental inputs and behavioral outputs. By systematically varying the social inputs, their effects can be observed on the response outputs, without the necessity of postulations about what goes on in the brain.[21]

The formation of schemata from the results of one's experience allows one to recognize classes of events, as well as unique events, and to anticipate their occurrence and reoccurrence from associated cues. Variation from what is anticipated or expected alerts one to discrepancies and enables one to take appropriately related action. Discrepancy is defined as the difference or differences between a perceived event and the infant's or child's schema for that class of events. Kagan formulates an hypothesis, which he calls the *discrepancy principle*. "The discrepancy principle states that an event that is moderately discrepant from the one that generated a schema (e.g., alterations in the temporal and spatial configuration of the original stimulus) will elicit longer fixations (attention) than minimally discrepant events or events that bear no relation to the schema." [22]

By the time the child is one year old, a new level or class of cognitive behavior is exhibited and begins to influence an infant's reaction to an event that is discrepant with his schema. This is called **hypothesis formulation** and is the interpreting of an event or stimulus figure by mentally relating the unusual event to a familiar form. The mental operation used in formulating the hypothesis is a cognitive structure used all through one's life. The scientific hypothesis is a highly sophisticated form of the child's hypothesis.

The formulation of an hypothesis to reconcile a cognitive discrepancy in an event by relating it to past familiar experience is the child's effort to assimilate the discrepant experience. Such efforts also produce changes in existing schemata and are one of the principal means by which schemata grow and become differentiated. This affirms an earlier idea of Piaget[23] that an infant attends to variations in experiences in order to assimilate these, the result of which is a further differentiation of cognitive structure. This process of behavior growth and differentiation can be viewed as a contribution to the child's growing independence from its parents

---

[21] This approach has some precedent in sociology. See, for example, George C. Homans, *Social Behavior: Its Elementary Forms* (New York: Harcourt, Brace and World, 1961); and John T. Doby, *Introduction to Social Psychology* (New York: Appleton–Century–Crofts, 1966), Chap. 7.

[22] Jerome Kagan et al., *Change and Continuity in Infancy* (New York: John Wiley & Sons, Inc., 1971), p. 62.

[23] J. Piaget, *The Origins of Intelligence in Children* (New York: International Universities Press, 1952).

through the socialization process. When we speak of the child's dependence upon its parents, we should distinguish several kinds of dependency. First, there is biological and physiological dependence, which is a physiological or developmental dependence and assumes warmth and nutritional, emotional, and physical security. There is also motor and cognitive skill dependence, which, in time, training, social interaction, and education will eliminate. Finally, there is a value and informational dependence on the family. These, assuming adequate social interaction, will also be eliminated in time by education, both formal and informal. The development of social competencies and the removal of these social dependencies is one of the major by-products of socialization.

Whatever the processes are that underlie the formation of schemata prior to the emergence of speech and sentences, clearly these processes are greatly augmented and facilitated by the use of language. Accordingly, it would seem that social experiences that are conducive to language development would facilitate the growth of cognitive structures.

The covariation between educational level of the parents and indexes of child growth and articulation in Kagan's study was consistently stronger for girls than boys. Quality of Embedded Figures Test and vocabulary performance were all more closely associated with parental social class for girls than for boys.[24] The middle-class girls showed more vacillation in a conflict situation and also showed more responsiveness to meaningful speech as contrasted to meaningless speech. The lower-class girls did not show the differential reaction to meaningful versus nonmeaningful passages. There are two possible explanations for the greater verbal responsiveness of young girls than young boys. One hypothesis is that since anatomical and physiological systems mature earlier in the girl than in the boy, language functions might also mature earlier in girls. At any rate, tests show a clearly more unified language–verbal factor among young girls than boys. A second possibility is that it could be true that mothers show more responsiveness to girls than to boys and that this stimulates verbal growth.

Until now we have emphasized the infant's development of behavior through self-initiated activity with respect to the environment nearby and the responses of the parents, particularly the mother to the child. This involves sensorimotor action such as crying, smiling, squirming, grasping, babbling, and by 18 to 20 months short sentences. With the development of language, a whole new environment opens up to the child as he or she learns that things have names and that people, including himself or herself, have names. Since the learning of short sentences usually occurs at about 18 months, it is assumed that this behavior pattern has to await

[24] Jerome Kagan et al., Change and Continuity in Infancy (New York: John Wiley & Sons, Inc., 1971), p. 183.

neurological maturation of the capacity for language. This does not assume a discontinuity in development—rather it suggests continuous development in the direction of increased complexity and differentiation.

A part of the increased differentiation deriving from language acquisition comes from the reflected evaluations, appraisals, and labelings by others of the child's qualities and performances. These *"significant others"* as G. H. Mead[25] called them, are socializers, and they provide a societal pressure for social competence, which helps to offset the child's self-centered or egocentric world. Mead suggests that the infant can only know whether he is competent after he has attained the symbolic capacities that go with speech and emerging selfhood. It is perhaps true that the self in the social sense does await the development of reflexive thought, which is dependent upon speech. More research is needed to fill in the gaps of knowledge in this area. For example, the infant is aware that its crying and smiling will elicit different kinds of responses from its parents. It is capable of initiating a wide range of behaviors long before language usage develops. The use of language gives the child another means of eliciting approval, and accordingly, he receives and understands another form of approval—in addition to a smile or being cuddled—namely, praise. We are assuming then that the internal development and functioning of the child, both physiological and psychological, are continuous functions, but that the environmental and particularly the social pressures exhibit discontinuities and sometimes inconsistencies. For example, the socializers do expect the child as it gets older to stop acting like a child while it eats and to begin to eat like an adult. The beginnings of self-discrimination through the reflections of others is as good a place as any to examine the influences that the family and its position in the class structure have on socialization.

SOME FAMILY INFLUENCES ON SOCIALIZATION

As was indicated in Chapter 3 one of the means of behavior control is social reinforcement. Parental reinforcement of child behavior may take the form of reward or punishment. Parental success in behavior shaping through the use of rewards and punishments will vary with the type, the degree, and the consistency of reward or punishment. In Chapter 13, it is shown that when social reinforcement and other means of social motivation fail, power is often exercised as a means of control. This also applies to parental control, though the reason may not necessarily be that it was a last resort. A

[25] G. H. Mead, *Man, Self, and Society* (Chicago: University of Chicago Press, 1934). See also Harry Stack Sullivan, *Conceptions of Modern Psychiatry*, 2nd ed. (New York: W. W. Norton & Co., 1953). For the significances of names in socialization, see the autobiography of Helen Keller, *The Story of My Life* (Garden City, N.Y.: Doubleday & Company, Inc., 1931).

Parental reinforcement is a major source for the formation of child sex roles and identifications.
(Courtesy Robert Rapelye, Photography International.)

lower-lower class father, for example, may use power as his principal means of enforcing his will. In summary, then, there are two principal means of parental influence on child socialization—these are social reinforcement and the parental exercise of power.

Let us now consider the different effects of these two principal sources of influence. Kelman[26] formulated a process of behavior shaping in terms of the degree of commitment of the person to the desired change. He identified three levels or processes and labeled them **compliance, identification,** and **internalization.** *Compliance is conformity to the expectations of another person in*

[26] H. C. Kelman, "Compliance, Identification, and Internalization: Three Processes of Attitude Change," in *Conflict Resolution,* 2 (1958), pp. 51–60; and H. C. Kelman, "Processes of Opinion Change," *Public Opinion Quart.,* 25 (1961), pp. 57–78.

order to gain a reward or avoid punishment. The conformity is outward in nature and is given as an act of expediency. One often notes automobile driving behavior change to a level of compliance when the driver discovers a policeman or patrolman nearby. In other words, the manifestation of compliance behavior depends upon the actor's ability to observe, or his knowledge of the proximity of, the influencing person.

Identification does not depend upon the presence of the influencing person. That is, the person being influenced or who accepts the new behavior does so both publicly and privately. Identification does depend, however, on the role that an individual takes at a particular time.[27] In other words, *the person adopts the behavior because he aspires to become like someone else* he particularly admires in some major way.

Internalization occurs when *one adopts a particular behavior pattern because it is consistent with his own values.* In this case, the content or behavior itself is rewarding. Kelman observes that the factors that determine which of these processes that actually occur are principally the *source* of the influencing agent's power, the manner in which he employs this power, and hence his effect on the learner's self-attitudes. To the extent that the individual is concerned with the *social effect* of his behavior, the influence will take the form of compliance; to the extent that he is concerned with vicarious learning or imitating another, the influence will take the form of identification; and to the extent that the new behavior is intrinsically satisfying and is congruent with the individual's own values, the influence will take the form of internalization.

In general, punishment is less effective in controlling behavior in the absence of the social control agent than is positive reinforcement. The main purpose of socialization has to do with causing people to become sensitive to and to take into account the *consequences* of their behavior not only for themselves but also for *others* affected. The evolutionary or adaptive reasons for this, in the case of man, should be obvious. Man adapts and meets his needs in a highly interdependent social system; hence the consequences of large amounts of adaptation through overly self-centered behavior would be a threatening of the stability of the system and hence survival. Thus, there is a necessity for balancing of stability and adaptability in a culture.

One of the unique consequences of human socialization at the level of internalization is the phenomenon of *conscience* and the related capacity to experience a *sense of guilt.*[28] The achievement of effective impulse control is most efficiently achieved in

[27] H. C. Kelman, "Processes of Opinion Change," *Public Opinion Quart.,* 25 (1961), p. 63.
[28] D. P. Ausubel, "Relationship Between Shame and Guilt in the Socializing Process," *Psychological Rev.,* 62 (1955), pp. 378–390.

Reinforcement is perhaps the best way of controlling behavior, although punishment is, at times, the most tempting method. ("Fatherly Discipline" by Honoré Daumier. Courtesy Chicago Art Institute.)

early childhood; therefore the family greatly influences, and is the principal source for, the development of the capacity for guilt feelings. Some would argue (for instance, Ausubel and Mowrer) that the socialization process would be ineffective without the aid rendered by guilt feelings.[29]

Socialization and Guilt

Guilt, according to Ausubel, is "a special kind of negative self-evaluation—a self reaction to an injured conscience."[30] Thus a feeling of guilt is a form of self-condemnation and self-punishment regardless of the social interaction situation. A more superficial form of reaction to one's own behavior is the reaction known as *shame*. Shame is uncomfortable or painful for an individual only if he is "found out" or "caught."

Children are taught to avoid certain things (avoidance learning), to refrain from some things (inhibition), and to be attracted to or desire other things (approach learning), and finally to perform certain kinds of activities and to do so in certain ways (role learning and habit formation). Animals learn in many ways similar to these—but they *do not* exhibit self-condemnation.

[29] D. P. Ausubel, *ibid.*, p. 378; and O. H. Mowrer, *Learning Theory and the Symbolic Processes* (New York: John Wiley & Sons, Inc., 1960), pp. 390–399.
[30] D. P. Ausubel, *ibid.*, p. 379.

The phenomenon of self-condemnation depends on language mechanisms, particularly the capacity for reflexive thought; that is, the organism must be capable of making its own behavior or anticipated behavior a *subject*, as well as object, of analysis and evaluation. Assuming then that one has acquired strong attachments to certain standards of conduct, he can then use these standards as anchors or guidelines for judging his *own* behavior, as well as the behavior of others. It will be shown below, in the section on internalization of norms, that the evaluation of one's own behavior and the resulting feelings that one experiences vary and change as one's status changes. The self-reflections and feelings also vary with the status variations and the judgments of others with whom one interacts. For example, one may tell a risqué joke to a group of peers and, as they laugh, he will be pleased and laugh with them. But suppose he suddenly looks behind himself and sees his Minister —then his laughter turns into chagrin and embarrassment. Why the change in his self-feelings? The answer is that in the latter situation, he is being socially reinforced *negatively* by a significant other, whereas before he was being reinforced positively by significant others. *Significant others* are defined as others with whom one interacts who have powers for social reinforcement.

Many pet lovers have reported instances of what appears to be shame in their pets and that this occurs only when the master catches the pet carrying out a forbidden form of behavior. Some researchers have claimed to demonstrate feelings of guilt in animals. Both these interpretations, however, appear to be instances of anthropomorphism, that is the interpretation of nonhuman characteristics in terms of human characteristics.

What kind of mechanism or experience causes an individual to judge himself by the standard of those to whom he gives allegiance? Ausubel offers the following explanatory answer[31]:

Behavior can first be regarded as manifesting moral properties when a sense of obligation is acquired. The central hypothesis of the present formulation is that this development typically takes place in children who are accepted and intrinsically valued by parents, and who thereby acquire a derived or vicarious status in consequence of this acceptance. By the fiat of parent acceptance they are provided with intrinsic feelings of security and adequacy despite their manifest dependency and incompetence to fend for themselves. They accordingly become disposed to accept parental values implicitly and unconditionally out of loyalty to the individuals to whom they owe their status and self-esteem.

In summary, shame is a reaction from fear of being caught and condemned by others. The person who is caught in a lie or

---

[31] D. P. Ausubel, "Relationship Between Shame and Guilt in the Socializing Process," *Psychological Rev.*, 62 (1955), p. 380.

stealing is likely to be ashamed. Guilt is self-punishment and leads to an individual's refraining from an act because he anticipates pangs of conscience or self-punishment.

There is no doubt that reinforcement through praise and healthy affection is an efficient source of social influence in the family's socialization effort. Punishment, on the other hand, has been much condemned because of its relative failure in experimental work and as a result of a partial misrepresentation of Freud.[32] It is therefore important to point out that punishment under certain conditions and when moderately administered is effective in establishing boundaries to behavior.

In discussing some results of research on the efforts of both rewards and punishments on childhood socialization, McCandless concludes[33, 34]:

Learning may occur in either of two ways: because right or correct or good responses are rewarded, or because poor or incorrect or bad responses are punished. Hartup, Moore and Sager (1963, *Journal of Consulting Psy.*) document this process of social reinforcement in terms of the pattern of rewards and punishments that are given, respectively to boys and girls for sex-appropriate behavior during their preschool and kindergarten years: little boys are punished for playing with girlish toys or indulging in sissy behavior, and are rewarded for playing with masculine toys or indulging in appropriate, male types of behavior. As a consequence, they seem to socialize, or sex-type, early, firmly, and quickly. On the other hand, girls apparently receive little or no punishment for tomboy behavior, but are rewarded for appropriate girlish behavior. The consequence appears to be, and several studies . . . agree on this, that girls sex-type much later in our society than boys. The reason for this, in terms of the economics of the laws of learning . . . is that when both rewards and punishments are administered, the child learns not only what he *can* do, but what he *cannot* do: double reinforcement, directionally speaking, is much more informative—extensive—than single-ended reinforcement. While the research evidence is not clear, it seems that a most effective learning occurs when the frequency of reward or positive reinforcement is substantially greater than that of punishment or negative reinforcement.

One of the difficulties with social reinforcement in the family is the inconsistency and uncertainty with which it is administered. From the general literature[35] on learning theory, it is quite clear that reinforcement, whether in the form of reward or punishment, will be more effective the *sooner* it is received following the response and the more *consistently* it is applied, that is, the more likely it is to always follow the response, provided the *amount* (of reward or punishment) is significant.

[32] Justin Aronfreed, *Conduct and Conscience: The Socialization of Internalized Control over Behavior* (New York: Academic Press, Inc., 1968).
[33] Boyd R. McCandless, "Childhood Socialization," in *Handbook of Socialization Theory and Research*, David Goslin (ed.), (Chicago: Rand–McNally & Co., 1969), pp. 801–802.
[34] For a good review of the literature on the effects of punishment on behavior see Helen H. Marshall, "The effect of punishment on children: A review of the literature and a suggested hypothesis," *J. of Genetic Psychology* No. 106 (1965), pp. 23–33.
[35] See S. Mednick, *Human Learning* (New York: Prentice–Hall, Inc., 1964).

We have shown that correct or appropriate responses can generally be expected when children and adolescents are in the presence of the socializing agents, particularly the parents or peer groups, and that incorrect or inappropriate responses can be expected when the socializing agents are absent, if the correct patterns of response have not yet been internalized. But face-to-face or primary group interaction covers only part of the span of human interaction. The symbolic capacity of man has made it possible for him to behave with considerable reliability even when the object of behavior is physically or temporally removed—that is, man can respond to the symbolic representations of experience and objects. Through symbolic representation, many, perhaps most, human norms are learned, for through the use of symbols man develops the capacity for reflexive thought and the ability to evaluate his own actions (and the actions of others) with respect to certain valued standards. Thus a major source of parental influence is in the area of the child's moral judgments and commitments to symbolic standards.

Parental Influences on the Internalization of Norms

The effect of parental influence on internalization of norms varies significantly with the social class background of the family.[36] The learning of and conforming to norms depends upon whether the behavior involved is socially reinforced. The *means* of reinforcement vary with the class position of the family. We may not approve of this and wish it were not the case—and some will claim that it is not true. Nevertheless the quality of education among all schools is not the same and one's social and economic opportunities are significantly affected by the school one attends. Social and economic opportunity of the family largely determines the amount of power, that is socially valued power, that the parents may have to use as reinforcement. Certainly love, affection, and parental appreciation are important sources of reinforcement, but there comes a time as the child grows older that these alone are not sufficient to control behavior.

The lower-class father with his limited economic resources has little power over his children and they know it. As a consequence, he tends to use physical power and, among the older children, this becomes a source of major disruption. The lower-class family structure is loosely organized and there are often few ties of intimacy and warmth to hold the family together. Hence it

[36] See James F. Short, Jr., R. Rivera, and R. A. Tennyson, "Perceived Opportunities, Gang Membership, and Delinquency," *Amer. Sociological Rev., 30* (1965), pp. 56–67. Also Wan S. Han, "Two Conflicting Themes: Common Values Versus Class Differential Values," *Amer. Sociological Rev., 34* (October 1969), pp. 679–689; Wan S. Han, "Discrepancy in Socio-Economic Level of Aspiration and Perception of Illegitimate Expediency," *Amer. J. of Sociology, 74* (November 1968), pp. 240–247.

tends to break up as soon as the children become old enough to get out of high school and move out on their own. Since they have little real normative identification with their family, these children are more influenced by the *peer* groups with which they associate.

The opportunity to demonstrate social competence in the socially valued activities of the society is the basis for self-esteem in our culture and in most cultures. Short *et al.* have contrasted the norms of Negro and white lower and middle-class teenagers. The findings of this study affirm the proposition mentioned above that lower-class teenagers tend to leave the family early. Many of these boys, white and black, join gangs and the gangs participate in a variety of illegitimate activities. As a consequence of these activities, the boys perceive more illegitimate than legitimate opportunity goals. The lower-class Negro boys who are not gang members perceive almost as many illegitimate as legitimate opportunities, whereas for lower-class white boys, who are not gang members, the perception of illegitimate opportunities, while relatively high compared to the middle class, is still quite lower than their perception of legitimate opportunities. For black middle-class boys, the ratio of perceived legitimate to illegitimate opportunities is more than two to one and for middle-class white boys the ratio is almost six to one. It is clear that Negro boys compared to white boys perceive fewer legitimate opportunities, that is, sources of means for adaptation. Most probably, this is due to the double handicap that the black has experienced, namely economic deprivation and institutional discrimination. Table 6–1 below summarizes the data of Short, Rivera, and Tennyson on opportunity perception of the groups just described.

TABLE 6–1

Total perceived opportunity score.

Negro gang members	2.1
White gang members	5.0
Negro lower class, nongang	7.1
White lower class, nongang	12.6
Negro middle class, nongang	13.6
White middle class, nongang	24.1

SOURCE: Summary of data from James F. Short, Jr., R. Rivera, and R. A. Tennyson, "Perceived Opportunities, Gang Membership, and Delinquency," *Amer. Sociological Rev.*, 30 (1965), p. 63.

The study just presented did not include females. There is no reason to think, however, that their opportunity perceptions would be significantly different, with the exception that perhaps black women may be more employable in today's affluent society than black men are. Two earlier propositions are also borne out by the data from the Short *et al.* study. The ties between adults and children are weaker in the lower classes than in the middle class, and as a result, the influence of the peer group will be stronger in the lower than in the middle class.

Of course, not all or even a majority of lower-class boys leave home, join gangs, and participate in patterns of delinquency; but a significantly greater percentage do than among the middle class and upper class. This suggests that the difficulties of adapting to economic hardship in an affluent society is a source of adaptive strain or pressure. Lack of economic opportunity and social security among the lower classes will explain the origin of the adaptive problem of the members of the lower classes, but it will not explain the *response* or responses made to this problem.[37] The great majority of lower-class youth are not engaged in serious delinquency and the difference in their relationships with their parents as compared to those who leave home and join gangs should be systematically studied.

One of the profound problems of socialization concerns the question: What causes the majority of people in the various social classes to feel that their achieved status in life is or is not about right for them, and that their share of life's goods is or is not a fair distribution? On the outcome of this dimension hinges the political stability of a society. This is not just a matter of the people becoming convinced by someone's rhetoric that there is an inherent justice in the status quo. If the people are to believe this for very long there must in fact be a substantial moral basis for the opportunity system and the system of distribution of rewards. In other words, the interaction process must validate the normative standards.

In the section on parental influences, we argued that childhood conscience was conditioned by early parental prohibition and parental identification resulting from parental reinforcement. However, as the child grows older and becomes a teen-ager and later an adult, such conditioning is not sufficient to maintain his conscience. The early prohibitions and reinforcements must be followed by later prohibitions and reinforcements that are correlated with his *new* status position as an adult, or else his conscience will fade significantly. This means that as one grows older and becomes involved in more and more complex matters, that is, as one moves from one status position to another in the social order, the norms

---

[37] For an interesting and partially successful effort to explain the response, see Richard A. Cloward and Lloyd E. Ohlin, *Delinquency and Opportunity* (New York: Free Press of Glencoe, 1960).

and rules of conduct become more abstract and the shades of meaning become more variable. And normative discrimination and differentiation becomes more complicated.

Additionally, we earlier argued that in regard to childhood normative conditioning, the child learns from the *consequences* resulting from his *actions*, that some things should and some should not be done. The baby learns, through parental reinforcement of his actions, what is "bad" behavior and what is "good" behavior. The more abstract norms that define right and wrong in the moral, economic, and political spheres are learned in essentially the same way, except that the order of events may be different. The young child will become *aware* of the norm as a *consequence of his behavior*, which is positively or negatively reinforced; the reinforcement allows for the discrimination and subsequent learning of the correct response. On the other hand, older children, and of course, adults may simply be *told* what the norm is, which may be sufficient to establish conformity. However, if this is not sufficient, then the others with whom he is interacting will apply sanctions to his misbehavior. To clarify the difference between these two modes of normative conditioning, we shall make the following distinction between *institutionalized social sanction* and *behavioral reinforcement*: We are using the concept of institutionalized *social sanctions* or *social reinforcers* to refer to the formal actions taken by a member or members of specialized organizations (courts, for example) following a deviation from a *social norm by* another member. The term *behavioral reinforcement* shall refer to reactions of others (1) to *behavioral deviations* that are noninstitutionalized and (2) to the behavior of children who are too young to comprehend norms verbally and who have to rely upon behavioral consequences for discriminating the presence of behavioral expectations. If a man robs a bank he is put in prison. The norm, in this case, prohibits robbery, and the sanction for this degree of violation, is imprisonment. Generally, a *norm* is an abstract and symbolic rule for an *expected pattern of behavior*. The pattern may be either a prescription or a prohibition, but herein it is recognized as a norm only if it is sanctioned. An act for which there is not a related sanction does not have a norm. The sanction may range all the way from judging someone as having poor taste in his choice of clothes or speech, on the one hand, to capital punishment for certain other kinds of offenses, on the other.

The sanctions may be symbolic or nonsymbolic; that is, they may be in the form of words of praise or condemnation, or they may be physical such as presenting or withholding food. It should be clear that since social norms are institutionalized means for defining social interaction, they would be empty symbols unless they were backed up by sanctions. Hence, sanctions and norms are re-

ciprocal elements that help define and make social behavior predictable. Norms evolve and change, and sanctions, which are part of
normative patterns, change accordingly. In this way, norms are reinforced continuously throughout the process of interaction and
during one's lifetime. In other words, at least in the long run, the
maintenance of moral commitment depends on subsequent sanctions. The internalization of norms must be the internalization of
sanctions, or there will be no normative commitment.[38]

Specific norms that define one's role vary with one's status
or place in the social structure; therefore, role aspirants can anticipate what will happen to them by observing what happens to others
who already occupy these roles. Also, since norms and moral commitment vary with one's social status, it follows that a change in
moral behavior is partially explainable by a change in status. The
relative constancy in adult moral commitment[39] can be explained in
part by the fact that one's adult status is relatively stable; thus the
social sanctions that reinforce his social environment are also relatively stable.

SOCIALIZATION AND ACHIEVEMENT ORIENTATION

One's perception of social opportunity, particularly higher educational and occupational opportunities, is conditioned by one's perception of the prevalence of those from one's own status background among those who have achieved higher status. Sewell's
study of "Community of Residence and College plans"[40] is a good
example. Residential communities, at least in the United States, are
reasonably homogenous with respect to social status levels. Sewell's
study showed that among farm boys of high intelligence and high
socioeconomic status 58 per cent planned to go to college. However, among sons of families in a large urban area who have equally
high status and intelligence, 83 per cent planned to go to college.
Moreover, of the farm boys with high intelligence and low status,
only 29 per cent planned to go to college. It is clear that one's status
background significantly affects one's status aspirations. It follows
from our earlier proposition on anticipatory socialization or aspiration that status background also affects one's normative commitment. In this study, the data on girls showed essentially the same
results. Some of the data in Sewell's study are so dramatic that it is
important to present them summarized in tabular form (see Tables
6–2 and 6–3).

[38] For a good discussion of the relationship of norms to learning and to sanctions, see John F.
Scott, *Internalization of Norms: A Sociological Theory of Moral Commitment* (Englewood
Cliffs, N.J.: Prentice–Hall, Inc., 1971), especially Chaps. 3–5.
[39] John F. Scott, *ibid.*, p. 190.
[40] William H. Sewell, "Community of Residence and College Plans," *Amer. Sociological Rev.*,
29 (February 1964).

TABLE 6–2

Percentage with college plans by place of residence, intelligence, and socioeconomic status (SES), for male and female high school seniors.

Place of residence	Low intelligence			Middle intelligence			High intelligence			Total[b]
	Low SES	Middle SES[a]	High SES[a]	Low SES	Middle SES[a]	High SES[b]	Low SES	Middle SES[a]	High SES[b]	
Males										
Farm	6.2 (195)	5.5 (127)	18.2 (55)	15.2 (125)	23.5 (119)	33.3 (69)	29.2 (89)	47.6 (84)	58.0 (69)	22.0 (932)
Village	5.9 (171)	20.3 (118)	24.0 (75)	18.6 (113)	30.1 (113)	54.2 (72)	34.3 (67)	49.0 (100)	73.4 (109)	31.8 (938)
Small urban	4.1 (170)	17.1 (117)	23.7 (97)	19.3 (135)	25.9 (135)	51.1 (139)	36.6 (82)	53.0 (115)	82.0 (245)	38.4 (1235)
Medium urban	7.4 (136)	14.6 (123)	38.1 (97)	18.5 (103)	36.3 (113)	58.8 (136)	38.4 (73)	57.5 (127)	81.0 (185)	41.7 (1093)
Large urban	6.1 (66)	27.7 (65)	36.8 (57)	30.4 (79)	40.6 (96)	65.1 (106)	34.0 (50)	62.5 (104)	83.1 (183)	50.7 (806)
Total rural	6.0 (366)	12.7 (245)	21.5 (130)	16.8 (238)	26.7 (232)	44.0 (141)	31.4 (156)	48.4 (184)	67.4 (178)	26.9 (1870)
Total urban	5.7 (372)	18.4 (305)	32.3 (251)	21.8 (317)	33.4 (344)	57.7 (381)	36.6 (205)	57.5 (346)	82.1 (613)	42.7 (3134)
Total	5.8 (738)	15.8 (550)	28.6 (381)	19.6 (555)	30.7 (576)	54.0 (522)	34.4 (361)	54.3 (530)	78.8 (791)	36.8 (5004)
Females										
Farm	5.1 (196)	17.4 (98)	23.4 (47)	12.5 (144)	22.1 (122)	29.3 (82)	21.1 (109)	37.2 (94)	61.4 (57)	21.1 (949)
Village	2.7 (187)	17.9 (106)	25.0 (60)	9.2 (109)	22.2 (99)	47.5 (101)	29.7 (64)	40.7 (91)	41.7 (115)	23.9 (932)
Small urban	2.7 (187)	9.9 (142)	39.0 (95)	7.1 (141)	24.8 (137)	48.1 (133)	17.6 (74)	38.0 (121)	72.0 (189)	29.5 (1219)
Medium urban	6.7 (179)	11.7 (120)	23.6 (89)	11.0 (127)	28.2 (131)	51.6 (128)	27.5 (69)	38.9 (139)	67.4 (245)	32.8 (1227)
Large urban	1.6 (123)	17.6 (108)	27.9 (68)	9.5 (95)	23.6 (106)	55.7 (140)	21.4 (56)	44.1 (111)	76.5 (183)	35.7 (990)
Total rural	3.9 (383)	17.7 (204)	24.3 (107)	11.1 (253)	22.2 (221)	39.3 (183)	24.3 (173)	38.9 (185)	48.3 (172)	22.5 (1881)
Total urban	3.9 (489)	12.7 (370)	30.6 (252)	9.1 (363)	25.7 (374)	51.9 (401)	22.1 (199)	40.2 (371)	71.5 (617)	32.4 (3436)
Total	3.9 (872)	14.5 (574)	28.8 (359)	9.9 (616)	24.4 (505)	48.0 (584)	23.1 (372)	39.8 (556)	66.4 (789)	28.9 (5317)

SOURCE: William H. Sewell, "Community of Residence and College Plans," *Amer. Sociological Rev.*, 29 (February 1964), pp. 24–38.
[a] Chi square significant beyond 0.05 level for males only.
[b] Chi square significant beyond 0.05 level for males and females.

An important implication of the Table 6–2 is the effect of reduced aspiration, as a function of lower social class background, on the development of the intellect. The sociological literature on social class and related differences in life styles, nutrition, and child-rearing practices describes differences in IQ that are related to differences in social class positions.[41] The Sewell data on educational aspiration would suggest that the life styles of youth in lower socioeconomic positions would lower their aspirations and hence their educational experience. This would negatively affect the development of intellectual potentiality, which, in turn, would affect the child's opportunity to demonstrate competence, which is the principal basis for self-esteem. Lowered self-esteem interferes with normative commitment to the action patterns associated with higher statuses.

One's anticipation of success in life is not only determined to a major extent by one's community of residence, but it is also significantly affected by the level of technological achievement and the general cultural themes of the larger society. A recent public opinion study comparing West German youth and Polish youth on "Preconditions for Success in Life" is illustrative (see Table 6–3).

If we assume the reliability of the sample statistics in Table 6–3, it is interesting to note the differences of emphasis that the Poles place on inherited characteristics (items 1 and 2) as compared to the Germans. This result is consistent with items 5 and 7. It seems that Poles emphasize the dependence of the individual on fate and on other uncontrollable conditions such as inherited characteristics and luck. The Germans emphasize individual control, education, and acquired characteristics. One might well expect a comparison of the modal attitudes of a relatively nonindustrialized society with those of a highly industrialized one to yield such results. In other words, the attitudes expressed are quite likely consistent with the modal personal experiences of the youth of the two countries.[42]

It is interesting to note that when the results of the opinion poll for the young Poles were compared with those for their older compatriots that the results were very similar. The same was true for older and younger Germans. In other words, the organizational and technological factors in the two societies that have conditioned opinion on "preconditions for success in life" have done so

---

[41] See James Coleman et al., Equality of Educational Opportunity (Washington, D.C.: U.S. Government Printing Office, 1966), Document No. FS5.238.38001; Steven R. Tulkin, "Race, Class, Family and School Achievement," J. of Personality and Social Psychology, 9, No. 1 (May 1968), pp. 31–38; also Sandra Scarr-Salapatek, "Race, Social Class, and I.Q.," Science, 174, No. 4016 (24 December 1971), pp. 1285–1295.

[42] For a detailed discussion of achievement motivation, see D. C. McClelland, J. W. Atkinson, R. A. Clark, and E. L. Lowell, The Achievement Motive (New York: Appleton, 1953).

TABLE 6–3

Preconditions for success in life.

	Young Polish (per cent)	Young West German (per cent)
1. Acquired characteristics, such as ambitions, diligence, and so on	46	73
2. Inherited characteristics and attributes	37	8
3. Fortunate circumstances, luck	25	16
4. The system blocks personal success	13	—
5. Education and professional know-how	10	32
6. Social skills	10	13
7. Moral qualities (honesty, kindness, and so on	9	27
8. Other answers	18	10
	168[a]	179[a]
Number of Cases	219	317

Source: Taken from a Radio Free Europe Pamphlet, Audience and Public Opinion Research Dept., "Preconditions for Success in Life in Poland and West Germany," (December 1971), Table 3, p. 8.
[a] More than 100% due to multiple answers.

with almost equal force for both the present generation of youth and their parents. It is quite likely that the differential rates of cultural and technological change in the two societies are highly correlated with their respective attitudes toward the prerequisites for success. Such a view is consistent with our concept of attitude as being *an evaluation* resulting from the consequences of behavior rather than a cause of behavior.

In the mid-1960's, Professor Robert Rosenthal, a social psychologist at Harvard, conducted an interesting experiment on animal performance as a function of the anticipations and expectations of their human trainers.[43] The rats were all from the same strain and exhibited the same levels of performance. However, the trainers were told, falsely, that some of the rats had been bred for high intelligence and the others were bred for dullness. The rats, all actually of equal intelligence, were randomly divided into the two falsely labeled groups, and the trainers were told to test them for performance. The "bright" group consistently showed high performance and the "dull" group consistently showed poor performance. It was Rosenthal's opinion that many minority-group children perform poorly because they are reinforced, as if they were poor performers, and that this conditions low self-esteem and low performance. He

[43] Robert Rosenthal and Lenore Jacobson, *Pygmalion in the Classroom* (New York: Holt, Rinehart and Winston, Inc., 1968).

One's aspirations and achievements are significantly affected by the level of one's experiences and rewards.
(Courtesy Wide World Photos.)

got a chance to test this out in a school in south San Francisco. This school had a sizable minority group of Mexican children, which was overrepresented in the "slow" track and underrepresented in the "fast track" school's three-track school system. In the spring of 1964, Rosenthal administered an IQ test to all pupils in the kindergarten and the first five grades. As in the animal experiment, he misinformed the teachers. In this case, they were falsely told that the test would show which pupils were due to "spurt ahead" academically. The teachers were given the names of 20 per cent of the student body, randomly selected from all grades and all three tracks, and were told that the pupils listed would improve dramatically within a year.

A year later, when all the children still in school were re-tested, the "spurters" showed an average IQ gain of 12.22 points, compared with 8.42 for a control group representing the rest of the student body. But the greatest gains came only in grades one and two—increases of 27.4 points in the first grade and 16.5 in the second grade for the "spurters." The control group rose only 12 points in the first grade and seven points in the second. Seventy-nine per cent of the "spurters" and 49 per cent of the control group showed absolute gains of 10 IQ points or more in the first two grades.

This study dramatically illustrates the principal thesis of this chapter that social reinforcers are major shapers of behavior and that one's self-image and hence his perception of his social competence is significantly determined by the evaluations of significant others, whether the behavior is moral or intellectual performance. While the "mind" is not totally a product of social forces, it is, as George H. Mead[44] so cogently argued, significantly determined by social forces.

The socialization processes involve not only the social and psychological making of individuals, but also the maintenance and remaking of society. It therefore encompasses such an extensive body of literature that the subject can only be selectively introduced in a single chapter such as this. The discerning student is already aware of this through his supplemental readings. But in conclusion we wish to point to certain significant areas that would have been dealt with had space permitted. The student is encouraged to read further in the areas that correspond to his or her interests. Some of these topics are (1) role change and behavior change; (2) effects of restricted rearing on stereotypic behavior; (3) the effects of nutrition deficiency on the brain and behavior development; (4) the effects of levels of cultural experience on cognitive growth; (5) authority and socialization; (6) language development and socialization; and (7) socialization and deviancy.

Summary

Socialization was conceived from the point of view of two interacting perspectives—first, the maintenance and continuity of society, and second, the development of social interaction competence of the individual. The social system was conceived as an adaptive system for the organization of diversity within the human population. The socialization process, when

[44] George H. Mead, *Mind, Self and Society* (Chicago: The University of Chicago Press, 1934).

operating efficiently, develops the potentialities of the individuals and allows for their placement into positions in the social system. This process was viewed first from the point of view of improved biological evolution through artificial selection and second through environmental improvement or euthenics. It was tentatively concluded that the increased genetic variability and hence adaptive capacity that results from randomized genetic assortment through a large number of subpopulations is preferable, given today's limited knowledge of human evolutionary processes, to systematic selection under conditions of inadequate knowledge.

Finally, the following additional topics relating specifically to individual development and adaptation were treated in some detail: (1) early experience and cognitive development; (2) early development of social behavior; (3) some family influences on social behavior; (4) socialization and guilt; (5) parental influences on the internalization of norms; and (6) socialization and achievement orientation.

Exercises

1. Compare and contrast the processes by which the offspring of social insects become socially mature and competent with those that effect the development of the offspring of human beings.
2. Assuming that a human offspring receives all the necessary physiological requirements for life and growth, but is deprived of all other social interaction, including speech, what types and levels of behavior development would be expected?
3. How does the socialization process help solve the problem of specialization in human society?
4. Explain the apparent paradox that the socialization processes contribute to the cultural continuity of a society and also contribute to social change in a society.
5. In what ways do differences in social class background affect behavior development of children?
6. Human reproduction provides a great range of diversity in native endowment: how does the human social system utilize and capitalize on this resource?
7. How does the "discrepancy principle" help explain the formation of new schemata?
8. According to Ausubel and Mowrer, the socialization process would be ineffective without the aid contributed by guilt feelings. How do guilt feelings stabilize socialization effects?
9. How does anticipatory socialization affect motivation and aspirations?
10. What are some effects that the anticipations or expectations of adults (particularly adults responsible for training children) have on the children's performances?

Selected Bibliography

Becker, Gary. *Economics of Discrimination*, 2nd ed. Chicago: University of Chicago Press, 1971.

Bernstein, Basil. "Sociolinguistic Approach to Socialization," in Frederick Williams, *Language and Poverty*. Chicago: Markham Press, 1970, Chap. 3.

Bronfenbrenner, Urie. *Two Worlds of Childhood: U.S. and U.S.S.R.* New York: Russell Sage Foundation, 1970.

Corothers, J., and Patrick Suppes (eds.). *Experiments in Second Language Learning*. New York: Academic Press Inc., 1967.

Flavell, J. H., et al. *The Development of Role-Taking and Communication Skills in Children*. New York: John Wiley & Sons, Inc., 1968.

Glass, David C. (ed.). *Environmental Influences*. New York: The Rockefeller University Press and Russell Sage Foundation, 1968.

Glass, David C. (ed.). *Genetics*. New York: The Rockefeller University Press and Russell Sage Foundation, 1968.

Gordon, Chad, and Kenneth J. Gergen. *The Self in Social Interaction*. New York: John Wiley & Sons, Inc., 1968.

Goslin, David A. "Standardized Ability Tests and Testing," *Science, 159*, 23 February 1938.

Hamblin, Robert L., et al. *The Humanization Processes: A Social, Behavioral Analysis of Children's Problems*. New York: Wiley–Interscience, 1971.

Heine, Patricke Johns. *Personality and Social Theory*. Chicago: Aldine Publishing Co., 1971.

Piaget, Jean. *Six Psychological Studies*, Anita Tenzer (transl.) and David Elkind (ed.). New York: Random House, 1969.

7

The Family as an Agency of Adaptation

In previous chapters the organization of human society has been examined in terms of the problems of survival and continuity. This chapter deals with one social institution, the family. Like other institutions, the family serves different purposes and takes many forms. Indeed the word "family" is often used when kinship, sexual union, clan, or some other term would be more exact. Like other parts of society, the family is changing in the modern industrial world; its functions and structure vary with the changes in society. Even so, certain fundamental purposes are still associated with the family. Society uses the family (1) to legitimize sexual behavior, especially sexual behavior leading to the birth of children, and (2) to define property rights and mutual obligations among the family members. Furthermore, society uses the family (3) as the primary means of socialization. In all three areas, the family operates to extend the society from generation to generation. The family provides much of the child's social as well as his biological inheritance.

Just as all societies must replace their members biologically, all societies must also replace their members socially; that is, a new generation must not only be born (biological replacement), it must survive with the aid of learned social mechanisms (social

In order to survive and function in a society, even the most technologically advanced society, a child must be fed, clothed, protected, educated, and socialized.
(Courtesy Robert Rapelye, Photography International.)

replacement) until it can bear children of its own if a society is to survive. Social survival depends on each generation's ability to use the resources available to it, and the skill in so doing must be acquired in large degree from an earlier generation. The process of acquiring that skill and the knowledge associated with it is called *socialization*. Socialization is a broad label that covers all the knowledge acquired by an individual; it covers formal learning as well as informal, factual material as well as beliefs and opinions.

Humans require a large amount of socialization, even where technology is not highly developed. Compared to many other animals, the human baby is a slow learner. In fact, chimpanzees learn some motor skills more rapidly than human infants when they are raised together.[1] As a proportion of the life span and in absolute years, the length of time necessary for the human infant to become able to care for itself is longer than for any other animal.[2] During this period the human child must not only be taught what

---

[1] Pioneering work in the study of primate learning is summarized in A. L. Kroeber, "Subhuman Culture Beginnings," *Quart. Rev. of Biol. III* (September 1928), pp. 328–330.
[2] A comparison among primates of different periods of dependency may be found in Weston La Barre, *The Human Animal* (Chicago: Phoenix Books, University of Chicago Press, 1954), p. 54.

he needs to know to survive, he must also be cared for by his society. He must be fed, clothed, protected, and educated. If a society fails to provide these necessary functions, it will cease to exist. Furthermore, if conditions change so that older skills no longer apply or are no longer sufficient, new patterns of socialization must emerge or the society ceases to exist. The enormous adaptability of human society is nowhere better illustrated than in the range of socialization mechanisms that have been devised under varying conditions.

In most societies, the family is the social unit that bears the major responsibility for socializing and caring for the child until he becomes an adult. The family serves other functions as well, but none of them is more important to the continuation and survival of the society. This responsibility to socialize and provide for the child is not restricted to the family, however, and the role of the family varies from place to place and over time.

There is no social or biological necessity for the important role assigned the family in human socialization. Although some

The ability of each generation to use the available resources, and the development of skills to do so, depend on the process of socialization. In most societies the family is charged with the major responsibility of socializing and caring for the child.
(Courtesy Robert Rapelye, Photography International.)

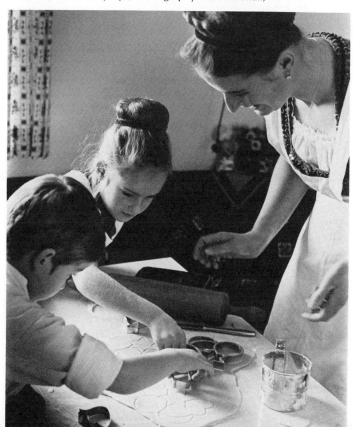

investigators argue for the "permanency of the family in our very biological nature," they are assuming that the procreational functions of a human pair-bond must imply some continuing pair-bond that in turn assumes responsibility for the infant.[3] That such a pattern is universal to some extent cannot be denied. That it is necessary is refuted by the use of social mechanisms such as orphanages to supplant the family when it fails. There is no reason to believe that a society where all children are raised in orphanage-like institutions could not exist. Even so, there are important reasons for assigning the child-rearing functions to the family.

When members of a society must devote large parts of their time to producing food, the opportunities for a specialized division of labor are few. Generally such societies will specialize primarily in terms of sex roles. Under such conditions, the husband–wife pairs are an effective economic unit as well as an appropriate sexual union. Since most of the population works at the same job and since each economic unit produces roughly the same surplus, caring for children bred in each household within that household is economically reasonable. At the same time, children have enormous economic value after their period of initial dependence. Even before their sixth birthday they can begin to help with the work of the household. In addition, parents look to their children for support during their own period of aged dependency, so that having many children is indeed a comfort in old age. Thus the economics of low levels of technology encourage the family.

Extended family ties seem to be a consequence of the technological base of the society, especially with respect to property rights. Any friend can be an ally; and when production is based mainly on hunting and gathering, sharing perishable goods equally among kith and kin is probably easily accomplished. Agricultural society and the idea of private property, however, pose the problem of who will share in surplus wealth and who will inherit goods at the death of the owner. Clear-cut rules of inheritance serve to reduce conflict over property, and kinship can serve as a means of defining such rules. Of course, kinship is only one way of defining the rules and many variations in how kinship is employed can be found. In some societies the eldest son inherits; in others all sons inherit; and in others all children. In some cases an individual can select his heir; in others he has no choice.

The role of the extended kinship system in the distribution of property and power is nowhere better illustrated than in the elaborate relations and rules employed by the European nobility. Though strong rulers often changed the rules, competing claims to power and property were couched in terms of kinship and the upwardly mobile hero of folk myth was a lost child of high birth.

---

[3] Compare, for example, Ernest R. Groves, *The Family and its Social Functions* (Philadelphia: J. B. Lippincott Company, 1940), pp. 1ff.

FORMS OF THE FAMILY

Marital forms and family forms are closely related. Marital forms are frequently classified as either **monogamous,** one male and one female, or **polygamous,** several males or females. Polygamy is further classified as *polygyny*, one male and several females, *polyandry*, one female and several males, or *group marriage*, several males and several females.[4] These different forms of marriage are not equally common. Even where polygamy is allowed, most of the population remains monogamous because of the additional expenses associated with polygamy. The mathematics of population work to restrict polygamy since either some imbalance in the sex ratio must exist in the society or polygamy and polyandry (unless practiced together) leave parts of the population unmarried. Though most families are monogamous, most societies allow some form of polygamy. Murdock examined records for 238 societies and found that 81 per cent of them allowed some type of polygyny, 1 per cent allowed polyandry, and 18 per cent were exclusively monogamous.[5] Each of these marital forms has many variations. For example, monogamous marriage may forbid or require remarriage at the death of a spouse. Marriages may be dissolved under different degrees of stringency, thus allowing for a sequential polygamy.

The important aspect of marital forms in relation to the family is that they lead to different family structures, which in turn determine different modes of socialization. These different modes are consistent with different forms of societal adaptation and levels of technology. Monogamy is associated with the **nuclear family,** a family that consists of a mother, a father, and their children. This simple family is a persistent grouping of the biological pair-bond (that is necessary for human reproduction) with its offspring. Because of the ubiquity of that pair-bond, it has been argued that the nuclear family is central to other types of families.[6] If this were true, polygamous families, for example, could be regarded as composed of a series of nuclear families with one person serving as a part of several nuclear families. The utility of such a view is questioned because the relation between parents and children in the regular nuclear family does not parallel that found in the separate pair-bonds of **polygamous families,** which consist of several males or several females and their children.

A third type of family is the **extended family,** which consists of either a nuclear family or a polygamous family extended to

---

[4] A thorough discussion of types of family and kinship organizations can be found in George P. Murdock, *Social Structure* (New York: The Macmillan Company, 1949). Murdock examined 192 societies and found that "47 have normally only the nuclear family, 53 have polygamous but not extended families, and 92 possess some form of the extended family" (p. 2).
[5] George P. Murdock, *ibid.*, p. 28.
[6] George P. Murdock, *ibid.*, pp. 1–22. Compare Ralph Linton, *The Study of Man* (New York: Appleton–Century–Crofts, Inc., 1936), pp. 154–155.

The persistence of the monogamous marital form is evident in this family portrait.
(Courtesy Russell Lee.)

include other relatives such as grandparents or aunts and uncles. Most societies recognize some form of the extended family for some purposes. The choice of residence by the newly married pair reflects the importance of the extended family. In modern America, the **neolocal** residence pattern is both typical and ideal. The couple establishes a new residence of its own. **Matrilocal** residence (with the family of the bride) and **patrilocal** residence (with the family of the groom) patterns are associated with greater extended family importance.

Thus far, the varieties of family have been examined, the importance of the family in maintaining the society has been discussed, and the need for some mechanism to care for and train the human infant has been stated. Though the family is universally responsible for some aspect of child bearing and the socialization of the child, the family need not be viewed as a singular or even an essential way to carry out these functions.

THE VARIETIES OF FAMILIES
AND TECHNOLOGICAL ADAPTATION

Both the structure of the family and the functions it performs for the child and for society vary with the technological base of the society. The variety of human social organization is so great that the relation between the type of family and technological organization is not simple—the same family structure is compatible with many technological structures. Some important features of the impact of technology on the family can be found with sufficient regularity to warrant examination, even if some exceptions render their interpretation probabilistic rather than absolute.

Whenever a society is sufficiently undifferentiated in its occupational structure to allow most men to exchange jobs with others without undue effort, the family can be the major teacher of occupational skills. For example, in the United States in 1850 most men were farmers and their sons could learn the occupation of farmer from them while their daughters learned from their mothers all they needed to know to be a farmer's wife. While a man could have learned farming from a farmer other than his father, few men did. Nonfarmers such as printers, blacksmiths, and tailors also learned their trade from their fathers in many cases, but often they served as apprentices to specialists who taught them the needed skills. For most people, however, the family was the source of occupational instruction; thus, in such a society, the family served adequately as the socializing mechanism for the occupational structure.

As the technological base of the society changed with the introduction of mechanized industry, the family had no occupational skill or knowledge to pass on to the new factory worker. Hence other socializers, such as the factory itself, became the major source of occupational knowledge. This development did not mean that traditional familial ties were removed by factory work. In fact, child labor was a major source of income in some families until that practice was made illegal. The factory system, by removing the important function of occupational training from the realm of the family, precipitated a change in the relation of the family to the child. Indeed, the factory system brought about a separation of the work and family roles of the father, and to a lesser extent of the mother, thereby changing many of the traditional relations among members of the family. Contact between sons and fathers was decreased, and the trend toward greater dependence on peer groups for friendship and socialization was begun. That trend was increased by other forces as well.

Continuing expansion of the technological base caused further changes in the role of the family. A growing demand for specialized education and a need for a literate population placed the child at a fairly early age in the hands of nonfamilial socializing agents. The school at first only added to the skills the family could offer. Soon it began to supersede the family in many areas. The morality of the school, the home economics of the classroom, the politics of the educated began to replace the traditional instruction of the family. Compulsory education was a major step in removing the child from socializing controls that had been long enjoyed by the family. Thus, in some instances, the new technological system *allowed* changes in the family's role in rearing its children, while in other circumstances, the system *required* certain changes. These changes were not necessary in an absolute sense, but they were necessary if the new technological system was to operate.

As more and more of the population came to depend on industrial jobs, residence with or near the family became less important. The industrial technology required large numbers of people at a single place as opposed to the farm's requirement of a few people in many places. The industrial system caused the family to move, and the moving in turn emphasized the *nuclear* family and *neolocal* residence to an increasing degree. Such new households cannot depend upon extended family ties to help in rearing children, so the intrusion of the school is viewed as an aid in child rearing. Furthermore, the school was welcomed because it offered social mobility and special advantage to the child in the industrial setting. The educated person has special advantages in industrial society because the increased complexity of the society can best be manipulated through the extensive knowledge that only education brings. The ability to read and to calculate mathematically is a great advantage in a society where most people are illiterate; and it is an overwhelming advantage in a society where all members must deal with industrial production. Thus technology requires that the family *move* and that it give up its children to *outside agencies for education*, thereby placing the family in a weakened position where the intrusion of the outside agency is welcomed. The family is rewarded by society for surrendering its children to the educational system because there the children receive social advantage, better jobs, and higher prestige.

The rather extensive changes in the role of the family as a socializing agent can be viewed as resulting from changes in the relation of the family to the system of production that was in turn induced by changes in the technological basis of that production. One word of caution should be employed. Although that interpretation is useful and helps to explain why the family has changed so much in the past hundred years, the extension of the argument to explain every change in the family as the result of the need to adapt to the new technology would be an error. Social adaptation is effective, though not necessarily efficient. The family changed enough to allow for the new technology. Some of those changes may not have been necessary or desirable. Many social conditions change in line with cultural preferences; some ideas, for many reasons, are resisted far more than others. Even so, strong evidence for the importance of the technological basis of these changes in the family is found in similar changes that have taken place in Japan, Africa, America, and Europe, when industrial production has become a predominant influence.[7]

THE LIFE CYCLE OF THE FAMILY

Because the family deals with developmental problems when it serves as a socializing agent for the child, distinctive stages in the socializing process can be identified. These stages, because they recur among families, define a life cycle from the formation of a family until the offspring of the family form a new family of their own. Typically this life cycle can be described in terms of a series of important events: marriage, birth of the first child, birth of the last child, marriage of the last child, and death of one of the marriage partners. These events are considered important because they represent significant changes in the adaptive and socializing functions of the family. Although these points have been listed in the order common in the United States, they often occur in another order in other societies. For example, in societies where high rates of mortality prevail, the marriage of the last child might typically follow the death of one of the parents.

   The new nuclear family is generally initiated by some form of socially defined ceremony or marriage. In some cases, this social recognition of the new family may take place after pregnancy or even after the birth of a child. In some societies, offspring are so important that proof that a union will not be barren is required before marriage is allowed. In addition to ceremonial and official approval of marriage, societies often extend social recognition to unions on informal bases, with or without the consent or even knowledge of the partners; for example, in the United States many localities recognize common law marriages.

   Although the life cycle of the nuclear family can be viewed as beginning with the marriage, such a view is an oversimplification. The life cycle is more properly seen as a cycle that repeats itself so that any point could be taken as the start. Moreover, the life cycle of the family is not simply a series of stages through which the family and its members pass. The life cycle represents

---

[7] The relation between technology and the family was examined closely in a pioneering effort by William F. Ogburn and Myer F. Nimkoff, *Technology and the Changing Family* (Boston: Houghton Mifflin Company, 1955). A contrasting view is presented by Gerald R. Leslie, *The Family in Social Context* (New York: Oxford University Press, 1967).

the changing adaptive functions of the family. The specific points of marriage, birth, and death identify the interstitial times when the family serves primarily sexual, reproductive, socializing, aging, and retirement functions. As will be seen, the lack of a common definition of the familial functions during the later stages of the cycle is associated with the rupturing of many nuclear families.

The period of courtship that leads to marriage takes many forms. Societies that regard marriage as a political and economic union of families often initiate marriages before the parties to the marriage have met or, in some cases, have even left their cribs. Generally, such societies focus on the procreational aspects of marriage but do not require sexual exclusivity by the married couple. Romantic love was something quite apart from marriage in the lore of ·Arthurian England, and the knight's lady fair might well be the wife of another as was the case with Lancelot's Guinevere. Only in comparatively recent times have romantic love and marriage been equated. Even so, the pursuit of romance often extends beyond the marriage. In spite of the myths of freedom of choice of mates, modern society imposes fairly strong constraints on who will marry whom. Though laws forbidding marriage among members of different races have been eliminated, the racial line is rarely crossed. Religious, educational, residential, and ethnic considerations reduce the choice of partners for most people, although exceptions are numerous and may be increasing. Research has indicated that early divorce is less common among those who have similar backgrounds, but the impetus to marry within socioeconomic groupings is probably more a result of propinquity and acquaintanceship than an assessment of the probability of divorce. Social groups such as country clubs, sororities, and church schools all serve to create a relatively endogamous system of mate selection.

The consequences of an endogamous mating system are only partly known. If genetic differences exist between the endogamous groupings, those differences will be perpetuated, but it is unlikely that such differences are very important in the endogamous groupings in the United States today. Even if they were, the rapid changes in the patterns of endogamy and the numerous exceptions to it nullify the long-range impact of the differences.

With the birth of the first child, the married couple is faced with the responsibilities of rearing children. The childless couple can act in many ways that are denied the couple with children. With the birth of the first child, the family begins its functions as a socializing agency for the child. From that time until the last child assumes adult responsibility, the parents will devote large amounts of their time and the resources of the family to the children.

When the last child has assumed adult status, the parents are freed of many obligations. Though they may continue their

The duties and obligations of an individual change as he moves through the life cycle of the family from child to parent to grandparent.
(Courtesy Annelise Rosenberg and Catherine Noren; from the forthcoming book *The Camera of My Family* by Catherine Noren. New York: Alfred A. Knopf.)

socializing functions as grandparents or as part of an extended family, their obligations morally and legally to their children have changed.

The death of one of the parents has little bearing on the function of the family if it occurs after the last child has become an adult. When such a death occurs earlier, the socializing functions may be impaired. Under such conditions, elaborate social mechanisms, such as required marriage by some member of the dead partner's family, adoption by some family member, or special homes, ensure care and socialization for the child.[8]

Because adaptive levels and mechanisms vary so much from place to place, the nature of the life cycle of the family also varies. Just as the family may have a greater or lesser role in the total socialization process under different conditions, the nature of the life cycle itself may also change. Thus in modern industrial society

---

[8] Children are more likely to be involved in divorce to an increasing degree. Between 1953 and 1966 the proportion of children under 18 affected by divorce rose from 6.4 to 9.5 per thousand; see Public Health Service, *Vital Statistics of the U.S., 1966* (Washington, D.C.: National Center for Health Statistics, 1969), Vol. 3, Table 2–1.

where other agencies account for much of the socialization process, the family can be subject to divorce or separation with less disruption of the socialization process. The life cycle of the family responds to changes in occupational career patterns, life expectation, fertility patterns, and technology.

During the past 70 years, several changes have taken place in the typical life cycle of the family in the United States. Though marriage is still the common experience for both men and women as shown by the relatively constant marriage rate, divorce is far more common than it once was. Thus more people will not complete the life cycle with their original mates. During the same period of time, the age at which marriage occurs for persons marrying for the first time has declined, with the decline being greater for males than for females. Thus, there has been a reduction in the average difference between the ages of the husband and wife. (See Table 7–1.) These changes are related to the relative ease of establishing a household in modern industrial society and a decreased need for the male to establish himself before marrying.

When taken in conjunction with increased life expectancy, the younger marriages imply that the time from marriage to its end is much longer than it was, if divorce or separation do not intrude. (Trends in divorce rates are shown in Table 7–2.) The reduction in the median age at marriage for men is especially important in this regard. Currently, life expectation for men is less at all ages than it is for women. The situation at the turn of the century was somewhat different. Medical technology at that time was not adequate to prevent many deaths during childbirth. This factor, coupled with larger sizes of completed families, greatly influenced the likelihood of the husband becoming a widower and reduced the average time a marriage would last. Thus, these factors, in conjunction with the fact that men usually established themselves before marriage and then married women who were considerably younger, tended to equalize the probability of widowhood for males and females. Medical developments and the tendency for males to marry younger females have increased the probability that a woman will live longer than her husband. More nearly balanced ages reduce that probability, but on the average, in a married couple, the wife is expected to outlive her husband by about seven years.

The extent to which changes in life expectancy and age at marriage have influenced the average duration of a marriage can be seen by comparing a typical couple married in 1900 at average ages of that period with couples married in 1970. In both periods, 98 per cent should survive to their 10th anniversary. Only 63 per cent of the couples of 1900 lived to their 25th anniversary, while 88 per cent of the 1970 couples should do so. Of the couples

TABLE 7–1

Per cent single by age and sex, 1890 to 1960, U.S. white population.

	Age 20–24		Age 30–34	
Year	*Males*	*Females*	*Males*	*Females*
1890	82.6	53.7	26.8	15.5
1900	79.7	53.5	28.4	17.1
1910	76.7	50.3	26.5	16.8
1920	72.6	47.5	24.4	15.4
1930	72.6	47.8	21.3	13.6
1940	73.4	48.7	20.8	15.0
1950	59.5	32.4	13.1	9.3
1960	52.6	27.4	11.3	6.0

SOURCE: U.S. Bureau of the Census Monograph by Irene and Conrad Taeuber, *People of the U.S. in the 20th Century* (Washington, D.C.: U.S. Government Printing Office, 1971), p. 284.

TABLE 7–2

Divorce rates in the United States, 1920–1966.

Year	Per 1000 in the population	Per 1000 married women
1920	1.6	8.0
1930	1.6	7.5
1940	2.0	8.8
1950	2.6	10.3
1960	2.2	9.2
1966	2.5	10.9

SOURCE: Public Health Service, *Vital Statistics of the U.S., 1966* (Washington, D.C.: National Center for Health Statistics, 1969), Vol. 3, Table 2–1.

married in 1900, 12 per cent reached their 50th anniversary, while 25 per cent of the couples of 1970 should celebrate their golden anniversary. This analysis shows how changes in life expectation influence the time available for the family life cycle, and is based upon the assumption that no divorce or separation takes place.

      Another important difference is in the age of mother at birth of her last child. Even for women who have the same number of children, the last child is born at an earlier age to the woman completing her childbearing in the decade of the 1970's. Since the average number of children born to each woman is smaller, final births typically occur by age 30 so that even with longer periods of familial dependency, the last child assumes adult status or leaves home for further education before his mother reaches age 50. Since she has many years of life expectation at that age, as does her husband, the family cycle has a much longer final stage than it did when women typically had their last child between the ages of 35 and 40. Society does not demand much from the family during this increasing part of the family life cycle, so the growing divorce rates at these ages should be expected.[9]

OTHER AGENCIES OF SOCIALIZATION

The modern nuclear family could not be expected to perform the functions of the extended family. The nuclear family needs industrial society just as industrial society requires the nuclear family. The nuclear family is well suited as an adaptation of the needs for biological reproduction, care, and socialization to industrial production. In Chapters 11 and 15, various aspects of socialization and the role of the educational system in human adaptation are examined. In this chapter, the consequences of changes in the function of the family for other agencies are the focus.

By allowing the educational system to instruct the child in many skills, the family loses control over a range of opinions, attitudes, and aspirations that would be reserved to it otherwise. Controversy over the school system is a necessary consequence of such changes. The schools, which have the child for large parts of its waking life, teach not only the skills necessary for life in an industrial society, but cultural values, religious views, and political attitudes. Moreover, a significant part of what the educational institution offers is apart from the instructional program. Though parents may control in some degree the formal program of the schools, the informal aspects of education are equally important. The school system has become increasingly organized by age groups. This organization limits contact between older and younger children to a startling degree. One study found, for example, that in a typical high school, over 90 per cent of the "best friends" of all children came from their own grades.[10] Such a structure limits the effectiveness of older children as socializers of the younger, as is the case within a family. It creates a strong "peer group" influence in

[9] The divorce rates among those with grown children have increased; however, at present nearly one third of divorces take place during the first four years of marriage, and only one fourth occur after 10 years of marriage; Public Health Service, *Vital Statistics of the U.S., 1966* (Washington, D.C.: National Center for Health Statistics, 1969), Vol. 3, Table 2–1.
[10] C. Wayne Gordon, *The Social System of the High School: A Study of the Sociology of Adolescence* (Glencoe, Ill.: The Free Press, 1955), p. 85.

the developmental years and leads to fads, conforming behavior, and isolation.[11] Thus the socialization of the educational system is related to the socialization of the peer group. Each is influenced by the other and both replace what might earlier have been effected by the family. Having reached school age, the child in industrial society turns outside the family for training and social support. He also receives companionship for recreation and social interaction outside his family. His friends are less likely to be the children of his parent's friends and may even be unknown to his family. In these circumstances, the expectations of the peer group become an important influence in molding the child's normative behavior patterns. The rules and distant sanctions of the family are less immediate and on occasion seem less painful than the disdainful reactions of his friends. Even as the family in industrial society needs the child less, so the child needs the family less.

The family serves to illustrate how the function of social institutions changes as the adaptive mechanisms of the society change. At the same time, changes in the adaptive mechanisms create demands that may have no parallels in earlier times. The industrial–technological development has made special demands of this type. Because the adaptive mechanism itself is subject to rapid rates of change, its demands on the society are also variable. Hence the society that successfully uses the technology must change the human skills in response to those changing demands. Jobs change, positions are redefined, and procedures elaborated at such a rate that, within a lifetime, training obtained as a youth becomes less useful. Obsolescence in personnel as well as in equipment characterizes such a society. Changes of such dimension, however, require not only newly learned techniques, but a new socialization in work habits, attitudes, and values. The socialization processes that were assigned to the family in earlier times and could be assumed to continue from youth throughout life can no longer be regarded as such. The technological adaptive mechanism requires that socialization continue throughout life; adult socialization becomes something to which most of society is subjected.

The extent to which the occupational structure will require more and more socialization has not been defined. Currently, the demand for retraining of engineers and health personnel is at a high peak. Other occupations may well follow in their path. As a rule, if jobs are highly specialized and the system technology is changing rapidly, skills may be expected to become out of date fairly rapidly. A society that seeks to reduce the rate of obsolescence

---

[11] The nature of the adolescent peer group has been subject to a great deal of study and some controversy. Riesman decried its influence in *The Lonely Crowd* (New Haven, Conn.: Yale University Press, 1961), but other investigators are more sanguine. See James S. Coleman, *The Adolescent Society* (Glencoe, Ill.: The Free Press, 1961) and Robert J. Havighurst, *Human Development and Education* (New York: Longmans Green and Company, Inc., 1953).

in occupational skills should emphasize generally applicable training in early years so that retraining will be limited to relatively few specifics. How the family life cycle will be affected by occupational obsolescence remains to be seen. Perhaps periods of retraining will become standard features of the family life cycle in the future.[12]

THE FAMILY AND SOCIALIZATION FOR OLD AGE

The reverence for old age that characterized many earlier societies has become a rare feature in modern industrial society.[13] Perhaps because the wisdom traditionally associated with long life is often out of date, youth may be contemptuous more of the attempt of age to apply outdated rules than of old age as such. Whatever the reason, the status of the old in industrial society is distinctive. The earlier agricultural economy assigned the old to work as long as they were physically able. After that, they typically lived with their family, doing what they could, cared for by their children and grandchildren. Industrial society finds the old of little value. Even before they are physically unable to work, compulsory retirement removes them from employment. After retirement, the family is unable to care for them in the same way. Housing units are smaller for the nuclear family; children are scattered in different parts of the country. Many retirees are capable of caring for themselves—they live productive lives and even begin new careers. Care for the aged who are unable to care for themselves is another function the family has transferred to other social agencies. The old folks' home has given way to retirement villages and special care centers. The aged are placed in an institution because their family is less suited to their care. That is not to say that the family has no responsibility for its aged members. Family ties define obligations to provide the institutionalized care, but the function of the family has changed.

The new status of old age requires socialization just as adult status did. The individual needs to prepare for and learn to live in retirement. The family often does little to provide this socialization. Modern society has not adequately defined the status of old

[12] Recently, for example, large numbers of aerospace workers in the United States have been retrained for positions in medical services and city planning under programs of the Department of Labor.

[13] Extreme reverence for age has been shown by the Chinese, as illustrated in the following: "Many generations of Chinese children were brought up on *The Twenty-Four Examples of Filial Piety.* Wu Mang, who let himself be eaten by mosquitos in order to divert them from his parents; Lao Laitze, who at the age of seventy put on his gaily colored child's clothes and played with toys to make his parents happy; Wang Hsiang, who during the summer fanned his father's bed and during the winter warmed it with his body, and twenty-one other equally filial characters were presented in this book as models for imitation." From Olga Lang, *Chinese Family and Society* (New Haven, Conn.: Yale University Press, 1946), pp. 24–25; quoted in Kingsley Davis, *Human Society* (New York: The Macmillan Company, 1948), p. 105.

The family of the present industrial society does little to socialize people for the status of old age. As a result the elderly feel little satisfaction in the role they must play.
(Courtesy Elsa Dorfman.)

age, nor has it established the appropriate role of the old person. Many old people feel they have lost any social usefulness and many of their children agree with them.[14] Modern industrial society has created the position of retiree, but has yet to socialize those who must take that role to the point that they feel satisfied in it. As life expectation at the older ages increases, and it will increase some—though not a great deal—the period of retirement will become more important. It remains to be seen if the adaptive system of industrial society can find useful positions for old people.

NEW FAMILY FORMS
AND SOCIAL EXPERIMENTATION

The decade of the 1960's saw the emergence of many new experimental forms of family formation and structure. Some of these forms were new only to the participants, having been observed historically in other instances. Others are without direct historical counterpart. While it is too early to say how these social experiments will influence the future and which, if any, of them will survive, several observations germane to the nature of the family can be made.

[14] The despair of old age, however, is more related to actual lack of activity than age *per se.* See Irving Rosow, *Social Integration of the Aged* (New York: The Free Press, 1967), pp. 102ff.

An enormous restructuring of sexual attitudes and behavior culminated during this period. Though sexual behavior outside marriage had been documented for some time, the moral evaluation of such behavior became positive, at least for part of the population, during this period. The factors contributing to these changes were many and probably included a higher level of education, a weakening of religious control over public morals, greater mobility in the population, the introduction of more effective contraceptives, greater knowledge of sexual behavior from earlier studies such as the Kinsey Report, and the examples set by well-known folk heroes such as movie stars and television personalities. Though the causes are obscure, the results have been both a number of experimental familial forms and considerable intellectual evaluation and justification for them. Three types of experiments can be identified: transitional efforts such as wife swapping and "swinging"; new family forms such as communes and corporate families; and the extension of the family to embrace deviant forms such as homosexual marriage. At this time, none of these has become typical for any significantly large part of the population. Evidence about them is impressionistic and the numbers involved are not known. Such experimental behavior, however, may lead to changes in the family and perhaps to new types of families in the future.

Summary

This chapter has discussed the family and the ways it serves the goals of human adaptation. The family was seen as a reproductive, economic, socializing unit with its function changing in response to technology, the life cycle, and social conventions.

Exercises

1. Consider technological and social forces acting on the family today in the United States and anticipate changes in the structure and function of the family in the future.
2. Examine divorce and marriage data from the *Statistical Abstract*. Can you find any support for the contention that marriage is becoming less popular?

3. List all your relatives by name and their relationship to you. Is your list as complete as others in your class? Is it as complete as one that might have been made 100 years ago? Why or why not?

4. Employing your own values, "design" an ideal family and marriage structure for an industrial nation.

5. What would be the consequence for the family if a society allowed no inheritance of property?

6. How might birth order influence the development of the child? In light of your argument, how might larger and smaller families differ?

7. What factors act to reduce and increase the influence the family exerts over the marital choices of its children? Can you cite historical cases?

8. In his book *On the Theory of Social Change* (Homewood, Illinois: The Dorsey Press, Inc.) Everett Hagen sees an important role for the family in economic development. Examine his argument. Are there other aspects of the family's influence on social change?

Selected Bibliography

Adams, Bert N. *Kinship in an Urban Setting.* Chicago: Markham Publishing Co., 1968.

Benson, Leonard. *The Family Bond.* New York: Random House, 1971.

Hughes, Helen MacGill (ed.). *Life in Families.* Boston: Allyn and Bacon, Inc., 1970.

Lewis, Oscar. *Five Families.* New York: Basic Books, 1959.

Wellmott, Peter, and Michael Young. *Family and Class in a London Suburb.* London: Routledge and Kegan Paul, 1960.

Examine the Census Monograph Series for the year 1960, and the vital statistics publications on marriage and divorce.

8

Stratification as an Organizational Device

It should be clear from the preceding two chapters that human societies have functioned by developing specialization of skills, efforts, and associations. Specialization, however, presents problems of a very practical kind; essentially, these problems involve creating social means by which a society *adapts to its specialized solutions*. In practice, then, any set of specialized differences must be organized—normally by *evaluation* of differences and by developing structures for implementing and institutionalizing (regularizing and justifying) evaluated distinctions (in short, stratification). Regardless of ideology and various standards of fairness or equity, this complex evaluation system is an apparently inescapable accompaniment—in some form—to social specialization.[1]

A BRIEF EXAMINATION OF FOUR DIFFERENT SYSTEMS OF STRATIFICATION

To appreciate the character and problems of socially evaluated differences, let us briefly examine the following four very different cases.

---

[1] See Bernard Barber, *Social Stratification* (New York: Harcourt, Brace and World, Inc., 1957), Chap. 1; Kingsley Davis, *Human Society* (New York: The Macmillan Company, 1949), Chap. 14.

Case 1. Caste in Indian Villages[2]

The traditional Hindu caste system was enormously complex and largely defies attempts at accurate description. Nevertheless, we may briefly examine the situation in two similar villages of Uttar Pradesh. In the absence of the Brahmin elite, the more prestigious set of families are the landowners (the Thakurs), who tend to have more formal education, larger families, and more farm animals. Then comes a trader caste—the Baniyas—who are fairly literate (because of business needs) and who have remained economically independent of the Thakurs. Somewhat lower in position are the Koiris, who are well-to-do vegetable producers and rather independent in attitude. On an approximately equal (or slightly lower) level are three groupings: The Ahirs, who are involved in cattle-herding and dairying; the Lokars, or blacksmith and carpenter category; and the Nonias, who own some land but primarily work as diggers of wells and channels. Finally, the Bhar-Chamar castes—numerically the largest—are the farm laborers, deep in poverty and illiteracy.

Traditionally, the dominant Thakurs controlled village life by owning the land and employing members of the "lower castes." Officially, caste restrictions have been removed, but the Thakur families still maintain a rather strategic position by levying taxes on villages, evicting tenants, overwhelming lower castes with lawsuits, lending money, and restricting formal educational opportunities. In recent years, the acquiescence of the lower castes has been replaced by resistance, challenge, and intergroup tensions. Social position is no longer clear or predictable, and the Thakurs fear the growing economic and political assertiveness of their former inferiors.

Case 2. Huxley's Utopia[3]

In the technologically advanced society projected by Aldous Huxley, science and rational (nonemotional) standards of efficiency promote a rigid and unyielding stratification system. This system has produced shudders and fears because of its "inhuman" features; but, more important to the sociologist, Huxley's "Brave New World" is impossible to sustain (as we shall explain in a later section). For the present, it is enough to describe the system as a *reductio ad absurdum,* an experiment in creating order out of diversity by means of strict genetic controls.

There is a seductive logic to such a system. Necessary specialization of skills depends on native abilities, appropriate motivations, and removal of extraneous values and sentiments. Consequently, each category of skill receives its proper quota of recruits

[2] K. K. Singh, *Patterns of Caste Tension* (Bombay: Asia Publishing House, 1967), Chaps. 2, 4–7; D. N. Majumdar, *Caste and Communication in an Indian Village* (Bombay: Asia Publishing House, 1958).
[3] Aldous Huxley, *Brave New World* (New York: Harper and Brothers, 1932).

through chemically controlled production of individually designed personalities. Instead of the normal processes of reproduction, followed by social training of the offspring, both "birth" and "training" are achieved by chemically controlled processes in test tubes.

The important tasks—scientific, professional, administrative—are assigned to properly produced Alphas and Betas. They constitute the natural elites. Only they can wear grey; only they are allowed the luxury of being childish in behavior (apart from their occupational responsibilities). And only Alphas and Betas may use the satisfying drug or narcotic called soma.

In descending order of chemically bred arrested development, there are the Gammas, the Deltas, and the Epsilons. The Gammas wear green and serve as semiskilled technicians—a bit superior to the Deltas, who may wear khaki and are limited to rather menial but not arduous tasks (such as operating or tending machines). Finally, the Epsilons—apparently without an assigned color of clothing—are the despised, uniformly ineffectual laborers, assigned to such necessary jobs as loaders and elevator operators.

In Huxley's chemically determined "caste system," each social category interacts with others only in productive tasks, not in informal relations or sexual contacts. Segregation is neither legislated nor imposed by force. Rather, it is infused before birth (or rather "decanting") by specific chemical processes designed especially for Alphas, Betas, Gammas, and Deltas. Thus, coordination by chemistry seems to require virtually no adaptive culture (for example, ideologies) or social organization (country clubs, Junior Leagues, labor unions, and so forth).

Case 3. A Meritocratic System[4]

Some years ago, a British sociologist, Michael Young, envisioned a strikingly possible stratification system in which social opportunities and levels of prestige were based solely on natural ability. In this setting, formal education was dependent on merit rather than income or family background. Consequently, an "upper class" of brainworkers (recruited from well-to-do and poor families) with similarly high ability and training was created to fill the most responsible positions in government, science, and the economic sphere. By contrast, those with limited talent were likewise restricted in education and thus were only able to fill manual jobs. Over time, the able elite were confirmed in their superior position, while those of the less able category, denied entrance to higher educational experience, were thereby certified as inferiors.

The lower status grouping resented their devalued or sub-

[4] Michael Young, *The Rise of the Meritocracy* (Baltimore, Md.: Penguin Books, Inc., 1961).

ordinate position because the finality of their location was clearly etched. In addition, continued mechanization greatly reduced the need for unskilled persons. Thus, those with limited ability and little education were slowly removed from the vital positions of the economic system. The eventual solution was to employ this growing labor pool in menial jobs—as service workers in restaurants, theaters, and so forth, and as domestic servants (maids, for example). Males in this category, however, were unable to find modern counterparts of the butler or footman tasks and, therefore, unemployment among unskilled males remained quite severe.

For some time, brainworkers and handworkers maintained a mutual segregation from one another that seemed to work. But ultimately the lower status category began to press for equality of opportunity, despite differences in ability. At the same time, the meritocracy was becoming virtually hereditary, since several generations of selection had greatly diluted the pool of natural ability in the lower categories. The confluence of merit and heredity, therefore, created a caste system that spawned dissatisfaction while, at the same time, it produced dissidents who, because of their deprivation, showed an inability to organize their grievances to bring about effective change in the distribution of opportunities.

Case 4. Urban Strata: Sophisticated Segregation

In the cities of industrialized societies (for example, the United States, Great Britain, Japan), the prominence of complex economic enterprises has resulted in major social distinctions that are symbolized in *occupational categories*.[5] Essentially, families with professional, managerial, and white collar occupations tend to have greater access to (and more success with) the traditionally valued experiences of their societies (higher education, health facilities, careers, community participation), as compared with those in unskilled and semiskilled occupations. For example, in 19th century Boston, sons of white collar fathers were almost twice as likely as men of blue collar families to enter and remain in white collar occupations. In addition, ethnic background conferred subtle social advantages—for example, Wasps with occupational backgrounds comparable to those of first generation immigrants (mainly the Irish), were more likely to rise occupationally than the first generation immigrants. To a lesser extent, the Wasps maintained this advantage over the more acculturated second generation of immigrants, as well.[6] Similarly,

[5] Stephen Thernstrom and Richard Sennett (eds.), *Nineteenth Century Cities* (New Haven, Conn.: Yale University Press, 1969); Margaret S. Archer and Salvador Giner (eds.), *Contemporary Europe: Class, Status and Power* (New York: St. Martin's Press, 1971).
[6] Stephen Thernstrom and Richard Sennett, *ibid.*, pp. 143–147; Peter M. Blau and Otis D. Duncan, *The American Occupational Structure* (New York: John Wiley & Sons, Inc., 1967), Chap. 6.

urban areas in most large nations have developed well-known patterns of residential specialization—determined by broad occupational differences, as well as by differences in income, nationality, race, and religion.[7]

Later in this chapter other important facets of urban stratification will be discussed. At this point, however, several distinctive features of urban social inequalities should be noted. First, urban inequalities tend to be relatively unplanned and unpoliced by central, powerful groups or structures (for example, the role of an entrenched ideological party). Second, many opportunities are "open" to overcome these inequities, legally and formally, with rather substantial amounts of enhanced achievement within and between generations. Third, and especially noteworthy and confusing, there are many bases for evaluating and acting upon social and cultural differences in urban areas. In addition to differences in occupation and income, there are differences in amount and source of education; location and type of housing; consumption and possession patterns; ethnic background; religious affiliation; speech and pronunciation patterns; political participation; involvement in nonpublic civic organizations; child-rearing practices.[8]

Typically, this variety permits two kinds of consequences. First, and the more obvious, the same individuals can be evaluated in quite different ways on each of several grounds. For example, one may be rated high in education, moderate in income, low in ethnic status. Consequently, urbanites tend to have somewhat "discrepant" or "inconsistent" sets of personal evaluations and thus of social opportunities. Except at the very top and bottom of social evaluation, then, one's social evaluation (position) may be very unprecise and subject to error or apparent injustice. But such a variety of criteria also permits selective "trade off" of one's "low" evaluations for another accessible position for which higher ratings are warranted. For example, disadvantaged or low-rated national or ethnic groups have often sought to capitalize on their personal strengths through professional sports (football, prizefighting, basketball, baseball) or professional crime—or less dramatically, through respectability in care of home or through religious excellence.[9]

[7] Sam B. Warner, Jr., The Private City: Philadelphia in Three Periods of its Growth (Philadelphia: University of Pennsylvania Press, 1968); Louis K. Loewenstein, The Location of Residences and Work Places in Urban Areas (New York: Scarecrow Press, 1965); Charles Tilly, Race and Residence in Wilmington, Delaware (New York: Teachers College, Columbia University, 1965); John Fine et al., "The Residential Segregation of Occupational Groups in Central Cities and Suburbs," Demography, 8 (February 1971), pp. 91–101.
[8] See, for example, W. Brandis and D. Henderson, Social Class, Language, and Communication (London: Routledge and Kegan Paul, 1970); George Fisk, Leisure Spending Behavior (Philadelphia: University of Pennsylvania Press, 1963), Chap. 4; Leonard I. Pearlin, Class Context and Family Relations (Boston: Little, Brown and Company, 1972); Bradley S. Greenberg and Brenda Dervin, Use of the Mass Media by the Urban Poor (New York: Praeger, 1970).
[9] Gerhard Lenski, "Status Crystallization: A Non-Vertical Dimension of Social Status," Amer. Sociological Rev., 19 (1954), pp. 405–413; Peter M. Blau and Otis D. Duncan, The American Occupational Structure (New York: John Wiley & Sons, 1967), Chap. 12.

Some Salient Aspects of Stratification Systems

Though these four cases of social stratification touch on only a small part of this widespread phenomenon, they provide important clues to the variety of human solutions in ordering diversity and specialization. First, these cases indicate that the organization and/or the creation of specialization are assumed by some strategic social category—large land holders, the Alphas and a corps of applied scientists, educational elites, and commercial–financial leaders. In short, stratification rests on some underlying advantage or special adaptive success.

Second, while strategic advantage (see the discussion of power later in this section) is basic to stratification systems, the way in which diversity is organized depends on some dominant set of criteria for ranking various roles and skills. In caste systems, ranking normally emphasizes control of land and insulation from the effects of other social categories. *Brave New World* and the meritocracy, on the other hand, evaluate persons and categories by level of intellectual achievement. The ranking system in urban stratification is much less clearly defined, though actual or anticipated material achievement seems to be a fundamental (if somewhat fuzzy) criterion. Perhaps the major issue in urban ranking (for participants, as

Symbols of distinctive skills or social abilities may be captured in special beaded garments and body ornaments, as well as in masks, housing, and trophies.
(Courtesy Mr. and Mrs. William Bascom.)

well as analysts) is to determine whether the most important arena of achievement is occupational success (or wealth) or participation in public decisions.

Third and closely related, stratification seems to be validated or legitimated for some time by some commonly held value system (ideology) or objective. Caste systems have been sustained by traditional religion, while urban ranking systems seem to reflect a long-term emphasis on productivity—an emphasis that is currently coming under serious question. Significantly, neither Huxley's utopia nor the meritocratic system contain a clear rationale for their ranking orders—an omission that perhaps explains the difficulties their architects have described.

Fourth, there is considerable evidence of friction, dissatisfaction, and conflict in these examples of stratification—regardless of ideology or source of control. With the exception of Huxley's "Brave New World," the practical difficulties of stratification seem to be triggered by *changes*—either in the larger society or by unanticipated effects of the stratification system itself. To a great extent, these difficulties do not appear to stem from rejection of the legitimating ideology, but rather from a perceived or actual inability to alter one's chances for higher ranking and rewards—in short, from blocked social mobility.

Finally, these cases indicate the changing significance of stratification as a social adaptive mechanism. Under certain conditions—primarily those of limited technology and social isolation—predominantly nonrational types of stratification may be adaptive. On the other hand, narrowly technical or rational criteria for organizing specialization may ultimately arouse serious social resistances that hinder effective adaptation for the larger community or society.

Tentatively, then, the practical problem of stratification is one of developing workable, flexible patterns of organization. In the preceding four examples, the patterns of organization were ultimately ineffective (maladaptive) because each society developed either rigidities or frustrating uncertainties. It seems likely that societies adapt to their specialized skills and responsibilities by developing (a) some rational criteria for allocation of rewards and (b) some nonrational means of controlling or mitigating the effects of rational distinctions. In the long run, societies cannot be scrupulously fair or outrageously unfair in distributing differential rewards—though either extreme may be feasible for short periods.[10] Consequently, complex societies operate with unavoidable tensions between standards, between social categories that benefit or suffer from in-

[10] Cf. Georg Simmel, *The Sociology of Georg Simmel* (New York: The Free Press, 1950), pp. 197–213; and Gerhard Lenski, *Power and Privilege* (New York: McGraw–Hill Book Company, 1966), Chap. 3.

consistent standards, and between proposals for maintenance and alteration of standards, opportunities, and costs.

Stratification, in practice, involves numerous *decisions* about priorities and *implementation* of social judgments. These rankings or priorities involve attempts at adapting to limited resources. Clearly, these require the ability to establish imposed connections between and among the behavior of specialized individuals and social categories—through positive supports **(coordination)** or limitation of rewards **(control).** Anticipating the discussion in Chapter 13, coordination and control are twin mechanisms of that pervasive phenomenon of social interaction: **power.** However, it is not useful to reduce stratification to the simple exercise of power, though this is a very tempting conclusion for those who prefer attractive slogans to understanding and careful analysis.

There is certainly an ineradicable component of power in any system of stratification—and in any social system (from peer group to nation–state)—though a significant portion of power in human interaction is converted into the more manageable form of **authority.** But the mechanisms of power in stratification systems are too complex and variable for a simple equation of power and stratification. Let us instead approach stratification in practice as a recurring series of problems of social adaptation. In each problem of stratification, we may then try to identify the form or forms in which power is expressed or is modified.

If we begin with the general notion of power as the extent to which a person or group effectively limits behavioral opportunities of others, then we must make the following two reasonable specifications about power. First, power varies in degree of successful application (whatever the reasons) and in given time periods. Absolute power—uncontested and incontestable—is probably a limiting case in human experience. Second, the phenomenon of power may be identified in several distinctive forms or transformations. Power that involves control of valued resources, facilities, wealth, and so on, is **economic power.** Another form concerns the ability to determine decisons about the use of resources in a social system —and this is **political power.** Still a third form can be found in the ability to transfer power from one base to another (for example, the use of an official position to obtain "inside information" about stock prices or needed land; or the use of wealth to avoid punishment for an illegal act). This may be called **privilege,** though "exploitation" has a somewhat similar meaning when the ideological element is removed. Finally, for our purposes, power may be converted into an accepted composite of judgments about the importance or worth of a given social category—this form is often called **prestige** or *relative status.*

BASIC SOCIETAL STRATIFICATION PROBLEMS

With these social mechanisms as essential tools, we may analyze stratification through a distinctive set of operational problems, both from the standpoint of the community or society and of individuals and subgroups. As Table 8–1 indicates, these problems are inter-related types of social difficulties; it is therefore necessary to approach stratification from both levels. For convenience, we shall first discuss each problem from the societal standpoint, and then we shall examine the impact of each problem on the experience of individuals and families in typical social situations.

TABLE 8–1

**Basic stratification problems
viewed from societal and individual levels.**

Problems from an individual or subgroup standpoint	Problems from a societal standpoint
1. Poverty; physical deprivation	1. Allocation of differential rewards
2. Inadequate participation in community decisions	2. Legitimation of standards of prestige
3. Inadequate development and recognition of personal ability	3. Motivation and use of each level of rewards and opportunities (styles of life)
4. Inadequate opportunities for the next generation	4. Replacement of vacancies in reward levels: vertical mobility
5. Unequal competition with other strata for resources and for channels of mobility	5. Provision of substitute rewards for immobility

Problem 1. Allocation of Differential Rewards and Opportunities

Given some minimal degree of specialization, how can we account for a particular system of social inequalities? Karl Marx concluded that control over the instruments of production conferred advantages to owners or entrepreneurs not only in income, but in possessions, prestige, political position, and legal status.[11] In short, in his analysis, Marx assigned a strategic role to complex economic skills (financing and administering production of marketable goods and services); thus, a lesser value and fewer opportunities were associated with those skills of lesser economic importance. According to

[11] Karl Marx and Friedrich Engels, *The German Ideology* (New York: International Publishers, 1939), pp. 7–18; T. B. Bottomore and M. Rubel (eds.), *Karl Marx: Selected Writings on Sociology and Social Philosophy* (London: Watts, 1956), Parts 3–5.

In order to achieve and maintain her status of beautiful-woman, society had to reinforce the means and ends of her achievement. Values must be commonly held in a society to exist.
(Courtesy Alfred Eisenstaedt, Life Magazine © 1972, Time Inc.)

Marx, economic skills therefore determine levels of social rewards (prestige).

Marx did not consider the question of *recruitment* to different levels of skill, however. Obviously, this is a matter of the amount and distribution of relevant abilities (genetic and learned) in a population—a subject involving continual controversy over fact and interpretation. Many years ago, Simmel contended that there is an *oversupply* of appropriate abilities for many of the responsible roles in society. Since there are relatively few of these responsible roles, many equally qualified persons are *arbitrarily* denied opportunities, thereby insulating the fortunate few from competition with apparent "equals." The result is a pragmatic hierarchy of strata that sustains social inequalities on the grounds of practicality rather than ideology or worth.[12] But Simmel does not explain why some among the equally qualified attain responsibilities while others are excluded.

[12] Georg Simmel, *The Sociology of Georg Simmel* (New York: The Free Press, 1950), pp. 300–303.

By contrast, Davis and Moore's famous "functional theory of stratification" asserts that there is normally a *shortage* of qualified persons for highly skilled roles and that such roles entail especially heavy demands on their personnel. Consequently, to assure proper motivation and dedication to difficult tasks, the small pool of qualified persons receives (or demands) distinctively higher levels of rewards and opportunities than are available to those persons with less valued and more easily supplied skills.[13] It is therefore assumed that social inequalities tend to be rationally developed and rationally revised with experience.

It would require the wisdom of Solomon and a massive set of facts to evaluate the relative fit of these theories with prevailing patterns of stratification in the United States and other complex societies. Who can ignore instances of ineptness and questionable motivations in various specialized fields and roles, for example, in government, business, education, entertainment, the military, and industry? And who can estimate the volume of unused or underrewarded abilities in each sphere of contemporary society? Perhaps the closest approximation to a reasonable judgment depends on a review of information concerning two questions: (1) To what extent are people of different abilities able *to use legitimate opportunities for access* to appropriate levels of responsibilities—for example, formal education? And (2) to what extent is the educational channel an effective means of developing abilities for proper levels of occupational responsibilities?

In answer to the first question, in the United States, and in western nations generally, there is clear evidence that entrance into and completion of higher educational programs are very weakly related to the intelligence of youngsters—assuming that IQ and similar tests are adequate measures of ability to learn.[14] The case of Wisconsin youth, carefully analyzed by Sewell and his associates, is especially revealing. For all males studied from 1957 to 1965, 47 per cent of those with high intelligence graduated from college, while 33 per cent of equally able girls completed college. However, only 20 per cent of the most able boys with lower class backgrounds completed college, while the same high level of ability in upper status families resulted in a 64 per cent graduation rate. In short, ability—bolstered by the extra advantages of family wealth and encouragement—was over three times more likely to receive the tan-

[13] Kingsley Davis and Wilbert E. Moore, "Some Principles of Stratification," *Amer. Sociological Rev.,* 10 (April 1945), pp. 242–249. See also Melvin M. Tumin (ed.), *Readings on Social Stratification* (Englewood Cliffs, N.J.: Prentice–Hall, Inc., 1970), Part 9.
[14] William H. Sewell and Vimel P. Shah, "Socioeconomic Status, Intelligence, and the Attainment of Higher Education," *Sociology of Education, 40* (Winter 1967), pp. 1–23; Patricia C. Sexton, *Education and Income* (New York: The Viking Press, 1961).

gible and untangible rewards of formal education in well-to-do, compared with poor, families.[15] (See also Table 8–2.)

TABLE 8–2

Estimated per cent of high school graduates who enter college in the United States, classified by high school grades (percentile rank in graduating class) and intelligence (Army General Classification Test—AGCT).

High school grades (percentile rank in graduating class) / AGCT score	1–20	21–40	41–60	61–80	81–100	Total entering college
155 and above	38%	45%	52%	59%	66%	66%
145–154	34	41	47	54	61	61
135–144	30	37	43	59	57	54
125–134	26	23	40	47	54	48
115–124	24	30	37	44	51	42
105–114	21	28	35	42	48	35
95–104	19	26	32	39	46	29
85–94	16	23	40	36	43	22
75–84	12	19	26	33	40	16

SOURCE: Dael Wolfle (ed.), *America's Resources of Specialized Talent* (New York: Harper & Brothers, 1954).
NOTE: Each percentage refers to a *single category* of high school students, that is, those combining a given grade and achievement scores. For example, the figure "38%" indicates that, in the lowest grade but highest score combination, only 38 per cent of such students actually entered college.

Before World War II, it might be argued, ability plus hard work could overcome limited formal education—this was the Horatio Alger theme exemplified so magnificently but unrepresentatively in the career of Andrew Carnegie. Yet studies of business and political leaders in early 20th century America clearly indicated that the amount of formal education tended to be crucial in developing opportunities and skills for key positions in economic and political spheres. Miller's analysis of 183 business leaders and 188 political leaders belies the Alger myth: 41 per cent of the business leaders and 55 per cent of the political leaders had either attended or completed college, while 37 per cent of the former and only 27 per cent

[15] William H. Sewell and Vimel P. Shah, *ibid.*; James N. Morgan et al., *Income and Welfare in the U. S.* (New York: McGraw–Hill Book Company, 1962), Chap. 2. The role of educational advising is described by Aaron Cicourel and John I. Kitsuse, *Educational Decision-Makers* (Indianapolis, Ind.: Bobbs–Merrill, 1963).

of the latter had ended their educations upon graduation from high school. Unfortunately, these studies do not—and could not—deal with the role of intelligence in these successful careers.[16]

Apparently, sheer ability is not an easy component to organize in societal allocation of responsibilities and rewards. Formal education seems to be a device for simplifying the selective process, but it does so with implicit or explicit biases that promote "unnecessary" (that is, not called for by objective differences in skills) inequalities.

Let us turn to the second question: How effective is educational experience in developing valued skills? Until very recently, such a question was considered almost sacrilegious or as having a self-evident answer. But it appears that our optimistic attitude about the practical effects of education is disturbingly untenable. Ivar Berg has treated this problem with skill and wit in his recent *Education and Jobs: The Great Training Robbery*. He discusses several studies by different business organizations (banks, the telephone company), which indicate that on the job experience (rather than formal education) is most closely connected with promotion into more responsible positions.[17]

Formal mass education gives certain information, but how effective is the educational experience in developing valuable skills?
(Courtesy Robert Rapelye, Photography International.)

[16] William Miller, "American Historians and the Business Elite," and "The Recruitment of the American Business Elite," in William Miller (ed.), *Men in Business: Essays on the Historical Role of the Entrepreneur*, Rev. Ed. (New York: Harper Torchbooks, 1962), pp. 309–337.
[17] Ivar Berg, *Education and Jobs: The Great Training Robbery* (New York: Praeger, 1970), pp. 16–18, 93.

Another approach to this question assumes that skill and responsibility are highly correlated with *level of earnings*. Thus, the problem is revised to account for differences in earnings between college graduates and high school graduates. Though education has a substantial relation to level of income, data on employed persons in California revealed that ability and motivation account for about 25 per cent of the income differences between the two educational levels.[18] The proper interpretation of these results remains a genuine problem for the sociologist. However, it is certainly unwise to conclude that social rewards are predominantly related to levels of performance or that equal opportunities to develop natural abilities are made available. Power, therefore, is a considerable part of the allocation process, in each of the four forms mentioned above.

Problem 2. Legitimation or Justification of Prestige

Short of intensive and extensive use of force, societies must find methods for solving the problem of achieving acceptance of the ways in which unequal social rewards are distributed. Earlier societies—and the simpler societies—typically develop fewer and clearer distinctions than are found in modern societies. Normally, inequalities in the former seem "reasonable" because of religious confirmation of "proper differences," or because of the demonstrated superiority of those with hunting, military, or persuasive skills. In highly specialized societies, the methods of sustaining consensus on reasonable (acceptable) inequalities must obviously be more complex—and perhaps more imperfect.

We have two kinds of evidence on this rather difficult and controversial issue. First and very basic, there is substantial agreement concerning the various levels of social reward (prestige) and the individuals and families that function at each such level—particularly for specific communities.[19] Second, using occupation as a convenient summary symbol of existing distinctions, there is very high and consistent agreement on the relative worth of over 90 occupational categories for at least 10 nations. The famous North–Hatt scale of occupational prestige (revised by Reiss and Duncan) reflects the collective judgments of many thousands of individuals, who express their learned evaluation of occupations.[20] We can assume that these judgments also draw upon their personal approbations of

---

[18] W. Lee Hansen and Burton A. Weisbrod, *Benefits, Costs, and Financing of Public Higher Education* (Chicago: Markham, 1969), pp. 18–19.

[19] Albert J. Reiss, Jr., *Occupations and Status* (New York: The Free Press, 1961); Robert W. Hodge, Paul M. Siegal, and Peter H. Rossi, "Occupational Prestige in the U.S., 1925–1963," *Amer. J. of Sociology, 70* (November 1963), pp. 286–302.

[20] Robert W. Hodge, Donald J. Treiman, and Peter H. Rossi, "A Comparative Study of Occupational Prestige," in Reinhard Bendix and Seymour M. Lipset (eds.), *Class, Status, and Power* (New York: The Free Press, 1966), pp. 309–321.

prestige distinctions between a dentist or minister and a mail carrier or a taxi driver. However, this kind of evidence does not allow us to conclude that the difference in actual rewards or social opportunities in these categories are acceptably related to their prestige rankings. In other words, the basic structure of social differences seems to be accepted, but the operation and the justice of that structure are matters for separate evaluation.

From a more personal or individual standpoint, justification or legitimation of a system of prestige levels concerns the judgment of one's opportunity to participate adequately in community (and wider) decisions. Simply stated, the issue is: Do those of higher prestige unduly dominate (or interfere with) important decisions that infringe on one's sense of self-worth—and on one's sense of belonging to the community? Clearly, one of the hazards of any structure of social inequality is the tendency to translate legitimate advantage into unwarranted exploitation and extension of privilege.

But the fundamentally reciprocal nature of social inequality seems to reduce the probability of either (1) untrammeled domination by favored social categories or (2) grieved and sulky attitudes of deprivation and oppression among abused social inferiors.[21] While there is considerable evidence of dissatisfaction with others and with "the system," it is very difficult to estimate the role of stratificational patterns in such objections and discontents. There is, of course, disquietude about racial discrimination, partisan political decisions, marital and sexual problems, alleged gaps and inequities between the generations, and numerous disputes about authority in work, education, and religion.

On the other hand, the response to participation in social class systems has been studied in several ways, with results that will not hearten the simpleminded or the opinionated. The first and most fundamental conclusion is that reaction to social inequities varies by nation and historical period.[22] The Dutch, for example, seem to be much less resistant to their elites than are the Italians and the Mexicans. In the United States, the historical record is heavily punctuated by uprisings, revolts, insurrections, movements, strikes against economic and social privilege (for example, Bacon's Rebellion, the Whiskey Rebellion, Shays' Rebellion). Farmer and labor parties were active expressions of a similar disaffection in the 19th and well into the 20th century. And yet the United States is generally thought to have a more "open" class system than those of western Europe.

However, indirect and less obvious responses to social

[21] Georg Simmel, *The Sociology of Georg Simmel* (New York: The Free Press, 1950), pp. 185–186. See also Peter M. Blau, *Exchange and Power in Social Life* (New York: John Wiley & Sons, Inc., 1964), Chaps. 5, 8.
[22] Arend Lijphart, *The Politics of Accommodation* (Berkeley, Calif.: University of California Press, 1968); Gabriel Almond and Sidney Verba, *The Civic Culture* (Princeton, N.J.: Princeton University Press, 1963), Chap. 13.

inequalities should not be ignored—though proper interpretation of these responses is in some doubt. One form of "dissatisfaction" is apathy or *acquiescence by default*, and is expressed by withdrawal or nonparticipation in political matters (registration, voting, exposure to political information, and the like). Such a condition has been more pronounced among low-income and lower occupational categories in the United States.[23] In the last few years, apathy or "dropping out" appears to be a special phenomenon of middle-class youth, who seem to be protesting *lack of meaning* rather than status inequities.[24]

A second form of dissatisfaction is expressed in feelings of powerlessness, distrust, and so on, and is symbolically identified as "alienation" by social scientists and laymen.[25] Again, these feelings are more prevalent among socially disadvantaged individuals and families, and are assumed to be the result of disheartening confrontation with direct or indirect restrictions from social superiors.

Still a third type of negative response can be discovered in selected varieties of deviant behavior, in which the proportion of participants of lower status is comparatively high.[26] For example, "blue-collar crimes" (theft, burglary, assault, and so on) and schizophrenic cases are both concentrated in low-income categories. It has been suggested that these types of behavior represent ways of rejecting the values and goals of those in socially advantaged positions. A classic example is Cloward and Ohlin's analysis of teenage gangs that seemed to adopt at least two different deviant means of reaction to social deprivation: a search for substitute status through "rumbles" or ritualistic feuding; and a direct attack on the allocation process by organized stealing. Parenthetically, a third form of reaction (about 1960) was drug usage, which seemed to represent a substitute for failure in other deviant skills.[27]

---

[23] Lester W. Milbrath, *Political Participation* (Chicago: Rand McNally & Co., 1965); Harold L. Wilensky, "Work, Careers, and Social Integration," *International Social Sci. J.*, 12 (1960), pp. 543–560; Scott Greer and Peter Orleans, "Mass Society and Parapolitical Structure," *Amer. Sociological Rev.*, 27 (October 1962), pp. 634–646.

[24] See the discussions in George A. Pettit, *Prisoners of Culture* (New York: Charles Scribner's Sons, 1970), Chaps. 7, 8; Bruce Cook, *The Beat Generation* (New York: Charles Scribner's Sons, 1971).

[25] Melvin A. Seeman, "On the Meaning of Alienation," *Amer. Sociological Rev.*, 24 (December 1959), pp. 783–791; Karl Marx, *Economic and Philosophical Manuscripts of 1844* (New York: International Publishers, 1964); Joachim Israel, *Alienation: From Marx to Modern Sociology* (Boston: Allyn and Bacon, Inc., 1971); Kenneth Keniston, *The Uncommitted: Alienated Youth in American Society* (New York: Harcourt, Brace & World, Inc., 1965); Joseph Nyomarkay, *Charisma and Factionalism in the Nazi Party* (Minneapolis, Minn.: University of Minnesota Press, 1967), pp. 114–150.

[26] Richard A. Cloward and Lloyd E. Ohlin, *Delinquency and Opportunity* (New York: The Free Press, 1960); John Lofland, *Deviance and Identity* (Englewood Cliffs, N.J.: Prentice–Hall, Inc., 1969); John P. Hewitt, *Social Stratification and Deviant Behavior* (New York: Random House, Inc., 1970); H. Warren Dunham, *Community and Schizophrenia* (Detroit, Mich.: Wayne State University Press, 1965); Paul M. Roman and Harrison M. Trice, *Schizophrenia and the Poor* (Ithaca, N.Y.: School of Industrial and Labor Relations, Cornell University, 1967).

[27] Richard A. Cloward and Lloyd E. Ohlin, *ibid.*, Chap. 7.

Finally, there is a small but growing fund of studies that suggests that *suicides* are specially affected by the operation of the stratification system in the United States. It is certainly unwarranted to view suicide as an extreme form of protest of social inequalities —but a sizable proportion of our suicides seem to be "skidders," or persons who have had damaging declines in occupational achievement. Furthermore, they are apparently unable to locate alternative routes for enhanced opportunities because those opportunities are largely limited to those in more favored or "upward moving" categories. Significantly, economic depressions do not encourage this variety of suicide; the suicidal thrust seems to be nurtured by apparent affluence in contrast to the subtle deprivations of a class system.[28]

Thus, in various implicit ways, the development of a system of ranked skills and rewards, plus a related scale of worth or prestige, presents continuing problems of understanding, adaptation, and concern with evidence of costly unworkability. But it is also important to note that despite these difficulties, social stratification persists—varying within narrow limits over generations. There are few instances in recorded history of dramatic, sudden, and sustained alterations in stratification systems,[29] though revolutions and less extreme forms of challenge punctuate the relatively short span of memorable human association. Objectively, then, stratification, with all its imperfections, works in complex society—or at least no adequate and persisting alternative has been found. But more positively, what enables stratification to function in view of its ever-present deficiences? The next few theoretical questions or problems provide important aspects of a satisfactory but correctable answer.

Problem 3. Sustaining Patterns of Social Distinctions— The Function of Distinctive Styles of Life

The prevailing set of inequalities or hierarchy of opportunities and rewards is also a set of cues to which people adapt in relatively distinctive ways. For most people at any given time, the full import of the pattern of inequalities is not recognized, nor is there an effective mechanism for perceiving the immediate implications of stratification. In general, humans are pragmatic and try to adjust their

[28] Warren Breed, "Occupational Mobility and Suicide Among White Males," *Amer. Sociological Rev., 28* (April 1963), pp. 179–188; Elton F. Jackson and Peter J. Burke, "Status and Symptoms of Stress: Addition and Interaction of Effects," *Amer. Sociological Rev., 30* (August 1965), pp. 556–564; Harold L. Wilensky and Hugh Edwards, "The Skidder: Ideological Adjustments of Downward Mobile Workers," *Amer. Sociological Rev., 24* (April 1959), pp. 215–231; Ezra Vogel, "Entrance Examinations and Emotional Disturbances in Japan's 'New Middle Class'," in Robert J. Smith and Richard K. Beardsley (eds.), *Japanese Culture* (Chicago: Aldine, 1962), pp. 140–152.
[29] This is the basic argument of Vilfredo Pareto, *Mind and Society* (New York: Harcourt, Brace and Company, Inc., 1934), Vol. 4, par. 2244–2254, 2487–2499, 2508–2512.

behavior to available resources—though failure and unwillingness to adjust are undeniable aspects of social experience. But, for the present discussion, the significant point is a tendency toward social and cultural separation of different prestige categories. The result is a fairly distinguishable variety of styles of life,[30] each of which involves a meaningful cluster of shared attitudes, focal interests, problems, expectations, and behavioral choices.

There is a long tradition in social science and in western literature that emphasizes the role of a style of life in understanding the behavior and motivations of specific persons and families. In social science, there are Le Play's studies of workers in France, Booth's monumental surveys of the poor in London, numerous studies in the 1920's and 1930's, of hoboes, lower-class delinquents, salesladies, and rooming house residents[31]; for recent years, mention should be made of Whyte's study of lower-class youth in Somerville, Mass., Mills's account of white-collar workers, Gans's analysis of Boston Italian families, and Oscar Lewis's much cited study of the "culture of poverty" in Mexico City.[32] Traditionally, the novel has been a rich source of description of life styles. We need only mention the major works of Dickens, Balzac, Sinclair Lewis, Faulkner, F. Scott Fitzgerald, John O'Hara, Thomas Mann, Proust, Orwell, and Steinbeck.[33]

The origins of particular life styles are difficult to trace, but it is now evident that given styles of life are learned from and reinforced by family interaction, neighbors, and work associates, and in recent generations, through the mass media. Thanks to many studies during the past 25 years, we have detailed information on several styles of life in a number of stratified societies. However, review and interpretation of this rich source of information is not feasible in this work. Perhaps a useful alternative is to select a few contrasting styles of life and to summarize the ways in which these are pursued by representative families.

A style of life organizes the experience and the behavior

[30] Hans H. Gerth and C. Wright Mills, *From Max Weber: Essays in Sociology* (New York: Oxford University Press, 1946), pp. 187–191.

[31] Charles Booth, *Life and Labour of the People of London* (London: Macmillan and Company, Ltd., 1892–1895), 6 vols.; Frederick Le Play, *Les Ouvriers Européens* (Paris: Imprimerie Imperiale, 1855); Harvey W. Zorbaugh, *The Gold Coast and the Slum* (Chicago: University of Chicago Press, 1929); Nels Anderson, *The Hobo* (Chicago: University of Chicago Press, 1923); Fredric M. Thrasher, *The Gang* (Chicago: University of Chicago Press, 1927).

[32] William F. Whyte, *Street Corner Society* (Chicago: University of Chicago Press, 1943; 2nd ed., 1955); Herbert J. Gans, *The Urban Villagers* (New York: The Free Press, 1962); Oscar Lewis, *La Vida* (New York: Random House, Inc., 1966); Oscar Lewis, *Five Families* (New York: Basic Books, 1959).

[33] Among the best examples by these writers are: Charles Dickens, *Bleak House, Hard Times*; Honoré de Balzac, *The Rise and Fall of Caesar Birotteau, The Middle Class*; Sinclair Lewis, *Main Street, Babbitt*; F. Scott Fitzgerald, *The Great Gatsby, This Side of Paradise, Tales of the Jazz Age*; Thomas Mann, *Buddenbrooks*; George Orwell, *The Road to Wigan Pier*; John Steinbeck, *Tortilla Flat, Cannery Row*.

of a social category; therefore, the means by which it accomplishes these effects are of obvious importance. Much research indicates that a life style operates in three ways[34]: (1) as a *connector* to available opportunities; (2) as a *filter* in the evaluation and use of opportunities; (3) as a *buffer* between insiders and outsiders in access to and use of opportunities.

More specifically, the ingredients of any style of life include such materials as complexity of speech patterns; amount, variety, and meaning of formal and informal associations; proportionate expenses for material items and services; emphasis on further social mobility; relative emphasis on the use of social mechanisms (such as violence, persuasion, diplomacy, and so forth); types of activities or resources that are veiled from outsiders; and a basic orientation toward change.

The "Stable Respectable Poor" Life Style in the United States

Undoubtedly, the key factor in this life style is limited formal education in a society that seriously views education as a major link to potential and actual opportunities. The result is an almost unalterable restriction to unskilled or semiskilled jobs, which are often dead ends and are marked by modest take-home pay. In general, adaptation to these limitations has taken two forms, for each which we have several kinds of evidence.

First, the stable poor life style is expressed in a meaningful cluster of attitudes or perceptions about the daily round of activities.[35] There is a notably low interest in higher education, in upward mobility or self-improvement, and in one's relative social position. Striving in the sense of greater effort or careful planning is considered unrealistic, though there is a lingering hope among some for owning a small business. More positively, the stable poor seem to compensate for externally imposed limitations by emphasizing certain kinds of personal interaction and, in many cases, by obtaining the psychological satisfactions of fundamentalist religions. On the other hand, there are some "inconsistent" attitudes that cannot be ignored. For example, working wives among the stable poor seek employment not only for the added income, but out of pride in extrafamilial achievement and for opportunities to associate with

---

[34] Alvin Boskoff, *The Mosaic of Sociological Theory* (New York: Thomas Y. Crowell, 1972), pp. 154–165.
[35] Lee Rainwater et al., *Workingman's Wife* (New York: MacFadden Books, 1962); Gerald Handel and Lee Rainwater, "Persistence and Change in Working Class Life Styles," *Sociology and Social Research,* 48 (April 1964), pp. 281–288; Lola M. Irelan (ed.), *Low-Income Life Styles* (Washington, D.C.: U. S. Department of Health, Education and Welfare, Welfare Administration, Division of Research, 1966), Publication No. 14; Mirra Komarovsky, *Blue Collar Marriage* (New York: Random House, Inc., 1964).

others. Also, at least among wives, there is a strong desire to live near people of superior opportunities, partly as an attempt at "reflected glory" and as a means of avoiding identification with the lowest or disreputable strata in the community.

The second major aspect of this life style is clearly reflected in *patterns of association*. Perhaps the dominant themes are *insulation* from the community and a *search for personal support and cohesion*. Insulation is achieved by nonparticipation in available voluntary groups, with the exception of religious affiliations and of those groups dealing with children's interests and activities; by relative disinterest in community issues, community information and resources, and voting; by a strong tendency to shop within a restricted radius despite better buys in more distant locations; by narrowing exposure to a few mass media (TV and radio primarily—with little regular use of books, magazines, and daily newspapers). To a degree that we can only estimate from interviews, these restrictions seem to mute the otherwise significant lack of social opportunities and perhaps to prevent the rise of painfully thwarted aspirations.[36]

On the other hand, as a counterweight to isolation, the stable poor possess several foci of cohesion. One is a rather firm dependence on one's parents and siblings, even though there is often a desire for "liberation" from early parental control and unhappy experiences in the parental household. Family visiting—rather than visits with neighbors and friends—is traditional and frequent. Yet there is also a tendency for the husband or wife to develop their own associational patterns. For one thing, the husband's working world is implicitly sealed off from the wife, who knows and cares little about that segment of dulled frustration. Husbands, however, enjoy participation in all-male cliques or crowds, which perhaps have the strongest hold on the older husbands, who have over time been able to balance the competing demands of home and congenial peers. The wives typically function with three sets of personal or emotional contacts: girl friends in one another's homes; young children; and fellow members of church-related activity groups.[37]

Most of these associations are "conservative" and inwardly oriented, with an emphasis on the familiar and the simple. Though it would be inaccurate to label these people as "resigned" or "adjusted," their acquired attitudes and values lead them away

---

[36] Bradley S. Greenberg and Brenda Dervin, *Use of the Mass Media by the Urban Poor* (New York: Praeger, 1970); Mirra Komarovsky, *ibid.*, pp. 34–36, 155; Arthur B. Shostak and William Gomberg (eds.),*Blue Collar World* (Englewood Cliffs, N.J.: Prentice–Hall, Inc., 1964).
[37] Mirra Komarovsky, *Blue Collar Marriage* (New York: Random House, Inc., 1964), pp. 24–26; Lee Rainwater et al., *Workingman's Wife* (New York: McFadden Books, 1962), p. 88; Elizabeth Bott, *Family and Network* (London: Tavistock, 1957).

from extremes in aspiration or frustration. They seem neither content nor alienated, neither passive nor violent.

The Striving Life Style of the
Newly Affluent or Those with Expectations of Affluence

A consuming interest in the behavior and values of upwardly mobile families is shared by laymen and social scientists, with numerous attempts to delimit and name this complex segment —for example, the new middle classes, "organization men," the new rich, the rising bureaucratic elite, and the newly successful strivers. The life style of this category is rather new and somewhat flexible; it also seems to involve several substyles that contribute some ambiguity to any discussion. However, in the United States at least, this life style is sufficiently developed to allow the tentative summary that follows.[38]

The major source of the strivers is the postwar economic expansion and its accompanying demand for professional and administrative skills. Consequently, the opportunity structure was quickly revised to activate college and university recruitment as a supplier of those skills and, not to be ignored, the government directly and indirectly subsidized the supply of jobs (through favorable taxation, for example) and the expansion of educational facilities (through the GI bill, research and training grants, and grants for campus buildings). Thus, the striver was and is essentially a product of an opportune shortage coupled with his preexisting ability to exploit the expanded educational channels of the 1950's and 1960's.

Analyzing the family origins of this rising category, we find that a substantial proportion were continuing to profit from advantages enjoyed by their parents (good schools, above average income, familiarity with middle-class cultural resources). But a significant proportion apparently overcame modest resources and acquired the necessary qualifications for occupational ascent. However, regardless of social origins, persons in this category are notable for their desire to exploit and generalize their opportunities or advantages to the fullest. Their dominant motivations and means for achievement are quite old—and to many now seem old-fashioned: these are continuous effort; accumulation of possessions; recognition and display.

This life style sets a pace that is almost incomprehensible to those with other life styles. Specifically, it demands[39]:

---

[38] Joseph A. Kahl, The American Class Structure (New York: Rinehart and Company, 1957), pp. 193–201; William H. Whyte, Jr., The Organization Man (New York: Simon and Schuster, Inc., 1956); Vance Packard, The Status Seekers (New York: David McKay Company, 1959).
[39] Joseph A. Kahl, ibid.

The newly affluent emphasize respectability and material rewards, as well as the opportunity to display them.
(Courtesy Robert Rapelye, Photography International.)

1. *Mobility*—The willingness to move rather frequently for occupational reasons, normally to suburban locations.

2. *Gracious home and possessions*—With home ownership as an early ideal and town apartments as an ultimate location.

3. *Consumer credit and budgetism*[40]—Strivers, particularly during the early married years, tend to plan significantly higher expenditures than current income would permit. Credit and revolving charge facilities are used extensively for travel, entertainment, clothing, home mortgages and renovations, and most recently for children's education.

4. *Voluntary associations*—Both for their intrinsic interest and for the social opportunities they provide, many civic and "cultural" organizations attract strivers to their membership. Studies continually show that those with relatively high income and education are most likely to belong and actively participate in voluntary groups in the community. While we can only guess that substantial numbers of these members are strivers, there are a few studies that specifically connect this life style with extensive voluntary group affiliations. For example, in an Atlanta suburb, a sample of strivers (called "attempted mobility" families) had somewhat more associations than other families. But more important, most of their voluntary

[40] William H. Whyte, Jr., "Budgetism: Opiate of the Middle Class," *Fortune, 53* (May 1956), pp. 133–137, 164–172.

groups were recent acquisitions; and though strivers had no perceived need or desire for such associations before moving to the suburbs, they seemed to exhibit (or intensify) their striving after moving.[41]

5. *Political behavior*—Since strivers emphasize effort, achievement, exploitation of opportunities, and the importance of education and knowledge, we would expect them to be especially interested in many facets of the political system. By inference from several studies of the past decade, those who might be fairly labeled young strivers are most active in voting turnout, membership in organized political groups, participation in local party activities, and (apart from wealthy businessmen) in financial support of political parties or candidates.[42]

6. *Exposure to mass media*—Strivers seem to have the most catholic interests in mass media, with the exception of television and radio, as evidenced by their interest in a broad spectrum of books, magazines, and newspapers. Information on politics and economic matters, cultural events, and so forth, is important for successful striving and perhaps, as a continuing means of identifying with other strivers (or, alternatively, distinguishing one's self from nonstrivers).[43]

The Established Elite Life Style

Sociologists have had understandable problems with this small and inaccessible stratum, with the result that our knowledge (as distinct from folklore) about the elite is largely drawn from novelists, newspaper reporters, magazine writers, and a few social biographers. Part of the difficulty stems from our inability to distinguish wealth from the character of its use. But there is perhaps enough information from varied sources to identify a distinctive cluster of rarefied features.

The hallmark of the elite style is socially inherited advantage—which precludes striving and assumes the ability to appropriate unbounded opportunities.[44] These advantages are necessarily

[41] Alvin Boskoff, "Social and Cultural Patterns in a Suburban Area: Their Significance for Urban Change in the South," *J. of Social Issues*, 22 (January 1966), pp. 86–89; Alvin Boskoff, *The Sociology of Urban Regions*, 2nd ed. (New York: Appleton–Century–Crofts, Inc., 1970), pp. 16–18, 181–182.

[42] Calvin J. Larson and Philo C. Wasburn (eds.), *Power, Participation, and Ideology* (New York: David McKay Company, 1969), Part 2.

[43] Bernard Berelson and Gary A. Steiner, *Human Behavior* (New York: Harcourt, Brace & World, Inc., 1964), pp. 529–535; Robert K. Merton, *Social Theory and Social Structure* (New York: The Free Press, 1957), pp. 406–413; Harold L. Wilensky, "Mass Society and Mass Culture: Interdependence or Independence?" *Amer. Sociological Rev.*, 29 (April 1964), pp. 173–197.

[44] The most revealing accounts include: E. Digby Baltzell, *Philadelphia Gentlemen* (New York: The Free Press, 1958); Stephen Birmingham, *The Right People* (Boston: Little, Brown and Company, 1968); Nathaniel Burt, *The Perennial Philadelphians* (Boston: Little, Brown and Company, 1963); Cleveland Amory, *The Proper Bostonians* (New York: E. P. Dutton and Company, Inc., 1947).

limited to a relatively small number of families in an area, since part of their value lies in their exclusiveness. In brief, superior advantage stems from continuous and respected family line and name, large sums of inherited wealth (property and income), unquestioned access to prestigious educational organizations, and assured entrée into a favored network of occupational, recreational, and social niches.

The elite life style assumes that its adherents unquestionably merit these advantages—not through effort or ability, but by birth. If opportunities do not *derive* from one's achievements, one's opportunities must be properly *translated* into responsible performance. The fundamental motivations are thus continuity of family position and responsibility for overseeing crucial forms of community activities. In addition, unlike the striver, one's advantages and contributions are "matter of fact" and not suitable for display, publicity, or external reward.

Specifically, the elite are expected to engage in productive administrative and "diplomatic" work—in governmental service, commerce, industry, the professions—to ensure continuity of wealth and to confer the fruits of their experience on important enterprises. An adult member of the elite may administer an industrial firm, a bank or investment house, a family foundation, a publishing firm, or an embassy—but not a junk yard or a tavern, however profitable. He is expected to be a generous and knowledgeable patron (financial, administrative, and advisory) of nonprofit (usually deficit) organizations, such as museums, symphony orchestras, opera companies, and universities. Another means of exhibiting social responsibility is through service in elective political posts (as mayor, governor), though this seems to be a suggested rather than a prescribed part of the elite value system.[45]

Styles of life require time to solidify, particularly if they are to be effectively transmitted to succeeding generations. The elite style is perhaps the oldest recognizable one in the United States and western Europe—about three generations in the United States, and five or six generations elsewhere. There is no mystery about the persistence of this life style; it is reinforced by social mechanisms that simultaneously offer it to the select few and effectively withhold it from "unworthy" imitators.[46] Unlike many other life styles, the elite variety possesses a sacred quality—that is, it is conceived to be unique, to reflect an ineffable power, and to require insulation from the grasp of inferiors.

---

[45] E. Digby Baltzell, *ibid.,* pp. 25–30.

[46] One of the earliest expressions of this theme is in Edmond Goblot, *La Barrière et le niveau* (Paris: Presses Universitaires de France, 1925), pp. 9–15. 105–108. A more recent and detailed discussion is in Lucy Kavaler, *The Private World of High Society* (New York: David McKay Company, 1960).

Established elite families do not raise questions about their privileges or their rewards, which are regarded by them as sacred rather than "earned."
(Courtesy Alfred Eisenstaedt, Life Magazine © 1972, Time Inc.)

The elite life style is upheld by social restrictions or subtle barriers. One form, noted many times in elite studies and novels, involves careful channeling of marriages among a small circle of "proper" families. This was especially visible in Boston, Philadelphia, Baltimore, and perhaps in Atlanta, Cincinnati, and New Orleans. In fact, when the marriage barrier is breached—as has happened among the Rockefellers—it receives wide coverage in the newspapers and magazines.[47]

All other barriers depend on implicit forms of segregation. Elite members tend to live in "exclusive" areas with locally meaningful and prestigious names. When residential "purity" de-

---

[47] This theme of marital selectivity is found in such well-known American novels as Christopher Morley, *Kitty Foyle* (Philadelphia: J. B. Lippincott Company, 1939), and J. P. Marquand, *The Late George Apley* (Boston: Little, Brown and Company, 1937).

clines through "invasion" of nonmembers, new residential locations become desirable. Likewise, a limited number of clubs, congregations, and resort areas are formed by—or come to cater to—the core families of the elite. The same stress on restricted access extends to the choice of colleges and professional schools, to retail services, and to some extent to preferential recruitment by prestigious firms.

The elite style of life requires, but does not guarantee, superior financial resources. Income is an assured tool, not a measure of worth or achievement. Consequently, the elite style seems irrational or even unjustly withheld—within apparent reach but seemingly beyond grasp (as the figures on Keats' Grecian urn). Yet the special significance of "higher" styles of life lies in the implied assumptions that decisive responsibility in complex systems is inherently exercised by a few in any generation and that the necessary qualities develop only with long nurturing in protected social environments.

Problem 4. Adequate Social Mobility: Allocation and Reallocation of Skills and Rewards under Changed Conditions

Mortality and alterations in resources and needs over time constantly challenge prevailing stratification systems, which are oriented to the past and to notions of blissful stability. From the standpoint of society as a whole, then, a major adaptive problem is the efficient replacement of persons who can no longer continue in positions of substantial responsibility (for example, as coordinators of several necessary roles). Clearly, this is a particularly demanding task because many individual "assignments" must be made with regard to a variety of skills and in various organizational settings. Errors and arbitrariness, then, are inevitable, though the *consequences* of misallocation can be evaluated in only very rough ways.

At the same time, the individual's stake in problems of social reallocation is likewise immense—in at least three respects. First, and least obvious to some, the smooth functioning of social mobility provides a basis for the necessary and desired goods and services that enable citizens to participate satisfactorily in complex society. Czarist Russia, the Weimar Republic of Germany, the Roman Empire in its decline, and the depression of the 1930's in the United States were classic instances of societies that developed great personal difficulties because of rigid or unresponsive stratification systems.[48] Second, change or reallocation of opportunities and

---

[48] See, for example, Hugh Seton-Watson, *The Decline of Imperial Russia, 1855–1914* (New York: Praeger, 1952); John R. P. McKenzie, *Weimar Germany* (London: Blandford Press, 1971); Theodore Abel, *Why Hitler Came to Power* (Englewood Cliffs, N.J.: Prentice–Hall, Inc., 1938); Michael Rostovsteff, *Social and Economic History of the Roman Empire* (Oxford: Clarendon Press, 1926); David A. Shannon (ed.), *The Great Depression* (Englewood Cliffs, N.J.: Prentice–Hall, Inc., 1960).

rewards is a desired consequence of personal achievement and increased skills or social qualifications. In other words, persons who have acquired more knowledge, more experience, more productivity (in their occupations or in the community) expect appropriate increases in prestige and in its material by-products (for example, more income, more leisure, and so on). This *intragenerational mobility* is a basic facet of what might be called the social biography of stratification.

Finally, persons and families are concerned with the processes and effects of *intergenerational mobility*—the changes in social rewards from parents to children to grandchildren. For those with relatively high positions, the practical problem is continuity through transmission of acquired advantages. But for families and individuals who endure perceived limitations or deprivations in opportunities (whatever the source), the prime motivation is often a search for social experiences that will adequately prepare offspring for entrance into and the efficient use of "channels" of mobility (education, marriage, selected job patterns, political contacts).

Turning again to the reallocation of rewards from the societal standpoint, the normal processes of social mobility are both intricate and subtle.[49] Our knowledge and understanding of social mobility are therefore partial and depend on our ability to reconstruct patterns from the short-term experience of categories of persons and from detailed "histories" of relatively small numbers of individuals. To assess or "measure" social mobility for some time period, it is essential to distinguish its major dimensions and the ways in which these dimensions interact in the social careers of families and individuals.

In very simplified terms, social mobility operates by "movement" of persons in four dimensions or facets of social experience. These are (1) changes in one's skills or effectiveness in occupational roles; (2) changes in one's participation in making key policy decisions in major organizational forms (a firm, a local government agency, an influential communication outlet, the federal government); (3) changes in values and perceptions concerning available or desirable social opportunities (that is, change in style of life); and (4) changes in access to and acceptance by more prestigious social categories.

Reallocation and re-recruitment require years and decades to develop and mature along the dimensions just noted. It is

---

[49] Among the most useful studies are Natalie Rogoff, *Recent Trends in Occupational Mobility* (New York: The Free Press, 1953); Seymour M. Lipset and Reinhard Bendix, *Social Mobility in Industrial Society* (Berkeley, Calif.: University of California Press, 1959); David Glass (ed.), *Social Mobility in Britain* (London: Routledge and Kegan Paul, 1954); Kaare Svalastoga, *Prestige, Class, and Mobility* (Copenhagen: Scandinavian Universities Books, 1959); Stephen Thernstrom, *Poverty and Progress: Social Mobility in a Nineteenth Century City* (Cambridge, Mass.: Harvard University Press, 1964).

generally assumed, with some justification, that changes in the first dimension (occupational skills) lead to succeeding changes in remaining dimensions. However, most of our knowledge of social mobility stems from students of *occupational mobility*. At this point, then, we must reserve judgment about the broader phenomenon.

Occupational Mobility

After almost 40 years of analysis, principally in western European nations and the United States, and most recently in selected Asian and Latin American countries, it is clear that the dominant trend, comparing sons with fathers, has been toward substantial *upward* occupational mobility.[50] Most studies indicate rather small improvements in occupational position for individuals, which suggests that the mechanisms of social mobility tend to operate gradually and conservatively. Furthermore, the most effective means or channel for occupational mobility is undoubtedly college and university education, plus the willingness to migrate from small towns to metropolitan areas. (See Table 8–3.) In many respects, the educational system serves as the crucial determinant of either limited or expanded career opportunities, though family status (particularly the educational level of parents) and family contacts likewise contribute to successful occupational movement.

TABLE 8–3

Per cent of males achieving intergenerational occupational mobility, by educational level (1962).

| | Educational attainment level | | | | | | | | |
| | Elementary (Years) | | | | High School | | College | | |
Amount and direction of mobility	None	1–4	5–7	8	1–3	4	1–3	4	5+
High, upward	2.1%	7.7%	10.0%	15.9%	18.4%	27.7%	31.1%	45.7%	53.1%
Moderate, upward	10.1	19.8	24.4	25.7	26.1	25.8	23.1	23.4	22.9
Stable	52.4	44.4	42.9	37.2	31.3	24.5	19.1	13.8	12.3
Moderate, downward	33.7	25.7	17.6	17.1	17.2	13.6	15.1	11.7	9.2
High, downward	1.7	2.3	5.0	4.2	6.9	8.4	11.6	5.4	2.5

SOURCE: Peter M. Blau and Otis D. Duncan, *The American Occupational Structure* (New York: John Wiley & Sons, Inc., 1967) p. 499.

[50] David Glass, *ibid.*; Natalie Rogoff, *ibid.*; W. Lloyd Warner and James C. Abegglen, *Occupational Mobility in American Business and Industry, 1928–1952* (Minneapolis, Minn.: University of Minnesota Press, 1955). See also Lawrence Stone, "Social Mobility in England, 1500–1700," *Past and Present* (April 1966), No. 33, pp. 16–55.

The significance of patterns of occupational ascent for the improved operation of social specialization and adequate coordination is far from clear. We cannot really determine if the mobile "replacements" in strategic positions are better, equal to, or inferior to their predecessors in ability.

On the other hand, the evidence of *continued* upward occupational mobility in various countries poses a very basic problem for students of contemporary society: what conditions promote this constant (though moderate) expansion of job opportunities? Undoubtedly, the most plausible explanation—apart from the "obvious one" of differences in birth rates—is the impact of technological invention and the resultant enlargement of skills and types of responsibilities, in both public and private organizations. Occupational mobility, by providing additional sources of trained (and retrained) persons, is therefore indispensable to the implementation of technical and informational advances.[51]

Nonoccupational Mobility

Occupational mobility rests on an expansive technology and economy; *social* mobility, in turn, depends on the ability to convert occupational success into greater opportunities for prestige and influence. However, because of the intrinsic exclusiveness of higher styles of life, and the strength of old associations, it requires some time to develop more prestigious affiliations and entrée into influential circles (public or private). Indeed, in some instances individuals appear to be content with improvements in occupation and/or income and fail to strive further for greater power, influence, or social responsibility.

But another aspect of mobility should be noted. A great many persons have managed to achieve greater occupational success than their educational level would normally permit. Others have had substantial increases in income without much change in skill or responsibility. Still others are earning *less* than expected, given their educational background, while some are in jobs that do not adequately use their formal education. These variations involve inconsistencies or discrepancies that, if perceived, tend to produce different kinds of concern about social mobility. For example, those with considerable achievements in jobs and/or income but with limited education have generally not sought greater prestige for themselves, though they tend to provide greater opportunities for their

[51] Kaare Svalastoga, *Social Differentiation* (New York: David McKay Company, 1965), pp. 126–136; Joseph A. Kahl, *The American Class Structure* (New York: Rinehart and Company, 1957), pp. 254–264; Dael Wolfle, *The Uses of Talent* (Princeton, N.J.: Princeton University Press, 1971).

children. The downwardly mobile—those with lower levels of income or jobs than their educational achievement would suggest—have been somewhat disturbed and have tended to insulate themselves from the channels of social mobility. Some seem to adopt simpler life styles, while others search for effective political protests or for "solutions" through drugs or suicide.[52]

The continuing process of reallocating opportunities and rewards involves very mixed results for the numerous participants in a system of stratification. If stratification sustains social inequalities, social mobility largely reproduces these inequalities—but it does so while holding out the possibility of *less* inequality. The phenomena of occupational and social mobility certainly involve, to a degree, recognition of and reward for ability, but a substantial amount of actual or potential ability is either undeveloped or unrewarded. What, then, are workable means for adaptation to the disappointments of social mobility for members of complex societies?

Problem 5. Provision of Alternatives for Social Immobility and for Limited Social Participation

The coordination provided by patterns of stratification and social mobility has its costs, which are perhaps unavoidable. The major cost is visible both in the short run and in long periods of societal operation. Essentially, this cost involves the internal threat of disaffection or alienation on the part of large numbers of the population who lose—or fail to develop—a clear stake in the future of their society or nation. Under normal or routine conditions, this lack of cohesiveness or devotion may be deplored, but it is not crucial. However in periods of crisis, such as war, deep depression, natural catastrophe, or conflict between subgroups substantial disaffection threatens the intricately designed pattern of technical and social specialization that nurtures a complex and dynamic society.[53]

Historically, the range of social mechanisms for dealing with blocked mobility is quite extensive. Perhaps the most direct form is the ancient one of "bread and circuses," in which societal leaders provide free entertainment and food to the most disadvantaged categories, presumably to blunt the edge of deprivation and effective protest. This was a device favored by some Roman emperors, and was also employed in Fascist Italy. Another mechanism, though perhaps not consciously designed by the leaders of society, is emigration of the urban poor or the landless rural persons to other

[52] Herman R. Brutsaert, "The Dynamics of Social Mobility: Analysis of the Relation Between Occupational Mobility and Selected Dimensions of Social Mobility," (Ph.D. thesis, Department of Sociology, Emory University, 1971) (unpublished).
[53] See Karl Mannheim, *Man and Society in an Age of Reconstruction* (New York: Harcourt, Brace and Company, Inc., 1940), Part 3.

nations—for example, the Irish in the mid-19th century and rural East Europeans in the late 19th century.[54]

However, there are more subtle mechanisms—which either are implemented by definite design or occur as largely unintended consequences—that soften the impact of vexatious social restrictions on immobilized families in urbanized societies. Beginning with Bismarck's Germany and up until the mid-1960's, the provision of government-sponsored services for the indigent and the marginal has been a significant component of modern stratification. Specifically, these services have at one time or another included free or low-cost medical care, disability insurance, unemployment compensation, low-cost housing, and supplementary education of various kinds.[55] It is generally agreed that these programs have not reduced inequalities to any marked extent—perhaps because such programs deal with symptoms rather than basic conditions of equality. Yet the recurrent creation of such programs—with new names and studied fanfare—cannot be fully attributed to ignorance of their limitations or to simple rascality. Perhaps beneath the political rhetoric, such programs are viewed as expedients and as social salves for immediate points of personal crisis and consternation.

Another social tool that merits consideration at this point (and also as one of the indispensable structures of modern society) is *consumer credit.* Certainly, loans for various purposes are available to a wide portion of the population. But during the last 20–25 years, a revolutionary part of the social economy of the United States (and to a somewhat lesser extent in England, Germany, and France) has been the quick availability of credit for clothing and expensive durable items among those with low (and foreseeably limited) incomes. (See Table 8–4.) The technology of mass production and the proliferation of credit and charge accounts make possible widespread sharing of articles and experiences once confined to a favored few (for example, television, automobiles, stereo phonographs, dozens of smaller electrical appliances, domestic and foreign travel, boats). In short, for many people some of the fruits of mobility can be enjoyed without striving for or achieving mobility. However, it is not clear that this imitation of mobility is fully satisfactory for the socially immobile. As we shall see in Chapters 12 and 16, these experiences have promoted a rise in expectations that cannot be placated solely by material means.

---

[54] A selected group of studies includes W. I. Thomas and Florian Znaniecki, *The Polish Peasant in Europe and America* (Boston: Richard Badger, 1918–1920; New York: Knopf, 1927); Arnold Schrier, *Ireland and the American Emigration 1850–1900* (Minneapolis, Minn.: University of Minnesota Press, 1958); G. F. Plant, *Oversea Settlement: Migration from the United Kingdom to the Dominions* (London: Oxford University Press, 1951).

[55] Harold L. Wilensky and Charles N. Lebeaux, *Industrial Society and Social Welfare*, Rev. ed. (New York: The Free Press, 1965), Part 2; Frances F. Piven and Richard A. Cloward, *Regulating the Poor: The Functions of Public Welfare* (New York: Pantheon Books, 1971).

TABLE 8–4

Amount of installment debt in the United States, by level of family income, 1968–1969.

	Installment debt							
	1969						1968	
Family income	*Have debt*	*$1–199*	*$200– 499*	*$500– 999*	*$1000– 1999*	*$2000 and over*	*Have debt*	*$2000 and over*
All families	51%	7%	8%	10%	13%	13%	51%	11%
Under $3000	22	72	6	3	...	1	17	...
$3000– 4999	37	10	9	7	6	5	40	4
$5000– 7499	60	10	12	13	15	10	56	11
$7500– 9999	65	6	8	14	19	18	62	14
$10,000–14,999	67	3	8	14	18	24	60	19
$15,000 and over	48	1	5	8	16	18	48	17

SOURCE: George Katona *et al., 1969 Survey of Consumer Finances* (Ann Arbor, Mich.: Survey Research Center, 1970), p. 22.

Finally, we should not ignore the importance of two prime alternative forms of mobility for members of occupationally blocked social categories (blacks, Puerto Ricans, and in earlier decades, Italians, Jews, Irish). Undoubtedly, professional sport has been a substitute stepping-stone for ethnic minorities in the United States (in baseball, boxing, football, and basketball). Perhaps blacks have profited most from this channel, given the immense success of such men as Jackie Robinson, Willie Mays, Bob Gibson, Wilt Chamberlain, Joe Louis, Jim Brown, Muhammad Ali (Cassius Clay), and many others with lesser reputation but with considerably higher incomes than they could command in the working world outside of sports. But as Daniel Bell has reminded us,[56] these sports previously provided opportunities for Jews (Benny Leonard, Max Baer, Sid Luckman, Hank Greenberg), Irishmen (Jim Corbett, Freddie Fitzsimmons), and for rural and small-town southerners before World War II. More recently, many who have profited from performing in professional sports have opened their own businesses (restaurants, bowling alleys, clothing stores), thereby establishing themselves as substantial entrepreneurs and public figures.

The world of entertainment, with its emphasis on individual talent (real or imagined) and personal flair, is perhaps the only

[56] Daniel Bell, *The End of Ideology* (New York: The Free Press, 1960), Chap. 7. See also Edwin B. Henderson, *The Black Athlete: Emergence and Arrival* (New York: Publishers Co., 1969); Wally Jones, *Black Champions Challenge American Sports* (New York: David McKay Company, 1972).

other legitimate alternative for the occupationally restricted individuals of modern society. Popular music, comedy, movies, night clubs, and television—as the major outlets—have provided numerous opportunities for minority groups (for example, Bill Robinson, Ethel Waters, Lena Horne, Duke Ellington, Count Basie, Cab Calloway, Pearl Bailey, Nat Cole, the Mills Brothers, Harry Belafonte, Bill Cosby, Flip Wilson, Jack Benny, George Jessel, Buddy Hackett, Danny Kaye, Kirk Douglas, Kim Novak, Danny Thomas, Smith & Dale, Gallagher and Shean, George Burns and Gracie Allen). Entertainers are generally viewed as "special" people by most of the rest of society, and they are generally permitted great latitude in behavior plus access to the most prestigious persons (the President, governors, foreign royalty) and often to important political leaders.

Stratification may be interpreted as a major social invention in response to problems of adaptation in minimally complex societies. Consequently, stratification has a sociological history and can be fruitfully studied not only in terms of its operation in a limited time span, but as an alterable, developing component of such societies. As Parsons aptly reminds us, in earlier, simpler stages of organization, a major form of coordination was the kinship system, which assigned rewards and privileges solely on the basis of membership in ranking and dependent families. This was clearly a "stratified" system, but one that *precluded* much specialization of skills.[57] However, with increasingly effective technology and expanded wealth, kinship as the sole basis of distinction became intolerable. Eventually, as in sixth century B.C. Greece and third century B.C. Rome, the monopoly of kinship was challenged and then partially overcome by independently achieved wealth and political power. Indeed, these new sources of power and prestige ultimately cracked (but did not demolish) the restrictive priority of kinship and liberated men for the quest of prestige and enhanced status through specialized achievements.

Thus, the differential evaluations or rankings of nonkinship forms of stratification were—in contrast to their predecessors—essentially a means of facilitating and organizing opportunities for categories that could contribute materially to the productive institutions (economic, political, administrative) of society. But in time the "rational" distinctions of relative worth and prestige were overlaid with attempts to sustain accumulated social advantages for succeeding generations—in other words, attempts to reassert kinship principles. Consequently, the fundamentally radical nature of stratification seems to be recurrently belied by misdirections in the general evolution of stratification systems. In another context, Karl Marx

[57] Talcott Parsons, "Evolutionary Universals in Society," *Amer. Sociological Rev.*, 29 (June 1964), pp. 341–345.

constructed a classic theory of social change and revolution on the "inevitable" tendency of class systems to rigidify or lag behind the expanded opportunities provided by technological development. In fact, Marx was so concerned with this inexorable lag that he argued for that most paradoxical of social innovations: a classless yet technically advanced society.[58]

RECENT CHANGES IN THE STRATIFICATION SYSTEM OF THE UNITED STATES

In recent decades—principally since 1940—there have been several changes in the stratification system of the United States, or in the attitudes of many about the validity of that system. Since most of our major institutional areas—scientific, economic, educational, political, governmental, religious, recreational, and familial—have likewise been marked by changes in resources, pressures, and opportunities,[59] our class system could not remain untouched. But as students of society, the question we must raise at many points is: To what extent are the alterations in stratification more or less adaptive than earlier forms?

Diversity of Ranking Criteria

Before World War I, the ranking of persons and the distribution of social opportunities were relatively simple and well understood. Occupational and income position were closely connected as the twin indicators of one's relative placement in the community. But the great depression, World War II, and the postwar economic boom obscured and complicated the indices of status by providing varied means of attaining or feigning social rewards. Formal education—particularly college and graduate education—became a social amulet or "open sesame" in a period of apparently limitless demand for skilled professionals and supervisory executive–administrative personnel. With increasing incomes and credit facilities, visible items were added to the status contest—notably housing style and location, clothing styles (the gray flannel suit), possession of expensive appliances, stylish and abundantly equipped automobiles (domestic and foreign). In addition, the role of participation in various "civic" associations and the more prestigious religious groups is becoming

---

[58] Karl Marx, *A Contribution to the Critique of Political Economy* (Chicago: Charles H. Kerr, 1904), pp. 11–12; Raymond Aron, *Main Currents in Sociological Thought* (New York: Basic Books, 1965), pp. 161–177.
[59] See Richard M. Abrams and Lawrence W. Levine (eds.), *The Shaping of Twentieth-Century America*, 2nd ed. (Boston: Little, Brown and Company, 1971); Bertram M. Gross (ed.), *A Great Society?* (New York: Basic Books, 1968), Chaps. 2, 6, 7, 11.

increasingly defined or interpreted as a supplement to the more obvious criteria of ranking (income and occupation).

This diversity serves to blur many of the previously sharp social distinctions; it is increasingly difficult for many to locate themselves confidently on the status scale or to compare their "worth" with their actual or imminent social opportunities. Perhaps the most definitely "placed" are the upper elite and the perpetually poor.

Status Discrepancies

Closely related to the preceding change is the possible inconsistency among criteria of relative status for specific individuals or families. It is unwise to infer inconsistency from a difference between two (or more) status criteria (for example, considerable formal education, but a low-paying job). But given the rapid changes in opportunities in recent decades, it is reasonable to conclude that many persons have faced problems of adjusting to the personal transitions of "movement" and differential degrees of achievement. Though the evidence is only suggestive at this point, it appears that many people are uncertain about their major social identification (for example, whether it is with occupation, race, nationality, local community, or political party, or something else). Some years ago, for example, this was noted in studies of voting, where the potential voters who faced such discrepancies (then called "cross-pressures") tended to be indecisive about political choices.[60] More recently, status discrepancies have been found in minority groups (for example, blacks, Puerto Ricans), with a consequent development of organized protest toward removing discrepancies (for example, in employment and residential location).[61]

Social Abdication

Systems of social stratification are largely informal and somewhat flexible, since coordination does not require rigidity and conscious coercion. However, the key to stratification lies in the dedication and confidence of strategic strata (that is, of those in the highest and above average social categories).[62] In recent years, those strata have

[60] Werner Landecker, "Class Crystallization and Class Consciousness," *Amer. Sociological Rev., 28* (April 1963), pp. 219–229; Paul F. Lazarsfeld et al., *The Peoples Choice* (New York: Columbia University Press, 1948).
[61] See, for example, Lewis Killian and Charles M. Grigg, *Racial Crisis in America: Leadership in Conflict* (Englewood Cliffs, N.J.: Prentice–Hall, Inc., 1964); Kenneth B. Clark, *Dark Ghetto: Dilemmas of Social Power* (New York: Harper Torchbook, 1965); Robert H. Connery (ed.), *Urban Riots: Violence and Social Change* (New York: Vintage Books, 1969).
[62] Crane Brinton, *The Anatomy of Revolution* (New York: W. W. Norton and Company, Inc., 1938); Lyford P. Edwards, *The Natural History of Revolutions* (Chicago: University of Chicago Press, 1927); Gilbert Murray, *Five Stages of Greek Religion* (Garden City, N.Y.: Doubleday & Company, Inc., 1955; orig. ed., 1925), Chap. 4.

been on a tricky social tightrope, trying to maintain their relative position and yet extend greater opportunities to less prestigious social categories. These incompatible goals cannot be accommodated in practice; consequently, some change in the system of stratification is beginning to emerge. One indication is a *relative* opening of channels of mobility—formal education, political office, public appointive positions. Another omen of change—whether temporary or permanent remains to be seen—is a widespread rejection of status advantages by youth and young adults from socially and economically comfortable families. This is expressed in dropping out of college, the search for nonrestrictive (and often poorly paid) employment, the immersion in socially isolated communal subcommunities, the extended dependence on hard drugs, and a refusal to work through established political channels for desired policy changes.[63]

Since a stratification system is not merely a pattern of unequal opportunities and rewards, but also one of different degrees of responsibility and accountability, these recent tendencies suggest a decline in the influence of presumably powerful categories or an abdication by members of these strata of the type of influence and power provided by these categories and an invitation to the lesser skilled or the underprivileged to fill the social vacuum. From a societal standpoint, stratification may be interpreted as constantly subject to improvements. But the crucial question concerning a change in stratification is the extent to which a changed source of recruitment to responsible positions is followed by better operation of diversified skills—an issue of larger scope than the narrower and more obvious considerations (both material and symbolic) of enhancement of rewards for deprived categories.

Changed Expectations

Comparison of different and changing expectations (produced by differences in stratification systems as they are influenced by technological and political changes) is extremely difficult, but the modern era (both in long established nations and the newly developing ones) seems to reflect not only greater resistance to the restrictive aspects of stratification, but also greater demands on, or higher expectations from, the more dynamic stratification systems. Compared with 100 years ago, contemporary societies offer infinitely greater opportunities for social, economic, and political participation to a wider range of citizens—through unions, education, credit, more

[63] Sherri Cavan, *The Hippies of the Haight* (St. Louis, Mo.: New Critics Press, 1972); Jack D. Dougles, *Youth in Turmoil* (Chevy Chase, Md.: National Institute of Mental Health, Center for Studies of Crime and Delinquency, 1970); William Hedgepeth, *The Alternative: Communal Life in New America* (New York: The Macmillan Company, 1970).

liberalized selection of elected officials, and expanded employment. But the relatively softened system of social allocation has also expanded the feasible range of potential achievement for many. In increasing volume, those who have tasted unanticipated satisfaction from new political strength, greater income, more travel, and better jobs want more of the same—not as a special dispensation, but as a normal right. This phenomenon of "rising expectations," nurtured by technology and economic prosperity in industrial nations and by independence and nationalism in the "new nations," seems to be an ineradicable challenge to stratification, and one important source of present and future alterations in that system.[64]

The rising expectations among females are one of many current threats to established patterns of social inequality.
(Courtesy Robert Rapelye, Photography International.)

[64] W. G. Runciman, *Relative Deprivation and Social Justice* (London: Routledge and Kegan Paul, 1966); Ted R. Gurr, *Why Men Rebel* (Princeton, N.J.: Princeton University Press, 1970); Jean-Francois Revel, *Without Marx or Jesus: The New American Revolution has Begun* (Garden City, N.Y.: Doubleday & Company, Inc., 1971).

The processes of social stratification—patterned rankings of specialized skills and resources—can be identified in virtually every aspect of complex societies (in any historical period). In such societies, however, it is difficult to understand stratification on the societal level alone. In fact, many of the discussions and studies of stratification contained in this chapter have directly or indirectly dealt with stratification in *specific communities*. In many respects, the community is a crucial focus for sociological analysis (if we continually search for the interconnections between communities and the larger society) because the essential structure and development of communities reflect specific processes of adaptation to definite land areas. In these processes, specialization of land use and allocation of resources and rewards (that is, stratification) are particularly clear. The next chapter, therefore, reviews the current state of knowledge of modern (mainly urban) communities as specialized subunits of societies.

Summary

Stratification is interpreted as a necessary but somewhat imperfect mechanism for ordering the specialized skills and responsibilities that mark a complex society. This coordination is achieved by ranking skills (either by force or by evolved consensus) according to their importance—that is, by controlling the amount and types of rewards to various skill groupings. As a major adaptive device, stratification systems have great importance from the standpoint of societies and nations, and from the viewpoint of individuals and families. To explore this dual significance, we have focused on a set of practical problems in stratification—how differential rewards are determined; how this allocation is justified or legitimated; how these patterns are maintained; how changes in these patterns occur; and how adjustments are made for those who benefit least.

An inescapable conclusion of these analyses is that contemporary stratification systems have become subject to unprecedented pressures. In particular, current stratification has developed subtle complexities of evaluation and personal location, which in part interfere with the coordination such systems are presumed to promote. Likewise, there seems to be a weakening of indispensable commitment to current stratification. Two sources for this problem are a disaffected favored category, who find their advantages meaningless or unworkable; and a recently ascending lower category, whose insistent "rising expectations" are at odds with the grudging adaptiveness of allocation mechanisms.

Exercises

1. Why is ranking of roles and categories a practical problem in human societies up to this point?

2. Under what conditions might social power be drastically reduced in highly specialized societies?

3. What problems of social adaptation in the modern world cannot be minimally solved by a system of equal social rewards and opportunities?

4. How does the evidence on unequal use of ability enable you to evaluate the explanations of social stratification by Davis and Moore and by Simmel?

5. In what specific ways is *ideology* important in the operation of stratification in the United States?

6. How can we account for the varied responses to social inequalities in our society?

7. How can we understand the operation of social power by analyzing the *style of life* of any social stratum or class?

8. Poverty has been a serious problem in most societies and historical periods. How would you account for poverty in preindustrial societies? What other factors are necessary to explain poverty in technologically advanced societies?

Selected Bibliography

Baltzell, E. Digby. *Philadelphia Gentlemen.* New York: The Free Press, 1958.

Bendix, Reinhard, and Seymour M. Lipset (eds.). *Class, Status, and Power.* 2nd ed. New York: The Free Press, 1966.

Blau, Peter M., and Otis D. Duncan. *The American Occupational Structure.* New York: John Wiley & Sons, Inc., 1967.

Coleman, James S., et al. *Equality of Educational Opportunity.* Washington, D.C.: Department of Health, Education and Welfare, 1966.

Dahrendorf, Ralf. *Class and Class Conflict in Industrial Society.* Stanford, Calif.: Stanford University Press, 1959.

Mills, C. Wright. *White Collar.* New York: Oxford University Press, 1953.

Schumpeter, Joseph A. *Imperialism and Social Classes.* New York: Augustus M. Kelly, 1951.

Sorokin, Pitirim A. *Social Mobility.* New York: Harper & Brothers, 1927.

9

Human Communities

      This chapter is concerned with the community, how it is organized, and how it serves society. In popular usage, the community may refer to a neighborhood or to a collection or grouping, such as the community of scholars or the community of nations. The essential idea is that the community consists of related parts joined by some common purpose, goal, or interest. Sociologically, the meaning of community is more restrictive, although even in this context the term may still refer to many different things.

      Human communities are social units organized in space. A community shows all the properties of social organization and differentiation of function that were discussed earlier. In ecological terms, a community is any bounded human settlement, any continuing organization of people in terms of geographic or areal considerations. A community may consist of only a few people or it may be a city of over a million. Community is a relative unit, used when the interrelated pattern of activity of people in a single geographic setting is to be emphasized. Thus communities within large cities can be identified for some purposes, while the whole city is treated as a community for other purposes. The community shares the problems of human society, the problems of survival, food, reproduction, socialization, and continuation. It solves or deals with these problems using the mechanisms defined for society. The unique aspect of analysis of the community is that such analysis

A community may consist of only a few people or it may be a city of over a million. In either case it serves as an adaptive mechanism for the human species, a unit in which society functions.
(Photo above, courtesy Robert Rapelye, Photography International; photo below, courtesy Photography International.)

emphasizes the relation between organization of a social system and organization of activities in space. The community is society in a setting; the community is society functioning.

When studying communities, it is important to distinguish between communities in abstract (the human community) and communities specifically (for example, Green Bay, Wisc.) In the abstract, communities are considered only in ecological terms; the community is an adaptive mechanism of the human species just as the colony is an adaptive structure for ants. At this level, analysis is not dependent on the characteristics of any special community, and findings are not limited to a single community but extend to all communities of a given type. In studying specific communities, however, many characteristics of the community may be historical remnants or result from the cultural basis of the society of which the community is a part. If the student confuses the two situations, he will view community life ethnocentrically, and if he extends his observations beyond the community he is studying, he is likely to misrepresent other communities. Many efforts have been made to determine the appropriate units for the abstract analysis of community, but only partial success has been achieved.[1] Students of human communities do not always agree on the basic elements of abstract analysis nor do they agree on the position of cultural and historical factors in the analysis of specific communities. This text will primarily use an approach to the human community that has been called the **ecological** approach. At a later point, the ecological approach will be extended.

Often it is convenient to separate communities into two groups: independent communities and dependent communities. As the name implies, the independent community is able to function without the services of other communities. It is essentially a complete society that grows its own food, makes its own tools, and deals with all the problems of social survival. Such communities are found only under primitive conditions because the development of specialization and the division of labor among communities are intrinsic to the development of civilization. Communities that specialize become dependent upon each other for certain goods or services, but collectively they become more effective producers through economies of scale (increased efficiency due to production of many items of a type at a single location) and the development of high levels of skill. As among people, an organizational structure of dependence and power emerges, so among communities there is a structure of dominance and subdominance. A community will have different characteristics not only because of its degree of independence, but because of its position in the hierarchy of dominance.

---

[1] One of the best efforts to define a community and its analytic components is found in Amos H. Hawley, *Human Ecology* (New York: The Ronald Press, 1950).

THE ECOLOGICAL VIEW OF HUMAN COMMUNITIES

Man's intimate relation with his environment has been commented on since ancient times.[2] The scientific minds of the 18th century recognized the need to preserve farm lands from the forces of depletion, even in the New World where land was relatively abundant.[3] Before the beginning of the 20th century, the Conservation Movement had been extended from Europe to America. Man had learned that continual abuse of his natural resources—an improper exploitation of his environment—spelled long-range disaster. Recent revival in environmental concern is new only in the range of abuses that have been identified and not in the idea of man's intimate dependency on nature.

At the same time that society was learning that conservation posed a serious question, biologists were learning that biological systems were closely interdependent. As part of the evolutionary mechanism, conditions that led to change in some species were also seen to lead a sort of chain reaction among other species. Moreover, under a constant environmental condition, a location was viewed as seeking its own ecological *climax*. That is, if an intrusion was temporary, its results would eventually be overcome and a natural climax or condition with certain plants and animals dominant over others would obtain.[4] This idea suggested to social scientists that the organization of human activity in geographic settings might also follow a general law. Certain types of land use patterns might be considered a direct result of a level of technology interacting with geographic factors. Robert Park, one of the fathers of human ecology, stated the problem in this fashion: "It is the interaction of these four factors—(1) population, (2) artifacts (technological culture), (3) custom and beliefs (non-material culture), and (4) natural resources—that maintains at once the biotic balance and the social equilibrium when and where they exist."[5] The works of these "classical ecologists," as they have been called,[6] were varied and focused on many aspects of the ecological structure; but common to most, if not all of these works, was a concern with the patterning of behavior in space and the factors that caused such patterns to change. From the earliest time, ecology thus was concerned with **process,** with change in human society.

[2] Some interesting speculation on how man learned to use the earth can be found in Julius E. Lips, *The Origin of Things* (New York: Fawcett Publications, 1956), pp. 55–68.
[3] Jefferson, for example, argued for the use of crop rotation and contour plowing to conserve the fertility of the soil.
[4] The idea of a natural climax has no implication of a preferable or more desirable state. It refers to what happens, not to what ought to happen.
[5] Robert E. Park, "Human Ecology," *Amer. J. of Sociology*, XLII (July 1936), p. 15.
[6] Different schools of human ecology are represented and compared in George A. Theodorson (ed.), *Studies in Human Ecology* (Evanston, Ill.: Row, Peterson, and Co., 1961).

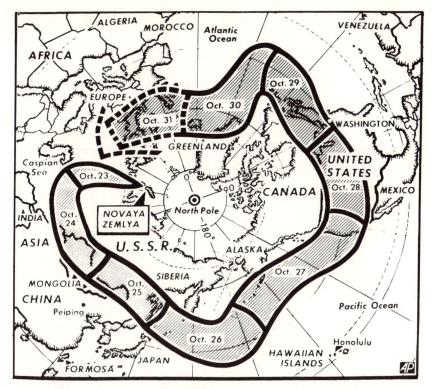

Man's interest in preserving his environment is not new—only the range of his abuses is new. On October 31, 1961 it was observed that the radioactive debris from a Soviet bomb explosion had, in ten days, made a nearly complete circuit of the earth.
(Courtesy Wide World Photos.)

The major substantive concern of the classical ecologists was the city and the processes that acted upon it. The example of the changing and growing American city led them to study what they felt was a unique American phenomenon. "All the manifestations of modern life which are peculiarly urban—the skyscraper, the subway, the department store, the daily newspaper, and social work —are characteristically American." This view expressed by Burgess suited most ecologists of the period.[7] Such a view limits the generality of their work, but does not obscure their contribution to a fundamental statement of the problem of community process.

The **growth of cities** (especially Chicago, since many of the classical ecologists were associated with the University of Chicago) posed several problems. First the rate of population growth was enormous. Second, the cities expanded geographically even more rapidly than their population grew. Third, most of the growth of the cities resulted from immigration; hence the population had

---

[7] Ernest W. Burgess, "The Growth of the City: An Introduction to a Research Project," in George A. Theodorson (ed.), *ibid.*, p. 37.

been socialized, at least in part, elsewhere. Fourth, the population came from many different racial and ethnic backgrounds, and these different groups arrived at different times. As a result of these conditions, within the context of the technological level and general culture of the United States at that time, certain results could be viewed as necessary consequences for the areal structure of the city. Specifically, the following were identified: growth of the city caused two immediate consequences—an expansion of the business district and an expansion of the outside boundaries of the city. The expansion of the business district coupled with the growth of the manufacturing district, which was located near the business district because of the proximity of transportation terminals, led to an increasing devaluation of adjoining residential property. This process created a zone of transition between the residential and the adjoining commercial and manufacturing areas. Since transportation for the public was limited, working men lived near their work and others with greater means lived farther out. The most elaborate residential areas, therefore, were those most distant from the central business district of the city. This idealized view gave rise to the "concentric zone" formulation of the pattern of land use in the city. The view was recognized as idealized by the formulators.[8] They also recognized that subbusiness districts would arise in the outlying areas to supply them with immediate needs.[9] Investigators have found some type of concentric pattern in many parts of the world. Nonetheless, in other places quite different patterns have been observed.

A reverse concentric zone with upper-class residences clustered around the central town square has been observed in older Latin American cities. The technological basis of land use patterns is illustrated by the fact that as modern modes of transportation are introduced in Latin American cities, the concentric zone seems to follow. Actual patterns deviate from the idealized model because of local influences. One Latin American city shows a layer-cake pattern with lower-class housing at the lowest altitudes, upper-class housing at higher altitudes, and lower-class housing again at the highest altitudes.[10]

It should be emphasized that the study of spatial dimensions of human activity is not directed toward the discovery and description of the areal patterns, as an end. Indeed, the primary importance of such a study is the analysis of areal patterns and their

[8] For example, see Ernest W. Burgess, ibid., p. 39.

[9] See Ernest W. Burgess, ibid., p. 40.

[10] A great many different international studies have been conducted. A classic is Theodore Caplow, "The Social Ecology of Guatemala City," Social Forces, XXVIII (December 1949), pp. 113–175. See also George A. Theodorson (ed.), Studies in Human Ecology (Evanston, Ill.: Row, Peterson, and Co., 1961), pp. 331–439; and Dennis McElrath, "The Social Areas of Rome," Amer. Sociological Rev., XXVII (June 1962), pp. 376–391.

relation to the organization of human activity and to social structure and social evaluation. Activities are assigned to space on the basis of their presumed value or importance.

The important aspect of the concentric zone theory is not the circular nature of the zones, but the processes associated with them. Several geographic patterns have been identified. All of them rest on the same basic processes that give rise to the concentric zone theory, although in different situations, these processes are manifested in different patterns. The processes themselves are of major concern; they are more general than the resulting patterns.

Examining the processes in light of the initial formulation of the ecological view of human communities shows the close interdependency of the fundamental ecological factors—population, environment, technology, and organization. An *increase in population* was associated with an *increase in productivity* and led in turn to an *increase in the geographic size* of the city. These increases caused a **redistribution** of land; generally residential land became commercialized for use by business and manufacturing. The resulting pattern was related to the technological basis of transportation as well. The commuters' zone, for example, could not exist unless there were facilities to support it. It should be noted that these processes are not recursive. On the contrary, they reenforce each other. A commuting pattern, once established, may be extended by appropriate technological expansion.

The patterns of *growth and redistribution* examined thus far have implications for human social life beyond the formation of neighborhoods and business areas. A related element in the experience of the American city was characterized by the early ecologists as **segregation.** They observed that racial and ethnic background of the inhabitants characterized different areas of the city. They identified German, Italian, Jewish, Chinese, and Negro areas in Chicago. Some of this segregation can be attributed to the processes of growth and timing mentioned earlier. Movement into the city by racial or ethnic groups occurred at different times for the different groups. When immigrants arrived, they tended to be alike in socioeconomic status, as well as cultural background. Most often, they were able to take over only the housing being abandoned by others, housing that was near the zone of transition if not part of it. Thus ethnic neighborhoods were created.

Socioeconomic homogeneity was not the only factor operating in this context. Other forces, such as racial discrimination, cultural preservation, and mutual support also acted to preserve these neighborhoods. The process that is integral to the creation of ethnic neighborhoods is not obscure, however, and it has been widely observed. The early ecologists characterized it in terms of **invasion–succession.** Although these terms have an invidious connotation, they should be understood in the sense in which their

The ethnic neighborhoods of New York City are numerous and varied. Since the early 1900's Italian immigrants have come to the tenements of Mulberry Street.
(Courtesy Library of Congress, Washington, D.C.)

originators used them. *Invasion* was borrowed from the plant ecologists and referred to the introduction of a new type of plant life to an area. This new life changed the ecological balance. If the new plant was more hardy than the one that lived there previously, that is, than the original dominant, then the new plant took over the area, or *succeeded*. The classical ecologists saw a parallel with changes in human neighborhoods—that is, new groups moving in tended to force older groups out. Unfortunately, the parallel could not be extended to explain or determine why some groups succeeded while others became part of the new ecological balance. Critics have pointed out that the position of "dominance" acquired by plants did not really apply to the succeeding human groups, who were generally dominated, blacks being a prime example. However, the analogy, though imperfect, focused attention on the changes in urban neighborhoods, and served a descriptive rather than an explanatory function—for, although the term invasion–succession does not *explain* why the process it names takes place, it does *describe* exactly what happens in many neighborhoods in American cities.

Criticisms of the early ecologists were many. Though some critics overstated their cases, their objections stemmed from a very real and basic problem—that human values and sentiments intruded in many ways in the patterns predicted by the ecologist.[11]

---

[11] Milla Aissa Alihan, *Social Ecology: A Critical Analysis* (New York: Columbia University Press, 1938).

Critics argued that human competition was not like that among animals or plants because human valuation was not always measured in terms of utility to survival but depended as well on cultural norms. Firey stated the case in its most extreme form: "Cultural factors mediate at every point between noncultural factors and the human community." [12] Other critics felt that the territorial aspect of community had been given exaggerated importance in the work of the ecologist. [13] These critics felt that the ecologist was making a false distinction in his effort to separate the territorial elements of social behavior—that is, community—from the social aspects. Furthermore, they believed this false distinction flawed his societal analysis because it caused him either to ignore the difference between the level of community and that of society or to fail to study important aspects of specific communities. The differences between the early human ecologists and their critics have not been resolved because they are fundamental to the idea of a social science. Ignoring some technical criticisms, the differences arise over whether human behavior can be meaningfully studied without reference to the values and sentiments of the persons involved. The ecologist says it can, in at least some contexts, though ecologists would differ on the limits of their theories. Critics of ecologists say human behavior cannot be meaningfully studied under such conditions, at least not in the manner formulated by the ecologists.

Later Ecological Studies

One major contribution of the early ecologists was that they focused attention on the differential distribution of people and acts in space, while relating those distributions to social structure and process. Students went further than the examination of segregation by race and ethnic grouping; they studied distribution of social classes, physical and mental illnesses, crime, commuting patterns, housing patterns, patterns of fertility, and differences in the sex ratio. [14] Moreover, the pattern that has emerged from such studies has been one of some consistency and generality. The zonal patterns found by the classical ecologists have been of relatively limited interest, but the general processes recognized as more or less universal by the basic ecological view have been identified in many countries. The associations or relations among the variables mentioned above have been verified in many cases, and changes in some variables, such as the distribution of blacks, are still generally associated with other variables, such as the distribution of certain types of crimes.

---

[12] Walter Firey, "Discussion of Hollingshead's 'Community Research: Development and Present Conditions,' " *Amer. Sociological Rev.*, XIII (April 1948), p. 152.
[13] Walter Firey, "Sentiment and Symbolism as Ecological Variables," *Amer. Sociological Rev.*, X (April 1945), pp. 140–148.
[14] Lists of representative studies can be found in the bibliographies of George A. Theodorson, *Studies in Human Ecology* (Evanston, Ill.: Row, Peterson, and Co., 1961).

Ecological correlational analysis has grown in sophistication and been advanced to a high degree. Accordingly, attempts to correlate certain factors that characterize the neighborhoods of modern American cities are undertaken with the understanding that although interdependence exists between these factors, the interrelations are often far more complex than the tenuous, superficial connections that might be suggested by a noncritical impression.[15]

There are a limited number of factors that are common to most modern American cities. Although the factors found in different studies may vary, the following, suggested by Shevky and Bell, are identified in almost every case: socioeconomic status, a factor that reflects the tendency of people with like education, occupation, and income to live in the same area; urbanization, a factor that reflects the clustering of different housing styles and fertility patterns in different parts of the city. This factor was labeled family style in some studies.[16] Third is segregation, which reflects the tendency of racial and ethnic groups to live in the same areas.[17] Though not completely independent of each other, these three factors act with a large degree of independence in most cities. Blacks are separate regardless of their family style or socioeconomic level, although their socioeconomic level is in large degree a function of their race.[18]

Examining correlations of this type poses some problems in logic that are often overlooked by the novice and sometimes by the professional. Consider the association between crime and blacks in a neighborhood. As with any correlation, care must be taken not to confuse the **association with causation.** *Association* simply characterizes the data; *causation* is inferred from a theory, which either coincides with or contradicts the association found in the data. At the same time, correlation based on data obtained from a neighborhood offers additional risk of misuse. The association may be true of the neighborhood but not of the individuals involved; that is, there may be more crime in neighborhoods where there are more blacks without blacks being involved in the crime. Such a case might exist if other ethnic groups found black areas good places to perform criminal acts. Such correlations have been labeled **"ecological correlations"** and the indiscriminate use of them for the inference of individual correlations has been called the **ecological**

[15] Jeffrey K. Hadden and Edgar F. Borgatta, *American Cities: Their Social Characteristics* (Chicago: Rand McNally & Co., 1965).
[16] Eshrev Shevky and Wendell Bell, *Social Area Analysis: Theory, Illustrations, and Computational Procedures* (Stanford, Calif.: Stanford University Press, 1955).
[17] See Otis Dudley Duncan and Beverly Duncan, "A Methodological Analysis of Segregation Indexes," *Amer. Sociological Rev.*, XX (April 1955), pp. 210–217, for measures of segregation.
[18] For a study of the urban blacks, see Karl Taeuber and Alma Taeuber, *Negroes in Cities* (Chicago: Aldine, 1965).

fallacy.[19] Such an error is not only the province of ecology, however; the error follows from using aggregate information to reflect individual behavior and can arise in many contexts. The user of any statistics should be careful to specify the units to which his data refer—that is, whether the data apply to individuals, families, households, census tracts, cities, counties, states, or nations. Then he should be certain that his analysis refers to those units or else he should make some adjustment in his interpretation. Often, especially in ecological contexts, the unit of interest is not the individual but the neighborhood, so the question, for example, of whether the blacks are involved in the crimes is not important—simply that the black *neighborhood* is involved is sufficient for the purposes at hand.

Relations Among Communities

Not only did the ecologist find that the community was organized in terms of areal patterns, but among communities he discerned an areal pattern, associated processes, and a structure of relations that suggested, once more, his favorite analogy with plant and animal ecology—dominance and subdominance.[20] Just as the presence of some species tends to characterize the ecological structure of a location, certain communities tend to dominate their environments. By providing services and maintaining economic control, these dominant centers organize their hinterlands. Within a region so organized, smaller centers provide similar services to smaller areas and hence are called subdominants. These centers, however, are not all alike even though they have similar functions. Some are financial dominants without being political dominants; some may dominate as service and distribution centers, while others are productive dominants or manufacturing centers. In the United States, for example, New York exercises financial and cultural dominance over most of the nation, while political dominance is centered in Washington. In each region, distribution centers such as Denver and Atlanta are regional dominants, with other cities depending on them. Efforts to measure dominance and influence among communities have been varied, but none is considered definitive. Newspaper circulation, store delivery zones, Federal Reserve Districts, commuting patterns, and transportation transfers have been used to define areas of dominance. These indices, as well as others, show

[19] For a lucid discussion of the problem, see Otis Dudley Duncan, Ray P. Cuzzort, and Beverly Duncan, *Statistical Geography: Problems in Analyzing Areal Data* (Glencoe, Ill.: Free Press, 1961), pp. 62ff.
[20] For a basic statement of the nature of dominance, see Donald J. Bogue, *The Structure of the Metropolitan Community* (Ann Arbor, Mich.: Horace H. Rackham School of Graduate Studies, 1949).

that in modern industrial society the division of labor extends beyond the individual to the community, even to large cities. It is a mark of the importance of technology in social organization that transportation and communication have to be developed to a high degree for this dominance to exist and for the complex interdependency among communities to be perpetuated.

The Location of Communities

Communities are not placed at random in a country any more than the areal pattern within the community is random. Although cities are not relocated easily, when conditions change, patterns of growth also change, and the result is very much like moving a city. Because it serves as a distribution center, the dominant city must be located in proximity to transportation routes. The cities of the United States, most of which were founded before the widespread use of rail transportation, are almost all located on the coasts or rivers because water transportation was the primary means of moving goods at that time. Moreover, the pattern of placement reflects the technology of transportation—that is, where goods had to be moved from one type of transport to another, a community was established. Ports were established for the change from sea to inland means of transportation. Inland cities were placed on rivers near the fall line where unloading goods was necessary. Some newer cities follow a different pattern, in response to a changed technology. The railroad freed cities from water transport, and cities grew where geography dictated that rail lines should cross. Even so, only two cities with over 1 million people, Atlanta and Denver, are without major water transportation or are above 1000 ft in altitude. Cheap air transportation may make cities possible in many parts of the country now considered unsuitable. Radical change in the pattern of communities should not be expected, however, because human adaptation employing new technology takes place in the context of existing community patterns. Therefore, the technology is usually employed to improve those patterns or to make them more efficient, rather than to replace them with others that might be more consistent with the technology.[21]

THE COMMUNITY IN DISASTER

In this chapter, the community as the unit of social adaptation has been stressed. The pattern of the community and the relations among communities is the mechanism by which human productivity is organized and the human society survives. The importance of the

[21] For a demonstration of how technological changes can influence communities, see Fred Cottrell, *Energy and Society* (New York: McGraw–Hill Book Co., 1955).

community in this context is well illustrated by examining the ways in which the community deals with uncertainty and disaster. Natural and man-made disasters affect both modern and traditional communities. During such times the community may draw on the resources of other communities and reorganize itself and its pattern of activities to meet the emergency. The floods in the eastern part of the United States in the spring and early summer of 1972 offer a grim illustration of forced evacuation, unsolicited aid, rerouting of transportation, and cooperation among communities. The ability of communities to cope with disaster is an unequivocal measure of their adaptability.

The enormous adaptability of the human community is nowhere better demonstrated than by its response to disaster. Modern societies rarely experience disasters as a whole, but communities within them are often completely disrupted by natural or man-made disaster. The resiliency of the human social order can be studied in the context of the community.

Disaster, whether natural or man-made, consists of four stages: **anticipation, onset, coping,** and **recovery.**[22] Disasters differ with respect to the length of these stages, as well as the effectiveness of social action during each of them. The extent of a disaster is a function of the disastrous event itself and the community's response to each of the stages. Examining each of the stages in turn will reveal how human communities respond differentially, as well as the dimensions of their resourcefulness.

Anticipation of Disaster

In one sense, communities are always anticipating disaster. Civil defense, fire protection, excess hospital facilities, and first-aid training are examples of long-range anticipation of disasters. Yet the time available to anticipate a specific instance of disaster is generally short, ranging from a few days to seconds, and the time in which the anticipation becomes certain is almost always short. A distinction can also be made between anticipation and *warning.* Warning should reduce the consequences of a disaster, but warning with anticipation, especially anticipation based on experience, seems most effective. Although there was adequate warning, Hurricane Audrey killed hundreds in southern Louisiana, while the anticipation of disaster engendered by that experience has reduced the loss of life in later storms.[23] Similar results were found for Edna, which

---

[22] Other phasing can be identified but these seem to be fundamental in that they are common to all disasters. Compare the specific stages used by Smelser for nuclear attack: Warning and Attack, Shelter, Emergence, Adjustment, and Recovery, in Neil J. Smelser, *The Social Dimensions of Nuclear Attack* (McLean, Va.: Human Sciences Research, Inc., 1964).

[23] C. W. Fogleman and V. J. Parenton, "Disaster and Aftermath," *Social Forces,* XXXVIII (1959), pp. 129–135.

followed Carol in New England by only 10 days. The anticipation created by the first storm rendered the population better prepared for the second.[24]

Anticipation may not always be effective in preparing a community for disaster. There are cases in which the approach of an army has caused panic within a population, though more often than not, populations react to attacks and sieges with considerable social cohesion. The long siege at Leningrad is a modern example. The population, facing almost certain defeat at the hands of an enemy whom they regarded with terror, continued to work productively and well, even when attack was immediate. That under such conditions they continued to work, eating a ration of food that was not sufficient to sustain life, indicates the deep resources of the human community.[25]

Onset of Disaster

The disaster itself generally lasts only a short period of time. During that period, the resources of the community are brought to bear to the extent that the community anticipated and prepared for the disaster. Otherwise, the individual faces the disaster without direct community support, except in the case of disasters such as war that are of long duration.[26] Injury and death during the onset period often remain unknown to those members of the community who would be concerned in normal circumstances. Activities during the disaster period are often focused on determining the fate of family, friends, and associates, in that order.

The Coping Period of Disaster

This period begins as soon as the onset period is over and activity at a socially organized level is again possible for most of the surviving members of the community. During this period, the community examines its resources, establishes internal communication, and begins to take care of the basic needs of its members. Medical care and the provision of food, clothing, and shelter dominate the programs of this period. (In some cases involving military action, defense may also play an important role.) During the coping period, many priorities established in normal conditions are changed. Medical care may go first to the less seriously injured because they are needed for work, and status may be accorded more readily to

---

[24] A. E. Prell, "Successive Hurricanes and Cultural Defense in a New England City," paper presented at the Annual Meeting of the American Sociological Society, Washington, D.C., 1955.
[25] See Leon Gouré, The Siege of Leningrad (Stanford, Calif.: Stanford University Press, 1962).
[26] Even continuing disasters such as war have repeated phases of intensity and might best be regarded as a series of related disasters.

authorities on the scene such as police and firemen.[27] Yet wider cultural values are not lost. One survivor of the nuclear bombing of Hiroshima recorded that he was preoccupied with the fate of the Emperor's portrait that had hung in his hospital.[28]

During the coping period of disaster, certain critically important conditions must exist if the disaster is not to be followed by social disasters. A study of 70 major disasters reveals that the early coping period is characterized by a *high degree of cooperation* among the members of the community, especially in aiding one another to locate family and friends.[29] At the same time, the study finds instances of riot and confusion in some cases and continued cooperation in others. The difference between these two developments is not simply a function of the horror of the disaster or the extent of loss of life and property, although minor disasters (if such exist) probably engender less danger of social disorganization because the return to normal conditions can be almost immediate. Though cultural factors may be involved, the major difference between the successful and the unsuccessful, or less successful, communities seem to lie in the ability of the former to provide unequivocal guides and authority during the later parts of the coping periods. Individuals left to themselves do not behave irrationally following a disaster, in that when questioned they can offer a clear means-to-ends evaluation of their behavior. Their collective action, however, seems irrational and has irrational consequences for the community. Generally, individuals prove willing to accept direction, and it is when that direction is lacking that social disaster becomes a likely consequence of the natural disaster.

War seems to follow a slightly different pattern, although not one without exceptions. Other man-made disasters are like natural disasters in that they are unintended, if not unanticipated. The Galveston harbor explosion and the Coconut Grove fire brought reactions like those to earthquakes and floods.[30] War is a deliberate attempt to destroy the community or to control it. Though single raids such as the bombings of Hamburg or the V-2 attacks on London may seem like natural disasters, the community's response is tempered by the protracted nature of war and the organizational structure imposed by it on the community. In war, the onset of disaster is intermittent so that coping becomes a much longer process for

---

[27] Examples of emergency priorities are discussed in W. T. Herzog, *Emergency Health Problems Study* (Durham, N.C.: Research Triangle Institute, 1963).

[28] Michihiko Hachiya, *Hiroshima Diary* (Chapel Hill: University of North Carolina Press, 1955), pp. 183–185.

[29] George D. Palmer and Saul B. Sells, *Individuals and Groups in Disaster* (McLean, Va.: Human Sciences Research, Inc., 1963).

[30] Dwight W. Chapman, "A Brief Introduction to Contemporary Disaster Research," pp. 3–22 in George W. Baker and Dwight W. Chapman (eds.), *Man and Society in Disaster* (New York: Basic Books, Inc., 1962).

some communities. That longer process might be expected to decrease social solidarity since prolonged coping periods following natural disasters lead to the most severe types of disorganization.[31] The nature of war seems to compensate for that tendency. The study of war-related disasters shows that the communities most affected by the war are least likely to suffer social upheaval and their populations are the least likely to complain. Analysis of the extreme cases of Leningrad (mentioned above) and Moscow suggest that one factor in this process may be the increased dependency of the population on authorities for their basic needs.[32] Yet the less severe case of London suggests that even when conditions are better and dependency on authority is proportionately less, considerable community solidarity can be generated in a city under attack. Indeed, this desire for community independence from direct outside control is so great that a different system of costs is employed. Natural disaster often generates programs of prevention and preparation based on their relatively smaller cost compared to the cost of repeated disasters. Wars often continue at great cost, even when the terms of peace would be much less costly.

Disaster and the Period of Recovery

Recovery, if begun soon, serves to adapt the community to immediate deprivation. The perception of a return to normal conditions enables the population to tolerate worse conditions than they would accept otherwise. Evidence seems to suggest, however, that this perception is relative to cultural background, as well as to the level of disaster and the rate of return to normal conditions. Studies of floods in Holland and in Mexican and American towns indicate that a cultural factor may influence the reaction to the speed with which recovery is begun.[33]

Panic and Rioting in Disaster

Panic or rioting has been observed at all stages of disaster. In large disasters, panic is restricted to certain locations, but in small or concentrated disasters, such as the Coconut Grove fire, panic may appear to be general. Panic results from the immediate efforts of individuals to save themselves during the onset of the disaster and is generally found where the freedom of movement of the group is

[31] This result may be due to a failure to meet expectations of a rapid return to normal following a natural disaster. War may reduce such expectations.

[32] For a study of Moscow in war, see Leon Gouré and H. S. Dinerstein, *Political Vulnerability of Moscow: Case Study of the October 1941 Attack* (Santa Monica, Calif.: The Rand Corporation, 1952).

[33] See R. A. Clifford, *A Comparative Study of Border Communities in Disaster* (Washington, D.C.: National Academy of Sciences—National Research Council, 1956), Disaster Study No. 7; and J. E. Ellemers, "General Conclusions," *Studies in Holland Flood Disaster, 1953* (Amsterdam and Washington, D.C.: Institute for Social Research in the Netherlands and National Academy of Science—National Research Council, 1955).

Unsolicited aid and cooperation in building emergency dikes to hold back the swollen Mississippi demonstrates the human community's tremendous adaptability in disaster.
(Courtesy Wide World Photos.)

restricted. Panic is short-lived and, unless additional disasters are anticipated, does not influence coping and recovery, beyond its contributions to the number of casualties at the onset of the disaster.

Rioting during the coping or recovery period is also rare, and its occurrence is probably engendered by the same sources of dissatisfaction that generate riots in other settings. Only where recovery is unduly delayed, or thought to be, are riots encountered. The human community will accept starvation without violence, if it is convinced that starvation is necessary.

Summary

This chapter has focused on the human community. The analysis of the human ecologists, which stresses the spatial aspect of the organization of the community, has been examined, and the community as an adaptive device has been emphasized. The organization of communities into systems of dominance and subdominance was discussed, and the technological basis of the structure of the community was emphasized. Finally, the potential of the community was illustrated by the responses of communities to crisis and disaster.

Exercises

1. The text discusses the idea of *segregation*. How many types of residential segregation other than racial can you identify? Can you devise a means of measuring segregation so that the degree of segregation in different places can be compared?

2. Evaluate from your own perspective the controversy between the classical ecologists and their critics.

3. Devise a land use pattern you think a modern city might develop if the constraints of history did not apply. What principles did you employ?

4. How does crisis differ from disaster in terms of the community structures involved?

5. Devise a means of measuring the dominance of one community over another? Do different measures lead to different patterns of dominance?

6. What justification can you offer for speaking of the black community or the Jewish community, if those groups are not spatially segregated from others in the society?

7. List some cases where the ecological fallacy could mislead an investigator. List others where the areal unit is really the unit of concern and the ecological fallacy does not arise. How do the two lists differ?

8. Examine a census tract report from the 1970 United States Census of Population and Housing. Use those materials to define social areas for a city. Compare your approach with that used by Shevky and Bell in *Social Area Analysis*.

9. Consider factors other than transportation routes that influence the location of communities? Do you think they will become more or less important in the future? Justify your view.

Selected Bibliography

Agger, Robert E., Daniel Goldrich, and Bert E. Swanson. *The Rulers and the Ruled: Political Power and Impotence in American Communities*. New York: John Wiley & Sons, Inc., 1964.

Alihan, Milla A. *Social Ecology: A Critical Analysis*. New York: Columbia University Press, 1938.

Banton, Michael. *The Policeman in the Community*. New York: Basic Books, 1964.

Hawley, Amos H. *Human Ecology: A Theory of Community-Structure*. New York: The Ronald Press, 1950.

Hunter, Floyd. *Community Power Structure*. Chapel Hill: University of North Carolina Press, 1953.

Jennings, M. Kent. *Community Influentials: The Elites of Atlanta*. New York: Free Press, 1964.

MacIver, Robert M. *Community*. New York: The Macmillan Company, 1920.

Saunders, Irwin T. *The Community: An Introduction to a Social System* (2nd Ed.). New York: The Ronald Press, 1966.

Stein, Maurice. *The Eclipse of Community: An Interpretation of American Studies*. New York: Harper Torchbooks, no date.

Vidich, Arthur J., Joseph Bensman and Maurice R. Stein. *Reflections on Community Studies*. New York: John Wiley & Sons, Inc., 1964.

Part III

Population and Technology: Consequences for Social Adaptation

10

Demographic Structure and Human Adaptation

The continuation of any human society depends on the ability of the society to reproduce itself biologically. Effective adaptation not only requires the birth of new generations, but it involves, as well, their distribution in space in such a way as to use the available technology to exploit the environment. If the population is not in balance with the technology and available resources, the environment may be adversely affected to the extent that it will be rendered unable to support even a much reduced population. If the population is reduced to the point that it cannot employ the technology, then some other technology, perhaps one much less effective, must be employed. Demographic problems are fundamental aspects of human society because they are so closely related to other social processes.

Like animal and insect societies, human societies are subject to limitations imposed by their size. The study of how the size of the population interacts with and influences other aspects of social organization is of great value, but it is necessary to understand *how* population size changes in purely demographic terms before examining *why* such changes take place and the *consequences* of such changes when they do occur.

Part photo: courtesy Jim Harrison.   273

Changes in the size of a population can be described by what has been called the **demographic equation**[1]:

$$P_2 = P_1 + B - D + I - E$$

This equation states symbolically that the size of a population at any given time (P_2) is equal to the population's size at some earlier time (P_1) plus the births that have occurred since that time (B), minus the deaths (D), plus those who have moved to join the population (immigration) (I), minus those who have left the population (emigration) (E). The difference between births and deaths is often called the **natural increase** in the population, and the difference between immigration and emigration is called the **net migration.** Those terms do not imply that births and deaths are more natural than migration; all demographic processes are natural and all are subject to scientific examination and prediction.

The demographic equation describes the mechanisms by which changes occur in the size of populations; it does not explain how such changes occur, nor does it show when demographic changes can be expected. To attempt that task, we have to examine the components of the equation. Changes in births and deaths, in migration and residence, must be examined to determine what factors are associated with changes in them.

A PROBLEM FOR STUDY

While most of the demographic history of man is locked in obscurity, there is every reason to believe that during the past two centuries the size of the human population has increased in an unprecedented fashion. Probably from 5 to 10 per cent of all people who have lived at any time during the history of the human species are alive today.[2] Such conclusions are speculative, for even today sound demographic data are not available for all the world's societies. Educated guesses place the population of the world in 1800 at about 1 billion.[3] Many thousands of years had passed before that figure was reached. A second billion was added by 1925 and a third by 1960.[4] Fairly conservative projections say that a fourth billion should be added by 1985 and a fifth before the end of the century. Even if these projections prove to be in error, the enormous growth

[1] Kingsley Davis, *Human Society* (New York: The Macmillan Company, 1949), p. 551.
[2] Nathan Keyfitz, "How Many People Have Lived on the Earth," *Demography*, III (1966), p. 581, gives an estimate that 4 per cent of all who have ever lived were alive in 1960.
[3] The difficulty in knowing population sizes before census taking became regular is very great. The decennial census of the United States dates from 1790, that of England from 1801.
[4] Dean Fraser, *The People Problem* (Bloomington, Ind.: Indiana University Press, 1971), p. 14; and Philip M. Hauser, "World Population Growth," in Philip M. Hauser (ed.), *The Population Dilemma*, 2nd ed. (Englewood Cliffs, N.J.: Prentice-Hall, Inc., 1969), p. 13.

can be expected to continue if only as a consequence of the huge "breeding stock" already living.

All parts of the world have not participated equally in this population explosion, nor have the rates of population increase in different places been constant over time. Some countries have experienced rapid population growth for a time followed by slow increases in their populations. Some populations have grown rapidly only in recent decades and continue to grow at a very high rate. These differences in rates of growth mean that the sizes of the populations of countries relative to each other are changing. Such changes influence the patterns of production and consumption, as well as the military and diplomatic postures of the nations concerned.

One basic difference in the demographic experience of nations is that between the industrially advanced nations and the "underdeveloped" nations. The industrialized nations with a little over 30 per cent of the total world population experienced about 33 per cent of the total increase in the world's population between 1920 and 1940. During that time the population balance between developed and underdeveloped populations remained almost stable, leading to the expectation that the spread of industrial organization would lead to improved levels of living in the underdeveloped world, as it had done earlier in the developed world. Current trends, however, show a different pattern. These same industrialized nations will receive only 13 per cent of the increase in world population anticipated for the period 1960 to 1980.[5] Such rapid growth of population in countries without an industrial base can be expected to have consequences far different from those that resulted from the smaller increases experienced by the industrialized nations.

The complex relation between time, place, economic basis, and population increase is a major scientific problem. Before examining the problem of how the factors are related, we must define the problem in terms of the *measures* available so that the concepts employed are *operationalized*. This definition will be made by referring to the components of the demographic equation. The equation states that there are two ways a population can grow: through natural increase and through migration. The total population of the world can only grow through natural increase, for the world is a **closed demographic system.** When the population of the world increases, the number of births must be greater than the number of deaths; in other words, the **crude birth rate** is greater than the **crude death rate.** The crude birth rate (CBR) is defined as the number of births during a year divided by the population at the midpoint

[5] Philip M. Hauser, *ibid.,* p. 22 passim.

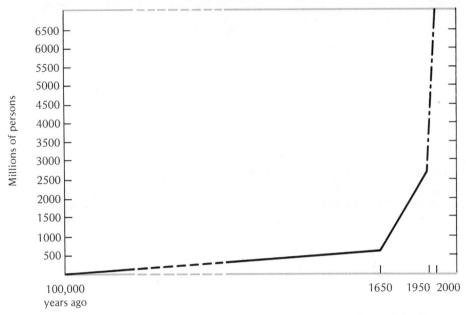

FIGURE 10–1   A schematic representation of the increase in numbers of the human species.
(Taken from William Peterson. *Population*, New York: The Macmillan Company, 1969, p. 10)

of that year and multiplied by a constant, generally 1000. The crude death rate (CDR) is defined as the number of deaths occurring in a year divided by the population at the midpoint of the year and multiplied by the same constant.[6] The difference between the CBR and the CDR is the **crude rate of natural increase** (CRNI):

$$CBR - CDR = CRNI.$$

These rates are called crude rates because they do not take into account the *demographic structure* of the populations to which they apply. For example, a population with a large proportion of old people that had the same CDR as a population with few old people would generally be regarded as having a lower "true" mortality rate. Demographers have many ways in which they try to control such factors. However, the crude rates are sufficiently accurate for an examination of world population trends.

There are two ways the natural increase in a population can become greater: births may increase or deaths may decrease (or both may change in some degree leaving a different balance). Most analysts agree that population was relatively stable without major increases until a few hundred years ago, as is shown schematically in Figure 10–1. Probably the birth rate was slightly higher than the

---

[6] Strictly speaking, these rates are not probabilities since everyone in the numerator is not in the denominator, and those in the denominator are not all exposed to the risk of falling in the numerator for the entire year.

death rate most of the time, but major epidemics, wars, and other disasters periodically raised the death rate to very high levels so that a general overall balance was maintained.[7] These birth rates were probably about as high as they could be—in the range of 40 to 60 per thousand persons in the population per year. From a period of very high fertility and equally high mortality, population increase could only have resulted from a decline in deaths, which is exactly what happened. Even the most elementary application of modern

During World War II, as in other catastrophes of major proportion, the death rate increased; but in the years that followed there was a rise in the birth rate, and the overall balance was restored.
(Courtesy Robert Rapelye, Photography International.)

[7] There were periods when population probably declined drastically, such as during the bubonic plague in Europe, when the population may have been halved.

Mortality responds to human invention and technology. The development of the antibiotic penicillin, from the penicillin mold, contributed to the low death rates of modern nations.
(Courtesy Berenice Abbott.)

medical practice causes enormous reductions in death rates. Modern nations experience death rates of 10 per thousand per year or lower. Such a low death rate (or even a rate approaching it), if found in a nation where fertility remains at the level necessary for the preindustrial society, will result in a population increasing at from 3 to 4 per cent per year. Such high rates of growth will double the size of the population in less than the length of a generation and quadruple it in two generations. Increases of that magnitude cannot continue beyond all bounds. Given finite space alone, not to mention other resources in short supply, some limit must exist for the total size of the population of the earth.

The problem of population increase is not confined to rapid growth alone. Earlier the differences in the rates of growth of industrialized and nonindustrialized nations were examined. Additional data for selected countries are shown in Table 10–1. These data reveal several important changes in population growth rates: the most industrialized nations had a rapid increase early and then began to have much smaller increases because their birth rates began to decline to the level of their death rates. This *demographic transition* is illustrated in Figure 10–2. The nations that are not industrialized have maintained their high rates of fertility even when their rates of mortality have fallen. Moreover, the decline in their death rates, and hence the increases in their rate of population growth, is far more rapid than that experienced by the industrial nations when they entered their period of rapid increase. The difference is easily explained because the later developing nations have, in a few years, adopted and implemented medical programs that took the industrialized nations decades to develop and implement. Thus, for nations of the underdeveloped world, medical technology is effective long before industrialization has developed to support their increasing numbers. These nations, then, are often unable to fit their increased population into traditional technologies; and the increase has come too rapidly for them to employ the technological adaptation that characterizes the developed world.

Additional problems of adjustment are posed by the nature of demographic growth. Though the world as a whole is a closed demographic system, population can be transferred from one part to another. During their period of rapid growth, the nations of Europe were able to export large numbers of people to the rest of the world. North America was able to absorb large numbers of Europeans without difficulty. Then the underpopulated parts of the world were the underdeveloped parts. The technology needed to develop the New World required large amounts of labor. Huge numbers of farmers were needed to support a relatively small number of industrial workers. None of these workers required elaborate training.

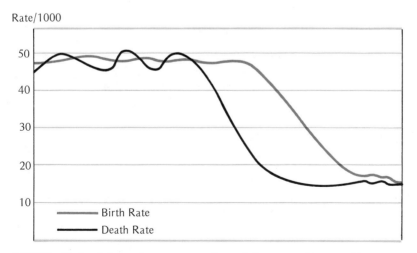

FIGURE 10–2 Schematic representation of demographic transition.

TABLE 10–1
Population information for 160 countries (1972).[a]

	Population estimates mid-1972 (millions)[b]	Annual births per 1000 population[c]	Annual deaths per 1000 population[c]	Number of years to double population[d]	Population projections to 1985 (millions)[e]	Annual deaths to infants under one year of age per 1000 live births[c]	Population under 15 years (per cent)[f]	Population over 64 years (per cent)[f]	Population in cities[g] of 100,000+[h]	Per cent of population in cities[g]	Per capita gross national product (US $)[j]
WORLD	3782[k]	33	13	35	4933	...	37	5		23	...
AFRICA	364	47	21	27	530	...	44	3		11	...
NORTHERN AFRICA	92	47	17	23	140	...	45	3		21	...
Algeria	15.0	50	17	21	23.9	86	47	L		14	260
Egypt	35.9	44	16	25	52.3	118	43	L		31	160
Libya	2.0	46	16	23	3.1	...	44	5		26	1510
Morocco[k]	16.8	50	16	21	26.2	149	46	L		24	190
Sudan	16.8	49	18	23	26.0	121	47	...		3	110
Tunisia	5.4	42	16	27	8.3	120	45	L		22	230
WESTERN AFRICA	107	49	24	28	155	...	45	2		7	...
Dahomey	2.8	51	26	27	4.1	149	46	L		6	P
Ghana[k]	9.6	47	18	24	14.9	122	45	L		18	190
Guinea	4.1	47	25	30	5.7	216	44	7		6	P
Ivory Coast	4.5	46	23	29	6.4	138	43	L		12	240
Liberia	1.2	50	23	26	1.6	137	37	L		N.A.	200
Mali	5.3	50	27	30	7.6	190	49	L		5	P
Mauritania	1.2	44	23	33	1.7	137	...	...		N.A.	140
Niger	4.1	52	23	24	6.2	148	45	L		N.A.	P
Nigeria	58.0	50	25	27	84.7	...	43	L		7	P
Senegal	4.1	46	22	29	5.8	...	42	L		15	200
Sierra Leone	2.8	45	22	30	3.9	136	37	5		7	170
Toga[k]	2.0	51	26	28	2.8	163	48	L		10	100
Upper Volta	5.6	49	29	35	7.7	182	42	L		N.A.	P
EASTERN AFRICA	103	47	22	28	149	...	44	3		5	...
Burundi	3.8	48	25	30	5.3	150	47	L		N.A.	P
Ethiopia	26.2	46	25	33	35.7	...	44	L		3	P
Kenya[k]	11.6	48	18	23	17.9	...	46	L		7	130
Malagasy Republic	7.3	46	25	33	10.8	102	46	L		6	110
Malawi	4.7	49	25	28	6.8	119	44	L		4	P
Mozambique[l]	8.1	43	23	33	11.1	...	42	L		4	210
Rhodesia	5.4	48	14	21	8.6	122	48	L		14	240
Rwanda	3.8	52	23	24	5.7	124	...	...		N.A.	P

TABLE 10–1 (Continued)
Population information for 160 countries (1972).[a]

	Population estimates mid-1972 (millions)[b]	Annual births per 1000 population[c]	Annual deaths per 1000 population[c]	Number of years to double population[d]	Population projections to 1985 (millions)[e]	Annual deaths to infants under one year of age per 1000 live births[c]	Population under 15 years (per cent)[f]	Population over 64 years (per cent)[f]	Per cent of population in cities[g] of 100,000+[h]	Per capita gross national product (US $)[i]
Somalia	2.9	46	24	32	4.2	190	...	...	7	P
Tanzania	14.0	47	22	27	20.3	162	44	L	3	P
Uganda[k]	9.1	43	18	27	13.1	160	41	L	4	110
Zambia[k]	4.6	50	21	24	7.0	159	45	L	11	290
MIDDLE AFRICA	**38**	**44**	**24**	**33**	**52**	**...**	**42**	**3**	**6**	**...**
Angola[l]	5.9	50	30	33	8.1	192	42	L	6	210
Cameroon	6.0	43	23	35	8.4	137	39	L	6	150
Central African Republic	1.6	46	25	33	2.2	163	42	L	11	130
Chad	3.9	48	25	30	5.5	160	46	L	N.A.	P
Congo (People's Rep. of)	1.0	44	23	33	1.4	148	42	L	21	220
Zaire (Dem. Rep. Congo)	18.3	44	23	33	25.8	115	42	L	7	P
SOUTHERN AFRICA	**24**	**41**	**18**	**29**	**34**	**...**	**40**	**4**	**29**	**...**
Lesotho	1.1	39	21	39	1.4	181	43	5	N.A.	P
South Africa[k]	21.1	41	17	29	29.7	138	40	L	32	710
ASIA	**2154**	**37**	**14**	**30**	**2874**	**...**	**40**	**4**	**16**	**...**
SOUTHWEST ASIA	**82**	**44**	**16**	**25**	**121**	**...**	**43**	**4**	**22**	**...**
Iraq	10.4	49	15	21	16.7	104	48	5	31	310
Israel	3.0	27	7	29	4.0	23	33	7	55	1570
Jordan	2.5	48	16	21	3.9	115	47	L	20	280
Lebanon	3.0	...	...	...	4.3	...	...	...	33	580
Saudi Arabia	8.2	50	23	25	12.2	...	...	...	14	380
Syria	6.6	48	15	21	10.5	...	47	L	31	260
Turkey	37.6	40	15	28	52.8	119	42	L	18	350
Yemen Arab Republic	6.1	50	23	25	9.1	...	...	...	N.A.	P
Yemen, People's Republic of	1.4	50	21	24	2.0	...	...	...	28	120
MIDDLE SOUTH ASIA	**806**	**44**	**17**	**27**	**1137**	**...**	**43**	**3**	**11**	**...**
Afghanistan	17.9	51	27	29	25.0	...	...	...	4	P
Ceylon	13.2	31	8	30	17.7	48	41	L	11	190
India[k]	584.8	42	17	28	807.6	139	42	L	10	110
Iran	30.2	45	17	25	45.0	...	46	L	23	350
Nepal	11.8	45	23	32	15.8	...	40	L	4	P
Pakistan[n]	146.6	51	18	21	224.2	142	45	L	10	110

TABLE 10–1 (Continued)
Population information for 160 countries (1972).[a]

	Population estimates, mid-1972 (millions)[b]	Annual births per 1000 population[c]	Annual deaths per 1000 population[c]	Number of years to double population[d]	Population projections to 1985 (millions)[e]	Annual deaths to infants under one year of age per 1000 live births[c]	Population under 15 years (per cent)[f]	Population over 64 years (per cent)[f]	Per cent of population in cities[g] of 100,000+[h]	Per capita gross national product (US $)[i]
SOUTHEAST ASIA	**304**	**43**	**15**	**25**	**434**	...	**44**	**3**	**12**	...
Burma	29.1	40	17	30	39.2	...	40	L	7	P
Indonesia	128.7	47	19	24	183.8	125	44	L	12	100
Khmer Republic (Cambodia)	7.6	45	16	23	11.3	127	44	L	10	130
Laos	3.1	42	17	28	4.4	...	...	...	7	110
Malaysia[k]	11.4	37	8	25	16.4	...	44	L	17	340
Philippines[k]	40.8	45	12	21	64.0	67	47	L	16	210
Singapore	2.2	23	5	32	3.0	21	39	L	100	800
Thailand[k]	38.6	43	10	21	57.7	...	43	L	8	160
Vietnam (Dem. Republic of)	22.0	...	...	...	28.2	...	...	...	11	P
Vietnam (Republic of)	18.7	...	...	...	23.9	...	...	...	13	140
EAST ASIA	**962**	**29**	**12**	**41**	**1182**	...	**35**	**4**	**20**	...
China (People's Republic of)	786.1	30	13	41	964.6	...	...	...	14	P
China (Republic of)	14.7	28	5	30	19.4	18	43	L	38	300
Hong Kong[k, l]	4.4	20	5	29	6.0	19	38	L	100	850
Japan	106.0	19	7	58	121.3	13	24	7	55	1430
Ryukyu Islands[k, o]	1.0	22	5	41	1.3	...	34	6	30	700
Korea (Dem. People's Rep. of)	14.7	39	11	25	20.7	...	...	...	17	280
Korea (Republic of)	33.7	31	11	35	45.9	...	40	L	33	210
Mongolia	1.4	42	11	23	2.0	...	31	6	27	460
NORTHERN AMERICA	**231**	**17**	**9**	**63**	**274**	...	**29**	**9**	**57**	...
Canada	22.2	17.5	7.3	41	27.3	19.3	30	8	49	2650
United States[p]	209.2	17.3	9.3	70	246.3	19.2	29	10	58	4240
LATIN AMERICA	**300**	**38**	**10**	**25**	**435**	...	**42**	**4**	**31**	...
MIDDLE AMERICA	**72**	**43**	**11**	**22**	**112**	...	**46**	**3**	**20**	...
Costa Rica	1.9	34	7	26	3.2	67	48	L	25	510
El Salvador	3.7	40	10	23	5.9	67	45	L	14	290
Guatemala	5.4	43	17	27	7.9	92	46	L	15	350
Honduras	2.9	49	17	22	4.6	...	47	L	10	260
Mexico[k]	54.3	43	10	21	84.4	69	46	L	21	580

TABLE 10-1 (Continued)
Population information for 160 countries (1972).[a]

	Population estimates mid-1972 (millions)[b]	Annual births per 1000 population[c]	Annual deaths per 1000 population[c]	Number of years to double population[d]	Population projections to 1985 (millions)[e]	Annual deaths to infants under one year of age per 1000 live births[c]	Population under 15 years (per cent)[f]	Population over 64 years (per cent)[f]	Per cent of population in cities[g] of 100,000+[h]	Per capita gross national product (US $)[i]
Nicaragua	2.2	46	17	24	3.3	...	48	L	18	380
Panama	1.6	38	9	24	2.5	41	44	L	30	660
CARIBBEAN[q]	**27**	**33**	**11**	**32**	**36**	...	**40**	**4**	**21**	...
Cuba	8.7	27	8	37	11.0	48	31	6	31	280
Dominican Republic[k]	4.6	49	15	21	7.3	64	47	L	18	280
Guadeloupe[k]	0.4	30	8	32	0.5	45	43	5	N.A.	540
Haiti	5.5	44	20	29	7.9	...	38	L	8	P
Jamaica[k]	2.1	33	8	33	2.6	39	46	L	28	550
Puerto Rico[l]	2.9	25	7	50	3.4	26	37	7	33	1410
Trinidad and Tobago[k]	1.1	23	7	63	1.3	37	42	L	N.A.	890
TROPICAL SOUTH AMERICA	**160**	**40**	**10**	**23**	**236**	...	**43**	**3**	**32**	...
Bolivia	4.9	44	19	29	6.8	...	42	L	15	160
Brazil	98.4	38	10	25	142.6	...	43	L	34	270
Colombia	22.9	44	11	21	35.6	76	47	L	35	290
Ecuador	6.5	45	11	21	10.1	91	48	L	21	240
Guyana	0.8	36	8	25	1.1	40	45	L	27	340
Peru	14.5	42	11	23	21.6	72	45	L	22	330
Venezuela	11.5	41	8	21	17.4	47	47	L	37	1000
TEMPERATE SOUTH AMERICA	**41**	**25**	**9**	**41**	**51**	...	**32**	**7**	**52**	...
Argentina[k]	25.0	22	9	47	29.6	58	30	7	61	1060
Chile[k]	10.2	28	9	37	13.6	92	39	5	37	510
Paraguay	2.6	45	11	21	4.1	67	46	L	19	240
Uruguay	3.0	21	9	58	3.4	49	28	8	53	560
EUROPE	**469**	**16**	**10**	**99**	**515**	...	**25**	**12**	**38**	...
NORTHERN EUROPE	**82**	**16**	**11**	**139**	**90**	...	**24**	**13**	**58**	...
Denmark	5.0	14.4	9.8	139	5.5	14.8	24	12	38	2310
Finland	4.8	13.7	9.5	174	5.0	12.5	26	8	24	1980
Iceland	0.2	19.5	7.1	58	0.3	13.3	33	9	N.A.	1850
Ireland	3.0	21.8	11.5	99	3.5	19.2	31	11	31	1110

TABLE 10–1 (Continued)
Population information for 160 countries (1972).[a]

	Population estimates mid-1972 (millions)[b]	Annual births per 1000 population[c]	Annual deaths per 1000 population[c]	Number of years to double population[d]	Population projections to 1985 (millions)[e]	Annual deaths to infants under one year of age per 1000 live births[c]	Population under 15 years (per cent)[f]	Population over 64 years (per cent)[f]	Per cent of population in cities[g] of 100,000+[h]	Per capita gross national product (US $)[i]
Norway	4.0	16.6	9.8	99	4.5	13.8	25	13	26	2160
Sweden	8.2	13.7	9.9	174	8.8	11.7	21	13	33	2920
United Kingdom	56.6	16.2	11.7	139	61.8	18.4	24	13	71	1890
WESTERN EUROPE	**151**	**15**	**11**	**139**	**163**	...	**24**	**13**	**45**	...
Austria	7.5	15.2	13.4	347	8.0	25.9	24	14	36	1470
Belgium	9.8	14.7	12.3	347	10.4	20.5	24	13	28	2010
France	51.9	16.7	10.6	99	57.6	15.1	25	13	40	2460
Germany (Federal Republic of)	59.2	13.3	11.7	347	62.3	23.6	25	12	54	2190
Berlin, West[l]	2.1	9.5	19.0	...	1.9	25.8	15	21	100	...
Netherlands	13.3	18.4	8.4	70	15.3	12.7	27	10	45	1760
Switzerland	6.4	15.8	9.1	70	7.4	15.1	23	11	33	2700
EASTERN EUROPE	**106**	**17**	**10**	**99**	**116**	...	**24**	**11**	**24**	...
Bulgaria	8.7	16.3	9.1	99	9.4	27.3	23	9	21	860
Czechoslovakia	14.9	15.8	11.4	139	16.2	22.1	24	11	16	1370
Germany (Dem. Republic of)	16.3	13.9	14.1	...	16.9	18.8	24	15	23	1570
Berlin, East	1.1	14.5	16.4	...	1.0	20.3	22	16	100	...
Hungary	10.4	14.7	11.7	231	11.0	35.9	21	11	24	1100
Poland	33.7	16.8	8.2	77	38.2	33.2	28	8	31	940
Romania	20.8	21.1	9.5	58	23.3	49.4	26	8	22	860
SOUTHERN EUROPE	**131**	**18**	**9**	**77**	**146**	...	**26**	**10**	**30**	...
Albania	2.3	35.3	7.5	25	3.3	86.8	...	...	10	430
Greece	9.0	16.3	8.3	87	9.7	29.3	25	10	34	840
Italy	54.5	16.8	9.7	99	60.0	29.2	24	10	29	1400
Portugal	9.7	18.0	9.7	87	10.7	58.0	29	9	24	510
Spain	33.9	19.6	8.5	70	38.1	27.9	28	9	33	820
Yugoslavia	21.0	17.8	9.0	77	23.8	55.2	28	7	28	580
USSR	**248**	**17.4**	**8.2**	**77**	**286.9**	**24.4**	**28**	**8**	**31**	**1200**
OCEANIA[q]	**20**	**25**	**10**	**35**	**27**	...	**32**	**7**	**49**	...
Australia	13.0	20.5	9.0	37	17.0	17.9	29	8	65	2300
New Zealand	3.0	22.1	8.8	41	3.8	16.7	32	8	46	2230
Papua–New Guinea[l]	2.5	...	...	...	3.6	...	43	L	N.A.	210

TABLE 10–1 (Continued)
Population information for 160 countries (1972).[a]

SUMMARY OF WORLD AND REGIONAL POPULATION (Millions).

	World	Asia	Europe	USSR	Africa	Northern America	Latin America	Oceania
MID-1972	3782	2154	469	248	364	231	300	20
U.N. MEDIUM ESTIMATE, 2000	6494	3777	568	330	818	333	652	35

SOURCE: Population Reference Bureau, *1972 World Population Data Sheet* (Washington D.C.: Population Reference Bureau, 1972).

[a] The table lists most U.N. members, and most geopolitical entities with a population larger than 200,000.
In the table, L indicates "estimated to be less than 5 per cent"; P—estimated to be less than U.S. $100; N.A.—not applicable: country has no urban community over 100,000; · · · — unavailable or unreliable.

[b] Estimates from United Nations, *Total Population Estimates for World, Regions and Countries, Each Year, 1950–1985*, Population Division Working Paper No. 34 (October 1970).

[c] Latest available year. Except for Northern American rates, estimates are essentially those available (January 1972) in *U.N. Population and Vital Statistics Report, Series A, XXIV, No. 1*, with adjustments as deemed necessary in view of deficiency of registration in some countries.

[d] Assuming no change in growth rate.

[e] Estimates from United Nations, *Total Population Estimates for World, Regions and Countries, Each Year, 1950–1985*, Population Division Working Paper No. 34 (October 1970).

[f] Latest available year. Derived from *U.N. World Population Prospects, 1965–1985, As Assessed in 1968*, Population Working Paper No. 30 (December 1969) and *U.N. Demographic Yearbook* (1970).

[g] Definition: Cities—Urbanized areas, metropolitan areas, and urbanized agglomerations as per Kingsley Davis, *World Urbanization 1950–1970, Volume I: Basic Data for Cities, Countries, and Regions* (Berkeley Calif.: University of California Press, 1969), Population Monograph Series No. 4.

[h] Estimates for 1970. Data from Kingsley Davis, *ibid.*

[i] 1969 data supplied by the International Bank for Reconstruction and Development.

[j] Total reflects U.N. adjustments for discrepancies in international migration data.

[k] For these countries, the U.N. estimates show a variation of more than 3 per cent from recent census figures. Because of uncertainty as to the completeness or accuracy of census data, the U.N. estimates are used.

[l] Nonsovereign country.

[m] Kuwait has a natural rate of increase of +3.6 and Malta has a natural rate of increase of +0.7. Their growth rate differs markedly from their rate of increase because their small base population is strongly affected by migration.

[n] Pakistan (West) 1972 estimated population 66.9 million.
Bangladesh 1972 estimated population 79.6 million.

[o] Reverted to Japan 15 May 1972.

[p] U.S. figures are based on National Center for Health Statistics, *Monthly Vital Statistics Rates, 20*, No. 12 (28 February), and Bureau of the Census, *Current Population Reports, Series P-25*, No. 476 (February 1972), Series D.

[q] Regional population totals take into account small areas not listed in the table.

Conditions have now changed. The relatively less crowded parts of the world are the developed nations, whose technologies require highly skilled workers. Therefore, these nations cannot help to reduce the problems of development in the underdeveloped world by serving as an escape valve for surplus population.[8] In fact, the developed nations are drawing the persons with the highest levels of skill from the underdeveloped world. This "brain drain" occurs between fairly well developed nations as well.[9]

Even if the possibility of emigration were not so limited, the difficulty for developing nations is compounded because rapid population increase leads to vast increases in the nonproductive parts of the population. Developing nations with their high rates of increase have proportionately more children. These children are nonproductive and require an increasing range of services, especially educational, if the nation is to seek development. These interactive processes—new technology requiring skilled manpower that is expensive to train, decreasing demand for immigrants in most of the world, rapid population growth—have led some investigators to the somber conclusion that parts of the world are doomed to increased misery and deprivations until their population growth is checked.[10] In fact, even that conclusion is optimistic to a degree. Because of the differences in the sizes of already living generations in a population that has gone through a period of rapid growth, such populations will continue to grow even if every mother in the new generation were to have only one daughter. The ratio of daughters to mothers is called the **net reproduction rate.** If every woman had only one daughter, the net reproduction rate would be one. Under those conditions, all other things being equal, the size of the population would *stabilize*, that is, it would neither decline nor grow. Table 10–2 shows what would happen in several nations if the net reproduction rate were to become one at once. From the table, it is easy to see that even if a reduction in fertility of an enormous magnitude were to take place, the population of the world would continue to grow rapidly. And the underdeveloped countries would have more increase than the developed countries.

---

[8] The developed nations are less crowded only in a relative sense. In absolute terms, the underdeveloped nations can be divided into an Asian group, which is very crowded, and an African–South American group, which is less crowded.

[9] For contrasting views, see F. J. van Hoek, *The Migration of High Level Manpower from Developing to Developed Countries* (The Hague: Mouton, 1970); and F. Bechhofer (ed.), *Population Growth and the Brain Drain* (Edinburgh: Edinburgh University Press, 1969).

[10] Fears of overpopulation are as old as Thomas Malthus (1766–1834), the eponym for *Malthusians*, or those who fear high fertility. His *Essay on the Principle of Population* (1798) is widely reprinted; for example, in Garrett Hardin, *Population, Evolution, and Birth Control* (San Francisco: W. H. Freeman, 1964), a book that also offers selections from modern Malthusians.

TABLE 10–2

Current and ultimate stationary populations, on the assumption that birth rates drop immediately to stationary level.

Country (Date)	Current population (× 1000)	Ultimate population	% Increase
Chile (1965)	8584	12,916	50.5
Colombia (1965)	17,993	29,786	65.5
Ecuador (1965)	5109	8518	66.7
Italy (1966)	53,128	62,189	17.1
Peru (1963)	14,713	23,080	56.9
United States			
(1966)	195,857	259,490	32.5
(1967)	197,863	267,096	35.0

SOURCE: Taken, with slight changes, from Nathan Keyfitz, "On the Momentum of Population Growth," *Demography*, 6 (1971), p. 72.

The discussion presented thus far suggests several major propositions. First, demographic processes vary in response to social adaptive mechanisms. The decline in death rates indicates that mortality responds to human invention and technology. The decline in fertility rates in developed nations shows that the level of fertility is not a biological constant but a function of the human social system. Second, to the extent that the adaptive mechanisms of society can be manipulated, demographic processes are subject to change and control. Once a certain level of technology becomes available to change adaptive mechanisms, demographic change will follow to the extent that the technology is actually employed in the society in question. Medical technology has been widely accepted and employed, though some resistance to it has been documented.[11] Practices to control fertility are less widely or readily accepted.[12] Third, many manipulations of adaptive mechanisms that have influenced demographic processes have had unanticipated consequences. (For example, introducing modern medical technology is intended to reduce misery in a population rather than to allow greater numbers to survive in misery.)

[11] Such resistance is often found in unexpected places. George Bernard Shaw opposed vaccination and ridiculed the practice in *Don Juan in Hell*.
[12] Resistance may come more from political and religious institutions than from individuals. Some illustrations are given in Richard L. Meier, *Modern Science and The Human Fertility Problem* (New York: John Wiley & Sons, Inc., 1959). Many studies have shown that official response to fertility control programs often lags behind popular attitudes. For example, see Mario Jaramillo-Gómez, "Medellin: A Case of Strong Resistance to Birth Control," *Demography*, V, (1968), pp. 811–826; this entire issue of *Demography* is devoted to fertility control.

CONTROLLING POPULATION GROWTH

In this section, two efforts to control the fertility of populations are considered. In one case, the efforts of several European nations to increase fertility are examined. In another, efforts by two nations to limit their births are compared.

Through most of modern history, European nations have equated a growing population with national strength and prosperity. The decline in the birth rates of these nations that began during the late 19th century was viewed as anything but an appropriate adjustment of the demographic process to the technology of industrialism. The nations of Europe felt that a calamity of prodigious proportions had overtaken them. As birth rates declined further, governments sought to change their demographic experience. Such concerns were not without precedents. Since the time of the Roman Empire, European nations had sought to encourage fertility. Augustus presented legislation that encouraged marriage, prohibited parents from keeping their children from marriage, allowed women with three or more children to wear distinctive dress, and gave fathers preferential treatment in appointment to public office.[13] In the early 20th century, European nations were following pronatalist policies of long precedent. In this century, however, the falling birth rate caused these incentives to be applied with unusual intensity in an effort to reverse a declining rate rather than to maintain an already high rate. Programs included family allowances, special honors for parents of large families, exemption from taxes and military service for fathers of large families, and marriage bonuses. Restrictions were placed on emigration to keep the population that had been produced within a country and on immigration to maintain a homogeneous population, then considered valuable.[14] The results of these efforts are difficult to measure, partly because adequate data are not always available and partly because it is not possible to say what would have happened to the birth rates in these countries if no programs had been in effect. One conclusion, however, is well substantiated: Programs had different effects in different places, and none was an overwhelming demonstration that government can increase fertility. Glass concludes that "an examination of the gross reproduction rates for France as a whole and for individual Departments [which are political subdivisions of the country], does not bring much evidence to support any contention that French population policy has succeeded in raising fertility."[15] By way of contrast, Germany was able to reverse the downward trend in its births.

[13] D. V. Glass, *Population Policies & Movements in Europe* (Oxford: Clarendon Press, 1940), pp. 86–87.
[14] D. V. Glass, *ibid.*, pp. 90–98.
[15] D. V. Glass, *ibid.*, p. 202.

Many of the same measures employed in France were used in Germany, but in Germany they may have been more effective. In addition the German government took strong steps to eradicate abortion, which was then one of the most effective methods of birth control available. Glass has shown that, though the program of encouraging births may have had some success, the increase in births in Germany could have been due entirely to the eradication of abortion, a claim made by the German government of the 1930's. The advent of World War II and the rapid return to fairly high levels of fertility in postwar Europe have confounded the influence of governmental policy on population growth. No clear-cut picture emerges because the effects of pronatalist policies are not themselves clear-cut. The overriding conclusion from the experience of European nations during the past century is that efforts to change the fertility patterns of the population by manipulating the behavior of individual families with rewards and sanctions have been of only limited utility. Changes in technology, such as the industrial revolution itself or the introduction of better medical techniques, cause more direct and dramatic changes in demographic processes.

An important question is raised by the European experience. Why did these nations have a declining birth rate? Why had they not continued with the high level of fertility from an earlier period and given themselves the increasing populations they desired? This question is important because it tests our knowledge of demographic processes. It also has important implications for nations that now seek to reduce their fertility.

During the decade of the 1960's, many underdeveloped nations realized that their then current rates of population increase were defeating their programs of national development. Economic and educational growth were unable to overcome the new burdens imposed by the growth of population. Perhaps for the first time in history large populations sought means to limit or control their increase.[16] These efforts reflected national policy rather than the desires of many individuals taken together, but evidence suggests that at least at the verbal, as opposed to the behavioral, level, the policies had widespread backing.[17] One precedent for such an effort began after World War II in Japan, where concern grew about whether a nation with limited land area and no further opportunity to expand at the expense of its neighbors could maintain an increasing population. Under the occupation army and the new Japanese government, programs were undertaken to limit the increase in the

[16] Controls such as allowing children to die from exposure had been practiced much earlier —in Sparta, for example.
[17] For a survey of current programs, see Dorothy L. Nortman, "Status of National Family Planning Programmes," *Population Studies, XXVI,* No. 1 (March 1972), pp. 5–18.

population. These programs consisted of legalized sterilization, induced abortion, and contraception.[18] On the face of it, the results are astounding. Japan had a birth rate of 30.2 per thousand persons per year immediately following World War II. This rate had declined to 17.2 per thousand by 1960.

The Japanese experience should be examined in a somewhat longer historical period. The postwar birth rate of 30.2 is fairly low compared with the underdeveloped nation's rate of over 40, which Japan had experienced earlier. Japan began to lower its birth rate to match its newly lowered death rate well before World War II, and the declining rates following the war can be regarded as a continuation of that process. It is essentially the same process that characterized the European countries following their industrialization. The governmental programs in Japan may have been only an incidental element in the urban–industrial process. Pointing out that the governmental program occurred after rates had begun to fall and that it was implemented through the private medical sector rather than through public agencies, Taeuber concludes that "the precipitant declines in the birth rate were products of the determination of most of the families of Japan to have only two children, not more and usually not less. The development came after almost a century of industrialization and urbanization. It accompanied a rate of economic growth even more miraculous than the rate of demographic transition." [19]

Since direct population policy does not seem to have been the causal factor in Japan or in Europe, the question of how other factors influence demographic change becomes more crucial. The Japanese experienced a very dramatic change in their demographic situation. The net reproduction rate can be used to illustrate this change. By 1956, the net reproduction rate had fallen below one in Japan. Such a reduced rate has continued until today. Ultimately, a net reproduction rate of less than one means that the population will cease to replace itself, although it may continue to grow for a while if there is a large proportion of young women. Japan, like the European nations of the 1930's, will be faced with the prospect of a declining population. Already some of her political leaders have suggested that a pronatalist policy may be needed in the future.

The Japanese example is illustrative of a principle: that a fall in fertility follows urban–industrial development, and that this decline is not limited to the culture of Western nations. This process, however it may be affected by cultural influences, extends from east to west, embraces different religious beliefs, and acts with and

[18] Irene Taeuber, "Population Growth in Less-Developed Countries," in Philip M. Hauser (ed.), The Population Dilemma, 2nd ed. (Englewood Cliffs, N.J.: Prentice Hall, Inc., 1969), pp. 46ff.
[19] Irene Taeuber, ibid., p. 49.

without the aid of governmental programs. These conclusions offer little evidence for optimism on the part of underdeveloped nations that feel they must control their population growth as a part of their efforts to encourage development. Yet investigators differ on their assessment of how effective such programs and policies have been. Bogue, who is among the most optimistic, states: "The years 1963–1964 very probably will go down in demographic history as one of the great landmarks of social science research progress. In the 12 months from June 1963 to June 1964 researchers in fertility control began to get a string of successes that leave no doubt that by planned intervention they have induced a downward change in the birthrate in high fertility populations." [20] Other views assign only an intensifying influence to such programs and emphasize that they are effective only where urban–industrial development is also taking place.[21] In any event, the rate of growth in the underdeveloped world has not been reduced overall, and more crowding is expected in the future in most of the world, regardless of how intensive the programs of population control may be. The effects of continued population growth will be examined in Chapter 11.

Thus far the influence of technology and social policy on population processes has been examined only with respect to fertility and population increase. These processes are basic in that their changes have influenced conditions in society to a considerable degree in recent years. The other element in the demographic equation, migration, has also been a subject of much concern to demographers because modern industrial technology is associated with changing patterns of migration. Migration offers a means of influencing population in an open demographic system that avoids the problems associated with increases in the dependent population that result when fertility is the means by which population increases.

MIGRATION AS A DEMOGRAPHIC PROCESS

Migration studies are generally divided into studies of **internal migration,** or that movement of populations which takes place within a nation, and **external migration,** or that movement which takes place among nations. External migration is fairly easy for a nation to control, although such controls are of fairly recent origin.[22] Internal migration is less subject to direct control, but technological change and the nature of the technology employed by a society influence the type and amount of migration that will take place.

[20] Donald J. Bogue, "Presidential Address," at a meeting of The Population Association of America, San Francisco, June 1964; and in *Principles of Demography* (New York: John Wiley & Sons, Inc., 1969), p. 824.
[21] For example, Dorothy L. Nortman, "Status of National Family Planning Programmes," *Population Studies*, XXVI, No. 1 (March 1972), points out that successes are limited to small areas such as Hong Kong.
[22] Thomas W. E. Rocke, *The Key in the Lock* (London: J. Murray, 1969) is a history of the English control of immigration.

External Migration

Efforts to control external migration may be simply described as the attempt to keep out undesirables and to attract desirables; however, the definition of what is desirable varies with the technological basis of the society and the size of the existing population. Throughout most of the history of the United States, a free immigration policy was in force—no restriction of any importance was placed on who could enter the country. By the second decade of the present century, however, fears that immigrants were "different" and undesirable were being voiced. Often the spokesmen for a restrictive policy argued that the new immigrants were Eastern and Southern Europeans, who were regarded as inferior to the earlier Anglo-Saxon and Northern European immigrants. Others argued that simply because the later migrants were different, they should be restricted in order to maintain a relatively homogeneous society.[23] It should not be overlooked that the country had become, for the first time in its history, predominantly urban, and the demand for unskilled labor had ceased to expand. The cultural objection to Eastern and Southern Europeans was voiced long after large numbers from those areas had entered the country. Thus the restrictive immigration policy of the 1920's is better regarded as a response to a changed demographic condition operating on a new technological base than as a cultural manifestation of anti-Eastern and anti-Southern European prejudice. The prejudicial aspects of the policy were incidental to the call for restriction.[24]

The liberalization of the immigration laws that occurred in the 1960's should be examined in the same light. The racial and national restrictions placed on immigration were removed; replacing them were "performance" definitions of desirable, highly skilled people, such as physicians, engineers, and so on; in other words, those whom the technology of the nation required were allowed to enter with little restriction. Thus the nation obtains exactly the kind of people it needs, while excluding those whose skills are less suited to the society. Here is an instance where public policy makers, regardless of the motives of the individuals involved, responded to the society's technological demands—a clear example of a culture's accommodation to technology.

Of course, external migration policy is not always rational. The degree of accommodation to technology may be small; a policy can be counterproductive. Indeed, accommodation to some phases of technology may be detrimental to some other phase.

[23] Some consequences of the Immigration Act are examined in Simon Kuznets and Ernest Rubin, *Immigration and the Foreign Born* (Washington, D.C.: National Bureau of Economic Research, Inc., 1954), Occasional Paper 46.
[24] The text in no way implies that prejudice was not a factor, but rather emphasizes that economic interest and prejudice generally go together.

Early in this century thousands of European immigrants flocked to the Promised Land of America. Later, immigration quotas were imposed to "refuse the refuse"—a popular outcry—and to admit only those with useful skills.
(Courtesy Ernst Haas, Magnum Photos, Inc.)

Nonetheless, even where control of demographic processes is as direct as in the case of immigration, technology rather than politics is the major ingredient.

Internal Migration

Internal migration may take any of several forms. Where nations control their people carefully, internal population movements may be nearly as closely regulated by governmental policy as immigration. In most of the world, internal migration is a *free* or *nearly free population movement,* where individuals determine for themselves whether they will move. Such decisions are not whims, however, and in the aggregate decisions to move are highly predictable. In fact, migration can be studied without reference to the motives and decisions of the individuals who move.[25]

One student of migration who does believe that the choices of individuals should be considered in a study of migration argues that free migration is a result of the balancing of the plus and minus factors of two different places.[26] When the attractions at the destination outweigh those at the origin, a move takes place. Pluses

---

[25] For example, the formulation of George K. Zipf, *Human Behavior and the Principle of Least Effort* (New York: Hafner Publishing Co., 1965), pp. 386–409.
[26] Everett S. Lee, "A Theory of Migration," *Demography, III,* (1966), pp. 47–57.

When weighing the attractions of a sweet, green California against the dust and hunger of Oklahoma and Arkansas, many farmers in the 1930's decided that the long westward trek was the only hope of survival.
(Courtesy Wide World Photos.)

and minuses are different for different people, which accounts for movement being more likely for some than for others, and explains why some areas exchange population with others. These differences in attraction are also a function of the level of technology. Industrial societies have a great deal of migration because opportunities (pluses) are frequently created by shifts in production.

Different pluses and minuses result from different levels of awareness of the potential movers, and from access to different lines of information. One implication of this aspect of the theory, therefore, is that migration should follow streams.[27] Moreover,

[27] Of course, the migrants themselves may become important sources of information and thereby help to perpetuate the stream by communicating with their friends and families.

these streams should be more specific when information is restricted. If informal lines of communication among people who know each other are the major or only sources of information, migration will take place between specific places. If general information about opportunities is available, migration from a given place will be to many different places. Under the assumption that whites have more sources of information than blacks, this theory predicts that white migration streams will be less specific with regard to destination than will black migration streams. Such was certainly the case in the United States in 1960 (see Table 10–3). That result is not unrelated to the actual as well as to the perceived distribution of opportunities. Since occupational opportunities are among the most important, this theory does indicate the extent to which the economic structure and its technological substructure influence free migration. Similar considerations can be applied to other *migration differentials:* age, sex, education, and occupation. As the opportunities vary within the nation and the knowledge of these opportunities is differentially available to a population that is unequally able to take advantage of them, migration occurs selectively and follows definable paths.

An additional element intrudes in migration in industrialized nations. A great deal of the population movement in such nations is routine and associated with transfers and regular career development within the corporate structure. Although such moves can be thought of as reflecting new opportunities for promotion and advancement, they can also be regarded as semiforced migration, in which the individual accommodates not to the changes in the technological base of society, but to the regular demands of the existing technology. Such analysis has not as yet been carried very far, but the implication is that additional development of the theory of migration is needed.

Summary

In this chapter, the basic processes by which population changes take place have been examined. Migration and natural increase have been examined as mechanisms of accommodation to a changing technology. The role of public policy in demographic processes has been examined, and the causes of changes in demographic factors have been considered. Some demographic indices have been introduced, and their applications illustrated. Several principles of demographic change have been discussed.

TABLE 10–3
Division of residence in 1960, by division of residence in 1955 and division of birth, for males five years old and over, by color (based on a 25 per cent sample).

Division of 1960 and 1955 residence, color, and sex	Total population, 5 years old and over[a]	BORN IN: New England	Middle Atlantic	East North Central	West North Central	South Atlantic	East South Central	West South Central	Mountain	Pacific
White—Male										
New England, 1960										
Total	4 430 662	3 329 155	271 369	66 123	28 833	51 118	15 909	16 945	8 838	18 056
New England, 1955	4 043 455	3 243 340	181 370	33 630	14 593	26 905	7 173	6 908	4 335	8 208
Middle Atlantic, 1955	101 746	17 292	67 168	3 166	1 170	2 486	566	566	331	745
East North Central, 1955	33 960	5 053	3 416	19 676	1 199	1 116	756	498	200	350
West North Central, 1955	12 063	1 849	805	872	6 747	357	185	391	124	241
South Atlantic, 1955	44 042	14 481	6 060	2 292	1 111	14 554	1 323	966	254	912
East South Central, 1955	7 563	1 571	593	401	188	554	3 610	229	34	121
West South Central, 1955	12 681	3 497	1 111	782	575	619	353	4 705	173	310
Mountain, 1955	7 678	2 033	781	677	496	340	132	423	2 139	330
Pacific, 1955	21 948	6 881	2 237	1 540	1 261	1 123	415	844	669	5 782
Abroad, 1955	63 956	13 936	5 074	2 100	1 123	2 303	1 127	1 135	469	864
1955 residence not reported	81 570	19 222	2 754	987	370	761	269	280	110	193
Middle Atlantic, 1960										
Total	13 626 055	235 861	10 449 538	233 565	75 847	234 153	47 800	42 591	21 126	38 388
New England, 1955	73 364	39 455	21 246	2 458	915	1 893	453	409	260	596
Middle Atlantic, 1955	12 775 362	180 376	10 212 434	167 042	52 830	176 051	31 888	26 256	13 856	23 497
East North Central, 1955	90 785	2 321	26 367	44 145	3 039	3 658	2 098	1 136	421	951
West North Central, 1955	22 055	553	5 679	2 035	10 079	702	298	656	320	444
South Atlantic, 1955	116 496	4 002	50 749	5 753	2 192	40 644	2 353	1 650	585	1 302
East South Central, 1955	17 909	474	5 673	1 124	393	1 457	7 254	431	109	226
West South Central, 1955	25 197	918	9 331	1 361	998	1 191	723	8 381	339	568

Mountain, 1955	13 618	420	6 006	950	755	500	189	443	3 229	487
Pacific, 1955	39 178	1 470	16 516	2 543	2 050	1 721	592	1 191	1 156	8 749
Abroad, 1955	224 018	3 416	36 602	3 873	1 800	3 613	1 266	1 479	661	1 112
1955 residence not reported	228 073	2 456	58 935	2 281	796	2 723	686	559	190	456
East North Central, 1960										
Total	14 470 283	78 704	489 846	10 922 515	469 119	343 018	619 166	152 764	46 961	57 383
New England, 1955	28 555	13 855	2 872	7 147	766	916	494	333	180	287
Middle Atlantic, 1955	117 871	2 755	78 477	18 422	2 456	3 691	1 420	950	423	785
East North Central, 1955	13 420 608	55 053	381 420	10 636 739	372 218	255 467	502 633	113 396	34 499	36 039
West North Central, 1955	117 745	726	2 700	31 004	68 808	1 559	2 784	3 625	1 226	1 239
South Atlantic, 1955	133 311	1 885	8 043	40 123	3 593	64 109	7 336	1 718	608	1 222
East South Central, 1955	117 613	404	1 761	17 666	1 889	4 205	86 350	1 767	336	430
West South Central, 1955	58 288	558	1 901	19 368	3 491	1 908	3 163	23 543	676	789
Mountain, 1955	29 166	376	1 190	13 833	2 613	946	1 103	1 062	6 145	768
Pacific, 1955	64 864	902	2 984	32 318	5 123	1 975	2 470	2 389	1 606	12 101
Abroad, 1955	146 722	1 348	4 883	42 672	4 370	3 993	4 318	2 235	811	1 202
1955 residence not reported	235 540	842	3 615	63 223	3 792	4 249	7 095	1 746	451	521
West North Central, 1960										
Total	6 447 026	20 151	67 596	361 285	5 269 715	46 420	66 403	181 313	60 672	53 073
New England, 1955	9 241	4 513	751	508	2 198	315	78	198	87	202
Middle Atlantic, 1955	23 317	645	13 875	1 587	3 906	712	305	368	182	264
East North Central, 1955	116 518	757	2 918	70 282	28 763	1 829	3 351	2 830	888	1 102
West North Central, 1955	5 940 975	11 174	41 175	267 577	5 092 836	26 878	47 300	130 647	42 951	35 062
South Atlantic, 1955	32 356	623	1 847	2 531	11 908	10 159	1 494	1 439	531	748
East South Central, 1955	17 162	155	488	1 232	4 374	696	8 370	985	201	184
West South Central, 1955	65 601	440	1 314	3 447	20 366	1 252	1 699	33 375	1 163	1 156
Mountain, 1955	39 978	281	860	2 765	18 687	638	611	2 695	10 980	1 363
Pacific, 1955	58 497	468	1 542	4 040	32 058	1 091	832	3 631	1 907	11 327
Abroad, 1955	54 084	824	2 074	4 239	25 428	2 200	1 582	3 072	1 134	1 271
1955 residence not reported	89 297	271	752	3 077	29 141	650	781	2 023	648	394
South Atlantic, 1960										
Total	8 819 164	168 015	642 829	424 114	141 006	6 355 688	404 451	116 143	32 248	57 922
New England, 1955 . .	84 677	54 787	8 487	2 780	1 329	6 894	1 215	834	333	942
Middle Atlantic, 1955	282 090	7 544	201 500	8 863	3 066	24 109	3 147	1 968	840	1 719
East North Central, 1955	237 772	2 788	13 152	145 848	7 385	34 224	13 006	3 003	998	1 711
West North Central, 1955	54 833	640	2 168	4 887	33 028	5 645	1 848	2 538	725	1 068

TABLE 10-3 (Continued)

Division of 1960 and 1955 residence, color, and sex	Total population, 5 years old and over[a]	BORN IN:								
		New England	Middle Atlantic	East North Central	West North Central	South Atlantic	East South Central	West South Central	Mountain	Pacific
White—Male (cont.)										
South Atlantic, 1960 (cont.)										
South Atlantic, 1955	7 535 240	88 696	378 864	225 671	74 097	6 130 483	270 962	56 207	14 673	24 712
East South Central, 1955	137 125	1 301	3 876	5 276	1 976	27 985	88 588	3 375	645	1 037
West South Central, 1955	73 177	1 249	4 072	4 678	3 299	16 432	5 627	32 610	1 190	1 576
Mountain, 1955	25 655	630	2 152	2 637	2 283	5 589	1 394	1 733	7 176	1 069
Pacific, 1955	78 645	2 737	6 954	7 455	6 090	19 316	4 623	5 205	3 008	19 381
Abroad, 1955	152 275	5 831	15 961	12 075	7 064	43 820	10 072	7 236	2 342	4 047
1955 residence not reported	157 675	1 762	5 643	3 944	1 389	41 191	3 969	1 407	318	660
East South Central, 1960										
Total	4 096 974	14 432	51 050	127 661	42 162	174 611	3 487 172	88 623	9 241	14 416
New England, 1955	7 164	4 282	436	231	188	399	1 071	117	27	89
Middle Atlantic, 1955	26 010	740	17 495	1 058	330	1 377	3 028	400	97	185
East North Central, 1955	94 364	420	1 958	36 460	1 910	3 139	46 239	1 567	294	416
West North Central, 1955	18 529	132	383	1 408	9 635	632	4 240	1 126	217	277
South Atlantic, 1955	91 846	1 135	3 530	3 794	1 543	41 968	34 375	2 237	450	753
East South Central, 1955	3 693 381	5 943	22 252	76 688	23 133	116 937	3 332 703	54 678	4 096	5 795
West South Central, 1955	51 924	325	1 017	1 830	1 611	2 436	19 766	22 854	479	537
Mountain, 1955	8 917	134	337	687	622	546	3 047	805	2 182	333
Pacific, 1955	22 329	337	829	1 563	1 356	1 474	8 475	1 733	774	5 114
Abroad, 1955	33 830	768	2 080	2 643	1 398	4 080	14 038	2 307	513	719
1955 residence not reported	48 680	218	733	1 299	436	1 623	20 190	799	112	198
West South Central, 1960										
Total	6 165 907	30 173	96 506	181 686	263 745	120 008	256 324	4 776 848	64 422	62 991
New England, 1955	15 108	8 970	1 187	564	376	530	331	2 078	154	249

1955 residence	Total	New England	Middle Atlantic	East North Central	West North Central	South Atlantic	East South Central	West South Central	Mountain	Pacific
Middle Atlantic, 1955	38 001	843	25 741	1 500	817	1 649	663	3 820	222	386
East North Central, 1955	74 069	579	2 408	41 926	3 937	2 216	4 029	14 701	652	701
West North Central, 1955	75 633	357	1 143	3 896	41 315	1 241	1 979	21 368	1 292	1 058
South Atlantic, 1955	66 990	1 417	4 386	3 756	2 599	30 085	5 585	14 763	819	1 264
East South Central, 1955	58 194	399	1 226	2 136	1 585	2 977	34 906	12 649	449	491
West South Central, 1955	5 508 927	14 231	51 049	113 221	195 666	70 164	197 441	4 580 177	42 524	35 959
Mountain, 1955	53 933	359	1 336	2 951	4 482	1 475	1 810	25 109	12 952	1 782
Pacific, 1955	80 460	789	2 278	4 153	6 138	2 420	2 678	38 431	2 866	17 873
Abroad, 1955	91 675	1 749	4 566	5 526	4 961	5 811	4 760	32 073	1 823	2 527
1955 residence not reported	102 917	480	1 186	2 057	1 869	1 440	2 142	31 679	669	701
Mountain, 1960										
Total	2 857 236	27 381	93 413	219 327	405 153	54 941	51 328	233 688	1 459 587	126 764
New England, 1955	11 111	7 078	1 011	504	340	252	188	193	697	228
Middle Atlantic, 1955	34 384	933	24 659	1 537	965	1 044	283	606	1 548	586
East North Central, 1955	79 238	597	3 242	55 251	5 438	2 110	2 726	1 931	3 297	1 073
West North Central, 1955	95 783	364	1 083	4 502	71 534	960	826	4 479	7 454	1 812
South Atlantic, 1955	32 336	787	3 138	2 853	2 206	13 775	1 775	1 711	3 602	1 315
East South Central, 1955	13 226	166	482	886	793	797	7 233	1 095	1 176	344
West South Central, 1955	80 705	594	1 617	3 478	5 671	1 869	2 427	52 501	7 610	1 994
Mountain, 1955	2 283 530	13 571	49 707	134 894	293 476	27 803	31 131	152 681	1 384 586	74 315
Pacific, 1955	127 287	1 649	4 606	9 148	16 320	2 963	2 419	11 679	31 302	41 604
Abroad, 1955	54 986	1 224	2 990	4 230	5 273	2 648	1 695	4 324	10 005	2 602
1955 residence not reported	44 670	418	878	2 024	3 137	720	625	2 488	8 310	891
Pacific, 1960										
Total	8 576 634	166 485	446 380	805 958	1 119 166	196 518	167 935	672 029	508 571	3 493 918
New England, 1955	52 283	33 897	4 374	2 154	1 595	1 461	588	874	652	2 895
Middle Atlantic, 1955	128 041	3 652	87 822	5 506	3 024	3 647	1 262	1 607	1 132	5 480
East North Central, 1955	221 412	2 140	9 546	151 857	12 681	5 797	7 694	4 560	2 710	9 055
West North Central, 1955	174 647	979	2 627	9 895	130 916	1 843	1 763	7 549	3 714	9 194
South Atlantic, 1955	114 684	4 990	12 143	10 830	7 411	47 074	5 696	5 980	2 854	12 312
East South Central, 1955	40 337	466	1 296	2 668	1 754	2 501	24 580	2 407	751	2 855
West South Central, 1955	150 003	1 323	3 654	6 574	8 881	3 654	4 473	93 360	3 989	12 260
Mountain, 1955	171 836	2 068	5 809	12 272	21 671	3 352	2 624	14 187	76 508	25 313
Pacific, 1955	7 108 159	110 799	304 378	582 908	907 672	116 255	111 790	518 240	403 778	3 363 878
Abroad, 1955	232 826	4 333	10 512	13 831	15 339	8 429	5 428	13 281	7 998	29 146
1955 residence not reported	182 406	1 838	4 219	7 443	8 222	2 505	2 097	7 684	4 485	21 019

TABLE 10–3 (Continued)

Division of 1960 and 1955 residence, color, and sex	Total population, 5 years old and over^a	BORN IN:								
		New England	Middle Atlantic	East North Central	West North Central	South Atlantic	East South Central	West South Central	Mountain	Pacific
Nonwhite—Male										
New England, 1960										
Total	111 253	41 447	5 311	1 651	645	32 319	5 769	2 566	140	866
New England, 1955	84 459	39 844	3 078	759	313	23 073	3 553	1 342	55	417
Middle Atlantic, 1955	3 641	239	1 520	50	17	1 074	147	72	16	50
East North Central, 1955	1 299	47	64	513	27	222	248	70	...	28
West North Central, 1955	370	33	19	26	139	39	30	36	4	8
South Atlantic, 1955	7 171	243	166	60	22	5 859	262	124	...	42
East South Central, 1955	1 240	47	17	4	18	93	988	21	5	...
West South Central, 1955	767	41	16	13	...	129	58	479	4	4
Mountain, 1955	205	17	8	13	8	54	28	27	24	7
Pacific, 1955	794	28	39	40	23	152	43	105	12	240
Abroad, 1955	4 908	189	200	84	45	692	236	184	13	47
1955 residence not reported	6 399	719	184	89	33	932	176	106	7	23
Middle Atlantic, 1960										
Total	1 182 216	5 154	507 776	11 518	3 485	409 204	57 500	15 191	795	4 204
New England, 1955	2 154	562	363	37	28	544	127	48	4	46
Middle Atlantic, 1955	1 041 855	4 263	493 464	8 693	2 728	354 320	48 532	12 302	627	3 103
East North Central, 1955	5 776	21	654	1 875	96	1 222	1 031	247	26	89
West North Central, 1955	916	...	134	27	335	109	122	43	3	22
South Atlantic, 1955	48 553	91	3 371	223	66	41 531	840	227	12	60
East South Central, 1955	5 947	8	309	64	9	386	4 854	39	...	12
West South Central, 1955	2 400	8	255	18	8	324	200	1 450	6	3
Mountain, 1955	490	8	150	4	4	108	46	54	71	16
Pacific, 1955	2 398	29	425	87	37	419	135	178	14	680
Abroad, 1955	18 123	46	1 284	202	60	1 822	459	270	22	86
1955 residence not reported	53 604	118	7 367	288	114	8 419	1 154	333	10	87

East North Central, 1960

1955 residence	Total									
Total	1 223 304	1 179	12 471	451 048	22 619	142 998	370 687	99 822	1 486	7 065
New England, 1955	775	184	26	128	13	133	127	43	14	21
Middle Atlantic, 1955	5 237	11	2 096	563	47	1 103	744	210	5	40
East North Central, 1955	1 077 780	886	9 500	439 616	19 545	127 772	327 785	87 982	1 105	5 579
West North Central, 1955	5 146	..	46	544	2 102	178	1 321	621	16	39
South Atlantic, 1955	13 262	26	141	1 007	79	9 885	1 360	235	8	63
East South Central, 1955	34 346	..	70	1 259	122	588	30 767	512	..	16
West South Central, 1955	10 123	8	41	601	62	199	1 086	7 659	5	40
Mountain, 1955	1 153	..	23	291	61	130	185	130	218	39
Pacific, 1955	3 224	23	63	678	54	221	564	405	32	936
Abroad, 1955	9 121	25	217	1 090	122	582	1 162	341	30	159
1955 residence not reported	63 137	16	248	5 271	412	2 207	5 586	1 684	52	133

West North Central, 1960

1955 residence	Total									
Total	265 970	235	1 508	7 087	137 188	6 283	44 556	43 593	1 365	2 131
New England, 1955	275	51	12	15	75	29	4	50	..	12
Middle Atlantic, 1955	1 198	8	517	35	78	272	92	49	3	26
East North Central, 1955	5 105	10	41	2 052	814	233	1 075	559	46	78
West North Central, 1955	227 281	135	616	4 443	132 235	3 571	37 246	35 712	691	1 197
South Atlantic, 1955	1 871	12	31	66	191	1 161	167	103	8	62
East South Central, 1955	4 667	..	13	66	182	102	4 013	144	..	6
West South Central, 1955	6 701	4	53	46	468	104	569	5 259	22	38
Mountain, 1955	1 307	..	15	5	335	74	70	221	497	25
Pacific, 1955	2 060	..	53	54	568	136	130	377	35	530
Abroad, 1955	4 058	8	117	188	476	471	373	336	7	118
1955 residence not reported	11 447	7	40	117	1 766	130	817	783	56	39

South Atlantic, 1960

1955 residence	Total									
Total	2 447 626	2 177	26 784	9 323	2 595	2 217 894	62 789	11 901	628	3 176
New England, 1955	1 900	482	93	45	12	882	52	40	8	63
Middle Atlantic, 1955	18 526	60	6 475	177	44	9 835	663	208	16	72
East North Central, 1955	8 842	14	183	2 978	179	3 099	1 518	343	..	57
West North Central, 1955	1 753	..	48	59	616	558	179	141	15	35
South Atlantic, 1955	2 311 580	1 437	18 517	5 226	1 423	2 170 897	46 505	6 836	351	1 423
East South Central, 1955	13 950	13	124	120	38	2 289	10 762	232	..	37
West South Central, 1955	4 950	8	68	58	46	1 434	429	2 706	13	28
Mountain, 1955	790	..	40	49	16	306	83	70	158	18

TABLE 10–3 (Continued)

Nonwhite—Male (cont.)

Division of 1960 and 1955 residence, color, and sex	Total population, 5 years old and over[a]	BORN IN:								
		New England	Middle Atlantic	East North Central	West North Central	South Atlantic	East South Central	West South Central	Mountain	Pacific
South Atlantic, 1960 (cont.)										
Pacific, 1955	3 786	32	153	109	83	1 223	257	403	48	999
Abroad, 1955	18 736	65	538	289	110	5 065	1 029	630	26	349
1955 residence not reported	62 813	66	545	213	28	22 306	1 312	292	13	95
East South Central, 1960										
Total	1 098 620	215	2 233	6 823	1 531	25 750	1 025 063	14 893	225	755
New England, 1955	213	35	8	4	4	40	109	4	...	...
Middle Atlantic, 1955	2 132	8	801	44	14	281	859	31	...	...
East North Central, 1955	8 102	8	21	1 884	84	266	5 470	196	4	65
West North Central, 1955	1 120	...	5	57	222	37	682	86	...	13
South Atlantic, 1955	7 391	27	75	50	33	4 382	2 467	154	5	8
East South Central, 1955	1 058 489	115	1 007	4 479	1 064	19 687	1 005 804	12 115	121	335
West South Central	3 835	...	29	29	19	101	1 757	1 825	12	12
Mountain, 1955	373	...	12	4	...	20	249	22	58	4
Pacific, 1955	1 187	...	25	24	8	47	647	84	28	260
Abroad, 1955	2 992	13	92	79	23	408	1 185	196	...	37
1955 residence not reported	12 786	9	158	169	60	481	5 834	180	9	21
West South Central, 1960										
Total	1 168 722	328	2 670	4 767	3 973	11 899	51 257	1 046 525	1 598	3 813
New England, 1955	447	138	15	9	4	103	42	101	...	8
Middle Atlantic, 1955	2 644	4	1 264	48	15	382	135	538	4	17
East North Central, 1955	5 624	8	61	1 882	106	247	847	2 223	16	53
West North Central, 1955	2 639	...	41	57	725	67	203	1 436	12	25
South Atlantic, 1955	4 669	15	172	42	22	3 058	363	795	12	46

	Total	New England	Middle Atlantic	East North Central	West North Central	South Atlantic	East South Central	West South Central	Mountain	Pacific
East South Central, 1955	7 915	...	23	72	20	250	6 167	1 197	8	11
West South Central, 1955	1 104 887	134	814	2 270	2 785	6 430	42 089	1 023 723	859	2 178
Mountain, 1955	2 326	...	33	41	53	106	129	1 332	550	35
Pacific, 1955	5 778	9	60	60	86	261	226	3 445	53	1 231
Abroad, 1955	5 519	20	137	173	92	682	534	1 918	12	144
1955 residence not reported	26 274	...	50	113	65	313	522	9 817	72	65
Mountain, 1960										
Total	142 656	181	1 158	1 940	4 241	3 587	5 316	23 870	87 423	4 350
New England, 1955	169	56	19	...	...	25	7	31	4	...
Middle Atlantic, 1955	833	9	421	21	11	172	63	31	8	24
East North Central, 1955	1 597	...	53	660	75	128	275	199	69	62
West North Central, 1955	1 825	...	22	70	853	46	115	433	153	39
South Atlantic, 1955	1 488	9	49	26	34	1 041	99	102	41	33
East South Central, 1955	1 211	...	9	13	11	66	956	80	26	9
West South Central, 1955	5 621	20	29	63	65	128	210	4 461	404	54
Mountain, 1955	118 756	64	347	824	2 837	1 303	2 995	16 927	84 592	2 608
Pacific, 1955	4 344	5	31	85	163	128	202	982	864	1 318
Abroad, 1955	2 853	14	141	119	88	420	240	289	182	136
1955 residence not reported	3 959	4	37	59	104	130	154	335	1 080	67
Pacific, 1960										
Total	833 401	1 471	8 519	16 535	15 096	27 554	48 427	171 612	12 684	368 872
New England, 1955	1 357	359	70	39	39	174	80	116	5	180
Middle Atlantic, 1955	6 336	45	2 819	155	96	1 126	382	307	30	602
East North Central, 1955	13 754	21	240	5 612	409	946	2 403	1 526	95	1 551
West North Central, 1955	5 705	12	33	139	2 975	145	502	1 054	56	461
South Atlantic, 1955	8 986	51	263	224	81	5 905	579	560	38	647
East South Central, 1955	9 332	9	44	132	51	305	8 008	298	7	218
West South Central, 1955	25 059	11	91	170	148	388	689	21 856	49	844
Mountain, 1955	6 929	16	82	147	231	287	309	1 455	2 634	968
Pacific, 1955	696 855	861	4 244	9 069	10 366	15 926	33 394	138 726	9 116	356 079
Abroad, 1955	30 087	64	408	463	326	1 628	1 040	2 102	213	4 669
1955 residence not reported	29 001	22	225	385	374	724	1 041	3 612	241	2 653

SOURCE: Bureau of the Census, U.S. Census of Population, 1960, Recent Lifetime and Migration (Washington, D.C.: U.S. Government Printing Office, 1960). Special Report.

a Includes persons for whom state of birth was not reported.

Exercises

1. A stable population could be obtained by having most women marry and have families with about two children. An alternative would be for fewer women to bear children, but for them to have larger families. What are some implications for these different patterns of fertility for society at large? For family life? For the genetic structure of the population?

2. What types of program would you employ to increase population?

3. What program would you employ to decrease the rate of population growth?

4. How many people should the United States have? How did you arrive at that figure? Would your answer be different for India? Why?

5. What immigration policy should the United States have? Should this policy be related to the policies of other nations? Why?

6. Migration can be regarded as a means of adapting the distribution of the population to changing environmental and technological conditions. Some migration can be regarded as dysfunctional. How can these differences be resolved within a single theory?

7. Using the demographic equation and population values for one state in the United States, project that population to the year 2000. What might cause your projection to be in error? How can it be improved?

8. Examine death rates for several countries. What might be some of the reasons that the rates in the United States are not the lowest in the world? Should they be expected to fall during the next decade?

9. Most birth control programs stress the idea of voluntary use of contraceptives or sterilization. Involuntary methods of control have been suggested, and new procedures might make governmental control of fertility without the consent of the population relatively easy. Evaluate such a program demographically and socially.

10. Why is life expectation at birth so much greater in developed nations than in underdeveloped nations, while the difference in life expectation at later ages is less pronounced?

Selected Bibliography

Barclay, George W. *Techniques of Population Analysis.* New York: John Wiley & Sons, Inc., 1958.

Carr-Saunders, A. M. *World Population: Past Growth and Present Trends.* London: Cass, 1964.

Davis, Kingsley. *The Population of India and Pakistan.* Princeton, N.J.: Princeton University Press, 1951.

Ford, Thomas R., and Gordon F. DeJong (eds.). *Social Demography*. Englewood Cliffs, N.J.: Prentice–Hall, Inc., 1970.

Freedman, Ronald (ed.). *Population: The Vital Revolution*. Garden City, N.Y.: Doubleday & Company, Inc., 1964.

Glass, D. V. *Population Policies and Movements in Europe*. Oxford: Clarendon Press, 1940.

Petersen, William. *Population*. New York: The Macmillan Company, 1969.

Shryock, Henry S., Jacob S. Siegel, and Associates, for the U. S. Bureau of the Census. *The Methods and Materials of Demography*. Washington, D.C.: U. S. Government Printing Office, 1971.

Taeuber, Irene B., and Conrad Taeuber, for the U. S. Bureau of the Census. *People of the United States in the 20th Century*. Washington, D.C.: U. S. Government Printing Office, 1971. A Census Monograph.

U. S. Bureau of the Census, *Historical Statistics of the United States, Colonial Times to 1957*. Washington, D.C.: U. S. Government Printing Office, 1960. See the *Supplement* to this as well.

Westoff, Charles F., and Raymond H. Potvin. *College Women and Fertility Values*. Princeton, N.J.: Princeton University Press, 1967.

11

Major Consequences of Population Changes

Using the terminology and framework that were defined and developed in Chapter 10, we will now focus on the ways that demographic processes affect society. This chapter differs from the previous one primarily in the way the variables described in Chapter 10 are employed, for here our concern is with the consequences of demographic processes. In the language of social scientists, we shall examine demographic factors here as independent variables.[1] Demographic causes and their consequences must be viewed as situationally determined and defined with respect to a given analytical purpose—*not as general laws* that describe a static situation in which one factor is always the cause and another is always its effect. For example, earlier the influence of social class on fertility was examined, and evidence was presented to show that social class influences fertility. In another context, it is possible that fertility may influence social class. Consider the case where a large family limits the educational opportunity for all the children because of fixed resources in the family. Under such cases, high fertility would likely lead to lower social class. To examine the second case is not

[1] Independent variables are the variables the researcher "sets" at different levels (or assigns different values) so that he can observe the changes in the dependent variables. In experimental research, the independent variable is manipulated by the researcher, but, in survey research, he must "find" the proper values. Independent variables are not necessarily causal variables.

to ignore the first, but to use a different emphasis. That sort of emphasis and an awareness of the complexity of cause and effect relations guide this chapter.

Generally, there are three ways in which demographic processes are studied. First, they are studied as they relate to each other. This case has been called **formal demography.**[2] Second, they are examined as results of other processes such as economic conditions or the psychological relations in families. Such study, as examined in Chapter 10, is sometimes called **population study,** though others prefer to call it **demography,** or **social demography, economic demography, biological demography,** and so on, depending on the area from which the independent variables have been drawn. The third type of analysis, where demographic factors are themselves the independent variables, is the basis of this chapter.

To say that demographic processes—fertility, mortality, morbidity, and migration can be predicted in many different ways for different purposes is only a partially useful conclusion. The advantage of such prediction rests on the consequences of demographic changes. If their consequences are vital, then it is necessary to be able to set them down, to indicate how demographic factors influence social life. Furthermore, perhaps more than one kind of consequence is involved. The exposition of the problem, however, is best obtained in terms of a *simple* scheme: Just as the factors influencing demographic variables were considered in terms of the components of the demographic equation, this chapter looks at the implications of demographic factors in terms of the demographic equation. Each of the elements of the equation has important consequences for the society. Since these elements are related to each other, some of their influences are indirect, for example, when illnesses that lead to deaths of young women also decrease the fertility of a population. One of the most crucial influences of demographic factors on society is through the effect of the total population size. Hence, in addition to the elements of change in the demographic equation—migration, fertility, and mortality—the combined result of those factors, total population size, will be examined separately. Accordingly, this chapter is organized in four major parts.

CONSEQUENCES OF MIGRATION

Though history is filled with examples of long and tedious migrations, from the wandering Jews to the trekking Boers, to the displaced millions following the Second World War, migration is, in some respects, a rapid process. Migration can change the size of a

---

[2] A good review of the scope of population study can be found in T. Lynn Smith and Paul E. Zopf, Jr., *Demography: Principles and Methods* (Philadelphia: F. A. Davis Company, 1970), pp. 1–17.

population almost as quickly as disaster and war, and unlike those processes, migration can increase, as well as decrease, a population. But, whether it be the movement of a whole nation or simply a change of residence by a family from one community to another, migration poses problems in the study of human adaptation. Since migration serves as a mechanism of adaptation in many different ways, it will have many different consequences. In some cases, a society may use migration to enlarge or diminish its unskilled worker population, or to obtain skilled persons that the society needs. In other cases, migration is an orderly means society uses to match the skills of its population to its needs for them as defined by a changing technology. In every case, certain problems or difficulties are encountered and must be overcome. The major source of these problems lies in the fact that migration, regardless of its form, in some degree or another places adult persons in environments and conditions for which they were not socialized or were only partly socialized. The migrant is either a stranger to a community or a newcomer to a strange land. Even the most routine residential change in modern industrial society involves meeting new people, learning new ways, dealing with new situations.

      Setting aside the case of movement into empty territory, a case of little recent historical importance and almost no importance at the present time, migration always involves some combination of *conflict, accommodation, acculturation,* and *dominance.*

There is much confusion and adjustment facing an immigrant to a new land.
(Courtesy Ernst Haas, Magnum Photos, Inc.)

Depending on the conditions, one or the other of these may be minimal or, for practical purposes, absent. Most residential changes in modern America carry with them only minimal conflict, although any school boy who has enrolled in a new school and any factory manager who has been moved to a new job will recognize that some conflict is inherent in being the new boy or the new boss. Even so, learning the new way, exercising cooperation, becoming acculturated, is relatively easy in most such cases. Although only in western movies and street gangs is the stranger required to prove himself by combat, serious problems can be generated and conflict may erupt even in a mobile society. The movement of blacks to large cities in America led to riots, and the so-called "hard-hat" reaction against black competition is important currently.[3]

The difficulty of such moves, however, especially for those who are not prepared for or used to them, cannot be overlooked. Homesickness and culture shock are real and affect most if not all migrants.[4] Though migration would not take place unless there were some advantage, real or imagined, to the migrant, migration also brings problems for the migrant. The consequences of migration, however, are not limited to the impact of new places, people, and things on the mover. The community he leaves (except in the case where everyone leaves together) and the community to which he moves must deal with changed conditions. Of course, one migrant is relatively unimportant, but hundreds and thousands pose serious problems for a nation, whether the migration is from that nation, to it, or within it.

The relocation of population in the United States between 1960 and 1970 will serve to show how great an influence is exercised by "normal movement" of the population in an industrial state. The United States began the decade of the 1960's with about one third of its population in large cities, that is, cities with populations of more than 50,000. That condition represented an enormous change in a nation that had been predominantly rural for most of its history. In fact, in 1960, the population was nearly equally divided into thirds: one third lived in large cities, one third lived in the urban areas surrounding those cities, and the other one third lived in the rest of the country.

By 1970, this distribution had been radically changed. The population residing in the areas surrounding the cities increased by 28 per cent or 16.8 million, while that in the cities themselves increased by only 5 per cent or 3.2 million. Most of the nation's

---

[3] The history of racial violence is covered quite well in Hugh Davis Graham and Ted Robert Gurr, *Violence in America* (New York: The New American Library, 1969), pp. 377–440. This is the report from the National Commission on the Causes and Prevention of Violence.
[4] *Culture shock* is a term used to label the disorganization and sense of discomfort experienced when a person is deprived of the expected signs and signals he receives in his usual habitat because he has been placed in another habitat.

increase in population during the decade was in the areas surrounding cities of 50,000 or more people.[5] This redistribution alone would be significant, because it resulted primarily from migration rather than differences in fertility. To compound the problem, movement from one metropolitan area (the large cities and their environs) to another was enormous. By 1970, nearly half the members of the population of the United States were living outside their state of birth. In the single year of March 1970 to March 1971, nearly 18 per cent of the population over one year of age changed residences, and 6.5 per cent moved from one county to another.[6] That pattern has been quite stable, as shown in Figure 11–1. Hence many communities are affected by changes in residence. New public facilities, new housing, new office space, new stores, and service companies have to be constructed in many places. Often such rapid growth taxes the resources of a community and conditions become worse rather than better. At the same time, some facilities may be unused or underutilized in areas that lose migrants rather than gain them. The countryside of many parts of the nation is dotted with abandoned houses, and the main streets of small towns offer empty stores no one wants to use. These consequences of migration are shown in the census reports. The number of small towns with populations of 2000 to 5000 has decreased; during the same periods, the number of places with populations of less than 1000 has increased because of the reduction in size of towns with 2000 to 5000 people.[7]

Even large cities experience some of the same problems, though not in the same dramatic degree. Of the 12 largest cities in the nation, 9 had a population decline during the decade. Though many of these places may extend their boundaries into the surrounding suburbs, which grew in every case, the shifts in population have reduced their residents, their voters, and their individual taxpayers, at least for a time.

Migration affects the migrant, the community of destination, and the community of origin. It can also extend its influence to other areas. One dramatic indication of how population movement can affect many distant places is offered by recent history in India and Pakistan. International conflicts must be viewed in

[5] Standard Metropolitan Statistical Areas (SMSA) are defined as cities of 50,000 or more population (or twin cities both of which are greater than 25,000) and the surrounding counties with which they are closely related. The political boundary of the city defines the "central city" and the rest of the SMSA is called the "ring" ("suburb" is often loosely used instead). These are the divisions on which the materials in the text are based.

[6] U.S. Bureau of the Census, *Current Population Reports: Mobility of the Population of the United States March 1970–March 1971* (Washington, D.C.: U.S. Government Printing Office, 1972), Series P-20, No. 235.

[7] A thorough examination of population redistribution can be found in Irene B. Taeuber and Conrad Taeuber for the U.S. Bureau of the Census, *People of the United States in the 20th Century* (Washington, D.C.: U.S. Government Printing Office, 1971), A Census Monograph.

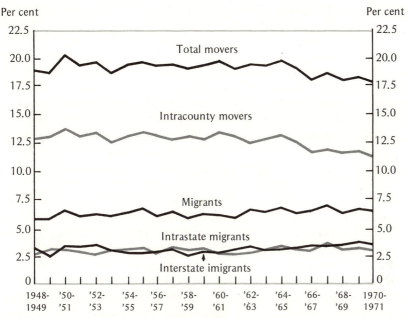

FIGURE 11–1   Movers by type of mobility as a per cent of the population one year old or over, for the United States, from April 1949 to March 1971.

terms of many causes and elements. As yet, no definitive history of the relations of India to Pakistan has been written. When it is written, Indian fears of Pakistan's alliances and Pakistan's fears of India's intentions will no doubt be cited as causes of the conflict, at least in some degree. Whatever the final verdict of history, the immediate cause of conflict was the movement of large numbers of the natives of East Pakistan into areas of India.[8] Their movement illustrates the nature of large population movements. Fleeing from conditions they found intolerable, they abandoned their homes and jobs to seek more favorable conditions elsewhere. A large number of migrants naturally increases the competition among them for positions in the community of destination. In this case, the re-sources of that community, which was in India, were so limited that conflict among the migrants and the native Indians became in-evitable. There were simply no places for so many. Whether India was morally justified in using force to return the migrants to Pakistan is beyond the scope of a work in sociology. The fact remains that migration induces conflict and does so in greater degree when eco-nomic accommodation is difficult. Some changes in the Indian community had to be made either to keep, return, or destroy the

[8] The movement was a result of internal conflict in East Pakistan, which later became the independent nation Bangladesh. Newspapers reported the population movement in the millions, but no exact figures are known.

guests they could not support. The war itself, though not necessary, is one of a class of results, all involving extreme conflict that had to occur.

Those consequences of the India–Pakistan conflict were not limited to a single nation or to the pair of nations involved. Distant people sent money, weapons, advice, ships, and food; great nations with little direct interest in the area were also brought to the point of conflict—all, in some degree, because migration has far-reaching consequences.

CONSEQUENCES OF FERTILITY

One obviously immediate consequence of high fertility is a large number of children. But along with the production of children, fertility has other consequences of immediate importance to the society. Pregnancy reduces the ability of women to perform certain tasks, and the presence of children requires that some agency, generally women and often the biological mother, be assigned to care for them during the period of dependency discussed earlier. Although the birth of the first child begins the period in the life cycle that is characterized by child care, the length of that period is determined primarily by the level of fertility. Large numbers of children influence the mother's health and the health of the children in families. Variations in fertility restrict or offer opportunities to each generation, while changing and timing demands made on communities for services. A case in point is the changing pattern of fertility in the United States during the past 50 years. Somewhat simplified, the pattern was one of relatively high fertility during the 1920's, with a decline in the 1930's that lasted until the post-World War II "baby boom"—a period of fairly high fertility, which began to decline about 1957.

The increased births between 1945 and 1950 imply an increase in primary-school-aged children between 1951 and 1956. Thus the change in fertility required community resources on a much larger scale for primary education. As the cohort aged, educational needs grew at each level, so that massive programs to expand educational resources were required. However, the lower birth rates of the 1930's are also important. Because those rates were low, the cohort of the 1930's was small. Hence the pool from which new teachers could be selected in the 1950's was also relatively small. Thus the variations in fertility created a demand and reduced the ability of the society to satisfy it. Moreover, the consequences of the pattern continue. The lower fertility pattern of the 1960's will produce relatively fewer children for education in the 1970's; at the same time, the numbers of people in their twenties will be large, and a great many of them have been trained as teachers.

Such a pattern affects any society with a changing fertility pattern. Members of the small cohort are courted by society with easy jobs and early promotion, while those of the large cohort must compete more intensively for the positions available.

Like other social processes, the pattern of human fertility is subject to moral evaluation by the human community. Fertility has become a subject for debate and discussion in almost every area of American society, and a major social movement has been raised to encourage the use of birth control. That social movement has engendered movements favoring and opposing abortion, as well as other associated legal and political decisions of far-reaching consequence.[9]

Fertility and the Labor Force

It is interesting to speculate on the number of ways societies could reduce the tendency of high fertility to restrict the participation of women in the labor force. It is certainly true that many factors, economic and social, influence the employment of women. Generally, however, women's participation in the labor force is infleunced by high fertility in two ways. First, women with many children are less likely to join the labor fôrce at all; second, when they do join, they join at different points in their lives, before and after rearing their children. At the same time, even women who continue to work while having children are absent from work for reasons associated with pregnancy. Though evidence from other societies indicates that time lost from work for childbearing need not be as great as it is in our society, the amount of time lost is clearly increased by bearing more children.[10] In the United States, the rate of participation in the labor force for women aged 24 to 44, the years of major responsibility for child rearing, increased steadily from 15.1 per cent in 1890 to 40.2 per cent in 1962. During that period, there was a general decline in fertility, the size of family, and a shortening of the childbearing years. Moreover, the rate of change in the labor force participation rate is lower during the periods of relatively high fertility.[11] Other nations experiencing declines in fertility also have larger numbers of women at work. It should be remembered that these forces influence each other.

[9] Many groups and approaches are involved in the birth control movement. Examples of efforts a current group is making are contained in Lawrence Lader, *Breeding Ourselves to Death* (New York: Ballantine Books, 1971).

[10] Other factors also influence women's availability for work. Weaning, for example, varies from about six months of age in the American middle class to over five years of age among the Chenchu tribe of India. See John W. M. Whiting and Irwin L. Child, *Child Training and Personality* (New Haven, Conn.: Yale University Press, 1953), p. 71.

[11] See U.S. Bureau of the Census, *Historical Statistics of the United States, Colonial Times to 1957;* and *Supplement to 1962* (Washington, D.C.: U.S. Government Printing Office, 1960; 1963).

The industrial technology provides jobs for women. In addition, women have reduced fertility so they are able to work; however, working may make reduced fertility necessary. Thus, as this sequence illustrates, cause and consequence influence each other.

Fertility and the Health of Children

The size of families has often been used to indicate an important source of social stability. Many early investigators felt that large families led to better adjusted children and more productive adults.[12] Some went so far as to condemn the single-child family as a major source of mental illness.[13] Later analysis has shown such views to be incorrect, and the example serves to demonstrate how frequently social science espouses the values of its times rather than developing views based on the results of scientific investigation. Recently, other aspects of the large family have come under examination. One such aspect subject to examination is high parity[14] and its consequences. Though fairly high rates of fertility can be maintained if childbearing occurs in the early years of a woman's life, generally high parity is associated with births in the later years.[15] Such births are known to have a greater chance of early death. There is also some indication that high parity children suffer more deformity and mental illness.[16] These conclusions regarding the effects of high parity require careful interpretation since some of these factors are associated with social class, which is also associated with fertility.[17] In any event, the outlook for children in a large family is not especially advantageous.

Consequences to Society of Changing Fertility

Though the level of fertility has implications for society, changes in that level have had important and immediate consequences in recent history. The immediate demographic result of a change in fertility is reflected in the age structure of the population. If fertility increases, the number of dependent persons in the population relative to productive workers is increased, a condition that continues for at least 15 years. For example, if an additional 500,000 children were

[12] Even early evidence was not favorable to large families. See John J. B. Morgan, *Child Psychology* (New York: Farrar and Rinehart, Inc., 1934).
[13] Alexandra Adler was one such proponent of multichild families. See Alexandra Adler, "The Only Child," in Alfred Adler, *Guiding the Child* (London: George Allen and Unwin, 1930).
[14] Parity refers to the number of children a woman has had or the birth order of the last child.
[15] High parity and a prolonged childbearing period extending to the later years are both related to education and income in the United States.
[16] One study of many in this area is J. Yerushalmy, "Neonatal Mortality by Order of Birth and Age of Parents," *Amer. J. of Hygiene*, XVIII (1938), pp. 244–270.
[17] Sir Dugald Baird emphasizes the role of social class in "Social Class and Fetal Mortality," *Lancet, II* (October 1947), pp. 531–535.

born in the United States each year for an indefinite period of time, it would be 18 years before the first of them would reach the ordinary age of high school graduation. Ignoring death among the group, during those 18 years about 9 million people would have been added to the group that would have formed the dependent population had the current fertility rates been maintained. In fact, such a change has historical precedent. The change in the number of live births between 1945 and 1946 was 553,000, and the number of births continued to increase until 1962, when it fell slightly; 1,410,000 more children were born in 1961, the peak year, than were born in 1945. Such large numbers of children posed problems in school construction. They indicated higher rates of housing construction, and greater demands for goods and services associated with children—toys, games, bicycles, and clothing.

On the other hand, when fertility declines, the dependent population decreases (except when increasing numbers of old people are present, as is the case now in the United States). Just as an increase in births will add an extra number to the dependent population, a decrease will reduce the burden. While the population of the United States is not likely to decrease in the near future, the number of people under 18 years old will decrease. If our births fall by 500,000 per year, which they may well do, then we can anticipate that, in 18 years, there will be about 9 million fewer persons under 18 years of age than would have been the case had the fertility rate remained at its current level. That is not to say that we would have 9 million fewer persons under 18 years of age than we now have since our births have not been constant for 18 years. But the number would be significantly smaller, and in fact much smaller than a projection of the increases of the recent past would have indicated. Fewer, rather than more, classrooms would be needed; toy manufacturers would need to produce for a smaller market, though that does not mean that they would have to produce less. There would be fewer jobs for teachers, and fewer playgrounds; and later, fewer new households would be formed. The economic consequences of such changes are great indeed. Some economists predict a depression if fertility falls too low,[18] while others take a more sanguine view—but no one denies the far-reaching changes that would take place in the economy and the society.

To this point, the discussion has been focused on the consequences of fertility, with an implicit assumption that the mortality rate was constant at least until adulthood. If that assumption is extended to equate changes in fertility with changes in population size, then the broader question of the consequences of

---

[18] See the early views expressed by D. V. Glass in *The Struggle for Population* (Oxford: Clarendon Press, 1936).

population size is broached. In a later part of this chapter, the relation between population size and land area—the influence of population density—is discussed. Another aspect of population size can be raised here since it is closely related to fertility. Earlier, the burdens of high fertility for the individual family and the society were discussed. In spite of those burdens, large populations are sought by nations for a variety of reasons. Historically, one of those reasons has been the military and industrial power represented by a large population. Although modern technology tends to increase the differences in the abilities of men to produce and to fight, such differences were not so great throughout history. Even now, although the most populous nations, China and India, are only relatively important industrially and militarily, most powerful nations have larger than average populations, and none can view without concern any indication of a decline in the size of its population. Thus historically and to some extent now, a changing population has both internal and external consequences for a community or a nation. The relative change in a nation's population becomes an indication of its importance, all other things held constant. An illustration of differential population growth is provided by the European experience in the 19th and 20th centuries. Earlier, the stability of the population of France and the rapid growth of the population of Germany was discussed. While international conflict is a result of many factors, population pressures certainly had an effect on the European situation. German political thinkers, as well as German demagogues, gave voice to the idea of *Lebensraum,* and her greater population gave Germany the military and industrial power to dominate Europe twice by conquest.[19] History proved France fortunate in her allies, if not in her leadership, but had the populations of the two countries been equal (40 million Germans and 40 million Frenchmen) at least one impetus to conflict would have been removed.[20] Repeatedly, in every process, demography is seen playing an important role in world affairs.

CONSEQUENCES OF MORTALITY AND MORBIDITY

Mortality and morbidity are discussed together because they have a common effect: both are processes that refer to the removal of a person from effective contribution to society.[21] Though the effects of mortality are permanent and those of morbidity are sometimes

[19] In 1871 and 1940, Germany dominated Europe although not every European country fell under German rule.

[20] The relation between demographic factors and war is not a simple one of cause and effect. A different type of relation was experienced by the United States, when the Korean War erupted at exactly the point when the small cohort of the 1930's reached military age.

[21] Mortality, of course, refers to death and morbidity to illness.

Elderly parents, experiencing a new life-stage called retirement, can and do lead healthy, useful lives if not shunted away in nursing homes.
(Courtesy Jim Harrison.)

not so permanent, high levels of death or illness reduce the effective size of a population, render it less able to adapt to the conditions it faces, and place increased burdens on the living and the healthy part of the population. In fact, the social costs of illness are greater than those of death—the sick must be cared for; the dead can simply be interred. One difference in these processes may be mentioned. Because all men must die, the important aspect of mortality is the age at which death takes place, whether it be early or late. All men need not suffer illness, so that illness can be removed to some degree, as well as postponed.

Consequences of Morbidity and Mortality to the Family

Just as changes in fertility have influenced family life, changes in mortality have been instrumental in restructuring the typical experiences of the human life cycle. Both men and women are less likely now than they were in 1900 to be widowed before their children become adults. Children are more likely to survive until their fathers' deaths, which renders one of the reasons for the desire to have many sons less important and less valid (although not necessarily weaker in those who have such a desire). Families are not so often called upon to care for the orphans of relatives and friends; thus the duties of the mobile family fortunately have been reduced just when such a reduction has become necessary. At the same time, the decline in mortality means that grandparents are more likely to be alive, even though life expectation in the later years of life has not increased as much as that at earlier years.

This result is not in keeping with the mobility of the family and the neolocal pattern of residence common in the modern industrial society. Thus, the modern family no longer feels a duty to take in its elderly parents, and retirement villages and homes for the aged have become the modern equivalent for the less acceptable old folks home of an earlier time. Increasingly, a new, nonproductive stage of the life cycle, *retirement*, is becoming the expectation for the period of life that extends from the curtailment of formal work to the death of the individual: a time when children are often distant and a stage in which a second neolocal residence is often established. In the United States, this result of increased life is shown in the formation of retirement areas and in the age structure of popular retirement locations, such as those in Arizona and Florida.[22]

Although the influence of modern medicine has been to increase life, partly by removing the effects of disease, modern man in some respects appears sickly. He spends more days in the hospital, on the average, than did his grandfather, and the costs to him and his family of being ill increase faster than almost any other item in his budget.[23] Because of the changes in the life cycle mentioned above, illness typically strikes when he is not with his family and is least able to pay for it. The pattern of morbidity, along with the development of medical technology, act to remove the family further from the care of the sick and to force greater reliance on social programs of insurance, public health, and governmental support.[24]

Consequences of Morbidity and Mortality to Society

The changing patterns mentioned above can be regarded as consequences for society of the pattern of mortality and morbidity, although in most cases the influence is indirect since it operates through the family. Other effects of these factors are perhaps more important, especially in the comparison of nations. Early death is expensive, regardless of the level of technology. The woman whose baby dies has been lost from productive labor for some time. The child who dies at age 10 has been supported by society for many years without contributing to the support of others. The young man who is killed in an automobile wreck may have consumed many

[22] In Florida, for example, 16.0% of the population was over 65 in 1970, as compared to the national figure of 9.9%. See Everett S. Lee, Martin L. Levin, William W. Pendleton, and Patricia D. Postma, *Demographic Profiles of the United States* (Springfield, Va.: National Technical Information Service, U.S. Department of Commerce, 1972).

[23] In 1972, the average cost per patient per day in hospital in the United States was just under $100.

[24] Physicians who were vocal in their opposition to federal medical care programs increasingly favor programs such as Medicare and Medicaid. John Colombotos, "Physicians and Medicare," *Amer. Sociological Rev., XXXIV* (June 1969), pp. 318–334.

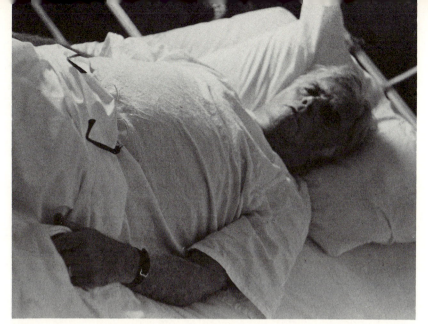

Illness is more costly than death. Although the family is removed from the direct care of the sick, it must still bear the emotional burden, and more recently, the awesome financial burden.
(Courtesy Elsa Dorfman.)

The consequences of a child's death are great for the society, as well as for the family. A child benefits from the society into which he is born and lives, and his early death prevents him from contributing to it.
("The Sick Child" by Edvard Munch. Courtesy Philadelphia Museum of Art. Photograph by A. J. Wyatt, staff photographer.)

thousands of dollars in goods and training, but has contributed little
to others. A society in which many die young carries a great burden,
one that some think is incompatible with economic development.[25]
Although high death rates at an early age may reduce the dependent population, the resources spent in rearing nonproductive persons to even an early death are wasted. When one adds human
grief and misery, periods of mourning, and the efforts expended on
folk remedies to prevent such deaths, the total cost of early mortality is clearly great enough to render a society far less adaptable to
changing conditions. Lower fertility rather than higher mortality is
not only a morally better solution to problems of excessive population, it is a more efficient solution, as well.[26]

Mortality and morbidity are closely related. Yet the
relative costs of morbidity seem to increase with the level of technology, while those of mortality (excluding rising cost of funerals)
seem to decline. Part of the reason for this is due to the rising costs
of more sophisticated treatments. Another part is due to the short
period before death, following the onset of illness in societies with
low levels of medical technology. Other aspects of ill health have
been identified as especially costly to societies at low levels of technology. This is the area of subclinical illness.[27] No one knows the
extent of such illness, even in developed nations where health surveys are common, but experience suggests that low levels of nutrition, chronic parasitic infection, and related phenomena may be a
primary cause of the lack of energy or laziness so often commented
on by European and American visitors to the underdeveloped
world.[28] If this is the case, then subclinical morbidity is especially
important in retarding development in those parts of the world, and
reliance upon psychological and motivational efforts to generate
social change may prove fruitless.

Striking examples of more immediate effects of death and
illness on human behavior can be found in studies of disasters and
plagues. Contrary to what is often supposed, these dramatic conditions rarely lead to panic or hysteria. They do lead to changes in
behavior and often to changes in the structure of society. Epidemics
lead to restrictions on the movement of population, to the destruction of goods thought to be related to the disease without respect

[25] The control of death alone, however, may also create problems. An examination of
some of the relations can be found in Arthur S. Miller, "Some Observations on the Political
Economy of Population Growth," Melvin G. Shimm (ed.), *Population Control* (Durham,
N.C.: Oceana Publications, 1961).
[26] Efficiency refers only to the relative costs of bearing children who will not survive, as
opposed to preventing their birth.
[27] Subclinical illness refers to disease that cannot be readily detected by a physical (non-
laboratory) examination.
[28] Such reports may, of course, be simply a result of Western ethnocentrism.

for the usual property laws, and to greater power for those expected to deal with disease. Often such efforts are counterproductive. In London during the Great Plague, cats were thought to be a cause of the disease. An extermination of cats followed, which allowed a greater growth of the rat population, the true vector.[29] Some of the greatest concentrations of death ever experienced in a short period of time took place during World War II in the London blitz, the bombing of the German cities, and the nuclear attack on the Japanese cities. In none of these cases was there a failure of the society to continue functioning or panic in the population. In all of them, the consequences of deaths were seen in broken families, relocation of resources, and changes in the structure of the population.

Consequences of Morbidity and Mortality for the Individual

There are special aspects of death or the anticipation of death and of illness that can best be viewed as the action of the demographic process through the social system on the individual. Death is universal and universally disliked, if not feared. Even those who believe that life after death is desirable, rarely seek death in preference to life. In fact, any society that taught people to seek death successfully would be unable to continue for long, unless it could restrict

The ritual of death in this Spanish village enables the grieving family to function again in the community. Every society must provide its members with a means of dealing with death.
(Courtesy W. Eugene Smith.)

[29] John F. D. Shrewsbury, *A History of Bubonic Plague in the British Isles* (London: Cambridge University Press, 1970).

such training to the old. Society must, however, provide its members with a means of dealing with death. The influence of the social system on the beliefs, attitudes, and outlook of the dying person is profound, especially when death is anticipated as part of a long illness. Only a few studies have been done on dying people for several reasons: their situation is delicate; certain questions would not be appropriate; and many cannot respond intelligently to questions because of the nature of their illness. Even so, limited research has shown that the initial sympathy offered the dying man is withdrawn or somehow changed by those who associate with him, including hospital personnel; as a result the dying person learns of his fate through nonverbal communication.[30] His ability to deal with the situation rests on resources of intellect and outlook that he has developed in his earlier life. In American society, dying is not made easy or dignified because life is one of the highest values. Though there are probably exceptions, the norms dictate that no one is allowed to die, if life can be sustained. Though euthanasia has had its proponents, it has not attained a legal standing at this time.[31]

Another related consequence that death has for the society is in the allocation of resources to prevent death. Treatment of illness is not available in the same degree or at the same level of sophistication to all members of society. The individual must reconcile his death and that of members of his family to the sure knowledge that some others may receive better or more treatment. When health and illness are in the hands of spirits, everyone has equal treatment; but when men treat other men, some will do a better job and some will be able to obtain better service. When treatment is very costly, such as the case of the artificial kidney machine, even wealthy societies cannot make them universally available when they are first developed.[32] If a society fails to provide adjustment mechanisms for these conditions of inequity, it can expect increased hostility on the part of those who anticipate that they will be the ones who suffer deprivation, hardship, pain, or death—the crueler manifestations of these inequities. In such cases new technology requires new social mechanisms to allocate on an acceptable basis the scarce but desirable products of the technology.

Illness is not only a condition, it is also a socially meaningful condition with important consequences for the individual. Sickness is a role and, like all roles, it gives status, rights, and obliga-

[30] Orville G. Brim, Jr., et al. (eds.), The Dying Patient (New York: Russell Sage Foundation, 1970), gives several studies of death.
[31] For a discussion, see A. B. Downing (ed.), Euthanasia and the Right to Death: The Case for Euthanasia (New York: Humanities Press, 1970).
[32] Availability and use of medical services generally vary by social class. See Time Lost from Work (Rockville, Md.: National Center for Health Statistics, 1972), Data from the National Health Survey, Series 10, No. 71.

tions.[33] Illness gives the member of society the right to take the sick role, to be excused from work or school, to receive medication and sympathy, to be less responsive and more grouchy than usual. Unless one is suffering the pains and miseries of illness, the sick role may be quite pleasant, as most school boys and not a few soldiers can testify. But the role is also constraining. The ill must not be too happy, though they can be cheerful; they cannot exert themselves; they must surrender their responsibilities to others and obey those who are often younger and perhaps less intelligent and less knowledgeable than themselves. For some, playing the sick role is difficult; in fact, some patients prolong their illness by refusing to accept the role of being sick. Being sick confers obligations, and morbidity is not to be taken lightly either socially or biologically.

CONSEQUENCES OF POPULATION SIZE AND DENSITY

The size of a population is not as simple a concept as it might appear. The size of the population of a city or a nation depends on boundaries, which may have artificial or irrelevant criteria. Using population density is one way to attempt to control the placement of boundaries, that is, to remove the influence of arbitrary definitions. At the same time, some importance can be attached to size, as such, because certain implications about social structure can be found in size. Principally, two consequences of size are often identified. First, a larger size allows for and in some degree requires a more complex division of labor. Second, increases in size require increases in secondary, as opposed to primary, relations. It is not known whether these trends are true for all types of population configurations, and it is doubtful that these changes are a linear function of size. There is no doubt, however, that, in general, numbers beyond a certain point imply a different kind of social organization and different patterns of interaction.

Though population density is of longstanding interest to students of demography, it has recently become a major concern of those who feel the world population is too large. Studies of the excessive crowding of rodents and insects show that whenever the animals are confined to a space, even if the food supply is maintained at an adequate level, they will increase their number to the point of overcrowding. The results of this overcrowding are shown in the biology and behavior of the animals. Aggression is increased,

---

[33] Sickness involves several different roles depending on the type and severity of the illness and the culture and social group of the individual. See Irving Kenneth Zola, "Culture and Symptoms—An Analysis of Patients' Presenting Complaints," *Amer. Sociological Rev.,* *XXXI* (October 1966), pp. 615–630.

Does overcrowding affect the mental and physical health of the city dweller? Is a country farmer less likely to be subject to the ills of modern society?
(Photo above, courtesy Russell Lee; photo below, courtesy Berenice Abbott.)

in some cases to the point of reducing the population; mutation rates become higher and abnormalities increase; sexual behavior becomes less frequent and random; and nonproductive behavior characterizes the increasing parts of the population.[34] Some students feel these findings can be extrapolated to the human population, though others have pointed to the difficulties in such an analogy. For instance, the conditions of crowding among the world's population today or in the future, if current growth rates continue, do not even remotely approach the intense crowding that occurs in such experiments. Other studies state that evidence has been found to show that population density is related to many indices of social disorganization, such as crime, divorce rates, mental and physical illness.[35] At least one recent study, however, shows that density and crowding are both unrelated to such factors and that the correlations observed are spurious—that is, they are due to other factors associated with the indices of social disorganization and density.[36] Social class, especially, was shown to have a strong influence. Upper-class areas, even when their density was high, scored low on the indices of social disorganization, and lower-class areas, even with low density, tended to score high. That result casts some doubt on the direct influence of density on social disorganization. That is not to say that population density has no importance in social analysis—for although social disorganization may follow from inadequate housing rather than from crowded housing, and although man is far removed from the crowding of fruit flies in a mason jar, density still affects life.

It is instructive at the gross level of cities and counties to examine what has been happening to population densities in the United States. Nationally, because there are more people, the density has increased, but that is not the case in the largest cities in the country. Manhattan attained its greatest population density in 1910, 102,711 persons per square mile, compared to a density of 67,160 persons per square mile in 1970. Philadelphia, Washington, D.C., St. Louis, and San Francisco all had greater densities in 1950 than in 1970. Boston had a greater density in 1930 than in 1970. Although these cities have been encircled by suburbs, the cities themselves have decreased their density. The cities mentioned above were selected because they changed their boundaries very little during the period of comparison, so the density refers to the same or nearly the same area in every case. The suburban areas are less densely

---

[34] For example, see John B. Calhoun, "A Behavioral Sink," in Eugene L. Bliss (ed.), *Roots of Behavior* (New York: Harper & Brothers, 1962); or Edward T. Hall, *The Hidden Dimension* (Garden City, N.Y.: Doubleday & Company, Inc., 1966).

[35] For example, E. M. Gruenberg, "Community Conditions and Psychosis of the Elderly," *Amer. J. of Psychiatry,* CX (June 1954), pp. 880–903.

[36] R. C. Schmitt, "Density, Health and Social Disorganization," *J. of the Amer. Institute of Planners,* XXXII (January 1966), pp. 38–39.

settled than the cities, so the total population of the metropolitan areas enjoys a lower level of density than did the urban dwellers of 20 to 70 years ago. Urban problems, whatever their source, are not a result of increasing population densities.

Summary

This chapter has examined some of the consequences of demographic processes on social behavior. Adaptive and maladaptive aspects of demographic processes have been considered. The student should remember that the interacting nature of the human ecological system renders the logic of linear statements, whose general form is "this variable causes that variable to behave as it does," valid only in limited cases for short periods of time. The complex interaction of demographic variables, mutually influencing each other while influencing and being influenced by other factors, defies simple causal models. The mode of exposition used here is not intended to obscure those interactions, but to serve to clarify them heuristically.

Exercises

1. Identify areas of the world where you think population pressure might lead to international conflict. What reasons can you give for your choice?

2. How might different sizes of generations cause intergenerational conflict? Do you see any evidence of such conflict in the United States and Europe?

3. How, and under what circumstances, do the demographic changes created by war affect society?

4. What are the likely consequences of some nations limiting their population growth while others do not?

5. Though large cities have experienced decreasing density in terms of their residential populations, do you expect this to be true for their "daytime" popualtions? Why or why not? Examine census reports to test your contentions.

6. Examine changes in the median age in the United States over the past 120 years. Is there an association between a low median age and political movements? Explain why or why not.

7. Examine the eugenics movement. Do you think the genetic structure of man can be improved deliberately? Why has the eugenics movement had such little success?

8. Contrast the consequences of the continued growth of existing cities with the establishment of new cities? Consider different ways existing cities might grow—for example, growth might be manifested in higher density or greater sprawl.

9. What can be expected to happen if the reproduction rate in the United States falls below replacement? Do you think this might happen?

10. Considering the consequences for every aspect of social life and individual well-being, how large do you think should a city be? What factors might cause your answer to change? Does the number of and relations among cities influence your answer? How?

Selected Bibliography

Eversley, D. E. C. *Social Theories of Fertility and the Malthusian Debate.* Oxford: Clarendon Press, 1959.

Glass, D. V., and D. E. C. Eversley (eds.). *Population in History.* Chicago: Aldine, 1965.

Gollin, Albert E. (ed.). *The International Migration of Talent and Skills.* Washington, D.C.: Bureau of Social Science Research, 1966.

Kulischer, Eugene M. *Europe on the Move: War and Population Changes 1917–47.* New York: Columbia University Press, 1948.

Malthus, Thomas R. *An Essay on the Principle of Population,* 7th ed. London: Reeves and Turner, 1872.

Petersen, William. *The Politics of Population.* Garden City, N.Y.: Doubleday & Company, Inc., 1964.

Spengler, Joseph J. *France Faces Depopulation.* Durham, N.C.: Duke University Press, 1938.

Thomlinson, Ralph. *Population Dynamics: Causes and Consequences of World Demographic Change.* New York: Random House, 1965.

Zimmerman, Anthony F. *Overpopulation.* Washington, D.C.: Catholic University of America Press, 1957.

12

Technological Developments and Problems of Social Adaptation

For the most part, early man's problems of adaptation focused on the constraints and dangers of his natural environment. His survival depended upon his ability to obtain the necessary sustenance from ready-made sources of nature. Therefore, early man's relationship to nature—that is, man in nature—was on a level similar to that of other primates. As was shown in Chapters 2 and 3, the invention of tools and a tool technology changed the relationship of man to nature for tools and technology gave him the capacity to bend nature to his will rather than simply to respond to it. Although this capacity has enabled mankind to solve many problems of adaptation, it has also produced some new problems because man is still dependent upon nature, and is an integral part of it, as well.

Man has lived approximately 99 per cent of his existence in an environment significantly unaltered by his behavior. In the past 5000 to 7000 years, the rapid growth and spread of the human species attests to man's adaptability. This rapid growth and concentration of population has resulted from the evolution of technology—the by-products of the technology and the waste products of the concentration of the population have significantly altered the environment.

Man-made products developed through advanced technology often have unanticipated side effects that require additional technology to control. (Courtesy Robert Rapelye, Photography International.)

The growth of technological adaptation, particularly through science, has resulted in the creation of man-made products whose unanticipated side effects have created new problems of adaptation. At the risk of some oversimplification, it is nevertheless accurate to say that man's man-made system of adaptation has itself become a problem of adaptation. Such a development is to be expected; at least, it should have been expected since the technological order or systems within a society are associated with the other subsystems of society. In particular, technological systems are associated with the economic, political, and educational institutions. In addition, they affect the quality of, and man's relation to, the ecological environment.

Changing forms of technology have been prime movers in changing the social structure of society. In fact, technological evolution has an impact on cultural evolution in a basic causal way similar to the effect of genetic mutation on biological evolution. The critical difference is that the principle or principles of selection that lead to progress in human adaptation are less clear in technological evolution than in biological mutation. It is assumed that survival is ultimately the basis for solution.

Leslie White argues with considerable force that the degree of cultural development, C, in a society is determined by E, the amount of energy harnessed per capita per year, and T, the quality or efficiency of the tools employed in the expenditure of the energy. He expresses this symbolically as[1]:

$$E \times T \rightarrow C$$

[1] Leslie A. White, *The Science of Culture* (New York: Farrar Straus & Cudahy, Inc., 1949), p. 368.

For example, a society with an energy system based on animal power could and did develop an agrarian social system with cities of a given size and with a population density considerably greater than that which existed in a hunting and gathering society based on man-power energy. Likewise, with the discovery and harnessing of fossil fuel, electricity, and later atomic energy, much larger amounts of power were generated; a society possessing these power resources, therefore, had the means for development of much larger populations and more complex social systems, such as industrial and large urban communities.

In a biological population, natural selection is effective and leads to evolution if there is (1) a sufficiently large population which is (2) divided into a large number of partially isolated subpopulations that (3) function as intrabreeding units. These conditions function to increase the genotypic variation in the population; biological evolution in turn depends upon genotypic variability and natural selection. The role that random processes play in increasing this variability is an extremely important question, and one that needs further inquiry. How dependent are biological evolution and cultural evolution on random processes? To what extent can random variation be replaced by systematic variation in both biological and cultural evolution, without hindering the adequacy of evolution and thus the continuance of effective adaptation?

As biological evolution is partially dependent upon the size of a species' population base, cultural evolution is dependent upon the size of the cultural base. The larger the cultural base, the greater the probability that invention or new combinations of traits will be produced. Also, the larger the cultural base, the greater the degree of social differentiation within the social structure. Social differentiation is necessary to activate, maintain, and promote continued cultural growth; the degree of differentiation or specialization within a society depends directly upon its level of technology, which in turn depends upon the level of energy the society is capable of harnessing. The increased variety of interests resulting from the increased specialization promotes competition and conflict, as well as cooperation, all of which stimulate cultural evolution or changes. Some of the changes are adaptive; presumably, these are the ones that are retained in the long run.

A society that depends upon human energy alone cannot develop very far. Certainly it cannot develop beyond a simple hunting and gathering type of social organization without discovering or borrowing new forms of energy. We find no highly developed societies that are powered by human energy alone. Horticultural and agricultural societies awaited the domestication of animals and plants, and industrial societies awaited the development of steam, fossil-fuel, and electric power.

The harnessing of more powerful and efficient sources of energy and the concomitant increase in the division of labor results in an increase in the supply of food and material goods, which in turn trigger an increase in the population of a society undergoing such changes. It is, of course, these processes that have led to the development of the great cities of the last few centuries. One of the by-products of this complexity and concentration of population, in addition to the sheer size of the mass, is the enormous volume of human, industrial, and commercial waste products. One of the more recent problems is from nuclear power plants—the nuclear power units have necessitated the construction of large cooling systems to return the water to the streams at normal stream temperature. The pollution of streams, oceans, air, and soil that results from these combined sources is of such magnitude that it threatens the welfare of the species and interferes with the processes of organic evolution. At such a critical point in technological development and social organization, the man-made environment has *itself* become a serious problem of adaptation. Under such a condition, man is no longer adapting with nature; rather, as a consequence of some of the by-products of technology, he has become a problem for himself and the rest of nature. It is precisely under such a condition of stress that values and ideologies begin to take on a new function in society with respect to both physical and social technology and planning. Prior to this condition, human social organization and supporting ideologies have functioned, for the most part, to implement, facilitate, and serve technological ends rather than to define and predetermine these ends. Furthermore, they have done so quite efficiently, and the capitalistic, socialistic, and communistic ideologies are each in different ways examples of this process. But continued efficiency calls for new coordination, far-range planning and the control of deleterious technological side effects, as well as curtailment of greed. In other words, man must learn to modify his man-made systems to control the consequences or effects of these systems upon his welfare. To do this he will first need to modify his value system.

In essence, the foregoing leads to the conclusion that the complexity of modern technology and social organization and the accompanying population concentration have reached a point of evolution where their interacting effects *need* to be *systematically* regulated and directed. Thus *purposive* selection has been added to *natural* selection as a means of human adaptation—but to accomplish this requires an adequate level of knowledge about biological and social evolution, knowledge that is presently insufficient. Therefore, our continued adaptation and evolution depend upon the development of adequate new knowledge and its guidance in ways that will minimize harmful man-made effects upon the natural world, for preservation of the balance of the natural world is essential to sustaining life in a healthy state. With this application of the role of values in adaptation, we have shown the interdependence of the four principal organizing concepts of the book—namely, knowledge, technology, organization, and ideology. Let us now turn to a consideration of the interaction of technology and social change.

TECHNOLOGICAL CHANGE AND SOCIAL CHANGE

As we have shown in Chapters 2 and 3, culture is an organized and integrated system of adaptation. For purposes at hand, however, we distinguished, in Chapter 1, four subdivisions of culture—namely, systems of *knowledge* such as folk knowledge and sciences; systems of *technology* which are composed of the physical and chemical instruments, together with the techniques of their use; systems of *organizations* by which man adapts to his fellows, and to nature; and, finally, *ideological* systems composed of beliefs, values, religion, philosophy, esthetics, literature, and art, which add a transcendental dimension to human life and presumably help guide the use of the instruments and raw materials.

The technological system is basic to all the rest, except for the great *interstimulation* between *modern technology* and *basic science*. The social system is fundamentally dependent upon the technological system. As Childe noted: "The bronze axe which replaces . . . the stone axe, is not only a superior implement, it also presupposes a more complex economic and social structure."[2] A more obvious example is the replacement of horse or animal power by steam and fossil-fuel power, in conjunction with the replacement of the agricultural or agrarian systems related to animal power by the industrial systems related to steam and fossil-fuel power.

It seems clear that technology is a major influence on social change, as noted by Francis R. Allen in his quote from William F. Ogburn. In the late 1930's Ogburn concluded that "the inventor of the automobile has had more influence on society than the combined exploits of Napoleon, Genghis Khan, and Julius Caesar."[3] The automobile has become the mode of transportation for whole societies, and, in the United States, a major focus of the economy and a major means for new life styles for the youth and the adults.

One of the principal effects of technological change is its contribution to a real increase in per capita income and level of

[2] V. Gordon Childe, *Man Makes Himself* (New York: Mentor Books, 1951).
[3] William F. Ogburn, *Machines and Tomorrow's World*, quoted in Francis R. Allen, *Technology and Social Change* (New York: Appleton–Century–Crofts, Inc., 1957), p. 107.

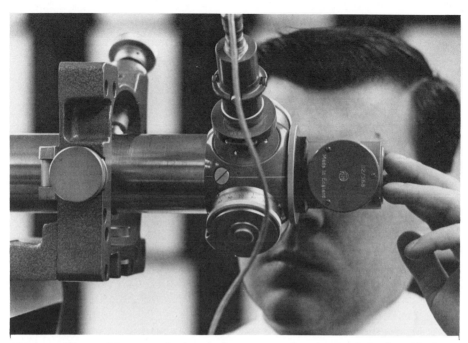

Man's problem-solving capacity is greatly augmented and extended when blocks to his perception are removed through improved instruments of observation.
(Courtesy Rene Burri, Magnum Photos, Inc.)

living. Economists of the early 19th century argued that this was an illusion. Their conclusion was based on the argument that a nation's economic growth is the result of its economic surplus being transformed into capital accumulation and that capital accumulation could not continue indefinitely. Also, any increase in real wages would lead to faster population growth. Therefore, they further argued that this combination means that wages could not remain above the subsistence level for long.[4] By this view, the only events that might lead to a wage above subsistence, temporarily, were war, famine, or some other major social crisis.

Subsequent events, however, have not borne out these predictions of the classical economists. Improved technological efficiency has in fact increased wages above the level of subsistence, as will be shown below. What the classical economists could not foresee or, at least, could not respond to, was the possibility of an increase in productivity beyond that provided by simply an increase of capital per worker or an increase in labor. There is a part of the increase in output that cannot be explained by increases in either

[4] See, for example, David Ricardo, *The Principles of Political Economy and Taxation* (New York: E. P. Dutton and Company, Inc., 1911).

capital or labor, but is instead a result of technological efficiency.[5]

Depending upon the basic assumptions that one is willing to make, one can view the increase in output per man to be due to either a relatively constant contribution of capital, labor, and technological change, or to the interaction of capital or labor and technological change. Is technological change neutral in its contribution to capital and labor or does it accrue differentially through time to one or the other? This is an extremely complex issue, and no attempt will be made here to argue that matter one way or another. For purposes of simplicity, we will assume as Solow does that technological change is neutral. Solow defines technological change as increased productivity corrected for capital increase. Thus, in terms of Solow's economic model, technological change is any shift in the production function over time. Furthermore, for innovations to become technological changes, they must be accepted and incorporated by the owners of capital into the capital framework or by the leaders of labor into the worker framework, and under some conditions by both. Thus Solow's model is not a causal or explanatory scheme, although it is a very useful way of identifying the sources of variation in productivity.

Increased productivity results in increased surplus capital and surplus wages, which in turn can be converted into new technology and still more new capital. Hence, the concept of *efficiency of productivity* is a useful consideration in understanding social change. The rate of social change in a society is correlated with the rate of technological change, and technological change depends primarily on capital to develop and promote it. For example, the American economy over the last century has grown at a very great rate. Increases in Gross National Product (GNP), capital, and real income in the United States were unprecedented in the world until the recent case of Japan. "Between 1870 and 1960, GNP experienced a 28-fold increase. Output rose from $17.65 billion in 1870 to $503 billion in 1960 (both in 1960 dollars); at the same time, income and output per worker rose precipitously over this period. Output per man increased 453 per cent; capital per man increased 274 per cent. The picture for the nation's agricultural sector is equally impressive. Although total output increased only 553 per cent over this period, the rise in productivity (output per man) is much higher, 949 per cent."[6]

The foregoing data are summarized in Table 12–1.[7]

---

[5] This is the initial assumption of Robert Solow, an economist at the Massachusetts Institute of Technology. For a discussion and evaluation, see Lester B. Lave, *Technological Change: Its Conception and Measurement* (Englewood Cliffs, N.J.: Prentice–Hall, Inc., 1966), pp. 11–92.

[6] Lester B. Lave, *ibid.*, p. 152.

[7] Lester B. Lave, *ibid.*, p. 153.

TABLE 12–1

Economic growth in the United States between 1870 and 1960.

	Series	Growth (percentage)
United States	GNP (Y)	2755
United States	Capital (K)	1830
United States	Labor force (L)	416
United States	Productivity: Y/L	453
United States	Capital per worker: K/L	274
United States	Capital output ratio: K/Y	−42
Agriculture	Y	553
Agriculture	Y/L	949
Agriculture	K/L	411
Agriculture	K/Y	−51
Appalachian agriculture	Y	353
Appalachian agriculture	K/L	674
Appalachian agriculture	K/L	344
Appalachian agriculture	K/Y	−49

SOURCE: Lester B. Lave, *Technological Change: its Conception and Measurement* (Englewood Cliffs, N.J.: Prentice–Hall, Inc., 1966), p. 153.

Notice that the total output in the agricultural sector increased only 553 per cent over this period while the increase was 2755 per cent for the entire economy; nevertheless the rise in productivity, output per man, is much higher in the agricultural sector —949 per cent, compared to 453 per cent. Thus, if prices for agricultural products had remained constant, the agricultural sector would be among the richest. Obviously, this did not occur; in fact, the drop in prices has contributed to what has come to be known as "the farm problem."

The development and diffusion of new technology is not just a matter of obtaining new knowledge and the capital means to convert the knowledge into applied functions; it is also a matter of educating and training of the workers so that they can use and apply the technology. In an industrialized society, this is primarily a problem of *continuing* adult education, but in an agrarian or nonindustrialized society, the impartation of new technology may mean the necessity to reeducate the labor force for an entire sector of the economy. In an underdeveloped society, this is difficult because of the high rates of illiteracy and the lack of a tradition of formal education for anyone except members of the ruling classes. Nevertheless, such a formal educational system must be instituted as a necessary condition for industrialization to occur.

The diffusion of technology from one culture to another assumes that the new technology is meaningful for adaptation to the members of the borrowing culture.
(Courtesy Cornell Capa, Magnum Photos, Inc.)

The highly efficient systems of communication and transportation available today to such industrial giants as the United States, Russia, Japan, West Germany, France, and Great Britain, and the competitive trade and political advantages afforded by these, make it extremely difficult for a currently underdeveloped nation to industrialize without great sacrifice. Where does such a society get the necessary surplus capital to invest? What products can it produce and successfully market on foreign markets? How can it educate and train its population to meet the skill requirements of the new technology? How can it transform the old belief systems and family practices into new ones that will permit the necessary changes in fertility patterns so that population increases will not outrun economic growth? And how can new attitudes toward authority and loyalties to new values be developed that are consonant with the rational needs of modern government? That is, how can the impulses to graft and vested interest, and the temptation to equate self-interest with public interest be controlled in a society in transition from a traditional system to a modern technological system? These and other related questions will be discussed in Chapters 15 and 16. The purpose in calling attention to them here is to indicate the correlation between technological change and social change. Often there is a time lag between one or more related elements in the change process. For example, a change may occur in the technology of health and medical practices in an agrarian society, resulting in a sharp reduction in the infant mortality rate. This would mean a sharp increase in the net natural increase, which would imply a subsequent decrease in fertility rates. Instead, the prevailing traditional fertility rates continue for quite some time after the decline in death rates. Such lags aggravate and often increase the problems and costs of adaptation. Consequently, it is desirable to *plan for the necessary related social changes* when technological change is introduced. However, the diffusion of new technological practices is easier than the diffusion of new social practices.

Technological and Social Change—and Their Diffusion

The study of the diffusion or the spread of the adoption of new ideas and practices is an important part of the understanding of technological change. The acceptance of new technology and its adoption for use are basic to the rate of technological change. Therefore, we shall examine some of the conditions related to diffusion.

First of all, the degree of social isolation of a society or a community affects the rates of technological and social change. Social contact is an extremely important source for new ideas and for discovery of the outmoded nature of one's own practices. The Golden Age of Pericles of Ancient Greece is well-known for its high rates of social change and for its mental mobility. It was also the crossroads of civilization for the then known world. The fact that Athens was the center of interaction on the world stage at that time brought the Athenians in contact with a great variety of cultural practices, which allowed for improved social and technological selection. The converse of this is also true; that is, social isolation reinforces old practices and reduces the pool of ideas available for selection. Second, the increased contact with other societies or communities enhances and increases the volume of economic exchange and, therefore, the rate of economic growth of the society. The adoption or development of new technology presupposes the necessary capital for its development. For example, if a country decides to mechanize its agricultural production, it must either buy tractors, reapers, corn pickers, and other equipment and educate the farmers to use them, or it must acquire the necessary know-how and skills to manufacture its own and educate its farmers to use them. Either way costs money, and the money, as well as the need, must be available.

Once the need for new technology is clearly recognized, and a recognized superior product, and the capital for its procurement, exist, then the likelihood of the rapid adoption of technology is very great. This implies, as stated earlier, that physical technology is likely to diffuse faster and be more quickly accepted than social technology. Its consequences, at least the short-range ones, appear to the potential users to be more clearly perceptible and predictable.

Whether this is true or not does not matter, for as long as the people believe it to be true, they will resist social change longer than technological change. In fact, most social changes, at least the more important ones, have come about as responses to very vexing conditions. In other words, they were more or less forced alterations of institutional practices that had already become outmoded. The Civil Rights Act outlawing racial segregation is such an example. On the other hand, technological growth and industrialization made the agrarian system obsolete, which in turn radically affected the previous status system and brought about the new emphasis on civil rights. The hotly contested changes are more visible, but the more profound and basic changes occur in an evolutionary way and are, therefore, less visible during their emergence.

The necessary conditions for rapid diffusion are well-illustrated in a study by Woodruff in 1962 (cited by Lave), which describes the rapid diffusion of the use of rubber. Charles Goodyear in 1839 invented a process called vulcanization, whereby natural rubber could be chemically stabilized against changes in temperature. Several people in Europe and England were experimenting on the process at the same time, which indicates the widespread interest and need for the new material.[8]

Goodyear's invention was diffused throughout Europe with great rapidity because of his need for capital. He sought this capital in Europe and then later on, Americans built European plants. There were a number of reasons for these plants. First of all, there was a boom in rubber that collapsed, leaving skilled workers and excess capacity in America. Secondly, Europe levied a high duty on imported rubber. The logical conclusion was that the American workmen emigrated to Europe. Indeed, all the secrets of the rubber industry were in the methods of production; thus, nothing short of the emigration of workmen would have been satisfactory. Finally, the joining of American skills and European capital speeded the diffusion.

If the discoveries that led to the process of vulcanization had been in small bits and had occurred in different countries, the process of diffusion would have been slower. Also, if the discovery had been at the level of basic science, rather than, as it was, in methods of production, diffusion would have been slowed down until the basic knowledge was converted into a workable technology. Finally, as a general rule, the more complex and difficult the basic discovery, the more expensive and difficult it is to convert to technology. This, of course, makes the technology more expensive and complicated, which in turn reduces the diffusion rate. The construction of atomic reactors is a good example.

[8] From Lester B. Lave, *Technological Change. Its Conception and Measurement* (Englewood Cliffs, N.J.: Prentice–Hall, Inc., 1966), p. 145.

One of the by-products of the accumulation of knowledge is the complexity of the emerging technology that requires an ever increasing level of skills and training if it is to be used efficiently.
(Courtesy Rene Burri, Magnum Photos, Inc.)

In summary, technological change presupposes the presence or availability of surplus capital to institute the new techniques and the availability of skilled workmen to carry out the processes. Moreover, the speed of diffusion of the new technology depends not only on these two factors, but also upon the complexity of the technology and the receptivity of the leaders of the interest or specialty groups in the proposed recipient societies. Finally, technological and social change presuppose that a society has the means for socializing or training its members in the new skills and new patterns of behavior that result from the two kinds of change. Therefore, as rates of change increase, the burden of socialization and resocialization increase. Some of these problems will be discussed below in the section "Technology and Socialization." *Before reading the next section, the student should review the basic chapter on socialization, namely, Chapter 6.*

TECHNOLOGY AND SOCIALIZATION

Socialization is the process by which a society equips its new members and reequips its old ones for effective participation in societal functions. The process involves supervised learning; the *amount of learning required varies directly with the level of technology* operating in the society. Furthermore, the *adaptive information is transmitted differently according to the forms of societal organization.*

For example, from the hunting and gathering through the agricultural societies, the information is primarily transmitted through the family. But in modern society, the differentiation of family and work roles makes this mode of transmission impossible. As a result, the educational institution has assumed a primary role in socialization in modern societies.

Thus it is clear that the problems of socialization are different for societies based on different levels of technology and social organization. Increases in the level and complexity of technology result in increased occupational specialization. The increased specialization in society necessitates specialized training or socialization to fill the new roles. For example, socialization in a hunting and gathering society consists largely of the children doing whatever the parents do or at least participating to some degree with the parents. By adolescence, the males and females are full-fledged participants, since participation is largely dependent upon motor skill, courage, strength, and motivation. The period of time required for maturation and development of the necessary technical and social skills and approved values and attitudes increases as the complexity of the technology and social organization increase. Hence the period of childhood and adolescence of modern man is much more extended than that of his ancient counterpart. In other words, it takes longer to acquire the necessary knowledge and skills to function effectively in the adult world of a modern society.

In periods of rapid and complex technological change, the values and attitudes necessary for efficient adaptive use of the new technology may not even be sufficiently in existence or evidence among the adult population for the new generation to learn them. In fact, the new technology may have consequences or potential consequences unforeseen by anyone except a very few of the creators of the technology themselves and sometimes not even by them. In this respect, Albert Einstein said, shortly before his death: "Our world faces a crisis as yet unperceived by those possessing the power to make great decisions for good or evil. The unleashed power of the atom has changed everything save our modes of thinking, and thus we drift to unparalleled catastrophe." In somewhat different words, H. G. Wells expressed the same problem as being one in which "civilization is a race between education and catastrophe."

In a relative sense, every major technical innovation, particularly in the area of weapons, generates threats of unperceived magnitudes. The crossbow, the machine gun, the bomber plane, chemical and atomic weapons are examples. However, thermonuclear power and weapons are of a very different order of magnitude. In fact, they represent a difference in terms of potential effects so great as to qualify them for a difference in kind. For example, weapons and weapon systems in the past have been capable of eliminating major portions of large populations; but they have not had the power to eliminate as well the systems of adaptation or the civilizations. Thermonuclear weapons are capable of destroying not only whole populations, but the entire technological and cultural subsystems associated with the populations. If such an atomic disaster were to occur, and given the accumulated depletion in the quality and quantity of the world's natural resources it would probably be impossible for future societies to rebuild at a level of technology equivalent to the present. Therefore, the present generations and generations to come, because of the potential consequences of modern war, are faced with the necessity of learning new attitudes and values toward war relative to the past—and this necessity is the direct consequence of atomic technology.

Clearly there exists a great lag between physical technology and the social means to regulate international disputes and to ensure the positive use of the technology. Given the presence of national armies and weapons systems in a world where no superior international equivalent force exists, such a danger will continue. Actually, the greatest danger today lies not so much in the availability of such weapons as in the *absence* of any real international power to enforce civil and moral behavior on national societies, as means for settling disputes.

The preceding clearly illustrates that technology, particularly new forms of energy and weapons systems, increases the power of a society. The control of the purposes and uses of such power and technology depend upon the kind of *organization* that controls the use, and on the ends or values that define the purposes or functions of the organization. In other words, social systems provide the direction, integration, and control of the uses of technology, however adequate or inadequate these controls may be. Consequently, any improvement in control and the direction of its use presupposes some social change in the related social systems. In other words, war is not the result of human instincts or aggressive drives, but instead derives from the social and cultural processes of human societies. Man obviously has the biological capacity for aggression and war, but the expression of these is socially determined. Moreover, the changing of attitudes toward war depends upon resocialization based upon the perceived new consequences of war.

The problem of the control of modern systems of *atomic weapons and international* disputes is only one of the major problems of adaptation to new technology today. Three other problem areas that have their origin in technological development and have major implications for social adaptation are (1) the interaction of

The products of technology have potentially harmful as well as beneficial effects; therefore, values and attitudes must be developed to insure their proper uses.
("The Motorist" by Henri de Toulouse-Lautrec. Courtesy The Art Institute of Chicago.)

man-made chemical pollutants with the ecosystem; (2) the interaction of automation and cybernetics with the economic system; and (3) crime. The first affects the quality of the natural environment on which man depends for survival; the second affects unemployment, the hours worked per week for employees, and the distribution of income; and the third affects man's attitude toward his fellows and his capacity to control himself without which adaptation is very unlikely.

The more complex the technology of a society, the more extended the period of time required for the youth to learn the technology, the greater the gap between the youth world and the adult world. This is most clearly evident when the socialization practices of simpler societies are contrasted with industrial societies. Societies

with relatively simple technology, such as pastoral and early agricultural societies, were characterized by tribal and clan organization
based on kinship ties. Social relations were also largely regulated on
the basis of the kinship ties. This mechanism worked very well as
long as the social units were small enough so that the social relationships could be personal. With the development of improved agricultural technology and an increasing food supply, clan and tribal
units grew large, and they tended to break up or fall apart because
the kinship system was no longer an adequate control mechanism or
a sufficient system for transmitting information. As a consequence,
specialized socialization or training organizations, such as appren-
ticeship systems and various forms of schools, were developed.

Furthermore, with the development of a surplus of food,
specialization was accelerated, which tended to produce social
classes with their in-group–out-group attitudes, thereby increasing
the difficulty of social control. Consequently, a new and more rational and centralized type of social organization was required to
control the much larger populations. Bureaucracy had its origin to
a significant extent in the early efforts of societies to cope with this
problem of control. The earliest forms of bureaucracy, one of which
originated in ancient Egypt, were associated with the development
of centralized government, particularly with its problems of tax collection, administration of armies, and problems of justice. This new
institution eventually evolved into the modern state requiring a
whole new scheme of socialization for the development of loyalties
to new types of leaders and authorities.

Socialization—that is, the conditioning of the new members of a society to the requirements of the society—involves three
interrelated but separate functions. These are (1) *cultural aquisition*
or the intergenerational transmission of culture; (2) behavior and impulse control, or *internalization*; and (3) *role training* or training for
social participation. These three were discussed in detail in Chapter 6. The purpose of reintroducing the concept of socialization in
this chapter is to call attention to the expanding set of processes
necessary for successful socialization in a society that undergoes
major technological change.

That an interdependence between brain development and
technological development characterizes the evolution of man's organic system, his personality structure, and his cultural system becomes apparent when man's evolution is viewed over long periods
of time. For example, the development of tool use, toolmaking, and
refined and advanced tools is accompanied by the development of
more elaborate hunting techniques, agriculture, and a concomitant
expansion of the cerebral cortex, as well as the development of
values and attitudes appropriate to the requirements of the social
systems in which one functions. But the means for developing the

necessary skills in a population must first be acquired before the populace can cope with the requirements of new social and technological systems. In this respect, let us turn now to an analysis of technological change and the labor force.

TECHNOLOGICAL CHANGE AND THE LABOR FORCE

According to the report of the National Commission on Technology, there were in 1955 only a few dozen electronic computers in the United States.[9] However, by the mid-1960's over 10,000 were being produced every year. Given the fantastic growth and accumulation of data necessary for operating business, industry, health and educational facilities, and government, the need for a more efficient system for data processing and analysis was critical. That the computer helped to meet this need was its great advantage. Also, such complicated feats, during the sixties, as landing on the moon and returning would not have been possible without computer directed flight. Like any other major technological innovation, the computer's adaptive advantages are great, but it also has some undesired side effects that need to be controlled. We will now discuss some of these.

The Bureau of Labor Statistics estimates that the average computer eliminates 35 clerical jobs and changes the kind of work for about 100 other white-collar workers. Based on the estimated 10,000 computers manufactured per year, the Commission Report extrapolates to indicate that 350,000 clerical jobs are eliminated per year and over a million more jobs require retraining. It is true that automation eliminates tasks that can be converted to an automated routine, but it also creates many new but different types of jobs requiring new kinds of skills. These dislocations within the labor force can cause serious economic hardship, unless the central government coordinates manpower retraining and reassignment programs. The displacement during the early 1970's of large numbers of aerospace scientists, engineers, and technicians, as a result of changing Federal priorities, is a significant example. It is significant not only because it involves economic and social hardships, but because it is also a waste of a highly skilled group of workers, most of whom were trained in colleges and universities on some kind of tax-supported fellowship or on the G.I. Bill.

Technological change and shifts in national priorities affect not only the employment/unemployment of certain categories of workers, but also the rank order of major categories of industry with respect to the national distribution of workers. In the United

[9] *Report of the National Commission on Technology, Automation, and Economic Progress. Appendix Volume VI. Technology and the American Economy* (Washington, D.C.: U.S. Government Printing Office, 1966), p. 45; hereafter referred to as the National Commission Report.

The vast amounts of information needed for solving problems in modern society require more efficient systems of data management and retrieval. The high speed computer is an efficient tool for this purpose.
(Courtesy Burt Glinn, Magnum Photos, Inc.)

States, for example, manufacturing, building, mining, agriculture, lumbering, and fishing constituted almost 63 per cent of the workers in the labor force in 1910 and the service industries accounted for approximately 35 per cent. By 1970, however, the service industries made up over 60 per cent, and the combined agriculture, manufacturing, and so on, had dropped to about 40 per cent. Table 12–2 gives a detailed version of these general trends. It is clear that technological growth changes the focus of economic activities and competition among nations.

In general, the proportion of the labor force still in agriculture may be regarded as an index of the degree of industrialization of a country. The advanced nations of the world have one third of the world's labor force, but they have 62 per cent of its industrial labor force. In India, for example, 70 per cent of its labor force is in agriculture, as compared to about 7 per cent in the United States and about 4 per cent in Britain.

Given the increased dependence of every member of the population of an industrial society on the economic growth of the society, relative *levels* of affluence clearly depend upon whether the economic growth is able to keep pace with or exceed population growth. Over the past few decades, the importance of national, regional, and local planning has taken on a new dimension of importance. Because of an increasing rate of social and technological change, the interaction of science, technology, and social patterns

TABLE 12–2

Per cent distribution of labor force in agriculture, industry, and services for the world and for selected countries, for 1960.

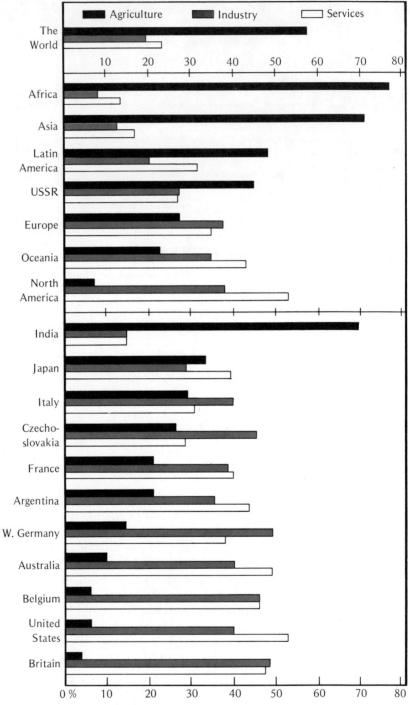

SOURCE: *Economist, 223* (1 April 1967), p. 55. Statistics taken from reports by the International Labor Office in Geneva, Switzerland.

has become more evident. This means that the national and state legislative bodies are faced with the problem of trying to understand the implications of science and technology for social change, of assessing their effects, and of deciding on courses of action. It also means that the government will have to utilize more effectively than it has in the past the vast array of scientific and technical expertise available for developing and executing public policy.

The accelerated rate of technological and social change implies the need for more efficient methods and facilities for the educating, training, and retraining of youth and adults. The tasks of educating and training in an industrial society call for many skills and a great variety of instructional techniques. Just as the computer has been a great aid to industry, science, and technology, it also provides great promise as a tool for information and data retrieval, as well as an aid for instruction. Time sharing in computer programming enables many individuals at remote access terminals to use a single computer. The same computer center that is handling many students is simultaneously servicing the faculty, administration, hospitals, and often many other activities. A computer-assisted instructional program can, when the student acquires the necessary computer language skills, provide a great deal of self-directed study for the student. These individualized efforts augment motivation and make learning more exciting.

One of the major adaptive problems of an advanced technological society is the expanding appetites and increased range of wants of the population. This increase is an important source of economic expansion, but it is also a major problem of social control for the large number of people who fail to regulate or correlate appetites with their personal resources. Failure to do so often leads to crimes against persons and property. Again we encounter an obvious, but important, interrelated problem of adaptation— namely, *systems adaptation* and *personal* or individual adaptation. This dual problem was stressed in Chapter 1 and has recurred throughout the book. For example, the chemical technology related to the production of detergents, pesticides, and industrial waste has adaptive effects on man's water and food supply, and is hence a *systems* problem of adaptation; a man who loses his job because of automation has a *personal* adaptive problem related to the advancement of technology and the improvement of economic productivity.

In other words, technological and social change may result in improved systems adaptability, while having negative side effects upon selected individuals in the population. This seems to be one of the unavoidable consequences of change. The solution, if there is one, lies in the willingness and capacity of societal leaders to anticipate the effects of change, and the plan to control or, at least, to minimize the undesired side effects (see Chapter 14).

Assuming that the opportunities of education are not denied to individuals or groups of individuals, most people are able to adapt to the vast number of technological changes that take place in an individual society.
(Courtesy Jim Harrison.)

For example, successful individual adaptation in a complex industrial society presupposes the capacity, motivation and opportunity to obtain the appropriate educational background necessary to acquire an adequate income. Not everyone has this capacity, and some who have the capacity have not had the educational opportunity. For the latter, the problem is to eliminate the obstacles to educational opportunity. However, once this is accomplished (assuming that it can be), there will still be a large number of people, who, for various reasons, have limited physical, mental, and social skills—and their incomes, as well as those general living conditions affected by income, will reflect these limitations. According to the 1960 Census of Housing, about 6.7 million households with incomes between $3000 and $4999 lived in units that needed either replacement or rehabilitation. (See Tables 12–3 and 12–4 below for 1970 housing data.) No adaptive system or mechanism is perfect. Adaptation is a matter of degree, and the degree of difficulty felt by members of a society increases as environmental changes occur that are related to the system. In an industrial society, most people, through appropriate education, are able to adapt to the changes in the technological environment. Their successful adaptation is manifested in adequate income, which allows for adequate accommodation. Thus, the great majority of people in an industrial society are well housed, although some are not.

TABLE 12–3

Average value of house by race in the United States for 1970.

	Non-Black	Black
1. Average value of house owned in the United States	$19,994.00	$12,294.00
2. Average monthly rent	$105.88	$76.77
3. Percentage of owner units lacking plumbing	3%	15%
4. Percentage of owner units with one or more persons per room	6%	16%

SOURCE: Everett Lee, Martin L. Levin, William W. Pendleton, and Patricia D. Postma, *Demographic Profiles of the United States* (Springfield, Va.: National Technical Information Service, U.S. Department of Commerce, September 1971), Vol. 1.

In the realm of human social behavior, an observer can easily confuse what *is* (that is, the empirical world) with what he believes should be. Physical reality on the contrary, is viewed as a part of nature, and any attitude on what it *should* be is viewed as absurd. In other words, it is assumed that man's knowledge of the physical world does not change the nature of that world, though it may change man's relationship to the physical world. For example, man's knowledge of gravity does not change gravity, but it has enabled him to build a technology that permits the control of some of the effects of gravity. In a similar sense, our knowledge about human nature may not change this nature, but it may allow us to control human nature. If we define human nature as *potential* behavior, then the human social system, particularly the legal system and ethical systems, is a means for regulating and controlling actual behavior. For example, if human greed and exploitation threaten the community welfare, they may be controlled through enlightened policies of taxation and equitable distribution of resources through public policy.

The foregoing suggests that we can change or modify human *behavior* through social control, conditioning, education, and regulation; but the changing of human *potential* is slow and results only over very long periods of time from biological and cultural evolution. The development of speech and language capacities in man did more to change human potential and eventually human behavior than any other evolutionary change thus far in man.

TABLE 12–4

Average value of house by race in the United States for 1970 by census region.

	Non-Black	Black
The North Central Region		
1. Average value of house owned	$19,022.00	$14,038.00
2. Average monthly rent	103.00	86.00
3. Percentage of owner units lacking plumbing	7.3%	6.7%
4. Percentage of owner units with one or more persons per room	7.1%	16.9%
The Northeastern Region		
1. Average value of house owned	$22,414.00	$14,769.00
2. Average monthly rent	109.00	91.00
3. Percentage of owner units lacking plumbing	2.3%	2.2%
4. Percentage of owner units with one or more persons per room	4.6%	9.6%
Southern Region		
1. Average value of house owned	$17,064.00	$10,228.00
2. Average monthly rent	94.00	58.00
3. Percentage of owner units lacking plumbing	10%	24%
4. Percentage of owner units with one or more persons per room	10%	19%
Western Region		
1. Average value of house owned	$23,301.00	$19,038.00
2. Average monthly rent	116.00	94.00
3. Percentage of owner units lacking plumbing	1.2%	1.7%
4. Percentage of owner units with one or more persons per room	6.8%	14.6%

SOURCE: Everett Lee, Martin L. Levin, William W. Pendleton, and Patricia D. Postma, *Demographic Profiles in the United States* (Springfield, Va.: National Information Service, U.S. Department of Commerce, September 1971), Vol. I.

The foregoing suggests that social reality contains within its sphere the capacity for self-awareness and hence the capacity to evaluate one's self and to reflect on the reasons for one's condition. The evaluation process often results in a person's alienation from the established systems of authority in society and all that this implies for recalcitrant behavior. Such alienation is often felt by those who experience severe and repeated failure in adaptation within the framework of the larger society. For example, Robert K. Merton[10] has formulated the cultural theory (1) that the value of success in an industrial society as measured by the accumulation of wealth is a *major* social value; (2) that the legitimate means for attaining this goal are effectively denied to many members of the lower class; and (3) that this adaptive problem leads to efforts among the lower class to achieve success by illegal means. In other words, a conflict of values pertaining to means–ends relationships is correlated with crime rates. The availability of means is differentially distributed, both socially and personally, in society. Consequently, the problem of adaptation associated with scarce means is differentially distributed—that is, it is more serious for some groups than for others. Hence the response to these inequities varies with the degrees of stress experienced, as well as with the perceived consequences of the response and the means available.

Poverty and Unemployment

Although we are the world's richest nation, we also have large numbers of the very poor. As indicated above, one of the major values in our ideological system is the achievement of wealth by individual effort. This is a very efficient system from the points of view of motivation and inducement. As technology advances, however, success becomes more and more difficult for those whose parents were also poor. The means for correcting the imbalance in opportunity is to improve the educational system for all, including the poor. This gives the children of the poor a better opportunity for economic advancement.

The results of our education system clearly show that not enough effort has been devoted to expanding the quality of education for all. Although the proportion of the population with incomes at the poverty level had been reduced between 1955 and 1965, it is still about 20 per cent of the population (see Tables 12–5 and 12–6 for the distribution of income in the United States by color for 1955 and for 1965, and Table 12–7 for the distribution of income by number of families in 1965).

A significant reduction in the proportion of the population at and near the poverty end of the scale presupposes equal

[10] Robert K. Merton, *Social Theory and Social Structure*, rev. and enlarged ed. (Glencoe, Ill.: The Free Press, 1957), pp. 161–194.

educational opportunity for all and an expanding economy. In particular, it assumes an increase in educational expenditures large enough to enable the lower classes to benefit occupationally as technology advances.

TABLE 12–5
Income by color for United States males, for 1955.

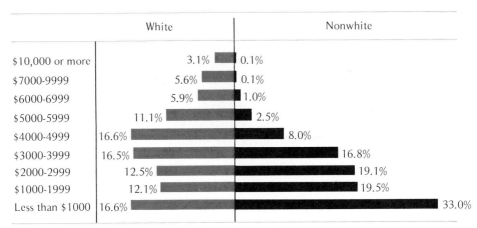

	White	Nonwhite
$10,000 or more	3.1%	0.1%
$7000-9999	5.6%	0.1%
$6000-6999	5.9%	1.0%
$5000-5999	11.1%	2.5%
$4000-4999	16.6%	8.0%
$3000-3999	16.5%	16.8%
$2000-2999	12.5%	19.1%
$1000-1999	12.1%	19.5%
Less than $1000	16.6%	33.0%

SOURCE: U.S. Bureau of the Census, *Current Population Report—Consumer Income*, Ser. P-60 (November 1956), Table 8.

TABLE 12–6
Family income by color in the United States, for 1965.

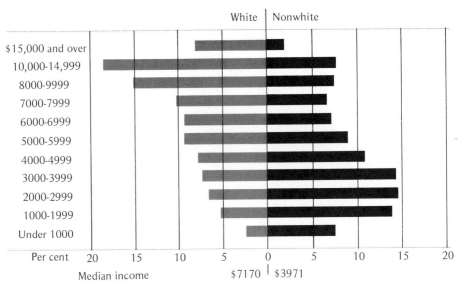

White | Nonwhite

$15,000 and over
10,000-14,999
8000-9999
7000-7999
6000-6999
5000-5999
4000-4999
3000-3999
2000-2999
1000-1999
Under 1000

Per cent 20   15   10   5   0   5   10   15   20
Median income $7170 | $3971

SOURCE: U.S. Bureau of the Census, *Current Population Reports*, Ser. P-60, No. 49 (10 August 1966), sample survey.

TABLE 12–7
Stratification of United States families by income, for 1965.

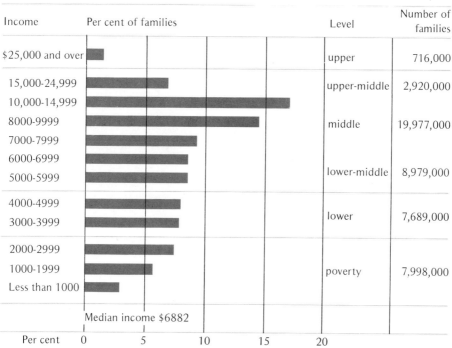

Income	Per cent of families	Level	Number of families
$25,000 and over		upper	716,000
15,000-24,999		upper-middle	2,920,000
10,000-14,999			
8000-9999		middle	19,977,000
7000-7999			
6000-6999			
5000-5999		lower-middle	8,979,000
4000-4999			
3000-3999		lower	7,689,000
2000-2999			
1000-1999		poverty	7,998,000
Less than 1000			

Median income $6882

Per cent   0   5   10   15   20

SOURCE: U.S. Bureau of the Census, *Current Population Reports,* Ser. P-60, No. 49 (10 August 1966), sample survey.

The report of the National Commission on Technology indicates that the needed increase has only partially taken place. For example, expenditures on technical research and development have risen 200 times since 1920, while educational expenditures are only 12 times as great.[11] In an advanced technological society, those who cannot get an adequate education, either from lack of opportunity or lack of ability, will end up on the unemployment rolls unless social policy is developed to control this. The disadvantages of excessive unemployment are serious and have been summarized by Edward Denison of the Brookings Institution.[12]

First, it discourages investment and research into new technology, which are two of the most important causes of our much needed economic growth. *Second,* it discourages workers from moving out of depressed areas and off farms, where they are either unemployed or underemployed, and seeking better jobs in new industries. *Third,* it increases union resistance to management's attempts to reduce wasteful labor practices, which increases opposition to more efficient production methods,

[11] *National Commission Report, Appendix Volume II,* p. 49.
[12] *National Commission Report, ibid.,* p. 49.

including labor saving machinery. *Fourth,* the high rates of unemployment lead to demands for higher tariffs to protect both industry and labor against goods produced more efficiently in foreign countries, therefore tending to hold up price levels at home.

Unemployment comes first to minority groups, particularly those at unskilled levels, to the young and to the returning war veteran. The National Commission Report describes some aspects of this situation[13]:

The unemployment of teenagers has long been over 15 per cent; Negro teenagers, 30 per cent; and residents of so-called depressed areas, from 50 per cent upward. Over a million young Americans between 16 and 21, although they would be expected to attend school, work in factories, or serve in the armed forces, are doing none of these. As school drop-outs, between 5 and 10 million American young people now face a future for which they are not prepared. There is no constructive place for them anywhere. . . . Since they are both out of school and out of work, they are especially bitter as they look for jobs that do not exist. They are often refused a job due to lack of experience, while at the same time they cannot get experience without a job.

Yet the demand is there. In one major city, over 2000 youths in one week registered for training, retraining, or any other way of winning a new lease on life. Many more are expected. Not one of the 2000 knew what he wanted to do. He just needed help. The U.S. Secretary of Labor says we have an "outlaw pack" of over 3½ million of these young people who cannot find jobs. The cost of this to the Nation is over $1000 per person every year in welfare and unemployment benefits alone, not counting the production lost by their unemployment or the cost of their possible crime of destructiveness. Seventy per cent of the recent crime increase has been in the 15–22 age group.

Our discussion of technological change and unemployment in relation to crime should be viewed as only *one* cause of crime under the condition of loose social control. There are, of course, other causes of crime, but unemployment is certainly one of the set when combined with a sense of alienation from the larger society.

Tables 12–8 and 12–9 show the crime rates by geographic region for 1956 and 1970,[14] and comparison of the two reveals the trend of increasing crime. While these figures are for urban areas, the same trend has occurred in rural areas, recently at an even more rapid rate. In commenting on the crime rates, the Federal Bureau of Investigation's (F.B.I.) 1970 *Uniform Crime Reports,* from which Table 12–9 was taken, states that since 1960, the rate for crimes of violence as a group increased 126 per cent and property crime rates rose 147 per cent.

[13] *National Commission Report, ibid.,* p. 49.
[14] For an interesting interpretation of regional variation in homicide rates, see Raymond D. Gastil, "Homicide and a Regional Culture of Violence," *Amer. Sociological Rev. 36,* No. 3 (July 1971), pp. 412–427.

TABLE 12–8

Urban crime rates, 1956, by geographic divisions (offenses known to the police per 100,000 inhabitants; population figures based on 1950 decennial census).

Division	Homicide	Robbery	Aggravated assault	Burglary	Larceny	Auto theft
United States	5.0	60.0	87.4	449.3	1228.4	233.5
New England	1.6	18.3	22.3	318.3	797.5	169.5
Middle Atlantic	3.0	50.1	75.6	360.4	786.0	167.4
East North Central	4.8	77.5	74.0	361.8	1154.7	189.1
West North Central	3.8	51.3	48.3	380.5	1312.9	212.6
South Atlantic	10.0	56.0	201.3	539.6	1370.8	285.6
East South Central	12.0	47.9	115.1	475.0	948.6	275.1
West South Central	9.4	46.6	101.3	608.7	1501.6	297.9
Mountain	3.8	65.9	52.3	624.2	2320.2	364.5
Pacific	4.0	99.9	109.2	757.2	2242.1	413.6

SOURCE: United States Department of Justice, Federal Bureau of Investigation, *Uniform Crime Reports for the United States,* XXVII, No. 2 (1956), p. 89.

TABLE 12–9

Urban crime rates by geographic region, 1970 (rate per 100,000 inhabitants).

Crime index offenses	North eastern states	North central states	Southern states	Western states
Murder	5.8	6.5	11.5	6.4
Forcible rape	12.7	17.0	18.0	28.9
Robbery	232.8	172.7	130.2	157.5
Aggravated assault	134.2	127.0	202.7	187.3
Burglary	1065.5	896.6	960.7	1541.8
Larceny	823.2	759.7	750.2	1269.3
Auto theft	571.0	419.3	327.1	570.2

SOURCE: United States Department of Justice, Federal Bureau of Investigation, *Uniform Crime Reports for the United States, Vol. 42,* August 1971), p. 6.

The effect of technology on social change is not in doubt, but does social change affect technology? The relationship between technology and social change is more accurately described as a feedback process rather than as the direct linear relationship that is often assumed. The fact that man is a language-using animal means that he can communicate about the past and the future in relation

Unanticipated and uncoordinated technological change can cause serious dislocations in the labor force.
(Courtesy Charles Harbutt, Magnum Photos, Inc.)

to the present. As a result, much of what man does is done in *anticipation* of its consequences. For example, President Roosevelt obtained passage of Social Security legislation in anticipation of an increase in the proportion of retired old people who would have no income without some form of forced collective savings. This measure is a form of social technology that, even with its limitations, has had far reaching effects upon the economy and on the stability of economic resources of many old people.

It is quite unlikely that the early forerunners of *Homo sapiens* would have survived to evolve into *Homo sapiens* if, somewhere along the way, advances in technology had not been made. These advances immediately set into motion a new mechanism affecting natural selection, namely, the increased survival rate of our forebears who possessed the technology.

TECHNOLOGICAL CHANGE AND CHANGING PATTERNS OF HEALTH

Neonatal Mortality Rate

Another major index of technological and economic development in a society is the **neonatal mortality index,** which is the age-specific death rate for babies from birth to one month of age. A low neonatal death rate is an important index to the successful adaptation of a population. This rate, as well as the infant mortality rate, has declined faster, for the Western nations of the world than for any other area. These are the nations, of course, in which technology has developed most rapidly.

Figure 12–1 shows a decline in the neonatal mortality rate in the United States from 44.4 per 1000 live births in 1915 to 18.5 in 1961, or a decline of nearly 60 per cent. In 1850, only three fourths of the newborn in the United States reached five years of age; in 1901, the same proportion reached 24; and in 1959, the same proportion survived more than 60 years.

The marked reduction in deaths of the young allows the population to sustain or increase its numbers with proportionately

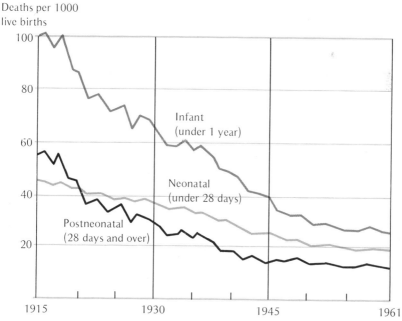

FIGURE 12–1   Infant mortality rates by age, in the United States, from 1915 to 1961.
(From various reports by the National Vital Statistics Division, U.S. Public Health Service. Compiled by Health Information Foundation. Chicago: University of Chicago Press.)

fewer births. The reduction in the death rate and the birth rate of the Western nations dramatically demonstrates this. In 1650 people of European ancestry made up about one sixth of the population of the world. By 1959, they constituted almost one third of the world's population.

Infant Mortality by Sex and Color in the United States

As indicated in the chapters on population, mortality at all ages in the United States has been higher among males than among females. In 1959, male infant mortality was 29.6 deaths per 1000 live births, some 29 per cent higher than the corresponding female rate of 23.0 per 1000.[15]

Infant mortality has traditionally been much higher among nonwhite infants than among whites. In 1915–1919 the non-white infant mortality rate averaged 149.7 per 1000 live births, about 61 per cent higher than the comparable figure for white infants of 92.8. Over the years, infant mortality has declined substantially for all, but in absolute terms the declines were greater for the non-whites. The nonwhite infant mortality rate dropped from 149.7 in the 1915–1919 period to 44.0 in 1959, and the corresponding figures for the white infants are 92.8 to 23.2. However, in *relative* percentage terms, the white decline was greater by 4 per cent, that is, a 75 per cent decline compared to a 71 per cent decline for the non-white infants.

These rates also vary by region. Infant mortality rates are currently lowest in the New England, Pacific, and West North Central regions. They were 16.8, 17.4, and 17.9 per 1000, respectively, in 1970 (see Figure 12–2 for the infant mortality rates by region for the United States in 1970).

To some extent the pattern of geographic variation in infant mortality is influenced by the racial and ethnic composition of the population in each region. These groups, particularly the blacks and Mexicans, have less access to adequate prenatal and post-natal medical care. The lowest infant mortality rate was among the white population of Utah—a rate of 15.3 in 1970. The highest comparable rate, 28.2, was in Mississippi and was undoubtedly affected by the large black population that resides there. Thus, the costs of differential institutional opportunity is dramatically reflected in these higher mortality rates.

Improved technology and the resulting improved economic conditions affect life expectancy at all ages. Let us now turn to remaining life expectancy for older people.

---

[15] These and other health statistics in this section were taken from reports by the Health Information Foundation, *Progress in Health Services,* The University of Chicago, Chicago, Ill., 1961.

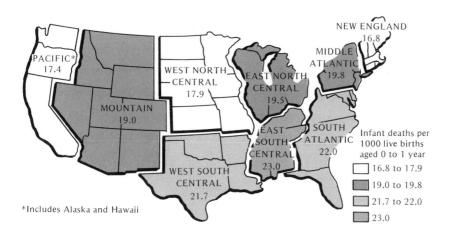

FIGURE 12–2   Infant mortality rates by geographic division for the United States in 1972.
(From various reports by the National Vital Statistics Division, U.S. Public Health Service.)

Trends in Remaining Years of Life for Older People by Sex and Color in the United States

Americans in the 1970's who are 45 have already lived almost as long as the average person born in 1900 could have expected to live. Today, these people have on the average about 30 more years of life remaining. In only a few countries in the world does the life expectancy of women at ages 45 and 65 exceed that of American women. However, there are many countries in which older men have a longer life expectancy than do American men.

Figure 12–3 shows the rank order of life expectancy in 14 selected countries for males and females at ages 45 and 65. As the infant mortality rate decreases and the life expectancy at all ages increases, the mortality rate from diseases of the heart increases. The increasing prominence of disability and death due to cardiovascular diseases is largely the result of technological and social progress made in the first half of the 20th century in controlling the communicable diseases. The increasing rate of heart disease is associated mainly with the middle and over age categories and more with males than females.

In 1900, about one fifth of deaths occurring in the United States were classified as resulting from cardiovascular–renal diseases. By 1925, the proportion had risen to about one third. By 1961, well

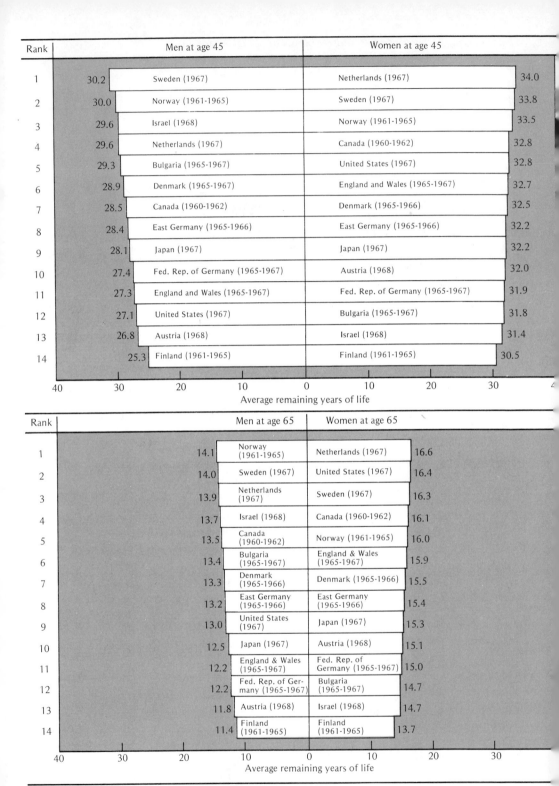

FIGURE 12–3 Average remaining years of life for males and females at ages 45 and 65, for 14 selected countries.
(From United Nations. *1969 Demographic Yearbook*. New York: United Nations, 1970, pp. 648–653.)

over one half of all deaths in the United States during the year were ascribed to this category. Most of this increase was due to the growing proportion of older persons in the population and to the improved procedures used for diagnosing and classifying causes of death.

In recent years, some reductions in heart disease mortality have occurred as a result of medical progress and improved surgical techniques. The largest reductions have been made in the childhood age group, and have resulted from progress against rheumatic fever and its frequent aftermath, rheumatic heart disease, and from the use of antibiotics to combat streptococcal infections. Nevertheless, in 1960, chronic rheumatic heart disease still accounted for 47.7 per cent of all deaths by heart disease at ages 15–24, and 37.5 per cent at ages 1–14. Hypertensive heart disease increases with advancing age; this is an increase not only in mortality rate, but also in the proportion of all deaths from heart disease attributable to hypertensive heart disease.

Heart Disease Mortality by Sex

An interesting sociological aspect of mortality from heart disease is the widening sex differential. This differential existed in 1900, but was much smaller than it is currently. In the first decade or so following 1900, the excess of male mortality averaged about 15 per cent. In 1960, it had reached 88 per cent. The hypothesis advanced to account for this attributes the widening sex differential to a combination of biological predisposition and sociological factors, particularly in the area of arteriosclerotic and coronary artery disease. It is believed that males are more predisposed to heart disease, and in addition, that they are more exposed to the social strains of modern life. The mechanism underlying these conditions that causes the effect or the disease is not clear. Moreover, the gap may be narrowed as the conditions of social life for women become more like

TABLE 12–10

Life expectancy by color and sex in the United States for 1929 and 1967.

Year	White		Nonwhite	
	Male	Female	Male	Female
1929	57.2	60.3	45.7	47.8
1967	67.8	75.1	61.1	68.2

SOURCE: *Vital Statistics of the U.S.* (Washington, D.C.: U.S. Government Printing Office, 1967), Vol. II, Sec. 5.

those for men. This point will be discussed in detail later in this chapter on "Technological Change, Social Change, and Crime Rates."

Many factors are undoubtedly involved in diseases of the heart and circulatory system. Social and environmental factors are only one of these. Nevertheless the increase in life expectancy in the United States from 1929 to 1967 is dramatic, as Table 12–10 reveals.

Nervous Breakdown by Sex, Age, and Education

The National Center for Health Statistics[16] estimates that approximately 5.4 million people in the United States consider that they have had a nervous breakdown and another 14.2 million have felt that they were going to have a nervous breakdown. As was indicated in earlier sections in this chapter, the degree of social and psychological stress varies in the population with the degree of difficulty in social and economic adaptation. For example, rates for nervous breakdown by educational level show a definite trend toward greater frequency among the less well-educated, particularly those with under nine years of education. This trend by sex and age is shown in Table 12–11.

TABLE 12–11
Joint relationships of sex, age, and educational level with per cent reporting a nervous breakdown for 1962.

Sex and educational level	All ages, 18–79 years	18–24 years	25–34 years	35–44 years	45–54 years	55–79 years
Both sexes						
Under 9 years	7.57	2.52	3.37	5.84	7.25	9.90
9 years and over	3.50	0.91	2.64	3.67	4.03	6.86
Male						
Under 9 years	4.34	3.26	1.36	3.71	4.52	5.20
9 years and over	2.46	0.95	1.87	3.40	1.86	4.40
Female						
Under 9 years	10.76	1.79	4.95	8.04	10.04	14.62
9 years and over	4.40	0.87	3.35	3.90	6.01	8.68

SOURCE: National Center for Health Statistics (Rockdale, Md.: U.S. Public Health Service, 1970), Ser. 11, No. 37, p. 15.

[16] National Center for Health Statistics, *Selected Symptoms of Psychological Stress in the United States* (Rockdale, Md.: U.S. Public Health Service, 1970), Ser. 11, No. 37, p. 14.

Thus, in nervous disorders, females show a higher rate than males, but as we indicated above, males have a much higher rate of coronary and cardiovascular disease. The social roles of the sexes vary so much that it is difficult to assess differential rates of illness between them. One of the most striking variations in behavior between the sexes that appears to have a causal base in the differential socialization of the sexes is crime behavior. This will be discussed next in relation to changing technology and social organization.

TECHNOLOGICAL CHANGE, SOCIAL CHANGE, AND CRIME RATES

A View of the Causes of Crime

This section will deal with two important variables—first, the increasing rates of crime, and second the wide gap between the frequency of crime among males and among females—and the relationship of these two to social and technological change.

The F.B.I.'s *Uniform Crime Reports for the United States* are the only national crime data available. They consist of voluntary reports by most local police jurisdictions in the country of offenses known to the police and arrests made. Judging from voluntary disclosures and the sizable number of undetected crimes, one may be sure that the *Uniform Crime Reports* significantly underreport the actual number of cases, although there is probably less underreporting concerning the categories of violent crimes, such as homicide, robbery, and assault.

Violent crime, at least in volume, is primarily a phenomenon of large cities. The 26 cities in the United States with populations of 500,000 or more contribute about one half of the total reported major violent crimes, but they comprise only one fifth of the total reporting population.[17] Moreover, violent urban crime is overwhelmingly committed by males. The reported male homicide arrest rate in large cities is five times the female rate, and the robbery rate is 20 times higher. Furthermore, and in spite of the numerous deficiencies in arrest data, true rates of violent crime by blacks appear to be considerably higher than rates for whites. Reported urban arrest rates are much higher for blacks in all four major violent crime categories, ranging up to 16 times as high for robbery and 17 times as high for homicide. If these data were correlated to reflect

---

[17] These and many other statistics in this section were drawn from Department of Justice, Federal Bureau of Investigation, *Uniform Crime Reports for the United States (1933–1968)* (The data were compiled from several issues); and from D. J. Mulvihill, Melvin M. Tumin, and Lynn A. Curtiss, *National Commission on the Causes and Prevention of Violence. Volume 11. Crimes of Violence* (Washington, D.C.: U.S. Government Printing Office, 1969).

differential social, economic, and educational opportunity among urban black and white groupings, these differences would be greatly reduced. The overall trends of individual violence in the United States are shown in Figure 12–4.

Let us examine some of the social and technological conditions associated with these rising crime rates. The single most important social condition underlying the causes of crime can be seen by contrasting the conditions of social life and the forms of social control in a simple primitive society with that of a modern society. The first factor relates to the size of the social units, and the resulting degree of acquaintance of everyone with everyone else. In the primitive society, where social units were very small, there was no anonymity. A second factor, and one related to the first, was the great dependence in the primitive society of the individual upon the band or clan for social acceptance, and for his personal safety and survival. If an individual were rejected by his larger social unit, he had no place to escape. Other clans or units were hostile to strangers. In other words, individual geographic mobility was virtually unthinkable. The whole social unit could and did move in nomadic fashion. If we contrast these conditions with those of modern social life, we are able to see more clearly the major conditions that bring about the weakening of social controls, and thus, those that create the *possibility* for escaping the consequences of committing a crime.

In the first place, the great geographic mobility possible today makes it difficult to apprehend and catch an offender; second, the offender can settle in another community many miles from the scene of the crime and begin life anew, without serious interruption of the normal social supports, such as a job, a place to live, recreation, medical care, and food. The great mobility and anonymity that so characterize modern society are important conditions for escaping social control. These conditions are, of course, associated with industrial organization and the free competition of workers for jobs in different parts of the nation. Thus the costs, both social and economic, of behavior control in an advanced society are enormously greater and more difficult than in simpler systems. The larger and more complex a society is, the more difficult it is to exercise effective social control. Third, in simpler societies one's welfare depends more on nature and less on the social system, with the exceptions of the necessity for cooperation and sharing. In modern society, one's welfare is significantly determined by his place in the social system; accordingly one's attitude toward the system depends to a high degree upon his social status. In a rapidly changing and mobile society one has high expectations that one day his fortune will improve. This is especially true in a society that judges success primarily on the basis of income and the acquisition of material

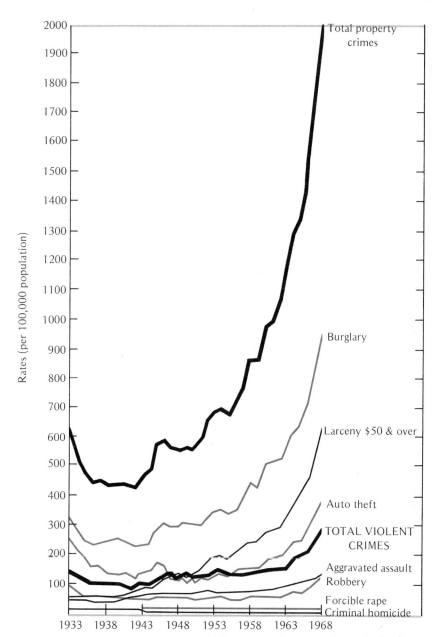

FIGURE 12–4   Levels and trends of individual violence in the United States. (From D. J. Mulvihill, Melvin M. Tumin, and Lynn A. Curtiss, *National Commission on the Causes and Prevention of Violence. Volume II. Crimes of Violence.* Washington, D.C., 1969.)

goods. If one has been unsuccessful in this attempt, his tendency to blame the system rather than himself largely depends upon his perception of the fairness of the system to all participants. If he blames the system for his failures, he can more easily justify acts of violence against it.

All individuals are potentially aggressive and violent—
that is, they have the *capacity* for aggression. Whether aggression or
violence is expressed depends upon the type of interaction that
occurs between or among individuals, and upon the nature and effectiveness of the social controls under which the interaction occurs.

Violence and Sex Differences

Much can be learned about aggression and violence by studying the
socialization of children. Though there are differences in temper-
aments of infants, a young child is "naturally" a nonconformist until
he is socialized into conformity. And the patterns of conformity vary
with the social organization of the society.[18] For example, women's
behavior becomes like men's when they occupy the same type of
social roles as men. Women who have been heads of countries have

TABLE 12-12

**The occupations of offenders arrested for major violent crimes in
selected cities in 1967.[a]**

Offender occupation	Major violent crime type (percentage)				
	Criminal homicide	Forcible rape	Aggravated assault	Armed robbery	Unarmed robbery
Executive	1.1	1.3	0.3	0.0	0.0
Manager	1.4	1.5	0.6	0.0	0.0
Secretary–clerical	1.8	2.9	2.8	0.3	1.7
Sales	1.0	0.8	0.7	0.0	0.0
Other services	2.1	4.3	6.4	1.4	2.0
Craftsman	0.0	1.6	0.8	0.0	0.0
Skilled laborer	5.3	5.4	5.1	5.3	1.5
Laborer	9.0	26.9	14.1	10.6	12.6
Farmer	0.0	0.4	0.0	1.0	0.0
Student	2.1	10.8	10.1	15.0	34.2
Housewife	5.8	0.0	3.0	0.5	0.6
Dependent	0.0	0.4	1.7	0.8	2.5
Other	1.6	1.2	2.8	0.5	1.5
Unemployed	5.4	7.9	6.4	13.5	7.1
Unknown	63.1	34.3	45.3	51.4	36.2
Total percentage	100.0	100.0	100.0	100.0	100.0

[a] Total number of offenders (statistical weights applied) 3790. Column figures
may not add up exactly to 100.0 per cent because of rounding.
SOURCE: D. J. Mulvihill, Melvin M. Tumin, and Lynn A. Curtiss, *National Commission on the Causes and Prevention of Violence. Volume 11. Crimes of
Violence* (Washington, D.C.: U.S. Government Printing Office, 1969), p. 96.

[18] For an interesting description of sex roles that differ from those in American society, see
Margaret Mead, *Sex and Temperament in Three Primitive Societies* (New York: Mentor
Books, 1950).

been as capable as men in performing tough administrative roles. One has only to think of Madame Gandhi of India and Prime Minister Golda Meir of Israel in the world today, and of Elizabeth I of England, Catherine the Great of Russia, and Margaret the First of Denmark in the past, as great examples of capable, courageous, and tough female leaders.

Although we find differences in the tendency to violence among different age, sex, and racial groups, there is no evidence to link these differences to genetic differences. Social and cultural conditioning and the socialization for specific sets of roles appear to be the determinants for the expression or suppression of aggression and violence. The female child is usually more supervised and controlled than the male; she is taught feminine ways and attitudes. The male, on the other hand, is taught that unless he expresses his aggression his manhood or masculinity may be in question. The male in the ghetto subculture is taught to be tough through socialization with peer gangs and teasing by adults. When the cultural roles of women and men become the same or similar, their rates of crime and violence also become similar. In fact, the current greatest increase in homicide rates is among females, though the relative rates are still much lower for women. Table 12–12 lists the percentage of violent crimes in selected cities in the United States in 1967 by occupation of the offenders arrested. It is clear that the rates of violence appear to be much greater for those of lower socioeconomic status than for those of higher status.

Variation in Reported Offense Rates
for Major Crimes of Violence by Region

As was shown above in the section on "Technological Change and the Labor Force," those most affected by unemployment are the young and the unskilled. This situation adds to the existing negative influences of the urban slums. Although there has been some improvement in recent years, unemployment for nonwhites is still about twice as high as that for whites; and although Negro family income in the cities has recently increased to a median of $5623, this figure represents only 68 per cent of the average white family income. For example, one third of the black families in cities lived on $4000 a year or less, while only 16 per cent of the whites did. Since the highest offense rates occur among the poor, both white and nonwhite, one would expect these rates to be higher in regions of lower median income and among the young.

Figure 12–5 summarizes this trend by region for the four major violent crimes combined (that is, the total numbers of rapes, robberies, and aggravated assaults). The highest homicide rate is in the South, with the other three regions fairly similar. Forcible rape

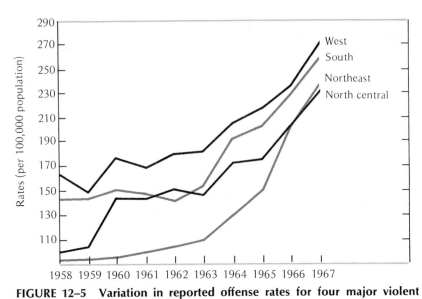

FIGURE 12–5   Variation in reported offense rates for four major violent crimes combined, by region, for 1958–1967.
(From United States Department of Justice, Federal Bureau of Investigation, *Uniform Crime Reports for the United States* (1958–1967), data compiled from various issues.)

is higher in the West than in the other three regions, which vary insignificantly from one another. Robbery is significantly higher in the West, the North Central, and the Northeast, than in the South. The data on aggravated assaults are conflicting; therefore it is difficult to tell which region is higher, although the Western region appears to be.

The percentage change in reported offense rates over the 10-year period, 1958–1967, is given by region in Tables 12–13 and 12–14, and by age in Table 12–15. Although the greatest percentage increase in homicide arrest rates occurred in the 10–17 year old age group, the greatest number of homicide arrests occurred in the 18–24 year old category.

In commenting on the causes of crime, the National Commission on the Causes and Prevention of Violence makes the following summary statement: "Combine poverty, deteriorated and inadequate housing, lack of good employment opportunities, economic dependency, poor education, and anonymous living with population density, social and spatial mobility, ethnic and class heterogeneity, reduced family functions, and broken homes—and an interrelated complex of powerful criminogenic forces is produced by the ghetto environment." [19]

---

[19] D. J. Mulvihill, Melvin M. Tumin, and Lynn A. Curtiss, *National Commission on the Causes and Prevention of Violence. Volume 11. Crimes of Violence* (Washington, D.C.: U.S. Government Printing Office, 1969), p. xxxiii.

TABLE 12–13

Variation in reported offense rates for four major violent crimes combined, by region, for 1958–1967 (rates per 100,000 regional population).

	1958	1959	1960	1961	1962	1963	1964	1965	1966	1967
Northeast	94.2	94.6	94.6	100.5	102.9	110.6	132.7	146.7	202.7	237.0
North Central	99.2	103.8	144.8	142.3	149.8	145.2	172.5	176.2	204.0	236.3
South	145.4	143.4	150.3	147.0	143.5	154.8	196.8	205.0	230.4	260.5
West	162.5	149.5	174.1	168.3	178.1	177.8	206.0	216.8	235.7	272.2

SOURCE: United States Department of Justice, Federal Bureau of Investigation, *Uniform Crime Reports for the United States.* Data were compiled from various issues.

TABLE 12–14

Percentage change in reported offense rates for four major violent crimes, by region, for 1958–1967.

Criminal homicide	
Northeast	+ 70.8
North central	+ 63.3
South	+ 5.6
West	+ 40.0
Forcible rape	
Northeast	+ 71.0
North central	+ 104.5
South	+ 53.7
West	+ 31.4
Robbery	
Northeast	+ 230.5
North central	+ 136.7
South	+ 127.7
West	+ 61.3
Aggravated assault	
Northeast	+ 109.8
North central	+ 151.1
South	+ 71.7
West	+ 81.5
4 major violent crimes combined	
Northeast	+ 151.7
North central	+ 138.2
South	+ 79.2
West	+ 67.5

SOURCE: D. J. Mulvihill, Melvin M. Tumin, and Lynn A. Curtiss, *National Commission on the Causes and Prevention of Violence. Volume 11. Crimes of Violence* (Washington, D.C.: U.S. Government Printing Office, 1969), p. 165.

TABLE 12–15
Percentage change in reported urban arrest rates for the four major violent crimes, by age, for 1958–1967.

Criminal homicide	
10–14	+ 150.0
15–17	+ 112.5
18–24	+ 76.2
25 +	+ 37.9
10–17	+ 121.1
All ages (10 +)	+ 55.4
Forcible rape	
10–14	+ 69.6
15–17	+ 19.8
18–24	+ 1.8
25 +	+ 26.5
10–17	+ 30.9
All ages (10 +)	+ 27.8
Robbery	
10–14	+ 192.9
15–17	+ 86.9
18–24	+ 38.1
25 +	+ 31.9
10–17	+ 121.3
All ages (10 +)	+ 71.8
Aggravated assault	
10–14	+ 290.3
15–17	+ 152.5
18–24	+ 62.0
25 +	+ 45.7
10–17	+ 197.0
All ages (10 +)	+ 68.7
4 major violent crimes combined	
10–14	+ 222.0
15–17	+ 102.5
18–24	+ 45.5
25 +	+ 41.1
10–17	+ 138.8
All ages (10 +)	+ 65.7

Source: D. J. Mulvihill, Melvin M. Tumin, and Lynn A. Curtiss, *National Commission on the Causes and Prevention of Violence. Volume 11. Crimes of Violence* (Washington, D.C.: U.S. Government Printing Office, 1969), p. 169.

There is no doubt that the foregoing factors are significant factors in the causes of crime, but whether they actually lead to criminal responses depend on other factors as well. There are many individuals in the ghettos who do not commit crimes of violence. How do these persons differ individually and socially from those who do? These cases of those who do not commit violent crimes need to be compared and contrasted with the offender cases. Moreover, while crime in the inner city has worsened, conditions in the inner city have generally improved. This also tends to suggest that other factors are involved.

We have argued in this book that attitudes are a consequence of behavior, rather than a cause of behavior. If one is able to commit crimes without serious consequences for himself, then there is no deterrence to criminal action through aversive conditioning. Neither the severity of the punishment nor the consequences of behavior can deter criminal behavior as effectively as the *certainty and swiftness of the negative consequence.* The implications of this are that we need more and better trained police officers for the inner city, and more efficient court action, *as well as* programs of social rehabilitation for the inhabitants. These are necessary because the areas of high crime rates have for so long been areas in which there are no effective established authorities or social controls that represent the conforming society for the youth to learn from or observe. The gangs that have arisen have provided the only consistent images available. Consequently, the regular presence of a stong but benevolent authority in these areas of high social disorganization is needed.

Summary

Technology was conceptualized to include the tools, techniques, and know-how by which man solves his problems of adaptation to his environment—both the man-made and the natural environment.

Improved and new technologies have extended man's abilities to adapt; as a consequence his species has increased in population at an exponential rate and has spread over the entire planet. The size of the human population, the complexity of the technology, and the interfered side effects of some of that technology on both the natural environment and man himself has made technology itself a new problem of adaptation. In the past, both man and his technology have evolved in a relatively *unplanned* manner. Current growth trends in population and industrial capacity obviously have finite limits, and these limits are determined by the ecological and biological support capacities of the planet and the capacity of the human population to govern itself constructively. That there are limits to both of these there is no doubt. But it would be foolhardy and catastrophic to discover these limits by experiencing their arrival. Therefore, planned and controlled growth and development are essential. Also, this new problem of adaptation transcends national borders and will therefore require international cooperation, planning, and policy development. As a result of these considerations, this chapter dealt with technology and adaptation in four interrelated problem areas. These were (1) the international control of armaments and international disputes; (2) the control of man-made pollutants to the ecosystem; (3) the correlation of technology, population growth, and economic growth, particularly the effects of automation on the economic system; and (4) the control of crime.

The *know-how* for controlling all of these either exists or can be developed. Whether or not agreement, both nationally and internationally, on policy and courses of action on these problems can be arrived at in time is a serious question. The problems are so complex and the solutions will require such major alterations from current practice that the resulting implied threat to power blocs and vested interests may block constructive effort. One example should suffice to show the nature of the sociological problem involved. To develop new technology to meet the economic and health needs of the population assumes continued economic progress. This in turn presupposes that the central government of the nation can control economic inflation, which is not possible unless the government has the power and the will to exercise the necessary controls on prices and wages. Given the great economic power blocs outside government, the development and implementation of such controls is difficult. One government official recently remarked that we in the United States have several "subgovernments" in the form of powerful labor and industrial organizations that frighten members of Congress from doing what is necessary for the general welfare. Unless this problem of decision making can be solved, then the problems of adaptation referred to above cannot be solved. Following a *general* discussion of the four areas of technology and adaptation referred to above, analyses were then made of particular problem areas—namely those of socialization, unemployment, health, and crime.

Exercises

1. Discuss the relationship of man-made tools and technology to man's adaptation. What changes have these made in man's relationship to his natural environment?

2. According to Leslie White, the degree of cultural development in a society is determined by what factors?

3. Discuss the similarities and differences between natural selection in biological evolution and the selection of ideas and values in cultural evolution.

4. What are the implications of the effects of modern technology and human waste products for planning for new technology and for controlling the effects of existing technology?

5. Consider the questions of rates of economic growth, increases in quantity and quality of energy supply, and technological growth on levels of living in modern society. Do these factors interact? Is continued growth in these three areas a necessary condition for continued improvement in levels of living?

6. What are the differences in the problems of socialization in a primitive society and in a modern society?

7. What are the differences in the problems of social control in a primitive society and in a technologically advanced industrial society?

8. Discuss the dependence of social change on technology.

9. Discuss some of the major effects of technological change on the labor force.

Selected Bibliography

Adelman, Irma, and Cynthia T. Morris. *Society, Politics and Economic Development: A Quantitative Approach.* Baltimore, Md.: Johns Hopkins Press, 1967.

Cole, Charles L. *The Economic Fabric of Society.* New York: Harcourt, Brace & World, Inc., 1969.

Commoner, Barry. *The Closing Circle: Nature, Man, and Technology.* New York: Alfred A. Knopf, Inc., 1971.

Galbraith, John K. *The New Industrial State.* Boston: Houghton Mifflin Company, 1967.

Helmer, Olaf. *Social Technology.* New York: Basic Books, 1966.

Jones, Martin V. "The Methodology of Technology Assessment," *The Futurist* (February 1972), pp. 19–25.

Kahn, Herman, Anthony J. Wiener, et al. *The Year 2000: A Framework for Speculation on the Next Thirty-Three Years. Volume II.* New York: The Macmillan Company, 1967.

Nuclear Energy Centers, Industrial, and Agro-Industrial Complexes. Oak Ridge National Laboratory Publication No. ORNL-4290 (November 1968).

Teich, Albert H. *Technology and Man's Future.* New York: St. Martin's Press, Inc., 1972.

Part IV

Social Regulation and Crises in Human Adaptation

13

Structures of Power
and Authority:
Control and Coordination

Almost every discipline or field of human interest (and interest in humans) has tried to deal with the eternal question of the practical connection between parts and wholes, freedom and order, specialization and coordination, creativity and responsibility, deviation and control, individuality and consensus.[1] Each field—religion, philosophy, art, the social sciences, the natural sciences—has developed its own tentative answers, though basically we can distinguish two opposing viewpoints. One approach, which may be called **romantic anarchism,** posits the superiority of creativity and the individual over the social and the organizational.[2] The other, while recognizing the importance of individual units or organs, emphasizes the crucial role of centralization and hierarchy (in short,

---

[1] Herbert A. Simon, *The Sciences of the Artificial* (Cambridge: MIT Press, 1969); David Bakan, *Disease, Pain, and Suffering* (Chicago: University of Chicago Press, 1968); C. H. Waddington, *The Ethical Animal* (New York: Atheneum Publishers, 1961).
[2] Joseph W. Krutch, *Human Nature and the Human Condition* (New York: Random House, 1959); Herbert Marcuse, *One-Dimensional Man* (Boston: Beacon Press, 1969).

---

coordination processes and structures) in social or collective adaptation—this, we call the **evolutionary "systems"** approach.[3]

There is no necessary antithesis between these positions; the first focuses on a short span of time and on relatively static conditions; the second considers behavior and its consequences over relatively long time periods, in which significant changes in resources, opportunities, and problems can be shown to occur. From our perspective, as described in Chapters 3 and 4, the second approach seems more fruitful. Instead of asking if coordination is necessary or desirable, we find that the more instructive question is how can we account for changes in the form and operation of social coordinative structures?

CONTEMPORARY PROBLEMS OF COORDINATION

Let us begin by reviewing a few contemporary problems in which coordination is a key difficulty.

Family Problems

Though the family is normally conceived as a cohesive group bound by affection and descent ("blood is thicker than water"), in problem families such bonds do not by themselves promote harmony or efficiency. Clearly, a major symptom of difficulty is the parents' inability to develop trust and respect in their children. This is reflected in the high proportion of juvenile court cases initiated by parents and relatives (10–30%), in the high rates of criminal behavior among young adolescents, and in the recently serious experimentation with drugs among adolescents.[4] It is also quite possible that early marriage (during high school, or in the first year of college) is in part an attempt to remove the weight of parental control. Several studies of lower-class wives, for example, have uncovered this reactive motive in many instances, as reported by the wives themselves. Incidentally, it is interesting to note that from 1940 to 1970, the age at marriage had been generally dropping for males and females (from 24.6 to 22 for males, from 21.2 to 20.6 for females).[5]

Another important facet of family problems is the eternally sensitive area of husband–wife relations. Legally and sym-

---

[3] Herbert A. Simon, *The Sciences of the Artificial* (Cambridge, Mass.: MIT Press, 1969), pp. 86–99; Piet Thoenes, *The Elite in the Welfare State* (New York: The Free Press, 1966), pp. 50–57; Donald McIntosh, *The Foundations of Human Society* (Chicago: University of Chicago Press, 1969), pp. 150, 272.

[4] Winston M. Ahlstrom and Robert J. Havighurst, *400 Losers: Deliquent Boys in High School* (San Francisco: Jossey–Bass, 1971); Richard S. Sterne, *Delinquent Conduct and Broken Homes* (New Haven, Conn.: College and University Press, 1964).

[5] Lee Rainwater et al., *Workingman's Wife* (New York: MacFadden, 1959), pp. 76–77; Mirra Komarovsky, *Blue Collar Marriage* (New York: Random House, Inc., 1964), pp. 24–28.

bolically, the husband is the head of the household.. But the long-term development of sexual equality and the husband's emphasis on his occupational responsibilities have often clouded the contours of family responsibilities and appropriate decision-making. In effect, each new marriage requires a definite personal understanding of each mate's spheres of influence and authority (for example, consumption patterns, personal allowances, responsibility for the children, vacation choices, the wife's employment). An overwhelming proportion of the family problems that eventuate in divorce or separation, or that are disclosed in family counseling sessions, stem from either (a) sharp disagreements about distribution of authority, or (b) the inability of either mate to handle some segment of family responsibility (for example, proper supervision of children, adequate use of family income, preparation of adequate meals).[6]

Organizational Problems: The University

The "campus" of colleges and universities is well-named; it originally referred to a field where military operations were concentrated. In recent years, the "military" or "conflict" aspect of higher education has become remarkably (and perhaps embarrassingly) obvious to the entire nation, if not to the world. Essentially, the problems of the university are variations on a common theme: where is the focus for responsible decision-making on key campus issues? Curriculum change (toward more "relevance" or for the interests of minority groups), dormitory privileges, parking, the proper emphasis on teaching and research, the relation between faculty research and governmental or corporate agencies, the grading system, granting or withholding of faculty tenure, the relation between undergraduate work and graduate and professional training are all problems that derive from challenges to existing authority and power, and which offer alternative solutions to "desirable" forms of campus decision-making.

   For some years, the patterns of authority in colleges and universities were largely unchallenged—in state institutions, the central administration and the state legislature were in a precarious dual command; in private universities and colleges, boards of trustees and key administrators (president, provost, or chancellor) established basic policies. Since World War II, however, the competition for academic power has become intense and complicated. Among the first major challenges were those from vocal alumni (who wanted winning football teams and/or the maintenance of traditional academic emphases) and from semiautonomous research institutes, funded by the federal government or private foundations. Almost

[6] Georgene H. Seward and Robert C. Williamson (eds.), *Sex Roles in Changing Society* (New York: Random House, Inc., 1970), Part 2.

simultaneously, the expansion of graduate programs and various professional schools (for example, medical and law schools) came into conflict with the space and faculty needs of undergraduate programs. During the late 1950's and early 1960's, the national shortage of qualified faculty members promoted a revival of long-dormant faculty power on many campuses. Most recently—largely since 1968 —college students have become vocal and sometimes effective in criticizing almost every aspect of the college community, through confrontation, violence, vandalism, and the institution of their own courses.[7]

As matters now stand, higher education in the United States is relatively free of the violent forms of internal power struggles—but the basic problem remains: Who in fact is willing and able to make crucial, practicable decisions about programs, goals, finances, and personnel? This question is one of particular urgency at this moment because the economics of higher education are marked by staggering deficits and menaced by uncertainties of future support.[8]

Modern Urban Regions

For most Americans, the most immediate illustration of apparent social chaos is the metropolitan complex or urban region (called the Standard Metropolitan Statistical Area by the Census Bureau and most students of urban areas). While cities have often been viewed in the past as efficient concentrations of populations and services, the actual operation of cities seems stultified, directionless, irresponsible, and even cyclothymic or manic-depressive—to borrow a well-worn psychiatric term. In many instances, for example, there is little or no cooperation between the governments of the central city and adjacent towns, suburbs, counties, and other administrative units (such as school districts, water districts, and so on.[9] Despite 40 or 50 years of local planning agencies, cities generally are unable to develop satisfactory connections between and among housing needs, transportation and highway needs, health and welfare needs, and formal educational needs. Large numbers of city residents are

---

[7] See, for example, Clark Kerr, *The Uses of the University* (Cambridge, Mass.: Harvard University Press, 1963); Harry Kidd, *The Trouble at L.S.E., 1966–1967* (London: Oxford University Press, 1969); Lewis B. Mayhew, *Arrogance on Campus* (San Francisco: Jossey-Bass, 1970); Robert A. Nisbet, *The Degradation of the Academic Dogma* (New York: Basic Books, 1971. For a picture of academic development and problems in another era, see Gordon Leff, *Paris and Oxford Universities in the Thirteenth and Fourteenth Centuries* (New York: John Wiley & Sons, Inc., 1968).

[8] James M. Buchanan and Nicos E. Devletoglon, *Academia in Anarchy* (New York: Basic Books, 1970); J. Victor Baldridge, *Power and Conflict in the University* (New York: John Wiley & Sons, Inc., 1971).

[9] Robert C. Wood, *1400 Governments* (Cambridge, Mass.: Harvard University Press, 1961); Oakland Task Force, San Francisco Federal Executive Board, *Federal Decision-Making and Impact in Urban Areas: A Study of Oakland* (New York: Praeger, 1970).

financially and culturally unable to enjoy the fruits of urban invention and affluence (theaters, museums, varied recreation areas, li-
braries, and so on). And neither private nor public sources have as
yet managed to provide adequate housing for an estimated 25 per
cent of a steadily increasing urban population.[10]

In addition, almost every major attempt at developing
more efficiency and more rational control of urban complexity has
been confronted by distrust, resistance, narrow group interests, and
even corruption. We have a number of well-documented accounts
of urban conflicts that successfully obstructed (or effectively marred)
a wide range of urban improvements, such as a new airport, im-
proved health services|and|location of hospitals, downtown renewal
projects, adequate highway or rapid transit systems.[11]

Likewise, there have been numerous attempts at developing more efficient *formal* structures of coordination in urban areas.
These include the "weak mayor" and "strong mayor" forms, the
commission form of city government, the city manager system, city–
county consolidation, metropolitan government, regional planning
bodies, and special contracts between the central city and surrounding communities for a particular service (for example, water supply,
fire protection). With few exceptions, these experiments in urban
coordination have been unworkable, primarily because voluntary
cooperation of crucial groups has been grudging, intermittent, or
tacitly withheld.[12]

The National Level of Organizational Difficulties

Throughout its history, but especially since World War II, the United
States has had some obvious continuing (and increasingly severe)
problems of administering its national services and programs. The
demand for federal support or subsidy to a multitude of interests and
groups has produced a gigantic patchwork of agencies (and entrenched personnel), which simply defies attempts at even modest
forms of coordination, regardless of the party in official control.
Essentially, the President, the Congress, and various regulatory agencies respond to the most immediate and powerful pressures from

[10] Jewel Bellush and Murray Hausknecht (eds.), *Urban Renewal: People, Politics, and Planning* (Garden City, N.Y.: Doubleday & Company, Inc. 1967); Robert H. Connery and Richard H. Leach, *The Federal Government and Metropolitan Areas* (Cambridge, Mass.: Harvard University Press, 1960); Lawrence M. Friedman, *Government and Slum Housing: A Century of Frustration* (Chicago: Rand McNally & Company, 1968).
[11] Edward C. Banfield, *Political Influence* (New York: The Free Press, 1961); Robert J. Mowitz and Deil S. Wright, *Profile of a Metropolis: A Case Book* (Detroit, Mich.: Wayne State University Press, 1962); Joan B. Aron, *The Quest for Regional Cooperation* (Berkeley, Calif.: University of California Press, 1969); Ralph W. Conant, *The Politics of Community Health* (Washington, D.C.: Public Affairs Press, 1968); Robert H. Connery et al., *The Politics of Mental Health* (New York: Columbia University Press, 1968).
[12] For descriptions and analyses of pressure groups, see Grant McConnell, *Private Power and American Democracy* (New York: Alfred A. Knopf, Inc., 1966); Betty H. Zisk (ed.), *American Political Interest Groups* (Belmont, Calif.: Wadsworth Publishing Co. Inc., 1969).

unions, oil companies, farm organizations, civil rights groups, manufacturers of durable goods, textile firms, trucking companies, major
airlines, the two or three largest airplane manufacturers, the timber
industry, drug companies, old age groups, the medical profession,
real estate developers, the banking and investment sectors, the
military services, and so on. Each "solution" or decision—in law and
administrative implementation—is thus an invitation to requests for
favored treatment for other groups or interests.[13]

As a result of decades of sequential dispensations to special interests, the national polity is increasingly incapable of developing well-reasoned, understandable, or workable networks of federal
programs. There are scores of dubiously connected services in each
of the following areas: health and welfare; housing and urban development; agricultural subsidies and financing; stimulation of
commercial and productive growth. Consequently, the effects of
governmental programs are difficult to evaluate, and the discrepancy
between promised benefits and limited or mixed results understandably encourages disillusionment, cynicism, and even disrespect for
persons in authority—and for authority itself.

Two examples from recent years may be briefly mentioned as symptoms of a national malady.

1. In August of 1971, President Nixon announced the
widely approved goal of halting serious inflationary pressures in the
American economy. The major mechanisms he proposed were wage
and price controls (the "freeze"). However, almost every affected
group (wage workers and their unions, industry, retailers, teachers,
civil service workers, and so on) pressed for exceptional treatment.
Wage and price boards, composed of representatives from business,
labor, and the public, had great difficulty in clarifying and implementing policies—and on several occasions, they altered their
judgments on specific cases. As a consequence, there was considerable doubt about the equity of controls (for example, interest rates
were not controlled) and, because specific groups were unwilling
to subordinate their demands to a genuine attack on inflation, the
results of the freeze brought about little improvement in economic
coordination or substantial containment of inflation.

2. Perhaps the most symbolic instances of national problems of coordination have been the intense controversies over the
appoinment of justices to the United States Supreme Court. Ideally,
the Supreme Court serves as the focal conscience of American society, as well as the court of ultimate appeal on fundamental (that is,
constitutional) issues. It therefore requires of the people a degree of
trust that no other official or public body can hope to approximate.

13 Robert H. Salisbury (ed.), Interest Group Politics in America (New York: Harper and Row
Publishers, Inc., 1970); Andrew M. Scott and Margaret A. Hunt, Congress and Lobbies:
Image and Reality (Chapel Hill, N.C.: University of North Carolina Press, 1966).

In recent years, however, candidates for this exalted position have been selected with minimal concern for the impartial moral stature that undergirds such a high level of trust. Several candidates were scrutinized and were found by the press and by the Senate to be vulnerable (that is, they seemed to have special biases on political and social issues—as do the common run of citizens). Two candidates were not confirmed—a rather rare event in American history. However, the validity of these evaluations is not important at this point. Much more revealing is the explicit conclusion that the rejected appointees personify the ruptures in legitimate coordination and the potential polarization of social and political differences in American society.

A BASIC DEFINITION OF REGULATION AND ITS MAJOR FORMS OF IMPLEMENTATION

The underlying difficulty in the preceding examples is the lack of effective and generally acceptable **regulation** of social diversity. This is a perennial problem in human organization, in part perhaps because the practical and theoretical implications of regulation are widely misunderstood. Either too much is expected of regulation, or regulation is viewed as an inherently repressive mechanism of unscrupulous despots. But these seem to be shortsighted—if not caricatured—viewpoints about a crucial phenomenon in human society. In fact, they tend to confuse *evaluations* with *conceptions* or descriptions of regulation, and thereby hinder or prevent the development of a reasonable understanding of the complexity and variability of regulation.

Let us begin, instead, with the notion of regulation as a universal social device that (a) responds to prevailing diversity by providing practical linkages between components of a social system and (b) tends to be altered in response to changes in the number and severity of practical problems derived from changes in social differentiation. In short, regulation is defined as an evolving, experimental, adaptive product of social interactions, of social achievements and frustrations.[14]

Regulation operates through distinctive social processes and mechanisms. In positive terms, regulation proceeds through direct or indirect **allocation** or assignment of resources, rewards, costs, and responsibilities among specialized or distinctive social

[14] Talcott Parsons, *Structure and Process in Modern Societies* (New York: The Free Press, 1960), Chap. 5; Talcott Parsons, *Sociological Theory and Modern Society* (New York: The Free Press, 1967), Chaps. 10, 11; Jan Pen, *Harmony and Conflict in Modern Society* (New York: McGraw–Hill Book Company, 1966); James G. March and Herbert A. Simon, *Organizations* (New York: John Wiley & Sons, Inc., 1958); Karl W. Deutsch, *The Nerves of Government* (New York: The Free Press, 1963).

The necessity for regulating competing streams of automobiles is widely accepted, though regulation of economic, political, and other differences is often hotly contested.
(Courtesy Robert Rapelye, Photography International.)

categories (classes, political subdivisions, ethnic groupings, communities, regions). But this rather general process of allocation or assignment may operate through emphasis on two roughly opposed forms of regulation.

Coordination

A major form of regulation emphasizes the positive or facilitative roles of regulatory positions and agents.[15] More specifically, coordination normally involves a set of indispensable tasks: (a) responsibility for "importing" resources from other social systems (for example, from state or federal sources to a city or a university); (b) developing regular distribution of resources to specialized units or divisions of a system; (c) encouragement and channeling of appro-

---

[15] Talcott Parsons, *Structure and Process in Modern Societies, ibid.*, pp. 33–44, 149–154; Amitai Etzioni, *The Active Society* (New York: The Free Press, 1968), Chap. 13; Donald McIntosh, The Foundations of Human Society (Chicago: University of Chicago Press, 1969), p. 150.

priate innovations from a part of the system to other related parts; (d) settlement of those differences between units that impede the expected operation of such units and that are judged to endanger important objectives of the system; (e) facilitation of an adequate flow of information among the various components of the system or organization; (f) consistent interpretation of the common values and practical interdependencies that characterize successful organization.

Control

At the other extreme of regulation is a series of control processes, which are more negative in character. In contrast to coordinative processes, control is exercised by restricting the flow of information and/or resources, by discouraging the transmission of innovations between parts of the system, by imposing settlements on contending subsystems, by emphasizing dominance and threats of force rather than necessary interdependence of parts, by favoring one specialized division (through assignment of resources) with a resultant (but not necessarily planned) reduction in the efficiency or contribution of some other specialized roles.[16]

The Roles of Coordination and Control

It is unwise to adopt a superficial *moral* approach to coordination and control processes (that is, that the former is desirable, while the latter is repressive, unfair, and so on). In practice, in all complex social structures, both processes are routinely used, but in varying proportions. Indeed, we can conveniently suggest a scale of regulation, from high concentration of controls to high emphasis on coordinative practices (see Figure 15–1). It is difficult to find examples for either extreme of this scale, perhaps because both forms are in some degree adaptive devices for complex social systems. The fundamental questions about regulation are therefore far from simple. We can begin by suggesting two. First, how can we account for major patterns of development in regulatory mechanisms? And second, how can we understand the relative achievements and difficulties of regulatory systems in specific societies or communities?

These are questions that have intrigued philosophers, historians, religious scholars, and various intellectuals for well over 2000 years.[17] However, only in the last half-century or so have the ingredients for promising answers been developed in the social sciences—particularly in sociology, social psychology, cultural or social

[16] Karl Mannheim, *Man and Society in an Age of Reconstruction* (New York: Harcourt, Brace, 1940), pp. 252–265; Richard A. Schermerhorn, *Society and Power* (New York: Random House, Inc., 1961), Chap. 1.
[17] See, for example, Robert N. Beck (ed.), *Perspectives in Social Philosophy* (New York: Holt, Rinehart and Winston, Inc., 1967).

anthropology, and political science. To a great extent, our understanding of regulation has accompanied analyses of the dynamics of
social power and authority—their social sources, key structures and
techniques, and practical and recurrent difficulties.

POWER AND AUTHORITY: NUCLEI OF REGULATION

Regulation may be defined as a specialized role (or roles) that (a)
develops in response to increasing division of labor and skills and
(b) is assigned to or is assumed by a definite position or social category. In practice, effective regulation works through decisions of
crucial actors, who communicate these decisions to persons in the
form of commands, orders, judgments, and so on, that are accepted
and acted upon by persons in given roles. While the practical need
for regulation is generally clear, the validity of such decisions and the
ability of regulators to achieve reasonable predictability of acceptance are among the most important issues in human social organization.[18]

Essentially, these issues in regulation have a common
base: the merited opportunity or responsibility of implementing
crucial social decisions. Normally, in every complex system, there
are roles (and appropriate individuals) that are widely recognized as
a rightful or legitimate focus for such decisions and for shaping behavior accordingly. These persons regulate social diversity by explicit **authority.** For example, a baseball manager has authority to
select and rearrange the members of the team for each game, to
dictate defensive and offensive strategies, to establish and punish
infractions of training rules, and to settle professional disputes
among team members.

But "authority" refers to *specified* matters for legitimate
regulation—matters based on social issues of some past period and
also on the assumption of stability in (a) social specialization and (b)
the practical problems of adapting to social and physical environments. From a realistic standpoint, however, regulation by authority
often sets limits that impede regulation itself.[19] For example, most
Presidents—Democratic and Republican—in this century have exceeded "constitutional" limits in engaging in military operations
without Senatorial approval—simply because modern political crises
require quick, decisive action. Likewise, many governmental executives (Presidents, governors, mayors) informally but effectively exert
pressure on private groups and subordinate officials to support im-
pending policies and potential candidates or appointees.

---

[18] Max Weber, *The Theory of Social and Economic Organization* (New York: Oxford
University Press, 1946), pp. 148–157, 324–329.
[19] Talcott Parsons, *Structure and Process in Modern Societies* (New York: The Free Press,
1960), pp. 190–194.

Regulation by force is an old but largely ineffective mechanism, as evidenced by the disaster at Kent State University.
(Courtesy Wide World Photos.)

These supplementary patterns of regulation may be usefully conceptualized as the social phenomenon of **power,** a term that is widely used, with varying shades of meaning. *In the perspective of this book, power may be defined as nonlegitimate or not yet legitimated processes of regulation,* which provide effective but limited means of mobilizing social behavior that cannot be handled by existing authoritative structures.[20] Obviously, **force** or coercion cannot be ignored as a third form of social regulation, but naked force has been relatively ineffective as a dominant means of regulation. Therefore, our major concern is to understand the conditions that encourage emphasis on these forms of regulation and, equally important, the processes by which changing emphases on authority, power, and force are created.

Problem 1.   Legitimation of Power

Since regulation is most visible in complex social systems (formal organizations, communities, nations), we can conveniently focus on

[20] Talcott Parsons, *Sociological Theory and Modern Society* (New York: The Free Press, 1967), pp. 297–317. See also the discussion and interpretation of Parsons' work in Alvin Boskoff, "Stratification, Power, and Social Change," in Herman Turk and Richard L. Simpson (eds.), *Institutions and Social Exchange* (Indianapolis, Ind.: Bobbs–Merrill, 1971), Chap. 18.

Traditionally, the political power of kings and emperors has been legit-imated by religious authority. Here King Boris III of Bulgaria is blessed by the Archbishop of Sofia.
(Courtesy Alfred Eisenstadt, Life Magazine © 1972, Time Inc.)

these. However, discovering the *sources* of power in such systems is often difficult. Such sources are well integrated into a system by the conversion of *power* into authority, which involves impor-tant social processes that are basic to the remaining problems of this chapter.

The first consideration is one not often recognized by lay-men and many professionals: power as a pattern of social interaction usually arises and develops within some existent social system, one with some prevailing patterning of authority. If regulation is to be maintained, then, authority and power processes must be adjusted to one another. One "solution" is found when persons in authority acquire supplementary power, as is quite common. In such cases, the power aspect of a regulator may be accepted informally but widely as a "zone of indifference" or as a necessary area of discretion and "judgment."[21] But such a solution requires *trust* in the character and responsibility of those in authority. Where such faith is questionable, or when persons in authority and their subordinates desire greater predictability in "power" decisions, the power aspects (if effective in practice) are transformed into rules, regulations, or procedural norms that bind all relevant parties through the legal mechanism of that social system.[22] For example, parents normally cannot expect their children to accept parental demands without connecting these to accepted and rather definite standards (on proper hours, household duties, weekly allowance, and so on). One difficulty in some families is simply the inability to *develop* binding rules because of irreconcilable interests or unwillingness to face power problems.

Another problem in legitimation arises when authority and power rest in different persons or social categories. At this point, we are only concerned with instances in which power sources *overcome* authoritative structures. Power *per se* tends to be based on personal rather than cultural or structural patterns; therefore, it is only vaguely bounded, is relatively unpredictable from the viewpoint of others, is without secure sources of support, and is subject to challenge from both external and internal influences. In short, comparatively speaking, unalloyed power is a vulnerable and marginal type of regulation and one that cannot function well without alteration. As Weber's classic discussion has shown, and as every major political revolution rediscovers, the early phases of power structures soon confront great difficulties in providing adequate regulation of diverse activities and organizations.[23] While authority operates with rather regular and automatic cooperation from specialized roles and groups, power without authority must simultaneously deal with resource problems and with a sociocultural vacuum (that is, the relative absence of valid rules, clear responsibilities, specific rights, and warranted rewards or sanctions). Since continued use of force is costly, and since trust is an essential element in effective social influence, power can be bolstered by crucial social arrangements that reduce widespread resistance and/or increase the likelihood of moral obligation to regulatory decisions.

One effective mechanism is a controlled sharing of responsibility with a "staff" of competent and sensitive advisors or

---

[21] James G. March and Herbert A. Simon, *Organizations* (New York: John Wiley & Sons, Inc., 1958), pp. 164–166; Chester I. Barnard, *The Functions of the Executive* (Cambridge, Mass.: Harvard University Press, 1938), pp. 167–171.

[22] John Thibaut and Harold L. Kelley, *The Social Psychology of Groups* (New York: John Wiley & Sons, Inc., 1959), pp. 128–138.

[23] Max Weber, *Theory of Social and Economic Organization* (New York: Oxford University Press, 1946), pp. 358–392; Crane Brinton, *The Anatomy of Revolution* (New York: Prentice-Hall, Inc., 1938), Chaps. 5, 6.

"experts." [24] This diffusion of power reduces the apparent arbitrariness of decisions and also permits a greater range of considerations in selecting goals and means for regulatory processes. It is well known in the field of administration (public and private) that inability to delegate authority inevitably impairs the effectiveness of most executives—and may even undermine their formal authority. However, newly achieved "authority"—following revolutions or the creation of new social systems (frontier or colonial settlements), or resulting from the conversion of great personal achievement into public prominence[25]—is also difficult to sustain without a network of "rational" intermediaries, who advise the centers of power and also interpret the intent and objectives of regulation for specialized social categories. Thus, a new government normally rests on careful selection of a cabinet; and, in a somewhat less serious realm, a new football coach usually begins by assembling four or five specialized assistants.

A second mechanism, the justification of the *structure of power,* is more positive and more time consuming. Since power contributes variant and somewhat unanticipated solutions to regulatory problems, "power" solutions *that do not rely on force* must become more predictable and more understandable, and, most important, must be endowed with a virtue that adequately replaces previous processes of regulation. Justification or legitimation of power is a major human enterprise—and a fascinating study in itself —but perhaps two aspects are especially relevant for our discussion.

Legitimation by Ideology[26]

It is regrettably true that questions regarding the best or most appropriate regulatory decisions (either power or authority) are seldom—if ever—rationally resolved or objectively evaluated. Instead, systems of authority rest on an implicit cluster of accepted (but largely unexamined) values. These have been called myths of authority, political formulas, rationalizations, derivations, social myths —but their common role is to furnish a meaningful and convenient reference point for questioned or questionable instances of authoritative action. The range of these "philosophies of power" is one evidence of man's inventive skills, for he has found justification for

---

[24] Hans H. Gerth and C. Wright Mills (eds.), *From Max Weber: Essays in Sociology* (New York: Oxford University Press, 1946), pp. 236–239.
[25] See Sigmund Diamond, "An Experiment in 'Feudalism': French Canada in the Seventeenth Century," *William and Mary Quarterly* (January 1961), pp. 3–34; reprinted in Werner J. Cahnman and Alvin Boskoff (eds.), *Sociology and History* (New York: The Free Press, 1964), pp. 170–190.
[26] Gaetano Mosca, *The Ruling Class* (New York: McGraw–Hill Book Company, 1939); Vilfredo Pareto, *Mind and Society* (New York: Harcourt, Brace, 1935), Vol. 3, Vol. 4, paragraphs 2181–2195; Georges Sorel, *Reflections on Violence* (New York: The Free Press, 1950); Karl Mannheim, *Ideology and Utopia* (New York: Harcourt, Brace, 1936), Chap. 3.

authority in such various sources as Divine Right; the will of the people; the public interest; racial purity; the sanctity of the nation; survival of the fittest; property as the fruit of robbery; black power; fear of the Yellow Peril; "what's good for General Motors is good for the U.S.A."; the master race; protection against political and religious heresies; resurgence of the Roman Empire; capitalist exploitation and oppression; Christian resistance to world communism.[27]

The technology of instilling the legitimizing ideologies of power is complex and in some respects imperfect. Indeed, the more specialized, diversified, or pluralistic a society, the greater the practical problems of creating and sustaining general moral approbation. In simpler societies[28] (for example, Carolingian France), the most frequently used device has been linkage of effective power to the prevailing religious system and its dominant officials. Modernization, secularization, and social heterogeneity have largely erased this source of legitimation. As many students of society have noted (Durkheim, Simmel, Fromm), a major source of societal problems is the relative absence of an alternative base for legitimation. This does not mean "the end of ideology" or the lack of ideological attempts to convert power into authority.[29] More accurately, these trends indicate that effective means for bolstering ideologies are still to be developed.

However, legitimation is not quite ready for its funeral rites. At the societal level, the focal power of economic and political notables has been rationalized in part by ideologies of national interest, national independence, or seductive notions of progress, which have been attractively diffused through the various mass media (newspapers, magazines, radio, and television). On the other hand, careful investigations of the impact of the mass media suggest definite limits to the social influence of these forms. Perhaps their greatest impact is in less differentiated societies, where competing

---

[27] Some examples of effective ideologies are discussed in Harold J. Laski, *The Rise of Liberalism: The Philosophy of a Business Civilization* (New York: Harper & Brothers, 1936); Herbert Butterfield, *The Englishman and His History* (Cambridge, England: Cambridge University Press, 1945); M. Morton Auerbach, *The Conservative Illusion* (New York: Columbia University Press, 1959); George L. Mosse, *The Crisis of German Ideology: Intellectual Origins of the Third Reich* (New York: Grosset & Dunlap, Inc., 1964); John G. Gagliardo, *From Pariah to Patriot: The Changing Image of the German Peasant, 1770–1840* (Lexington, Ky.: University of Kentucky Press, 1969).

[28] Charles Petit-Dutaillis, *The Feudal Monarchies in France and England* (London: Kegan Paul, Trench, Trubner, 1936), Book 3.

[29] Emile Durkheim, *The Division of Labor in Society* (New York: The Free Press, 1947), preface to the 2nd ed., pp. 287–290; Emile Durkheim, *The Elementary Forms of the Religious Life* (New York: The Free Press, 1947), pp. 427–431; Georg Simmel, *Conflict and the Web of Group Affiliations* (New York: The Free Press, 1955), pp. 162–163, 191–195; Erich Fromm, *Escape From Freedom* (New York: Rinehart, 1941); Daniel Bell, *The End of Ideology* (New York: The Free Press, rev. ed., 1962); Daniel Boorstin, *The Genius of American Politics* (Chicago: University of Chicago Press, 1953).

forms of communication are lacking. In these nations (in Turkey, for example), the relative novelty and speed of communication techniques (radio, television) seem to lend special credence to their contents or messages.[30]

Mass media play a more subtle role in the legitimation of power in the more urbanized, technologically developed societies. Advertising and public relations have often used one or more of these media to create favorable "public images" for power figures, or to lessen the impact of controversial actions by wielders of power (for example, John D. Rockefeller, Andrew Carnegie, Juan Perón, Joseph Stalin and the cult of personality). But this "impression management" is neither easy to accomplish nor durable, because of the effects of continued differences in social perceptions and conflicting sources of information and interpretation.[31] In fact, suspicion of manipulation through ideologies is an understandable by-product of such campaigns in recent decades.

Legitimation by Laws

The apparatus of law—as distinct from custom—is a social invention of immense but changing importance. Essentially, law has had a *sacred* character—first as communicated by the supernatural to charismatic individuals (Solon, Moses, Mohammed), and in recent centuries as a socially remote creation of prestigious specialists (legal scholars, jurists, and elderly legislators).[32] "The Law" or the legal realm should be distinguished from specific laws, since legislation and its application reduce the gap between the largely inaccessible legal order and a given population. Consequently, the basic problem in converting power into authority through law is: How does a society employ the sacred aspect of laws without reducing the general acceptance of legal sanctity?

This form of legitimation of power normally develops by a rather general legal mandate—such as a constitution or charter, or a prestigious commission report and recommendations—which becomes a sacred reference for types of responsibilities or decisions, rather than a justification of specific power groups.[33] The document

[30] Cf. the results of the following: Joseph T. Klapper, *The Effects of Mass Communication* (New York: Free Press, 1960); Marshall McLuhan, *Understanding Media* (New York: McGraw–Hill, 1964); Marshall McLuhan and Quentin Fiore, *The Medium Is the Message* (New York: Random House, Inc., 1967); Everett Rogers and Lynn Svenning, *Modernization among Peasants: The Impact of Communication* (New York: Holt, Rinehart and Winston, Inc., 1969); Daniel Lerner, *The Passing of Traditional Society* (New York: The Free Press, 1958).
[31] Ernest Dichter, *The Strategy of Desire* (Garden City, N.Y.: Doubleday & Company, Inc., 1960); Jacques Ellul, *Propaganda* (New York: Alfred A. Knopf, Inc., 1965).
[32] Max Weber, *On Law in Economy and Society* (Cambridge, Mass.: Harvard University Press, 1954), Chaps. 5, 7.
[33] Henri Pirenne, *Early Democracies in the Low Countries* (New York: Harper Torchbook, 1963; orig. ed., 1915), Chaps. 2, 3; Henri Pirenne, *A History of Europe* (Garden City, N.Y.: Doubleday & Company, Inc., 1958), Vol. 1, pp. 197–209, 238–256; John R. Commons, *Legal Foundations of Capitalism* (Madison, Wisc.: University of Wisconsin Press, 1959; orig. ed., 1924), Chap. 9.

Directly or indirectly, monitoring and control of news media are important mechanisms of wielding power in modern, technologically advanced societies.
(Courtesy Robert Rapelye, Photography International.)

is effective as a material reflection of the sacred, and also as a flexible set of conferred "powers," whose ambiguities make it difficult to find adequate leverage for attack.

From this base, the legitimated power of new governments or new leadership inevitably confronts practical problems of authority in general, and "new" authority in particular. New "regimes" tend to have a regulatory "honeymoon" of short duration (for example, the 100 days of the New Deal), in which the sacredness of the document of mandate is unquestioned and a flow of specific "enabling" laws is largely accepted. However, after that brief period, there is the distinct danger that a number of specific laws will exhaust the initial fund of legitimation. Frequency of laws and regulations inspires notions of the routine and the ordinary, in contrast to the sacred. And specific laws, rather than specific decisions, tend to be (or to seem) expedient and without understandable interconnections, thus further exposing the chinks in the armor of legitimacy. Consequently, legitimation of power by legal means is a continuing process,[34] one that is constantly vulnerable to tacit withdrawal of moral obligation in complex social systems.

[34] Max Weber, *Theory of Social and Economic Organization* (New York: Oxford University Press, 1946), pp. 363–373, 382–392.

Problem 2.   Understanding the Relative
Effectiveness of Regulatory Structures

The essential task of regulation is management of the major diversified roles and skills so that each role can be maintained and yet
make an acceptable contribution to the larger system (organization,
community, or society). As we have already noted, the basic ingredients of regulation include the structures of power and authority,
and processes of coordination and control. However, the *implementation* of these ingredients poses increasingly difficult problems for
modern societies. Theoretically and practically, then, how can we
understand and explain differences in the success or effectiveness of
contemporary patterns of social regulation? More specifically, what
kinds of social and social psychological factors help to explain the
achievements and limitations of regulation?

The Recruitment Process

Many perceptive thinkers (Pareto, Mosca, Mannheim,
Toynbee, Merton, Barnard)[35] have observed that regulation depends
on the abilities and skills of those who achieve positions of authority and power. In recent years, studies of experimental groups and
formal organizations strongly suggest that power positions tend to
be developed by persons who possess one or more of the following assets: a charismatic personality; strategic control of relevant
resources (money, credit, land); a superior fund of information or
knowledge; and special skills in effective communication.[36] But
these are clues to "ideal" processes of recruitment, and they are
limited to the "power" aspect of regulation. The crucial question
remains: What features distinguish the more effective regulators?
And, closely related, what *trends* in the recruitment of regulators
can be identified and explained?

In communities and societies, the regulators for which
we have the most relevant information are key political figures, high

---

[35] Vilfredo Pareto, *Mind and Society* (New York: Harcourt, Brace, 1935), Vol. 4, esp. paragraphs 2482–2507; Gaetano Mosca, *The Ruling Class* (New York: McGraw–Hill Book Company, 1939), pp. 51–66; Robert K. Merton, *Social Theory and Social Structure* (New York:
The Free Press, 1957), Chaps. 7, 10; Karl Mannheim, *Man and Society in an Age of Reconstruction* (New York: Harcourt, Brace, 1940), pp. 86–96; Arnold J. Toynbee, *A Study of
History*, abridged ed. (New York: Oxford University Press, 1947), pp. 209–239; Chester I.
Barnard, *The Functions of the Executive* (Cambridge, Mass.: Harvard University Press, 1938),
pp. 159–160, 220–226.
[36] Harold D. Lasswell and Abraham Kaplan, *Power and Society* (New Haven, Conn.: Yale
University Press, 1950), pp. 203–244; Dorwin Cartwright (ed.), *Studies in Social Power*
(Ann Arbor, Mich.: Institute for Social Research, University of Michigan, 1959; John
Thibaut and Harold L. Kelley, *The Social Psychology of Groups* (New York: John Wiley &
Sons, Inc., 1959), pp. 126–136; Barry E. Collins and Harold Guetzkow, *A Social Psychology
of Group Processes for Decision-Making* (New York: John Wiley & Sons, Inc., 1964), pp.
144, 167–173; Gerhard Lenski, *Power and Privilege* (New York: McGraw–Hill Book Company, 1966), Chap. 3.

Hitler rose to power, and retained it for a dozen years, because of his charismatic appeal to frightened and bewildered Germans.
(Courtesy Photography International.)

administrative officials, successful business executives, revolutionary elites, and perhaps most recently, community decision-makers.[37] One can assume that a fundamentally common set of tasks confronts each of these leaders and that the normal recruitment processes are somewhat similar. However, it is quite necessary to distinguish the *initial qualifications* of regulators from the actual manner in which these persons function in regulatory structures.

Most of the research on regulators focuses on their backgrounds and their potential abilities to cope with the responsibilities of high level authority or power. A substantial cluster of studies of American business leaders, for example, indicates that they are well qualified for complex economic responsibilities—in the amount and breadth of their formal education, in their derivation from business and business-related families, in their adaptability to urban environments, and in their long-term familiarity with (and some participation in) the governmental sphere. Similar findings—but from a more limited number of investigations—appear to be applicable to high

---

[37] Harold D. Lasswell and Daniel Lerner (eds.), *World Revolutionary Elites* (Cambridge: MIT Press, 1965); Mabel Newcomer, *The Big Business Executive* (New York: Columbia University Press, 1955); W. Lloyd Warner and James C. Abegglen, *Occupational Mobility in American Business and Industry* (Minneapolis, Minn.: University of Minnesota Press, 1955); Floyd Hunter, *Community Power Structure* (Chapel Hill, N.C.: University of North Carolina Press, 1953); Alfred Stepan, *The Military in Politics: Changing Patterns in Brazil* (Princeton, N.J.: Princeton University Press, 1971); David T. Stanley *et al.*, *Men Who Govern: A Biographical Profile of Federal Political Executives* (Washington, D.C.: Brookings Institution, 1967); Willis D. Hawley and Frederick M. Wirt (eds.), *The Search for Community Power* (Englewood Cliffs, N.J.: Prentice–Hall, Inc., 1968).

public officials (on the national level).[38] In the past, these qualifications were not found among revolutionary leaders (in Europe between the two World Wars), though the newer nations of Africa and Asia are notable for the high status (in education, travel, and so on) of their embryonic political elites.[39]

It is extremely difficult to evaluate regulators on their qualifications alone. In the business and industrial realm, for nations like the United States, Japan, and Germany, the managerial and administrative leaders have been generally successful in encouraging high productivity and substantial levels of profit. There have also been monumental instances of disastrous regulation—as in the case of the Pennsylvania Central Railroad.[40] The key leaders in metropolitan management have not been more than erratically successful in regulating urban development, for reasons that will be examined later. Finally, the new political elites in the developing nations present highly varied patterns in the translation of their personal abilities into effective development of traditional political and economic systems. Two indications of their limited success should be mentioned, though they require continued study. These are (1) the use of force and coercion, through one-party systems, military campaigns against dissidents, and the repeated use of political assassination; and (2) *corruption,* as a reflection of both (a) inadequate recruitment to responsible positions, and (b) ineffective surveillance of and/or meager knowledge about major segments of the society.

Since corruption in its various forms is a perennial (and perhaps an increasing) problem for systems of authority and power, it deserves close attention and in-depth understanding. By corruption, we generally mean the behavior of persons in responsible positions that betrays the substantial trust normally assigned to those positions. Why do apparently qualified persons abuse their due privileges? Glib answers, such as "power corrupts," or "it's human nature," are much too simple—particularly when we consider several crucial factors.[41]

[38] W. Lloyd Warner and James C. Abegglen, *ibid.,* pp. 34–35; Seymour M. Lipset and Reinhard Bendix, *Social Mobility in Industrial Society* (Berkeley, Calif.: University of California Press, 1959), Chap. 4; David T. Stanley et al., *ibid.,* pp. 17, 36, 47, 79.
[39] P. C. Lloyd (ed.), *The New Elites of Tropical Africa* (London: Oxford University Press, 1966); Marvin Zonis, *The Political Elite of Iran* (Princeton, N.J.: Princeton University Press, 1971.
[40] News and financial magazines gave extensive coverage to the Penn Central case during 1970–1971. See, for example, the accounts in *Business Week* (June 27, 1970) and (October 17, 1970); and *Newsweek* (January 17, 1972).
[41] Ronald Wraith and Edgar Simpkins, *Corruption in Developing Countries* (New York: W. W. Norton and Company, Inc., 1963); Arnold J. Heidenheimer (ed.), *Political Corruption: Readings in Comparative Analysis* (New York: Holt, Rinehart and Winston, Inc., 1970); Neil J. Smelser, "Stability, Instability, and the Analysis of Political Corruption," in Bernard Barber and Alex Inkeles (eds.), *Stability and Social Change* (Boston: Little, Brown and Company, 1971), pp. 7–29.

First, the evidence from the political realm suggests that corruption is concentrated in middle and lower levels of authority. Second, corrupt officials are likely to be poorly paid, upwardly mobile persons from lower-class or lower middle-class status categories. In other words, misuse of power and authority in government reflects the recruitment of socially marginal persons who have little previous experience in responsible positions.[42] But there is also evidence of corruption at relatively high levels of power or authority—for example, the corrupt state and municipal "machines" or boss systems in the first half of the 20th century in the United States. Rogow and Lasswell, following an intensive analysis of 30 political bosses, conclude that these bosses generally shared a deprived boyhood and adolescence (either in social prestige or economically) and developed various patterns of corrupt behavior as compensation for earlier personal restrictions.[43]

Finally, one of the anomalies of complex authority systems is the apparent ignorance of subordinate corruption among persons in the highest levels of authority. For example, Warren Harding was supposedly unaware of the machinations of several Cabinet members in the Teapot Dome scandal of the early 1920's; and President Eisenhower believed his administration was as "clean as a hound's tooth" until the exposé of his top assistant, Sherman Adams. President Grant likewise was completely shocked by the classic corruption of administrators and Congressmen during his stay in the White House. These cases suggest another facet to the recruitment problem in positions of high authority: persons with limited practical experience in political authority (that is, military leaders or unknown mediocrities such as Senator Harding) are incapable of administering complex systems efficiently and with adequate knowledge of potential points of vulnerability in authoritative networks.

Techniques and Resources of Regulation

Power and authority function effectively—or otherwise—through the development (or creation) of adaptive social mechanisms. There seems to be a fundamental, practical difficulty in social regulation—almost a contradiction built into the normal operation of such regulation—that defies direct or permanent solutions. On the one hand, regulation is necessary for ordering and facilitating specialized roles in some reasonable, efficient manner.

[42] Arnold J. Heidenheimer, *ibid.*, pp. 247, 327, 433, 492.
[43] Arnold Rogow and Harold D. Lasswell, *Power, Corruption and Rectitude* (Englewood Cliffs, N.J.: Prentice–Hall, Inc., 1963), pp. 50–59. Studies of corruption in American cities and on the national level are too numerous to include, though major ones would include the Crédit Mobilier scandal, Teapot Dome, the Tweed Ring, and Tammany Hall. For a very recent illustration, see Walter Goodman, *A Percentage of the Take* (New York: Farrar, Straus and Giroux, Inc., 1970).

But the visibility of power and authority tends to accentuate existing differences in opportunities and limitations between the regulators and the regulated.[44] To the extent that such differences are not understood, or are only partly justified by ideology or practice, exercise of power or authority is interpreted as intrusion upon, rather than a beneficial supplement to, one's role or roles. Clearly, the matter of trust (to which we referred earlier) is recurrently crucial, since the personal threat of visibility is limited by the fund of merited trust in the regulatory structure and/or specific regulators.

Part of the effectiveness of regulation stems from patterns that either maintain trust or that guard against erosions in these nonrational perceptions of regulation. But these patterns may impede the regulators, while appeasing or placating the regulated. Consequently, effective regulation entails rather artful and imaginative use of varied, two-edged structures—which tend to receive periodic review and reevaluation to ascertain whether (a) effectiveness is being obtained at the price of reduced trust or (b) if the maintenance of trust is resulting in perilously depressed effectiveness.

A major set of adaptive mechanisms minimizes visibility of regulation by controlled dispersion of power and authority. Collectively, these are sometimes called "delegation" or "decentralization of lines of authority."[45] However, this widespread type of adaptation "from above" is especially necessary in highly complex systems. First, it permits variation in decision-making in line with particular problems and resources at different "locations" in the system. Second, it gives access to less fearsome foci of authority, thereby providing multiple opportunities for developing understanding and trust (and, to be sure, misunderstanding and hostility) of regulators. Third, delegation, decentralization, and other such mechanisms tend to reduce the direct interaction (and thus the visibility) between central power and authority and various specialized segments of the system.

These mechanisms are adaptive but never provide fully satisfactory adaptation; they produce mixed results and permit problematical variations in the relations between regulators and the regulated. For example, delegation may promote multiple and competing nodes of power around "localized" officials, with resulting emphasis on specialized roles or divisions, rather than the problems of regulation. In universities, this is found in the nonlegitimated influence of particular schools, institutes, or departments that effectively counters the operation of the central administration. Furthermore, delegation may so reduce (or disguise) the necessary

---

[44] Peter M. Blau, *Exchange and Power in Social Life* (New York: John Wiley & Sons, Inc., 1964), pp. 132–140, 224–233.

[45] Talcott Parsons, *Structure and Process in Modern Societies* (New York: The Free Press, 1960), pp. 151–154, 195–198; Chester I. Barnard, *The Functions of the Executive* (Cambridge, Mass.: Harvard University Press, 1938), pp. 159–160, 220–226.

information base of central regulators that they either become incapable of appropriate decisions or become dependent on the loyalty and information of strategically located administrators, lieutenants, or representatives. The ultimate result, without adequate use of countermeasures, may be an informal feudalism that is simply insupportable in modern societies.[46] Indeed, it is interesting to note that advanced feudal tendencies have been on a definite decline since World War II, except in the regulatory nightmare of metropolitan governance.[47]

An important but largely ignored set of adaptive mechanisms operates to mask or blur regulatory processes in several ways. One means involves statements that point to real or alleged practical limitations on the power–authority of specific officials or leaders. This denial of *decisive* ability to regulate seems to emphasize the "human," "personal" aspects of regulation rather than the objective, unresponsive, "dominance" aspects. A closely related technique focuses on the enormous pressures, the multiple difficulties, and the personal sacrifices that accompany high levels of power and authority. Certainly, responsibility for social regulation is most demanding. But this technique gives the impression that the burdens are equal to or greater than the satisfactions. Thus, long working hours are emphasized, partly symbolized by hurried, unappetizing lunches and the bulging briefcase or attaché case that extends working time into the sanctity of the home.[48] Or much attention is given to the homey or rustic vacation retreats to which the regulator frequently returns (with suitable publicity) for mental and physical regeneration.

Still a third technique for reducing the visibility of power–authority is perhaps used less frequently than it once was: this is the choice of a Spartan, ascetic style of life, far from the contamination of the costly, the esoteric, or the luxurious. For example, crafty regulators in the past have maintained residences in modest quarters and developed reputations for moral insulation from rich food, intoxicating beverages, sex, and modish clothing.[49] This may well be an outmoded technique in more affluent societies and communities, where such perverse abstinence could be interpreted as hypocritical rather than a mark of simplicity or the prosaic. Currently, few regulators in the United States seem to veil their positions by this

[46] Chester I. Barnard, *ibid.*, Chaps. 8, 10. See also G. Bingham Powell, *Social Fragmentation and Political Hostility: An Austrian Case Study* (Stanford, Calif.: Stanford University Press, 1970).

[47] Robert C. Wood, *1400 Governments* (Cambridge, Mass.: Harvard University Press, 1961), pp. 113–124.

[48] John Thibaut and Harold L. Kelley, *The Social Psychology of Groups* (New York: John Wiley & Sons, Inc., 1959), pp. 232–235.

[49] See, for example, biographies of Rockefeller and Nasser—Allan Nevins, *Study in Power: John D. Rockefeller* (New York: Charles Scribner's Sons, 1953), 2 vols.; Robert St. John, *The Boss: The Story of Gamal Abdel Nasser* (New York: McGraw-Hill Book Company, 1960).

method. In less urbanized and industrialized nations, however, powerful figures still employ this method, particularly those with a military or ecclesiastical background.

Cooptation

When visibility of power–authority cannot be substantially reduced, adaptive mechanisms then tend to deal with the problem of enlarging or confirming trust in regulators. Public relations, ideology, and so on comprise one type of solution to this problem, but the widespread nature of these techniques tends to *raise* the visibility of power–authority. An alternative approach selectively shares responsibility for regulation with a few representatives of significant social segments. This process of *cooptation*,[50] in short, involves recruiting actual or potential dissidents to key positions, with the dual consequence of (a) removing capable leadership from areas of resistance and (b) developing a more comprehensive approach to regulation among persons with previously narrowed social allegiances.

Cooptation is revealed in several social patterns: intermarriage; recruitment into political parties and high appointive offices; and admission into policy-setting councils. Historically, cooptation through intermarriage has been frequently used—mainly by marriage of the newly rich (merchants or successful entrepreneurs) with the aristocracy or its equivalent (in Greece, the Roman Republic, late medieval Europe, 18th and 19th century England, and in the United States in the past 80 years).[51] In the governmental realm, most obviously in the United States, cooptation has been ethnic and religious in nature, normally in response to increasing concentration of ethnic categories in specific communities (for example, New Haven, Milwaukee, St. Louis).[52]

Since 1964, a major attempt at cooptation, aimed at raising the level of trust among disadvantaged social categories, has been made in urban areas—with very mixed results. This approach, known as "citizen participation," formally requires representation of neighborhoods in official planning boards and local administrative structures. Officially, the justification for this apparent sharing of responsibility is concern for both local perception of specific needs and goals, and the "discovery" that authoritative decisions are more

---

[50] Philip Selznick, *TVA and the Grass Roots* (Berkeley, Calif.: University of California Press, 1949); Vilfredo Pareto, *Mind and Society* (New York: Harcourt, Brace, 1935), paragraphs 2179, 2309, 2482–2484.
[51] Sylvia M. Thrupp, *The Merchant Class of Medieval London* (Ann Arbor, Mich.: University of Michigan Press, 1963; orig. ed., 1948).
[52] Robert A. Dahl, *Who Governs? Democracy and Power in an American City* (New Haven, Conn.: Yale University Press, 1961), Book I; Bayard Still, *Milwaukee: The History of a City* (Madison, Wisc.: State Historical Society of Wisconsin, 1965).

likely to be implemented when affected citizens have a substantial role in developing and overseeing community policies.[53]

The principal illustrations of this approach can be found in two federally designed but locally administered structures: the Community Action Program (CAP) of the Office of Economic Opportunity (OEO), and the Model Cities Program. Studies and observations of these citizen participation systems clearly indicate the novelty and exploratory character of local cooptation. Citizens in poverty areas are often overwhelmed by these new opportunities for sharing authority; they also lack experience in developing agreement among themselves. Furthermore, in most cases, urban regulators (mayors, boards of aldermen) have been extremely cautious in extending cooptation beyond the limits of the conference table.[54]

On the other hand, a very special case of cooptation is now in process in New York City, where the vast and complex enterprise of public education has been restructured to include neighborhood administration of schools. Previously, a centralized and virtually autonomous Board of Education and an entrenched bureaucracy operated a cumbersome network of about 900 schools and over a million students from a symbolic site in Brooklyn—110 Livingston Street. Since 1969, about two dozen "local" education districts have been formed, each with its own governing board and superintendent. At present, however, the local boards are legally limited in selection of teachers and principals, in the determination of instructional materials and curriculum, and in making financial decisions. This experiment is set in a context of ethnic conflict, a notorious local conflagration over control in the Ocean Hill–Brownsville area, a bitter teachers' strike, boycotts by black parents, and tremendous pressure from teachers unions against local participation.[55] Consequently, cooptation is a grudging, slow, and irregular process, marked by reciprocal and well-founded fears. The extremely ambivalent nature of this experiment in cooptation is not hard to fathom. It rests on a demonstrable need for cooptation and decentralization; but the unusually wide extension of cooptation constitutes a perceived threat as malignant as the continued conflicts that prompted such a solution.

---

[53] Ralph M. Kramer and Harry Specht (eds.), *Readings in Community Organization Practices* (Englewood Cliffs, N.J.: Prentice-Hall, Inc., 1969).

[54] Neil Gilbert, *Clients or Constituents?* (San Francisco: Jossey-Bass, 1970); Edward M. Kaitz and Herbert H. Hyman, *Urban Planning for Social Welfare: A Model Cities Approach* (New York: Praeger, 1970); Richard E. Edgar, *Urban Power and Social Welfare* (Beverly Hills, Calif.: Sage Publications, 1970).

[55] David Rogers, *110 Livingston Street* (New York: Random House, Inc., 1968); Mario Fantini et al., *Community Control and the Urban School* (New York: Praeger, 1970), Chaps. 5, 6, 8; Jewel Bellush and Stephen M. David (eds.), *Race and Politics in New York City* (New York: Praeger, 1971), Chap. 5; Marilyn Gittell (ed.), *Educating an Urban Population* (Beverly Hills, Calif.: Sage Publications, 1967), pp. 205–239.

Response to Crisis and Change

Increasingly, the effectiveness of power–authority structures depends on ability to adapt the social system to altered opportunities or limitations. This is so crucial in complex systems that a detailed discussion of the dynamics of decision-making in crisis periods is given an entire chapter (Chapter 15). At this point, however, a few conclusions about regulation and processes of change merit some consideration.

First, the pressure for change on the part of those in regulatory positions varies considerably. In the case of relatively autonomous organizations, competition with other organizations and the normal attempt to maintain organizational identity seem to encourage great sensitivity to practical problems of adaptation through change. Normally, regulators either design innovations or implement selected innovations from key roles in the organization. This has been repeatedly demonstrated in studies of business firms, large medical-health facilities, and "service" organizations[56] (such as the YMCA, the Polio Foundation). However, in highly entrenched bureaucratic systems (for example, the New York City public school system, the French federal administration), the absence of external competition and rather rigid tenure provisions greatly reduce the organization's vulnerability to objectively needed processes of change and adaptation. The situation is much more complex and varied on community and national levels. Often, regulators are confronted with multiple and largely contradictory pressures for change, so that the *net* pressure is low and postponable for long periods.[57]

Clearly, the more diversified a social system, the greater the opportunities for deficient coordination and the more numerous the possibilities for perceived inequities. Consequently, regulators cannot long avoid the practical necessity for promoting and implanting changes designed to meet the crucial operational problems of efficiency, identity, and allegiance. Power–authority *structures,* however, provide general opportunities to develop policies toward change. The key to actual responses lies in the dominant characteristics of persons in regulatory positions.

We need to be reminded that relatively few persons in any generation have the opportunity to achieve (and maintain) positions of crucial power–authority in modern society. Thus, experience with high level responsibility is extremely limited. In fact, there is little formal preparation for exercising power–authority effectively. At present, in the United States, perhaps 2000–3000 persons consti-

[56] James G. March and Herbert A. Simon, *Organizations* (New York: John Wiley & Sons, Inc., 1958), pp. 175–189; James D. Thompson, *Organizations in Action* (New York: McGraw–Hill Book Company, 1967), pp. 46, 119, 140–157; Michel Crozier, *The Bureaucratic Phenomenon* (Chicago: University of Chicago Press, 1963).
[57] Cf. Edward C. Banfield, *Political Influence* (New York: The Free Press, 1961).

tute a pool of regulators—good, bad, and indifferent—in the crucial political, economic, and scientific–technological realms. Most of them have limited regulatory responsibility—for a corporation, a network of federal programs, a powerful labor union, a metropolitan community, a state government. Thus, we can confidently expect considerable uncertainty and inexperience in regulators, as well as an understandable resistance to such regulators on the part of alert and somewhat disillusioned subordinates.

Failure to meet requests for adaptive changes is a critical problem for those in power–authority positions. Frustrated groups are now more willing to seek public sympathy for their cause, as in this instance of pickets from CORE (Congress of Racial Equality) who chained themselves to columns of the Federal Courthouse in New York City.
(Courtesy Wide World Photos.)

Unfortunately, those features of regulators that tend to promote adaptive changes in complex social systems are difficult to identify. Michels' famous "iron law of oligarchy" asserts that people in strategic power–authority positions—whatever their prior values and abilities—tend to emphasize the maintenance of power and a general resistance to change.[58] But there is some evidence that change-oriented regulators tend to be of above average status in newly rationalized social systems. Under these conditions, (a) regulators are secure enough to concern themselves with problems of coordination (that is, of adaptation to the environment) rather than with problems of control (internal adaptation); and (b) the general

---

[58] Robert Michels, *Political Parties* (New York: Dover Publications, Inc., 1959; orig. ed., 1915), Part 6.

emphasis on improving system rewards (rather than specialized satisfactions) encourages bold attempts at reallocation of resources and facilities for probable increases in measurable returns (for example, increased GNP, higher profits, greater ability to exercise national independence).[59]

Increasing complexity, it seems, places appalling practical restrictions on the adaptive potential of regulators, as Thompson and others have recently concluded. By inference, regulators must be capable of recognizing the following paradoxical fact: while centralization of power–authority tends to accompany increasing complexity, the actual adaptive efficiency of centralized authority tends to *decline* with certain levels of social complexity.[60] This seems to require persons in regulatory positions to be personally capable of participating in rather new coalitions of interdependent regulators, coalitions that are (or can be) permitted to experiment with correctable changes. While this appears to be a highly idealistic conception, it is objectively necessary and within the technical capacities of modern societies. Adaptation is certainly not inevitable; we are concerned with identifying the mechanisms that increase the probability of social adaptation.

Problem 3.   The Evolution of Power–Authority Systems

As human society has painfully developed and evolved toward greater complexity and greater adaptive capabilities, power–authority structures have also changed in rather visible and significant ways. Certainly, these changes have often been irregular, somewhat delayed, and even hotly contested; and perhaps they have been achieved at unduly high cost to many humans. But the evidence of the overall development from informal, focused structures to complex formal systems is relatively clear.

Essentially, changes in power–authority appear to be responsive to changes in technology, population, dominant ideologies, and the character of social organization. In the earliest (and subsequent "primitive") human societies, simple technology and limited population size present few practical problems for regulation. Consequently, authority was located in a small number of prominent or especially capable persons, whose primary responsibility was the coordination of interfamily or clan relations in significant community affairs, such as religious ceremonies, warfare, and settlement of disputes. Under these circumstances, the distinction between public and private, between types of activities (for example, religious,

---

[59] Cf. Mason Haire et al., *Managerial Thinking: An International Study* (New York: John Wiley & Sons, Inc., 1966); Harold D. Lasswell and Abraham Kaplan, *Power and Society* (New Haven, Conn.: Yale University Press, 1950); Lucian W. Pye, *The Spirit of Chinese Politics* (Cambridge, Mass.: MIT Press, 1968), pp. 206–227.
[60] James D. Thompson, *Organizations in Action* (New York: John Wiley & Sons, Inc., 1968).

familial, and economic), and between coordination and control as social mechanisms, were barely perceived. The responsibilities of power–authority were often considered greater than the rewards to the regulators. Therefore—and quite to the contrary of some contemporary theories about the "power drive"—leaders were reluctant to serve for lengthy periods and viewed their responsibilities as disposable burdens.[61] Let us call this the **informal, semifocused** level of power–authority.

A second phase of power–authority became apparent in the technologically advanced communities of the classical civilizations (India, China, Greece, Egypt, Mesopotamia, Rome), beginning about 2500 B.C. and extending to approximately 400 B.C. The key developments were a revolution in food production (the so-called "agricultural revolution"), the clustering of populations in permanent settlements (villages, towns, and cities), and the emergence of trade. These trends produced numerous semiautonomous communities, with an incipient separation of economic from kinship and religious activities. Power–authority tended to shift to more formalized positions, usually filled by religious dignitaries, who perhaps provided the only common basis for regulation in their stewardship of knowledge about the supernatural.[62]

However, at this phase, formalized rules or laws were embryonic; the basis for regulatory decisions was arbitrary but increasingly contestable—for example, in the case of interpretation of oracles or the auspices. The major regulatory problem was often one of competition or conflict between family lines, each seeking to convert its military or economic achievements into public responsibility. One consequence of this conflict was the increasing emphasis on the control mechanism of regulation, primarily to limit access to strategic positions (as in the case of ostracism and assassination).[63] In retrospect, then, we may point to a "Balkanization" of regulation, with a growing number of similarly developing polities, which we may call the **formal, dispersed** phase of power–authority.

The third distinguishable stage is a long and irregular one historically—from the city-states and urban empires, and after the feudal hiatus in Europe, to the emergence of the nation–state in the 17th through the 19th centuries. Several crucial cultural and social changes during this phase successfully challenged the earlier type of

---

[61] Robert A. Dahl, *Who Governs? Democracy and Power in an American City* (New Haven, Conn.: Yale University Press, 1961), pp. 282–286; Margaret Mead (ed.), *Cooperation and Competition Among Primitive Peoples* (Boston: Beacon Press, 1961; orig. ed. 1937), pp. 458–511.

[62] V. Gordon Childe, *Man Makes Himself* (New York: Mentor Books, 1951), Chaps. 7–9.

[63] Antony Andrewes, *The Greeks* (London: Hutchinson, 1967); W. G. Forrest, *The Emergence of Greek Democracy* (London: World University Library, 1966).

Resistance to power and authority has a long history in democratic societies. In recent years, a revival of that resistance is expressed in anti-war demonstrations and in demands for civil rights.
(Courtesy Elsa Dorfman.)

regulation. First, increased military effectiveness (close, disciplined infantry formations, the long bow, iron weapons, and then gunpowder) destroyed local autonomy and led to concentrated or centralized government based in a few urban nuclei. Second, increasing opportunities for trade encouraged not only improved agriculture but manufacture of marketable commodities. Third, trade developments stimulated migration to towns and cities, thereby creating more heterogeneous populations.[64]

Management of such novel complexity was the underlying practical problem of the entire classical era. The great empires (Persian, Chinese, Egyptian, Carthaginian, Roman, Hindu) successfully solved this problem by creating political and legal innovations (in varying degrees), which in effect produced **formalized concentration** of power–authority.[65] Those that were unable to implement such innovations (Athens, Sicily, the Hebrews) remained isolated or were engulfed in neighboring empires.

[64] Max Weber, *General Economic History* (New York: The Free Press, 1950), Part 3; Henri Pirenne, *A History of Europe* (Garden City, N.Y.: Doubleday & Company, Inc., 1958), pp. 183–221; Josiah C. Russell, *Medieval Regions and Their Cities* (Bloomington, Ind.: Indiana University Press, 1972).
[65] S. N. Eisenstadt, *The Political System of Empires* (New York: Free Press, 1963); Karl Wittfogel, *Oriental Despotism* (New Haven, Conn.: Yale University Press, 1957).

The components of formalized concentration can be iden-tified in varying strength in the early Roman Empire, in 17th century England and France, in the United States in the early 19th century, and in the German Reich of the Hohenzollerns, 1870–1914). Most important, from our vantage point, was the virtual conversion of au-thority from kinship and/or religious bases to civil or "professional" grounds. Though nepotism and hereditary succession were never fully discarded, regulation became a full-time career for specially competent administrators and officials (in short, a bureaucracy). This reached its earliest peak in the formal examination and educa-tional systems of China, England, and Germany.

But bureaucracy as a new form of authority was bolstered by two major innovations in formal regulation: legal systems and reg-ularized taxation. Formal law, with extensive application to popula-tions, largely developed from two types of practical problems: the growing heterogeneity of populations as a result of migration; and, somewhat later, the needs of merchants, traders, and financiers in increasingly complex commercial transactions. Roman law and then urban legal systems of the late medieval period (14th and 15th cen-turies) provided regularized means of dealing with the interests of various social categories (merchants, workers, the Church, peasants, serfs). At the same time, formalized law legitimated and centralized a network of public taxes, through which (a) citizens were obligated to express their interdependence in community or nation and (b) the apparatus of formalized regulation could be sustained. In time, au-thority to tax became the cardinal component of regulatory sys-tems.[66] And, as historical studies clearly demonstrate, major crises in regulation stemmed from resistance to taxation policies—for ex-ample, the English revolutions of the 17th century, the American revolution, and various revolts in the period preceding the French revolution.[67]

However, it would be inaccurate to attribute the develop-ment of a formalized concentration of power–authority to bureau-cracy, law, and taxation alone. In each of the evolving formalized entities—the Roman Empire, the Egyptian Empire, the Byzantine Em-pire, Britain, France, Russia, the United States, Germany, Italy, the Meiji Restoration in Japan—authority was undergirded by a uni-versal ideological system that justified or sanctified the emerging power–authority structure. One ideological form was a universal religion: the Islamic religion of the Moors; Catholicism in France;

[66] Henri Pirenne, *Medieval Cities* (Princeton, N.J.: Princeton University Press, 1925), pp. 121–167; Max Weber, *On Law and Economy in Society* (Cambridge, Mass.: Harvard University Press, 1954), pp. 96–105, 122–132, 144–154, 267–275.
[67] Crane Brinton, *The Anatomy of Revolution* (New York: Prentice–Hall, Inc., 1938), Chap. 2; Ralph W. Greenlaw (ed.), *The Economic Origins of the French Revolution* (Boston: D. C. Heath and Company, 1958).

Anglicanism in Britain; the Greek Orthodox Church in Russia; Buddhism and Shintoism in Japan. Religion was increasingly supplemented by a second ideological form—ethnic or national identity, or nationalism.[68] National interest or national destiny—in more recent decades, self-determination and independence—have been powerful instruments for mobilizing support for centralization among diversified populations, even in the face of local and economic differences.

Formalized concentration of power–authority, in varying degrees, has been functioning for the past four centuries with a degree of success that is remarkable. It accompanied the flowering of science and technology, the various arts, literature, educational systems, medicine, and the development of man's goals for universal enjoyment of these achievements. In contemporary terms, this phase of power–authority is "the establishment," with all that is implicit in that concept. But there are clear indications that such a system is reaching the point of diminishing returns in the eternal pursuit of social adaptation to a complex and changing environment.

First and foremost, formalized concentration is increasingly incapable of regulating social complexity, except by using control and coercion. There are several reasons for this condition, though they vary in strength in different nations. Perhaps the most obvious factor is social and cultural differences themselves, which have not been (or cannot be) understood to the degree necessary for the difficult task of making intelligent regulatory *decisions*.[69] A second condition is a visible decline in universal ideologies as motivating influences among diversified social categories. Nationalism in long-established nations has not retained its former emotional appeal, particularly after devastating wars, and functions primarily as a justification of political and economic bargaining among the regulatory elites of various nations. Likewise, the religious basis of contemporary regulatory systems has been weakened by the routine of religious operations and by denominational diversity, despite numerous religious "crusades" or revivals and the ecumenical movement of the past 25 years.[70]

Third, the effectiveness of the larger authority systems in dealing with the incessant and multiplying interactions among nations has become a source of widespread anxiety and cynicism

[68] Louis L. Snyder, *The Meaning of Nationalism* (New Brunswick, N.J.: Rutgers University Press, 1954); Louis L. Snyder, *The New Nationalism* (Ithaca, N.Y.: Cornell University Press, 1968); Carlton J. H. Hayes, *The Historical Evolution of Modern Nationalism* (New York: The Macmillan Company, 1948); Carlton J. H. Hayes, *Nationalism: A Religion* (New York: The Macmillan Company, 1960).

[69] Charles Lindblom and David Braybrooke, *A Strategy of Decision* (New York: The Free Press, 1963).

[70] Bryan R. Wilson, *Religion in Secular Society: A Sociological Comment* (London: Watts, 1966); David A. Martin, *The Religious and the Secular* (New York: Schocken Books, Inc., 1969).

among citizens. Costly wars, "international incidents," the uncertainties and tensions of a long "cold war," inconclusive negotiations
on arms limitations, and so on, have generated open criticism (where
permitted) and even political defeat of major leaders and parties
(the Labor government in Britain, the dramatic withdrawal of Lyndon
Johnson from a second full term in the Presidency).

Fourth, the formalized concentration system in several societies has come to be a social anachronism, with its mechanisms
geared to relatively modest attempts at coordination precisely when
technological ability and popular philosophies encourage ever rising
social expectations.[71] For example, in the United States, there is
widespread concern for more accessible and reasonably priced
health services, more variety of housing in various locations, greater
availability of higher education, enlarged facilities for the aged, more
adequate training and child care facilities for disadvantaged minorities, more equitable opportunities and rewards for females, and a
new and intensified regard for safety and beauty in our despoiled
environment—all at the same time, all with legitimate claims to
public attention and action, and all with dubious possibilities of significant achievement. Yet all such goals are (or seem to be) within
our technical and financial powers. But the prevailing structure of
power–authority is implicitly designed to segregate formal authority
from direct activation and forceful monitoring of laudable but highly
complex policies and decisions. Instead, the formalized concentration system serves as a magisterial umpire, which merely surveys the
half-hearted or irregular play of implicated interest groups and implicitly allows the intricacies of the game to supersede its crucial objectives—all of which results in stalemate or feckless compromise
rather than worthwhile achievement.[72]

In short, given the novel cultural capacity and the expanded social objectives of the last 50 years, the prevailing regulatory system creaks with indecision and sputters with missed
opportunities. Its adaptive effect is declining and its legitimacy is
close to precarious. On the other hand, elements of a new, experimental, and more serviceable form of regulation can be vaguely discerned, though it must be remembered that major restructuring of
human societies has always been a long and wearisome process. Perhaps the most interesting development in recent decades is an un-
heralded supplementation of the traditional regulatory system by

[71] Michel Crozier, *La Société bloquée* (Paris: Editions du Seuil, 1970); Marilyn Gittell (ed.),
Educating an Urban Population (Beverly Hills, Calif.: Sage Publications, 1967), pp. 205–239.
[72] Edward C. Banfield and James Q. Wilson, *City Politics* (Cambridge: Harvard and MIT Press,
1963); David Rogers, *The Management of Big Cities* (Beverly Hills, Calif.: Sage Publications,
1971); Jean L. Stinchcombe, *Reform and Reaction: City Politics in Toledo* (Belmont, Calif.:
Wadsworth Publishing Co., Inc., 1968); Theodore J. Lowi, *The End of Liberalism: Ideologies,
Policy, and the Crisis of Public Authority* (New York: W. W. Norton and Company, Inc.
1969).

several tentative forms of coordination, especially in the United States and Britain.

Focusing on the United States first, we must remember the rather recent development of the formalized concentration system—probably from 1940 or so. During the preceding generation, formal and informal power–authority was diffused through state governments, municipal bosses and machines, and perhaps 200 key financial and manufacturing firms. Concentration in regulation partly emerged in the late 1930's (with federal economic programs aimed at unemployment and depression) and expanded with the compelling demand of the war, in the form of numerous federal

Criticism of governmental authority is sometimes presented in symbolic form, as in this ceremony of burning President Nixon in effigy for unpopular policies.
(Courtesy Wide World Photos.)

bureaus, a complex military bureaucracy, the solidification of strategic labor unions, and the economic dominance of four or five sets of manufacturers (automobiles, steel, oil, electrical appliances, and food processing).

The new candidates for regulatory responsibility seem to evade, rather than challenge, the existing structure. For example, such private foundations as the Ford Foundation have tried to encourage local and national experiments in policy formation and implementation (in urban planning, poverty, delinquency), thereby shifting considerable responsibility to professionals and neighborhood residents. Significantly, several Congressmen have interpreted these activities as unwarranted intrusion in public affairs and have tried (unsuccessfully) to remove the tax exemption for such foundations.[73]

Likewise, an important response to concentrated authority may be interpreted in the dramatic migration of city dwellers to suburban and fringe areas, and the apparent refusal of long distance migrants (usually transferring to new jobs) to choose city residence within metropolitan regions. Though there are varied motives for suburbanization, the relevant consequences for regulation have been reduced ranges of official authority in our major urban areas. In fact, by resisting annexation to cities, and by incorporating suburban and fringe areas, the typical urban regulatory structure has come to be a mosaic of conflicting or parallel authorities.[74]

A third form of supplementation involves various attempts at local option—in determining the desired composite of local needs or in translating national directives and guidelines in accord with local conditions. An earlier example of this approach was the boss system, which was replaced by federal programs and authority, not for moral reasons but because of the expedient of greater efficiency of service on the federal level. More recently—mainly in the 1950's and 1960's—local option was organized by coalitions between public officials and a shifting cadre of influential and active businessmen, the so-called "community power structure" (for example, in Atlanta, New Haven, St. Louis).[75] The significant

---

[73] Commission on Foundations and Private Philanthropy, *Foundations, Private Giving, and Public Policy* (Chicago: University of Chicago Press, 1970), Part 2, Chaps. 5–7; Thomas C. Reeves (ed.), *Foundations Under Fire* (Ithaca, N.Y.: Cornell University Press, 1970), Part 3.

[74] Oliver P. Williams, *Metropolitan Political Analysis* (New York: Free Press, 1971); Amos H. Hawley and Basil G. Zimmer, *The Metropolitan Community* (Beverly Hills, Calif.: Sage Publications, 1970). Cf. the viewpoints in Charles E. Gilbert, *Governing the Suburbs* (Bloomington, Ind.: Indiana University Press, 1967); Alvin Boskoff and Harmon Zeigler, *Voting Patterns in a Local Election* (Philadelphia: J. B. Lippincott Company, 1964), Chaps. 5, 6.

[75] Floyd Hunter, *Community Power Structure* (Chapel Hill, N.C.: University of North Carolina Press, 1953); Robert Dahl, *Who Governs? Democracy and Power in an American City* (New Haven, Conn.: Yale University Press, 1961). See also Alvin Boskoff, *The Sociology of Urban Regions,* 2nd ed. (New York: Appleton–Century–Crofts, 1970), Chap. 12 for a review of various urban power structures.

aspect of this innovation was its attempt to develop positively coordinated decision-making in a wide range of issues (health, housing,
transportation, education, land use) on a predominantly local basis.
However, local public officials no longer depend on business influentials, primarily because federal funds are distributed in most
cases through formal municipal agencies. The "power elite" are
therefore imminent casualties in the restructuring of regulation.

At the same time—largely in the last 10 years—many local
and neighborhood experiments in mobilizing citizen action for immediate and officially neglected problems have been launched.
Though these vary in scope and success, they point to a common
technique of combining private concerns with dramatically created
public mechanisms to work in the neglected crevices of existing authority.[76] In the Hyde Park–Kenwood area of Chicago, for example,
"grass roots" concern for racial and housing problems prompted
organized action without outside assistance or legitimation. Most
residents have come to invest their loyalty in the local "authority"—
not simply because it is local, but because it has been effective in
obtaining visible, tangible improvements. In other cities, similar
"improvement" groups (usually in poverty areas or in racial ghettos)
are facing and partly resolving problems of (1) achieving results of
sufficient number and importance to warrant authority, and (2) acquiring the degree of authority necessary to implement common
definitions of needs.

Turning now to developments in Great Britain, we find increasing dissatisfaction with the prevailing power–authority system,
but only rather tentative and equivocal attempts at remedial forms.
First, a venerable mechanism—the influential parliamentary commission—has been applied as a responsible and heeded critic of bureaucracy and of established values. The Wolfenden Commission
report on homosexuality and the Seebohm report on deficiencies in
welfare services reflect significant sources of discontent that have
not been adequately met by political parties or elections. Second,
the development of an official ombudsman or administrative umpire
may be interpreted as an attempt at redressing irresponsible acts of
public bureaucracy. However, after a few years of operation, the
position of ombudsman appears to offer a rather limited challenge
to centralized authority. Finally, a third indicator of potential
change is a proliferation of vocal and increasingly effective pressure
groups, or citizen groups—representing consumers, various professionals, social welfare interests, the poor, and students. While Britain's basic political system is far from being a creature of these
special interests, close observers of government policy detect gen-

---

[76] See, for example, Peter H. Rossi and Robert A. Dentler, *The Politics of Urban Renewal*
(New York: The Free Press, 1961); Robert S. Tyler, "Atlanta's West End: A Study of Neighborhood Participation in Urban Renewal" (Master's thesis, Emory University, 1969) (unpublished).

The authority crisis is partly a reflection of citizen distrust of public leaders. Increasingly, citizens desire adequate information and greater participation, and—that elusive public commodity—honesty.
(Courtesy Wide World Photos.)

uine concern for and definite consideration of the viewpoints of varied groups in that nation.[77]

The "authority crisis"[A] in contemporary societies is probably the single greatest impediment to human adaptation—and the most significant challenge to human ingenuity and inventiveness. The more "advanced" societies are straining through a lengthy period of transition in power–authority, in which tentative mixtures of two mechanisms may be considered preludes to a new, fourth stage of regulation: that of **selectively formalized planning networks.**

As the international economist, Albert Hirschman, has suggested,[78] regulatory systems normally emphasize one of two typical reactive responses to regulatory processes. One pattern of response is passive rejection or evasion of cooperative behavior—the so-called "exit option" of withdrawal or nonparticipation. This is the typical response of autonomous persons who act as "consumers" rather than participants. The alternative pattern, which Hirschman calls the "voice option," involves responsible criticisms of authority by persons and categories with great loyalty to the system (organization, community, or nation). If we analyze the stages of power–authority in the context of these "options," we may plausibly characterize the *informal, semifocused type* as having no exit and little

[77] Ben Whitaker (ed.), *A Radical Future* (London: Jonathan Cape, 1967); Ian Gilmour, *The Body Politic*, rev. ed. (London: Hutchinson, 1971), Part 3; M. Donald Hancock and Gideon Sjoberg (eds.), *Politics in the Post-Welfare State* (New York: Columbia University Press, 1972), pp. 117–181.
[78] Albert O. Hirschman, *Exit, Voice, and Loyalty* (Cambridge, Mass.: Harvard University Press, 1970), pp. 4, 40, 59, 77–86, 123.

voice options; the *formal, dispersed type* as having both exit and voice options; and the *formal, concentrated type* as having exit and some voice options.

From this standpoint, the authority crisis may be described as a consequence of an excess of the exit option and a deficit in the voice option. In effect, the supplementary structures we discussed earlier in this section are symbolic of attempts to deny exit and promote greater participation or "voice" in the regulatory process. Sociologically, the emerging stage of regulation seems to require a *balancing* of exit and voice mechanisms. Strategically, given the high levels of complexity in social and cultural patterns, control mechanisms stifle complexity and yet are necessary to contain or reduce the exit option. On the other hand, maximum use of the voice option tends to impede the coordinative processes of regulation. Finding the proper or appropriate balance for these opposing mechanisms that will allow them both to function effectively within a single system is the essential dilemma of modern social adaptation. Thus, the basic theoretical specification for satisfactory or effective authority structures is that they should rationally produce *appropriately changing emphasis on exit and voice, on control and coordination.* While it would be foolish to wager on the probability of such a creation, the future of human societies (as we have known them in recent centuries) certainly rests on the extent to which this form of readaptation is approximated.

But, as is quite evident, the processes of social regulation in modern societies are repeatedly hindered by intense disagreements, actual or threatened violence, and shifting or uncertain commitments to common objectives. In short, conflict in various forms is an undeniable and critical challenge to social adaptation—and one that requires careful analysis and thought, rather than the simple horrified reaction of the smug conservative or the passionate approbation of the untutored and impatient social critic. The next chapter, therefore, examines social conflict and the major means by which conflicts are handled (adaptively or otherwise) in contemporary societies.

Summary

In complex human societies, adaptation largely involves practical problems of regulating various roles and activities. This is a major issue in such widely divergent areas as family problems, operation of universities, urban development and crises, and national policies and politics. However, regulation involves two complementary processes (a) *coordination*, or the facilitation of proper performance by specialized roles; and (b) *control*, or the attempt to limit or restrict the interference of certain roles or subgroups with the operation of the larger social system.

　　　Both coordination and control are normally the responsibility of a limited number of designated roles, which have either legitimate tasks (authority) in social regulation, or nonlegitimate ones (power), or some combination of these. Consequently, to understand regulation as an indispensable adaptive process, it is important to examine (a) the methods by which power is converted into authority; (b) how power–authority achieves varying degrees of effectiveness; and (c) how power–authority evolves in response to technological, demographic, and ideological changes.

　　　Currently, prevailing forms of power–authority are unequal to the problems of regulation. The explicit and implicit need for alternative forms of regulation is therefore a major concern—and a source of considerable social experimentation—of participants and analysts of modern complex societies.

Exercises

1. Review instances of crisis, conflict, tension, or disagreement in any group or community (for example, family, sports team, a city agency). In how many instances can these be described as challenges to authority or power?

2. What are the essential differences between coordination and control in human groups?

3. Under what circumstances is control more appropriate (more adaptive) than coordination?

4. What conditions lead to the development of power, when authority is relatively well established in a group, an organization, or a community?

5. How can developments in law be understood as reflections of practical problems of sustaining coordination and/or control?

6. What is a helpful way of understanding the continuing phenomenon of political corruption, despite changes in systems of social regulation?

7. What specific factors help to account for power–authority systems that are able to adapt to changed conditions or problems?

8. Evaluate any new public policy or program (local, state, or national) as a development toward more "voice" or more "exit" in problems of social regulation. Does this policy or program produce more efficient regulation? Less conflict? Greater trust of existing authority?

Selected Bibliography

Barnard, Chester I. *The Functions of the Executive*. Cambridge, Mass.: Harvard University Press, 1938.

Blau, Peter M. *Exchange and Power in Social Life*. New York: John Wiley & Sons, Inc., 1964.

Burnham, James. *The Managerial Revolution*. New York: John Day, 1941; Bloomington, Ind.: Indiana University Press, 1960.

Gerth, Hans H., and C. Wright Mills (eds.). From *Max Weber: Essays in Sociology*. New York: Oxford University Press, 1946, Part 2.

Lasswell, Harold D. *Politics: Who Gets What, When, How*. New York: Meridian Books, 1958; orig. ed. 1936.

Lenski, Gerhard. *Power and Privilege*. New York: McGraw–Hill Book Company, 1966.

Oppenheimer, Franz. *The State*. Indianapolis, Ind.: Bobbs–Merrill, 1914.

14

Social Conflict and Systems of Adaptive Resolution

This chapter is devoted to an examination of some of the causes and consequences of conflict in human society. Every society deals with some degree of internal conflict and most face conflict with other societies. A society's failure to manage the conflicts it faces leads ultimately to social collapse; therefore, conflict resolving and reducing mechanisms are among the most important adaptive mechanisms. To understand how these mechanisms operate in society one must examine three aspects of the problem: the sources of conflict, the relation between conflict and violence, and the resolution of conflict. Accordingly, this chapter deals with all three topics.

Conflict is often regarded as a failure of human social institutions. In such views, conflict results when the proper or the normal social procedures are inadequate for dealing with new conditions or when evil persons act to subvert the moral system. Conflict is unusual, abnormal, and short-lived—a pathology to be treated or excised. The sociologist has a somewhat different view of conflict. Like other words that refer to human behavior in general usage, conflict has several meanings and different colorations. Sociologically, conflict refers to the *conditions of struggle or effort attendant upon the mutual incompatibility of different goals*. It must be understood that *goals* refers to a wide range of wishes and desires in this context. Some goals are immediate and others far removed. Some represent ends; others are means to ends. Goals may be either general (such as striving for "human betterment") or specific (such as owning a new car). When members of society feel differently about goals or have different goals towards which they are striving, conflict is the result. This definition implies that conflict is natural in society so long as all goals are not commonly held. Most sociologists regard conflict as natural, as a regular and expected part of the human condition. Social pathologies can be identified and related to conflict, as will be seen later in this chapter. Social conflict, *per se*, is no more pathological than other social processes and conditions, such as social mobility, social differentiation, and education.

This definition also implies that conflict is inevitable. Though some conflicts can be averted and some forms of it certainly can be avoided, conflict itself seems to be inevitable, at least until a society agrees on all goals. There is no example of such a society, though some societies are in much greater agreement than others, and some goals generate more consensus than others.

Goals, values, and ideologies are all closely related in human society. Goals are states or conditions toward which action is directed. Values define the importance of goals (and other social objects and conditions), while ideologies organize values into a pattern and seek to justify and rationalize the values. Regardless of the content of the ideology, it establishes relations among values that define the relative importance of the values with respect to each other. Thus ideology establishes a hierarchy of values. This hierarchy has two related but distinct dimensions that can be labeled *specificity–generality* and *relative importance*. Like goals, values can be specific or general in their form. Very specific rules, such as "don't eat with your fingers," are called norms; these are the rules of behavior, although not every act is governed by a norm. Thus norms may require a man to wear trousers, but they do not indicate whether he should put them on before or after he dons his shirt. In addition to being specific or general, values differ in their importance or the intensity with which they are held by the members of the society. Taking the two dimensions together suggests four types of values: *important–general, important–specific, less-important–general*, and *less-important–specific*.[1] In studying conflict, goals can be associated with the different types of values; the types and intensities of conflicts between goals depend on the types of values involved. Goals associated with values at higher positions in the structure of value are generally agreed upon, while goals of lower order, especially those associated with the specific means of attaining higher-order goals, are more likely sources of conflict. Thus the

[1] These distinctions may appear complicated, but they are actually a simplification since they ignore several salient aspects, such as whether values are applied without respect to person or in terms of the individual's paternity or race or other inherited characteristics.

goal of providing for the general welfare can be widely agreed upon, but the agreement may decrease with respect to goals of having a national Department of Welfare, a guaranteed income for everyone, or aid for unmarried mothers. As disagreement over goals increases from the general to the specific, the likelihood of conflict also increases. However, a second relation between conflict and the hierarchy of goals exists: although the likelihood of conflict increases at the lower levels of the hierarchy, the intensity of conflict will be less at those lower levels. This balance between likelihood and intensity of conflict is a major source of stability in the face of social change.[2]

An additional variable is related to the hierarchy of goals. The more likely a conflict is to take place, the more social structures there are to resolve it. Hence, not only is conflict at the lower levels of the hierarchy less intense, the effective resolution of such a conflict is more likely because social resources are available for that purpose. In order to see how these principles apply to different societies, a typology of conflict can be employed. At least four different types of conflict can be identified, and each type has certain distinct characteristics.[3]

Internal conflict refers to conflict that takes place within an individual. Since the goals held by an individual are acquired during his socialization and come from other parts of society, internal conflict is related to conflict in society and stems in many cases from differences among goals that lead to conflict at other levels, as well. Whenever the goals of society are less clear or more in disagreement, more internal conflict should be in evidence.

Conflict among individuals can better be distinguished from **conflict among groups** by degree rather than by absolute kind. Conflict among individuals has a special characteristic, however. Unlike other types of conflict, it involves no major ideological component. The goals of the participants are generally immediate—one man's wife or wallet—and the values concerning these goals are agreed upon. The distinction is useful because conflict among individuals, even when there is a component of group sanction or organization, is more easily controlled and directed by society and, though often quite intense, is generally of limited duration. Conflict among groups in society often extends over many generations and can become the basis for rebellion and revolution, the most drastic type of intrasocietal conflict.

A fourth type of conflict is here designated **extrasocietal conflict** to emphasize the international and external nature of such

---

[2] If such were not the case, society would be plagued by frequent, intense conflicts, and social stability would be impossible. Certain types of frequently encountered conflict become so routine that they are treated as normal or merely as competition. See, for example, the works of Herbert Spencer, such as *The Study of Sociology* (London: Appleton, 1874).

[3] This typology is simpler than the more complete one used in Ralf Dahrendorf, *Gesellschaft und Freiheit* (Munich: R. Piper and Co., 1962), p. 206.

The agony of violence is individual as well as social, but the horror of violence does not serve to prevent it.
("Wounded" by Otto Dix, 1916, etching and aquatint, 7¾" × 11⅜". Courtesy The Museum of Modern Art, New York, and Abby Aldrich Rockefeller.)

conflicts. Although nations can be regarded in some contexts as supergroups, conflict among nations has many distinguishing characteristics when compared with conflicts among groups within a single nation.

𝒳 These four types of conflict require four levels of analysis: the individual, the interpersonal, the intergroup, and the intersocietal. Because of the variety of groups and nations some investigators increase the list to account for conflict among cultural groupings (societies) within a single nation, as distinct from conflict among groups or that between nations, especially large nations.[4] Such complexity is increased if the typology is extended to include conflicts among different international groups, such as communists or fascists, as both extranational and intergroup possibilities. Such elaboration is not necessary for this exposition, but the student should remember that those complexities do arise.

A typology of conflict does not explain the process of conflict. Like other typologies, it is only a means for ordering ideas and serves at best as a heuristic device. To use this typology, two other dimensions of conflict need to be employed. All forms of conflict can be classed as *violent* or *nonviolent* with respect to (a) the means employed to conduct the conflict and (b) the types of resolution the conflict allows. Tables 14–1 and 14–2 show the result of imposing

[4] Rolf Dahrendorf, *ibid.*, is a case in point.

TABLE 14–1

Means of conflict by level of conflict and type of conflict.

Level	Violent	Nonviolent
Internal	Self-destruction or injury	Self-hatred or mental illness
Interpersonal	Assault	Office politics or attacks on reputation
Intergroup	Riot or guerrilla war	Political and legal action
Intersocietal	War	Diplomacy

TABLE 14–2

Means of conflict resolution.

Level	Violent	Nonviolent
Internal	Death or treatment	Treatment or compartmentalization
Interpersonal	Act of authority or death of one party	Action by authority or a third party
Intergroup	Revolution or control by authority	Negotiations or action by authority
Intersocietal	Victory or defeat	Negotiation or international law

the violent versus nonviolent dimension on the typology of conflicts with regard to the means of *conflict* and means of *conflict resolution.* Thus, violent internal conflict leads to self-destruction or injury and will be resolved by death or treatment, either of which removes the conflict between goals that engendered the internal struggle. The charts show the comparisons for each type of conflict. Examining these charts suggests an important contrast in the resolution of conflicts. Some conflicts can be resolved by the means employed in the conflict, although not only by those means. Other conflicts are resolved by means external to the conflict itself. External resolutions are generally the least costly in terms of human life and effort. However, great variation and unpredictability in the mechanisms available to bring about external resolution are what render large scale violent conflicts, such as war and revolution, so very costly.

Often conflict will change from violent to nonviolent prior to resolution. Thus war is only rarely resolved by a complete victory coupled with unconditional surrender. Generally a stage in the conflict is arranged in which violence is suspended such as an armistice, so that means of nonviolent conflict resolution can be brought to bear. Even riots and civil disturbances where the degree of organization by some of the participants is relatively small, are often settled or partially settled by resort to nonviolent channels of negotiation.

An understanding of conflict must rest on the several considerations mentioned above—the varieties and types of conflict must be separated; the role of violence in conflict must be identified; and the means of conflict resolution available must be considered. An additional factor will also be considered; this is the conditions that lead to conflict or to a change from one form of conflict to another, especially the transition from violent to nonviolent conflict. As a first step toward achieving this sort of understanding, differences among societies with respect to the types of conflict and the levels of violence they display, will be examined.

DIFFERENCES AMONG SOCIETIES

If conflict is defined as a consequence of differences in goals, societies will differ from each other in the level of conflict only if their goals are in greater or smaller agreement. More important, differences among societies will be found in the ways in which they resolve conflict and the means employed by them to carry out conflict-associated behavior. This section of the chapter considers factors that lead to consistency in goals, easy conflict resolution, and nonviolent behavior in response to conflict.

Factors That Tend to Reduce Conflict Among Goals and Means

Divergent goals within a society are a function of the complexity of the society, which in turn depends upon the level of the technology on which the society is based and the size of the population of the society. The higher the level of the technology and the larger the society, the greater will be the divergence of goals within the society, all other things being equal. There are other sources of divergence in goals, such as the cultural diversity of the population and the relative degree of isolation of various segments of the society. It seems true however, that for a given technology and social organization, the level of conflict among goals is fixed, and potential conflict is thereby determined.

This formulation suggests that large industrialized nations should have nearly the same degree of potential conflict and that conflict should be greater than that observed in small nonindustrialized societies, which does indeed seem to be the case, though actual conflict and acts of violence do not follow the same pattern.[5]

---

[5] Violence, for example, has a large cultural element and can be found high and low at all levels of technology. See, for example, Charles Tilly, "Collective Violence in European Perspective," in Hugh Davis Graham and Ted Robert Gurr, *Violence in America: Historical and Comparative Perspectives. A Report to the National Commission on the Causes and Prevention of Violence, June 1969* (New York: The New American Library, 1969), pp. 4–42.

Why, then, are similar potentials for conflict differentially realized in different situations?

Modern industrial societies are characterized by many separate conflicts and varying coalitions are formed for each of them. If that were all that is involved, conflict would not vary from situation to situation at the same level of technology. However, goals are not simply in conflict with each other; the degree of conflict and the intensity of the conflict among social groupings may also vary. Reduction of the level of conflict in society by reducing the differences among goals, then, is often accomplished by varying the intensity of conflict rather than by reconciliation of goals. Some examples may serve to make the point clear.

The case of workers and employers offers an instance where there is conflict engendered by the divergence in goals with respect to the distribution of the returns to the business. Each group wishes more for itself and less for the other; these types of goals differ in every worker–employer situation. Even so, the intensity of the commitment of different groups of employers or workers to the goal of increasing their own share of profits varies. Although a lack of awareness of the alternatives may play a part in some instances, differential intensity is more often related to the influence of other more important or more immediate goals. Some workers and employers may embrace to a greater extent a common goal of increasing profits, or some may be subjected to external goals, such as the demands of a nation at war. Under those circumstances, the conflict is still present, but it is less intense. Individual goals may also reduce conflict between groups by imposing restrictions on the participation of part of a group in the general goal; in fact, to obtain certain individual goals, some groups may even accept a limited benefit from the general goal. For example, some workers might prefer lower wages without conflict with management to higher wages with greater conflict. Thus, a divergence of goals within one party to a conflict will reduce the intensity of the original conflict.

Differences Among Societies in Conflict Resolution

Clearly, less intensive conflicts, even when they stem from the same basic differences in goals, are more easily resolved. One social mechanism for resolving or managing conflict is to appeal to higher values or to point to the dangers that are posed to important goals by the conflict. In politics, appeals may be made to national enmity in the face of external threats, real or imagined. In some cases, a part of society may be singled out to serve as a scapegoat, thereby reducing the divisions in the rest of society. Such steps were taken in Germany during the 1930's and proved very effective. Fear of Communism and especially of Russia together with an irrational hatred of the Jews served to overcome the differences among other parts of German society. While political differences were multiplied in France and parties proliferated with each government, Germany became one of the most united nations in Europe.

Niccolo Machiavelli was perhaps the greatest analyst of methods a ruler might use to reduce internal conflict. Machiavelli argued that love and fear of the ruler were important in maintaining the position of the state, but that fear was more important and more effective and therefore to be preferred when a choice had to be made.[6] Machiavelli also emphasized the importance of symbolic behavior and religious beliefs in reducing conflict. He suggested that the wise leader would give his authority to miracles, even false miracles, because they increased unity by strengthening religion.

However, political programs designed to increase national solidarity need not be cynical, nor must they rest on persecution of selected groups. The national goal of economic growth and power coupled with the individual goal of savings and advancement through work have been joined in the Japanese society to produce not only a uniquely high rate of economic growth, but a degree of integration of goals that is not found in most industrial societies.[7] National goals, such as space exploration or the extension of education to larger parts of the population, can serve to reduce the intensity of conflict within the society. Such goals cannot simply be proclaimed. They must truly be widely held before they can serve to reduce the intensity of conflict; and competing national goals may well reduce or remove any effect they might otherwise have had.

Violence as a response to conflict is relatively unusual when compared with other responses. Most conflicts are dealt with through some form of accommodation. Compromise, exchanges, rules, tradition, and law combine to render most conflicts nonviolent. The natural or expected form of human conflict is the nonviolent form. With the hundreds of differences in goals that exist in society, human social life would be impossible if violence were the common means of conflict resolution. However, because the degree of violence varies from time to time and place to place and the results of violence are often dramatic, violence is often viewed as the extreme form of the general process of conflict. It is not true that the more extreme the conflict the more likely it is to lead to violence unless violence is accepted as a definition of extreme conflict. Violence is most likely to occur when other means of conflict resolution are not available or do not work. Violence often takes place when the resolution of differences between goals seems rather easy

---

[6] Several translations of his work are available, including Niccolo Machiavelli, *The Historical, Political and Diplomatic Writing of Niccolo Machiavelli*, Christian E. Detmold, transl. (Boston: James R. Osgood and Co., 1882).

[7] See Herman Kahn and Anthoney Wiener, *The Year 2000* (New York: The Macmillan Company, 1967), p. 161, for estimates of future Gross National Product per capita for Japan.

Human societies have developed nonviolent devices for dealing with conflict. The United Nations, for example, since its inception in 1945, has done much to avert international violence.
(Courtesy United Nations.)

and the intensity of goal conflict relatively slight. For a case of the first type, consider wars of religion that have been fought over an *iota*.[8] The second type is illustrated by the violence often suffered by the innocent bystander to some mob action or crime.

Violence must be distinguished from force, though in the popular vocabulary they are often interchangeable. Force and violence both refer to physical coercion that may lead to injury or death. Force describes those actions that are reserved to the state or the officials of society and are hence legal applications. Violence refers to acts that are not regarded as legitimate. Society at large disapproves of violence, although it regards force, even with the same consequences, as proper.

Recent studies have examined the differences in violence over time and between nations. Some of the results of these studies are shown in Table 14–3. While data on crimes of violence and use of police force are subject to considerable variation in accuracy, the

---

[8] In fourth century Greece, the orthodox Christians felt that Christ was identical to God the Father (homoousios), while the Arians, who lost the war and became heretics, believed Christ and God were similar (homo*i*ousios). It took 200 years of conflict to resolve the difference.

TABLE 14–3

List of polities, total magnitude of strife (TMCS) scores, 1961–1965, and groupings.

Polity	TMCS[a] Score	TMCS[a] Rank	Economic development[b]
Congo-Kinshasa[c]	48.7	1	Medium
Indonesia[c]	33.7	2	Medium
South Vietnam	32.8	3	Low
Rwanda[c]	28.2	4	Low
Yemen	23.6	5	Low
Angola	22.1	6	Low
Dominican Republic	21.9	7	Medium
Iraq	20.5	8	Medium
Venezuela	20.3	9	High
Sudan	20.2	10	Low
Algeria	19.5	11	Medium
Syria	17.8	12	Low
Colombia	16.9	13	Medium
Rhodesia	16.4	14	Medium
Uganda	15.6	15	Low
Zambia	15.5	16	Medium
Bolivia	15.2	17	Medium
Cuba	15.2	18	Medium
Kenya	15.0	19	Medium
Guatemala	14.5	20	Medium
Israel[c]	14.0	21	High
Burma	13.9	22	Medium
Nigeria	13.8	23	Low
Argentina	13.2	24	High
Ethiopia	13.2	25	Low
Camerouns	13.1	26	Low
Italy	12.3	27	High
Peru	12.3	28	Medium
France	12.1	29	High
Tunisia	11.8	30	Medium
Greece	11.6	31	Medium
Malawi[c]	11.6	32	Low
Singapore	11.5	33	Medium
Papua–New Guinea	11.3	34	Low
India	11.0	35	Medium
Burundi	10.9	36	Low

SOURCE: Hugh Davis Graham and Ted Robert Gurr (eds.), *Violence in America: Historical and Comparative Perspectives. A Report to the National Commission of the Causes and Prevention of Violence, June 1969* (New York: The New American Library, 1969), pp. 600–606.

[a] The TMCS score is a composite of several measures of violence. The definition of TMCS is given in Graham and Gurr, pp. 598–599 (see source note below).

[b] Economic development level was assessed on the basis of conditions in the late 1950s and early 1960s.

[c] These scores are believed to be unrealistically high because of data estimation procedures used.

TABLE 14–3 (Continued)
List of polities, total magnitude of strife
(TMCS) scores, 1961–1965, and groupings.

	TMCS[a]		Economic develop-ment[b]
Polity	Score	Rank	
Belgium	10.5	37	High
Nepal	10.3	38	Low
Thailand	10.3	39	Medium
South Korea	10.2	40	Medium
United States[d]	10.2	41	High
Ecuador	10.1	42	Medium
South Africa	10.0	43	High
Mozambique	9.8	44	Low
Guinea	9.5	45	Low
Panama	9.5	46	Medium
Nicaragua	9.4	47	Medium
Portugal	9.3	48	Medium
Iran	8.4	49	Medium
Honduras	8.3	50	Low
Mali	8.3	51	Low
Philippines	8.3	52	High
Ceylon	8.2	53	Low
Jordan	8.1	54	Medium
Ghana	7.9	55	Medium
Somalia	7.9	56	Low
Haiti	7.8	57	Low
Dahomey	7.7	58	Low
Brazil	7.4	59	Medium
Chad	7.2	60	Low
Morocco	6.7	61	Medium
Liberia	6.6	62	Low
Sierra Leone	6.5	63	Low
Libya	6.3	64	Low
Pakistan	6.3	65	Low
Tanganyika	6.2	66	Low
Uruguay	6.2	67	High
Japan	5.9	68	High
Lebanon	5.8	69	Medium
Niger	5.8	70	Low
China	5.7	71	Medium
East Germany	5.5	72	High
El Salvador	5.4	73	Medium
United Kingdom	5.4	74	High
Czechoslovakia	5.3	75	High
Spain	5.2	76	High
Senegal	5.1	77	Low
Paraguay	5.0	78	Medium
Turkey	5.0	79	Medium
Canada	4.9	80	High
Chile	4.9	81	High
Mexico	4.7	82	High
West Germany	4.6	83	High

[d] The United States is ranked on the basis of 1961–1965 civil-strife data. On the basis of June 1963–May 1968 data, it ranks 24th, with a TMCS score of 13.6.

TABLE 14–3 (Continued)
List of polities, total magnitude of strife
(TMCS) scores, 1961–1965, and groupings.

| | TMCS[a] | | Economic develop- |
Polity	Score	Rank	ment[b]
Malaya	4.5	84	Medium
Togo	4.1	85	Low
Bulgaria	3.9	86	High
U.A.R.	3.9	87	Medium
Cambodia	3.8	88	Low
U.S.S.R.	3.6	89	High
Poland	3.3	90	High
Yugoslavia	3.3	91	High
Austria	3.1	92	High
Puerto Rico	2.9	93	High
Hungary	2.8	94	High
Costa Rica	2.7	95	Medium
Australia	2.6	96	High
Ireland	2.3	97	High
Finland	2.1	98	High
Afghanistan	2.0	99	Low
Ivory Coast	1.8	100	Low
Jamaica	1.5	101	Medium
C.A.R.	1.3	102	Low
Switzerland	1.2	103	High
Saudi Arabia	1.1	104	Low
China-Taiwan	.0	105	High
Denmark	.0	106	High
Hong Kong	.0	107	Medium
Malagasy	.0	108	Low_
Netherlands	.0	109	High
New Zealand	.0	110	High
Norway	.0	111	High
Romania	.0	112	High
Sweden	.0	113	High
Volta	.0	114	Low

generalization that violent acts tend to come in waves seems sufficiently well supported. National variations also seem real, although they are to a degree dependent upon national reporting practices. Even so, the rough ordering of nations with respect to the levels of violence found in them is probably generally correct, though the exact order should not be taken as conclusive. These data suggest that, although our theory indicates that *conflict* should be greater in the more advanced nations, *violence* is high and low in nations at virtually every level of industrial development. The sources of violence, then, are not to be found in the sources of conflict, but in the area of conflict management.

One aspect of the ability of societies to manage conflict without violence is only partially understood, but its importance is widely recognized. A tradition of violence or a tradition of non-violence can play an important part in determining the probability of a violent response to conflict. Violent behavior, like other behavior, is learned. A tradition of violence can persist long after any legal basis for it has disappeared. Fighting becomes a way of life during many conflicts so that former soldiers, especially if they are displaced by the conflict, turn to lives of violence. This condition becomes traditional and may be passed on from generation to generation. When this happens, the violence takes on ritualistic aspects and some elements of legitimization, at least among the violent group. Violent behavior is then governed by rules, and although it lacks the sanction of the state, it assumes some of the forms of force.

VIOLENT RESPONSE TO CONFLICT

A Case of Traditional Violence—Colombia

Recent Colombian history offers an instructive case of the development of a tradition of violence and the efforts of a society to deal with that tradition. Violent confrontation has been a part of Colombian history since the Spanish conquest of the native inhabitants of the area in a manner that was especially brutal even for those times. During the period of revolutionary wars for independence, Colombia first gained and then lost her independence in bloody wars before she became finally free from Spanish rule.[9] During the years that followed, stable government was rare, as borders were changed and government followed government, more often by extralegal means than by constitutional procedures. In general, only under strong men who exercised dictatorial or nearly dictatorial powers were there periods of stability and economic growth.[10] Against such a background, violent actions were expected to be frequent. *Machismo* combined with tradition to influence individual behavior, as well as the behavior of political groups. Interpersonal disputes were often settled with a machete, just as political disputes were settled with arms—and the loser in both cases was frequently not available to complain afterward. Even under these conditions, the level of violence was often low, and most of the time and for most of the people, violence was not a major concern.

The specific case of violence that will be recounted here is actually a *series* of violent outbreaks that began in 1948 and has

[9] First independence was declared in 1810, but the second republic was not established until 1819. Spain recaptured the capital in 1816 and began a period called the "period of terror." Hundreds of rebels were executed during the "reconquest."
[10] Civil wars were fought in 1829, 1854, 1860, 1876, 1885, 1895, and 1899.

continued in some degree until the present time.[11] The Colombians have named this outbreak simply *La Violencia*.[12] In 1948, Colombia was experiencing a political crisis in which the traditional Liberal and Conservative parties were vying for power. In addition, new voices representing the workers and peasants were being raised in the political arena. One of the most outspoken of these new leaders was Jorge Gaitán. Gaitán was popular, and his assassination on April 9, 1948 was a major cause of the initial outbreak of violence in the country. That event alone, however, was not the single cause of violence. The change of government in 1946 had left much of the country unhappy, and acts of sabotage were frequent throughout the country. The Ninth Panamerican Conference, where George C. Marshall, then Secretary of State, represented the United States, had a session interrupted when a bomb was found in one of the meeting rooms.[13] The assassination of Gaitán was a major immediate cause, however, of what followed. His cry to his followers is represented thus[14]:

> Si avanzo, seguidme;
> si retrocedo, empujadme;
> si os traiciono, matadme;
> si muero, vengadme.

His followers accepted the last line fully. Violence followed, mostly in the city of Bogotá where Gaitán was killed, but also in other parts of the country. The confusion surrounding the death of Gaitán was great. Charges of interference from other nations, of Communist plots, and of attempted revolution were in the air, and even today a clear history of what happened has not been prepared.[15] There is general consensus that immediately following the assassination, there was a period of increase in tension anticipating the elections of 1949. Following that period there was a period of intense violence that lasted until the Dictator Gustavo Rojas Pinilla seized power in a popular move that restored order. As Rojas became more and more

---

[11] The materials are taken from Alonso Moncada, *Un Aspecto de la Violencia* (Bogotá: Alonso Moncada, 1967) and German Guzman, Orlando Fals Borda, and Eduardo Umaña Luna, *La Violencia en Colombia* (Bogotá: Editiones Tercer Mundo, 1963, 1964), Vols. I and II.

[12] "The Violence."

[13] German Guzman, Orlando Fals Borda, and Eduardo Umaña Luna, *La Violencia en Colombia* (Bogotá: Ediciones Tercer Mundo, 1963), Vol. I, pp. 35–36.

[14] German Guzman, Orlando Fals Borda, and Eduardo Umaña Luna, *ibid.*, p. 36. Translated, the verse reads|

> "If I advance, follow me:
> If I retreat, push me,
> If I betray you, kill me,
> If I die, avenge me."

[15] See John Martz, *Colombia, A Contemporary Political Survey* (Chapel Hill, N.C.: University of North Carolina Press, 1962), pp. 33ff for an account.

the dictator and less and less the popular hero, agitation for his replacement became stronger, and by 1954 more violence became common. Violence took the form of skirmishes between armed groups of supporters of different political factions, including the supporters of Rojas, and the form of banditry, or encounters between unarmed people and the political groups. In many villages the members of one party were able to kill or drive off all members of the other party; raids by Conservatives on Liberal and Liberals on Conservative villages were frequent, with thousands of deaths the result. Rojas was replaced in 1959 by a National Front in which Liberals and Conservatives were united under an agreement to share power in all governments and to rotate the national Presidency. This agreement led to a relative reduction of the violence, but a period of continued killings followed. This period of *La Violencia* illustrates the force of tradition in violent behavior. Exact data on the number of killings are lacking, but estimates range from 200,000 to 500,000[16] for the entire period of the violence. Two sets of estimates of deaths for the period of interest, 1958–1961, are shown in Table 14–4.

The violence was spread over most of the country, though rural areas suffered most.[17] In addition to raids on villages, buses and trains were ambushed and often the riders were killed to a man.[18] Though the history is far more complex than can be indicated here, with the many declarations of independence by certain areas, urban terrorists, and Communist infiltrators within the criminal as well as political spheres, the ritualistic elements are strong. Although they are extreme examples, the *consignas* and *cortes,* as described by one author, suggest the nature of ritualistic violence[19]:

Picar para tamal is to reduce the human body to the small pieces of meat used in the popular dish. . . . *Bocachiquiar* is a torture that receives its name from a very spiny fresh water fish called *bocachico.* In preparing the fish, one makes fine cuts in it to make it ready to eat. The torture consists of making small cuts in the body of the victim and allowing him to bleed to death slowly. Sometimes small children are charged with this task. . . . *El corte de franela* consists of making a deep wound in the throat near the trunk of the body. This is done without striking a blow but by drawing a sharpened machete rapidly across the back of the neck. . . . *El corte de corbata* consists of making a cut in the front of the throat and passing the tongue of the victim through the slit so that it rests on his neck.

[16] Several estimates are given by Alonso Moncada, *Un Aspecto de la Violencia* (Bogotá: Alonso Moncada, 1967), p. 8.
[17] The coastal areas remained relatively quiet. See German Guzman, Orlando Fals Borda, and Eduardo Umbaña Luna, *La Violencia en Colombia* (Bogotá: Ediciones Tercer Mundo, 1963), Vol. I, pp. 118ff.
[18] Some of these attacks appear to be nothing more or less than robbery.
[19] German Guzman, Orlando Fals Borda, and Eduardo Umaña Luna, *La Violencia en Colombia* (Bogotá: Ediciones Tercer Mundo, 1963), Vol. I, pp. 226–230. The first two have no direct translation, the third is "the throat cut," and the last "the necktie cut" for obvious though macabre reasons.

TABLE 14–4

Numbers of deaths from "La Violencia," 1958–1961, as estimated by different men.

Year	Estimate of Charry Samper, Minister of Justice	Estimate of Gutierrez Anzola, based on records of the National Police
1958	3798	3796
1959	2264	2550
1960	2013	2557
1961	2488	3186

Source: Alonso Moncada, *Un Aspecto de la Violencia* (Bogotá: Alonso Moncada, 1967), p. 8.

The ritualization, not only in the acts themselves, but in their names, indicates that a form of violence and cruelty became a way of life and an integral part of the experience of the people involved. The participation of children and young people indicates that a regular socialization process took place involving the same mechanisms used in other types of socialization; therefore, a generation was raised knowing as normal a form of activity that other generations would have considered unusually violent. Thus, in parts of Colombia, there arose a whole generation for whom violence was a way of life. It is not surprising that they continued their violent activities, often for different causes, and sometimes without any cause at all, for years after the original causes were removed.[20]

Ultimate Sources of Violence

Two factors seem to predict the likelihood of violence: (1) cultural conditioning and traditions of violence and (2) the absence of non-violent means of conflict resolution. Even the most peaceful cultures allow violence under some conditions and may face violence-inducing situations when placed in contact with other cultures. The Hopi, an Indian tribe of the Southeast, are among the most peaceful of the cultures that have been studied. Even so, they killed missionaries who offended them too often.[21]

Violence is an appealing solution to conflict because it offers an immediate and perhaps final solution to the conflict. The costs of violence are more social than individual, at least for the victor. However, not only are times and cultures differentially likely to produce violence, but at the same time within a culture, some

[20] German Guzman, Orlando Fals Borda, and Eduardo Umaña Luna, *La Violencia en Colombia* (Bogotá: Ediciones Tercer Mundo, 1963), Vol. II, pp. 381ff.

[21] See Ernest Beaglehole, "Notes on Hopi Warfare," in *Hopi of the Second Mesa*, American Anthropological Association, Memoir No. 44 (1935), and Richard Brandt, *Hopi Ethics* (Chicago: University of Chicago Press, 1954).

individuals are more prone to violence than others. Some may be subject to greater degrees of conflict, but this alone probably does not account for all of the individual differences in tendencies to violence. Several theories that attempt to account for individual differences in violence have been advanced, but none seems to account for all the differences that have been observed. Probably such differences can and do arise from a multitude of different causes so that no single explanation can be expected to be sufficient. A brief review of some of these theories and their inadequacies and utilities will serve to place them in context.

1. **Theories of aggressiveness** generally posit some type of aggressiveness based in drives or instincts that are simply differentially distributed in the society. Such a view cannot account for changes in the total amount of aggression in society, because genetic predispositions do not change in short periods of time. Indeed, to the extent that aggression is a function of innate drives, levels· of violence would be expected to remain constant with the parameters imposed by social conditions. One recent finding has shown that chromosomal formations do indeed seem to predict certain types of violent behavior on a statistical but not on an individual basis, but the interpretation of that result remains in doubt.[22]

2. **Theories of imperfect socialization** stress that some individuals simply do not learn the rules of behavior and the control of impulses that govern most people, and therefore they are more likely to engage in violent behavior.[23] Some of these theories assume that violent behavior is more natural and hence takes place in the absence of civilized rules. Others refer to competitive socialization that encourages violence in some subcultures. The former theories are probably wrong since violence is not more characteristic of primitive man than of civilized man. Though there is little evidence to suggest that civilized man is more violent, certainly modern technology allows civilized man to be more efficient in his violence and to inflict his violent acts on large numbers in ways no primitive could even imagine.[24] The latter set of theories, in maintaining that some subcultures may heighten propensities toward

[22] A brief discussion can be found in I. Michael Lerner, *Heredity, Evolution, and Society* (San Francisco: W. H. Freeman and Company, 1968), pp. 118–119.

[23] There is a great deal of evidence that shows the human is fundamentally aggressive and that conditions channel his aggressive tendencies. See Elton B. McNeil, "The Nature of Aggression," in Elton B. McNeil (ed.), *The Nature of Human Conflict* (Englewood Cliffs, N.J.: Prentice–Hall, Inc., 1965), pp. 14–41.

[24] See Hugh Davis Graham and Ted Robert Gurr, *Violence in America: Historical and Comparative Perspectives. A Report to the National Commission on the Causes and Prevention of Violence, June 1969.* (New York: The New American Library, 1969), p. 567, for measures of civil strife by level of economic development. Thirty-seven nations ranked high on economic development suffered 1.7 deaths per million persons from causes of turmoil, conspiracy, and internal war, while 38 countries ranked low had 841 deaths per million from those causes during the period 1961–1965. The United States had a comparable figure of 1.1 during the period 1961–1968.

violence during their socialization processes, merely locates the problem within a separate group, while failing to determine the reasons for the emergence of violence within that subculture.

3. **Theories of situational violence** assume a constant degree of aggressiveness for most or all people but argue that violence-inducing situations are uncommon. Therefore, most people are not subjected to them even in the course of a lifetime.[25] These theories argue that most people do not kill in the ordinary course of their lives, but when placed in violent conditions, such as those of war, will kill without any hesitation. Experiments have shown that people generally are quite willing to inflict pain, even the risk of death, on others, if they feel that there is sufficient justification. The justification does not have to be compelling. Students, when instructed to administer electric shocks to others, were quite willing to do so even when the others showed signs of being in great pain, provided the students felt they were doing a socially acceptable act, namely, participating in an experiment.[26] That result may account for so many atrocities being committed by those who seem otherwise mild mannered and peaceful. It is probably true that most people respond to situations rather than initiate them; for this reason, a situational theory of violence has much to recommend it. It does not explain, however, why these situations arise, nor does it describe or delineate the conditions that tend to inhibit them. Thus, a situational theory cannot account for the various levels of violence in society.

Riots, Rebellion, and Revolution

Violence on a large scale involving many persons has posed a problem for the student of human society. Why do men rebel? Why do crowds riot? Can these events be predicted? Though the extreme responses of riot, rebellion, and revolution might be expected to be the result of extreme provocation or serious deprivation, the historical record does not support that contention. Riots are not most likely in the worst slums; rebellion is not most frequent among the poorest colonies; revolutionaries are not found primarily among the most exploited classes. Most students of revolution feel that objective conditions interact with the expectations of the population and that interaction leads to aggressive behavior. Whether the

[25] For a view that regards violence as unusual in human behavior, see Fred R. Crawford, "Reducing Violence," in Fred R. Crawford (ed.), *Violence and Dissent in Urban America,* SNPA Foundation Seminar Books (Atlanta, Ga.: Southern Newspaper Publishers Association Foundation, 1970).

[26] Several experiments have shown the extent to which responses are a result of a social situation rather than the individual's moral code. Some anthropologists distinguish between "guilt" cultures, where internal ideas of right and wrong control behavior and "shame" cultures, where ideas of right and wrong are based on the responses of others to the act in question.

Once liberated, the oppressed may wreak more violence than the hated oppressors. This is the hypocrisy of revolution.
("With or Without Reason" by Francisco Goya. Courtesy Museum of Fine Arts, Boston.)

aggression is rioting or rebellion depends on the degree of organization of the population in question. As long as the population expects little, poverty and deprivation do not lead to rebellion. When their expectations increase, but their objective condition remains the same, frustration results, which is converted into action unless the disparity between expectations and conditions can be reduced. Davies argues convincingly that such differences occur when "a prolonged period of rising expectations and rising gratifications is followed by a short period of sharp reversal, during which the gap between expectations and gratifications quickly widens."[27] He shows that such a trend characterized the American Revolution, the American Civil War, the Nazi Revolution, and the Black Rebellion in the United States.

International Conflict: Diplomacy and War

Conflicts among nations and societies have profound effects on the course of human history. Not only is the course of power changed

---

[27] James C. Davies, "The J-Curve of Rising and Declining Satisfactions as a Cause of Some Great Revolutions and a Contained Rebellion," in Hugh Davis Graham and Ted Robert Gurr, *Violence in America: Historical and Comparative Perspectives, A Report to the National Commission on the Causes and Prevention of Violence, June 1969* (New York: The New American Library, 1969), p. 671.

by war, but some theorists see in war the origins of social stratification and the nation state.[28] Throughout most of history, warfare has
been glorified and the warrior has been accorded a high place in
society. While war has been an unhappy time for parts of the population in most instances, only recently has war been condemned as
a means of following and insuring national interests. Even so, most
of the world accepts war as necessary, if not desirable, and warfare
is unlikely to end in the near future.

The sources of war are easily seen in greed; but participation in war is often for the highest motives, and the actual gain by
warfare is sometimes difficult to measure. War probably has many
elements in common with other forms of violence. Although war is
usually regarded as a legitimate use of national power, it is more
akin to intrasocietal violence than force, since it is not sanctioned
by or exercised by an authority greater than the participants. Warfare is rarely uncontrolled. Wars are fought by rules, and although
cultural differences may render the behavior of one side barbaric to
the other, these rules subject all participants to some restraints.

Some nations are regarded as warlike to a greater degree
than others, just as some societies are regarded as more prone to
violence. Studies show that war is more frequent in the history of
some nations than of others. Though it is difficult to count wars
because of differences in intensities, durations, and geographical
extent, one investigation counted the years a country was at war
between 1800 and 1925. Separate wars in the same year counted as
additional years at war. The results from some European countries
were: France 134, England 128, Austria–Hungary 37, Italy 27, and
Germany 18.[29] One striking thing that emerges is that the nations
generally regarded as peace loving have fought more wars than the
others. Perhaps the number of wars a country is likely to fight is
related to the size and power of the country rather than its love of
war. One observation can be offered: war does not seem to be
simply a function of ideological, cultural, or religious differences.
Catholic fights Catholic as readily as he fights Protestant, and Russian
fights Russian as quickly as he fights German. Wars often start over
seemingly trivial events while serious actions may pass without any
response whatsoever. Perhaps the most socially significant thing
about the course of war is the enormous societal cost, which is related to the tendency of wars, once begun, to grow if they do not
end in a quick victory for one side. Indeed war shares with other
forms of conflict a social meaning in its own right that goes beyond

---

[28] Such a view has been advanced by Ibn Khaldun, Gustav Ratzenhofer, and Lester Ward.
For example, see Howard Becker and Harry Elmer Barnes, *Social Thought from Lore to Science*, 2nd ed. (Washington, D.C.: Harren Press, 1952).
[29] Pitirim A. Sorokin, *Social and Cultural Dynamics* (New York: American Book Company,
1937), pp. 383ff.

the causes of the dispute or the immediate points of issue. When conflict becomes intense, the failure to win or at least to preserve some parity is perceived, often rightly, as leading to losses beyond the immediate issue. Thus, nations may dispute claims to relatively small areas of land, not because the land itself is important, but because a failure to maintain a claim might lead to further demands of a more serious nature or a weakening of the nation's position in other areas.

Wars have tended to become greater in geographic extent as transportation has become more efficient. The machines of warfare have become more effective and war has involved larger and larger parts of societies. In modern war, the distinction between the workers who manufacture weapons and the soldiers who use them has been reduced, and civilian populations are often regarded as military targets. Nuclear weapons have reduced, if not eliminated, any advantage to a victor in a large scale war, and the balance of terror may have worked to eliminate such wars during the time between 1946 and the present. Even so, some recognition should be made of the fact that weapons of war have previously been considered so horrible as to end war for all time, the first such instance

As the devices of war become more sophisticated and effective, war is extended to greater parts of the population.
(Courtesy Wide World Photos.)

being in the 15th century.[30] Nations have fought wars that were more costly than any victory could reward, and the causes of war are so poorly understood that simplistic faith in the rationality of war is probably ill placed.

The Chain of Violence

War shares with other forms of violence what might be called the **chain of violence.** In the chain, violence is linked to violence and continues until some event breaks the chain. It is not clear why the chain begins, why some conflicts forge the first link, but after the initial stage, the rate of growth appears to increase rapidly until a major event—defeat, disaster, or despair—acts to break the chain.

The chain begins with the conflicts engendered by different goals. It continues with events in which conflicts cannot be resolved, and one side seeks to coerce the other. As soon as force is brought to bear, the side being forced must either surrender or resort to force in sufficient scale to deter the further application of force by the first side. Not only do the sides weigh the value of force and the issue at hand, they also consider the other costs of defeat—additional demands, their position in other disputes, and even intangibles such as prestige and honor. Even a weaker nation may resort to force against a stronger one in the belief that the stronger might not find the fight worth the cost or potential gain. As a war continues, each side proceeds with greater and greater interest in victory and makes additional efforts with increasing ease. Thus wars flow not so much from the often small events that lead to them, but the increasing chain of violence that causes each action by one side to be met with an increased reaction by the other until one or the other is totally committed to the conflict with everything to lose in defeat. Generally, the stronger party to the conflict can break the chain better than the weaker because it has less, relatively, to lose by doing so; but often such a cost is still too great, and a resolution on the battlefield is the outcome, regardless of the even greater cost of that course.

CONFLICT, VIOLENCE, AND ADAPTATION

Although this chapter has stressed the naturalness of conflict in human society, the functional aspects of violence and conflict are easily missed because they seem wasteful and inefficient. Moreover, the obvious uses of conflict to eliminate the weak or those less effective in employing violence has been overly emphasized in a form of social Darwinism that tends to justify any social conditions that

---

[30] At that time, the Papacy felt that the crossbow was so terrible a weapon as to render war unacceptable to civilized nations.

Conflict often increases feelings of solidarity. In the case of a campus demonstration, the opposing parties cooperate for their mutual benefit to limit and control the means of conflict.
(Courtesy Wide World Photos.)

arise.[31] The importance of conflict, and even violence, is subtly defined in terms of positive contributions to society. The existence of such contributions does not mean the conflict is either good or bad, but only that conflict contributes to the operation of society as society is currently organized.

Perhaps the major function of conflict is its contribution to social change and to the adaptation of society to changing conditions. Conflict becomes more intense when methods of easy resolution are not available, as in times of rapid change. A new technology, such as the developments of the industrial revolution, can lead to conflict because the decision-making procedures of the nonindustrial society are no longer effective. The conflict that results, for example, between labor and management, creates different patterns of decision that are more suited to the new conditions. While one might argue that the prolonged conflict with periods of intense violence that accompanies change can be averted or limited by more moral or more clever participants, such interpretation does not reduce the importance that conflict plays in the emerging social

[31] Social Darwinism is not always a simple-minded application of biology to social systems. See Howard Becker and Harry Elmer Barnes, *Social Thought from Love to Science*, 2nd ed. (Washington, D.C.: Harren Press, 1952), pp. 69ff.

structure. Partially because conflict cannot extend itself beyond certain points without destroying society, it serves to encourage new accommodations and hence adaptation to social change.

A second function of conflict is to increase social solidarity. Not only does the threat from the other group of competitors draw the conflicting groups closer, opposing groups are often forced to deal with their common interests in order to define and resolve their differences. This process is delicate. When conflict becomes very intense, common interests are obscured. Generally, however, conflict groups in society experience cooperation that is itself important to the integration of the society. An example of how such cooperation comes about is seen in the conflict between campus demonstration groups and the rest of the university community. Though early demonstrations often led to arrests, disorganization, and even violence, as time passed both demonstrators and the university began to cooperate in organizing, structuring, and limiting demonstrations. Such cooperation was viewed by both groups as advantageous; as a result, to some degree these groups were more closely integrated with each other than before.

A third function of conflict can be mentioned. Conflict offers a means of social mobility to individuals and groups in society. Successful participation in conflict and its resolution results in greater participation in later decisions. Thus the union leader who organizes a successful strike will gain credence, prestige, and power with both management and labor.

"Was it for this you were born?" by Francisco Goya.
(Courtesy Museum of Fine Arts, Boston.)

Summary

This chapter has dealt with conflict and violence in human society. Conflict has been viewed as the result of the differences in values and goals in the society or among societies. Conflicts can be reduced by changing goals, but the level and intensity of conflict can be influenced by many other mechanisms, among which are external threats and scapegoating. Violence is seen as a response that often has traditional, ritualistic elements. Several views of violence were examined, and war as a type of international violence was analyzed in terms of the chain of violence that leads to war. Conflict is often a source of social crisis, and the management of crisis and the resolution of conflict are closely related processes. In the next chapter, the question of crisis and social response to crisis will be examined.

Exercises

1. How might violence toward others, such as murder, and violence toward the self, such as suicide, be related? Examine data for several countries or one country over a period of time to see if your prediction is correct.

2. What effect should the introduction of intensive educational programs have on the level of violence in an underdeveloped nation? How might other factors influence the results of that effect?

3. In what countries would you expect a rebellion or revolution to take place in the near future? Why?

4. If an organization has a high level of intensive conflict, what steps could be taken to reduce the conflict? Is reducing the conflict always desirable from the point of view of the organization? From the point of view of individual members?

5. How effective is fear as a means of social control? When would you expect it to be most effective? When would it be least effective?

6. Is modern society more or less susceptible to disruption by violence on the part of relatively small groups?

7. Extend Sorokin's analysis of participation in wars to the current date. What problems do you have in counting the years of participation in war? Include the United States in your analysis and evaluate your results.

8. Violence can take many forms: riots, lynchings, political assassination, and so on. List as many types as you can and state what factors might increase and decrease the incidence of each. Do these factors differ from case to case?

Selected Bibliography

Abel, Theodore. *The Nazi Movement.* New York: Atherton Press, 1965; orig. ed. 1938.

Brinton, Crane. *The Anatomy of Revolution*, Rev. ed. New York: Vantage Books, 1965.

Dollard, John, et al. *Frustration and Aggression.* New Haven, Conn.: Yale University Press, 1939.

Graham, Hugh Davis, and Ted Robert Gurr (eds.). *Violence in America: Historical and Comparative Perspectives. A Report to the National Commission on the Causes and Prevention of Violence, June 1969.* New York: The New American Library, 1969.

Lubasz, Heinz (ed.). *Revolutions in Modern European History.* New York: The Macmillan Company, 1966.

Lorenz, Konrad. *On Aggression.* New York: Harcourt, Brace & World, Inc., 1966.

15

Planning and Decision-Making in Periods of Crises

Although it is increasingly difficult to separate "normal" from "unusual" or critical periods, our focus in the last two chapters has been on the more normal aspects of social organization. The major thrust of all social organization—implicit and explicit—is to regularize and normalize experience, to furnish ready answers to anticipated problems, tasks, issues, needs, and pressures. In short, adaptation through social organization has been changing or evolving slowly, grudgingly, and with apparent emphasis on past adaptive systems.

Yet an essential and perhaps inescapable feature of complex societies (and "modernizing societies," which seek complexity) is the emergence of rather severe threats to either the *efficiency* or the *survival* of complex societies. These threats may well be called *social crises* and can be considered major clues to potential alterations in the heritage of adaptive mechanisms.[1]

[1] Karl Marx, *Economic and Philosophical Manuscripts of 1844* (New York: International Publishers, 1964); Friedrich Engels, *Herr Eugen Duhring's Revolution in Science (Anti-Duhring)* (New York: International Publishers, 1939); Karl Mannheim, *Man and Society in an Age of Reconstruction* (New York: Harcourt, Brace and Company, Inc., 1940); Karl Mannheim, *Diagnosis of Our Time* (London: Routledge and Kegan Paul, 1943); Pitirim A. Sorokin, *Man and Society in Calamity* (New York: E. P. Dutton and Company, Inc., 1942); Leonard Binder et al., *Crisis and Sequences in Political Development* (Princeton: Princeton University Press, 1971).

In the simplest terms, a social crisis is an identifiable and prolonged discrepancy between the real or assumed requirements of a recurring practical social issue and the effective application of existing social and cultural solutions.[2] Crises, therefore, may derive from newly acquired pressures (whatever the source) or from significant declines in the actual efficiency of workable structures (whatever the reason)—or both. But proper and timely identification of crises by most participants has been rare, perhaps because faith in the prevailing mechanisms has been well cultivated, or because—until recently for most people—alternative solutions have not seemed possible.

Historically, human societies have had an erratic record of success in responding to social crises. But it would require a revolution in method and focus to analyze societies as evolving consequences of meeting, avoiding, solving, or yielding to identifiable social crises—thus providing a societal "batting average" for crisis confrontation. Some years ago, the historian, Arnold Toynbee, tried such an approach, but with enormous difficulties and highly controversial results.[3] For our purposes, it is perhaps only necessary to recall a few famous crises and to examine the key features of past crisis management as a prelude to contemporary patterns.

During the classical period of Western civilization (1500 B.C. to 400 A.D.), two cardinal crises seem unusually instructive. In the fourth century B.C., when Grecian culture was highly developed but fractionated politically, the basic crisis was the growing inadequacy of the city–state form in the face of external aggression. The Peloponnesian War was an early indication that neither the leading city–states (Sparta and Athens), nor fragile confederations of city–states, could adequately coordinate military and economic resources on the Grecian peninsula. The emerging threat of Macedonia under Philip was clearly recognized by Demosthenes and others, who pleaded for genuine and lasting alliances with various peoples. Athenian leadership embarked on a tragedy of tactical errors; instead of expanding political and military organization, neighboring allies were successively alienated and then plucked by Macedonian armies. Thus, crisis became catastrophe when Philip overwhelmed Greece and effectively destroyed Greece as an autonomous cultural entity.[4]

---

[2] William I. Thomas, *Source Book for Social Origins* (Chicago: Chicago University Press, 1909), pp. 16–21.

[3] Arnold J. Toynbee, *A Study of History* (London: Oxford University Press, 1935–1954), 12 Vols. The abridged edition by D. C. Somervell (New York: Oxford University Press, 1947) is very useful, particularly Chaps. 13–16.

[4] J. B. Bury *et al.*, *Cambridge Ancient History* (New York: The Macmillan Company, 1925), Vol. 3, pp. 549–552, Vol. 4, pp. 62–65, 139–153, Vol. 5, pp. 107–109, 348–349; Thucydides, *The Peloponnesian Wars* (New York: Modern Library, 1934), Books 4, 6.

Normally, society encourages faith in the accepted routines and mechanisms—the military traditions, for example—particularly, but not exclusively, among the young.
(Courtesy Jim Harrison.)

Centuries later, the extensive Roman Empire developed a prolonged and deep-seated crisis of interlocking dimensions—political, administrative, and economic. Essentially, the oldest aspect of crisis was irregularity of imperial succession, which came to be a contest between candidates from different army units throughout the empire. This in turn was aggravated by intense economic difficulties, which derived both from costly wars of expansion and from a localized, inefficient agricultural system that stifled trade and encouraged uncontrolled migration to cities and towns. The recurrent crisis was further magnified by desperate taxation policies, which ruined a vast network of urban officials, who in effect had been the major source of coordination in the empire. By the fifth century A.D., the point of no return had been reached; in place of the former empire, there were only a series of loose political fragments that came to form the basis of feudalism.[5]

The roll call of subsequent social crises is long and perennially fascinating.[6] We can only mention a few: the religious and

[5] Michael Rostovtzeff, *Social and Economic History of the Roman Empire* (Oxford: Clarendon Press, 1926), pp. 103, 122–123, 351–355; Tenney Frank, *Rome and Italy of the Empire* (Baltimore: Johns Hopkins Press, 1940), pp. 303–306.
[6] Jerome Blum et al., *The European World*, 2nd ed. (Boston: Little, Brown and Company, Inc., 1970), Part 2; R. R. Palmer, *A History of the Modern World*, 2nd ed. (New York: Alfred A. Knopf, Inc., 1961), Chaps. 9, 12, 17.

social impasse that preceded the major revolts in 17th century England; the enclosure movement and controversies of the 18th century; the problems of English urbanization and industrialization in the middle of the 19th century; the frustrations of the rising middle classes in prerevolutionary France; the slavery issue in the United States in 1840–1860; the conflict between farmer–labor groups and corporate business giants of the 1870's to the 1930's; the severe economic crises of the 1920's and 1930's; the competition of extremist political ideologies in Germany, France, and Italy; the crises of polarization between East and West in the 20th century; the multiple problems of contemporary urban–metropolitan growth; the painful attempts to reduce the effects of past discrimination against blacks in the United States.

In retrospect, it is reasonably clear that many of these crises were handled with little understanding, with parochial concern for consequences, with continued absence of creativity, and with limited resources or knowledge. Indeed, continued failure to provide adaptive solutions to crisis was normally followed by severe conflict and violence, which often intensified crisis (and incidentally *clarified* the difficulties). We might almost conclude that man seems to have learned little or nothing from previous failures in dealing with social crises. On the other hand, despite incredible fumbling in crisis, in very few instances has such social ineptitude resulted in severe problems of mass physical survival or loss of societal identity.

The atom bomb was both a triumph of science and technology and an omen of our reduced possibilities for arriving at maladaptive solutions to social crises.
(Courtesy Wide World Photos.)

Most frequently, in the past, maladaptive solutions to social crises have either delayed a society's ability to evolve more fruitfully (that is, with greater complexity and overall efficiency) or allowed a competitive advantage in social development to be usurped by (or transferred to) another society (for example, from Spain to England; from Greece to Rome; from France to Germany in the 19th century; from Russia to Japan after 1905).[7]

It may well be that the era in which nonadaptive solutions to crisis could be devised with impunity is coming to a close.[8] The margin for error was in practice quite wide—until 1945—because the destructive capacity of complex societies and the pressure of collective, nonrational violence were limited. Since 1945, however, cultural complexity, technological efficiency in human and environmental destruction, and effective reservoirs of irresponsible social intervention have developed to such a degree that errors in analyzing and resolving major crises can be lethal on a scale previously unknown. Theoretically and practically, then, an understanding of social crises and of the effective means of handling crises is indispensable for human adaptation.

TYPES OF SOCIAL CRISES

In line with the earlier definition of social crises, the probability of crisis and the variety of crises would be far greater in complex societies and in rapidly changing societies. During the last 10 years, in fact, social scientists have studied the intricate careers of the modernizing nations (in Africa, Asia, and Latin America) as attempts to cope with five major crises[9]: identity crises, legitimacy crises, participation crises, distribution crises, and penetration or program-coordination crises. It is assumed that such crises occur in the sequence just noted, at least for developing or modernizing nations. For our purposes, however, it may be helpful to simplify this useful approach by classifying crises by the major adaptive dimensions of society.

Technological Crisis

A technological crisis occurs when the available knowledge and technological equipment are unable to cope with or satisfy a persistent level of social needs or aspirations for a given society. In

[7] R. R. Palmer, *ibid.*, Chaps. 3–6, 13.
[8] Karl Mannheim, *Man and Society in an Age of Reconstruction* (New York: Harcourt, Brace and Company, Inc., 1940), pp. 44–51; H. G. Wells, *Outline of History* (Garden City: N.Y.: Garden City Press, 1920), p. 1100.
[9] Leonard Binder, *et al., Crisis and Sequence in Political Government* (Princeton: Princeton University Press, 1971), pp. 21–25; Lucian W. Pye, *Aspects of Political Development* (Boston: Little, Brown and Company, Inc., 1966), pp. 51–66.

other words, inadequate resources (natural and human) interfere with reasonable levels of efficiency, or with survival itself. For example, India has been suffering from a recurring technological crisis: an agricultural system that cannot produce enough food to avert famine and malnutrition in significant portions of the population of 450 million people. Another technological crisis created considerable anxiety in the mid-1950's, when Soviet technological achievements (and related training programs) came to overshadow American capacities in the realms of weaponry and space probing. This technological discrepancy between competing nations was defined as a severe threat to national survival and was followed by extensive attempts to improve scientific education and recruitment.[10] Still another example of technological crisis was the so-called "brain drain" of the 1960's in Britain. The fact that many highly competent scientists migrated to the United States indicated an imminent decline in scientific development, which likewise reduces further capabilities for adaptation in civilian and military spheres.[11]

In general, technological crises seem more problematical in societies with simpler, or newly developed, levels of technology. However, the conditions of such crises and the necessary means for resolving them tend to be clear and generally accepted. The major mechanisms—financial resources, specially trained manpower, and specifically required inventions—are likewise clear.

Ideological Crises

The essence of ideological crisis is incompatible differences between (a) the basic or common values of a social system and the values or interests of some significant subgroup, or (b) the values of two or more significant subgroups, for these differences impede the practical solution of some societal problem.[12] Such crises are not solely valuational; they produce (or represent) troublesome deficits in allegiance to the welfare of the larger system, and an unwillingness to cooperate with related subcategories in resolving normal problems of the community or nation.

There has been a tendency in recent years to underestimate the existence and importance of ideological differences in

[10] David D. Van Tassel and Michael G. Hall (eds.), Science and Society in the United States (Homewood, Ill.: Dorsey Press, 1966), Chaps. 6, 8; Jerome B. Wiesner, Where Science and Politics Meet (New York: McGraw–Hill Book Company, 1965), Part 2.
[11] Committee on the International Migration of Talent, Modernization and the Migration of Talent (New York: Education and World Affairs, January 1970); F. J. Van Hoek, The Migration of High Level Manpower from Developing to Developed Countries (The Hague: Mouton, 1970).
[12] F. S. C. Northrop, The Meeting of East and West (New York: The Macmillan Company, 1946); Leonard G. Benson, National Purpose: Ideology and Ambivalence in America (Washington, D.C.: Public Affairs Press, 1963).

In today's society, ideological differences are not simply philosophical arguments or subjects for formal debate. They are urgent realities that frequently erupt in violence because there are few feasible alternative means of managing such conflicts.
(Courtesy Leonard Freed, Magnum Photos, Inc.)

complex societies.[13] But this judgment may simply refer to the fact that ideologies have become the property of large numbers, rather than the monopoly of "professional" elites, who are by training and circumstance more adept at sharpening and dramatizing special or variant perspectives. It is difficult, for example, to locate currently contrived and reasonably clear meanings of such value systems as democracy, liberalism, conservatism, communism, atheism, fascism,

[13] Daniel Bell, *The End of Ideology*, Rev. ed. (New York: The Free Press, 1962); Seymour M. Lipset, *Political Man* (Garden City, N.Y.: Doubleday & Company, Inc., 1960); Daniel J. Boorstin, *The Genius of American Politics* (Chicago: University of Chicago Press, 1953); Daniel J. Boorstin, *The Decline of Radicalism* (New York: Random House, Inc., 1969); Mostafa Rejai (ed.), *Decline of Ideology?* (Chicago: Aldine–Atherton, 1971).

and unionism. Yet various kinds of opinion surveys (on voting, public issues) strongly suggest that people's answers to poll and interview questions can be clustered and interpreted as reflecting an underlying ideological viewpoint (for example, political cynicism, economic or political conservatism, racism).[14] In addition, we cannot ignore the recent outpouring of strongly ideological positions, such as Black Power, Women's Liberation, citizen participation, student protest, homosexuality, and the Wallace movement.[15]

In any case, ideological crisis is perhaps more serious than technological crisis. Ideological crises are less overt for long periods, and therefore are more difficult to detect and confront. Likewise, for most people, the connection between values and behavior remains elusive, perhaps because few people have the opportunity to examine these carefully through prolonged observation and investigation. Consequently, for most people, ideological crisis goes unrecognized until advanced phases of development are reached; and the climate for dealing with ideological crisis therefore tends to be lukewarm, unsettled, or even unfavorable.

Perhaps the most compelling aspect of ideological crises, comparatively speaking, is the essentially *nonrational* character of the differences that provoke such crises. Apart from force or coercion, the only means of reducing the impact of conflicting value systems is by asserting their subordination to a "higher" value or goal. Certainly, the validity of the higher value cannot be demonstrated or derived by logical arguments. We need only recall the interesting but futile efforts to do so by such intellectuals as Rousseau, Hegel, Kant, Marx, and Toynbee.[16] In practice, two impediments to the resolution of ideological crises seem particularly strong and distinctly nonrational. One difficulty is the limited experience and the narrowly defined interests of social categories (peasantry, small businessmen, bureaucrats, and so on), which serve as persisting blinders to objective comparison and constructive doubts. This pervasive condition is not ignored by successful politicians, who seek support by catering to as many specific interests as possible. The second

[14] See, for example, Samuel A. Stouffer, *Communism, Conformity, and Civil Liberties* (Garden City, N.Y.: Doubleday & Company, Inc., 1955); Angus Campbell et al., *The American Voter* (New York: John Wiley & Sons, Inc., 1960); Robert Lane, *Political Ideology* (New York: The Free Press, 1962).
[15] Among the continuing mass of relevant works, see Stokely Carmichael and Charles V. Hamilton, *Black Power* (New York: Vintage Books, 1967); Betty Friedan, *The Feminine Mystique* (New York: W. W. Norton and Company, Inc., 1963); John Murphy, *Homosexual Liberation* (New York: Praeger, 1971); Seymour M. Lipset and Philip G. Altbach (eds.), *Students in Revolt* (Boston: Houghton Mifflin Company, 1969).
[16] J. J. Rousseau, *The Social Contract* (available in many editions; for instance, New York: E. P. Dutton and Co., 1947); G. W. F. Hegel, *The Philosophy of the State and History* (Chicago: S. C. Griggs, 1892); Karl Marx and Friedrich Engels, *The Communist Manifesto* (available in many editions; for instance, New York: International Publishers, 1948); Immanuel Kant, *The Doctrine of Virtue* (New York: Harper Torchbooks, 1964).

impediment is the phenomenon of *alienation*, or the absence of trust or faith in the larger system, in key positions in that system, or in current personnel in those positions.[17]

Apparently, the only "rational" means of dispelling ideological crisis is the real or assumed threat of external aggression and the consequent need for intensified morale and allegiance. Religious and political leaders of the charismatic type—who normally arise in periods of ideological crisis—have frequently dealt with such crises by identifying one or more external enemies or heresies and then embarking on "defensive" or "just" wars to preserve the identity of the nation or church. French monarchs of the 17th century are prime examples, as are such men as Hitler, Mussolini, Stalin, and Nasser. Many years ago, William James developed a much quoted analysis of this very phenomenon and called for an adaptive "moral equivalent for war." Regretfully, after two generations, no feasible solution has as yet been offered.[18]

Organizational or Structural Crises

If the previous crises are basically problems of resources or allegiance, organizational crises may be distinguished as crises in *social efficiency*. The primary indicators of such crises are repeated failures in coordinating the roles and skills of important social segments, the lack of effective mechanisms for handling disputes, the lack of regular, predictable methods for allocating material rewards, and failure to convert authoritative decisions (policies) into feasible, concordant patterns of behavior. Obviously, organizational crises are more likely in highly complex social systems, or in systems that are in the process of rapid change toward complexity. Perhaps the major frustration in such crises is the knowledge that high capabilities (skills) and relatively clear objectives are useless if not mocking achievements without the catalyst of relevant social forms. In the simplest terms, such crises may be described as the result of combining costly ingredients without a definite and tested recipe.

Organizational difficulties erupt into crises with considerable frequency—and sometimes with remarkable persistence—in contemporary societies. Metropolitan regions in the United States are perhaps prime examples of organizational chaos and resultant

[17] For general discussions, see Frank P. Besag, *Alienation and Education* (Buffalo, N.Y.: Hertillon Press, 1960); Bernard Murchland, *The Age of Alienation* (New York: Random House, Inc., 1971); Fritz Pappenheim, *The Alienation of Modern Man* (New York: Monthly Review Press, 1967). More specific analyses may be found in Michael Aiken et al., *Economic Failure, Alienation and Extremism* (East Lansing, Mich.: Michigan State University Press, 1968); Kenneth Keniston, *The Uncommitted: Alienated Youth in American Society* (New York: Harcourt, Brace & World, Inc., 1965); Jon M. Shepard, *Automation and Alienation* (Cambridge: MIT Press, 1971).

[18] William James, "The Moral Equivalent of War," in his *Memories and Studies* (New York: Greenwood Press, 1968; orig. ed. 1910), pp. 267–296.

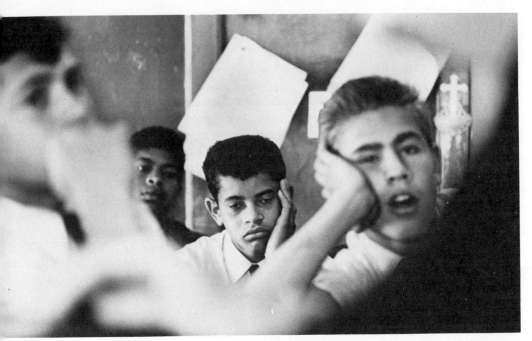

A frequent expression of organizational crises is the obvious inability to recognize or use individual talents. Restlessness or boredom are understandable reactions from those who derive little satisfaction from educational organizations.
(Courtesy Charles Harbutt, Magnum Photos, Inc.)

frustration in virtually every major area of public planning (housing, transportation, crime control, and so on). This is the indigestible fruit of hundreds (and in the largest metropolitan areas, thousands) of separate political units, autonomous districts (education, parks), and specialized boards (transportation, sewerage), each of which has to some extent unique combinations of financial support, operational authority, and geographic responsibility. In the past 50 years, four or five organizational solutions have been tried or suggested (for example, city–county consolidation, metropolitan government, extensive annexation), but fundamental organizational changes have not been possible thus far.[19]

Since the 1930's, the federal government has developed numerous specialized programs and agencies, both civilian and military, both domestic and foreign in their impact. The proliferation of agencies created an organizational crisis during the early years of United States' participation in World War II, when inadequate orga-

[19] Hugh LeBlanc and D. Trudian Allensworth, *The Politics of States and Urban Communities* (New York: Harper & Row Publishers, Inc., 1971), Chaps. 9–12, 16, 17; Michael N. Danielson (ed.), *Metropolitan Politics* (Boston: Little, Brown and Company, Inc., 1966), Parts 3, 4.

nization delayed mass production of military equipment for at least one year. Soon after the war, a major organizational crisis was recognized in the wasteful competition among the three military services. The crisis was met by the formal development of a strong Department of Defense and by scientific accounting and purchasing procedures (the McNamara reforms).[20] In recent years, the maze of programs in welfare and housing has reached new highs in confusion and uncertainty, with understandable criticisms from consumers, local governments, various professions, and politicians. These organizational crises were finally confronted by reshuffling related programs into two gargantuan departments—The Department of Housing and Urban Development, and The Department of Health, Education and Welfare.[21] From an administrative and an operational standpoint, many of the previous difficulties have not been removed. At present, federal operations and consequences are so complicated that we cannot reliably describe or evaluate the degree of efficiency or adaptive results these changes have produced. Paradoxically, the underlying crisis in federal services and programs lies in our *inability* to identify organizational crises in reasonably objective terms and at strategic points in that awesome structure.[22]

PLANNING AND ADAPTATION TO SOCIAL CRISES

As Karl Mannheim observed many years ago,[23] human society has been marked by long-term alterations in methods of resolving collective difficulties, crises, or catastrophes. The oldest and most primitive approach was *chance discovery* of solutions by random individuals. This probably accounts for such ancient and rather unfathomable practices as specific incest taboos, food preparation, dietary regulations or prescriptions, and selection of particular objects or animals as religious foci. Essentially, chance discovery was (and is) highly unpredictable, dubiously effective, and antagonistic to the development of knowledge or technical skill for manipulating the environment. If societies had not evolved solutions beyond chance discovery, in all probability there would be few (if any) humans to study.

[20] James M. Roherty, *Decisions of Robert S. McNamara: A Study of the Role of the Secretary of Defense* (Coral Gables, Fla.: University of Miami Press, 1970).
[21] See John B. Willman, *The Department of Housing and Urban Development* (New York: Praeger, 1967); *Handbook on Programs of the U. S. Department of Health, Education and Welfare* (Washington, D.C.: U.S. Government Printing Office, 1965).
[22] Charles L. Schultze, *The Politics and Economics of Public Spending* (Washington, D.C.: Brookings Institution, 1968); Alice M. Rivlin, *Systematic Thinking for Social Action* (Washington, D.C.: Brookings Institution, 1971).
[23] Karl Mannheim, *Man and Society in an Age of Reconstruction* (New York: Harcourt, Brace and Company, Inc., 1940), pp. 150–155.

A vastly improved method of meeting physical and social difficulties can be traced back 30,000–50,000 years, though it remains as an increasingly anachronistic method in many parts of the world today. Mannheim calls this method *inventing*, by which he means the practice of devising single tools and specialized organizations and norms for limited problems. Most of our current social and cultural apparatus are products of inventing; some examples are laws, rules, peer group culture, the corporate form, money, interest rates, credit, military weapons, books, buildings of every description and use, automobiles, bureaucracies, religious denominations, sports, curricula, styles of dress, and so on.

In retrospect, the inventive form of adaptation or problem solving has produced the notable achievements of the last 5000 years—agricultural improvements, mass production of varied commodities, urban structures, the common law, the university, the nation, the major religious systems, hospitals, universal suffrage, the political party, the train, the automobile, the airplane, representative government. But these expressions of human ability and collective achievement eventually developed defects that rivaled their virtues. And, in one form or another, the utility and desirability of the inventive approach are being severely questioned.

Fundamentally, invention has been a technique for identifying specific problems or difficulties and then creating workable solutions (usually technical, but sometimes organizational or ideational–valuational), without concern for the further consequences of applying specific solutions.[24] In the simpler, more static societies and communities of the past (that is, until 1800–1850 in Western Europe and North America), the method of invention was largely successful because social units (families, occupations, communities) were relatively self-contained and the technology of communicating influence (ideas, usages, styles, aspirations, indirect costs) was as yet undeveloped.[25] In general, under these conditions, difficulties were perceived as concrete and localized; crisis, as we have defined it, was either ignored or was reduced to limited problems that could receive rather immediate and often impressionistic attention. Thus, the typical solutions of the inventive phase are special bits of *legislation* (for or against every meaningful activity or group) and the *appliance* or *gadget*.

The 19th century paved the way for two revolutionary pat-

[24] David Braybrooke and Charles E. Lindblom, *A Strategy of Decision: Policy Evaluation as a Social Process* (New York: The Macmillan Company, 1963); Charles L. Schultze, *The Politics and Economics of Public Spending* (Washington, D.C.: Brookings Institution, 1968), Chaps. 3, 4; Robert A. Dahl and Charles E. Lindblom, *Politics, Economics, and Welfare* (New York: Harper & Brothers, 1953).
[25] Karl Mannheim, *Freedom, Power and Democratic Planning* (New York: Oxford University Press, 1950), pp. 7–14; Godfrey Wilson and Monica Wilson, *The Analysis of Social Change* (New York: Oxford University Press, 1945), pp. 24–30, 83–88.

terns that are inescapably part of the 20th century. First, we can mention the development of *intricate interdependence* of institutions, social categories, communities, and regions within nations, and increasingly—whether we like it or not—between and among a growing number of nations. Clearly, this set of complementary impacts or influences was generated by unanticipated but nonetheless crucial effects of science and technology, the expansion of a market system into economic and noneconomic spheres (for example, in education, government, recreation, and sports), the centralization of authority in national or federal systems, the immense growth of population, and the multiplication of highly valued social and cultural needs.

Second, and closely related to the preceding patterns, complex societies have been beset by social crises with disturbing frequency and pungency. To a great extent, these crises arise from (a) the increasing opportunities for making unworkable or narrowly conceived decisions on issues of collective importance (for example, transportation, taxation, zoning)[26] and the rather quick reverberation of such decisions through the experiences of directly and indirectly related groups, social categories, communities (for example, the effects of college curriculum changes on size and use of faculty, on recruitment of students, on competition for space and budget; the effects of lending policies on production of expensive housing and the consequent difficulty of developing adequate low-income housing); and (b) the understandable but misleading presumption that complexity means social ability to serve an infinitely expanding burden of needs, demands, pressures, and expectations.

Disappointing and bitter experiences of the last half-century lead to an unavoidable conclusion: the combination of heightened interdependence and the recurrence of social crises cannot be effectively managed by the method of invention. The inventive approach implicitly assumes a clear-cut, easily isolated problem, a direct "rational" solution, and relatively common acceptance of the solution. In short, the inventive form is primarily suitable for *technical* problems; it is not applicable to the organizational or ideological difficulties that characterize complex social systems.

Neither discovery nor invention is capable, by itself, of providing solutions to the crucial problem of interdependent systems—the problem of the practical necessity of *regulating* or *monitoring* such systems in order to forestall or quickly reduce the severity of social crises. In other words, recalling the discussion in Chapter 13 (Response to Crises and Change), discovery and invention become maladaptive because each form essentially ignores the emerging necessity of creating adequately complex power–authority

[26] See J. Kenneth Galbraith, *The Affluent Society* (Boston: Houghton Mifflin Company, 1958).

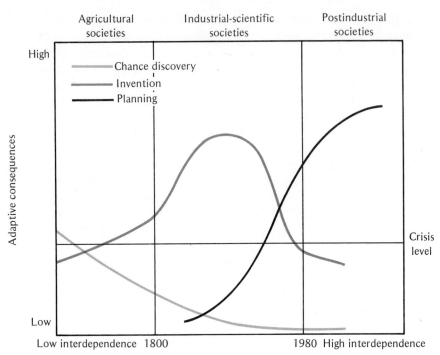

FIGURE 15–1 Adaptive consequences of major social mechanisms in simple and complex societies.

systems. During earlier historical phases, when discovery and invention were dominant forms, power–authority systems largely operated by methods of control and coercion, or by fitful emphases on facilitating *specific* programs (for example, military aggression, competition for export markets, intensive development of such internal resources as coal and metals, subsidization of agriculture, protection of specific home industries, construction of roads, canals, bridges, and "welfare" payments to disadvantaged social categories). Such power–authority systems are now obsolete as adaptive devices in two respects: they cannot handle social crises—in fact, they even intensify crises; and their continued ineffectiveness has progressively undermined the legitimacy of existing authority among large segments of contemporary populations.

The third and most recent social mechanism for meeting and averting social crises is the *social planning* orientation,[27] a pattern that is developing slowly and irregularly in complex societies. Though there are intimations of planning in earlier eras and in portions of contemporary society,[28] the most significant indications of

[27] Karl Mannheim, *Man and Society in an Age of Reconstruction* (New York: Harcourt, Brace and Company, Inc., 1940), pp. 152–164.
[28] Lewis Mumford, *Technics and Civilization* (New York: Harcourt, Brace and Company, Inc., 1934); Lewis Mumford, *The Culture of Cities* (New York: Harcourt, Brace and Company, Inc., 1938).

the trend toward planning can be noted in scores of attempts throughout the world to deal with accumulated problems at the level of communities, regions, and nations. The distinguishing features of a planning approach are not yet fully evolved, nor do many so-called planning structures share very similar strategies or similar degrees of effectiveness. Because of the genuine novelty of the planning approach, we shall begin with an analysis of planning that reflects its direction and readjustments through time. In the next section, specific case studies of planning will be surveyed to discover the achievements and the limitations of this radical but embryonic social response to contemporary social crises.

Social planning involves a general goal or philosophy and a network of direct and indirect social influences, as does every social mechanism. The explicit objective of planning is to maximize the benefits and minimize the costs and frictions of the various resources and skills that are available to a definite population. Planning as a social mechanism (directed by specific actors) seeks to follow this objective by developing several typical operations and organizational patterns:

1. The most basic operation is the use of relevant knowledge and social techniques to regulate or coordinate the relations and mutual effects of key roles, resources, and social products within a defined social system. Since the practical significance of these components may change over time, planning also involves reordering or altering the strategy of regulation to take account of such changes. For example, planners may try to coordinate the supply of jobs, housing, and capable workers in an area so that there are limited shortages or excesses of each component. If people tend to live at greater distances from their jobs than at an earlier period, the problem of coordination then becomes one of (a) encouraging or facilitating adequate transportation for longer distances (if residence at a greater distance is more desirable) or (b) developing more housing facilities at lesser distances (if current housing shortages induce workers to move to outlying areas).

2. Such regulation (and alteration in regulation) requires that regulatory decisions be made at strategic points in social systems.[29] The very notion of strategic points is inseparable from complex systems, and the continued operation of complex systems is generally assumed to depend on the nature of action or effort at those points. Essentially, "strategic points" refer to a limited number of roles or subsystems whose operation largely determines (facilitates, orders, limits) the capabilities and performance of remaining parts of the system and thus is essential to the successful functioning

---

[29] Karl Mannheim, *Man and Society in an Age of Reconstruction* (New York: Harcourt, Brace and Company, Inc., 1940), pp. 362–366.

The assembly line is designed to regulate production of cars by strategically combining previously manufactured parts. When mistakes are made, "quality control" is supposed to locate these. If not, such cars have to be recalled from consumers. Even in technological matters, strategic points do not always assure satisfactory regulation.
(Courtesy Erick Hartmann, Magnum Photos, Inc.)

of the entire system. For example, in the contemporary society of the United States, the national economy and thus the effective operation of economically tinged activities clearly depend on (a) four or five major commercial banks; (b) the three biggest producers in the automobile industry; (c) the steel industry, mainly in the top four firms; and (d) four or five major oil producers—regardless of constitutions, political ideologies, or the dominant political party. These strategic points channel either key commodities or focal sources of credit and consequently determine the level of productivity, of employment, and disposable funds for major societal enterprises.[30]

3. At these strategic points, planning requires the intervention of authoritative systems, each of which is linked with a central authority that determines (a) overall perspectives and objectives and (b) the implementation of those objectives in specifically appropriate ways at each strategic point. Obviously, many people are op-

[30] Maurice Zeitlin (ed.), *American Society, Inc.* (Chicago: Markham, 1970), Parts 1, 4; C. Lowell Harriss, *The American Economy*, 3rd ed. (Homewood, Ill.: Richard D. Irwin, 1959), Chaps. 6, 7.

posed to centralized authority, since it has often been abused in the past. Central authority does not guarantee planning, but planning as a genuine social mechanism is impossible without centralized authority.

4. Centralized authority in planning structures ideally works by making *strategic choices or decisions at strategic points* about necessary actions directed toward anticipated achievements and predictable difficulties.[31] Structurally, strategic choices depend on a preexisting system of indispensable ingredients: adequate and up-to-date information about strategic points and their impact on other subsystems; unambiguous specifications of authority; adequate operational agencies for monitoring and coordinating strategic points and other related segments of the larger system; adequate participation from various subsystems to provide subtle information and needs, as well as sufficient motivation for cooperation from those subsystems.

5. Less visibly but of undoubted importance, social planning involves mechanisms designed to translate sharp emotional and valuational differences in the population into areas of "rational" and "technical" analysis and policy—the so-called "depoliticization of issues." [32] Cynics can easily point to the immense obstacles this process must inevitably face and fail to dislodge. However, in the last 30 years there is some evidence of a *reduction* in the power of purely political or parochial considerations on certain issues. There is, for example, more acceptance of national responsibility for rational surveillance of wages, prices, employment, and credit, for collective approaches to improved and more accessible health facilities and services, for coordinated protection of the physical environment. This is also reflected in the common practice of creating prestigious (and presumably) objective commissions to survey and make recommendations on crucial public issues (crime, student violence, racial discrimination and conflicts, child care, the aged). England developed this technique *before* the ambitious planning program of the postwar Labor Government, with very important contributions to the informational base and policy-making aspects of British urban planning in the late 1940's and thereafter.[33]

[31] J. K. Friend and W. N. Jessop, *Local Government and Strategic Choice* (London: Tavistock, 1969), pp. 88–89, 110–118, 135.

[32] Karl Mannheim, *Man and Society in an Age of Reconstruction* (New York: Harcourt, Brace and Company, Inc., 1940), pp. 360–363; Richard L. Meier, *Developmental Planning* (New York: McGraw–Hill Book Company, 1965), Chap. 21. Contrast these with the viewpoint in Friedrich A. Hayek, *Individualism and Economic Order* (Chicago: University of Chicago Press, 1948), pp. 78–88.

[33] George M. Young (ed.), *Country and Town: A Summary of the Scott and Uthwatt Reports* (London: Harmondsworth, 1943); J. B. Cullingworth, *Town and Country Planning in England and Wales* (Toronto: University of Toronto Press, 1964); Beverley J. Pooley, *The Evolution of British Planning Legislation* (Ann Arbor, Mich.: University of Michigan Law School, 1960), pp. 14–27.

Though many intergroup differences in goals and perceptions are resistant to rational mechanisms for accommodation, social planning does not require stultifying conformity or authoritative intervention in every type of organization or activity in a community or nation. The basic structure of planning involves *selective* controls (when necessary) in line with strategic coordination or facilitation processes. Ideally, then, there is considerable opportunity for variety in details among the subsystems—if there is fundamental agreement on overall goals, basic strategies of planning programs, and a meaningful distribution of costs and adaptations among those subsystems. Totalitarian planning systems (in the Soviet Union, Fascist Italy, Nazi Germany) have largely substituted coercion and control for the more "rational" mechanisms of planning—as previously described—with a consequent emphasis on rigid procedures, which greatly limits the adaptive potentialities of an admittedly novel social device.

EXPLORATIONS IN PLANNING

Planning as a response to genuine social crisis is rather recent and therefore also somewhat experimental. Examples of planning, on the other hand, are numerous and confusing. On the national or societal level, we should include national mobilization for major wars; peacetime economic and social planning; and in varying degrees, programs for modernization in underdeveloped nations.[34] During the last 30 years, but with accelerated interest and organized ventures during the last 10 years, many metropolitan areas have established planning structures, but with limited success thus far. It may be helpful at this point to summarize and analyze a few selected "case studies" of planning as a prelude to some tentative conclusions about planning in practice.

The New Deal [35]

As the first major peacetime planning venture in the history of the United States, the New Deal was an audacious attempt to meet the accumulated crises of the Great Depression with little prior experience, with hastily devised structures, and with inadequate knowledge of the functioning of strategic points in American society. But the crises were unbearably severe: 13 million unemployed (25 per

[34] John D. Millett, *The Process and Organization of Government Planning* (New York: Columbia University Press, 1947); Peter Marris and Martin Rein, *Dilemmas of Social Reform* (London: Routledge and Kegan Paul, 1967); Charles Hitch, *Decision-Making for Defense* (Washington, D.C.: Brookings Institution, 1965).
[35] Basil Rauch, *The History of the New Deal, 1933–1938* (New York: Creative Age Press, 1944); Frank B. Freidel (ed.), *The New Deal and the American People* (Englewood Cliffs, N.J.: Prentice–Hall, 1964); Ellis W. Hawley, *The New Deal and the Problem of Monopoly* (Princeton: Princeton University Press, 1966).

cent of the labor force); plummeting farm prices; rising numbers of farm and home foreclosures; declining industrial productivity; paralysis on the part of most local and state authorities; increasing strength of radical movements (Communist, KKK, Nazi Bund groups, rightist reactionary groups such as the Coughlin movement); hesitant and ineffective use of authority on the federal level. In short, when Roosevelt began his administration on 4 March 1933, there were simultaneous and interlocking crises in organization, ideology, and to a lesser extent, technology. And during the election campaign and the four months that followed, the attack on these crises was merely verbal, without strategy or structure.

It is possible to give only a highly condensed (and perhaps unbalanced) summary of New Deal planning from 1933 to 1939; the rapid spawning of programs, policies, legislation, and bureaus, and the impact of partisan, personal, and interest group pressures yielded a density of details that is still being probed by historians and biographers. For our purposes, the fundamental notion of the New Deal was to cope with all presumed strategic points simultaneously and with breath-taking speed. Most of these points were diagnosed as needing financial aid (pump priming), social control or limitation, or encouragement of greater activity. It was assumed that (a) significant changes at strategic points would percolate with beneficial effects throughout the nation; and (b) changes at one strategic point would facilitate or supplement changes at other strategic points.

More specifically, New Deal planning selected three points for attack: agriculture; business and industry; and the labor force. In agriculture, farm surpluses, low prices, and heavy debts were countered by subsidies and loans to reduce farm acreage, by export subsidies, somewhat liberalized credit, and attempts to aid small or marginal farmers to resettle in other areas and occupations. Industry was encouraged to develop wage and price levels, presumably to maintain wages and stabilize prices. Federal agencies likewise supplemented private industry by providing funds and jobs for construction projects. Finally, the worker was shored up through three sets of complementary programs: encouragement of organized labor and collective bargaining; social security programs for the aged and the disabled; welfare payments for the unemployed.

From an organizational standpoint, New Deal planning was not well-structured: programs were not suggested and implemented by a single responsible agency; instead programs were competitively devised by a succession of presidential advisors and by representatives of potent interest groups in agriculture, industry, and finance. There was no monitoring of programs and results, and virtually no change in operational techniques during a seven-year period. Only one agency (the National Resources Planning Board) seemed to develop a needed informational base for planning; but it did not (or could not) enter into the informal network of decision-making.[36]

The results of these New Deal programs are clear and instructive. Agricultural planning did not reduce farm surpluses (since farmers intensified production on smaller acreages), nor were surpluses disposed of abroad (because government-supported prices decreased our competitive position in the world market) or for domestic use (except on a small-scale through "food stamp" distribution to welfare families). But farm subsidies—mainly to the large producers—forced many black tenant farmers from the land, into Southern and Northern cities, for which they were economically and culturally unprepared. Industrial supports and programs largely stabilized prices, but provided few additional jobs in the private sphere. Major increases in employment—in public projects (such as the Public Works Administration and the Works Progress Administration)—did not substantially lessen the pool of unemployed, 5 million of whom were receiving welfare payments.

By 1937–1938, industrial production and sales were largely unimproved, because the various welfare, agricultural, and financial programs did not produce significant increases in purchasing power. In fact, the consequences of agricultural and industrial planning were contradictory: farm supports increased food prices for urban workers and the unemployed, while the stable production levels and controlled prices for industrial products constantly reduced the value of returns to most farmers. During the late 1930's, too, the growing strength of labor unions and bargaining power likewise resulted in wage settlements that were quickly transformed into higher prices.

The strategic points, then, were handled without coordination and without sufficient authority (from Congress and the operational government agencies) to obtain conformity with specific planning goals. In retrospect, the New Deal was an experiment in multiple interventions without clear strategy in decision-making. But it reduced the severity of ideological crises (the three-term administration of Roosevelt, despite opposition from most newspapers, indicates a degree of consensus that is unparalleled in free societies) and provided a set of rough organizational tools for approaching the pervasive organizational crises of the 1920's and 1930's (that is, discovering a workable mix of public and private devices for integrating economic, educational, familial, and "cultural" spheres). These tools —taxation, social security programs, fiscal and credit manipulation, federal grants to certified state and local programs, and so on— became the basis for postwar attempts at national planning. However, the scope of contemporary (that is, from 1950 to date) difficul-

---

[36] John D. Millett, *The Process and Organization of Government Planning* (New York: Columbia University Press, 1947), pp. 18–24.

ties is considerably greater, precisely when the financial resources for genuine planning are perhaps adequate for the first time in the history of the United States.

Urban Planning: Stockholm, Nagoya, and Pittsburgh

For most major cities from the late 19th century to the present, uncontrolled growth has been accompanied by a repertory of problems that are all too well-known—in housing, transportation, public education, racial difficulties, taxation sources, slum environments, water and air pollution, and so on. Fundamentally, most of these problems have developed from inadequate organization and diffused authority, which permitted the technological and ideological difficulties of rapid expansion to ripen into familiar urban crises. These crises have been largely averted by planning in Stockholm, which deserves some attention as a possible model for community planning in other nations.[37]

Stockholm began urban planning about 300 years ago, with the distinctive advantage of public ownership of land. The older suburbs were part of an overall plan in the 17th century, well before traffic problems developed. In recent decades—though *private* ownership of land has replaced the earlier system—planning has continued to be tied to a basic strategy of linking and balancing the central city and suburban developments. In the central city, the business district has been continually renovated for greater efficiency (through constructing level streets, pedestrian malls, underground crossings at busy intersections). Housing needs have been pursued through a planned series of suburban communities—now about 22 such areas have been built—the most famous of which is Vällingby. Each suburb is designed with a complete transit system (usually rail) linked with the inner city, fairly extensive retail facilities, but with limited local employment.

Currently, Stockholm has the common urban problems of continued immigration and the pressure of population on a previously well-designed transportation system (roads, rail lines, and a subway). Its metropolitan planning system is authorized to limit further construction in the city and the existing suburbs. The next likely step is coordination of further growth with adjacent rural areas.

By contrast with Stockholm, cities that have only recently developed urban planning programs face more difficult problems of implementation.[38] Nagoya, the third largest city in Japan, began its

[37] Kell Astrom, *City Planning in Sweden* (Stockholm: Swedish Institute for Cultural Relations with Foreign Countries, 1967); Goran Sidenbladh, "Stockholm; A Planned City," in *Sci. Amer., 213* (September 1965), pp. 107–118.
[38] "Planners Easing Nagoya's Growth," *New York Times* (April 11, 1965); "Pittsburgh Renewal Plan Completes Major Phase," *New York Times* (November 30, 1970); Roy Lubove, *Twentieth Century Pittsburgh* (New York: John Wiley & Sons, Inc., 1969).

comprehensive planning program in 1946, after the extensive destruction of World War II. Essentially, its planning is aimed at providing physical and economic development with concern for
carefully limited population growth. The key mechanism is central
allocation of land for modern heavy industry and for exceedingly
broad (150 ft) roads in the core of the city. However, rapid development has vastly increased land values and seems to encourage growth
at the periphery. Unless population size is effectively halted within
the next decade or so, the familiar problems of congestion and traffic
delays may undo the planning of the last generation.

Pittsburgh began its planning in the mid-1950's, after a
prolonged crisis marked by smog, dirt, and despair. The symbol of
Pittsburgh's difficulties had been its downtown industrial slum. Consequently, urban planning was built around the revival of that area, in
the hope that the economic and social deficiencies of the city (poverty, unemployment, poor public education, and so on) would be
reversed by the fruits of a downtown renaissance. Briefly, the thrust
of planning was supplied by a small corps of influential business and
industrial leaders, who achieved four strategic objectives: (1) They
achieved substantial reduction of smog and smell, and (2) development of the downtown "Golden Triangle" from a gray zone of
blight to a set of imposing office buildings, apartments, and a park;
(3) furthermore, they convinced major firms to remain in Pittsburgh
rather than relocate in the suburbs; and (4) they initiated a careful
study of varied needs for further economic and social planning. But
after more than 15 years, belated urban planning for a typical industrial city has barely touched the organizational issues that men-
ace modern urban regions.

PROBLEMS OF TRANSITION

The consequences of a planning approach for social adaptation are
inherently temporary, no matter how intelligent the conception and
coordination of a given set of programs, for social organizations and
related forms of decision-making are normally oriented to the past or
to a future with limited and predictable change. Indeed, one fascinating type of "planning"—the literary utopias of the last 200 years—
assumes that social crises can be resolved by *planned societies* in
which further significant change is arrested.[39] But in real societies
and in the real world of social and physical environments, cultural

[39] Some of the more famous utopias include: Samuel Butler, *Erewhon*; Edward Bellamy,
Looking Backward; George Orwell, *1984*; Aldous Huxley, *Brave New World*; B. F. Skinner,
Walden Two. General discussions of the significance of utopias may be found in Lewis
Mumford, *The Story of Utopias* (New York: Boni and Liveright, 1922); Robert C. Elliott, *The
Shape of Utopias* (Chicago: University of Chicago Press, 1970); Arthur E. Morgan, *Nowhere
was Somewhere* (Chapel Hill, N.C.: University of North Carolina Press, 1946).

Modern society is in constant motion, actually and metaphorically, and its basic processes of invention and evaluation cannot be slowed down (as frames in a movie film can) by the desires and actions of isolated individuals. (Courtesy Jim Harrison.)

and social innovations are not halted by declaring a moratorium on change or by commiseration on the annoyances and difficulties of change. Social complexity and differentiation facilitate and even encourage innovations, with or without planning. Consequently, *in practice* social adaptation in complex societies requires *readjustments* to inevitable processes (not specific instances) of change, not the pursuit of and fixation on a completed and unalterable social system. A planned society or a planned community is in fact the end of planning and the exhaustion of adaptation—as the tortuous history of planning in the Soviet Union (until about 20 years ago) demonstrates.[40]

Planning as a developing and still imperfect adaptive tool therefore faces all or most of the practical difficulties of the human quest for collective solutions. Nevertheless, the significance of this most complex adaptive social mechanism is its potential superiority over the discovery and inventive forms. But planning not only has limits imposed by external or environmental restraints; there are also *internal* obstacles to efficient planning. Experiments in planning suggest the following three recurring and interrelated impediments to successful planning.

[40] Robert J. Osborn, *Soviet Social Policies* (Homewood, Ill.: Dorsey Press, 1970); Erich Strauss, *Soviet Agriculture in Perspective* (London: Allen and Unwin, 1969); Robert Holt and John E. Turner, *The Soviet Union* (New York: Holt, Rinehart and Winston, Inc., 1962).

Contradictory Values and Perceptions

The most pervasive aspect of complex societies—contrary to the conclusion that these are "mass societies" [41] with essentially uniform goals, values, and experiences—is a diversity of judgments about the nature and resolution of social crises. This conflict of diagnosis and effective remedies is quite common in crises or near crises in urban communities—for example, fluoridation, school bonds, zoning controversies, location of highways, housing, poverty programs, needed governmental changes.[42] On such matters, for example, there are considerable divergences between residents of central city and suburban areas, blacks and whites, low-income and above-average-income families, the young and the middle-aged, those with limited education and those with considerable formal education, those with local concerns and those with broader social orientations.

The facts of pervasive and complex differences in attitudes and perceptions also point to significant underlying orientations to crisis and to the dimensions of crisis—differences that persist not only among citizens, but also among leaders and professional analysts of community problems. For example, business and financial groups regard growth and expansion as paramount goals for urban areas, while wage workers and professionals tend to emphasize stability and better services to various disadvantaged social categories. Likewise, there is considerable controversy about the *causes* of urban social crises. City residents—particularly blacks—claim that white middle and upper classes are not concerned with overall urban development and, therefore, settle in suburban areas to avoid social and financial responsibilities. On the other hand, whites insist that urban difficulties derive from uncontrolled migration of blacks, who are not adapted to urban patterns and who therefore develop deviant behavior that menaces "law-abiding" citizens. Some social scientists and political leaders account for urban problems by pointing to the critical inefficiency of weak and uncoordinated urban and metropolitan governments. Others, notably Raymond Vernon, an economist, and Edward Banfield, a political scientist, boldly assert that no genuine urban crises exist, that many "problems" are simply the reflection of eccentric and subjective interpretations by well-to-do persons, who are annoyed by difficulties to which other segments are rather well-attuned (for example, in transportation and housing), that urbanites actually live more com-

[41] William Kornhauser, *The Politics of Mass Society* (New York: The Free Press, 1959); Harold L. Wilensky, "Mass Society and Mass Culture: Interdependence or Independence?" *Amer. Sociological Rev.*, 29 (April 1964), pp. 173–197.
[42] See for example, Robert L. Crain, *The Politics of School Desegregation* (Chicago: Aldine, 1968); Robert L. Crain et al., *The Politics of Community Conflict: The Fluoridation Decision* (Indianapolis: Bobbs–Merrill, 1969); Richard F. Babcock, *The Zoning Game* (Madison, Wisc.: University of Wisconsin Press, 1966).

fortably than ever before, and that if crises in urban areas were genuine, people would have spared no effort or cost to resolve them.[43]

In addition, there are great differences—and perhaps a great deal of confusion—about the *strategies and solutions* for this patchwork of diagnoses. Businessmen and land developers appear to favor rebuilding the central city—with attractive apartments, office buildings, and civic centers—to encourage resettlement of middle-income families in inner zones. Urban officials and some planners tend to emphasize the necessity of expanded jurisdiction through annexation of suburban areas. Some city and state officials flatly assert that massive federal funds to urban areas provide the only possibility of meeting urban crises. And still other solutions involve a long and difficult process of promoting social and economic equalities among metropolitan residents.[44]

The Conservatism of Quantity

With few exceptions, complex society and its past achievements encourage a belief in the efficacy of *more*—more effort, more money, more education, more business, and so on. Certainly, if annexation, or a sales tax, or social security provided past solutions—and some resultant problems as well—then it would *seem* reasonable to aim for more annexation, higher sales taxes, and expanded social security payments. But this is the *inventive* approach, which still is easier to understand and requires fewer alterations in basic knowledge or values. Furthermore, the "quantity" approach reduces the necessity of making selective decisions, and thus avoids decisions that would generate more dissension and conflict. Consequently, the tenor of most proposed (and enacted) laws (in state and national legislatures) is simple—more taxes, more expenditures, more buildings and facilities, more employees, more specific guidelines and regulations. In fact, coordination and planning are not only dismissed as unnecessary or undesirable; they become increasingly impossible without painful surgery on the cancerous tissue of accumulated enactments and agencies.

Brinkmanship: From Crisis to Crisis

The mechanisms of planning face an underlying and widespread resistance from a subtle perspective in much of Western Europe and

---

[43] Edward C. Banfield, *The Unheavenly City* (Boston: Little, Brown and Company, Inc., 1970); Robert C. Wood, *The Necessary Majority* (New York: Columbia University Press, 1972); Raymond Vernon, *The Myth and Reality of Our Urban Problems* (Cambridge, Mass.: Joint Center for Urban Studies of MIT and Harvard University, 1962).
[44] Herbert J. Gans, *People and Plans* (New York: Basic Books, 1968); John V. Lindsay, *The City* (New York: W. W. Norton and Company, Inc., 1970); Henry W. Maier, *Challenge to the Cities* (New York: Random House, Inc., 1966).

the Western hemisphere. In simple terms, this is a kind of social paralysis that is expressed in (a) inability to recognize imminent crisis or to act decisively in early stages of social crisis and (b) apparent inability to learn the practical lessons derived from previous crises. The French sociologist, Michel Crozier, has described this pattern for contemporary France in studies of specific bureaucratic organizations and of politics and government in France generally.[45] Likewise, in the United States since World War I, the dominant style of most leaders and officials has been remarkably consistent—that is, they ignore problems as long as public indignation will allow; belatedly apply superficial measures under intriguing or mystifying labels; blame political opponents or international conspiracies for inadequacies of these measures; and confront the reappearance of crises as though such crises had never occurred before.[46]

A prime example is the problem of slums and slum housing, which can be traced back to the 1890's in major urban areas of the United States.[47] The criticisms of reformers were largely unheeded until about 1920, when several cities began tentative plans to contain inadequate housing by zoning regulations. For the next 15 years, studies of poor housing documented living conditions that remained beyond the sphere of public recognition and policy. In the New Deal period, federal funds for public, low-cost housing were a distinct break with tradition, although the resultant slum clearance and rehousing was a slow process, with long waiting lists of needy families. Essentially the same housing program—with more funds—was continued after World War II, but with more verbal concern for relocating families displaced by slum clearance.

Since 1954, federal housing legislation has resulted in about 400,000 public housing units, as against an estimated need of 10 million. More important, public housing continues to be delayed by cumbersome and expensive processes of negotiation, design, complex financing, and multilevel administration (complicated by federal regulations). Furthermore, design and location of public housing have remained virtually unchanged: high-rise, high density apartments in deteriorated inner city areas. In many cities, considerable portions of cleared areas have been used for commercial purposes (motels, office buildings) and expressways, rather than for low-cost housing. Perhaps the only "new" development in public housing is a growing rate of default in rent payments (despite a re-

[45] Michel Crozier, La Société bloquée (Paris: Editions du Seuil, 1970).
[46] Edward C. Banfield and James Q. Wilson, City Politics (Cambridge, Mass.: Harvard University Press, 1963).
[47] Jewel Bellush and Murray Hausknecht (eds.), Urban Renewal: People, Politics and Planning (Garden City, N.Y.: Doubleday Anchor Books, 1967), Parts 2 and 3; William Wheaton et al. (eds.), Urban Housing (New York: The Free Press, 1966); James Q. Wilson (ed.), Urban Renewal (New York: The Free Press, 1966); Roy Lubove, The Progressives and the Slums (Pittsburgh: University of Pittsburgh Press, 1963).

cent program of federal rent supplements) and the assumption of ownership by the Department of Housing and Urban Development of local housing projects. At this point, housing for poor families is still critical, although the stock of substandard housing had declined from a national total of 17 million in 1950 to about 6 million in 1966.

Despite much legislation, failure to develop genuine planning for low-income housing has marooned many families in physical conditions that belie our affluence and our presumed sensitivity to human dignity.
(Courtesy Bruce Davidson, Magnum Photos, Inc.)

The capacity for innovation and further specialization in complex societies almost ensures the development of problems in coordination of efforts and rewards, and of substantial differences in values and goals. *Repeated crises*—that is, failures to reduce the severity of community and national problems—indicate socially dangerous delays in the construction of appropriate (that is, adaptive) organizational forms and supporting value systems and in the combination of capacity for development with responsible attention to anticipated costs or difficulties. In the long past of social adaptation in societies and communities, man's innate ability and his social organization have often enabled men and women to devise long-lasting (but imperfect) means of organizing effort with greater efficiency. Family structures, age grades, councils of elders, occupational guilds, corporations, and centralized governments were perhaps all indispensable instruments of *previous* social adaptation.

Currently, many societies and communities are uncomfortably placed in a crucial *transitional phase*, a structural crossroads of social organization and evolution. One direction, a continuation of social mechanisms shaped in the last 300 years, follows the path of multiple inventions and erratic, partial regulation. The major result has been—and promises to be—uncontrolled and bewildering social change. Less clearly—because it involves an uncharted course —another direction entails intelligent anticipation of social crises and more rational attempts to deal with such crises, through planning orientations and structures. Potentially, then, rather than serving as pawns of social change, societies will be capable of guiding change.

If the future development of human societies hinges on structural alterations evolved for controlling social change, the nature and complexities of social change must be understood. The problems of social change have long been of interest to students and interpreters of social phenomena. However, the heritage of explanations and predictions of social change is exceedingly varied and confusing.[48] Therefore, in the final segment of this book (Part V), contemporary knowledge and conceptualization of social change will be reviewed in terms of two crucial sets of relevant phenomena: the dynamics of successful innovation, and the coordination and regularization of significant innovations in advanced stages of social change.

Summary

Social crises in communities and societies present continuing problems and threats to power–authority systems, and to the operation of the larger social systems. Such crises, which may be primarily technological, organizational, or ideological, tend to occur when additional demands are made on social organization or when existing forms of organization are allowed to deteriorate. Examples from classical Greece and Rome indicate that inadequate responses to social crises can endanger complex societies and even alter their basic organization and identity.

Historically, responsible efforts in handling social crises were

---

[48] See Alvin Boskoff, *The Mosaic of Sociological Theory* (New York: Thomas Y. Crowell, 1972), Chaps. 10, 11; Wilbert E. Moore, *Social Change* (Englewood Cliffs, N.J.: Prentice–Hall, Inc., 1963); Kenneth E. Boulding, *A Primer on Social Dynamics* (New York: The Free Press, 1970); Hollis W. Peters (ed.), *Comparative Theories of Social Change* (Ann Arbor, Mich.: Foundation for Research on Human Behavior, November 1966).

based on underlying strategies that were in part a reflection of the fund of knowledge available to key segments of society. *Chance discovery*, the oldest method for dealing with social crises, was prescientific and of limited effectiveness. In the major civilizations of antiquity and the present, however, the method of *invention* provided specific and relatively practical solutions to social difficulties of various kinds. In fact, the major achievements of human societies thus far have resulted from applying the inventive approach. With the development of advanced levels of social complexity, and the emergence of unparalleled technological capacity for human destruction, the practical limitations of invention have become increasingly visible. The emerging but incomplete mechanism for adapting to crisis under these conditions is *social planning*. Essentially, planning involves attempts to create social forms for more efficient regulation, by making authoritative decisions at a limited number of strategic points in complex systems. As contemporary experience with planning demonstrates—for example, the New Deal and instances of urban planning—the planning approach is subject to great internal dissidence on appropriate goals and policies. Modern societies, then, seem to operate in a cultural and organizational transition, in which they must choose between invention and planning in trying to develop greater capacities for controlling social change.

Exercises

1. What are the distinctive characteristics of social crises—both in past societies and currently?

2. Compare the impact of technological crisis and ideological crisis on social adaptation in contemporary societies.

3. What is the relation between modern social crises and alienation?

4. Evaluate the notion that organizational crises are the key to the difficulties of modern societies (for example, the United States).

5. Why is the method of invention essentially maladaptive in dealing with crises of modern societies?

6. Review the necessary conditions for planning as a form of social adaptation. What *changes* in socialization, stratification, and community organization would be required in practice to make planning an effective tool of adaptation?

7. How would you evaluate the following programs or proposals from the standpoint of planning? (a) the negative income tax; (b) desegregation of public schools; (c) the national highway program; (d) federal aid to higher education.

Selected References

Etzioni, Amitai. *The Active Society.* New York: The Free Press, 1968.

Gans, Herbert J. *People and Plans.* New York: Basic Books, 1968.

Mannheim, Karl. *Man and Society in an Age of Reconstruction.* New York: Harcourt, Brace and Company, Inc., 1940.

Mayer, Robert R. *Social Planning and Social Change.* Englewood Cliffs, N.J.: Prentice–Hall, Inc., 1972.

Mumford, Lewis. *The Culture of Cities.* New York: Harcourt, Brace and Company, Inc., 1938.

Mumford, Lewis. *The Myth of the Machine: The Pentagon of Power.* New York: Harcourt, Brace, Jovanovich, Inc., 1970.

Part V

Continuity and Change: An Overview of Broad Patterns in Social Adaptation

16

Cultural and Social Change in Modern Societies

This chapter is concerned with the general phenomenon of social change with emphasis on how it occurs and how it affects social adaptation. Chapter 17 deals with a special source for potential social change, namely, creativity and innovation, and Chapter 18 deals with problems of implementing and integrating innovations within existing social structures.

Man's environment, though relatively stable for periods of time, is nevertheless always undergoing some degree of change. Accordingly, if he is to adapt to these changes successfully, he must be able to modify his present adaptive systems and responses. His adaptive problems are always conditioned by his biological needs, but his responses and systems for adaptation are cultural and social. As was shown in Chapter 12, the principal source of man's capacity for change is the level of his technology. Accordingly, Chapter 12 should be reviewed, or at least kept in mind, while considering the problem of social change. Some have claimed that since man is capable of creating his own environment through culture, he is free of biological restraints. It is true that technological change has freed man of many biological restraints, particularly in the areas of health, disease, and food; but each new modification produces new selective pressures that affect man on both biological and cultural levels.

Part photo: "DANCE" by Henri Matisse, 1909, oil on canvas, 102⅜" x 152¾."
Courtesy The Museum of Modern Art, New York
and Gov. Nelson Rockefeller in honor of Alfred H. Barr, Jr.

For example, the average life span has almost doubled in industrial societies during the past century. However, related to this are increases in the rate of metabolic diseases of the aged and in the social problems of the aged. In other words, man is always in the state of becoming, and his problems of adaptation change as his environments (natural and man-made) change.

This chapter will concentrate on processes of social change in industrial societies, but agrarian and earlier forms of societal organization as they illuminate our understanding of change in modern societies will also be considered. Two processes of human adaptation that have been repeatedly emphasized are the transmitters of human heritage, namely, genetic transmission and natural selection, and cultural transmission and social selection. These are the sources of both continuity and change in human society. An organism may be perfectly suited to its environment, and natural selection will operate to keep it that way, assuming there is sufficient genetic variability over time. Not all change is adaptive, but through change man improves his adaptive capacity; therefore, the limitation

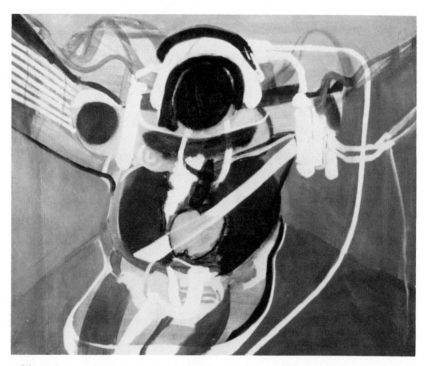

Although man in space is freer than any creature has ever been, he is still tethered to thousands of earthly systems and devices. He is, as never before, dependent on his fellows.
("Man's New Dimension" by Hans Cremers. Courtesy NASA, Washington, D.C.)

of change, either genetic or cultural, imposes a limitation to adaptation by limiting selective alternatives.

Before social selection, and hence social change, can occur, alternatives must be present in the population's repertory of possible behaviors; these necessary alternatives allow differential reinforcement to act and hence selection to occur. In other words, social change develops from the existing intellectual, social, and cultural resources and potentialities of a society. Thus social change assumes that the creative solutions needed are available from the innovative sources in the society.

In the broad sense, cultural and social changes may occur in an evolutionary or unplanned way, or they may occur through planned, guided, or systematic means. The first occurs largely in an unconscious manner and as a result of the normal stresses and strains of everyday social interaction. The second or planned variety occurs through the systematic introduction of new ideas, technology, and new systems of social organization. Both evolutionary and planned change arise from several sources. The first of these is the impact of *cultural contact* and cultural diffusion from other cultures. For example, the introduction of Western technology, including new forms of political and economic organization, into Japanese society following World War II stimulated major social changes in Japan. A detailed analysis of the Japanese example is found in Chapter 18. The second source is the impact of new technology from *within* a society; thirdly, the competition and conflict among groups in a society for differential advantage in the struggle for scarce resources, including power; and fourth, the degree of reward and recognition for innovation in a society. The third source, especially the conflict factor, is difficult to assess because it often results in a revolutionary change in the personnel who hold or exercise power, without any significant or real changes in the institutional systems by which the society adapts. The many military coups in Latin America afford some examples.

The ubiquitous character of cultural and social change is self-evident. It is both a *means* of adaptation and a *cause* of new problems of adaptation. For example, the introduction of modern communicable disease and sanitary technology in traditional types of societies (underdeveloped) was a means of reducing the infant mortality rate; however, the resulting increase in the rate of growth of the population exceeded the rate of economic growth and thus caused a new problem of adaptation with regard to levels of living. In modern society, the need for systems of transportation more rapid and efficient than horse-drawn vehicles was solved by the invention and mass production of the automobile. However, the tremendous growth of the cities and the concomitant increase and concentration

When the first ships brought man to fellow-man, not only his physical capacities were expanded but also his ideas.
(Courtesy Alfred Eisenstaedt, Life Magazine © 1972, Time Inc.)

of the number of automobiles and trucks on the streets and highways have combined to produce two new major problems of adaptation, mainly, traffic congestion and air pollution from exhaust fumes. These are simply two examples among hundreds of a similar sort that could be given. The reader can supply many similar illustrations of his own. The point is existing problems of adaptation are solved by the development of new means for coping with the problems. These means may be cultural, social, or technological. Often the new means have unanticipated side effects, which constitute a new problem (the field of pharmacology or drug use in medicine is an obvious example).

At this point, the distinction in Chapter 15 between invention and planning should be noted. At least some of the undesired effects of discovery and invention can be controlled through adequate pretesting and planning. The use of computers today, particularly simulation procedures, is very helpful in screening out the "bugs" in new programs and thus in controlling undesired effects.

The adaptive problems that result from the unintended and unanticipated effects of either planned or unplanned previous change suggest for their control the following analyses (1) extensive pretesting of proposed changes of new technology to ascertain, insofar as possible, the side effects; (2) examination of current evolving trends and problems, and in addition, of existing knowledge and anticipated new knowledge to estimate the probable new problems of adaptation in the future. With knowledge about the anticipated new problems of adaptation in the future, (3) action could be initiated early to prevent the forecasted undesired things from happening and to permit planning for desired courses of action. In summary, social and cultural changes, in general, are characterized by a two directional causal system. For example, an increased food supply in a nonindustrialized type society will, with sufficient time, result in an increased population, which in turn will stimulate a further increase in food supply. In more general terms, *A* affects *B*, and after a sufficient time span, *B* then acts upon *A*. This complicates the analysis of social and cultural change because in practice it becomes very difficult to disentangle the *direction* of causal effects among the set of variables that presumably produce the outcome or outcomes.

Until now it has not been necessary to provide a technical definition of cultural and social change, but before we go further it is necessary to do so.

THE CONCEPTS OF
CULTURAL AND SOCIAL CHANGE

Cultural change can be distinguished from social change only with great difficulty. The two are related and represent different foci of emphasis or interest, as will be shown below. We will begin the distinction by indicating the function or purpose of the concept of culture. First, we should note that there are patterns of behavior and guides to behavior such as norms, beliefs, and values that are peculiar to a generation, a group, or an individual, but are *not* transmitted or passed on to the next generation or even to succeeding new members in the current group. On the other hand, there are behavior patterns and guides to behavior that *are transmitted* in varying degrees of completeness to the new members of current groups and often to succeeding generations. Culture refers to those learned patterns of behavior, beliefs, and values that *are transmitted from one population to the next.* Thus culture is primarily, though not completely nor necessarily, transgenerational rather than generation specific. Behavior patterns that are institutionalized within a generation or a group may change within as well as between generations. The central idea is that once behavior has been standardized for succeeding generations or for new members, it has become culture. The reader will no doubt notice the conceptual similarity between the view of culture given here and the concept of instinct given in biological discussions. The concept of instinct refers to those behavior patterns in certain species that are transmitted from one generation to another through genetic transmission. In other words, the central feature of the concepts of culture and instinct is that they refer to the *transmission of behavior patterns across generations.* An interesting distinction, though, in the transmission of man's cultural heritage, as contrasted to the genetic transmission of an insect's genetic heritage, is that man's cultural heritage changes and *accumulates* within as well as between generations. *Cultural change,* then, refers to the *extinction* of prescribed or proscribed ways of doing things, and their replacement by new standards, which are then maintained and transmitted.

Social change refers to alterations in the *patterns of interaction* or social behavior among individuals and groups within a society. As was indicated earlier, the distinction between cultural and social changes is largely one of emphasis. Cultural change refers to changes in the rules, standards, or guides to conduct or ways of living, and social change refers to changes in the position or relationships of individuals and groups to one another over time. Since cultural change and social change are interrelated, they cannot be separated clearly and distinctly. For example, the invention and diffusion of the automobile as a new form of transportation was a cultural change. It, in turn, sharply affected dating practices among young people, recreation patterns within the family, and residential patterns within the city. Two more examples should help make clear the distinction. The development of systems of labor union organization in Europe and America in the late 19th and 20th centuries was a cultural invention, but it radically altered the position of power of industry officials over the working class in democratic societies, and hence the patterns of social interaction of labor and management representatives. Finally, changes in the system of peasantry in Germany provides an excellent example of both cultural and social change. Prior to the late 1840's, the peasant was rewarded for his

Accessibility of transportation has resulted in unprecedented geographic mobility, social heterogeneity, and social indifference.
(Courtesy Robert Rapelye, Photography International.)

labor by a share of the goods he produced. It did not make much difference how much he produced since his share did not vary a great deal. The indebtedness of the landowners, taxes, and inefficiency in the work and low motivation of the peasants forced the landowners to try other methods of inducing improved productivity. The practice of hiring the peasant and paying him wages for time worked was introduced and was an almost instant success. As a consequence the landowners began to free the peasants, who then gained the status of wage earner. This was a *cultural change* from the customary way of rewarding the peasant with a share in kind of the crops to rewarding him with wages or money. This gave the peasant some incentive, for the more he worked the more he received, and it allowed him to exchange his earnings for things other than crops. *His new status relationship with his landowner was the social change.* In this respect, he had changed from a relationship of *fixed status* to his lord to one of *free status* based on a contractual arrangement, or as Sir Henry Maine so dramatically phrased the idea "from status to contract."

As with genetic mutations, not all cultural and social innovations are adaptive. George Foster[1] cites an interesting fable of a monkey and a fish in showing the importance of the cultural context when evaluating proposed changes in a society. As the story goes, a monkey and a fish were once caught in a great flood. The monkey had climbed a tree to safety. As he surveyed the raging waters, he saw a fish struggling against the swift current. Filled with compassion to help the less fortunate one, he reached down and lifted the fish from the water. To the monkey's surprise, of course, the fish was not very grateful for his ill advised good intentions. Don Adams, whom Foster was citing, was an educational advisor to Korea, and with the monkey and fish fable in mind he concluded: "The educational adviser, unless he is a careful student of his own culture and the culture in which he works, will be acting much like the monkey; and, with the most laudible intentions, he may make decisions equally disastrous." A better known example, perhaps, is the Aid to Dependent Children act, which, although designed to strengthen families, had the unanticipated effect of producing more fatherless families.

CHANGE AND ADAPTATION

Looking ahead and correctly anticipating the consequences of evolving future conditions or planned changes is perhaps currently man's most difficult and urgent problem. Change in a primitive society is very slow, but to carry out conscious change in such a society generally involves the consent of the entire population. Moreover, there is very little social differentiation within primitive societies; hence when change does occur, it affects most everyone in the same way, which is why most of the adults are involved. A modern industrial society, on the other hand, is so specialized and differentiated that change can occur within a sector without the members of other sectors being aware of the change at the time; or if they are aware of it and oppose it, they may not be able to do anything about it. After a sufficient lapse of time, the effects of change in one sector may be experienced in others. The more specialized a society is, the more quickly the effects of change in one sector are felt in another. For example, a national strike in the transportation industry can result in the closing down of other major industries because of depletion of supplies and raw materials, which often have to be transported to centers of production over very great distances. This, of course, quickly has serious consequences for the general welfare and na-

[1] George M. Foster, *Traditional Cultures: and the Impact of Technological Change* (New York: Harper & Brothers, 1962), p. 1, cited from an original article by Don Adams, "The Monkey and the Fish: Cultural pitfalls of an Educational Adviser," *International Development Rev.,* 2, No. 2 (1960), pp. 22–24.

tional security of a nation and, of course, soon becomes a political problem for the central government. Governmental efforts to control inflation during World War II, and recently by President Nixon in 1971, clearly reveal the complexities involved when change differentially affects large, but competitive groups. Too tight a system of controls seems to stimulate a black market and loose controls are not effective in controlling inflation. The alternatives are some position in the middle range in the severity of control, which is a relatively slow process, or to control very tightly both wages and prices for all groups and to be prepared to deal swiftly and sternly with attempted black marketing. However, the latter alternative is unpalatable in a democratic society, but, with continued increased differentiation, it may become necessary to protect the general interest from excessive competition and conflict among special interests.

A grave crisis in a society can focus public opinion, galvanize a social movement toward the common good, and bring about a new consensus without centralized force, if the society is not polarized on the issue or issues. In other words, if public opinion on an issue is not too evenly and strongly divided, a crisis situation that transcends the individual interests or the several competing groups can provide the motivation for major social change; for even in the darkest periods of crisis in a society's history it is its *existing* institutions that enable it to survive. Men of strong conviction are always present, but in addition, a central value focus is needed to provide cohesion for cooperative action.

Some social change derives from planned change of institutional arrangements, such as the Emancipation Proclamation by President Lincoln, although in this change force was also involved, and the Civil Rights Act of 1964 under President Johnson, which earlier involved a good deal of social agitation. This type of change is an alteration of institutional norms or regulations by the central regulating agency (the State) and has the effect of *subsequently* changing the behavior of participants. Another type of change *begins with* a change in the behavioral practices of individuals or groups and, as the number of individuals who exhibit the new behavior increases, it reaches a "critical mass" and becomes the basis for a new norm. This, it seems, is one of the bases for fads and fashions—for example, consider the recent rise in the popularity of beards among the formerly beardless.

Some change is symptomatic of hidden but emerging patterns. Other change is the result of the accumulation of several factors, and often is not noticed until it suddenly seems to appear. In addition, what often appears at the present to be change or to herald change is simply "noise in the system." Often one hears some public figure today, frequently a self-styled intellectual, analyzing some current behavior, claiming it to be the wave of the future. It is easy to confuse one's wishes, biases, and incomplete pictures of things with reality, and it is sometimes difficult to distinguish fads from emerging new reality.

Organic evolution is too complex and the present state of the biological sciences too inadequate to look ahead and discern even the dimmest outline of man in the far distant future. When one contemplates the probabilistic basis of human genetic developments, the complexity and difficulty of such forecasts becomes obvious. Each human zygote, through bisexual reproduction, receives 23 chromosomes from each of the parents. Each chromosome contains many genetic potentialities. Furthermore, no *fixed* pattern restricts the pairing of maternally and paternally derived chromosomes. Each cell resulting from meiotic division contains some chromosomes from each parent. Since man has 23 pairs of chromosomes, there are 2^{23} or 8,388,608 equally likely combinations. It is equally or more difficult to discern the structural outlines of sociocultural systems in the far distant future.

As in biological evolution, the social and cultural changes that are of interest are changes that are adaptive. As we stated earlier, not all change is adaptive. Some changes have no adaptive consequences, some have maladaptive effects, and, of course, some are adaptive. We are interested in avoiding maladaptive change and encouraging improved adaptive change. But how does the expert recognize which is which until after the fact? In biological evolution, change is proven to be adaptive only after natural selection has occurred. In the realm of cultural and social change, it is possible to conclude on a short-term basis that some changes are adaptive. For example, we have good reason to assume that the control of radiation exposure or hazards is adaptive. The difficulty is that the criteria for judging whether a cultural or social change is adaptive for a population are much less clear than the criteria for evaluating the adaptive worth of biological changes. Genetic selection is judged adaptive if it results in increased population growth of a species or at least a stable population. Judged on this basis, man has obviously over long periods of time shown great adaptive capacity; furthermore, his greatest population increases have occurred as a function of cultural and social change.

Though we do not always have enough knowledge about cultural and social change to allow us to make decisions in advance as to which course is the more adaptive, we nevertheless make decisions in the present that greatly affect our future adaptive capacities and conditions. Natural selection is ultimately the arbitrator of these as it is of the genetic changes in biological evolution. The task then is to improve our information concerning the processes about which we must make daily decisions, so that we can better and more wisely choose among the alternatives. If we assume that the primary long-range policy is to maintain and improve the quality of the species of man, then it appears that there are at least two major sources of power upon which this policy depends. The first is the control of sources of *energy*, for it is through the harnessing of energy that culture and technology, both physical and social technology, are advanced. In other words, man's capacity to maintain his position in nature is dependent upon the energy and technological resources available to him, including technology to assess and control the effects of technology on the rest of nature. The second form of power or control is the capacity of man to *control and regulate himself* so that he will not destroy his own kind, either by war or by the unwillingness to compromise on decisions affecting his relationships to the ecosystem or other systems within society itself. This includes eventually population control, waste control, and the monitoring of the effects of advanced technology on human genetics and on the natural environment, as well as the control of war as an instrument of national policy. Instead of man's basic problem of adaptation being one of conflict between warring instincts as Freud contends, it is the conflict between the need for a system (necessary restraint for organization) and man's capacity to exceed the bounds of his self or his socially constructed systems. Social systems cannot operate without rules, but rigid and unchanging rules are maladaptive; at the same time, unregulated self-interest leads to unbridled conflict and chaos.

Man's biggest threat is man himself.
(Courtesy Catherine Noren.)

In other words, in the long run, man's adaptive capacity depends on his means to control his environment, or at least to adapt, and to control himself for the betterment of the general welfare. In the earlier history and prehistory of man, the control of elements in his natural environment such as disease, famine, and pestilence were his foremost threats to survival. However, on the contemporary scene, the most dangerous threats to man's survival are his own actions or potential actions toward his fellows and his own man-made environment. Perhaps from a vague recognition of this come the questions that are being asked about what determines the quality of human life and the human environment. What are the indices to the quality of social life? How does one measure the quality of social adaptation? These questions are now begging for an answer, and man's long range survival may very well depend upon the quality of our answers.

Obviously, if we cannot ask the right questions or formulate them in a precise way we cannot get valid answers. Perhaps the first question is: What are the determinants of the quality of infant health at birth? How is maternal health and maternal care related to the quality of the fetus? The fetal environment is very important to the maintenance of genetic quality. A second logical question pertains to the quality of neurological stimulation and life supports after birth, that is, during infancy and childhood? A third set of questions concerns the development and training of human capacities and the efficient placement of individuals in the social system. All of these presuppose the solving of problems related to opportunities for development and adaptation. For example, the risk of being or becoming disadvantaged in the midst of abundance is greater for some groups than for others. "In 1966 about 30 million Americans, or 15 per cent of the population were living in households below the poverty line using the Social Security Administration definition. The incidence was 12 per cent for whites and 41 per cent for nonwhites. Among the aged it was 54 per cent for whites and 77 per cent for nonwhites. In terms of numbers, however, far more poor persons are white than nonwhite, are young than are old." [2] A fourth set of questions concerns a rather nebulus area which might be called "quality of life style." These refer to matters that transcend levels of consumption, job security and health, but of course, presuppose these. Just as bare subsistence living is a poor way of life, so is hedonistic conspicuous consumption. How are one's attitudes toward others, appreciation of nature, music, and art elevated? How does one come to feel that his life is useful and that he is needed? These are questions that relate to factors and conditions that make life worthwhile rather than just bearable.

[2] Eleanor B. Sheldon and Wilbert E. Moore (eds.), *Indicators of Social Change* (New York: Russell Sage Foundation, 1968), p. 18.

In retrospect, change in human systems of adaptation is adaptive if it increases survival or stability of the population, improves the physical and mental health of the members, and increases the stability of the societal and community social systems. It is quite likely that much change has nothing to do with improved adaptation, but instead reflects noise and dissatisfaction among certain members. One of the characteristics of life in a modern society is the accelerating rate of change. As a consequence, change itself has become a problem of adaptation.

SOCIAL AND TECHNOLOGICAL CORRELATES OF RATES OF CHANGE

Social life is made bearable and psychologically stable by values that define situations for us. The relationship of unsolved problems of adaptation to the development and change of the basic social values of a culture is an important question. The fact that these values vary among societies is well-known. To help appreciate these differences, it is useful to experience the consequences and difficulties of moving from one system to another. "In the words of a young American doctor in a Bombay hospital, 'I just wasn't psychologically attuned to the problems I would have to face. Back in the United States a doctor never has to ask himself: Why try to keep this baby alive? He concentrates all his knowledge and will power on the need to save a child and give him a chance for a normal life. But here in India, maybe two or three hundred million people will never experience a single day free of hunger or sickness in their entire lives.' "[3]

Very rapid change in a society creates a condition of uncertainty and bewilderment akin to that experienced by the young doctor, that is, people lose their moorings or anchors and become confused in their orientations to life and problems of adjustment. Many of the student movements in the 1960's were motivated by a vague feeling that things were wrong, but there were no accompanying clear values to guide action to improve conditions. Very rapid change in the social and cultural systems of a society produces a crisis of values in relation to unsolved or poorly solved problems. Given the breakdown in common orientations, and the experience of sharing common problems, cognitive reflection gives way to expressive action when large numbers interact with regard to their common problems. These are the underlying factors of social movements and collective behavior, both of which are often the forerunners to social change.

[3] George M. Foster, *Traditional Cultures: and the Impact of Technological Change* (New York: Harper & Brothers, 1962), p. 7.

This tenant farmer's wife endures her poverty in an affluent and ever-changing society.
(Courtesy Walker Evans.)

Because we live in a period of rapid invention, we are likely to think that our culture is largely self-created. The role of diffusion and contact with other cultures in the development of a culture is simply enormous. A dramatic appreciation of the role of cultural contact can be glimpsed by comparing an isolated society with others that are not isolated. The slow cultural growth of societies left to their own abilities is well-illustrated by the Tasmanians. Ralph Linton states[4]:

These people were cut off from the rest of mankind at least 20,000 years ago. When they reached their island they seem to have had a culture which, in its material development at least, corresponds roughly to that of Europe during the Middle Paleolithic. They were still in this stage when Europeans first visited them during the eighteenth century. During the long period of isolation they had no doubt made minor advances and improvements, but their lack of outside contacts was reflected in a tremendous culture lag.

Isolated areas in the United States provide another, but much less extreme, example.

[4] Ralph Linton, *The Study of Man* (New York: D. Appleton–Century Co., 1936), p. 325.

Linton suggests that there is probably no culture in existence today that owes more than 10 per cent of its total elements to inventions made by members of its own society. He dramatically describes the indebtedness of American society to other cultures in the following[5]:

Our solid American citizen awakens in a bed built on a pattern which originated in the Near East but which was modified in Northern Europe before it was transmitted to America. He throws back covers made from cotton, domesticated in India, or linen, domesticated in the Near East, or wool from sheep, also domesticated in the Near East, or silk, the use of which was discovered in China. All of these materials have been spun and woven by processes invented in the Near East. He slips into his moccasins, invented by the Indians of the Eastern woodlands, and goes to the bathroom, whose fixtures are a mixture of European and American inventions, both of recent date. He takes off his pajamas, a garment invented in India, and washes with soap invented by the ancient Gauls. He then shaves, a masochistic rite which seems to have been derived from either Sumer or ancient Egypt.

Returning to the bedroom, he removes his clothes from a chair of southern European type and proceeds to dress. He puts on garments whose form originally derived from the skin clothing of the nomads of the Asiatic steppes, puts on shoes made from skins tanned by a process invented in ancient Egypt and cut to a pattern derived from the classical civilizations of the Mediterranean, and ties around his neck a strip of bright-colored cloth which is a vestigial survival of the shoulder shawls worn by the seventeenth-century Croatians. Before going out for breakfast he glances through the window, made of glass invented in Egypt, and if it is raining puts on overshoes made of rubber discovered by the Central American Indians and takes an umbrella, invented in southeastern Asia. Upon his head he puts a hat made of felt, a material invented in the Asiatic steppes.

On his way to breakfast he stops to buy a paper, paying for it with coins, an ancient Lydian invention. At the restaurant a whole new series of borrowed elements confronts him. His plate is made of a form of pottery invented in China. His knife is of steel, an alloy first made in southern India, his fork a medieval Italian invention, and his spoon a derivative of a Roman original. He begins breakfast with an orange, from the eastern Mediterranean, a canteloupe from Persia, or perhaps a piece of African watermelon. With this he has coffee, an Abyssinian plant, with cream and sugar. Both the domestication of cows and the idea of milking them originated in the Near East, while sugar was first made in India. After his fruit and first coffee he goes on to waffles, cakes made by a Scandinavian technique from wheat domesticated in Asia Minor. Over these he pours maple syrup, invented by the Indians of the Eastern Woodlands. As a side dish he may have the egg of a species of bird domesticated in Indo-China, or thin strips of the flesh of an animal domesticated in Eastern Asia which have been salted and smoked by a process developed in northern Europe.

When our friend has finished eating he settles back to smoke, an American Indian habit, consuming a plant domesticated in Brazil in either a pipe, derived from the Indians of Virginia, or a cigarette, derived from Mexico. If he is hardy enough he may even attempt a cigar, transmitted to us from the Antilles by way of Spain. While smoking he reads the news of the day, imprinted in characters invented by the ancient Semites upon a material invented in China by a process invented in Germany. As he absorbs the accounts of foreign troubles he will, if he is a good conservative citizen, thank a Hebrew deity in an Indo-European language that he is 100 per cent American.

[5] Ralph Linton, *ibid.*, pp. 326–327.

The discovery of the existence of a new cultural element either by contact with another culture or through invention is not sufficient to assure its incorporation into a culture. The culture must have the resources necessary to incorporate the new element; and in addition, the new element must have sufficient support by members of the society to assure its adoption. It is something of an oversimplification, but one that contains a substantial grain of truth, to say that for each new planned cultural change there are those who oppose it as well as those who support it. In other words, the distribution of resources within all societies is necessarily unequal and hence power and interests are unequal. Accordingly, there is always tension between the members whose greatest interests lie in the status quo and those who would seek to form some kind of a new status quo.

There is no systematic theory of social change in sociology. The successful formulating of one would be a scientific contribution of very great importance. In classical sociology, Spencer and Durkheim wrote within the evolutionary tradition of the late 19th century and formulated a crude "theory" of social change based on specialization, differentiation, and integration. However, they did not adequately account for the processes and conditions that control these basic aspects of social change. Modern versions of evolutionary theories of social change are provided by Wilbert Moore, Neil Smelser, and Marion Levy.[6] They conceive of modernization of a traditional society as the " 'total' transformation of a traditional or premodern society into the types of technology and associated social organization that characterize the 'advanced,' economically prosperous, and relatively politically stable nations of the Western World. . . . In fact, we may . . . speak of the process as industrialization." [7]

Thus technology, which utilizes inanimate sources of power (fossil fuel, electricity, and so on), coupled with economic development and a decreasing dependence on agriculture as the principal means for the gross national product (GNP), characterize the modernization process. Economic resources, human resources, and technology are, of course, the principal means for social change —but how are the goals and priorities for change decided upon? How is consensus for one policy achieved, or, at least, how are deci-

[6] Wilbert E. Moore, Social Change (Englewood Cliffs, N.J.: Prentice–Hall, Inc., 1963); W. E. Moore and Robert M. Cook (eds.), Readings in Social Change (Englewood Cliffs, N.J.: Prentice–Hall, Inc., 1967); Neil J. Smelser "Toward a theory of modernization," in Amitai and Eva Etzioni (eds.), Social Change (New York: Basic Books, 1964); Marion J. Levy, Modernization and the Structure of Society (Princeton, N.J.: Princeton University Press, 1965), 2 Vols.; Talcott Parsons, Societies: Evolutionary and Comparative Perspectives (Englewood Cliffs, N.J.: Prentice–Hall, Inc., 1966); "Evolutionary Universals in Society," American Sociological Rev., Volume 29 (June 1964), pp. 339–357.
[7] Wilbert E. Moore, ibid., pp. 89, 91–92.

sions made to implement one policy rather than another? These questions we cannot answer. It is relatively easier to explain how decisions are made to maintain existing structures, but the explanation of the forces that wittingly or unwittingly produce change is more difficult. For example, in an agrarian society controlled by an agricultural elite, opposition by this group to almost any change in the direction of industrialization is to be expected, since such change would undermine that group's position of power.[8] Economic development is generally pushed by classes and groups interested in a new economic order, and opposed by those interested in the status quo.[9] In the long run, the forces (witting and unwitting) that stimulate change have generally succeeded, rather than those forces attempting to maintain the status quo.

Change and Self-Fulfilling Prophecy

Among the unique determinants of human social behavior and social change are man's *beliefs* and *theories* about human behavior. Theories about thermonuclear action do not affect the behavior of atoms, but they do affect man's relationship to the atom. The behavior of men, however, is *not* independent of the theories of human behavior that men adopt.[10]

If men believe that some groups are innately inferior, they are likely to treat them as such. If they believe that the nature of the economic order is cyclical and self-regulating, then their economic policies and actions will be in accord with that belief, and, of course, the result will be great cyclical variability in the economic system. In other words, belief helps shape actuality in human affairs because of the self-fulfilling-prophecy character of social beliefs. A tragic example of this in modern times is seen in the Nazi beliefs and related policies prior to and during World War II. In varying degrees, beliefs and theories about human nature affect the development of all human institutions, since institutions are based on human conceptions, and human conceptions are guided by implicit or explicit theories. Accordingly, change is affected by the emergence of new beliefs and theories. It must be said then that the study of social change is significantly a study of how man wittingly or unwittingly makes himself. Two models of how man attempts to shape his future consciously will be discussed below. The first of these is the Bell and Mau model, and the second is that of Donald Schon. Schon's will be used as the model for the chapter.

[8] See A. F. K. Organski, *The Stages of Political Development* (New York: Alfred A. Knopf, Inc., 1965), p. 144.
[9] For a discussion of this idea, see Paul A. Baran, *The Political Economy of Growth* (New York: Monthly Review Press, 1957).
[10] Roy G. Francis, "The Nature of Scientific Research," in John T. Doby (ed. and coauthor), *An Introduction to Social Research*, 2nd ed. (New York: Appleton–Century–Crofts, Inc., 1967) pp. 5, 20.

The Bell and Mau Model

The industrialized nations of the world today are exhibiting a rate of change greater than that of any other time in history. The accelerating rates of social and cultural change, and the resulting problems of adaptation in the social, biological, and psychological areas produced by such accelerated rates, raise questions about the subjective and objective limits to change. By subjective limits we mean the limits of individual tolerance or adaptability to change; by objective limits we are implying that there may be external plateaus beyond which human resources and capacities will not allow man to go. We will come back to this point in a later discussion. Just now we wish to present a more integrated and systematic summary of how social change occurs. One such summary is provided by Bell and Mau[11] and is reproduced schematically in Figure 16–1.[12] The basic notion in the Bell and Mau formulation is that social change is explained in terms of a feedback decision model, or in their words, a "cybernetic–decisional model." It treats the process of change as a feedback cycle resulting from the cumulative interaction between information and action.[13]

Motivated individuals, acting as individuals or members of groups, their images of the future, and their resultant behaviors are the key elements that keep the system moving and bring a future into being in the present. The behavior is viewed as largely the result of decisions (or in some cases as decisions not to decide), which are essentially choices among alternative futures. Hence the use of "decisional" in the label. Images of the future are of critical importance in influencing which of the alternative futures becomes present reality.

From Figure 16–1, it is clear that the authors are emphasizing decisions about present or anticipated unsolved problems; furthermore, they maintain that these decisions are conditioned by present knowledge, beliefs, and images of the future, plus the capacity of the members of society to recognize alternative courses of action and to implement the chosen course. The formulation includes unintended as well as intended consequences. This omnibus clause means, of course, that the propositions about unintended consequences can never be tested since they will never be known until after the fact. If, however, the system is dynamic, it can *subsequently* recognize and cope with these unintended consequences. The Bell and Mau scheme is interesting and probably basically correct. It is, however, too complicated and insufficiently simplified for fruitful use in its present state.

[11] Wendell Bell and James A. Mau (eds.), *The Sociology of the Future* (New York: Russell Sage Foundation, 1971).
[12] Wendell Bell and James A. Mau (eds.), *ibid.*, p. 21.
[13] Wendell Bell and James A. Mau (eds.), *ibid.*, p. 18.

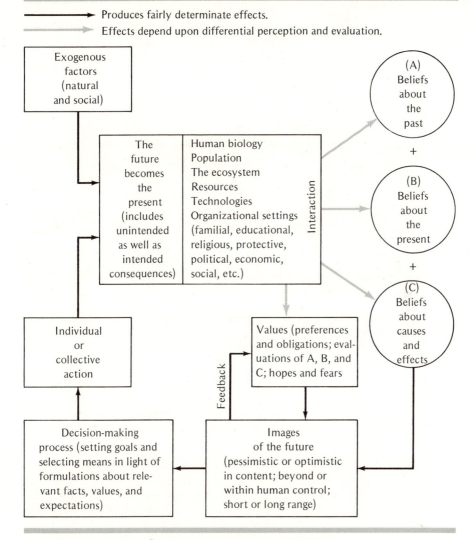

Produces fairly determinate effects.

Effects depend upon differential perception and evaluation.

Exogenous factors (natural and social)

The future becomes the present (includes unintended as well as intended consequences)

Human biology
Population
The ecosystem
Resources
Technologies
Organizational settings (familial, educational, religious, protective, political, economic, social, etc.)

Interaction

(A) Beliefs about the past

+

(B) Beliefs about the present

+

(C) Beliefs about causes and effects

Individual or collective action

Values (preferences and obligations; evaluations of A, B, and C; hopes and fears)

Feedback

Decision-making process (setting goals and selecting means in light of formulations about relevant facts, values, and expectations)

Images of the future (pessimistic or optimistic in content; beyond or within human control; short or long range)

FIGURE 16–1 Cybernetic-decisional model of social change.
(From Wendel Bell and James A. Mau (eds.). *The Sociology of the Future.* New York: The Russel Sage Foundatoin, 1971, p. 21.)

The Schon Model

Our thesis is that social change occurs when the challenges of unsolved problems are met by the decisions and actions of key people (scientists, industrialists, political and governmental leaders, educators, and so on) coupled with the commitment of their followers necessary to implement the chosen course of action, and to modify it, as new feedback information dictates. The key element is the *unsolved problem or problems.* How does one react to an unsolved problem? First of all, it depends upon the problem itself, how central it is to the welfare of those concerned, and the number

Man's future conditions are significantly determined by his present image of the future.
("Space Conversation" by Franklin McMahon. Courtesy NASA, Washington, D.C.)

of people whose welfare is involved. Our attention to a problem, or even our willingness to admit publicly that one exists, depends upon the relationship of the problem to the individual or group concerned. Dust from a stone quarry seems a necessary by-product to the stone company, but a vexing problem to the people who happen to have to live nearby. In other words, we are both selectively attentive and selectively inattentive to information emerging from our environment. Second, the reaction depends upon whether there are theories, ideas, or information available or presently obtainable to permit a solution. Of course, some information exists on the effects of the problem or it would not be noticed at all, but there may be little if any information on how to solve it or to control its effects. In such a circumstance, there is uncertainty as to how to respond. If the whole community or society is uncertain about its proper response, then the *system* is plunged into uncertainty and action may be postponed. As Schon quite correctly notes: "The most threatening changes are the ones that would plunge the system into uncertainty." [14] Third, reaction may take the form of a resigned response, of doing nothing at all, because of a belief that the problem is beyond human effort or that the "cure" is worse than the problem.

We stated earlier that the rate of social and cultural change was extremely slow in ancient times and that it has accelerated steadily toward the present. The slowness of change in the past

[14] Donald A. Schon, *Beyond the Stable State* (New York: Random House, Inc., 1971), p. 13.

gave societies ample time to adjust. The problem then was that change often did not occur in time to be of aid to the many who needed help. These differential rates of change are reflected today when industrialized societies are compared to traditional societies on selected variables. Figure 16–2 below shows rates of vital statistics for selected developed and underdeveloped regions. It should be noted that the growth rate of the underdeveloped areas is currently approximately two times as great as the developed regions. (Developed nations of today once had a high birth rate, but with industrialization of these nations the rate dropped.) The high rate of population growth of these underdeveloped regions seriously interferes with their economic growth or with improvement of their living standards. In Latin America, for example, while the gross national product has about doubled in the two decades or so since 1945, the general economic condition of the region has nevertheless improved only very slowly because of a more than 45 per cent increase in population.

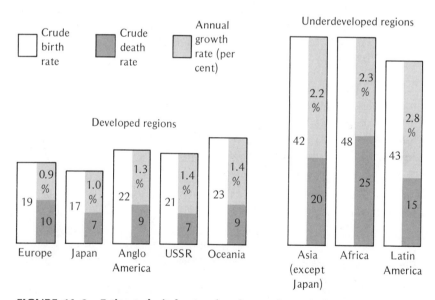

FIGURE 16–2 Estimated vital rates for the earth's principal regions, separated into the less developed and more developed groups.
(From Glenn T. Trewartha, Arthur H. Robinson, and Edwin H. Hammond. *Elements of Geography,* 5th ed. New York: McGraw-Hill Book Company, 1967, p. 527.)

In many of the underdeveloped countries, population increases have exceeded increases in food production. For example, in the Fast East during the five-year period ending with 1964, the population increased 10 per cent while food production increased by 8.5 per cent. In Latin America during this period, the population rose

11.5 per cent while the food supply only increased 6.5 per cent.[15] Recently, there has been an increase in food production in some parts of the underdeveloped world though this increase is probably temporary.

The comparative rates of population growth and food production on a worldwide basis are shown in Figure 16–3. The increase in food production has been offset somewhat by population growth. As a consequence, per capita food supply has barely held its own, or perhaps has even declined.

As a result of the dissemination of birth control information and the development of fertility control programs by under-developed nations, by the end of this century birth rates among these nations are expected to decline faster than death rates. Even so, with the natural increase rate of nearly 19 per thousand expected to be reached by the year 2000, a doubling of population numbers over a span of about 37 years is still anticipated. Clearly a substantial reduction in fertility will not be sufficient to solve many of the problems of the underdeveloped nations. The tremendous increase in world population is the direct result of rapid cultural and social change—that is, change in medical practice, food production, and methods of social organization—especially in nations or cultures unaccustomed to and unprepared for these rapid changes.

One way of illustrating the acceleration in the rates of change is to note the time required for diffusion or spread of inventions. Schon notes that "curves showing the length of time required for technological innovations to spread broadly throughout populations of users, suggest an exponential rate of shrinkage."[16] For example, see the four inventions listed below:

Invention	Time required for diffusion in years
Steam engine	150–200
Automobile	40–50
Vacuum tube	25–30
Transistor	about 15

One of the problems in responding to very rapid and pervasive change is that the population members are uncertain or in

[15] See Glenn T. Trewartha, *A Geography of Population: World Patterns* (New York: John Wiley & Son, Inc., 1969), p. 55.

[16] Donald A. Schon, *Beyond the Stable State* (New York: Random House, Inc., 1971), p. 24. An exponential curve describes a population that increases or decreases at a constant rate with each generation. For example, a bacterial cell grows to a certain size and divides to become two cells; the two new cells repeat this process to become four; the four become eight, and so on. Thus, one cell can be expressed as 2^0 cells, two cells can be written as 2^1 cells, four cells as 2^2 cells, and so on. Such progressions in populations are called exponential growth, or logarithmic growth.

Index: 1952-1956 = 100

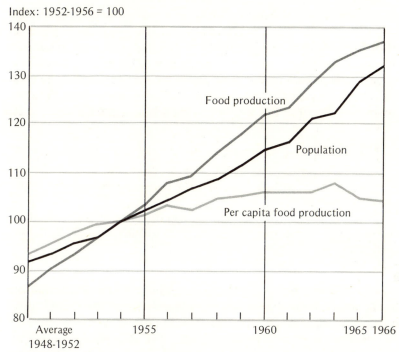

FIGURE 16–3   Rates of world food production, population growth, and per capita food production.
(From *Population Bulletin,* December 1968.)

conflict about which of the many factors are the ones of true concern. For example, if next year is to be significantly different from this year, then planning for next year is difficult unless one knows in advance what the conditions will be. In other words, one cannot soundly plan for new and unknown future conditions, unless, as in the past, one can base his plans on present conditions and assume a relative steady state of the system. As Schon argues, the response to social and cultural change has traditionally assumed continuity of structure and process through time, or what he calls a "stable state." In the past, a stable state assumption could be made for even a century or more, and the error involved would not be too great. This is no longer the case in modern society. In the area of technology, exponential growth curves seem to characterize all forms and types of technological growth, and, of course, technological growth is a main source of social change. In fact, technological systems assume a high dependence upon given forms of social organization and vice versa. Furthermore, it should be clear that what will sustain the function and vitality of an institution at one era of time will not suffice at a later time. As Schon notes, the American Labor Movement achieved its goals of the 1930's and was a dynamic force in meeting the competitive needs of labor with industry and hence serving the larger society as well. But presently, it is not a dynamic force for social change, but simply another bureaucratic institution, itself in need of changes, or as the late Walter Reuther said, a new mission.[17]

Schon's own summary of his theory of social change is a fairly accurate picture of the view expressed in this chapter, as well as the schematic view of Bell and Mau. Schon's view is based on the assumed realization of the two following adaptive goals:

1. If our established institutions are threatened with disruption, how can we invent and bring into being new or modified institutions capable of confronting challenges to their stability without freezing and without coming apart at the seams?

2. If we are losing stable values and anchors for personal identity, how can we maintain a sense of self-respect and self-identity while in the very process of change?

The above two questions pose the problem of adaptation to social and cultural change quite accurately, and the implied solution is to formulate clearly the image of the future that is *desired* by the population and then to create the conditions necessary for its realization. Such an approach must be a dynamic one, subject to revision in accordance with information feedback. Furthermore, it proceeds on the following assumptions as stated by Schon, with slight modification:

1. The loss of the stable state by a society means that the society and all of its institutions are in continuing processes of transformation. In our own society, for example, we cannot expect new stable states that will endure even for our own lifetimes.

2. We must learn to understand, guide, influence, and manage these transformations. We must make the capacity for undertaking them integral to ourselves and to our institutions.

3. We must become able not only to transform our institutions, in response to changing situations and requirements, but we must invent and develop institutions that are "learning systems," that is, systems capable of bringing about their own continuing transformation.

Moreover, the foregoing task requires that we first be able to answer the following questions:

1. What is the nature of the process by which organizations and societies transform themselves?

---

[17] Donald Schon, *ibid.*, p. 17.

2. What characteristics have to be built into social systems to give them a "learning systems" capacity?

3. What are the forms and limits of knowledge that can operate within social-systems learning? (This is, as we indicated in Chapter 3, a different problem and condition of learning than that of individual learning. The conditions and constraints of interperson and intergroup learning involves more and different parameters than simple individual learning. Of course, the processes that go on inside the brain are the same, but the context and conditions of decisions and action are quite different. They must, for example, take into account the beliefs, needs, and values of the others involved.)

4. What demands are made on a person who engages in this kind of learning?

On reflection, clearly the rate and scope of modern social change is too great and too difficult to manage on a crisis to crisis basis. Chaos, accumulation of unsolved problems, and frightening uncertainty are the likely outcomes of such an approach from now on. Today, the major sources of social change derive from major centers of action composed of industrial and laboratory complexes operated in conjunction with the central government, which helps to finance these centers of technology and often helps to man them. Such centers are fairly well removed from large numbers of the population; as a consequence, the people are unable to understand proposals for action because they have insufficient information. This in turn makes it difficult to elicit sufficient local cooperation.

In the past, innovations came from a great variety of sources, often from the works of individuals—for example, Watt's steam engine, McCormick's reaper, and Edison's electric light. The laboratories of modern technology cost millions and hundreds of millions and employ hundreds and even thousands of technicians and scientists. The facilities of the past were basement laboratories and small facilities in universities and private firms. Moreover, the diffusion or spread of innovations, whether social or technical, was, in the past, on a missionary or salesman basis—that is, one-man type shows. Therefore, though there may have been several individuals in different places trying to sell their ideas or products at the same general time, diffusion proceeded at a very slow rate and on a very small scale.

Today, on the other hand, whole new programs suddenly spring forth on a nationwide basis either from government or industry—for example, The Economic Opportunity Act, Price and Wage Controls, Social Security Programs, change of automobile models, new ways of packaging food, and so on.

Since the rate of spread or diffusion of products throughout a population has accelerated so rapidly, it is important to take a look at the diffusion process, both in the present and in the past, as a source of social change. But before we turn to a discussion of the diffusion of new ideas and products, an explanation of what is meant by the loss of the "stable state" is useful for purposes of clarity. By loss of the stable state, we do not mean that *all* values, for example, have become empty and are in need of change, for there are some values, it can be argued (though not easily demonstrated), that are of proven universal worth. For example, no social system based on the duplicity of each and all of its members could endure. Behavior would be unpredictable and, therefore, coordination and integration, which are fundamental to any social system, would be impossible. The same universality applies to societal standards regarding murder. No society could long survive if all disputes were handled personally. In time, a jungle of aggression would emerge, with leaders of factions warring continually with each other until some institution similar to the "state" or government arose to solve conflict impersonally among the members. The same is true in respect to the values that define the rights and property of others. The point is that the difference between the jungle and civilization is the respect for the rule by law, written or unwritten. Thus in our discussion of the loss of the stable state, we are referring primarily to man's attitude toward change and to the need for bringing what has been largely an unconscious process under more conscious and rational control. This means we must learn how to change our institutions as well as ourselves, and we must recognize the necessity for educating the public for dealing with change. It does not mean, however, that all traditions and values of the past are changed, but rather that, in many cases, conditions for realizing or perfecting these are improved.

PROCESSES OF CHANGE
IN TRADITIONAL AND MODERN SOCIETIES

We have already seen in the previous section that every culture borrows or receives many more elements from other cultures than its own members create. Let us take a look at some currents of social change in the United States and examine some of the underlying conditions. According to Schon, the United States during the last 30 years has experienced three distinct but interacting currents of social change. These are[18]:

1. A growing awareness and intolerance of the imbalance in our society between the production of consumer goods, to which the major thrust of the economy has been devoted, and the critical public systems, such as transportation, housing, education, and waste disposal, which have taken a poor second place.

[18] Donald A. Schon, *Beyond the Stable State* (New York: Random House, Inc., 1971), p. 16.

2. A growing dissatisfaction with the relatively powerless position in American society of many minorities—not only racial but more broadly, the poor, rural families, the aged, the sick, prisoners, the mentally ill. . . . It includes demands for participation, decentralization, and more local control. . . .

3. A growing disenchantment, expressed most vigorously by the young, with the goals and values of social progress, as these have remained relatively intact since the eighteenth century.

These three dissatisfactions presently are more of the form of poorly coordinated but rather isolated social movements and protests rather than full-fledged social changes. Considerable emphasis has been directed in each of the three areas especially in the last decade or so and evidence indicates further emphasis in the future. What seems to be new about these social pressures is not

The social conscience of the sixties and seventies dictates that the powerless minorities must be freed and fed and healed. This social movement is not new, only the gusto with which it is pursued is new.
(Courtesy Jim Harrison.)

that the problems themselves are new, but that there is an intensity of feeling and increased strength of belief that more should be done about them.

But modern industrial society is not the first instance of accelerating technology. It is the *nature* of technology to accelerate. Contemporary technology stands on the technology of the past.[19] It is cumulative and its added thrust arises from this very fact. Consequently, many societies have experienced new technological plateaus and peaks, and the related disruptions and major social changes—for example, Greece during the Hellenistic period, Europe in the Renaissance, and Japan in the 19th and 20th centuries. Thus the exponential growth of science and technology is characteristically not new. DeSolla Price makes this same point by noting that[20]

. . . the 80 to 90 per cent currency of modern science is a direct result of an exponential growth that has been steady and consistent for a long time. It follows that this result, true now, must also have been true *at all times in the past,* back to the eighteenth century and perhaps even as far back as the late seventeenth. In 1900, in 1800, and perhaps in 1700, one could look back and say that most of the scientists that have ever been are alive now, and most of what is known has been determined within living memory. In that respect, surprised though we may be to find it so, the scientific world is no different now from what it has always been since the seventeenth century. Science has always been modern; it has always been exploding into the population, always on the brink of its expansive revolution. . . .

Interdependence of Technological Development and Ideology

While it is true that technological growth accumulates and accelerates through time, it is not true that technological innovation leads inexorably to its implementation and application. The laissez-faire assumption of technological inevitability, given the presence of the necessary knowledge, is true only if a society operates on this value assumption. A different value assumption or policy would lead to a different outcome. The development and use of technology has never been independent of the context of other institutions in society. It has in the past been accorded an overwhelming role in Western society because of its value in coping with the problems of adaptation associated with disease, scarcity of food, and means for production. But an analysis of Western ideology and values of the past makes this quite understandable. For example, given the frontier conditions in early American society, an ideology of extreme individualism was very adaptive. Individualism in extreme form is

[19] For an interesting and brilliant spoof on this subject, including a witty parody on quasi-scholarship, see Robert K. Merton, *On the Shoulders of Giants: A Shandean Postscript* (New York: The Free Press–Collier–Macmillan Co., 1965).
[20] Derek DeSolla Price, *Big Science, Little Science* (New York: Columbia University Press, 1963), pp. 14–15.

much less adaptive in modern urban society. Likewise, given the size and concentrations of the population today, unregulated technological innovations and their applications can have dangerous side effects. Accordingly, Robert Lynd's question "Knowledge for What?" is quite appropriate. It is presumed here that the assumed or actual consequences of a technological innovation will determine the attitude of the members of a society toward the potential use of the innovation.

Some Cultural Factors That Inhibit Change

When considering diffusion, investigators of social change find it useful to think of factors that stimulate change and factors that inhibit change. Social change is a process by which a society confronts or deals with its changing situations or problems of adaptation. Some constraints on these efforts derive from the culture, some from the social structure, and some, of course, from the natural environment. The cultural constraints are in the form of current limits to available knowledge and technology, and resistance to change through the psychological and social effects of traditional beliefs.

Conflict of Cultural Traits. Often a new trait with which the members of a society come into contact is logically in conflict with an existent trait of their own. In such an event, the members of the population will resist the new trait. American Foreign Aid advisors reported difficulty with tractor maintenance efforts by natives of India. The Indians were not greasing the tractors because they thought that the grease was animal fat, a taboo in their culture. Foster reports a study on the Navaho by Reichard, which indicates that the Navaho's abhorrence of death made it very difficult for them to comprehend Christianity, which is based on the concept of death and resurrection.[21]

Incompatibility of Technology. Before a complex pattern of technology can diffuse to another culture, the receiving culture must have an existing technology that is at least compatible with the new one. It would be impossible to diffuse atomic technology to a society without an adequate number of its members being skilled in advanced mathematics and physics.

Societies with simple or primitive technology are at a great disadvantage in competing with societies that have advanced technologies. In the past, contact between such societies led to

[21] George M. Foster, *Traditional Cultures: and the Impact of Technological Change* (New York: Harper & Brothers, 1962), p. 79.

political domination by the society with the superior technology, often in the form of colonialism or some form of mercantilism. Today a similar form of domination takes place when an underdeveloped nation imports technology from an advanced industrial society, only to find itself unable to operate the technology. It must then resort to "inviting" large numbers of technical assistants and advisors from the modern nation.

Models of Diffusion

In noting the increasing complexity of technology and the resulting new ways in which it is diffused, Schon formulates two models of diffusion. These two models are labeled *The center–periphery model* and *the proliferation of centers model.*

The Center–Periphery Model. This model involves essentially three elements. These are the existence of (1) a new idea, that is, the innovation; (2) someone or someones who know about the new idea and have an interest in communicating or selling it; and (3) another someone or someones who do not know about it and are potential users. One of the early and perhaps earliest diffusion agents was the priest; some of the modern examples of agents of center–periphery model change are the agricultural extension agent, the public health nurse, the doctor, drug salesmen, and teachers.

Schon schematically illustrates this model as follows[22]:

The effectiveness of the center–periphery system depends first upon the level of resources and energy at the center, then upon the number of points at the periphery, the length of the radii or spokes through which diffusion takes place, and the energy required to gain a new adoption. The diffusion capability of an agricultural extension agent, for example, depends upon his own energies and skills, the number and location of the farmers he serves, and the time and effort he must devote to work with each farmer.

[22] Donald A. Schon, *Beyond the Stable State* (New York: Random House, Inc., 1971), p. 82.

The success of the center–periphery system depends on two factors: First, the availability and use of local substructures to work through in reaching the potential users, and second, the capacity of the center to induce and to manage effectively feedback from the would-be or actual users. For example, the agriculture extension people used committees composed of local farmers elected by their neighbors to represent them. This committee structure not only provided a social structure for decision making and action, but it also afforded an excellent means for feedback.

Schon identified two varieties of the center–periphery model—the "Johnny Appleseed" type and the "magnet" type.[23] In the Johnny Appleseed type, the primary center is a moving or roaming one, which travels a territory spreading a message. Some examples are traveling scholars, saints, artisans of the Middle Ages, Voltaire, Thomas Paine, Karl Marx, or the late Martin Luther King. The "magnet" model attracts agents of diffusion *to* it; for example, the universities and the capitals of the major nations of the world serve as centers of influence for developing nations.

Each of these varieties of the center–periphery model has its own advantages and limitations.[24] The magnet model allows for closer supervision and tighter control from the center and greater efficiency in the use of change agents; but it has less control over what happens afterwards and permits less variation of doctrine to suit particular cultural needs at the outposts. This doctrinaire rigidity often characterizes efforts to diffuse ideologies.

The Johnny Appleseed model allows the teaching to be adapted to the special conditions of the territories. Saint Paul the Apostle was quite adept at this process to cite an ancient example. But the Appleseed model provides less of an opportunity for the development of a critical mass at the center capable of attracting new followers.

When the center–periphery system exceeds the resources at the center, it experiences failure in feedback and distortion of messages from the center by its agents. For example, a salesman or social worker who have too many customers or clients to call on cannot give sufficient time to any; in addition they do not have adequate time to receive instructions and new information from the head office—hence, the whole system is threatened. The same is true of a teacher who has too many pupils for adequate individual attention. When the system of diffusion and influence becomes so large and complex that the center–periphery model is no longer adequate, it is often transformed or elaborated and thus becomes the *proliferation of centers* model.

[23] Donald A. Schon, *ibid.*, p. 83.
[24] The discussion of these models borrows freely from Schon.

The Proliferation of Centers Model.   This system retains the basic center–periphery structure, but differentiates primary from secondary centers, as illustrated schematically below.

The secondary centers carry out the diffusion efforts and the primary center supports and manages the secondary centers. As Schon quite correctly notes, "the proliferation of centers makes of the primary center a trainer of trainers." [25] The limits to the capacity and effectiveness of the new system depend now on the primary centers resources and its ability to generate, manage, and support the new secondary centers. The modern corporation is, of course, an excellent example of the proliferation of centers model, but the Roman Army and early Christian Church were among the first and most important examples. In each case, there was a centrally established doctrine and a centrally established method of diffusing it.

Schon notes that the late 19th and early 20th centuries were marked by the flowering of a cluster of highly developed models along the lines of the proliferation of centers. Some of the major examples are industrial expansion, the Communist Movement, and Imperialism. The Coca Cola Company and IBM are examples of the industrial type on a worldwide basis. The same model is found in the field of medicine and health care under the label of "centers of excellence." The idea in this case is to develop centers of medical research and teaching whose purpose is to serve peripheral rings of community physicians. [26]

Except perhaps for the structure by which religion is often diffused, change in traditional societies has been along the lines of the center–periphery model. With respect to religion, proliferation of clusters model has often been the means of the extension of influence from outside. Of course, in modern times, traditional soci-

---

[25] Donald A. Schon, *Beyond the Stable State* (New York: Random House, Inc., 1971), p. 85.
[26] Donald A. Schon, *ibid.*, p. 94.

eties are undergoing major transition as a result of their contact with industrial societies, and the mechanisms of influence, for the most part, follow the proliferation of centers model just described. Nevertheless, it is informative to examine one case of change in a traditional society where the change derives from internal influences.

The late Professor Ralph Linton describes the effect of institutional change on the Tanala, a hill tribe of western Madagascar.[27] Prior to approximately 200 years ago, the economic basis of their life was the cultivation of rice in dry areas, that is, dry rice growing. This was done by cutting and burning of the jungle to provide fertile soil, a method that yielded a good crop the first year and a moderately good one for a few years afterwards. After this, the land had to be abandoned and another site located and the process repeated. Since their subsistence centered around and depended upon rice, they necessarily had to migrate as the land was depleted. Furthermore, since the cleared and burned jungle area produced the best crops, the natives used all of the area possible for the crops and located all the huts in a village pattern in the center. When the land wore out, the village as a whole moved to the next site. Under these conditions, there was no opportunity for individual ownership of land to develop. The village as a whole held a territory within which it moved from site to site.

Joint families[28] owned the crops growing on jungle land that they had cleared, but the division of land for this use was an equitable one. The village elders staked out equal frontage of land to be cleared by each joint family. The family members working as a group could clear back from the front as far as they thought necessary.

The Tanala clans came into contact with the Betsileo, who were cultivators of wet rice. Some of the Tanala borrowed the wet rice practice, although it began as a simple adjunct to dry rice—that is, they planted naturally wet places in the valleys. Since this operation was a small task, it started as work done by households rather than joint families. Later small systems of terraces were created, also borrowed, and once again on a household rather than a joint family basis. Since the maintenance of the terraces and their cultivation was a year around activity, and since it was done for the most part by a household, the terraced lands never reverted to the village for reassignment. Also, since the irrigation system tended to replenish the soil, movement to a new location was no longer necessary. Thus individual households began to lay claims to the tracts they cultivated. Accordingly, a system of private property developed and, in time, what had been a classless society became a society of class

---

[27] Ralph Linton, *The Study of Man* (New York: D. Appleton–Century Co., 1936), pp. 348–350.
[28] A joint family is a conjugal group that includes in its social system the additional households created by the marriage of the sons. Even though the daughters marry out of the family they still cooperate with the original family group.

based on landholding. With this came a weakening of the joint family form of social organization. Loyalty to this unit had been maintained largely by the economic interdependence of its members and their constant need for cooperation.

At first, the rise of land ownership did not seriously affect those who did not have land. They simply farmed land as before—that is, dry rice growing—by going farther out from the village. Finally, this became so inconvenient that they began to develop sleeping quarters and granaries on the farming sites. These distant fields also soon became household rather than joint family enterprises, and as a consequence the joint family pattern soon broke down. Thus there developed the landowning class, which cultivated wet rice and had an investment in a specific locality and, therefore, would not move with the landless ones, who had to move as was the clan custom. Thus the village split; with this emerged a new form of social organization. Clearly major change can come about, though slowly, in a traditional society, as a result of internal contact or interaction and borrowing by the members themselves. In other words, there were no change agents other than the consumers or family members themselves to decide what should be diffused.

An interesting modern contrast to this is provided by Schon.[29]

In 1960 a group of consultants proposed to the Whirlpool Corporation that they produce a "solvent washer" which would be, in effect, a home drycleaning machine for all kinds of garments. Whirlpool, it turned out, already had a version of the idea. But its market studies had convinced it that women would resist any increase in the amount of ironing they had to do; home dry-cleaners would simply produce more clothes to be ironed.

In the early sixties, however, "wash-and-wear" gained acceptance. And wash-and-wear fabrics could in most cases be "finished" acceptably without ironing. The introduction of wash-and-wear released the idea of the coin-operated dry-cleaner, which had been on Whirlpool's shelves. Norge had the same idea, and Whirlpool and Norge raced to be first on the market with the "coin-ops."

The introduction of the "coin-ops" confronted traditional private dry-cleaning establishments with a new form of competition. The result was to force such companies either to set up "coin-op" concessions, to turn themselves into more industrialized dry-cleaning establishments better able to meet the new competition, or to specialize in "craft" work highly geared to the needs of particular customers, so that in special areas they could outperform the "coin-ops."

In the meantime, people were cleaning their clothes in common equipment at room temperature. Bacterial problems arose which created the "need" for new bacteriostats that could function effectively in coin-ops.

A striking point in this case as contrasted to the Tanala is the sudden and almost simultaneous involvement of an extensive

[29] Donald A. Schon, *Beyond the Stable State* (New York: Random House, Inc., 1971), pp. 71–72.

"If men define things as real, they are real in their conse-
quences." W. I. Thomas.
(Courtesy W. Eugene Smith.)

network of different groups, all of which were forced to make sudden changes in their activities or go out of business. This is virtually
the hallmark of modern change in industrial societies.

There are many new and good ideas that emerge on the
scene in modern societies; there are also, as always, crack-pot ideas,
many more of them, in fact, as well as pathologies of thought that
are thrust upon the public for attention. Social selection does not
seem to sift them out easily except in the pragmatic and objective
areas of science and technology. Some of the old ideas that are
socially maladaptive but are still around in various guises are racism
and related doctrines of supremacy. The prevalence of such ideas
and their augmentation by systems of instantaneous and societal,
even worldwide, electronic communication makes for difficult problems in socialization. How, for example, does a new generation sift

the grain from the chaff? For many of the types of activities and products to which they are exposed, most people are not able to perform this discriminatory task because they do not have the necessary technical know-how. For example, most people know that vitamins are necessary for maintenance of health; vitamin pills and supplements are advertised as a means of filling this need and people are urged to buy them just to be safe. What people do not know is that one can take a harmful overdose of some vitamins and that a normal diet contains all the necessary vitamins anyway. Consequently, in modern society, some organization has to be responsible for sifting the claims of manufacturers and informing the public. A recent Federal law establishing penalties for false advertising is a step in this direction. The point is that without some form of public protection, the public is at the mercy of the complexity of modern communication and technology.

SOCIALIZATION IN TRADITIONAL AND MODERN SOCIETIES

It is true that each generation of technology is a source of new change and growth, a property unique to technology. How is this age of technology different from other ages? There are two differences that seem to be distinctive to our age. The first is the all *pervasiveness* of technology in modern society.[30] There is no area or aspect of modern life that is free from the effects and influence of technology. Moreover, the electronic mass media (radio and television) confront entire societies, indeed on occasions the entire world, with events and happenings that stimulate simultaneously the conflicts and passions of all groups. This stimulation of the entire mass has the effect of producing an instant public, but a public of short-lived stability, whose orientation is subject to rapid changes precipitated by exposure to the next set of events. It reminds one of the saying "we must get with the *zeitgeist*" (spirit of the age), to which one sociologist, Lewis Coser, has wittily replied: "He who weds the zeitgeist will surely experience a quick divorce." Change has been rapid for several centuries, but never so *pervasive* as now. The second feature of modern change is the level of complexity achieved by modern technology. As John R. Platt[31] asks, how much faster is it possible for an airplane to fly and still be able to land within the nation? In other words, are there practical as well as adaptive limits to levels of technology? The application of computers to automation and improved organizational practices have resulted in a reduction of the number of hours in the work week. As Platt correctly notes, it is not the elimination of the hours worked

[30] Donald A. Schon, *ibid.*, p. 25.
[31] John R. Platt, *The Step to Man* (New York: John Wiley & Sons, Inc., 1966).

Can mankind learn to cope with the onslaught of technology or must he suffer a sense of alienation and helplessness?
("Melancholia," by Albrecht Dürer. Courtesy Francis Gray and Fogg Art Museum, Harvard University.)

per se that produces the adaptive problem. The problems associated with the 30-hour or the 10-hour week, or with no work at all, are related to self-identity, self-respect, economic distribution, and idleness and boredom with respect to all the remaining hours in the week when one does not work. Answers to these problems will have to be found, or we may find that social stability is no longer possible.

It has been estimated that paleolithic man doubled his population every 30,000 years. Today the world population doubles every 30 or 40 years—roughly 1000 times as fast.[32] What are the implications of such speed of change for socialization and adaptations?

---

[32] John R. Platt, *ibid.*, p. 194.

Socialization in Traditional Societies

We have shown that social change is gradual in traditional societies and therefore easier to integrate into existing structures. The cultural values of traditional societies are more or less uncritically accepted, so that the child grows into adolescence generally accepting whatever is around him. A boy follows almost literally in his father's footsteps and as a result identifies with his father's activities and acquires his skills as he grows up. The adolescent in a traditional society is not likely to experience an identity crisis.

In a traditional society where the ideal status was restricted to the warrior status, as in the Comanche and some other Indian tribes, men whose personalities were completely uncongenial to the warrior role were in difficulty unless the society made special provision for them. This is in fact what happened. These men were given a special status, that of *berdache*. They wore women's costumes and performed women's activities, although their status was distinct from that of women. For example, they continued to hunt and they were expected to be somewhat more competent than women even at women's tasks.

Ralph Linton, in commenting on how misfits are socially defined in different societies, noted that "in pre-Islamic Arabian literature the greatest heroes are nearly always represented as epileptics. . . . Many an individual who is at present an inmate of one of our asylums would not only be free but 'sitting on top of the world' if he had happened to be born in some other society."[33]

In traditional cultures fatalism and beliefs in magic play an important part in socialization because traditional societies have a very low degree of mastery over nature. Drought, floods, and famines are looked upon as reactions of the gods or evil spirits, whom man can propitiate but cannot control. Accordingly, part of a young man's or young woman's learning involves the mastery of techniques for "righting" oneself with these spirits. Much modern behavior is of a similar nature, except in this case individuals perform certain actions to gain favor with powerful figures in their community.

In summary, the socialization of youth in traditional societies is almost wholly a function of the family. The family is an extended group, including several households of blood relations. Given the fact that almost all of the problems of adaptation in a traditional society, except defense against outside enemies, are solved by the family or joint families, one would also expect this group to guide socialization.

Socialization in Modern Society

From the point of view of social organization and adaptation, the characteristic that most distinguishes modern society from tradi-

---

[33] Ralph Linton, *The Study of Man* (New York: Appleton–Century Co., 1936), p. 481.

tional society is the very high degree of differentiation and specialization in the social structure of modern society. This increased differentiation, specialization, and the concomitant high rates of change are the principal conditions that make socialization a much more difficult and complex process in modern society.

In modern society, the children's early socialization occurs largely within the family, and is for the most part centered around the mother. In many families, however, this function is soon shared with nursery schools, day care centers, and kindergartens. Therefore, by two to four years of age, the child is thrust into a setting with several other youngsters of his age and supervised by some adult. By age six he is in regular school, and will continue to be so on into adolescence. In other words, the modern child soon moves into a greatly extended sphere of social influence outside the family—a world of peers, school, and mass media, all of which offer many different conceptions of life. Contrasted with the child in the traditional society, the modern child experiences a much wider scope and variety of experience that he must integrate; furthermore, he also experiences a discontinuity between childhood socialization and adult roles. This discontinuity produces problems of self-identity.

Another very important difference in socialization in modern societies is the necessity for adults to upgrade continually their fund of knowledge and skills in order to perform their adult roles adequately. This means that not only children but adults, as well, have to adapt to changing conditions and to *change itself*. Accordingly, the effort to establish a sense of identity is not only difficult for the child and adolescent, but also for the adult. The changing of careers by adults in midlife today is not unusual.

In modern society, the pervasiveness of centers of power makes it increasingly difficult for individuals to make decisions of great import. The number of regulations and constraints increase as the system's complexity and the number of people involved increase. Restrictions are further increased as the decisions of representatives or leaders of nations begin to affect other nations. The effects that decisions will have on the other nations becomes another check of growing importance on decision-making. These restraints and limitations accumulate and contribute to a feeling on the part of the members of the general public that governments, as well as they themselves, are helpless. Such a feeling, of course, creates anxiety; as more and more people who have this feeling interact, the anxiety is intensified and accentuated, and becomes the large and very real problem of alienation.

The solution to the problem of alienation and feeling of helplessness was implied in our discussion of models of change or diffusion in the section "Processes of Change in Traditional and Modern Societies." The solution suggested was to formulate in advance the goals of the institution and its related organization and to design the structure to attain these goals. The structure should include feedback processes to enable the system to "learn" or adapt to error or miscalculation. In other words, the social system would be redesigned to include a learning system, which implies that the members of the population would be continuously resocialized to the continuing change in their relations to the systems.

Aspects of these processes already exist in modern society in the areas of private industry and government, but not in the public areas that relate to the population at large, where the need for such procedures is even greater. Centers and procedures for involving and informing the affected public on the issues that influence their adaptation are as necessary for the successful operation of a modern society as they are for the success of a large corporation. In addition, some feedback process to political elections is essential to enable the population to adapt to the necessity of a more planned type of social system. In other words, informal socialization, which was sufficient in traditional societies, no longer suffices in modern societies—nor do the school systems as now constructed. Some forms of continuing formal adult education are also needed.

One of the most important changes that man is now undergoing, in terms of its implications for modifying his present behavior, is the increasing interaction, planning, and tolerance among all societies. Apparently, we are moving, whether we like it or not, in the direction of a single coordinated mankind. The geographically isolated and competing groups of mankind of the past are being bound together by modern technology. The question is whether our understandings of our own nature, values, institutions, and emotions will rise to meet this challenge of one humankind. Success in dealing with a challenge of such great magnitude could result in man's liberation from his own tyranny—and failure could bring about his own demise.

Summary

In this chapter, we considered change both from the evolutionary and the systematic or planned sense. Given the present state of knowledge, we suggested that random selection is still man's safest procedure for organic evolution. On the other hand, cultural and social evolution can profit from systematic selection and technological and social planning because errors can be corrected rather quickly. Such a procedure assumes the inclusion of an adequate feedback and learning system for self-correction. Moreover, socialization of the population to prepare the members for a dynamic social state rather than a stable social state is also assumed.

Following this, we considered Schon's models for change or diffusion—namely, the center–periphery model and the proliferation of centers model. We suggested that the proliferation of centers model could be applied to public affairs as it has so successfully been used in the private sector. In this case, the electronic mass media would have to be used differently than they are at present, or at least their role would have to be expanded to include their use for educational purposes. They could not possibly continue to serve simply as an instant mirror of all the difficulties in the world, which offers no constructive guidance for solutions.

Finally, we considered problems of socialization in traditional and modern societies. These were contrasted, but the traditional society type was not analyzed under the condition of transition from the traditional to the modern state. Perhaps an application of the proliferation of centers model could be used here to aid in the transition. The difficulty would be the shortage of middle-class or skilled personnel necessary to make such a planned system work.

Exercises

1. Give illustrations of planned social change and evolutionary or unplanned social change.
2. Distinguish and illustrate cultural change and social change.
3. Contrast social change in traditional and modern societies. What are the implications of the differences for socialization?
4. There has been a relative loss of the so-called "stable state" property of modern society. What are some of the implications of this loss for adaptation to change?
5. Is man's basic problem of adaptation today one of conflict between warring instincts as Freud contended, or is it a conflict between the need for a system of rules and man's capacity to evade rules? Discuss your answer.
6. List and discuss factors that facilitate and factors that impede social and cultural change.
7. Describe and list the basic assumptions of Schon's model for social change.
8. Technological change has always been, relatively speaking, rapid. What primarily distinguishes modern technological change from that of the past?
9. Discuss the adequacy or inadequacy of the assumption of technological inevitability, that is, that technological development proceeds independently.
10. What creates the focus of the creative impulse during any era in a society?

Selected Bibliography

Allen, Francis R. *Socio-Cultural Dynamics: An Introduction to Social Change.* New York: The Macmillan Company, 1971.

Barber, Bernard, and Alex Inkeles (eds.). *Stability and Social Change.* Boston: Little, Brown and Company, 1971.

Bauer, Raymond A. *Social Indicators.* Cambridge, Mass.: M.I.T. Press, 1966.

Drucker, Peter F. *The Age of Discontinuity: Guidelines to our Changing Society.* New York: Harper & Row Publishers Inc., 1968.

Duncan, Otis Dudley. "Social Forecasting: The State of the Art." *The Public Interest,* 17 (Fall 1969), pp. 88–118.

Ferriss, Abbott L. *Indicators of Trends in the Status of American Women.* New York: Russell Sage Foundation, 1971.

Johnston, Denis F. "Forecasting Methods in the Social Sciences," *Technological Forecasting and Social Change,* 2 (1970), pp. 173–187.

Mead, Margaret. *Continuities in Cultural Evolution.* New Haven: Yale University Press, 1964.

The President's Commission on National Goals. *Goals for Americans.* Englewood Cliffs, N.J.: Prentice–Hall, Inc., 1960.

17

Creativity and Innovation: Potentials of Human Adaptation

Innovation and social change are intimately related processes, yet they can be usefully distinguished. Innovation refers to the source and development of new ideas and practices, while change refers to the incorporation of those ideas into the fabric of society. Innovation may occur without change, although historically innovation is often evident to the investigator only through the changes it has wrought. Change may take place without innovation, as is the case when nations are conquered or when natural disaster reduces or destroys a population. Innovation creates a potential for social adaptation, a potential for meeting new conditions. Together the processes of innovation and change have influenced the recent history of modern society in an unprecedented way; a major portion of modern social change has arisen from innovation and from the consequences, often long range and unforeseen, of the adaptation by whole societies at an ever increasing rate to the results of innovation. This chapter is devoted to innovation—technological, cultural, and social. Chapter 18 will deal with social change. Together they form a unit. The separation of the processes is merely academic and pedagogic, for, in modern society, innovation and change interact with and stimulate each other.

Creative minds, working in an atmosphere that rewards and values innovation, will produce an abundance of ideas and hence, an abundance of goods.
(Courtesy Berenice Abbott.)

The emphasis in this context is on *modern* society. Though primitive and traditional societies have shown innovative behavior, typically they resist change and new ideas. A society in which survival is precarious and hunting and agriculture are bound in superstition is a society in which change represents great risk and hewing to the tried and true has great adaptive value. Only where surpluses exist can innovations that are not essential to the present or immediate future be encouraged. Only in modern society has change become common and expected. Modern man, and he only in limited contexts, seeks new ideas for their own sakes and expects new practices to be better than the old. In the United States, the desire for the "new" is so great that manufacturers have found it advantageous to counterfeit new products, since much of the public prefers new tooth paste, new soap, new vitamins, and new looks in magazines, packages, and even politicians. New religions, new morals, new marriage contracts, new politics, new universities, and even new traditions show that the demand is not limited to goods. Even though much of what is called new is really quite old, and sometimes historically discredited, the mood of the country clearly favors the new.

Man may yet have to examine the advantage of the new, but the rate of invention, at least as represented by the number of patents awarded, has been increasing steadily; in the area of consumer products, the time between the development of the idea and the availability of the product in the market place has been steadily decreasing. Interestingly enough, the trend with respect to modern weapons systems is different. There the time between the basic idea and actual deployment of the weapons seems to be increasing. Perhaps as other systems become equally sophisticated, a reversal of the process will take place in all sectors of society.[1] Innovation will be considered under three headings: the cultural sources of a creative mind; innovation and social organization; and innovation and technology. These topics will serve to show how certain settings stimulate the creative mind to enormous efforts; how certain organizational structures create a setting in which innovation is most likely to take place; and how technological innovation serves to increase other types of innovation in a society. Innovation is a method of adaptation that allows man to relate to a changing environment. At the same time, innovation acts to change the environment, which in turn necessitates further innovation. Ideas do not only stimulate new ideas; they establish conditions in which new ideas *must be found*, or the level of society will regress, populations decrease, and culture degenerate. The process of developing new ideas, of finding new ways, of applying old techniques to new problems characterizes the innovative society. As modern society becomes more innovative, its adaptive problems multiply. It has been suggested that the rate of innovation has already become so great that society cannot cope with it.[2] Scientific journals have proliferated to such a degree that even within a single field no one person can read all that is published. One result of this proliferation is some duplication of effort, which, though inefficient, can be tolerated. Another possible result is that man may become inundated with material he cannot understand and with practices that he cannot adapt to as an individual. If that occurs, innovation becomes maladaptive, and society must, if it remain an adaptive mechanism, seek an adjustment. Since the consequences of the adoption of innovations are often unforeseen, the consequences of radically reducing the rate of innovation might also be unforeseen. In the near future, at any rate, innovation will be an increasing part of human life.

[1] A private conversation with Eugene Wigner indicated that the increasing complexity of weapons systems may be a critical factor. Traditionally, weapons systems have been more complicated than other aspects of technology.

[2] Many popular studies have indicated that change in the modern world is too great for man's traditional ways of dealing with change. For example, see Charles A. Reich, *The Greening of America* (New York: Random House, Inc., 1970).

THE CULTURAL SOURCES OF A CREATIVE MIND

In the history of man, a few men stand out as geniuses. Generally these men are regarded as possessing special biological endowments of great mental or creative abilities. Yet ages of genius seem to indicate that something more than native ability is involved, that sometimes genius labors at uncreative tasks and spends itself in the mundane. Why should a single high school system in Hungary produce within a few years five of the most brilliant physicists in the Western World? Surely this is not simply the result of an accident of genetics.[3] Why should the rate of innovation proceed at two to three times the rate of population increase in the United States? Surely the genetic quality has not improved at that rate.[4] Genius prospers and innovation flourishes when culture is receptive to new ideas.

Moreover, the areas in which innovation is encouraged will be the areas of greatest change and the areas where genius will be found. The Greeks during the Golden Age encouraged innovation in ideas, but not in practice. They stimulated new mathematics, new drama, and new education, but only in Syracuse did their culture move toward new engineering and new weapons of war. In fact, the Greeks invented an engine run by steam, but sought no practical use for it.[5] The Romans, on the other hand, were quick to seek new engineering practices, often acquired from Greeks, and to apply them to construction and especially to the technology of war. But the Romans were not receptive to innovation in every department. They made little change in the practice of agriculture, though the basic knowledge for such change was available to them. It remained for the conservative Middle Ages to employ the horse collar and the moldboard plow, innovations that led to a veritable revolution in agricultural production and set the stage for the population increases in Europe that have occurred during the past 900 years.[6] It is important to realize that our knowledge of the rate of innovation in the past is not always independent of the adoption of the

[3] The quality of Hungarian education was high at the time. See Eugene P. Wigner, "An Appreciation on the 60th Birthday of Edward Teller," in Hans Mark and Sidney Fernbach (eds.), *Properties of Matter Under Unusual Conditions* (New York: John Wiley & Sons, Inc., 1969).
[4] It cannot be said definitely whether genetic change plays any important part in modern adaptive mechanisms in human society because such change takes place over many generations. There is no evidence to indicate that genetic changes have been important in recorded history, though some small changes may have occurred whose adaptive significance has escaped the efforts of investigators thus far.
[5] The invention of a steam engine by Heron of Alexandria was the climax of an age of invention and discovery by the Greeks, which included knowledge of some properties of electricity and of the nature of vacuums. Some historians feel that cheap labor prevented the application of these inventions to a much earlier industrial revolution.
[6] Population growth was not continuous during the period. The innovation of a more urban social system brought with it increases in disease, and plagues often reduced population enormously for short periods.

There are some innovations that unalterably change our lives and pervade our existence. The camera allows man to cross the boundaries not only of space but also of time.
(Courtesy Catherine Noren, from the forthcoming book *The Camera of My Family.* New York: Alfred A. Knopf.)

innovation. Ideas that came into play in the Middle Ages might have been available for hundreds of years, but they may not have been mentioned in the surviving documents or recounted in the oral histories. If so, the use of these ideas must have been the result of reinvention. Many ideas seem obvious, though what we know will work is generally obvious. However, if there had been a social and cultural demand, surely some Greek or Roman could have thought of the moldboard or the horse collar.

All the examples above serve to indicate that it is not genius that guides invention, but culture. Genius follows the path set for it. Genius moves beyond the thoughts of others, but only a short way beyond. Clocks are a good example of culture eliciting an invention. Time and a means of identifying different days and parts of days have been important to most societies. Accuracy was probably always important, and some of the water clocks of the ancient world were quite accurate indeed. Yet the invention of a clock that would keep truly accurate time awaited the demand of

Technological innovations have often required man to re-evaluate his ideas and concepts. Perhaps the most shattering scientific innovation was Galileo's assertion that the earth is not the center of the universe. This revelation forced man to re-examine his position in the master scheme.
("The Ptolemic system" by Gassendi, 1658. Yerkes Observatory Photograph, University of Chicago, Williams Bay, Wisconsin.)

navigators who had to cross oceans for a timepiece that would aid them in fixing their position. To meet this demand, contests to find more reliable timepieces were sponsored by kings, and as a result accuracy was improved. Even today, the technological development of transportation from rail to air, from piston to jet engine to rocket propulsion, has been accompanied by a demand for better and better timepieces; and the resulting innovations—which range from a better escape mechanism at first to the vibrating crystals used today—likewise reflect an ever-increasing technological sophistication.[7] These innovations obviously required many intermediate innovations and the development of many technologies.

Culture also influences innovation by its variety and richness of ideas. If a culture is varied in its content, the permutation of ideas that can be combined with others is increased since innova-

[7] The historical process is discussed by Lloyd A. Brown, "The Longitude," in James R. Newman, *The World of Mathematics* (New York: Simon and Schuster, Inc., 1956), pp. 780–819.

tion is primarily the combination of old ideas to form new ones. A culture that knows of alloys will quickly explore dozens of combinations, just as a culture that understands breeding will be able to produce specialized breeds for different purposes.

　　Though many ideas or concepts cannot be combined into a meaningful innovation, the increasing influence of ideas as their number grows can be illustrated by examining the number of possible combinations of *n* things that result as *n* increases. The number of such combinations increases more rapidly than does *n* in a way that parallels the growth in the number of innovations that results from an increase in ideas and their interactions.

　　When the cultural pattern of a society is varied and receptive to innovation, one should expect the rate of innovation to be high. Cultural stimulants to innovation, however, are usually specific —that is, they usually apply differentially to different areas in the society. There is, however, a tendency for innovation in one area to influence practices in another. In the United States, the enormous receptivity to innovation in the industrial and medical sectors probably led to innovations in the religious, and perhaps the political, sectors. The tendency has been for religious views to give way to the more empirically based scientific views, but elaborate social innovation has been necessary in the process. Institutions of higher education, for example, became creators of scientific knowledge and practice and reduced their role as educators of clergy. State-controlled institutions where little religious influence was allowed replaced the religiously supported private school as the major force in higher education. The curriculum expanded and traditional fields of liberal arts gave way to courses in agriculture and business administration. Though the old titles of Bachelor of Arts and Doctor of Philosophy were generally retained, they came to represent quite different skills as social innovation accommodated technical and scientific change.

INNOVATION AND SOCIAL ORGANIZATION

Social organization influences the process of innovation in several ways. The size of the society, the relations among the parts of the society, the relations of the society to other groups, and finally, the diversity of the society all have an effect on innovative behavior, and on the amount and type of innovation, in the society.

Size and Innovation

The general axiom is that the more ideas available and the more able the minds to combine them, the greater will be the rate of innovation. A larger society, all other things being equal, should have more ideas available. It should be underscored, however, that simply being larger does not imply that more ideas are available. Though innovation and population increase have proceeded together in the Western World, large populations with low rates of innovation existed for many years in the past and exist in parts of Asia and Africa today. Even in western countries, where innovation is practically a way of life, some fairly large populations contribute little or nothing to the process and resist it in every way they can.[8] Therefore, the idea of size must be taken in context, that is, in the setting of the innovation. For example, 10 physicists who interact with each other may produce more new ideas than each of them would if working entirely alone, but 10 other men may produce fewer than one of them would alone. Moreover, the interaction is between ideas, not men. Through reading, a single mind can be in contact with the ideas produced by hundreds—it is the availability of those hundreds that counts.

Size of population also influences the number of superior minds that are available. To the extent that genius is genetic, large populations should offer more of them than small populations. The question of the genetic influence on intelligence is not settled, but there is some reason to feel that the level of performance of most members of society is far below the limits imposed by their biological makeup. To some degree, the genius may not be better endowed than others, but he may be more able to use what he has.[9]

Social Relations and Innovation

The structure of a society will greatly affect the innovative behavior of the society. If the assumption that genius has a large biological component is accepted, a society that allows only some of its members to participate in the exchange of ideas and the educational program would seem to be at a disadvantage. That the disadvantage seems only slight when Europe and the United States are compared may beg the question, though it does not close it. The proportion of the European population that obtains a higher education is about one eighth of that of the United States.[10] That such a difference does not render the United States eight times as innovative as Europe seems without question. But both areas might be more innovative and even more sophisticated in the nature of their innovations if they were able to educate the most capable parts of their

[8] Everett M. Rogers, *Diffusion of Innovations* (New York: The Free Press, 1962), pp. 57ff.
[9] Defining genius is difficult in other than "performance" terms so the "quality" of genius is usually inferred. Some of the problems associated with measuring intelligence are discussed in J. P. Guilford, *Intelligence, Creativity, and Their Educational Implications* (San Diego: Robert R. Knapp, 1968). See also his *Nature of Human Intelligence* (New York: McGraw–Hill Book Company, 1967), for a more extended discussion.
[10] European educational systems are not all alike, of course, but European nations do not send a very large part of their population into higher education. At the same time, they do select extensively, on terms of ability, most of those who are to be educated, especially in scientific and technical fields.

population, gentleman and commoner, rich and poor, black and white, and male and female. Evidence does indicate that none of these groups is generally superior to the other in all if in any forms of innovation.[11]

Access to education is only a part of the question of access to ideas. Other forms of isolation may also affect the amount of innovation available in subgroups of society. Segregation of any kind reduces the communication and the exchange of ideas that lead to innovation. Several studies have shown that black college students received ideas later in life than white students and in some cases did not receive them at all.[12] Educational systems differ and some students receive a more stimulating education than others. The contribution of the group that receives the less stimulating education, even if the ability of its members is as high, will be smaller than that of the other group. The structure of the educational system can especially influence the innovative behavior of students in the development of the habit of innovative thought.[13] The student who is told repeatedly that new ideas are bad or that only the ideas of his text are worthy will soon learn not to be innovative. Even when he has good ideas, he will probably not express them. Accordingly, the rest of the class will not benefit from his ideas, though they will be spared his bad ideas. Actions that reduce the sharing of ideas must reduce the level of innovative behavior. In the broader context of the rewards system, the society that rewards innovation can expect to have more. Patent offices are a structural expression of this fact. (Ironically, there was a short-sighted suggestion to close the United States Patent Office in the late 19th century because "everything had already been invented.") Rewards for the inventor are a basic means of increasing his output. At the same time, sanctions can be applied to discourage the innovator whose ideas or devices are considered undesirable. Innovation per se is not socially desirable, at least in the minds of most people, and innovative frauds and inventive quacks are often severely dealt with, though most unproclaimed inventors are faced with ridicule rather than prison.[14]

Rewards may also be differentially available in a society.

---

[11] Of course, if some groups lack contact with the full range of ideas available in a culture, those groups will be less innovative.

[12] For example, see Russell Middleton and John Moland, "Humor in Negro and White Subcultures: A Study of Jokes Among University Students," *Amer. Sociological Rev.,* 24 (1959), pp. 61–69.

[13] The influence of the school alone, however, should not be over emphasized. Recent studies show that other factors influence educational performance, and probably, creativity more than does the school system. See for example, Lee J. Croubach and Patrick Juppes, *Research for Tomorrow's Schools: Disciplined Inquiry for Education* (New York: The Macmillan Company, 1969).

[14] Social innovation often receives the most severe reaction. Innovators in the areas of morals and religion are especially likely to receive a strong reaction. Galileo found trouble with the Inquisition only when his innovative behavior entered the theological sphere.

Agrarian society typically offers rewards only to a select few of its members. Under such conditions, innovation is likely to be restricted to those whose social position makes it acceptable for them to be rewarded. Yet those persons, secure in their positions, are the least likely to be inclined to innovations, especially social innovations, that might change their status. For that reason, such societies are not generally characterized by high rates of innovation.

A final aspect of reward for the innovator should be mentioned. The society cannot afford to offer rewards for innovation unless it is organized to capitalize on the innovation. Innovations in technology, especially, must be timed properly if they are to be of value sufficient to encourage societial use. A steam boat before vessels of the size necessary to support so heavy an engine offers the inventor little practical return. A society organized to use and anticipate the use of new inventions can afford to stimulate their development.

A society, as it becomes less able to use new ideas, reduces in its population the willingness to produce new ideas. In this mechanism may be found the key to slowing a rate of innovation that has outgrown the ability of a society to deal with it. The social mechanism for reducing innovation, therefore, may be found in the decreasing value of new ideas.

Intersocietal Contacts and Innovation

As modern science has developed its character as an international community or series of communities, the distinction between inter- and intrasocietal contacts has become less important. None the less, during most of history, innovation was most characteristic of the nexus where lines of travel and hence lines of communication crossed. The intersection of trade routes formed the first international scientific conferences, for it was there that different cultures and large numbers of people met and exchanged ideas. In this context, Becker distinguished between physical and mental isolation.[15] Societies can be isolated mentally while maintaining some degree of contact with other societies. Modern nations, however, even in areas where most of their population is uneducated, have been able to employ radio and television to reduce greatly the degree of mental isolation, even among those who are geographically remote from population centers. Studies have shown such programs to be highly effective in changing behavior. The conservatism of peasants, at least that of some of them, may be a function of the limited availability of ideas and not a stubborn resistance to change.[16]

[15] Howard Becker and Harry Elmer Barnes, *Social Thought from Lore to Science*, 2nd ed. (Washington, D.C.: Harren Press, 1952), pp. 6ff.
[16] Daniel Lerner, *The Passing of Traditional Society: Modernizing the Middle East* (Glencoe, Ill.: The Free Press, 1958), *passim*.

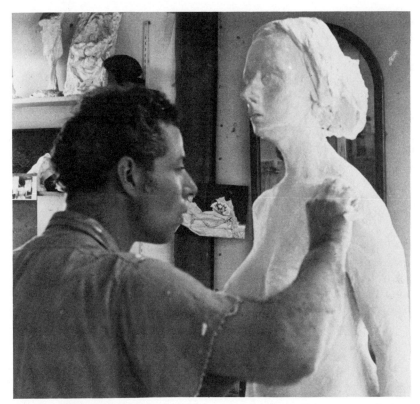

Man the innovator brings into existence that which did not exist before. He is a collector of the ideas of many cultures.
(Courtesy Elsa Dorfman.)

Diversity in the Society and Innovation

It was remarked above that diversity in a society when coupled with segregation does not lead to innovation. At the same time, societies that have a diverse population based on many cultures, where there is communication among the different groups and where no one group dominates the others to the point of eradicating their differences, should have relatively high rates of innovation. Innovation of this sort is limited to the areas in which the cultures can effectively exchange ideas. In modern society, these areas are the fine arts and entertainment rather than science and technology, where cultural diversity seems irrelevant.[17]

Other sources of diversity also play a role in innovation. Competing groups, whether they are culturally similar or different, create a diversity within a society and probably spur innovative behavior. The role of competition in society has received attention

[17] The role of different groups in American Society is examined in Nathaniel Weyl, *The Creative Elite in America* (Washington, D.C.: Public Affairs Press, 1966).

from many social philosophers and their verdicts are contradictory. Some argue that competition is inefficient, while others feel that it is useful in obtaining the best efforts from each party. Historical examples can be given for both cases, and many other examples do not support either side.[18] Innovation is a means to success in competition and is probably stimulated by it. The nature of modern technology, however, is such that no competitor can remain far ahead of another purely in terms of the technology used, so that innovation in other areas, such as advertising, is probably more important in the modern competitive system. Several groups working on the same task or related tasks may work harder and will probably be able to exchange significant ideas more readily than a single large group, if only because there are points at which a single group becomes too large for its members to act together efficiently and productively.[19]

There is one final comment on the role of diversity in innovation. Differences can be engendered in the educational system if it is geared to many specific programs without their mutual isolation. Examples of men who have moved from one field to make major contributions in another are legion—and specialized education, so long as it does not preclude communication with other fields, is an important source of this type of cross-fertilization.

INNOVATION AND TECHNOLOGY

During the preceding discussion, the special role technology has played in the innovations of modern society has been mentioned. Here the specific nature of that role is examined. Technology, the application of technology, and the growth of modern science are the major themes in this section. The industrial revolution was the age of the practical man. Inventions were supposed to lead to immediate application. Theory was a late development and received special recognition outside scientific circles only after World War II, when man learned that a theory could destroy a city. At least one investigator has seen the basis of this enormously innovative age in the development of new sources of energy.[20] Through most of human history, man had relied upon the strength of his own body and in more recent time the strength of domesticated animals to do his work. Hence, the surplus energy he could generate was small.[21]

[18] An examination of the development of industrial production in various nations from England to Japan reveals a variety of levels and types of competition, all of which led to rapid economic growth.
[19] Efforts by more than a few people must be coordinated, and patterns of communication must be established to avoid confusion. Such coordination generally involves establishing related subgroups or individuals who can proceed on different parts of a problem. The number of people who can work effectively together as a single group probably varies with the problem or area in which they are working.
[20] Fred Cottrell, *Energy and Society* (New York: McGraw–Hill Book Co., Inc., 1955).
[21] Fred Cottrell, *ibid.*, pp. 15ff.

With the development of new sources of energy, the rate of innovation increased. Man was thrust from the waterwheel to jet propulsion in only a few centuries.
("Moment of Lift-Off—Apollo 11" by William Thon. Courtesy NASA, Washington, D.C.)

Most of his efforts could only sustain life. At those levels of adaptation, only small parts of a population could become educated, exchange ideas, and speculate on new and better ways of doing things. Necessity was a long time in giving birth to invention. It was the basic changes in the sources of power that enabled man to begin the innovative age and those changes rested in a technological revolution. No innovation of art, no invention of politics could have caused the enormous changes that followed the development of new sources of energy. Thus the freedom to seek new ideas, the stimulation for their application, the materials for their transformation into devices, the cycle of idea following idea were all a result of the new and more abundant sources of energy.

To be sure, the increases in the sources and amounts of energy available to man closely paralleled increases in innovation. At the same time, much of the innovation was directed toward increasing the sources of energy and the ways of using the energy productively. Each process stimulated the other. Thus we see that the influences of increases in energy and innovation may not always be easily distinguished. Yet the predominance of the force of the technological area is seen in its contrast to other areas such as religion, theater, and music, in which there has been no comparable development and expansion. Furthermore, changes that have taken place in those areas have often been the adaptation of existing forms to the new technology—for example, electronic instruments, drive-in churches, and moving pictures. Relatively few changes in technology have been made because of changes in those other areas. Only politics, where little change has taken place, is able to guide and direct technology, and there guidance is more often imaginary than real. Technology has its own direction, and only recently have societies begun to realize that the direction of technology is not always progress.[22]

The relation between innovation in basic sciences and in technology is not fully understood. Frequently, technology has been developed without reference to theoretical science.[23] Recently, programs such as the Manhattan Project and the Space Program have been designed to apply principles of basic science to technological ends. Even the Space Program is primarily composed of technology and the applications of technology, though some of its projects are designed to advance basic science.[24] One fact is now certain—rapid developments in basic science do not lead directly to rapid technological innovations. Most new procedures are applications of basic principles well-known for a long time. Probably the lag between basic research findings and their application to technology will always be fairly long, while the time between new applications and their availability in the society will continue to shorten.

Technological change probably will not decrease in modern society simply because basic research is reduced. A reduction in basic research probably leads to a channeling of technological change—that is, technology would have to follow established paths (which might prove expensive) because with reduced basic research comes a decrease in the ability to seek alternative paths. For example, a failure to solve the basic problems associated with the development of fusion reactors to generate electric power might cause a greater than necessary dependence on fossil fuels and fission reactors in the future. The costs and difficulties cannot be determined exactly, but either a higher rate of pollution or a lower rate of expenditure of energy might well be one consequence. Thus technological growth probably would not slow as a result of less basic research; but it might follow less effective paths and result in more expensive uses of resources than it would if full programs of basic research were maintained.

A final type of innovation might be mentioned in the con-

[22] The rise of the idea of progress and changes in views of progress are examined in Sidney Pollard, *The Idea of Progress* (New York: Basic Books, 1968).

[23] Edison, for example, though one of the most prolific of inventors, worked almost without reference to formal scientific theory.

[24] Although most of the space program did involve applications of technology rather than scientific innovation, the entire program was to a large degree devoted to scientific discovery through making the observation of events and conditions in outer space more precise. Thus the contribution of the program to basic science is enormous.

text of science and technology. The innovations of science have been so powerful, so useful, and so rewarding that imitations of science have been encouraged by society. For instance, society does not always distinguish between scientific medicine and chiropractic, social scientists have been guilty of aping the formulas of science rather than its basic methods; and more has been claimed in the name of science than could possibly be developed.[25] Such pseudo-innovations, though not new ideas, may be a necessary result of true innovation. Many combinations of ideas, though they result in new ways of thinking or describing experience, are just empty combinations rather than innovations. A new geometry may be a basic advance or only a contradictory system, without utility or even intellectual merit.[26] Science, like other social institutions, has the problem of distinguishing between the innovative man and the proponent of pseudoinnovation. Science has rewarded the false, as well as condemned the true innovator; but the final verdict is often not reached until those to whom rewards are due and those who confer rewards have passed beyond the reach of society.[27]

THE ROLE OF INNOVATOR

The last topic for this chapter is the role of the innovator. Although innovation, as has been seen, is a socially induced response, the innovator is not randomly selected from society. The role of innovator can be examined as a special case, without viewing the innovator as one who uniquely bestows gifts on society, gifts that, without him, society would be denied.[28] Innovators are recruited and trained for their roles. Though ability may render some unfit for the role and others especially able, the innovator, contrary to popular belief, is a product of society rather than a rebel against it. An innovator, especially one whose innovations are social rather than technical, may be viewed and view himself as a revolutionary or one outside society; but the source of his ideas is the society and its store of information. Timothy Leary may seek a new religious experience he feels is beyond the ken of other men, but he does so in response to the technology and even the mores of society. His invention is simply an

[25] A strong criticism of social science was voiced by Pitirim A. Sorokin in *Fads and Foibles in Modern Sociology and Related Sciences* (Chicago: Henry Regency Company, 1956).
[26] Creativity is not simply a combination of old ideas, but a combination that has meaning or utility. See the discussion of W. W. Pouse Ball, "Calculating Prodigies," in James R. Newman, *The World of Mathematics* (New York: Simon and Schuster, Inc., 1956), pp. 467ff.
[27] It is important to recognize that the idea of reward is quite broad. Many innovators find rewards in personal satisfaction and in the process of innovation itself. Direct financial rewards are only a part of the whole mechanism of reward.
[28] Exactly how and to what extent different parts of society influence innovative behavior has not been established. For a study of the difficulties in determining how social practices influence performance, see Lee J. Cronbach and Patrick Suppes, *Research for Tomorrow's Schools: Disciplined Inquiry for Education, Report of the Committee on Educational Research of the National Academy of Education* (New York: The Macmillan Company, 1969).

application of existing drug techniques and his interpretation nothing more than mystical religion.[29]

The role of innovator is cast in several types, and changes among these types are part of the transition from traditional to innovative society. The first type of innovator might be called the **independent innovator.**[30] His efforts often seem to be historical accidents because he is neither trained nor formally selected by society to be an innovator. In many cases, the independent innovator is not recognized and often his innovation may be rediscovered several times. History records the story of the farmer in Scotland who derived, or at least gave evidence of having derived, many basic mathematical relations, some unknown to mathematicians of the time, without having any knowledge of formal mathematics.[31] Doubtless his experience has been repeated in other cases that remain unrecorded. The independent innovator, because he is unlikely to have an impact on society, demonstrates that simply creating the new within an individual mind is not always socially defined as innovation. An outstanding example of the independent innovator is Gregor Mendel, who examined the properties of genetic inheritance. Mendel's work was unknown to geneticists until it was independently rediscovered many years after his death. Because of his isolation, his discovery of the principles of heredity was actually without any social significance.[32]

A second type of innovator might be called the **charismatic innovator.**[33] He is the independent innovator who makes good. Though his ordinary position is not that of innovator, he is accorded special authority, perhaps through the marvel of his innovation. This type of innovator is rare because most innovations cannot be viewed with the degree of marvel required. Some innovations in religious thought appear to be of this type, but religions often hide their origins to make their founders appear more innovative.[34] In traditional societies where innovations are regarded with

[29] Compare the analysis of mysticism in William James, *The Varieties of Religious Experience* (New York: Modern Library, 1929), pp. 376ff.
[30] The use of the term independent does not imply that this innovator exists in isolation from society or that his inventions are not related to his social experience.
[31] Many mathematical prodigies are independent inventors. For examples, see Fred Barlow, *Mental Prodigies* (New York: Philosophical Press, 1952), or W. W. Pouse Ball, "Calculating Prodigies," in James R. Newman, *The World of Mathematics* (New York: Simon & Schuster, Inc., 1956), pp. 467ff.
[32] Mendel's results were independently rediscovered by de Vries, Correns, and Tschermak. See C. P. Oliver, "Dogma and the Early Development of Genetics," in R. Alexander Brink (ed.), *Heritage from Mendel* (Madison, Wisc.: University of Wisconsin Press, 1967).
[33] Charisma is often used to mean personal appeal or a compelling way. In this context, it has a more precise and somewhat different meaning. Charisma is a characteristic imputed to an individual by a group or society that allows that individual, because of that characteristic, to violate certain norms or rules of the group.
[34] For example, early Christianity sought to deny the Jewish elements in its own practices and to increase the newness of the religion.

distrust and anyone who advocates changing patterns and procedures is subject to ridicule, a charismatic innovator is the only type
that could have strong impact. The unknown inventors of the horse-
shoe and the spinning wheel must have had extraordinary personalities if they survived the suspicion and hostility of their neighbors.[35]

The **incidental innovator** is the third type to be considered. His innovations take place as a result of other activities,
without any intention on his part to innovate or at least to innovate
in the area of his discovery. Innovations such as the fermentation of
fruit juice and the making of butter were the products of the incidental inventor. If the behavior that leads to the incidental result is
common, the discovery will be made frequently in the society, as in
the two cases above. Incidental innovation may be the result of activities that are not engaged in frequently or not engaged in by many
people. Indeed, incidental elements are often part of a formal innovative process, as is reported to be the case in the invention of safety
glass and the discovery of penicillin.[36]

The **formal innovator** is one who is trained and selected
by society to innovate. Though certain men have played this role
throughout history, from the engineers who constructed the pyr-
amids to the alchemists, in modern society the formal innovator has
become the major source of the new. Often his innovations are applications of known techniques to only slightly new cases, such as
the use of nose cone material for cooking vessels, but the sum of his
efforts creates the culture of innovation and supports the rapid developments and social change characteristic of modern society.[37]
Formal innovation is rarely dramatic and often involves taking the
large innovative ideas, such as that of a rotary engine, and making all
the innovative steps necessary to produce a working model. Formal
innovation can become a source of stability, for although it is associated with change, it is also predictable. This idea is explored in the
next chapter.

The final type of innovator to be considered is the **innovative genius.** There are men who are able to take great leaps in
intellectual innovation. Although innovation is a socially engendered process, certain minds respond to social stimuli with radically
new formulations that set the direction for human thought and in-

[35] In many cases, the myth that attributed the invention of discovery to gods may have been
an effective social mechanism to protect the inventor.
[36] The casual contamination of a culture that led Fleming to his discovery should not be
taken apart from the entire process. Fleming was trained to innovate. He knew what meaning to put on his observation, and the process of testing and retesting, using different molds,
and so on, was far from an accident. For an account of the discovery, see J. D. Ratcliff,
Yellow Magic: The Story of Penicillin (New York: Random House, Inc., 1945).
[37] It should be noted that the formal inventor has a predictability in his actions because he
follows lines laid out by society for innovation in those areas in which society accepts innovative behavior.

novation for decades or centuries. Newton was such a man. Yet others of his day were approaching the same thoughts and concepts and had he never finished his work, another would have done so.[38] But only a few minds could follow his presentations, and fewer still could have made their way without his instruction.

This typology of innovators suggests that the role of the individual in the process of innovation is varied. Indeed it is more varied than the typology indicates since pure types rarely exist. Innovators are combinations of the types presented. Some students feel that to describe innovation as a product of society and social systems is to lower the importance of the innovator and to reduce the contribution of the individual. That is not the case. The innovator is a rare person, and his importance and value are not lessened by the fact that society seeks and stimulates his skills.

In the next chapter, the problem to be addressed is that of social change. There the emphasis will be placed on the adoption of innovation, the diffusion of ideas, and the consequences these have for society.

Summary

This chapter has been concerned with the process of innovation. Cultural, organizational, and technological sources of innovative behavior were examined. The influence that the size of the population, the diversity of the culture, and the structure of rewards have on innovation was discussed, and a typology of innovators was presented. Innovation was viewed as a social process that increased the adaptive resources of the society. At the same time, certain maladaptive aspects of innovative behavior were examined.

Exercises

1. Examine the life of some well-known inventor, such as Leonardo da Vinci or Thomas Edison. How would you classify him as an innovator? How did society influence his behavior?

2. Some innovations, such as the automobile or immunization procedures,

---

[38] Simultaneous inventions that may be independent support the contention of the text. Some examples are discussed in Robert K. Merton, "Priorities in Scientific Discovery: A Chapter in the Sociology of Science," *Amer. Sociological Rev.*, 22 (1957), pp. 635–659.

have important implications for society. Others are of less consequence, such as Metrecal or chewing gum. List some recent inventions or discoveries and evaluate their likely consequences.

3. How would you define the practical limit beyond which the rate of innovation in a society cannot go? Do you need to distinguish between innovation and adoption in your response? Why?

4. Examine several social innovations of the past 100 years. To what extent is each of them a response to changes in technology? Is there a basis on which you can distinguish those closely related to technology from the others? Could you find examples of purely social or cultural innovation?

5. Choose an area such as transportation or agriculture and examine changing practices and methods for the past century. Does the adoption of a procedure at one time restrict the nature of innovation later? Do you see practices following blind roads and returning to older patterns? Does your answer relate to the idea of progress? How?

6. If innovation is basically the combination of existing ideas, what accounts for the differences in innovativeness between individuals? How might you predict whether one applicant for a job or scholarship might be more innovative than another?

7. Examine the development of some modern innovations, such as nuclear weapons, jet aircraft, television, rock and roll music, student governments, or the like. Can you identify the innovator or innovators? What problems are encountered?

8. What programs might be formed to stimulate, direct, or decrease innovative behavior? Examine some research and development programs, such as those in the Federal Government, to see how they fit your suggestions.

Selected Bibliography

Barnett, H. G. *Innovation: The Basis of Cultural Change.* New York: McGraw–Hill Book Company, 1953.

Bright, James (ed.). *Research Development and Technological Innovation.* Homewood, Ill.: Richard D. Irwin, Inc., 1964.

Butterfield, Herbert. *The Origins of Modern Science*, Rev. ed. New York: The Free Press, 1957.

Childe, V. Gordon. *Man Makes Himself.* New York: Mentor Books, 1952.

Getzels, Jacob W., and Philip W. Jackson. *Creativity and Intelligence: Explorations with Gifted Students.* New York: John Wiley & Sons, Inc., 1962.

Katz, Elihu, Martin L. Levin, and Herbert Hamilton. "Traditions of Research on the Diffusion of Innovation," *Amer. Sociological Rev., 28* (1963), pp. 237–252.

Ogburn, William F. *Social Change*. New York: The Viking Press, Inc., 1938.
Rogers, Everett M. *Diffusion of Innovations*. New York: The Free Press, 1962.
Schon, Donald A. *Technology and Change: The New Heraclitus*. New York: Delacorte Press, 1967.
Wilford, John Noble. *We Reach the Moon*. New York: Bantam Books, 1969.

18

From Innovation to Social Change: Problems of Integrating Adaptive Solutions with Existing Structures

As the last chapter demonstrated, the development of more complex societies generates increased opportunities for a variety of new ideas, techniques, and activities. But it is extremely important to recognize that inventions are only *potential* adaptations, and that inventions do not necessarily lead to significant change in the operation of human societies. We therefore face one of the most perplexing and momentous issues of modern society—both in theory and practice: How is superior adaptive capability (a prime characteristic of highly evolved societies) converted into the organized implementation of that capability? Or in simpler but perhaps too general terms: How can we explain patterns of successful versus obstructed social change?

A few years ago, a widely read and discussed best seller, provocatively entitled *Future Shock*, aroused popular interest in change as an inevitable and almost unmanageable phenomenon in contemporary American society.[1] Alvin Toffler, the author of this disturbing work, presented four main conclusions. First, the pace of innovation is incomparably more rapid than ever before. Second, this rapidity is well beyond our current ability to regulate, organize, and profit from the welter of cultural novelties. Third, many people are fundamentally disturbed by this continued failure to develop satisfactory adaptations to incessant innovations (that is, they are experiencing, or suffering from, "future shock"). Finally, as a response to future shock, people have turned to various substitute means of "adaptation" in the attempt to dispel future shock—such as drug addiction, mysticism, vandalism and violence, and nihilistic politics.

Fifty years ago, but with considerably less dramatic intention, the same analysis of modern society was proposed by William F. Ogburn.[2] Essentially, Ogburn concluded that complex societies tend to produce more technological inventions than can be controlled by prevailing values and organizational forms (especially government). This imbalance was called "cultural lag," a term that has since been widely used to account for virtually every social difficulty—criminality, marital problems, inefficient government, urban sprawl, crises in public education, modern wars, and so on.[3] Ogburn's concept of cultural lag in effect was an attempt to interpret the *barriers* to social change and it inferentially raised the question of the *dynamics* of genuine social change. Toffler, on the other hand, asserts that radical changes have already occurred and that many people are in fact trying to reduce the impact of these changes by reverting to simpler or "earlier" forms of behavior.

This apparent difference in approaching the phenomenon of social change illustrates the necessity for developing a comprehensive framework for the identification and analysis of social change, as it occurs in functioning human communities and societies. This is an important but difficult task because, customarily, variation and deviations are confused with change, and inventions in ideas or values and in technology are somehow assumed to be equivalent to significant organizational changes.[4] In the next section, a simplified orientation to social change will be outlined—not for sale but for trial. It will attempt to answer only a few crucial questions about change: (1) How can we distinguish change from continuity? (2) What social processes link innovation to change? (3) What are the varied consequences of social change for modern complex societies and currently modernizing societies?

---

[1] Alvin Toffler, *Future Shock* (New York: Random House, Inc., 1970).
[2] William F. Ogburn, *Social Change* (New York: B. W. Huebsch, 1922), pp. 200–214.
[3] Cf. Marshall B. Clinard, *The Sociology of Deviant Behavior*, 2nd ed. (New York: Holt, Rinehart and Winston, 1963), Part 1; F. James Davis, *Social Problems* (New York: The Free Press, 1970), Chaps. 1, 2; Parts 2, 3.
[4] Alvin Toffler, *Future Shock* (New York: Random House, Inc., 1970), pp. 379, 395.

The impact of change is overwhelming for some individuals, as suggested by the concept of "future shock." This problem has been acknowledged and symbolized in art for several generations.
("The Shriek" by Edvard Munch, 1896, lithograph, printed in black, $20\frac{5}{8}$ × $15\frac{13}{16}$. Courtesy The Museum of Modern Art, New York and the Mathew T. Mellon Fund.)

A SOCIOLOGICAL ANALYSIS OF SOCIAL CHANGE

System as Context

The most elementary premise in any discussion of change is the prior existence of some social order or organization, or social system —simply because it is impractical to identify change without an appropriate basis for comparison. If we say that workmanship is less reliable than it used to be, or that morals are more liberal than in

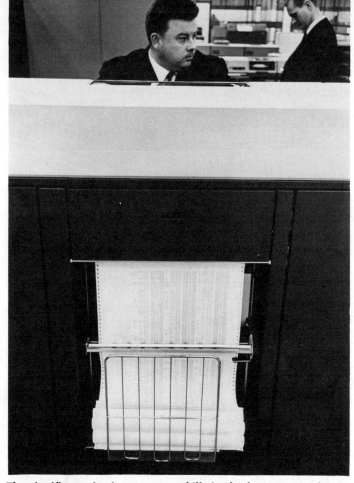

The significant rise in computer skills in the last 15 years is not simply a technical improvement, but an omen of the decreasing social value of persons with lesser or less efficient skills.
(Courtesy Leonard Freed, Magnum Photos, Inc.)

earlier generations, we are assuming not only a reference point in time, but the location of the change in some organized population or category of artisans, mechanics, repairmen, craftsmen in a set of enterprises, or some age category with identifiable moral qualities. In fact, when we cannot identify either a base period or a base population, any statement about change (or lack of change) is irresponsible and immune to reasonable discussion. For example, the statement "human nature hasn't changed much" is so vague that it can neither be accepted nor rejected on any demonstrable grounds. First, we do not know the time period on which the comparison is based: 1973 versus Cromagnon man? 1973 versus 600 B.C. ? 1973 versus A.D. 1400 in Western Europe? Second, we do not know if the implied comparison includes all known human societies, or some selection of societies from given historical periods (for example, classical Athens, Renaissance Florence, colonial Virginia, or metropolitan

Chicago in 1968). In addition, of course, since there is little agreement on the definition of "human nature," the question of change in that phenomenon remains unanswerable.

What is Change?

A second consideration of a fundamental sort, once a definite social base is identified, is the distinction between change and normal variation in social behavior and organization. Clearly, most people do not precisely repeat past behavior or maintain static attitudes toward their social experiences. We learn rough sets of expectations about friends, relatives, co-workers, clients, repairmen, salesmen, clerks, physicians, and so on. And each type of social contact is therefore broadly predictable. But normal observation will indicate that on some days people are more alert, or more impatient, more irritable, more worried, or more efficient in specific roles. Likewise, accidents, contingencies, and unexpected pressures are found in almost every group, association, or organization—for example, a shortage of cash or supplies, the sudden emergence of a competitor, an unanticipated gift, a lapse in otherwise dependable persons, a revised time schedule that interferes with other responsibilities.

In many instances, these variations are barely or briefly noted by the persons involved; in fact, minor adjustments in behavior normally enable people to absorb such unforeseen conditions without permanent rearrangement of responsibilities, rewards, or values. For example, schools and colleges continue to function with little visible change in overall results, despite new teachers, illness among teachers, the use of substitutes or shifting assignments among other teachers, varying amounts of absenteeism among students, days lost because of bad weather, or the introduction of new courses or teaching techniques.

In contrast to variations, which have temporary and rather slight impact on the operation of some group or organization, *change* may be defined as sustained adjustments in the organization of a social system that result in new or different social products and consequences.[5] One major form of change is substantially increased social specialization, which usually promotes increased technical efficiency and greater opportunities for useful and problematical variations. However, a second important type of change involves the radical reallocation of values, opportunities, or rewards, without alterations in the degree of specialization. This type of change is significant because it alters the *distribution* of social outputs rather than

[5] Alvin Boskoff, "Functional Analysis as a Source of a Theoretical Repertory and Research Tasks in the Study of Social Change," in George K. Zollschan and Walter Hirsch (eds.), *Explorations in Social Change* (Boston: Houghton Mifflin Company, 1964), pp. 213–218, 224–225.

the *amount* of socially useful returns. These two kinds of change may be combined in practice, as has been the case in Western societies from the medieval period to the present; however, developmental change does not insure reorganizational change—as the newer nations have discovered.[6]

How, then, do the phenomena of change differ from variation? Or in other words, what is it that *changes* when social change occurs that does not change when variation takes place? This is not a simple question, nor is there crystallized agreement on the most useful answer. But it is much more satisfactory to work with an arbitrary answer than a vague or slippery one. And a clear definition of a phenomenon must precede any serious attempt to explain its dynamics and course.

First, we can identify several familiar *dimensions* of variation in a social system. These are[7]:

1. Population variations—in size, density, age and sex distributions, birth and death rates, migration patterns.
2. Technological variations—in cost and efficiency of tools, machines.
3. Cultural variations—in shared values, norms, knowledge, symbols, and so on.
4. Interactional variations—in patterns of transmitting influences, information, goods and services, both within and between systems.
5. Environmental variations—in climate, soil quality, supply of flora and fauna, and in natural or induced "crises" in environment (for example, flooding, avalanches, earthquakes, and so on).
6. Intersocietal variations—in contacts with hostile, friendly, or neutral societies.

Second, we must recognize that these types of variations occur simultaneously or nearly so, in numerous combinations during any significant unit of time for a community or society. But the *joint effect* (if any) of these composite variations is more important—from our standpoint—than the individual effects resulting from a new method of manufacturing gas from coal, a new religious cult, a new imposition of taxes, an increased proportion of elderly persons, and the circulation of new magazines.[8] Essentially, we want to know if

---

[6] Lucian W. Pye, *Aspects of Political Development* (Boston: Little, Brown and Company, 1966); Warren F. Ilchman and Norman T. Uphoff, *The Political Economy of Change* (Berkeley, Calif.: University of California Press, 1969).

[7] Bryce F. Ryan, *Social and Cultural Change* (New York: Ronald Press: 1969), Chaps. 1, 2; Robert M. MacIver, *Social Causation* (Boston: Ginn and Company, 1942), Chaps. 10, 11; Richard T. LaPiere, *Social Change* (New York: McGraw–Hill Book Company, 1965), Chaps. 7–11.

[8] *The New York Times*, June 5, August 4, and August 20 (1971).

these numerous variations cancel each other, or if they somehow cumulate to produce *altered social effects that could not be anticipated from patterns of activities and values that existed before the operation of such variations.* Variations that do not materially affect predictions or anticipations, therefore, do not allow us to identify the phenomenon of social change.

What is the crucial criterion of change in social systems? In line with the orientation of this work, and in view of the limitations of available definitions, change can be approached as the identifiable increase (and decrease) in *adaptation* (1) of social systems to their environment and (2) of subcategories or subgroups to the operation of particular communities or societies. In short, what is assumed to change is the *structuring* of humanly contrived solutions to sets of common problems.[9] Thus social change becomes visible when structural alterations result in meaningful differences (positive or negative) between patterned features of a social system at two or more time periods. For example, the influence of labor unions since the 1930's is a result of legal encouragement and organizational efforts. This relatively recent level of effective union power can be gauged by local and national impact on election of public officials and by relative success in obtaining legislation favorable to workers.

Definition and Measurement of Change

Social change is conceived of as a complex phenomenon of social systems, as expressed in revisions in the processes and forms of specialization and regulation, and as reflected in definable increases or decreases in successful adaptation to, or mastery of, available resources. The "measurement" of social change must therefore consist of two kinds of evidence: (1) significant or potentially significant restructuring of the basic social organization of a community or society; and (2) reliably altered levels of achievement (or frustration), which can be attributed to such restructuring.

Measurement of social change becomes a morass of dubious data unless evidence on *both* components of social change is used, since these components may be independent of one another. For example, an apparent structural alteration may lead to little or no increase in social adaptation. This conclusion was vigorously championed by Vilfredo Pareto a half century ago in his famous discussion of the "circulation of the elites."[10] Pareto simplified the vicissitudes of national leadership throughout history as the structural alternation

---

[9] See Chap. 4; see also L. T. Hobhouse, *Social Development* (New York: Henry Holt & Company, Inc., 1924), pp. 14, 78–89; Gerald E. Caiden, *Administrative Reform* (Chicago: Aldine, 1969), Chap. 3; Hollis W. Peter (ed.), *Comparative Theories of Social Change* (Ann Arbor, Mich.: Foundation for Research on Human Behavior, November 1966), pp. 15–16, 320–323.
[10] Vilfredo Pareto, *Mind and Society* (New York: Harcourt, Brace and Company, Inc., 1935), Vol. 4, pars. 2274–2278, 2300–2309.

of two types of regulation: one form was characterized by skills in applying force or coercion, while the second involved the successful use of manipulative, inventive social skills. To Pareto, the changing recruitment of elites (from previous elite categories, as well as from the non-elite) produced minor or short-lived "changes" (in productivity or in control of opposition). In the same vein, Robert Michels found that replacement of middle-class leaders by those from working-class backgrounds and ideologies does not produce greater democracy or equality of participation in organizations. His explanation is that the "iron law of oligarchy" necessarily restricts the functioning of leadership categories, regardless of the way in which they are selected.[11]

On the other hand, adaptive changes in achievement can occur with only minor or insignificant structural changes. The classic case is the Western Electric studies at Hawthorne (Illinois) in the 1920's and early 1930's.[12] These studies were designed to explore the techniques that might promote higher output levels among semi-skilled workers. Surprisingly, virtually every minor change in physical conditions (better lighting, and so on) led to higher productivity. Perhaps the only "structural" change was identifying selected work groups for study. This seemed to produce a heightened morale that encouraged better performance regardless of the type of innovations to which they were exposed.

What are the principal sources of relevant data on the identification of social changes? In Table 18–1, measurements or indicators of social change are derived from two prior considerations: (1) interactional innovations and (2) presumed or potential changes in the adaptive performance of given social systems (see columns 1 and 2 respectively). Social change is therefore estimated by making periodic comparisons of each indicator or dimension, and by searching for developments in the profiles of such indicators. For example, we might attempt to describe the extent and character of social change for a community (or nation) by monitoring the alterations in the following indicators[13]: participation in voting by selected residential or occupational categories; membership and participation in organized interest groups; use of informational mass media by

[11] Robert Michels, *Political Parties* (New York: Dover Publications, 1959, orig. ed. 1915), Parts 2, 6.
[12] F. J. Roethlisberger and W. J. Dickson, *Management and the Worker* (Cambridge: Harvard University Press, 1939); L. Urwick and E. F. L. Brech, *The Making of Scientific Management: Volume 3, The Hawthorne Investigations* (London: Pitman, 1952), Chaps. 3, 5. See the reinterpretations of this study by Henry A. Landsberger, *Hawthorne Revisited* (Ithaca, N.Y.: Cornell University Press, 1958); and Alex Carey, "The Hawthorne Studies: A Radical Criticism," *Amer. Sociological Rev.*, 32 (June 1967), pp. 403–416.
[13] Eleanor B. Sheldon and Wilbert E. Moore (eds.), *Indicators of Social Change* (New York: Russell Sage Foundation, 1968); Otis Dudley Duncan, *Toward Social Reporting: Next Steps* (New York: Russell Sage Foundation, 1969); Raymond A. Bauer (ed.), *Social Indicators* (Cambridge, Mass.: MIT Press, 1966).

TABLE 18–1

Major dimensions of social change and adaptive consequences, with selected indicators of each dimension.

(1) Major dimensions of structural innovation (social change)	(2) Adaptive results (illustrative possibilities)	(3) Sample empirical indicators of structural innovations
1. New or revised roles	Greater efficiency	Changes in occupational structure
2. Changed access to opportunities for specific social categories	Greater competition and initially greater efficiency	Changes in illness rates, residential patterns, voting participation rates
3. Reallocation of resources and prestige levels	Greater equality and more cooperative efforts in preserving environment	Changes in incidence of taxation; employment rates
4. Changed responsibilities for socialization	Inconsistency in values and growing problems of social adaptation	Changes in reported sources of beliefs, opinions, tastes for specific age groups, minorities, and so on
5. Changed opportunity for variation, deviation, and so on	Greater use of talents and increased efficiency	Changes in rates of patents; formation of experimental communities
6. Changed means of handling conflicts	Greater use of resources for physical and social adaptation	Changes in incidence of strikes, boycotts, and so on; changes in litigation rates

selected social categories (use of newspapers, news magazines, TV documentaries, and so on); occupational composition; availability and use of health and welfare services for disadvantaged social categories; and rates for specific types of crime and problem behavior (for example, robbery, fraud, murder and manslaughter, suicide, and alcoholism) among different strata and areas. But such a profile—repeatedly obtained—is of limited value unless (1) we explore the interconnections between the indicators (for example, we should attempt to determine what the relation is between change in political participation and changes in crime and problem behavior rates) and (2) we can explain the changing profiles by establishing practical links between decisive social processes and the behavioral and organizational developments that are recorded in such empirical indicators of change.

Innovations such as television gradually became part of the established routine through acceptance by neighbors and peers.
(Courtesy Bruce Davidson, Magnum Photos, Inc.)

MAJOR PROCESSES OF CHANGE

These indicators of social change are important—but only as *descriptive* summaries of completed products. Accurate description is indispensable, of course, but description can only provide clues to a reasonable explanation of the complexities of social change. If social change is a set of potential consequences that emerge through time from the stimulation of innovation(s), the basic problem in analysis is to account for successful and unsuccessful translations of innovative challenges into incorporated patterns of significant change. Fundamentally, this task involves the redefinition of social change as a rough sequence of crucial social processes that act as links between potential and accomplished social changes.

The discussion of the sources of innovation (see the section entitled "Innovation and Social Organization" in Chapter 17) should be recalled and perhaps reviewed at this point. To a large extent, many innovations constitute an initial annoyance, or threat, or perhaps an unanticipated challenge to many members of a social system. Thus, some degree of passive or active resistance to innovation is quite normal, whatever the qualities or content of the new value, technique, interpretation, or organizational form. The first practical problem is therefore one of *entrance* into an existing set of practices and social rewards.

Diffusion and Trial Processes

Since innovations are quite varied, no single explanation of "acceptance" can be adequate. However, most studies of attempted diffusion indicate that successful introduction of an innovation usually involves: (1) clear (and often a personal) presentation of the innovation; (2) attempts to relate the innovation to existing goals or aspirations, almost always without intending to "revolutionize" behavior or the functioning of the social system; and (3) some supplementary information or practices that facilitate early trial of the innovation.[14]

Obviously, all patterns of human behavior began as innovations, though many of these patterns have not been (or cannot be) traced to their respective periods of trial and basic acceptance. We have, however, an extensive fund of studies on this issue for such innovations as the city-manager system, hybrid corn, new drugs for medicinal use, fluoridation of water, "progressive education," the parliamentary form, school desegregation, modern diplomatic and ambassadorial systems, and modernization programs in underdeveloped nations.[15]

In general, diffusion processes depend on the relative contributions of the innovators, inventions, agents of transmission, and the adopters themselves—although there is some uncertainty about the relative importance of these four ingredients. Successful adoption seems to be facilitated by informal "leadership" categories, for they are able to influence their peers and then wider social categories to try a new technique or product—as in the case of new drugs among physicians, hybrid corn among farmers, progressive education among school administrators and teachers, new appliances (for example, air conditioners) among neighbors.[16] However, some inventions are imposed on initially unwilling categories—as has been the case with desegregation of local schools—with prolonged difficulties in the trial process.

[14] For a general discussion, see Bryce F. Ryan, *Social and Cultural Change* (New York: Ronald Press, 1969), Chap. 6. For examples of diffusion studies, see James S. Coleman *et al.*, *Medical Innovation: A Diffusion Study* (Indianapolis, Ind.: Bobbs–Merrill, 1966); Everett Rogers, *Diffusion of Innovations* (New York: The Free Press, 1962).

[15] Richard S. Childs, *The First 50 Years of the Council-Manager Plan of Municipal Government* (New York: American Book–Stratford, 1965); Harold A. Stone *et al.*, *City Manager Government in the United States* (Chicago: Public Administration Service, 1940); Bryce F. Ryan and Neal Gross, "Diffusion of Hybrid Seed Corn in Two Iowa Communities," *Rural Sociology, 8* (March 1943), pp. 15–24; James S. Coleman *et al.*, *ibid.*; Robert L. Crain, "Fluoridation: The Diffusion of an Innovation Among Cities," *Social Forces, 44* (June 1966), pp. 467–476; George L. Haskins, *The Growth of English Representative Government* (Philadelphia: University of Pennsylvania Press, 1948); Garrett Mattingly, *Renaissance Diplomacy* (Boston: Houghton Mifflin Company, 1955); Harold Nicolson, *The Evolution of Diplomatic Method* (London: Constable, 1954); Lawrence A. Cremin, *The Transformation of the School* (New York: Alfred A. Knopf, Inc., 1964), Part 2; C. A. Bowers, *The Progressive Educator and the Depression* (New York: Random House, Inc., 1969); Benjamin Muse, *Ten Years of Prelude* (New York: The Viking Press, 1964).

[16] Elihu Katz and Paul F. Lazarsfeld, *Personal Influence* (New York: The Free Press, 1955); William H. Whyte, Jr., *The Orgzanization Man* (New York: Simon and Schuster, Inc., 1956), Chap. 24.

Legitimation Processes

Informally adopted inventions in practice have short careers because continued use is often affected by personal whim and the pressures of alternative practices and competing activities. Specific fashions in clothing, entertainment, and public issues are good illustrations of the fleeting nature of inventions that lack clear and continuous forms of social support—and are expected to be replaced frequently. But inventions that ultimately contribute to social change must become sufficiently regularized to make an irreversible impact on the functioning of a definable social system. The processes of regularization are among the most important phenomena in the operation of human societies, but these processes are also the indispensable links between social stability and potential change on the one hand and genuine social change on the other hand.

Regularization *may* be imposed by force or coercion. However, that procedure is a costly and generally inefficient means of insuring continued use of specific inventions. Much more effective is a set of integrating or legitimating processes, which provide means for (1) developing widespread commitment to given inventions and (2) fitting such innovations into the prevailing network of obligations and social influences. It should be fairly clear that the earlier analyses of power–authority (the section entitled "Legitimation of Power" in Chapter 13) are especially relevant at this point. But we may delineate the operation of power–authority for this problem by identifying five vital processes of legitimation or institutionalization.

Rule- and Norm-Making Processes

A new practice normally reaches potential adopters accompanied by minimal information about its use or its consequences. Perhaps part of the initial attraction of novelty is the opportunity to experiment with different applications and to devise individualized patterns of use. This has undoubtedly been a crucial aspect of the spread of various kinds of drugs among adolescents in recent years. But after a period of early experimentation and substantial acceptance, continued use of an innovation generates several practical problems that require commonly accepted standards, norms, or rules. Often, there is a problem of obtaining adequate resources and/or services for the new practice, as well as determining "proper" occasions for its use. In addition, some arrangements must be made for rescheduling other activities.

The development of new rules and norms around innovative practices is a rather complex process; furthermore, to provide an explanation of this process that applies to all kinds of innovations is impossible. However, there seems to be a tendency to develop rules or norms that implicitly deal with matters of efficiency or expediency, rather than morality or ethics. For example, innovations in formal administrative practices for specific firms and organizations are often followed by informal agreements among co-workers on changing means of handling clients and on sharing or exchanging responsibilities.[17] In the case of technical innovations for which individual adaptation is predominant, rules seem to develop in households and also within neighborhood units. Boating, television, and so on, have been incorporated in family life styles by informal norms on appropriate times and places, and on sharing of responsibilities or choices. More specifically, families have developed rules about the amount of television viewing for children, for location of the first and additional sets, and of timing meals with viewing.[18]

Developing or Extending Authority

New rules or norms related to a new set of practices are facilitators of adoption and trial; these norms do not, however, deal with the desirability or rationale of the innovation, nor with the problem of promoting interest among the apathetic, the marginal, or the resistant. Successful innovations must therefore receive the blessing or impetus of a relevant source of authority, or, with somewhat more difficulty, such innovations may encourage newly devised forms of authority.[19] In either case, authority not only *legitimizes* the innovation (that is, defines the innovation as necessary to the operation of a social system), but it provides continued rewards (material and symbolic) for acceptance and earnest practice.

This process is perhaps taken for granted in most instances. But it is clearly revealed in the extensive popularity of public junior colleges or community colleges during the last two decades. Though established colleges and universities were lukewarm or hostile to the innovation, state and local educational authorities perceived the junior college as a major instrument for expanding educational opportunities. Through their influence and prestige, the importance of two-year programs was emphasized for large, untapped pools of students—and for the crucial consideration of state legislatures. Rather quickly, networks of accessible junior

[17] Peter M. Blau, *The Dynamics of Bureaucracy* (Chicago: University of Chicago Press, 1955); Esther Stanton, *Clients Come Last: Volunteers and Welfare Organizations* (Beverly Hills, Calif.: Sage Publications, 1970).
[18] See, for example, Wilbur Schramm et al., *Television in the Lives of Our Children* (Stanford, Calif.: Stanford University Press, 1961), Chaps. 3, 6.
[19] Robert M. MacIver, *The Web of Government* (New York: The Macmillan Company, 1947), pp. 294–298.

colleges were established in many states and in time these educational innovations were able to feed their graduates into senior colleges and universities.[20]

Processes of Socialization and Indoctrination

Innovations become established through repeated use, although the significance or personal importance of innovations is not insured by mere frequency of application. In addition to *individual* perceptions of their worth—which may be varied and ephemeral—innovations that survive require complementary social supports. These are often formulated as myths, traditions, ceremonials, ideologies, or slogans, all of which are effectively transmitted through either formal or informal associations.[21] Essentially, these processes of socialization–indoctrination are the primary objectives of the advertising industry. Each product or service is—or was—an innovation in consumer life style, attractiveness, or technical efficiency (in the home or workplace). Consequently, advertising campaigns try to develop familiarity with the symbolic content of the product—as well as the product itself. For example, cigarettes may be presented as an emblem of a rustic but fictitious "Marlboro Country," or a leading soft drink is obliquely labeled as "the real thing," and in recent months, as a liquid symbol of international amity and brotherhood ("if I could give the world a Coke . . .").

Problem-Solving and Conflict-Reduction Processes

Inevitably, continued practice of innovations generates problems of competition for time, resources, commitments—despite the facilitating processes we have noted. Some of these problems derive from unanticipated effects of using innovations; some from the *number* of adopted innovations; and some from differences in the motives and skills of the adopters. Whatever the reasons, the continued impact of an innovation depends on some mechanisms for handling disputes, for refurbishing motivations in the face of difficulties or unanticipated costs, and for solidifying or justifying these solutions. Again, existing or revised structures of authority serve as crucial links in the social careers of innovations, mainly with respect to changes in the evaluation of given innovations over a period of time.

---

[20] Leland L. Medsker *et al., Breaking the Access Barriers: A Profile of Two Colleges* (New York: McGraw–Hill Book Company, 1971), Chap. 2; Burton Clark, *The Open Door College* (New York: McGraw–Hill Book Company, 1960).

[21] On the role of advertising, see Ian Lewis, "In the Courts of Power: The Advertising Man," in Peter L. Berger (ed.), *The Human Shape of Work* (New York: The Macmillan Company, 1964), pp. 113–180; Joseph Bensman, *Dollars and Sense* (New York: The Macmillan Company, 1967).

Innovations that survive and proliferate do so not simply because of repeated use but because of affirmation and support by the structures of the society.
(Courtesy Robert Rapelye, Photography International.)

In the complex career of the innovations designed to achieve school desegregation,[22] the role of authority or authorities has been so inconsistent and mercurial that the fate of desegregation remains dubious at best—and perhaps the intended innovations will be discarded. The first authoritative sanction for desegregation was the Supreme Court decision in 1954. Thereafter, with considerable regional and local variations, school boards either delayed implementing the innovation, or developed partial applications of desegregation policy. In recent years, the Department of Health, Education, and Welfare has added its authority to the process of settling local disputes about reassignment of pupils and teachers, and to the controversial issues of transporting students over substantial distances (the "busing issue"). The "structure" of authority has been complicated by contradictory decisions by state and federal courts, by pronouncements of governors, and by numerous public statements from competing organizations (teachers unions, taxpayers groups, school boards) that seek either to validate their current authority or to obtain some semblance of authority out of the temporary chaos in authority on this focal issue.

The busing controversy illuminates the basic instability of any innovation for which consistent and focused authority has not been developed. Indeed, the prime test of power–authority in complex systems is its ability to regulate the career of innovations with responsible concern for (a) short-term and long-term effects on the larger system and (b) the varied impacts of subcategories that favor

22 Cf. Horace Barker, *The Federal Retreat in School Desegregation* (Atlanta, Ga.: Southern Regional Council, December 1969).

or resist those innovations.[23] In short, the critical points in social change seem to occur in specific decisions (favorable, hostile, or apathetic) of key figures in strategic power–authority structures. Diffusion or dispersion of power–authority seems to delay (and often confuse) the necessary processes that guide innovations beyond the shoals of conflicts and uncertainties—or, equally important, it can likewise delay the alternative processes that halt the spread of and commitment to given innovations.

Processes of Solicited Readjustments

One of the authentic clues to potentially advanced phases of social change is the attempt to encourage *supplementary* innovations—that is, innovations that clarify or facilitate the use of earlier innovations. Although supplementary. innovations may develop slowly and erratically from the perceptions and skills of individuals in a given society, change is more likely when legitimizing groups directly or indirectly "sponsor" additional innovations in order to promote a cumulative chain of social effects. (See section entitled "Japan's Meiji Restoration" in this chapter.)

Legitimizing and institutionalizing innovation in simpler societies does not often result in significant change, perhaps because there is little prior experience with the desirability and feasibility of supplementary innovations or because cultural and social resources for supplementary innovation are inherently limited. However, in relatively complex societies, the capacity for creating supportive innovations is sufficiently high to encourage motivations and pressures for such "planned" innovations.[24]

In general, the more advanced the processes of legitimation, the more evident are the demands for limited types of supplementary innovation. With considerable frequency historically, the process of solicitation has been launched by crucial power–authority groups—that is, kings or emperors (Augustus, Peter the Great), dominant strata (the upper samurai of Japan, urban bourgeoisie of late medieval Europe), charismatic leaders (Franklin D. Roosevelt, Ataturk, Castro), and, more recently, prestigious private foundations (Rockefeller, Ford, Carnegie). In the last century in Western civilization, another source of pressure can be found in the influence of intellectuals and professionals, such as scientists, engineers, economists, planners, educators (men like John Dewey, J. Maynard Keynes, Harry Hopkins, Sigmund Freud).

Although a careful analysis of solicited innovation in processes of social change is not yet available, several tentative con-

[23] See Chaps. 12 and 14.
[24] S. N. Eisenstadt, *Essays on Comparative Institutions* (New York: John Wiley & Sons, Inc., 1965); Guy Benveniste and Warren F. Ilchman (eds.), *Agents of Change* (New York: Praeger, 1969).

clusions seem plausible. First, there are considerable differences in the abilities and decisiveness of sponsoring authorities. Augustus was probably more objective in his program for directed change than either Hitler, Stalin or Sukarno. Second, the process of developing sponsored innovation takes time and may be frustrated by changes in the power structure or in the dominance of key individuals in that structure. Solicited innovations in the United States, for example, are constantly subject to the disorganizing impact of elections and the uncertainty of financial support and encouragement from sensitive or vulnerable public agencies. Third, there are rather different problems in soliciting and managing the three major types of innovation (technical, organizational, and valuational-ideological). The latter two types present great difficulties—as supplementary innovations—for both the inventor and the sponsoring authority. Finally, the sponsoring authority must often deal with confounding factors—for example, the competition of unsolicited and yet attractive innovations; the rather quick and yet unanticipated adjustments made by early adopters; and the imperfect practical meshing of solicited inventions with earlier inventions. In short, in the past, solicited invention has often been fitful and impressionistic, rather than intelligently and persistently planned (see the discussion of planning in Chapter 15, particularly the section entitled "Explorations in Planning").

Derivative Consequences

While legitimating processes are often intended to *consolidate* the presumed gains or advantages of given innovations, the actual consequences of innovations and their institutionalization may be so extensive and "unpredictable" that identifiable social change can be traced, pondered, and—most difficult and controversial—evaluated. In other words, accepted innovations tend to encourage further adjustments—directly, among the adopters themselves, and indirectly, among those who are affected (positively or negatively) by the behavior of adopters. Thus, when well-to-do urban families adopted the innovation of suburban residence, the less affluent families were able to resettle in the vacated houses and apartments, which ultimately altered the concentration of poor and marginal families in inner urban zones.[25]

An extremely important principle of social organization must now be noted, although it has been implicitly used at various points in this book (see especially pp. 150–155). Very briefly, human behavior develops and is expressed within imperfect but nonetheless identifiable social systems. In social systems, as in systems throughout nature, we recognize a minimal regularity of interaction

[25] Leo F. Schnore, *Class and Race in Cities and Suburbs* (Chicago: Markham, 1972).

Human social systems are composed of interactions that are regular but not very visible or recordable. By contrast, human ingenuity can produce complex technical systems, such as this Saturn V rocket system, that are spectacularly intricate and tangible.
("VAB Bay" by Lowell Nesbitt. Courtesy NASA, Washington, D.C.)

among the various components or parts. The primary components of social systems are roles and positions, and the prescribed or expected relations among these roles describe those systems in time and space. Social systems, therefore, "work" through more or less intricate networks of interchanges or interactions. Consequently, any alteration in a major interchange will require *some adjustment* in one or more portions of the network, because the network is based on past contributions (resources, controls) that evoke previously "appropriate" responses in behavior. When the type or amount of such contributions changes, the meaning and efficacy of past responses likewise change, and persons therefore seek adjustments that *simulate* the basic pattern of preexisting relations.

As an example, let us examine the case of a familiar social system—the modern nuclear family. Though many external changes typically impinge on families, there is one constant internal development that challenges that system, with results that are perhaps always in some doubt—this is the growth of children into adolescence and young manhood or womanhood. Typically, this "innovation" is followed by some extension of freedom and responsibility to the teen-ager, less parental overseeing, a separate room perhaps, or a larger one than formerly, access to the family car, and so on. But in most instances, these changes infringe to some extent on the family resources available to the parents or to other children. Consequently, to retain harmony (and perhaps sanity), an informal scheduling of space and materials is necessary—not without some friction, bargaining, and compromise. In addition, as a consequence of increasing independence, the young people tend to make judgments about leisure, morality, education, career, and so on, through interactions with peers, rather than parents. Obviously, delicate readjustments by parents are increasingly necessary, in recognition of these changes, and also for the prevention of open and irreconcilable conflicts within the family. As we can see from the figures on runaways, adolescent crime, and adolescent personal disorders, some family systems do not succeed in developing viable adjustments to change. And, in some cases, the preexisting system seems too fragile to permit effective readjustments to change or crisis.

Since legitimated innovations normally lead to a range of social effects—anticipated and unforeseen by innovators, leaders, and many subcategories of the population—it is necessary (1) to develop some orderly approach to these effects and (2) to estimate the relative connection of such effects to overall patterns of social change. This is a very complicated task because rather long time periods must be studied and the roles of specific innovations, of various strategic social categories, and of continuing social processes are often difficult to disentangle when one attempts to explain specific patterns of effects. In addition, variations in patterns of social effects between processes of *unregulated change* and the relatively infrequent processes of *directed or planned change* must be considered.

Whatever the source or content of accepted innovations, however, the major derivative effects can be classified in a tentatively simple manner. But these effects should be viewed as potential rather than inevitable; and we should resist the temptation to search for a single "necessary" sequence of derivative effects in processes of social change.[26] With these cautions, then, the following typical kinds of derivative effects can be identified:

[26] Alvin Boskoff, "Functional Analysis as a Source of a Theoretical Repertory and Research Tasks in the Study of Social Change," in George K. Zollschan and Walter Hirsch (eds.), *Explorations in Social Change* (Boston: Houghton Mifflin Company, 1964), pp. 235–238; Bryce F. Ryan, *Social and Cultural Change* (New York: The Ronald Press, 1969), Chap. 10.

1. Development of new skills or reevaluation of preexisting skills.

2. Changed emphasis on available resources (land, minerals, etc.).

3. Changed (expanded or reduced) opportunities for achievement within the affected system.

4. Changes in the pattern of population distribution and population composition.

5. Increases in (or reemergence of) conflicts between and among status categories and economically based categories.

6. Alterations in the number and/or content of value systems or ideologies.

7. Changes in the relative prestige assigned to identifiable social categories (occupations, minorities).

8. Changes in the structure of strategic decision making.

9. Changes in the relation of the social system to the social and physical environments.

Derivative consequences may be viewed as possible but often irregular ripples that respond to the intrusion of either casual or strategic innovations. Therefore, to identify, measure, and evaluate social change, we must trace societal ripples over an extended time period—through generations and even centuries. In addition, we must search for recurrent *obstacles* to derivative consequences, because social systems and their agents do not easily yield long established structures to the rational incursions of efficiency and logic. Despite the sensational statements of magazine writers and enthusiastic apologists and detractors, genuine social change (as distinct from upheaval) tends to be a prolonged and difficult set of social processes and intermediate products.

SUCCESSFUL VS. UNSUCCESSFUL SOCIAL CHANGE: TWO INSTRUCTIVE CASES

Let us examine two contrasting instances of social change: first, the widely acclaimed, successful accomplishment of societal change in Japan during the period 1870–1920; and then the rather limited extent of social change in selected nations of the Far East.

Japan's Meiji Restoration:
Guided Social Change and its Consequences

After numerous civil wars and bloody replacements of emperors, Japan in the early 17th century stabilized into a 200-year, semifeudal and partly centralized regime, known as the Tokugawa period. Although there were both local discontent and sporadic signs of agricultural and educational development, Tokugawa Japan seemed to be adequately regulated by powerful shoguns, figurehead emperors, a small central bureaucracy and an imperial court, and by dependent regional lords. However, the unforeseen intrusion of a United States naval force in 1854 served as a truly shocking innovation to the Japanese polity. This rupture of a "splendid isolation" was recognized as irreversible and potentially disruptive of the entire Japanese system. Consequently, a crucial adaptive innovation occurred—that is, the overthrow of the Tokugawa rule by powerful nobles from two provinces and the creation of an aggressive central government around a revived imperial system (the Meiji Restoration) in 1867.[27]

The aim of political innovation—and of subsequent innovative forms—was national adaptation through measures and policies aimed at significantly increased productivity and military capacity. From 1868 to 1900, Japanese leaders (mainly the newer nobility and selected groups of aggressive merchants) engaged in the dual processes of legitimating the initial political–administrative change and of stimulating a bewildering number of derivative consequences. The details of this remarkable transformation have been fully reported by economic and political historians during the last 15 years.[28] For the present purposes, it is only necessary to supply a representative sample of the means by which social change was accomplished in little more than a generation.

The first set of practical problems in achieving genuine change was legitimating the new regime. To a large extent, this required handling of dissident groups and provinces and also the creation of a new ideological system. With no hesitation, the Meiji oligarchy of leading nobles suppressed several peasant revolts and decisively defeated local rebellions by disgruntled samurai (warrior) groups during the period 1874–1877. At about the same time, the prevailing Buddhist religion was largely replaced by a revived emperor-worship system (the Shinto religion). Positively and negatively, then, the Meiji government had monopolized the sources of legitimacy with startling efficiency.

Thereafter, the major innovative efforts were shifted to direct and indirect measures designed to promote productivity and

---

[27] John Whitney Hall, *Japan: From Prehistory to Modern Times* (New York: Delacorte Press, 1970), Chaps. 13, 15; John Whitney Hall, *Government and Local Power in Japan, 500 to 1700* (Princeton, N.J.: Princeton University Press, 1966); Albert M. Craig, *Choshu in the Meiji Restoration* (Cambridge: Harvard University Press, 1961); E. Herbert Norman, *Japan's Emergence as a Modern State* (New York: Institute of Pacific Relations, 1940).

[28] E. Herbert Norman, *ibid.*, pp. 50–61, 161–171; Thomas C. Smith, *Political Change and Industrial Development in Japan: Government Enterprise, 1868–1880* (Stanford, Calif.: Stanford University Press, 1955), pp. 11–32, 85; William W. Lockwood, *The Economic Development of Japan: Growth and Structural Change, 1868–1938* (Princeton, N.J.: Princeton University Press, 1954), pp. 10, 61, 495–507; Bernard Silberman, *Ministers of Modernization* (Tucson, Ariz.: University of Arizona Press, 1964), pp. 3–8, 16–37; Johannes Hirschmeier, *The Origins of Entrepreneurship in Meiji Japan* (Honolulu: University of Hawaii Press, 1964), pp. 46–58, 112–122.

receptivity to the experience of more advanced nations. A fundamental group of innovations involved the radical conversion of lower and middle samurai from warriors and gentlemen of leisure to entrepreneurs. This was done by transforming government stipends to the samurai from rice to money or negotiable bonds and by facilitating the investment of these funds in commercial and industrial enterprises. Traditional taxation was likewise converted into monetary form, thereby compelling commitment to manufacture and commerce in modern terms. In addition, the government dissolved the old merchant guilds, with their restrictive policies, and developed crucial reforms toward viable national legal and currency systems, as well as policies specifically aimed at encouraging and subsidizing extensive foreign trade.

The Restoration stimulated a herculean redirection of skills and ideas by funneling the fruits of agricultural surplus (largely developed by government efforts) into industrial development; by modernizing and extending public education well before its adoption in Western nations; and by subsidizing foreign travel so that students might digest the technological and cultural achievements of England, Germany, the United States, and other nations.

As a result, the dominant emphasis in Japanese society came to be urban and capitalistic, with a consequent alienation of peasant communities and a sharpening of rural–urban distinctions. In contrast to Tokugawa days, labor power became a valuable resource. Understandably, the ancient practice of infanticide was vigorously discouraged, perhaps because population growth was believed to be a positive contribution to economic development. Most important, however, was a decided shift in prestige that occurred during the formative decades of a modernizing Japan. In place of the traditional focus on the warrior nobility and ancient family lines, Meiji Japan and subsequent generations placed the highest levels of opportunity and social reward on successful industrialists and bankers, a selected number of educational leaders, and on central governmental administrators.

By the turn of the century, the innovations and subtle structural alterations in Japanese society had vastly increased its organizational and productive efficiency—to the point where Japan was able to challenge and defeat Russia in 1905. However, the major derivative consequence of this process of social change was a new ideology of imperialism that culminated in a prolonged and ultimately unsuccessful war with the United States.

Arrested Social Change in
Thailand, Burma, Malaysia, and Other Nations

A number of colonial peoples in the Far East and Africa, as well as several underdeveloped nations in the Near East and Africa, have embarked on programs of "modernization" during the last 10–40 years. By contrast with Japan, their inability to achieve significant levels of change has been evident to a corps of sympathetic investigators in the social sciences. In particular, studies of the processes of "arrested social change" in Thailand, Burma, Malaysia, and Turkey are sufficiently detailed to allow a number of widely applicable conclusions.[29] Indeed, the common features of these experiments in modernization confirm our basic notion that innovation cannot produce social change without definite and cumulative processes of institutionalization.

In many instances, external pressures (from other nations or private foundations, or international assistance bodies) furnished the initial source of innovation; this was true for Malaysia, Burma, and Thailand. But, clearly, such innovations were predominantly limited to narrow forms of economic improvement—for example, better agricultural methods and large sums for industrial investment. In Burma, Thailand, and Malaysia, the major difficulty has been the immovable position of the governmental bureaucracy, which in effect neutralized most innovations.[30]

Essentially, development has been impeded by the failure to shift legitimacy from traditional groups to new leadership. In Thailand, despite aggressive individual efforts, both the monarchy and an expanded bureaucracy has retained enormous prestige, even though their power was reduced. The traditional class structure based on landed privilege was also untouched. Consequently, the predominantly high status members of the bureaucracy continues to assert the privilege of initiating change, while initiative for change is fundamentally perceived as a threat to their position—as was true of the Malaysian bureaucracy.

Lacking the ability to compete with established status categories, key political leaders could not implement technical and organizational innovations derived from foreign commissions or consultants, nor could radical changes in norms (toward efficiency, productivity) be firmly established in large segments of the population. Though educational opportunities have been expanded in Thailand and Malaysia, students flocked to bureaucratic positions (rather than to commerce, industry, or science), because high status remains entangled with officialdom. In addition, in Malaysia, ethnic competition between Malays and Chinese constantly interferes with projected innovations in the economy. Consequently—and paradoxically—without genuine transfer of legitimacy, the early innovations in modernized education and financial–industrial policies

[29] Milton J. Esman, *Administration and Development in Malaysia* (Ithaca, N.Y.: Cornell University Press, 1972); William J. Siffin, *The Thai Bureaucracy* (Honolulu: East–West Center Press, 1966); Fred W. Riggs, *Thailand: Modernization of a Bureaucratic Polity* (Honolulu: East–West Center Press, 1966); Robert E. Ward and Dankwart A. Rustow (eds.), *Political Modernization in Japan and Turkey* (Princeton, N.J.: Princeton University Press, 1964); Lucian W. Pye, *Politics, Personality and Nation-Building* (New Haven, Conn.: Yale University Press, 1962).
[30] Fred W. Riggs, *ibid.,* p. 56; William J. Siffin, *ibid.,* p. 252.

have tended to strengthen internal resistance to further and more far-reaching processes of modernization.

RETHINKING SOCIAL CHANGE

Human social systems (groups, communities, and societies) constantly mix established usages and variant practices in a tentative and unplanned manner, in an effort to deal with the recurrent problems of human association (see Chapter 4). Thus, they usually seek to adapt by unspoken strategies of retention and substitution of learned patterns of behavior. Because of this mixture of the old and potentially new, social systems seem to be repeatedly on the threshold of change, and also on the borders of greater or more efficient adaptation. However, possibilities of change and desire for change do not eventuate in social change without effective processes of translating innovations into a set of approximately cumulative and reinforced social mechanisms.

There is a continuing and unavoidable paradox in the study of—and participation in—modern social systems. On the one hand, social and cultural complexity allows (and perhaps encourages) varying degrees and kinds of innovation. But that very same complexity may interfere with the spread and derivative effects of innovation, especially when social complexity is not accompanied by considerable practical interdependence among component groups, communities, and organized activities. Of course, the degree to which interdependence is weak or lacking limits the extent to which we can speak of a "system" at all.

However, paradoxes are way stations to new directions in conceiving, thinking, and acting. The ambivalent character of social complexity compels us to search for mechanisms and social processes that ultimately produce change out of the turmoil of variation, innovation, and dubious coordination. There is a long tradition in social and political thought—in which many contemporary actors have firm belief—that the major means of overcoming this ambivalence and of producing change is violence and revolutionary movements sustained by force of arms.[31] This is an adaptive form that has been asserted to be of crucial importance in social change. And yet the social effects of violence and revolution have not been seriously analyzed in a reasonably objective manner.

In the absence of such a careful investigation, what is a useful, tentative approach to this highly significant issue? We must first face the sobering fact that relatively few historical instances of

---

[31] See the analyses by Henry Bienen, *Violence and Social Change* (Chicago: University of Chicago Press, 1968); H. L. Nieburg, *Political Violence* (New York: St. Martin's Press, 1969); Monica Blumenthal et al., *Justifying Violence: Attitudes of American Men* (Ann Arbor, Mich.: Institute for Social Research, 1971).

violence, revolt, rebellion, revolution, and so on, have produced—
or facilitated the development of—clearcut social changes.[32] The
French Revolution, for example, did not "change" French society;
later industrialization and reaction to incompetent military operations in the Franco–Prussian War probably account for the fundamental and especially gradual pattern of French social change.[33]

But when revolution does lead to social change—as in selected phases of Russian society following the Bolshevik Revolution
—violence and force by themselves do not appear to be the key
mechanisms of change; rather they appear to serve as means of creating a *structural precondition* for effective change. A major practical difficulty in complex systems, as we have already noted, is a
tendency toward multiple innovations without adequate processes
of coordination and cumulation of derivative social effects. In other
words, change is impeded by either lack of a decision-making structure or by one that actively insulates innovations in their respective
settings.[34]

Effective revolution and violence, then, serve to impose a
new or revitalized *hierarchical structure* that facilitates (1) legitimation processes and (2) the production of a pattern of derivative
social consequences—where preexisting stalemated processes and
countervailing influences had neutralized the potential effects of innovation.[35] The Japanese "restoration" was a classic case of revolutionary violence as a catalyst of social change. Violence may also
be applied to replace "obstructive" persons in critical positions of a
formal social–political hierarchy, as frequently happens in "palace
revolutions" in Latin America and the Near East. However, a *coup
d'état* often involves merely a *substitution of persons* rather than any
genuine difference between the aims and abilities of the new tenants
of power–authority and the old.

Violence and revolution may be viewed as attempts to accelerate the evolution of social systems so that they may better adapt
to or control their environments. But we should clearly distinguish
the *ideology* of violent movements from their practical social consequences. Revolutionary movements that seek social change cannot in practice produce such change by developing "classless" or
radically egalitarian structures of decision making—although leaders

[32] Pitirim A. Sorokin, *Social and Cultural Dynamics* (New York: American Book Company, 1937–1941), in 4 Vols., Vol. 3, Chaps. 11, 14; Harry Bienen, *ibid.*, pp. 69–80, 104–106.
[33] See Alfred Cobban, *The Social Interpretation of the French Revolution* (Cambridge, Eng-land: Cambridge University Press, 1964), pp. 75–79, 167–169.
[34] Edgar S. Dunn, Jr., *Economic and Social Development* (Baltimore: Johns Hopkins Press, 1971), p. 104; Eugene V. Walter, *Terror and Resistance: A Study of Political Violence* (New York: Oxford University Press, 1969); Martin Needler, *Political Development in Latin America* (New York: Random House, Inc., 1968), Parts 3, 4.
[35] Herbert A. Simon, *The Sciences of the Artificial* (Cambridge, Mass.: MIT Press, 1969), pp. 86, 98–99.

and propagandists may employ ideologies of equality as a means of gaining adherents.[36] Social change, at least those varieties that promote more complex adaptations for relatively large populations, requires *strategic inequalities* to manage the indispensable processes of legitimation and control of derivative effects.

Of course, social change processes may also operate in the direction of lesser complexity—that is, comparatively fewer goals or lower levels of aspiration, or organization of social efforts for a narrower range of participants. This has been called a "reduction in scale" and has been a perennial recommendation from persons and groups who question the adaptive capacities of human societies.[37] In fact, however, reduction in scale has been a rare phenomenon in human history. The feudal period in Western Europe was perhaps the prime experiment in social simplification, but feudalism was constantly challenged by political and technological innovations that ultimately transformed it into the imperfect but more complex adaptive systems of centralized, bureaucratic government and national–international networks of capitalistic enterprise.[38]

EMERGING ALTERATIONS IN SOCIAL CHANGE

Perhaps the major difficulty in understanding the operation of social change is a basic alteration in the character of social change, mainly during the last two generations or so in the United States and in other Western nations. In the preceding millennia of societal development, social changes were explicit or implicitly addressed to problems of adaptation to physical environments, to questions of scarcity and deficit. Under such circumstances, social change tended to favor production of technologies and specialized social skills. Conflict between social categories (classes, and so on) derived from substantial differences in adaptive needs and was largely expressed in competition for information, technical means, land, and ideological prominence. The net result was slow, erratic, and often inconclusive social change.

By contrast, the more recent forms of social change rest on relative independence of restrictive physical environments and on an emerging preeminence of social organizations that are capable of directing social changes in a more cumulative and rapid

---

[36] James C. Davies (ed.), *When Men Revolt and Why* (New York: The Free Press, 1971), Parts 3 and 4; Louis H. Masotti and Don R. Bowen (eds.), *Riots and Rebellion: Civil Violence in the Urban Communty* (Beverly Hills, Calif.: Sage Publications, 1968), pp. 157–165, 187–199.

[37] See the analysis of scale by Godfrey and Monica Wilson, *The Analysis of Social Change* (Cambridge, England: Cambridge University Press, 1945), Chaps. 2, 4. Arguments for reduction of scale are discussed by Henry David Thoreau, *Walden* (New York: Dodd, Mead and Co,. 1946); Morton and Lucia White (eds.), *The Intellectuals Versus the City* (Cambridge: Harvard University and MIT Press, 1962); Lewis Mumford, *The Conduct of Life* (New York: Harcourt, Brace and Company, Inc., 1951).

[38] Robert S. Lopez, *The Birth of Europe* (New York: Evans, 1967), Book 2; Henri Pirenne, *A History of Europe* (Garden City, N.Y.: Doubleday & Company, Inc., 1958), Vol. 1, Books 5, 6.

manner. Consequently, the adaptive focus of current and future social change is increasingly the social environment and its organizational components. Change thus becomes a process of pursuing different (and to some, "better") patterns of distribution of "social luxuries" rather than the means of coping with hostile environments. Certainly, conflict does not disappear in modern social change processes—but conflict changes in severity and kinds of consequences. With a few obvious and important exceptions (student protests, the black movement), conflict tends to shift toward tactical matters and questions of appropriate means—rather than the emotional and stressful competition for central power–authority. And perhaps as important, such conflicts do not effectively promote social change; instead, they reflect disagreements about certain by-products of change (for example, this sort of conflict is evidenced by the passive participation of some groups, by limited concern for amenities).

Change as Physical and Social Adaptation

Societies and nations differ in the relative strengths of the problems of adaptation to the physical and to the social environment and the corresponding two types of social change. It is therefore particularly necessary to identify the key features of the adaptive situation of a given society before we try to understand how social change develops and how its adaptive effects are perceived and managed. With a preliminary emphasis on simplicity, let us classify adaptive structures and adaptive results into four types, as described in Table 18–2. Historically, societies have developed from *A* to *B*, and then either to *C* or *D*. But the movement from *B* to *C* or *D* appears to be the most intriguing and challenging adaptive change in human social history.

TABLE 18–2

Types of societal adaptation by dominant form of orientation to environments.

Adaptive structure \ Level of adaptive results	Relatively high	Relatively low
Primary adaptation to the physical environment	*B* Transitional "capitalistic"	*A* "Primitive" societies
Primary adaptation to the social environment	Planning societies *C*	Bureaucratic corruption *D*

The shift from environmental dependence to relative autonomy and to adaptation of a predominantly social nature suggests a corresponding change in the *problems* of social change. Earlier social change was based on the ability to develop specialized skills and multiple nuclei of power and authority. Change, therefore, tended to promote lesser coordination and unequal and incompatible consequences, as Marx and others have indicated. In short, social change was an indirect and variably adaptive result of cultural innovations.[39] But the newer form of social change (facilitated by societal reorientation toward the social environment) entails a complex set of problems that are as yet barely identified.

Tentatively, then, the emerging form of social change is (or will be) characterized by organizations specifically designed to promote widespread social change. This is based on the vast fund of previous experience with ineffectual social change (and difficulties of adaptation to the social environment) in societies that operate with multiple and relatively unaccountable social nuclei of change (for example, science, business, administrative decisions, pressure groups). As one perceptive political observer has concluded,[40] pluralism or old-fashioned liberalism has been a disappointing failure in practice because such a system cannot govern (coordinate) and cannot plan in the advanced nations of the Western world. However, it is also difficult to create and sustain an adequate "change organization," one that is both broadly *responsible* and sufficiently *flexible* to alter processes of social change in line with adaptive problems. At present, in central planning bodies at the federal level, politicians, statesmen, and various intellectuals are trying to devise a reasonable facsimile of a change organization, with only limited success thus far.

A second feature of the newer social change complex is a renewed danger of maladaptation to the physical environment, which results from uncontrolled technological achievements and uncoordinated applications of technology and wealth to the physical setting. Here it is only necessary to mention modern weaponry, power blackouts, and erosion as examples. In short, as a result of either disinterest in the ultimate limitations of the natural environment, or of delusions of social mastery, the ancient problems of survival are again approaching center stage. This adds another dimension to social adaptation—and a new dilemma: a choice between major emphasis on physical adaptation and survival, at the

---

[39] Karl Marx, *A Contribution to the Critique of Politcal Economy* (Chicago: Charles H. Kerr, 1904), pp. 11–12; Emile Durkheim, *The Division of Labor in Society* (New York: The Free Press, 1947), Book 2, Chap. 5; Book 3; Godfrey and Monica Wilson, *The Analysis of Social Change* (Cambridge, England: Cambridge University Press, 1945), Chaps. 4, 5.
[40] Theodore J. Lowi, *The End of Liberalism* (New York: W. W. Norton and Company, Inc., 1969), Chap. 7.

This juxtaposition of simple and advanced technologies presents a sharp contrast in adaptation. The simpler peoples must cope with their physical environment, while the societies that produce planes and efficient means of destruction must come to terms with the social environment and its contemporary dilemmas of social regulation.
(Courtesy Cornell Capa, Magnum Photos, Inc.)

price of past social and cultural achievements or luxuries, or pursuit of more complex social arrangements and more issues concerning intrasocietal adaptation, at the cost of a despoiled or even lethal environment.

Third, we can anticipate a special problem in the relation between social change and conflict. Unlike earlier forms of change, the new form seems to operate on the principle of immunity from the arena of social conflicts—that is, conflict does not *cause* or promote specific processes of social change. Instead, the change organization or structure should be capable of determining appropriate, adaptive forms of change. Whatever the validity of this hope, it is still quite probable that inadequacies in creating and legitimating social change will encourage some differences in expected rewards, some dissatisfactions, and social conflict. But conflicts vary in type and significance, as outlined in Chapter 14. The major difficulty, then, may well be the ability to restrict conflicts to those of a constructive sort, as one means of *clarifying* the various costs and benefits of proposed innovations and subsequent social change.[41] In retrospect, the development of law and constitutional government during the past 300 years represented attempts to restrict or "civilize" conflicts during a period of accelerating mastery of the physical environment.[42] And these attempts were moderately successful— until now. However, traditional philosophies of legality and compromise (the value system that underlies "liberalism" and "pluralism") are being challenged, sometimes cavalierly, sometimes righteously. To the extent that these mechanisms for the management of conflicts become unworkable, adaptive alternatives will be required in order to transform further innovations into genuine social change.

Finally, the newer social change will face somewhat different problems of power and social inequality. Comparatively, power–authority will be more centralized and presumably more effective in implementing innovations. But centralization of power–authority also reduces responsibilities beyond the favored circles of societal decision making. Likewise, centralization serves to magnify errors, inadequacies, or technical failings in sustaining or promoting adaptive solutions to either physical or social environments. Consequently, social change can be expected to place unprecedented burdens and strains on the key social roles of the imminent future (the roles of regulators or planners). In addition, given these circumstances, while inequalities will not (and cannot) be erased, the continuation of irrational or arbitrary inequalities will be challenged with a vigor and effectiveness that surpasses all previous attempts. This is already evident in embryonic form in movements for racial and sexual equality. But such movements are based on *ideologies of fairness*, which are inherently open to differences in interpretation. As the newer form of social change and its special adaptive problems become more prominent, the pressure for greater social equalities can be expected to swell from actual or alleged *maladaptive effects* of specific inequalities.[43] In the past, dominant social categories have dealt with protests against inequalities either by repres-

---

[41] Lewis A. Coser, *The Functions of Social Conflict* (New York: The Free Press, 1956), pp. 121–137.

[42] Karl Mannheim, *Man and Society in an Age of Reconstruction* (New York: Harcourt, Brace and Company, Inc., 1940), pp. 327–335.

[43] See, for example, the analysis of racial discrimination from this general standpoint by an economist—Gary S. Becker, *The Economics of Discrimination*, 2nd ed. (Chicago: University of Chicago Press, 1971).

sion or by limited (and sometimes symbolic) reductions in inequality (for example, by extension of citizenship, voting, greater educational opportunities). Neither of these mechanisms is very practical under the emerging structure of social change. Therefore, those in power–authority positions will have to devise innovative responses to presumably new internal social demands.

THE RENEWED ROLE OF SOCIAL AND IDEOLOGICAL CREATIVITY IN ADAPTATION

If human adaptation is to continue (and advance), social change processes (as we have summarized them in this chapter) will likewise require careful cultivation. But equally important, processes of social change will require greater attention to the consequences of various innovations for the adaptive situations of several social categories. Without such concern in the future, the foundations of social organizations (an ancient and valuable adaptive network) can become critically weakened, by destructive conflicts and by ineffectual socialization of substantial numbers. Human societies depend not only on the adaptive contributions of knowledge and technology, but on those of social organization and ideology. The latter two show definite signs of wear and practical insufficiencies. In the future—if not the present—human evolution will depend on renewed innovations in forms of human relationships, as well as in systems of beliefs and values.

Though social and cultural evolution have spawned fabulous varieties of experience, social types and categories, and material achievements, the basic problems of adaptation now before us clearly suggest that fundamental *similarities* within a population (and between populations) need greater recognition. Quite probably, workable innovations in social organization cannot be created without this recognition, and without the development of thought systems to interpret these similarities for the benefit of social innovators. In short, the role of modern intellectuals assumes a new character: they serve not primarily as critics, but as continual and responsible gatekeepers of adaptive social change—through identifying and clarifying the ideologies that both reflect general adaptive needs and function as blueprints for organizational invention and implementation. We thus return to a repeated and still hotly disputed notion in the history of sociological theory[44]: that intellectual development is the essential basis of social evolution—perhaps even an evolutionary necessity.

[44] Pitirim A. Sorokin, *Contemporary Sociological Theories* (New York: Harper & Brothers, 1928), Chap. 8; Pitirim A. Sorokin, *Society, Culture and Personality* (New York: Harper & Brothers, 1947), Chaps. 39, 43, 46.

Summary

Analysis and understanding of social change in human societies are very important and difficult tasks, especially since innovations do not necessarily lead to social change. Another source of difficulty is the variety of ways in which variation may occur: in population features, technological efficiency, knowledge and value systems, environmental structure, as well as the interactional or organizational developments that are the focus of social change. Essentially, it is necessary to trace the effects of such variations (and innovations) on organizational developments and on the changed adaptation of societies to their environments.

Description of changes (in population, technology, and so on) entails the use of quantitative indicators that record experience on important dimensions of social behavior over certain periods of time. However, to *explain* the effects of these variations (derived from specific innovations), social change is approached as a rough sequence of social processes, in which the impact of innovation is guided by crucial social decisions. The first process involves diffusion and trial of innovations; this is significantly affected by a second process (or set of processes)—that of legitimation, in which key persons develop facilitating norms, means of influencing potential adopters, management of practical conflicts and difficulties, and even encouragement of supplementary innovations. Thirdly, social change results from processes of developing unanticipated readjustments (cultural and social) to accepted innovations.

These readjustments or derivative consequences, although difficult to identify in their early stages, constitute a large portion of the phenomenon of social change. Briefly, derivative consequences include changes in content and significance of social skills, in opportunities for achievement and mobility, in composition and distribution of populations, in cooperative and competitive relations between social categories, in patterns of social decision making, and in adaptation to physical and social environments.

After brief case studies of social change in Japan, and arrested social change in selected underdeveloped nations, a major paradox in social change was discussed: the apparent conflict in modern societies between immense capacity for innovation and yet limited social change. The role of violence in promoting social change seems rather restricted unless violence is replaced by a hierarchical social structure that can convert innovations into change by means of the change processes analyzed earlier.

But social change is also related to the kinds of societies and adaptive situations in which they operate. Historically, human societies were adapting, in the main, to restrictive environments, and social changes favored social categories that could best monopolize technology and property. However, technological achievements have shifted societal problems from those of adaptation to the physical environment to emphasis on social adjustments. This shift allows greater opportunities for effective social change, on the one hand, and yet is marked by greater societal dangers and a rather new pressure for social equality, on the other. Paradoxically, success in physical or material adaptation has come to emphasize practical necessities in social adaptation that were once perhaps desirable ideals, but that now seem to be of prime importance for human adaptation. The direction of social change also promises to depend on an ideological creativity that encourages subsequent adaptation to both physical and social environments.

Exercises

1. Why is it necessary to distinguish *innovation* from *change*?

2. Is social change equivalent to social adaptation? In what ways are these similar and different?

3. What are the most important means of ensuring the diffusion of specific innovations?

4. What are the crucial parts played by authority and power in processes of social change?

5. Why does successful diffusion of innovation encourage additional (and often unanticipated) innovations?

6. Under what conditions does violence promote social change? How can we explain violence as an obstacle to, or delayer of, social change?

7. What is the value of the much-quoted French saying: "Plus ça change, plus c'est la même chose" (the more things change, the more they turn out to be the same)?

Selected Bibliography

Barber, Bernard, and Alex Inkeles (eds.). *Stability and Social Change*. Boston: Little, Brown and Company, 1971.

Boulding, Kenneth E. *A Primer on Social Dynamics*. New York: The Free Press, 1970.

Eisenstadt, S. N. (ed.). *Readings on Social Evolution and Development*. (London: Pergamon Press, Inc., 1970.

Moore, Barrington. *Social Origins of Dictatorship and Democracy*. Boston: Beacon Press, 1966.

Nisbet, Robert A. *Social Change and History*. New York: Oxford University Press, 1969.

Ryan, Bryce F. *Social and Cultural Change*. New York: Ronald Press, 1969.

Schon, Donald A. *Beyond the Stable State*. New York: Random House, Inc., 1971.

Wilson, Godfrey, and Monica Wilson. *The Analysis of Social Change*. Cambridge, England: Cambridge University Press, 1945.

Index